READER'S DIGEST

ATLAS OF THE WORLD

THE READER'S DIGEST ASSOCIATION, INC.

Pleasantville, New York • Montreal

READER'S DIGEST

ATLAS OF THE WORLD

Project Editor: Joseph L. Gardner
Project Art Editor: Richard J. Berenson

READER'S DIGEST GENERAL BOOKS

Editorial Director: John A. Pope, Jr.
Managing Editor: Jane Polley
Art Director: Richard J. Berenson
Group Editors: Norman B. Mack, David Trooper (Art),
Susan J. Wernert

A World of Wonders

Based on the research and design concept
of Mary Jane Hodges

Produced by
Toucan Books Limited, London

Directors: Robert Sackville West, Adam Nicolson
Art Editor: John Meek
Consultants: See page 240.

INTRODUCTION

Next to a dictionary, perhaps, an atlas is the most useful and most often consulted reference book in a home library. Every member of the family will turn to its pages—to locate unfamiliar place-names suddenly in the news, to help with homework assignments, to plan vacations, or to daydream over armchair travel to faraway and exotic climes.

And for all these reasons, the maps that form the core of an atlas must be comprehensive, up-to-date, and legible. To ensure that the maps in READER'S DIGEST ATLAS OF THE WORLD met all these requirements, we went to America's foremost mapmakers, Rand McNally & Company, and asked them to produce the stunning series that appears in "The World in Maps," pages 64–192. The bold topography—exclusive to this atlas—uses a combination of elevation tints and hill shading to achieve a three-dimensional effect without sacrificing detail or legibility.

An introduction to mapmaking and a complete list of maps appears on pages 64–65, followed by the legend that explains how to use the maps and the locator that shows the areas covered. The maps themselves begin on page 68. Following the world reference maps are four pages of charts and statistics and an index to more than 40,000 place-names.

An atlas, however, should be much more than a book of maps. Preceding the maps in this volume is "A World of Wonders," 60 pages of breathtaking art, photographs, and informative text especially created for READER'S DIGEST ATLAS OF THE WORLD. Each of its full-spread features explains and examines in depth a separate story in the unimaginably long journey from the origin of the universe some 15 billion years ago to the choices for managing the planet mankind faces as we approach the 21st century of the present era. The contents listed opposite summarize the wealth of provocative, stimulating information offered in this section.

Together, these beautiful, accessible maps and the cornucopia of encyclopedic information contained in the introductory thematic section guarantee that this volume will be among the most handsome and treasured volumes in your library.

—The Editors

Global vegetation changes between May and August
show up in this composite of satellite images.

CONTENTS

A World of Wonders
pages 4–63

The World in Maps
pages 64–192

Universe: From the Big Bang to an Uncertain Future

Space is swelling around us. Many billions of cubic miles of new space appear between the galaxies every day, sweeping our galaxy apart from its neighbors and creating the cold void we see as the blackness of the night sky. Until this century it was thought that the universe was eternal and unchanging; but astronomers now know that the universe has a life history.

When the American astronomer Edwin Hubble examined many distant galaxies in the 1920's, he discovered that the distance between us and those galaxies is constantly on the increase. But Hubble's discovery went further. Not only were the galaxies moving away, but the speed at which they were doing so was greater the farther they were from us.

If we backtrack to an earlier time, it is clear that the galaxies were closer together. The further back we go, the closer they must have been. At the beginning of the universe, some 15 billion years ago, all the material in the galaxies we now see must have occupied a single point. The latest research into the early moments of time suggests that the building blocks of our universe were created immediately after that first instant — the big bang — as the universe began its explosive expansion from a single point.

Since then, the universe has expanded through time to the vastness we can observe today. The farthest objects that astronomers have observed — the superbright cores of distant galaxies called quasars — are about 10 billion light-years away. (A light-year is the distance traveled by a ray of light in one year — at a speed of about 186,000 miles (300,000 km) per second.)

Astronomers cannot be certain about the future of the universe. It will either collapse again under its own gravity to a single point or continue its expansion forever, becoming cold, empty, dead, and dark.

THE BIRTH AND GROWTH OF THE UNIVERSE
Our universe began in a single point about 15 billion years ago. The illustration reconstructs its past and peers into alternative futures.

1. At the big bang — the moment of creation — the universe is concentrated into a single point, infinitely hot and dense. This is the beginning of space and time.

2. During the first billionths of a second, the universe goes through a brief phase of accelerated expansion, growing from the size of an atomic nucleus to the size of a volleyball.

3. After a millionth of a second, the primeval universe is a violently expanding fireball, about 10 billion miles in radius. It is filled with protons, neutrons, and electrons — the building blocks for atoms — as well as billions of tiny particles called neutrinos.

4. After one minute the universe, about a million billion miles across, has become a giant thermonuclear reactor, building the nuclei of helium atoms from the hydrogen nuclei created in the big bang. At a few billion degrees, it is still too hot for complete atoms to form.

5. After a few hundred thousand years, the temperature of the universe has sunk to about 4,000°C, no hotter than the surface of the sun. The bright mixture of matter and radiation is now cool and dispersed enough for atoms to form. The universe darkens, and matter begins to clump together under the force of gravity.

6. After a few billion years, the galaxies are born as vast clouds of gas begin to contract, triggering an epidemic of star formation.

DARK MATTER: THE SECRET BULK OF THE UNIVERSE

The dark matter that may constitute most of the substance in the universe, but is invisible to us, has not yet been positively identified. One strong candidate, however, is the tiny, almost massless particle called the neutrino. For a long time it was assumed that neutrinos had no mass, but recent research has suggested that they do have a tiny weight, about 0.005 percent of an electron — which is itself only 0.05 percent of the mass of an atom. Not surprisingly, neutrinos have been called the nearest thing to nothing yet conceived of by physicists.

Neutrinos are almost impossible to detect because they interact very weakly with other matter. Millions of them are at this moment streaming through your head and through this page. They could pass straight through many light-years of lead with only a small chance of knocking into an atom. Physicists have calculated that vast numbers of neutrinos — about 10^{90} (10 followed by 89 zeros) — were produced in the big bang, but none of these cosmic neutrinos has ever been or is likely to be observed.

TOWARD THE BIG CRUNCH. If the bulk of matter in the universe is in something other than stars and galaxies, the future will take a different shape. It may be that around each galaxy in a vast halo is a form of matter that is invisible from earth. This dark matter could perhaps constitute 99 percent of the stuff of the universe. The gravitational force of this unseen matter may eventually halt and reverse the cosmic expansion. The galaxies will then begin to fall back on each other and eventually collide. The temperature will rise, and the universe will accelerate toward its catastrophic fate, when in the final gravitational collapse it will again return to a single point and complete obliteration. Some physicists have speculated that another universe might then be born, in which case the whole process could begin again.

LOOKING INTO THE PAST

Light takes time to cross interstellar space, traveling 5,878 billion miles (9,460 billion km) in a year. Therefore, when you look out into the night sky, what you are seeing is not the present but the past. Telescopes are timescopes. Light from the moon takes just over a second to reach us and from the sun about eight minutes. Proxima Centauri, the nearest star to the solar system, is about 4.3 light-years away, and light from distant galaxies may not reach us for many billions of years after it was emitted.

But there are limits to our ability to look into the past. The light now arriving at the earth from one of the most distant and ancient objects yet discovered — the quasar PKS 2000-330 — set out more than 10 billion years ago. That is almost as far as we can see. Any light coming from a point only a little farther away would have set out at a period in the universe's history when neither stars nor galaxies had yet been formed. The universe at that time was suffused with light in which no distinct sources could be identified. That epoch sets the limits on the universe that we can observe.

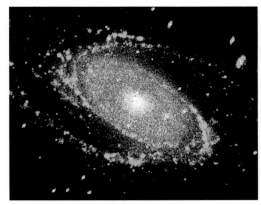

LIGHT-YEARS AWAY. We receive the light from the spiral galaxy M81, in Ursa Major, more than 18 million years after it was emitted.

EXPANSION INTO A FROZEN FUTURE. If the universe consists mainly of the luminous gas and stars that astronomers can see and there is no great bulk of dark matter, the inward pull of gravity will not be enough to stop the expansion set in motion by the big bang. The universe, in this case, will continue to grow forever. The stars will go out, because their nuclear fuel will be exhausted, creating a universe without light. Many stars and galaxies will collapse into black holes. The cosmos as we know it will have disintegrated.

7. Today the galaxies are gathered in superclusters, 100 to 400 million light-years apart, in great sheets and filaments with darkness between them. The explosive heat of the big bang has dwindled to a faint background radiation.

Our Neighborhood in Space

We live near the outer edge of a spiral galaxy, a giant Catherine wheel, glowing with the light of 100 billion stars and stretching 100,000 light-years through space. The whole galaxy is turning on its axis (the sun takes more than 200 million years to complete a single revolution) and, over the 12 billion years the galaxy has been in existence, that rotation has flattened into a disc the region where new stars form.

This is our neighborhood in space, but from our position inside the galaxy, 28,000 light-years from the center, we have no more than a sideways view. Like a plate seen edge on, we see our galaxy compressed into the band of stars we call the Milky Way.

To obtain a complete image of the galaxy presents many problems. It surrounds the earth on every side, and from any one point on the surface of the earth large parts of the galaxy are obscured. Astronomers from the Lund Observatory in Sweden, however, have overcome this difficulty by constructing a mosaic of photographs taken from several different places around the world. In this way they have been able to unfold the sky and lay it out flat, to make a map of the celestial globe.

The Lund map (below) shows the positions of about 7,000 stars, all of them visible with the naked eye and most of them within about 10,000 light-years of us. Although within the Milky Way, many of the stars in the plane of the galaxy are much farther away,

and their images are too faint and too near each other to be seen individually.

Nevertheless, we can deduce something about the nature of the galactic disc. Were it not for the thick lanes of dust that, wound round in the spiral arms, lie between us and the center and cut out virtually all the light, the view toward the center would be bright with the tightly packed stars of the core. The dust appears on the photograph as dark, almost starless blotches.

Many of the images outside the plane of the disc come from sources outside our own galaxy. For example, the two bright spots beneath the Milky Way on the right-hand side are satellite galaxies, called the Small and Large Magellanic Clouds.

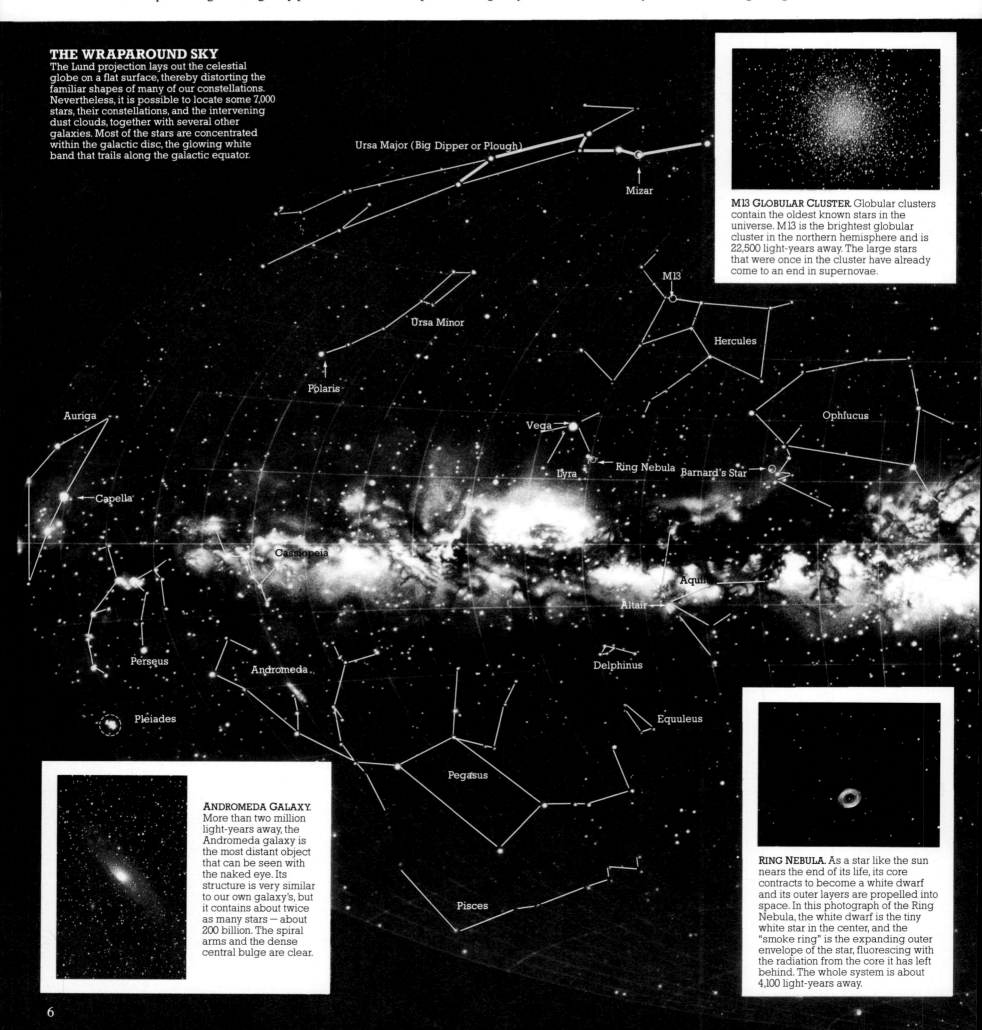

THE WRAPAROUND SKY
The Lund projection lays out the celestial globe on a flat surface, thereby distorting the familiar shapes of many of our constellations. Nevertheless, it is possible to locate some 7,000 stars, their constellations, and the intervening dust clouds, together with several other galaxies. Most of the stars are concentrated within the galactic disc, the glowing white band that trails along the galactic equator.

M13 GLOBULAR CLUSTER. Globular clusters contain the oldest known stars in the universe. M13 is the brightest globular cluster in the northern hemisphere and is 22,500 light-years away. The large stars that were once in the cluster have already come to an end in supernovae.

ANDROMEDA GALAXY. More than two million light-years away, the Andromeda galaxy is the most distant object that can be seen with the naked eye. Its structure is very similar to our own galaxy's, but it contains about twice as many stars — about 200 billion. The spiral arms and the dense central bulge are clear.

RING NEBULA. As a star like the sun nears the end of its life, its core contracts to become a white dwarf and its outer layers are propelled into space. In this photograph of the Ring Nebula, the white dwarf is the tiny white star in the center, and the "smoke ring" is the expanding outer envelope of the star, fluorescing with the radiation from the core it has left behind. The whole system is about 4,100 light-years away.

GALACTIC ARCHITECTURE

The shape of the galaxy is based on a delicate interplay between two cosmic forces. The centrifugal effects of rotation tend to scatter the stars into outer space, and the pull of gravity tries to drag them in toward the center. Balanced between these two forces, and molded by them, the galaxy makes its slow and stately progress through the universe.

In the central bulge, 30,000 light-years in diameter, gravity has concentrated the stars very thickly. If the earth were orbiting a star there, night would be made as bright as day. Bulge stars are old and orange-red. At the very center, there may be a small black hole. The matter falling into this might be the

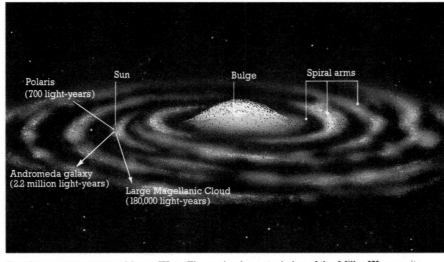

source of power for the radio waves that spread out from the galactic center.

Surrounding the bulge is the great disc of younger stars like the sun, part of a second generation that formed from the enriched gas and dust clouds that were the end product of the earlier stars. In the disc, less than 3,000 light-years thick, there are four ragged spiral arms extending from the nuclear bulge and coiled around each other. Stars and dust clouds are not fixed in these arms, but move through them as they orbit the center of the galaxy. The arms themselves are produced by the dynamics of rotation, like the ridges in a whirlpool, and over time the pattern slowly spirals outward as the galaxy rotates. As the arms move through the interstellar clouds of the gal-

axy, they concentrate the dust and gas there, triggering the formation of new stars in bright bands along the inner edges of the arms.

Above and below the disc is the halo, a nearly spherical region 150,000 light-years or more across. The halo preserves the shape of the early galaxy before it contracted and flattened to a rotating disc. The halo is filled with widely separated single stars and with about 500 massive globular clusters, each containing hundreds of thousands of stars.

Astronomers have not been able to establish the size of the halo with any precision, nor its constituents. Gradually diminishing into intergalactic space, it may be filled with dead stars, stars of very low mass, or large numbers of subatomic particles, none of which can be seen.

THE STRUCTURE OF THE MILKY WAY. The main characteristics of the Milky Way are its bulge, disc, spiral arms, and halo. As a guide to the Lund map and to the scale of the night sky, our sun and the star Polaris have been located, together with features outside the Milky Way, such as the Large Magellanic Cloud and the Andromeda galaxy.

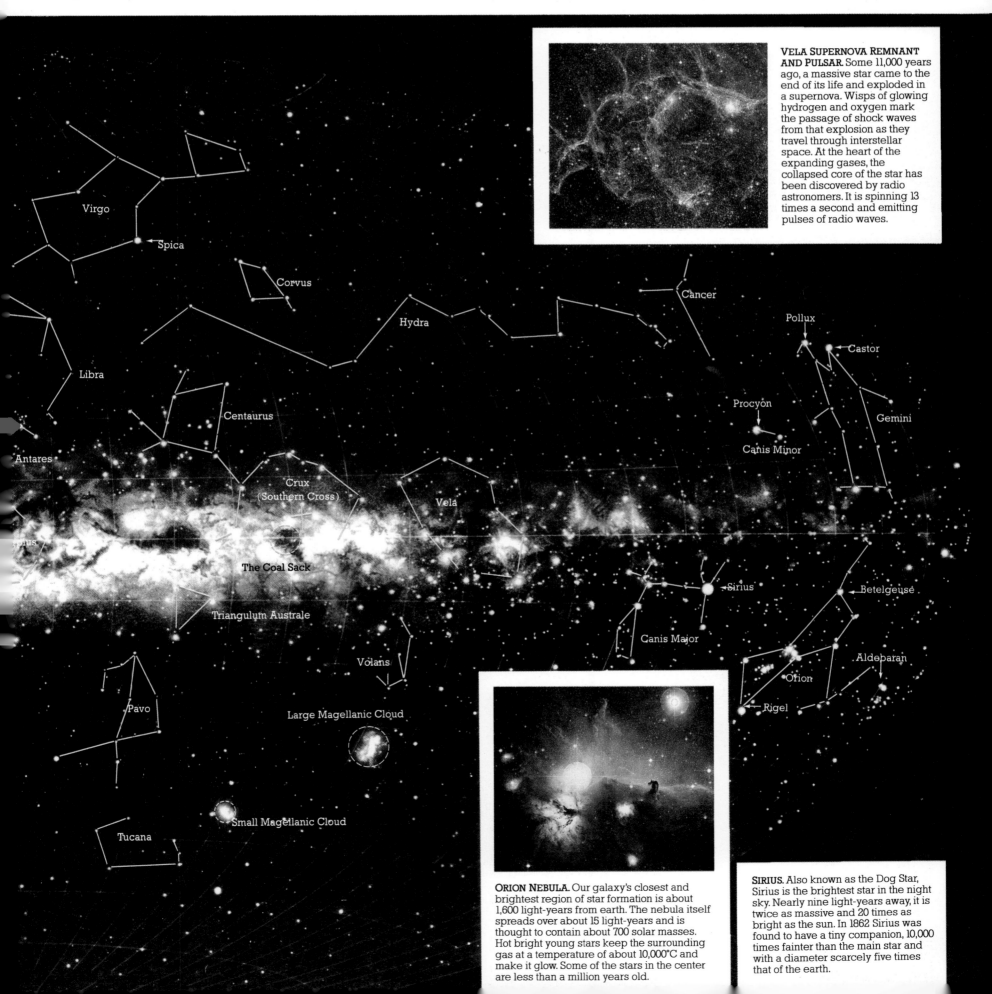

VELA SUPERNOVA REMNANT AND PULSAR. Some 11,000 years ago, a massive star came to the end of its life and exploded in a supernova. Wisps of glowing hydrogen and oxygen mark the passage of shock waves from that explosion as they travel through interstellar space. At the heart of the expanding gases, the collapsed core of the star has been discovered by radio astronomers. It is spinning 13 times a second and emitting pulses of radio waves.

ORION NEBULA. Our galaxy's closest and brightest region of star formation is about 1,600 light-years from earth. The nebula itself spreads over about 15 light-years and is thought to contain about 700 solar masses. Hot bright young stars keep the surrounding gas at a temperature of about 10,000°C and make it glow. Some of the stars in the center are less than a million years old.

SIRIUS. Also known as the Dog Star, Sirius is the brightest star in the night sky. Nearly nine light-years away, it is twice as massive and 20 times as bright as the sun. In 1862 Sirius was found to have a tiny companion, 10,000 times fainter than the main star and with a diameter scarcely five times that of the earth.

Stars: Cosmic Dust to Nuclear Furnace

Our sun is an average star — middle-aged and middle-weight, leading a steady, settled life in the suburbs of an ordinary galaxy. It is, for the time being, in perfect balance. The inward pull of gravity exactly counteracts the heat and pressure of the nuclear furnace at the core, which would otherwise explode the star. We should be grateful. Only in the neighborhood of such a reliable and long-lived body is it possible to find the constant conditions of warmth and light that are necessary for life.

A star much smaller than the sun will never become hot enough for nuclear burning to start in the core, and a planet circling such a star would be in constant twilight and frost. A star much more massive than the sun will lead a more hectic life, burning very fiercely and exhausting its fuel in 10 million years or less. If the earth had been the satellite of a massive star, there would have been no time for the complex evolution of life to occur.

Nevertheless, these massive stars do play a crucial part in the formation of life. Every atom on earth was once fused either in the burning heart of such a star or in the massive supernova explosion that ended its life, scattering into interstellar space the heavy elements from which the sun and the planets began to form. In the infancy of the galaxy there was a brief and brilliant generation of massive stars. Most of them have now disappeared, but we live off their legacy.

Man has never observed the life history of a single star, because the time scale is so vast. However, by combining observations of different stars at different stages in their lives, we can reconstruct the evolution of our sun. Parts of this story are retold in the sky every night: in the wispy remains of the Vela supernova, in the recently formed stars of the Orion Nebula, in the red supergiants such as Betelgeuse, in the white dwarf that accompanies Sirius, and even in our own solar system.

THE STRUCTURE OF THE SUN

The architecture of the sun consists of a series of nested shells, one inside the other, like the layers of an onion.

At the very center and stretching a quarter of the way to the surface is the core. The temperature is about 15 million °C, and the density of the compressed gases is 12 times that of lead. A pinhead of this turbulent matter would be hot enough to kill a man at a thousand miles. These conditions are extreme enough for nuclear fusion to occur. Every second, millions of tons of hydrogen are fused into helium. In the process about 4.5 million tons of matter is converted into energy, which then radiates out from the core.

The radiative zone surrounds the core and extends four-fifths of the way to the surface. The gamma rays, X-rays, and photons produced in the core fight their way outward through the dense solar gases. It is a slow journey, and a single ray can take a million years to cross this zone.

In the outermost fifth of the sun, energy is moved in large bundles of gas, driven by the heat from within. This convective zone consists of layers of cells, each smaller than the one below. Each of the cells in the outer tier is about 600 miles (1,000 km) across and is bordered by an area in which the gas is rising and dark where it is sinking.

This pattern of rising and falling gas gives the sun's surface, called the photosphere, a mottled and granulated appearance, bright where gas is rising and dark where it is sinking. The photosphere is no more than a few hundred miles thick and is usually marked by sunspots, which are often the size of the earth in diameter and about 2,000°C cooler than the surrounding surface. The spots mark kinks in the sun's magnetic field, where it has been twisted and contorted by the rotation of the gases and by the turbulence in the convective zone. Spots often occur in pairs, each with an opposite

EVOLUTION OF THE STARS
Drawing on observations from the night sky, this illustration charts the development of our sun, from its birth among the remains of a massive star of a previous generation, and predicts its likely future. The stages in this evolution are not to scale.

6. SUPERNOVA. Eventually the core is hot enough to fuse helium into carbon, which in turn is fused into heavier elements in successive phases. The end is reached when iron has been produced in the core. Thereafter, no more energy can be produced in the core by nuclear fusion, and the middle of the star collapses catastrophically under its own gravity. This collapse releases energy into the outer parts of the star and results in the most violent explosion known in the universe, a supernova. For a short time a single star becomes as bright as a whole galaxy.

5. RED GIANT. After 10 million years all the hydrogen in the core of the star has been exhausted. With no outward-thrusting force to counteract its gravity, the core contracts and heats up. Hydrogen continues to fuse into helium in an outer shell and the star expands to a red giant.

BLACK HOLES: TERMINAL COLLAPSE

Very large stars, more than 15 times the mass of the sun, may not end in the catastrophe of a supernova but will probably collapse in relative quiet. Under the inexorable forces of gravity the dying star will be squeezed into one of the most bizarre forms that matter can assume in the universe — a black hole. As gravity begins to take absolute control, the laws of physics that regulate the rest of the cosmos change dramatically. All possible structures are smashed. The building blocks of matter disintegrate. Even light cannot escape the intense gravitational field. Nothing can emerge from the black hole and, in effect, the matter there has retreated out of the universe. Space and time are bent into a tight circle and eventually crushed to a single point. The universe is full of such black holes. They are inevitable features of a gravity-powered cosmos.

We can, of course, never *see* a black hole, but the matter falling into one releases large amounts of energy, particularly in the form of X-rays. It is this energy source that may lie at the heart of quasars and help to explain how the brightest and most distant objects known, although only a few times bigger than the solar system, can emit more energy than a whole galaxy.

7. AFTER THE EXPLOSION. The supernova sends shock waves and clouds of gas into space. From this gas a new generation of stars will form, enriched with elements from the supernova and, in the case of the sun, surrounded by planets on which life can evolve.

NEUTRON STAR. After the supernova only the central core survives, an object of extraordinary density perhaps only a few miles across. The vast gravitational pressures crush everything into neutrons packed tightly together. This neutron star spins very quickly, up to 30 times a second, and emits strong radio beams, concentrated at the magnetic poles. As they sweep through space like the beams from a lighthouse, they are visible to radio astronomers on earth as pulses. For this reason, neutron stars, when they were first detected in 1967, were called pulsars.

NEUTRON STAR

THE CUTAWAY SUN

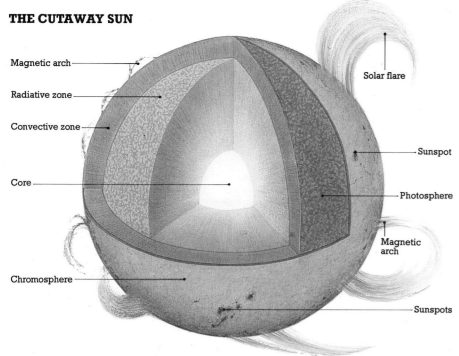

- Magnetic arch
- Radiative zone
- Convective zone
- Core
- Chromosphere
- Solar flare
- Sunspot
- Photosphere
- Magnetic arch
- Sunspots

SOLAR ARCHITECTURE. The distance from the sun's core through its various layered zones to the surface is about 432,500 miles (696,000 km) — 109 times the radius of the earth.

magnetic polarity. The lines of magnetic force emerge at one spot to reenter the surface at the other.

Beyond the surface of the sun, the sun's atmosphere, or chromosphere, is a few thousand miles thick. Here the sun's magnetic field arranges the gases in long "hedges," like the iron filings around a magnet. Above them giant braided arches loop between sunspots — sometimes hanging there for months at a time, sometimes for a few minutes — bursting in flares and prominences up to several hundred thousand miles out into space.

More constant but less dramatic is the faint halo of white light called the corona. In places, particularly above the sun's magnetic poles, gaps appear in the corona and the light glows less intensely. These holes are the sources of the solar wind, a great stream of atomic particles that have escaped the sun's magnetic grip and slipped out into space, bathing the solar system and sweeping past the earth.

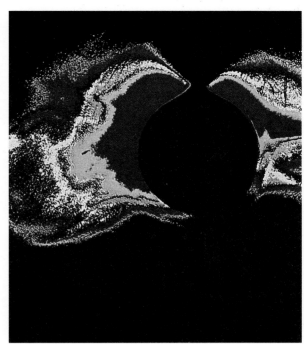

SOLAR DISPLAY. Flaring streamers in the corona may climb more than 400,000 miles (about 640,000 km) above the sun's surface. In this image, taken from the U.S. space station Skylab, gaps in the corona above the sun's poles are clear.

4. MATURITY. Another 50,000 years later the massive star is stable. It has reached a hot maturity in which the outward pressure of the light from the nuclear fusion of hydrogen into helium is counterbalanced by the inward pull of the star's own gravity.

3. NUCLEAR BURNING. After 50,000 years the center of the star has become so hot that nuclear burning begins. The young reddish star churns with massive convection currents, while the outer reaches of the gas cloud are blown off in a hot wind.

2. EMBRYO STAR. The gas in a cloud fragment clumps together under its own gravity. A dense core, the embryo star, begins to form, surrounded by a halo of infalling gas perhaps 60 times more massive than the sun.

1. GAS CLOUD. A cold, dense cloud of gas is struck by an arm of the galaxy, and breaks up into fragments.

8. COLLAPSING CLOUD. During the formation of a star like the sun, one of these cloud fragments may take about a million years to contract to the size of the solar system. As the cloud collapses still further, the release of gravitational energy heats up the core, which begins to glow.

9. SPINNING DISC. A million years later the young sun is twice its present width and about one and a half times its present brightness. Low-grade thermonuclear reactions have begun in the core. The contracting cloud is flattened by rotation into a spinning disc. Dust and gas in the disc begin to coalesce into "planetesimals," or embryo planets.

10. EMBRYO SOLAR SYSTEM. After another 30 million years the sun has reached maturity, almost as it is now but a little darker and a little cooler. In the core the temperature has risen to 10 million °C and the great nuclear furnace, turning hydrogen into helium, has started to burn. The planetesimals have now grown massive enough to sweep up nearly all the surrounding particles, coalescing into the nine planets of the solar system but leaving a debris of asteroids, meteorites, and comets.

11. TODAY. Now, 4.6 billion years after its birth, the sun has become a yellow star, with a temperature in the core of 15 million °C.

12. EXPANDING SUN. In about 4 billion years' time the hydrogen in the core of the sun will be exhausted, leaving almost pure, very dense helium. Hydrogen burning will spread into the outer region of the star — which, as a vast red giant, will expand, engulfing the earth and the inner planets.

13. HELIUM FLASH. In about 5.5 billion years from now, the helium core will become hot and dense enough to burn. This will happen quickly, and the star will flare up in a "helium flash." Helium burning gives the star a new lease on life, but when the helium in the core is exhausted, burning will continue only in the outer shells. The complex processes of nuclear burning in the layered shells of an aged red giant lead to a phase in which the forces of expansion and contraction get out of step. The star may begin to oscillate, alternately shrinking and expanding, and possibly shedding some of its outer layers into space.

14. RING NEBULA. Once the helium in the core is consumed, the core will contract and heat up. It will never become hot enough to burn the heavier elements. The end, therefore, will be gentler than a supernova's: the outermost layers of unused hydrogen will expand into space to form a "ring nebula," leaving a residual core that will become a small but very bright white dwarf star.

15. BLACK DWARF. Eventually the white dwarf, which is no more than a fossil star, will cool down to become a cold, dense black dwarf, no longer radiating energy and invisible to astronomers.

Earth

Mars

Asteroid belt

Mercury

Venus

Sun

Solar System: Empire of the Sun

Some 4.6 billion years ago, a spinning cloud of cosmic dust and gas contracted to form a young star and its retinue of planets. What emerged was the highly ordered structure of the solar system.

The star, our sun, weighs almost 1,000 times as much as the rest of the system put together. Its massive gravitational force guides the nine planets, dozens of satellites and comets, and hundreds of thousands of asteroids — lumps of rock that never coalesced into planets — around the sky. The path of each planet around the sun is determined by a balance between the inward pull of the sun's gravity and the orbital speed of the planet itself, which tends to propel it outward. Planets closer to the sun, where the inward pull is stronger, move faster than those farther out.

The influence of the sun is all-important. As well as controlling the orbital velocities of the planets, it has shaped their characters, so that their chemical composition and mass vary according to their distance from the sun (see CHARACTER ANALYSIS). Despite their subjection to the sun, the individual planets

have their idiosyncracies. Unlike the earth and the other planets that rotate on their axes from west to east, Venus and Uranus spin in the opposite direction. Uranus's axis of rotation is tilted almost into the plane of its orbit.

It is less than 60 years since Pluto, the ninth planet, was located. And there is still speculation over the existence of a tenth planet in our solar system. Some astronomers are convinced that the slight wiggle in the orbits of Uranus and Neptune is caused by the

gravitational pull of a very dim and distant planet beyond Pluto.

It is almost certain that our solar system is not unique. The motion of several nearby stars — including Barnard's Star, 5.9 light-years away — suggests that they may be perturbed by the gravitational force of planetary companions. Astrophysicists reckon that around each of about 20 billion of the stars in our galaxy there is likely to be at least one planet at the right distance for life to emerge.

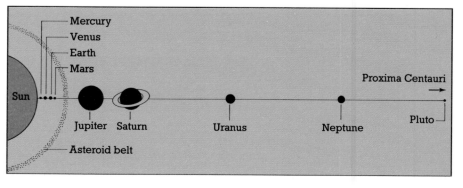

Sun — Mercury — Venus — Earth — Mars — Jupiter — Saturn — Asteroid belt — Uranus — Neptune — Pluto — Proxima Centauri

DISCOVERING DISTANT WORLDS. In this diagram the relative distances of the planets from each other and from the sun are shown to scale. The nearest star, Proxima Centauri, would be 660 yards (600 m) away.

Jupiter

Uranus

Neptune

Pluto

Saturn

Comet

SUBJECTS OF THE SUN

All the planets orbit the sun in the same direction and in more or less the same plane, spinning on their axes as they go. Satellites such as our moon, floating in the plane of its planet's equator, indicate the tilt of its planet's axis. A comet — a ball of dust, water, and rock that has frozen into a dirty iceberg — races in from the outskirts of the solar system. As its eccentric orbit brings it closer to the sun, some of the icy mass is converted into a gaseous tail. In this illustration of the solar system perspective has distorted relative distances, but the relative sizes of the planets are to scale.

CHARACTER ANALYSIS OF THE PLANETS

The chemical composition and other characteristics of the planets are determined by their distances from the sun. In the original chaos of the solar system the heavier elements, such as the metals, condensed and solidified around dust particles at the higher temperatures nearest the sun. For this reason, the inner planets (Mercury, Venus, Earth, and Mars) are denser and more "terrestrial" than those farther out. Lighter elements, such as hydrogen and helium, remained as gases because they condense into a liquid only at temperatures close to absolute zero; they were flung out from the inner regions of the solar system to form the "gaseous" bodies of Jupiter and of Saturn, which is of such low density that it

	Time taken to orbit the sun in earth years	Average orbital velocity in miles/second (km/sec)	Angle between orbit of planet and orbit of earth	Time taken to rotate on axis in earth time	Tilt of axis to perpendicular of orbital plane	Average distance from sun in astronomical units*	Average surface temperature in °C	Density relative to water	Equatorial diameter relative to earth diameter†	Mass relative to earth	Escape velocity in miles/second (km/sec)	Number of known moons	Number of known rings	Date of discovery
Mercury	0.24	29.8 (47.9)	7.00°	58 days 15 hr 36 min	0°?	0.39	+350° (day) −170° (night)	5.4	0.38	0.06	2.64 (4.25)	0	0	These planets are all visible to the naked eye.
Venus	0.62	21.7 (35.0)	3.39°	243 days	178°	0.72	+475°	5.3	0.95	0.82	6.43 (10.36)	0	0	
Earth	1.00	18.5 (29.8)	—	23 hr 56 min	23.45°	1.00	+22°	5.5	1.00	1.00	6.95 (11.18)	1	0	
Mars	1.88	15.0 (24.1)	1.85°	24 hr 37 min	24°	1.52	−23°	3.9	0.53	0.11	3.12 (5.02)	2	0	
Jupiter	11.86	8.1 (13.1)	1.30°	9 hr 55 min	3°	5.20	−123° (at cloud tops)	1.3	11.2	318	37.06 (59.64)	16	1	
Saturn	29.46	6.0 (9.6)	2.49°	10 hr 40 min	27°	9.54	−180° (at cloud tops)	0.7	9.4	95	22.0 (35.41)	17	Extensive system	
Uranus	84.0	4.2 (6.8)	0.77°	16 hr	98°	19.2	−218° (at cloud tops)	1.7	4.1	15	13.3 (21.41)	15	10	1781
Neptune	164.8	3.4 (5.4)	1.77°	18 hr	29°	30.1	−228° (at cloud tops)	1.8	3.9	17	14.61 (23.52)	2	1	1846
Pluto	248	2.9 (4.7)	17.2°	6 days 9 hr	50°?	39.5	−230°?	1.1	0.25	0.002	0.6 (1.0)	1	0	1930

*One astronomical unit is 92,956,000 miles (149,598,000 km). †Earth's diameter is 7,926 miles (12,756 km).

would float on water. The wide orbits of these two planets allowed them to sweep up large quantities of gas, making them massive. This, in turn, increased their escape velocity — the speed needed for an object to escape from the planet's gravity. A great deal of the

matter attracted by Jupiter and Saturn did not become part of those planets themselves but took the form of miniature planetary systems, each a whirlpool of gas that eventually became satellites and rings. One theory contends that, because Jupiter took up so

much gas, the supply for the planets beyond it was reduced. Saturn is smaller than its giant neighbor, and the three outermost planets — Uranus, Neptune, and Pluto — are smaller still, as are their masses, escape velocities, and their retinues of moons and rings.

Partners in Orbit

Less than a century ago, people thought that Venus was a steaming tropical swamp and that Mars was inhabited by creatures intelligent enough to construct canals. They did not even suspect the existence of Pluto. Today such ideas are as dead as the notion that the earth is flat. For, over the past few decades, our knowledge about the earth's neighbors in space has been transformed.

The thousands of photographs of Mercury and Venus transmitted by the U.S. Mariner 10 in 1974 were the first detailed pictures of two planets that previously appeared featureless when viewed through earthbound telescopes. Then, in 1975, the Soviet spacecraft Venera 9 and Venera 10 survived the pressure of Venus's atmosphere to land intact and send back the first photographs of that planet's surface. The unmanned U.S. Vikings 1 and 2 went into orbit around Mars in 1976. Their landers separated from the orbiting craft and touched down safely, enabling a tiny laboratory on board to test soil samples for signs of life. In 1973 and 1974 the U.S. Pioneers 10 and 11 flew past Jupiter — eight times farther from the earth than Mars — on their way to interstellar space. They blazed the trail for the "grand tour" of the U.S. Voyagers. Voyager 1, having flown by Jupiter and Saturn, has already left the plane in which the planets orbit the sun and is journeying through uncharted regions toward the boundary of the solar system. By the end of the 1980's, Voyager 2 will have encountered Jupiter, Saturn, Uranus, and Neptune before heading off toward Sirius, 8.7 light-years from earth.

We owe these achievements to rapid developments in the technology of interplanetary space probes. Atlas Centaur rockets blasted Pioneers 10 and 11 away from earth at 16 times the speed of a rifle bullet. Although this is faster than the earth's escape velocity — the speed needed to escape from the earth's gravity — it would not have been sufficient to enable the Pioneers to escape the sun's gravity and end up between the stars of the galaxy. To accomplish this, scientists used split-second timing to exploit the gravitational effects of the planets themselves. In 1973, Pioneer 10 was the first probe to be dragged along by the gravitational pull of Jupiter and hurled on its journey toward Pluto and interstellar space.

MERCURY

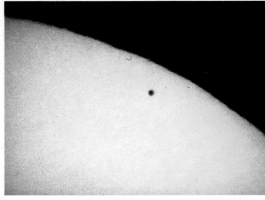

In this photograph the fastest-moving planet in our solar system flits across the face of the sun. Very little was known about Mercury before Mariner 10 made the first of its three fly-bys in 1974. The photographs transmitted back to earth by the spacecraft were pieced together in a giant jigsaw puzzle that revealed a world very similar to our moon. Bombardment by meteorites has scarred the surface, forming craters and hurling up concentric rings of mountains around them. The planet's core has contracted, and the surface has puckered and creased into ridges. Mercury is too small to retain a protective atmosphere. As a result, it is a planet of extremes: scorched by the sun during the day and frozen by night.

VENUS

What may appear in our skies as a beautiful and beguiling object is, on the surface, a scene of desolation: a wasteland of rocks roasted by the highest temperatures of all the planets in the solar system. The early Soviet space probes — Veneras 4, 5, and 6 — were crushed by the intense pressure of the planet's atmosphere (90 times that of the earth) as they attempted to land. Later Veneras, however, were more successful. From them, from Mariner 10 (which flew by on its way to Mercury), and from the U.S. Pioneer Venus (which has been in orbit since 1978) we have learned more about the planet. Venus's atmosphere is composed mostly of carbon dioxide, which traps more heat than it radiates, creating pressure-cooker conditions. Volcanic eruptions belch clouds of sulfur dioxide into the skies.

MARS

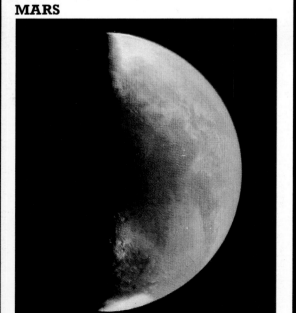

Because of its superficial similarities to the earth, scientists assumed until recently that there might be life on Mars. The length of its day and the tilt of its axis are almost identical to those of the earth; there are even ice caps at its poles. However, exhaustive tests of the rust-red soil and scans of the salmon-pink skies have indicated that the essentials of life are absent: the planet's limited supplies of surface water are frozen; there is very little oxygen; and no ozone layer protects the planet from the sun's ultraviolet radiation.

JUPITER

Of all the planets in our solar system, Jupiter is the one that most nearly became a star. Its mass has attracted at least 16 satellites, such as Io which, in this photograph, floats in front. A vast bulk of gases wreathes the planet in a kaleidoscope of swirling clouds. Voyagers 1 and 2 have also returned spectacular photographs of Jupiter's Great Red Spot, a cloud system three times the size of the earth. Beneath it, hydrogen and helium are so compressed by the force of gravity that they behave like liquid metals in the ocean surrounding Jupiter's rocky core.

Pluto's orbit.

Jupiter.
Pioneer 10 fly-by;
December 4, 1973.

Pioneer 10

Earth.
Viking 1 launch;
August 20, 1975.

Earth.
Voyager 2 launch;
August 20, 1977.

Jupiter.
Pioneer 11 fly-by;
December 3, 1974.

Earth.
Voyager 1 launch;
September 5, 1977.

Earth.
Viking 2 launch;
September 9, 1975.

Venus.
Venera 9 landing;
October 22, 1975.

Earth.
Mariner 10 launch;
November 3, 1973.

PROBING THE PLANETS

In this chart of the solar system, the paths of the interplanetary space probes are plotted against the orbits of the planets themselves. Scientists time the launch of the probe to minimize the distance it will have to travel in order to fly by its moving target.

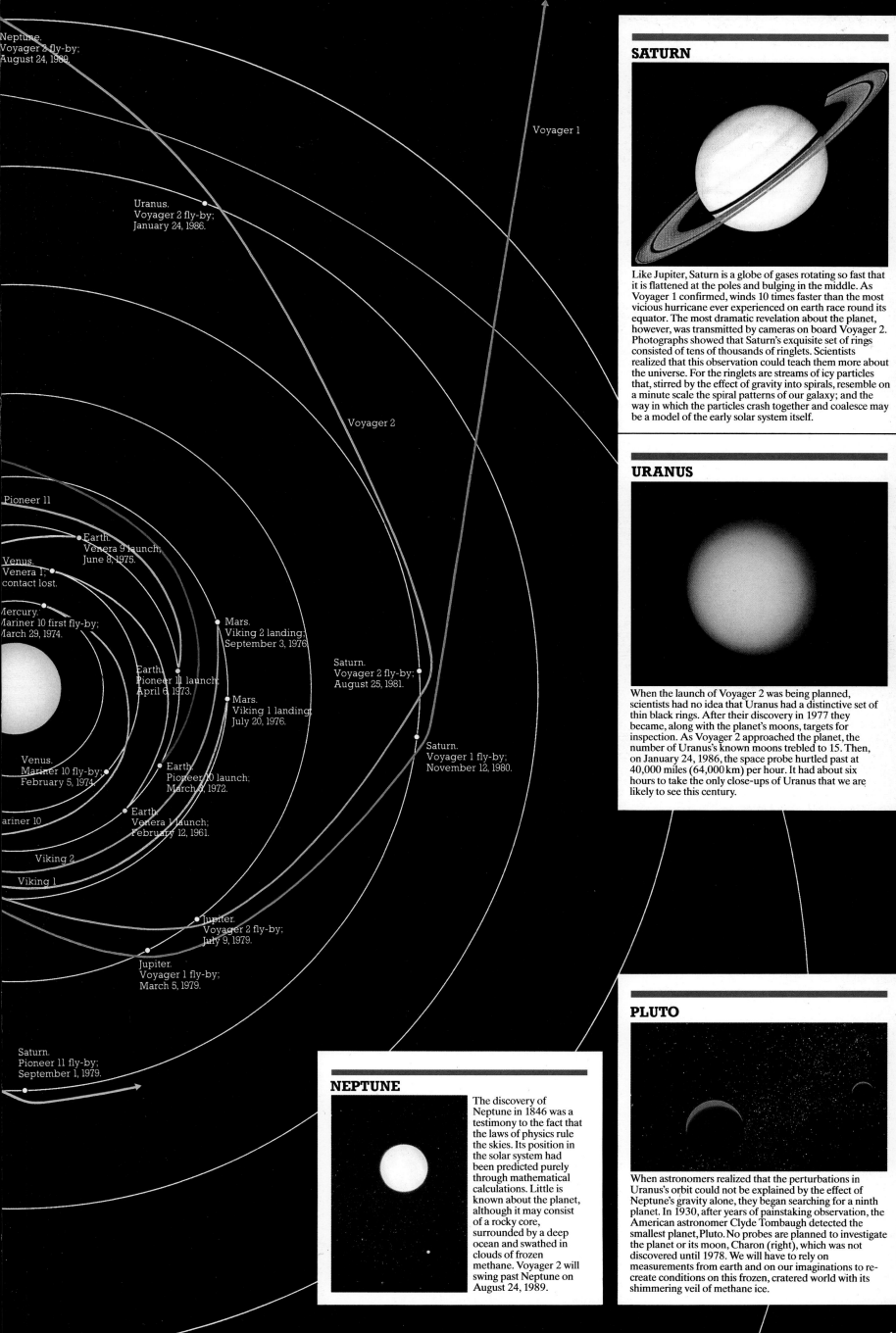

Neptune.
Voyager 2 fly-by;
August 24, 1989.

Voyager 1

Uranus.
Voyager 2 fly-by;
January 24, 1986.

Voyager 2

Pioneer 11

Earth.
Venera 9 launch;
June 8, 1975.

Venus.
Venera 1;
contact lost.

Mercury.
Mariner 10 first fly-by;
March 29, 1974.

Mars.
Viking 2 landing;
September 3, 1976.

Saturn.
Voyager 2 fly-by;
August 25, 1981.

Earth.
Pioneer 11 launch;
April 6, 1973.

Mars.
Viking 1 landing;
July 20, 1976.

Saturn.
Voyager 1 fly-by;
November 12, 1980.

Venus.
Mariner 10 fly-by;
February 5, 1974.

Earth.
Pioneer 10 launch;
March 3, 1972.

Mariner 10

Earth.
Venera 1 launch;
February 12, 1961.

Viking 2

Viking 1

Jupiter.
Voyager 2 fly-by;
July 9, 1979.

Jupiter.
Voyager 1 fly-by;
March 5, 1979.

Saturn.
Pioneer 11 fly-by;
September 1, 1979.

SATURN

Like Jupiter, Saturn is a globe of gases rotating so fast that it is flattened at the poles and bulging in the middle. As Voyager 1 confirmed, winds 10 times faster than the most vicious hurricane ever experienced on earth race round its equator. The most dramatic revelation about the planet, however, was transmitted by cameras on board Voyager 2. Photographs showed that Saturn's exquisite set of rings consisted of tens of thousands of ringlets. Scientists realized that this observation could teach them more about the universe. For the ringlets are streams of icy particles that, stirred by the effect of gravity into spirals, resemble on a minute scale the spiral patterns of our galaxy; and the way in which the particles crash together and coalesce may be a model of the early solar system itself.

URANUS

When the launch of Voyager 2 was being planned, scientists had no idea that Uranus had a distinctive set of thin black rings. After their discovery in 1977 they became, along with the planet's moons, targets for inspection. As Voyager 2 approached the planet, the number of Uranus's known moons trebled to 15. Then, on January 24, 1986, the space probe hurtled past at 40,000 miles (64,000 km) per hour. It had about six hours to take the only close-ups of Uranus that we are likely to see this century.

NEPTUNE

The discovery of Neptune in 1846 was a testimony to the fact that the laws of physics rule the skies. Its position in the solar system had been predicted purely through mathematical calculations. Little is known about the planet, although it may consist of a rocky core, surrounded by a deep ocean and swathed in clouds of frozen methane. Voyager 2 will swing past Neptune on August 24, 1989.

PLUTO

When astronomers realized that the perturbations in Uranus's orbit could not be explained by the effect of Neptune's gravity alone, they began searching for a ninth planet. In 1930, after years of painstaking observation, the American astronomer Clyde Tombaugh detected the smallest planet, Pluto. No probes are planned to investigate the planet or its moon, Charon (right), which was not discovered until 1978. We will have to rely on measurements from earth and on our imaginations to re-create conditions on this frozen, cratered world with its shimmering veil of methane ice.

The Moon: A Fossil Planet

Unlike the earth — a dynamic planet where weather has eroded the shifting surface and erased the record of early history — the moon has hardly changed. Its main features have been fossilized in time. Its gravitational force — only a sixth of that of the earth — is not great enough to grasp or retain an atmosphere. As a result, there is no water, no weather, and no wind.

Until recently three competing theories attempted to explain the origin of the moon, some 4.5 billion years ago. The "fission" theory claimed that the early earth was rotating so fast that a chunk of it broke away and was flung out into space to form the moon — leaving, it was even suggested, a scar on the earth's surface in the form of the Pacific Ocean. The "double planet" theory contended that the twin bodies of earth and moon formed independently from the same primordial cloud of dust and gas. And the "capture" theory proposed that the moon formed elsewhere in the solar system and was pulled into orbit by the earth's gravity as it flew past the earth. None of these theories, however, was confirmed by the Apollo missions of the late 1960's and early 1970's. The Apollo findings showed that the chemical compositions of earth and moon are very different — that, for example, there is little or no iron, water, or sodium on the moon. These discoveries raised more questions than they answered.

Over the past few years a fourth theory, which has been tested by computer simulations, has been gaining strong support from scientists. The "giant impact" theory argues that the moon was created when a planetary body collided with the early earth. In the crush, hot jets of vapor were blasted into space, where they cooled, coalesced, and eventually condensed into a "protomoon." Iron from the two bodies stayed within the earth, and volatile materials, such as water and sodium, simply boiled away.

Soil samples collected by the Apollo astronauts record subsequent phases of the moon's development. The highlands were the first areas to form as the lighter materials in the interior of the molten moon floated like scum to the surface, where they cooled to form a primitive crust. Giant meteorites bombarded the moon, scarring the highlands and blasting out great basins in the surface. Although they are waterless, these basins reminded the early astronomers of oceans, and each of them is still known by the Latin word for sea, *mare*. Between 3.9 and 3.2 billion years ago, lava welled up from the interior of the moon. These volcanic outpourings flooded the basins and filled them with layers of dark basaltic material that then solidified into the gray plains of today. Even after the volcanic activity had died down, meteorites continued to pound and remodel the surface.

MOONS OF THE SOLAR SYSTEM

Our moon, which has often been described as a sister planet to the earth, is just one of more than 50 planetary satellites in the solar system. It is the sixth largest.

All of the planets, with the exception of Mercury and Venus, have moons revolving around them. The investigation of these satellites has been one of the most interesting features of the space probes in the past few years. This collage of recent photographs examines a selection of other moons and compares them with our own.

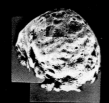

PHOBOS 14 miles (22 km) in diameter. It is shown here in a mosaic of images taken by Viking 1.

DEIMOS 8 miles (13 km) in diameter.

PHOBOS AND DEIMOS The cratered surfaces of Phobos and Deimos are dark gray. Like our own moon, they are dusted with a loose coating of pulverized rock known as the regolith.

OUR MOON. 2,160 miles (3,476 km) in diameter. Since our moon takes the same time to rotate on its axis as it does to orbit the earth, the same hemisphere is always facing earth. With the naked eye it is possible to distinguish the dark, waterless seas, such as the Mare Imbrium, and the bays, such as the Sinus Roris, from the brighter highlands around them.

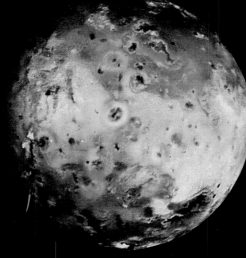

IO. 2,255 miles (3,632 km) in diameter. Although Jupiter's Io was discovered by the Italian astronomer Galileo in 1610, little was known about it until the Voyager fly-bys in 1979. Vividly colored photographs revealed that it is the only body in the solar system, other than the earth, known to be volcanically active today.

WALTZING WITH THE MOON

The moon's gravity causes our planet to wobble slightly in its elliptical path around the sun. In gravitational terms, earth and moon operate as a single mass, whose center of gravity still lies within the earth, but well out from the center. The two bodies weave about each other in their orbit, like partners waltzing around a ballroom.

The moon has no light of its own and shines only by the light it reflects, mostly from the sun. Its phases are simply what we on earth can see of this reflected sunlight at different times during its orbit. When the new moon lies between the earth and the sun, no sunlight falls on the side of the moon facing the earth. It is dark and invisible. As it proceeds along its orbit of the earth, a growing or waxing crescent of reflected sunlight illuminates its eastern edge. At the first quarter, just over a week after the new

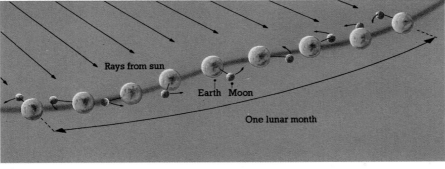

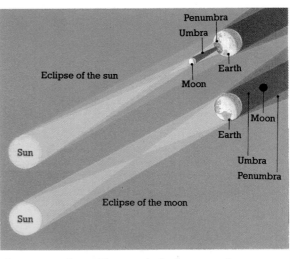

PHASES OF THE MOON. The moon completes one cycle of phases every lunar month, or 29.5 days.

| New moon | Waxing crescent | First quarter | Waxing gibbous | Full moon | Waning gibbous | Last quarter | Waning crescent | New moon |

SHADOWS IN SPACE. The moon's shadow on earth causes a solar eclipse; earth's shadow on the moon a lunar eclipse.

moon, half of the moon's illuminated hemisphere is visible from the earth. This portion waxes, or grows, until the moon's face is fully illuminated. It now begins to wane, going through its phases in reverse. By the end of the lunar month, the moon is back in its original position relative to the earth and the sun.

If, at new moon, the plane of the moon's orbit crosses the plane of the earth's orbit around the sun, the long, cone-shaped shadow cast by the moon plunges an area of the earth into the darkness of a total solar eclipse. However, because both earth and moon are constantly on the move, this phenomenon never lasts longer than seven minutes in any one place. Surrounding areas escape the dark shadow, or umbra, and fall within the moon's lighter shadow, or penumbra, witnessing only a partial eclipse. If, at full moon, the sun, the earth, and the moon are aligned in exactly the same plane, there is a lunar eclipse. As the moon passes through the earth's shadow, it disappears from sight.

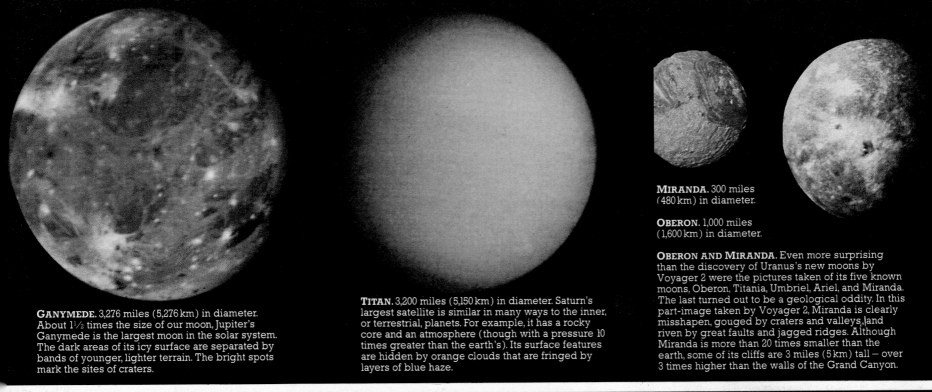

GANYMEDE. 3,276 miles (5,276 km) in diameter. About 1½ times the size of our moon, Jupiter's Ganymede is the largest moon in the solar system. The dark areas of its icy surface are separated by bands of younger, lighter terrain. The bright spots mark the sites of craters.

TITAN. 3,200 miles (5,150 km) in diameter. Saturn's largest satellite is similar in many ways to the inner, or terrestrial, planets. For example, it has a rocky core and an atmosphere (though with a pressure 10 times greater than the earth's). Its surface features are hidden by orange clouds that are fringed by layers of blue haze.

MIRANDA. 300 miles (480 km) in diameter.

OBERON. 1,000 miles (1,600 km) in diameter.

OBERON AND MIRANDA. Even more surprising than the discovery of Uranus's new moons by Voyager 2 were the pictures taken of its five known moons, Oberon, Titania, Umbriel, Ariel, and Miranda. The last turned out to be a geological oddity. In this part-image taken by Voyager 2, Miranda is clearly misshapen, gouged by craters and valleys, and riven by great faults and jagged ridges. Although Miranda is more than 20 times smaller than the earth, some of its cliffs are 3 miles (5 km) tall — over 3 times higher than the walls of the Grand Canyon.

EARTHRISE OVER THE MOON

The earth "rises" above the highlands in this idealized lunar landscape. There is no wind to disturb the layer of shattered rock known as the regolith, and no atmosphere to blunt the shadows cast by the crater walls.

Stages in the making of the moon are recorded by features in the moonscape. The sinuous rille (1) was once a channel of lava meandering downhill; when its roof of congealed crust collapsed, a hollow trench was left behind. Bright streaks of ejected rock radiate from the site of a meteorite impact, forming a ray crater (2). A wrinkle-ridge (3) has formed where the originally molten surface of the moon solidified and puckered. The terraced walls (4) of the large crater enclose a group of peaks (5), probably created by the rebound of rocks ejected during impact. A lunar fault (6) has developed where one block of crust slipped apart from another under the force of gravity. The cinder cones (7) that stand in front of the mountain ranges (8) are the remains of small extinct volcanoes.

The Making of the Earth

We know little about the very earliest days of the earth. During the 4.6 billion years of its existence, the continents have shifted continually, many of the oldest rocks have disintegrated, and rivers have moved whole mountain ranges into the sea. Much of the record has been wiped clean.

Scientists have attempted to reconstruct the way in which the primeval cloud of dust and gas, from which the solar system is formed, evolved into the earth of today. Under the influence of gravity, the original mixture of elements in the churning cauldron of the early earth separated into different layers. Heavy materials sank to the core, lighter materials rose upward, and the lightest of all were expelled as gases

to form the first atmosphere. The conditions that prevailed at certain stages in this evolution are recorded in the rocks that were created at the time. The fossilized remains of living organisms act as markers of the successive ages of geological time.

The interior structure of today's earth is revealed by seismology, the study of shock waves as they pulse through the different layers of the planet: core, mantle, and crust. Other techniques that help us to understand the interior of our planet include drilling into the upper crust, and the study of fragments of the upper mantle and lower crust that are forced to the surface during the great upheavals that produce mountain belts.

4. THE FIRST SPARKS OF LIFE (3.8–2.5 BILLION YEARS AGO).

The gases that billowed out of the hot interior contained water that had been locked up in minerals. These gases cooled and condensed into clouds that blanketed the earth. In massive thunderstorms, rain poured down to fill the early oceans. Lightning discharges from the violent electric storms forged the elements within the primitive atmosphere and ocean into more complex molecules. By now the crust was thick enough in places to withstand the meteorites. The first streams and rivers appeared, eroding the volcanic rocks and laying down sand and mud as the first sedimentary layers on the sea floors. As the rains fell, they washed down the molecules that were to form the basic building blocks of life. The first organisms, blue-green algae, were able to trap the energy from sunlight in a process known as photosynthesis. They used this energy to convert carbon dioxide from the sea water into carbon for food and oxygen, which was then expelled as a waste product.

5. THE AIR THAT WE BREATHE (2.5 BILLION–600 MILLION YEARS AGO).

By 2.5 billion years ago, the crust had strengthened and thickened into mobile belts that resemble the continental crust of today. The continents began to drift, amalgamate, and split on their long wanderings across the surface of the globe. By about 1.9 billion years ago, the oxygen expelled by the primitive organisms began to accumulate in the atmosphere and to replace carbon dioxide as the second most abundant gas, after nitrogen, in the air. Some of this oxygen was converted into a layer of ozone, which screened the earth from the sun's harmful ultraviolet radiation. It made the surface waters safe for the emergence of a more sophisticated form of life.

6. LAYING THE FOUNDATIONS FOR THE MODERN WORLD (600 MILLION YEARS AGO).

What we know about the inner structure of the earth comes from the study of seismic waves created by earthquakes or nuclear explosions. As these waves travel through the earth, their speed and direction are altered by the composition of the materials through which they pass. Gravity has arranged materials of different densities into separate layers, the structure of which has changed little in the past 600 million years.

At the center is the inner core, as big as our moon. It is composed mostly of iron, with temperatures of up to 6,000°C. Next comes the liquid metal outer core, stretching up to about half the radius of the earth. This, in turn, is surrounded by the mantle – a layer of hot rock comprising the bulk of the earth and made up predominantly of silicon, magnesium, iron, aluminum, and oxygen. At a boundary known as the Mohorovičić discontinuity, after the Yugoslav scientist who discovered it, the mantle interfaces with the solid crust. To us, on its surface, nothing seems as solid and substantial as the crust but, compared with the rest of the earth, it is as thin as an eggshell.

Heat from the core provides energy for massive convection cycles, or cells, in the mantle. In each of these, hot but solid rocks rise in some places and sink in others. The cells operate in a region of the mantle called the asthenosphere, between about 60 and 250 miles (100–400 km) beneath the surface, where some of the rocks are partly molten. Magma from the mantle emerges at ocean-floor ridges, driving the lithospheric plates on either side apart. The plates consist of both crust and upper mantle. Over the last 600 million years, these movements have propelled the continental plates across the surface, shaping the geography of the globe today. Where two of the rigid plates collide, one of them sinks back toward the asthenosphere.

Atmosphere

Mantle

Outer core

Inner core

Oceanic crust
Continental crust
Lithosphere
Magma
Asthenosphere

3. THE CRUSTED EARTH
(4.2–3.8 BILLION YEARS AGO).

As the earth started to cool, the molten rock congealed on parts of the surface to form a primitive and brittle crust. Where falling meteorites punctured this crust, magma surged up to the surface and spread out in vast sheets. Seething lava erupted from massive volcanoes and solidified to form the first true continental crust, floating and moving on the denser mantle below.

2. THE MELTING POT
(4.6–4.2 BILLION YEARS AGO).

As the earth's interior compacted under gravity, heat from the radioactive elements within caused it to melt. Iron, being heavier than the elements around it, sank toward the center, where it formed a liquid iron core. Buoyant, lighter materials, such as the silicates, created an outer layer, or mantle, of partially molten rock. The liquid surface belched out hot gases — such as carbon dioxide, nitrogen, and steam — radiating the heat of the interior out into space.

1. THE COLD DAWN OF EARLY EARTH
(4.6 BILLION YEARS AGO).

Along with the other planets, the earth was born some 4.6 billion years ago out of a cloud of gas surrounding the early sun. Particles of dust in this swirling cloud collided and coalesced to create our embryonic world. Because the sun was still too young to radiate large amounts of heat and light into the solar system, the atmosphere was cold and dark. Meteorites constantly bombarded the earth.

RECONSTRUCTING THE EARLY EARTH

Over the past few decades, many geologists have begun to focus their attention on the story of the early earth. The rocks they have uncovered can be seen as a trail of clues, providing circumstantial evidence for stages in the first 4 billion years of the earth's history. As a result, we can begin to construct conditions on earth at various times and even to imagine how the earth might then have looked if seen from space.

MILESTONES IN EARTH HISTORY

Evidence for the formation of the earth's crust comes from the world's oldest known rocks — gneiss (granite that has been twisted under great pressure and heated to great temperatures). Such rocks have been found in Greenland and date from over 3.8 billion years ago (see THE CRUSTED EARTH).

The existence of sedimentary rocks, some 3.8 billion years old in Greenland and some 3.5 billion years old in southern Africa, indicates that the great rains, which weathered the rocks and washed many layers of sediment onto the ocean floors, had begun. Some microorganisms more than 3.5 billion years old, which have been found as fossils in Australia, are our earliest records of plant life. Between 3.5 and 2 billion years ago, their poisonous waste product — oxygen — was absorbed by the iron dissolved in the oceans and formed banded ironstones that are found in rocks of this age on all continents (see THE FIRST SPARKS OF LIFE). As a result, these early cells were not killed off by their own excretions.

Rusted "red beds" of rock, some 2 billion years old, in southern Africa mark the appearance of free oxygen in the atmosphere, as surface materials began to oxidize too.

Fossil evidence from southern California dates the first microorganisms capable of sexual reproduction at around 1.3 billion years, and evidence from Australia dates the first multicellular organisms, such as early sponges, at around 700 million years old.

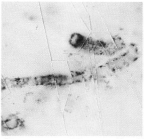 

ANCIENT AND MODERN. Fossil remains, found in Western Australia, of oxygen-producing microorganisms, some 3.5 billion years old (left), are similar to some of the blue-green algae found in Baja California today (right).

ARCHAEAN GNEISS. These 3 billion-year-old outcrops of granitic rock, or gneiss, in west Greenland date from a period in geological history known as the Archaean.

Earth in Space

The earth is the ideal place to live. Its continents and islands, its oceans, lakes, and rivers, support an amazing abundance and variety of life — several million plant and animal species and man himself. How does science account for this richness?

Life as we know it — perhaps the most important criterion being the ability of the organism to reproduce itself — can evolve and flourish only under certain conditions and limitations, and according to a strict sequence of events. Our planet provides the ideal incubator and shelter.

Water is essential to life because it moderates extremes of temperature and transports nutrients to where they are needed. Among the planets of the solar system, only the earth has water available in its three forms: solid, liquid, and vapor. This global interchange system of glacier-ocean-atmosphere maintains a comfortable environment that supports life-forms from the polar bear to the tropical orchid. Earth is close enough to its shepherding star, the sun, to receive warmth, light, and energy, and far enough away not to burn up.

EARTH'S RADIATION SHIELD

The great magnet in the earth's core wraps the planet in a vast curved envelope of magnetic force. This protective cocoon, the magnetosphere, wards off the lethal stream of ionized, or electrically charged, particles blown off the sun.

As the earth and its magnetic field plow through this solar wind, a shock wave builds up in front of them, just like the shock wave that precedes a supersonic jet. The charged particles are slowed down and diverted around the magnetosphere. On the sunward side of the earth, they compress the magnetopause, the boundary of the magnetosphere; but on the other side, they stretch it out in a teardrop-shaped tail up to 500 earth diameters long. Although most particles are deflected around the magnetosphere, some are trapped and concentrated in the two doughnut-shaped rings within, known as the Van Allen radiation belts after the U.S. scientist Dr. J.A. Van Allen, who discovered them.

The solar wind varies in its strength, however. During violent eruptions on the sun's surface, bursts of high-speed particles surge through the solar wind. Some of these may reach the earth within a couple

THE NECESSITIES FOR LIFE

The evolution of earth from cold stellar debris to spinning dynamo and the gradual build-up of a protective atmosphere may be unique in the universe. No other planet in the solar system, at least, shows any sign of life. Only two of the known planetary satellites — Jupiter's Europa and Saturn's Titan — hold any hope of meeting the prerequisites of producing and sustaining life.

Of the four building blocks for life, hydrogen was created in the first second of the universe; carbon, nitrogen, and oxygen were fused in the great nuclear core of a massive star that exploded before our sun was formed. It was the energy of our sun, however, that forged these elements into the complex molecules from which life developed. But, as well as being a giver of life, the sun can also be deadly, and the earth requires protection from its lethal rays.

	Mercury	Venus	Earth	Moon	Mars	Europa	Titan
Structural building blocks, such as carbon, hydrogen, nitrogen, and oxygen.		√	√		√	?	√
A liquid medium, such as water, with a large temperature range for chemical interactions.			√			?	?
An appropriate temperature range to support life-sustaining chemical reactions and to permit bonding and breakdown of molecules.			√			?	
A source of energy to spark life, aid growth, and provide food and warmth.	√	√	√	√	√	√	√
Protection from harmful cosmic radiation.		√	√			?	?

THE EARTH'S JOURNEY THROUGH THE YEAR

The seasons are caused by the fact that the earth's axis is not perpendicular to the plane of its orbit but tilted at an angle of 23.5°. At the summer solstice, the North Pole is tilted toward the sun. The sun's rays hit the Tropic of Cancer (23.5°N) directly, warming the northern hemisphere more than the southern hemisphere. At the winter solstice, the positions are reversed. The South Pole is tilted toward the sun, and the sun's rays are concentrated over the Tropic of Capricorn (23.5°S) and spread more thinly over the northern hemisphere. At the two equinoxes, the earth is tilted neither toward nor away from the sun.

VERNAL EQUINOX
On or around March 21 in the northern hemisphere, the vernal equinox signals the beginning of spring.

LIFE-SUPPORT SYSTEM
Scientists have determined that, within the solar system, the basic life-support zone stretches some 80 million miles (130 million km), with earth near its center. Although Venus is on its inner edge and Mars on its outer, both planets are lifeless.

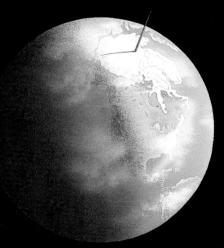

SUMMER SOLSTICE
On or around June 22, the northern hemisphere has its longest day — 24 hours of light at the Arctic Circle — and the southern hemisphere its shortest. In July the earth reaches aphelion, the most distant point from the sun in its elliptical orbit. It is now over 3 million miles (5 million km) farther away than at perihelion, its nearest point, in January. This difference is minute in celestial terms and accounts for a variation in irradiation (light and heat emitted by the sun) of only about 3 percent, keeping the earth's temperature within a stable range.

THE WATER PLANET
To a visitor from outer space, earth would appear to be the only inviting planet in our solar system. Torrid Venus is trapped beneath its cover of oppressive clouds; Mars is a rocky, red desert. Earth, described by the Apollo astronaut James Lovell as a "small oasis in the vastness of space," is the watery planet, retaining water as liquid, solid, and vapor. Almost an entire hemisphere is ocean; the globe is wreathed in clouds; ice covers both poles. With a different geological history, liquid water would never have formed; closer to the sun, it would have blown away; with a different tilt or orbit, it would have frozen.

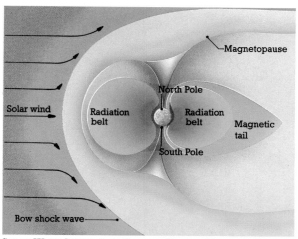

SOLAR WIND SHIELD. A shell, created by earth's magnetic field, protects us from the stream of particles flowing from the sun.

of days and penetrate the shield. They are funneled by the earth's magnetic lines of force down into an oval area surrounding each of the poles. Here, on hitting the top of the atmosphere, they form a curtain of brightly colored lights rippling in the darkness of the night. This brilliant display is known as the aurora borealis in the northern hemisphere and the aurora australis in the southern hemisphere. It is likely that the aurora borealis — or the northern lights, as it is also known — inspired several Biblical descriptions of celestial apparitions, such as the one from the Second Book of Maccabees of "horsemen running in the air in cloth of gold."

NORTHERN LIGHTS. The bands of brightly colored lights in the night sky above Fairbanks, Alaska, are caused by high-speed solar particles entering the earth's upper atmosphere.

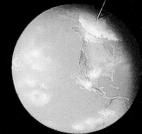

THE AIR PLANET
Gravity clutches the atmosphere — the essential water as well as the air we breathe — to our sphere. Within its protective membrane, an umbrella or "para-sol," known as the ozone layer, absorbs the sun's lethal ultraviolet radiation — the cause, even in its diluted form, of sunburn.

WINTER SOLSTICE
On or around December 22, the northern hemisphere has its shortest day — commonly regarded as the first day of winter — and the southern hemisphere its longest. The ice cap at the North Pole spreads with the increasing cold before beginning to contract once again during the spring and summer.

OUR QUIET STAR
A modest second-generation star, the sun has been stable for some 4.6 billion years — long enough for life-forms to develop and evolve on earth — and will remain so for another 5 billion years. Smaller stars have longer lives (up to 100 billion years) but have too small a mass for an extensive life zone. Massive stars radiate vast amounts of energy and have extensive life zones but burn out in 10 million years at most.

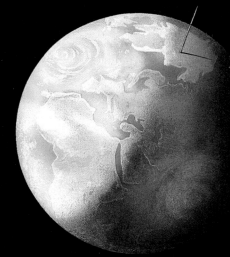

THE EARTH PLANET
The outer planets of our solar system — far enough away from the sun to retain their gases — are, in effect, giant balls of seething gas. By contrast, the inner, or terrestrial, planets are denser than those farther out because their low-density gases were blown away by the solar wind. The density of earth provides a surface that interfaces with its atmosphere — so that, quite literally, our feet can be on the ground and our heads in the clouds.

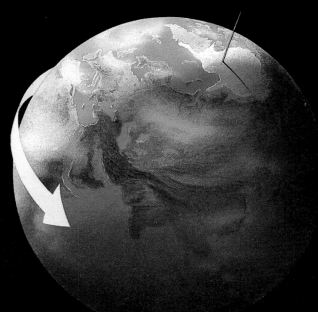

AUTUMNAL EQUINOX
On or around September 22, at the northern autumnal equinox — literally "equal night" in Latin — the sun is directly over the equator. Day equals night in both northern and southern hemispheres.

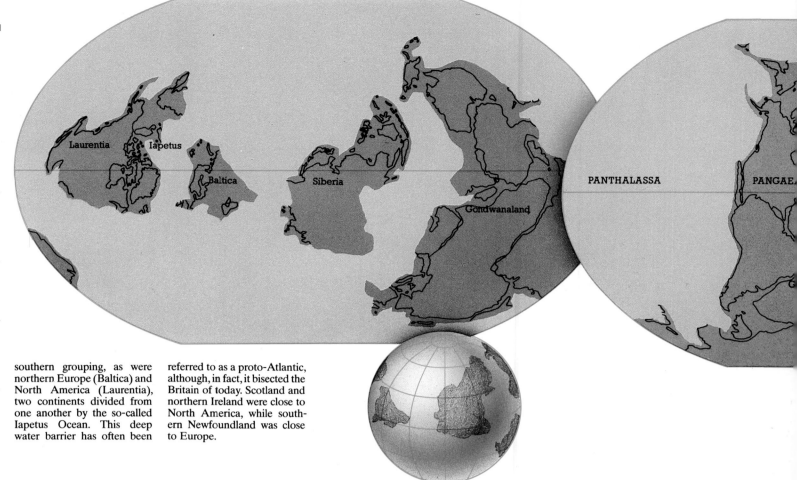

THE JIGSAW TAKES SHAPE (560 MILLION YEARS AGO)

Some 560 million years ago, the continents were barren deserts, arranged in a pattern that seems startling to the modern eye. All of the major land masses are identifiable, although many of them, including Britain, Scandinavia, Siberia, parts of Australia, and much of North America, would have been veiled by seas.

Clustered together in a single continent called Gondwanaland are the future shapes of South America, Africa, southern Europe, Antarctica, and Australasia. Notice India, too, nestling among them — not for hundreds of millions of years will the subcontinent be propelled on a collision course toward Asia. The continental shelves of the different pieces of the puzzle would have slotted together even more snugly than the coastlines themselves.

At this time Asia (Siberia) was entirely detached from the southern grouping, as were northern Europe (Baltica) and North America (Laurentia), two continents divided from one another by the so-called Iapetus Ocean. This deep water barrier has often been referred to as a proto-Atlantic, although, in fact, it bisected the Britain of today. Scotland and northern Ireland were close to North America, while southern Newfoundland was close to Europe.

The Continental Mosaic

Ancient mapmakers may have labeled dry land *terra firma* — "firm earth" — but in reality the land beneath our feet is moving. Mounted on the rocky plates of the earth's outer shell, the continents are adrift, gliding about the globe, driven and lubricated by titanic heat flows in the semi-molten mantle below.

The plates move at speeds which may seem modest enough, rarely exceeding six inches (15 cm) a year. But the results have been dramatic. Over millions of years, plates have collided head on, causing land masses to buckle and form mountain ranges. Earthquakes and volcanoes periodically devastate areas where plates grind past one another.

"Plate tectonics" is the name given to the modern theory of these massive movements. It is a relatively new field of study, which won acceptance only in the 1960's, but it incorporates earlier ideas of a so-called continental drift. You need only glance at a world map to see how neatly the eastern coast of South America might be fitted, jigsawlike, into the west coast of Africa. The English scientist and statesman Sir Francis Bacon noted the "fit" as early as 1620, though he could offer no explanation. The question continued to baffle scientists. Then, in 1912, the German meteorologist Alfred Wegener suggested that all of the present continents had at one time been joined in a single supercontinent. He called it Pangaea, from the Greek for "all lands," and proposed that its two main components — Laurasia (Europe, North America, Greenland, and Asia) and Gondwanaland (South America, Africa, India, Australasia, and Antarctica) — began to drift apart about 200 million years ago.

Since 1912 Wegener's theory, which initially met with derision, has been confirmed by a wealth of evidence. It now forms the basis of our understanding of the continental mosaic and has been used to produce the computer reconstructions and projections on these pages. The hemisphere beside each of the maps records how the world might have looked from space and highlights the main earth-shaping events caused by the drifting continents.

FOSSILS THAT RECORD THE DRIFTING CONTINENTS

Some of the most persuasive evidence for the theory of continental drift comes from the fossil record. Why, for example, should there have been, more than 500 million years ago, two quite separate and distinct communities of shallow-water sea creatures flourishing on the continental shelves of Europe and North America? And why, 400 million years ago, should these communities have mingled, and the differences between them begun to vanish? The most logical explanation is that during the earlier period they were kept apart by some natural barrier, such as deep sea water, but that later the barrier vanished. Following this line of reasoning, scientists believe that, more than 400 million years ago, North America collided with Europe, closing the Iapetus Ocean, so that the communities were able to mix.

Fossils of a plant called Glossopteris, which evolved 280 million years ago and thrived in the cold conditions surrounding the south polar ice cap, have been found in South America, South Africa, India,

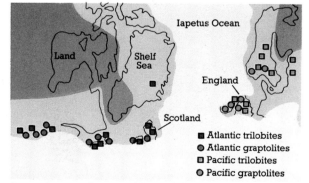

OCEAN BARRIER. Prevented from mixing by the deep waters and strong currents of the Iapetus Ocean, marine organisms such as the trilobites and graptolites evolved into distinct Atlantic and Pacific communities.

- ■ Atlantic trilobites
- ● Atlantic graptolites
- □ Pacific trilobites
- ○ Pacific graptolites

and Australia. Since Glossopteris was a land plant, its fossil distribution strongly implies a former land connection among the four continents at the time of Pangaea.

A similar tale is told by the aquatic reptile, Mesosaurus, remains of which are found in both Brazil and South Africa. As the creature was adapted to swimming only in freshwater shallows, it can hardly have negotiated the full width of the present-day Atlantic. The clear implication is that the Atlantic barrier did not exist 200 million years ago.

MESOSAURUS. The fossil remains of Mesosaurus show a reptile 3 feet (1 m) long, with a narrow head and tail and a mouth crammed with pointed teeth.

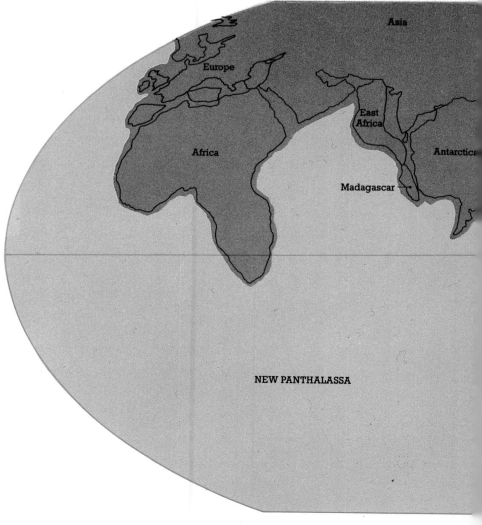

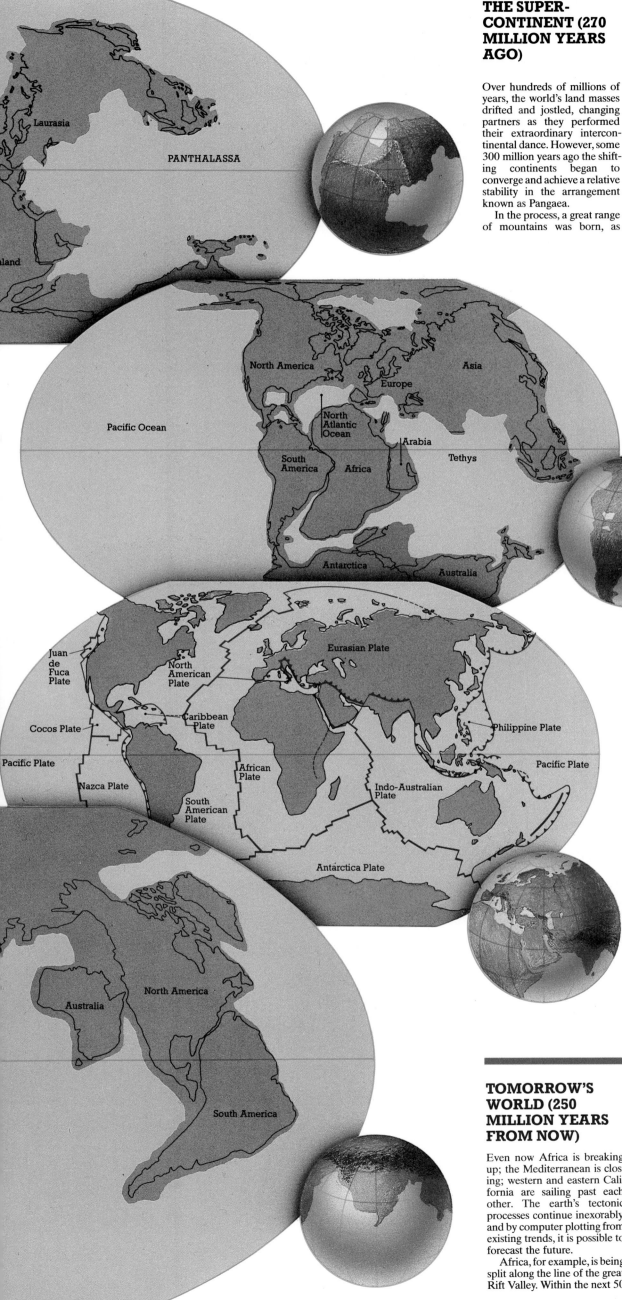

THE SUPER-CONTINENT (270 MILLION YEARS AGO)

Over hundreds of millions of years, the world's land masses drifted and jostled, changing partners as they performed their extraordinary intercontinental dance. However, some 300 million years ago the shifting continents began to converge and achieve a relative stability in the arrangement known as Pangaea.

In the process, a great range of mountains was born, as North America crashed into Europe and the Iapetus Ocean was closed. These mountains stretched down the line of the present North Atlantic Ocean from Spitsbergen, Greenland, and Scandinavia in the northeast, through Newfoundland to the Appalachians in the southwest. Today's Grampian mountains in Scotland, for example, are the eroded remains of part of this chain.

As Europe bumped into Asia, the Ural mountains were pushed up. This chain, which snakes up and down the middle of Eurasia, marks the closure of the ocean that had divided Baltica from Siberia.

The supercontinent created a land connection between all of today's continents. Its existence prevented currents in the world ocean — Panthalassa (from the Greek for "all sea") — from circulating along the equator. Long before the emergence of Pangaea, vegetation had colonized much of the earth. Although an ice cap still covered much of Antarctica, Australasia, India, southern Africa, and South America, there were swamps and temperate forests to the north. Farther north, Europe, North America, and northern Africa were covered by extensive deserts and high plains.

THE BREAKUP (130 MILLION YEARS AGO)

Over the last 200 million years, Pangaea has disintegrated. The process, which began with the westward drift of North America, continued as South America was ripped from the coast of Africa. Among the tectonic dramas that followed, India split off from Antarctica and, mounted on its plate, hurtled north — in geological terms — toward Asia.

At the beginning of this period, the world's major oceans were the Pacific and Tethys, which stretched as a giant seaway from Spain to southeast Asia, separating Europe from Africa. However, the Indian, Atlantic, and Antarctic oceans of today began to form as the rifts that split Pangaea widened. By about 160 million years ago, new ocean floor was being generated beneath the Atlantic. Tethys, on the other hand, was squeezed by the African and Arabian plates as they swung toward southern Europe so that eventually it was closed off and formed the early Mediterranean Sea.

THE CONTINENTS TODAY

Two of the world's greatest mountain-building upheavals have happened within the last 40 million years. The Alps were formed as the African and Eurasian plates collided, and the Himalayas as India slammed into Asia.

The drift of continents continues today. Most scientists acknowledge at least 12 main plates (though some of the boundaries are uncertain) and the plate margins, or meeting points, fall into three main types: constructive, destructive, and conservative.

At constructive margins, plates are moving apart. The sea floor is spreading, allowing semi-molten rock to well up between the two diverging plates. In the mid-Atlantic, Europe and North America are being forced apart at roughly an inch (2 cm) a year.

Destructive margins occur where plates are forced together. When two continental plates collide, giant mountain ranges are thrust up. When an oceanic plate meets a continental plate, part of its load of crust is subducted, or carried down, into the mantle beneath the more buoyant continental crust. When two oceanic plates collide in this way, a volcanic island arc, such as the Marianas Islands in the Pacific, is built by molten rock rising from the subduction zone.

At conservative margins, no new crust is generated or destroyed, but there can be disastrous earthquakes. Plates grind side by side, creating a "transform fault." Most of these "side-slip" faults are to be found at sea, cutting from east to west across the mid-oceanic ridges, but occasionally they appear on land as, for example, in the San Andreas Fault in California.

PLATE BOUNDARIES OF THE WORLD

-----Uncertain   ——Constructive   ▲▲▲ Destructive (Collision)
▲▲▲ Destructive (Subduction)   ——Conservative

TOMORROW'S WORLD (250 MILLION YEARS FROM NOW)

Even now Africa is breaking up; the Mediterranean is closing; western and eastern California are sailing past each other. The earth's tectonic processes continue inexorably, and by computer plotting from existing trends, it is possible to forecast the future.

Africa, for example, is being split along the line of the great Rift Valley. Within the next 50 million years, a long tract may be ripped from its eastern flank to become an immense offshore island. Meanwhile, the main body of Africa will converge with Europe so that the Mediterranean closes, crumples, and is uplifted to form a new mountain range. Elsewhere, Australia is in the process of colliding with Indonesia, adding an extension to the Himalayas so that a chain of mountains might well reach all the way from Spain to southeast Asia. And a sizable portion of California, carrying Los Angeles, will embark from the North American mainland and proceed northward.

This projection is based on the assumption that, as at present, the Atlantic Ocean will continue to widen. However, another long-term prediction proposes that it will start to close up again in about 100 million years, dwindling to such an extent that the Americas are brought back into union with the Old World. By 250 million years from now, it is suggested, another Pangaea will have come into being: a land mass surrounding the residue of the South Atlantic.

Volcanoes and Earthquakes: The Shuddering Earth

On the morning of August 27, 1883, a cataclysmic eruption blew the heart out of Krakatoa, a volcano lying in the Sunda Strait in Indonesia. The fallout of volcanic dust showered an area of 290,000 square miles (750,000 sq km) and caused an ink-black night to engulf much of the neighboring islands of Java and Sumatra. The terrific blast was heard even in central Australia 2,500 miles (4,000 km) away. And for years afterward, fine dust from Krakatoa circulated in the earth's upper atmosphere, diffusing the sun's rays so that extraordinary sunsets were seen as far away as London.

The Krakatoa detonation is just one illustration of the ferocious power pent up beneath the surface of the earth. For some time, people have known that volcanoes and earthquakes tend to occur in clearly defined belts around the world—in particular around the Pacific "Ring of Fire." However, it is only recently, with the theory of plate tectonics, that scientists have begun to understand why the earth shudders and leaks fire in these zones more than in others.

PLANET IN MOTION
Earthquakes and volcanoes are the most spectacular evidence of the great cycle of the earth, creating and destroying the ocean floor at the ragged boundaries of continental plates.

Focus of earthquake

THE RESTLESS EARTH

Deep beneath the surface of the planet, the earth is in motion. Vast, slow convection currents (1), moving through the semi-molten rocks of the mantle (2), are driven by the heat coming from the earth's core. Where these currents rise toward the surface, magma (3), a hot mixture of molten rocks and gases, wells up at a mid-ocean ridge (4) and is expelled in floods of basaltic lava. Older crust (5) is pushed aside, and new oceanic crust is formed at the ridge. The old crust does not move aside easily, and deep

flaws in the crust appear, called transform faults (6), the site of many shallow earthquakes (7).

The oceanic plates (8 and 9) are driven apart by the formation of the new crust. They are relatively rigid and glide along above the rocks of the upper mantle, which flows like hot toffee. Where a plate passes over a constant "hot spot" (10), molten basalt forces its way through to the surface. The lava flows out in sheets and creates a broad-based, gently sloping edifice known as a "shield volcano" (11). The passage of the plate over the hot spot leaves a trail of volcanoes (12), which one by one

become extinct as they are carried away from the source of their heat and power.

Where one oceanic plate meets either another oceanic plate (13) or a continental plate (14), it sinks and is carried down into a subduction zone (15), creating a deep ocean trench (16). As the slab of ocean crust sinks under a continent, a mound of sediment is scraped off to form an "accretionary prism" (17). Sometimes the prism rises above sea level, creating offshore islands from continental debris and slices of material from the ocean floor.

As the crust is pulled down

toward the heat and pressure of the mantle (18), massive earthquakes occur and, on the continent, the layers of the crust are buckled and distorted (19). The rocks of the descending plate, which carry vast amounts of seawater down with them, become partly molten and buoyant with the heat. Magma rises toward the surface, where it erupts, often explosively, in the strato-volcanoes (20) either of an island arc (21) or of the great mountain ranges on the rim of the continents (22).

The cones of these volcanoes, rising around a central vent, consist of layers of hard-

ened lava and fallen tephra, or pulverized rock, that have been generated by repeated eruptions. A turbulent *nuée ardente* (23) — French for "glowing cloud" — sometimes accompanies the eruption. It is an incandescent cloud of gas, ash, and rock fragments. The welded rock formed from the deposits of the cloud is called an ignimbrite.

Behind the active volcanic arc, parallel lines of islands and ridges often extend toward the edge of a continent. They are formed by a process known as "back-arc spreading." The volcanic arc periodically rifts as a result of a small-scale

version of sea floor spreading (24). The volcanoes nearer the continent (25) become extinct as they are pushed farther away from the active zone. The basin formed between the extinct and active volcanoes is known as a "marginal basin" (26).

Earthquakes (27) may occur anywhere above the descending plate. The farther they are from the trench, the deeper their focus. No earthquakes, below depths of 430 miles (700 km), where the temperature is too high and conditions too plastic for any friction to build up.

PATTERNS OF VIOLENCE

Volcanoes are among the great scene-setters of planet earth. They form majestic mountains on land and, beneath the sea, spew forth the fabric of the ocean floor. Volcanic gases are among the constituents of the earth's atmosphere, and volcanic ashes enrich its soil. Nevertheless, it is for their destructive powers that volcanoes are chiefly known. Although no two volcanoes are precisely alike, the most violent eruptions are usually produced by the strato-volcanoes found in island arcs above subduction zones. The explosive mechanism is essentially like that of a champagne bottle popping its cork. A plug of pasty lava stops the vent, so that gases build up under pressure that eventually becomes intolerable.

In trying to forecast eruptions, scientists first study a volcano's history. The existing layers of lava and tephra, for example, give clues to the strength and frequency of past explosions. For more detailed predictions, readings from a seismograph are invaluable: almost all eruptions are preceded by tremors, the earth shuddering as magma forces its way up from below. In fact, by using three seismographs it is possible to pinpoint the focus, or center, of the tremor and thereby locate the rising magma with precision.

As magma wells up from below, it can alter the gravity, magnetization, and electrical resistance of neighboring rock. Instruments can register such changes and so help in forecasting. Other apparatus includes the tiltmeter (to record changes in the slope of the

volcano), and laser-ranging devices (to detect any new swelling or lumps in the cone).

A coming eruption may be suggested also by changes recorded at local hot springs and fumaroles — small vents common in volcanic areas, which give off vapors and gases. Here, rising temperatures and changes in gas content, especially increases in sulfur dioxide and hydrogen sulfide, are warning signs. Finally, scientists may make use of satellites orbiting the globe. Infrared radiation emitted by rising magma is revealed on their scanners.

One of the most thoroughly studied detonations of recent times was the eruption on May 18, 1980, of Mount St. Helens in the Cascade Mountains of Washington State. Lying on the Pacific "Ring of Fire," the volcano had been dormant since

MOUNT ST. HELENS BEFORE. Vulcanologists identified a mile-wide bulge on the north face of the cone as the probable site of eruption. Indeed, they even landed by helicopter on its quivering surface to take their readings.

MOUNT ST. HELENS AFTER. The anticipated cataclysm came on May 18, 1980, when an earthquake shook the bulge loose and it slumped from the summit in a giant landslide. Pulverized rock was hurled 12 miles (20 km) up into the atmosphere.

1857. But from 3.47 p.m. on March 20, 1980, earth tremors were detected by a local seismological station. It was this advance warning that enabled the authorities to impose a 20-mile prohibited zone around the mountain, perhaps saving many lives.

FRONTIERS OF DANGER: HOW AN EARTHQUAKE WORKS

Earthquakes are often experienced, along with volcanoes, at the point where two plates are forced together (see THE RESTLESS EARTH). However, many occur at transform faults, where plates grind and scrape past one another and no upsurge of magma is involved.

If the rocks at the plate boundaries are sufficiently slippery — as schists are, for example — the slabs merely slide past one another in a process known as "creep." Brittle slabs of crust, however, may interlock temporarily through friction. Rock has some elasticity and will tolerate a certain amount of push and pull. But as the pressure of the subterranean forces accumulates, perhaps over hundreds of years, and the strain becomes intolerable, the slabs are ripped apart in one juddering paroxysm. The point of rupture, usually many miles underground, is known as the focus of the earthquake. Above it, at ground level, is the epicenter.

The sudden release of energy sets up shock waves, traveling outward from the focus, that can shake cities to their foundations. Some of the world's greatest cities lie on or near these dangerous faults: Tokyo, Lisbon, San Francisco, among others.

Seismographs measure the amount of energy released on a scale named after C. F. Richter, the U.S. scientist who introduced it. Magnitudes of 0–3 on the Richter scale create no damage and may pass almost unnoticed, while a magnitude exceeding 8 can flatten a city. The great San Francisco earthquake of 1906, in which over 500 people were killed, measured 8.25. Yet here, as elsewhere, it was noticed that the structures built on hard rock survived remarkably well. Those built on soft ground succumbed to catastrophe.

SUDDEN RELEASE. Pressure gradually builds up along a fault until released in one destructive earthquake.

ROAD HAVOC. The overpass to the Golden State Freeway in California collapsed during an earthquake in 1971.

CAN SCIENTISTS PREDICT EARTHQUAKES?

On July 27, 1976, an earthquake devastated Tangshan, an industrial city in northern China, and some 650,000 people were killed. That it struck without warning — despite the

complex seismographic equipment — illustrates the difficulty of predicting earthquakes.

Nevertheless, modest successes have been achieved in interpreting early warning signs. Seismographs sometimes detect small tremors as foreshocks. There are also various instruments which either record telltale changes in land levels and contours or

register the strain that builds up in rock before a rupture.

Some of the most promising research is concentrated on primary, or P, shock waves. These are the fastest seismic waves, traveling by compression and dilation like the bellows of an accordion. (Slower S waves ripple up and down.) Research suggests that the speed at which the rock

transmits P waves changes before an earthquake strikes.

Scientists have also studied the length of time between major earthquake episodes. Violent earthquakes sometimes come in cycles at plate edges, strain building up during long periods of quiet. Where gaps in seismic activity are recorded, there is high potential for catastrophe.

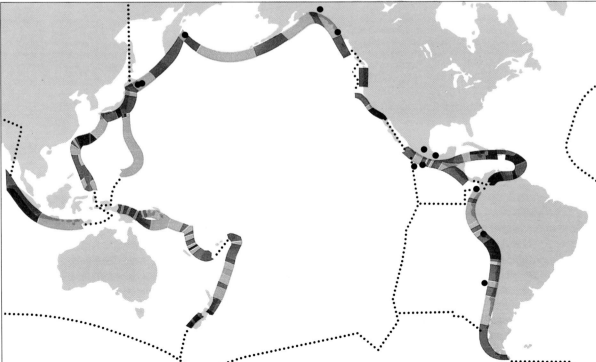

- ••• Plate boundary

- ■ High seismic potential (site of great earthquake over 100 years ago)

- ▨ Medium seismic potential (site of great earthquake between 30 and 100 years ago)

- ■ Low seismic potential (site of great earthquake within past 30 years)

- ▢ Historical record incomplete

- ▢ No historical record

- ● Sites of successful forecasts

GAP MAP. The concept of seismic gaps suggests that large earthquakes are most likely to occur where they have happened 100 years or more ago. High-risk areas include Chile, California, Taiwan, Sumatra, and the Caribbean.

Mountain Building: Forces that Shape the Earth

Mountains are for many people symbols of eternity, soaring toward the heavens as they have done, it seems, since time began. But that sense of timelessness is false. Only a few tens of millions of years ago — not a long span by geological reckoning — the material from which Mount Everest and the sky-raking peaks of the entire Himalayan range are made lay beneath the sea. Trapped in the layers of folded rock which form the Himalayas lie marine fossils, the debris of islands, even slivers of oceanic crust.

In the 19th century geologists had little idea that mountains were created by vast forces within the earth. They reasoned that the earth must be shrinking, and likened its mountain ranges to the wrinkles on the skin of a dried apple. Today the concept has been replaced by the theory of plate tectonics.

Modern earth scientists believe that the Himalayas, the Rockies, and the Alps — indeed all of the world's major mountain ranges — started life at the edges of continents. Heat currents within the earth cause the ocean floor to spread, so that oceanic crust can act like a slow conveyor belt, bringing continents, volcanic chains, and seamounts into collision.

"Orogenesis" is the technical term for the process of mountain building. Although a range starts at a continent's edge, the finished product may end up far inland, either sandwiched between converged land masses or bulwarked from the sea by the gradual buildup, or accretion, of blocks of sedimentary rock. Tens of millions of years elapse before a young range reaches maturity. Nevertheless, the pressure of the moving plates is remorseless — capable of pushing seabeds to the roof of the world.

THE HIMALAYAS – CRASH OF CONTINENTS

When one continent collides with another, the impact tends to throw up a mountain system of great complexity. Some 40 million years ago, India crashed into Asia at the geologically breakneck speed of 4 inches (10 cm) a year. The collision created the Himalayas — mountains welded together by warped and shattered rock, interlocking to form the highest chain on earth.

As the intervening ocean closed up, India slid some 310 miles (500 km) beneath Asia. It then continued to plow northward for another 930 miles (1,500 km), with some parts sliding in sheets over Asia while others were driven sideways along gigantic horizontal, or strike-slip, faults. The resulting folds and overfolds of lay-ered rock account only partly, however, for the double thickening of the earth's crust that is found in the Himalayas. For huge quantities of magma, or molten rock, have welled up beneath the crust, especially under the high plateau of Tibet. This has created surface volcanoes in places.

Sutures, or narrow seams, in the earth's surface have been found in the Himalayas and indicate a vanished ocean. They are often distinguished by sequences of rock, known as ophiolite complexes, that orig-inated in the oceanic crust and were trapped when the conti-nents converged. The rem-nants of island arcs have been found in the Karakoram range, for example. Sutures surround the Transhimalaya area — sug-gesting that it was once an island off India, trapped in the vicelike convergence of the continents.

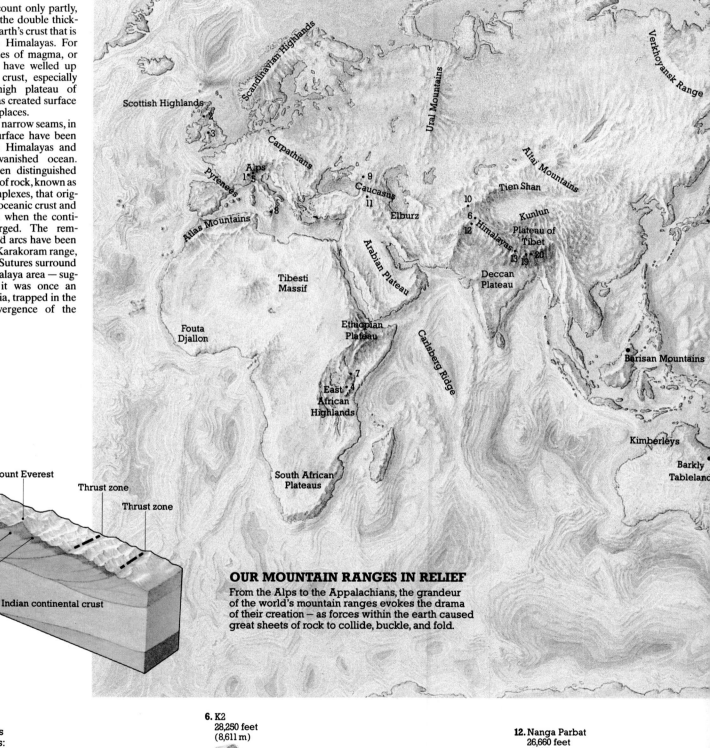

OUR MOUNTAIN RANGES IN RELIEF

From the Alps to the Appalachians, the grandeur of the world's mountain ranges evokes the drama of their creation — as forces within the earth caused great sheets of rock to collide, buckle, and fold.

Block diagram labels: Rising magma · Tibetan Plateau · Transhimalaya · Suture zone · Mount Everest · Thrust zone · Thrust zone · Asian continental crust · Indian continental crust · Layers of folded rock

A PEAK PROFILE OF THE MOUNTAINS OF THE WORLD

This panorama of jagged peaks encompasses the highest mountain in each of the continents: Kilimanjaro in Africa, Mount Elbrus in Europe, Mount Everest in Asia, Mount Cook in Australasia, Mount McKinley in North America, and Aconcagua in South America.

1. Mont Blanc
15,771 feet
(4,807 m)

2. Ben Nevis
4,409 feet
(1,344 m)

3. Mt. Snowdon
3,560 feet
(1,085 m)

4. Kilimanjaro
19,340 feet
(5,895 m)

5. Matterhorn
14,688 feet
(4,477 m)

6. K2
28,250 feet
(8,611 m)

7. Mt. Kenya
17,058 feet
(5,199 m)

8. Etna
10,902 feet
(3,323 m)

9. Mt. Elbrus
18,510 feet
(5,642 m)

10. Communism Peak
24,590 feet
(7,495 m)

11. Mt. Ararat
16,945 feet
(5,165 m)

12. Nanga Parbat
26,660 feet
(8,126 m)

THE COASTAL RANGE – A PATCHWORK QUILT

In the early days of plate tectonics, scientists assumed that the great mountain systems were all formed either by the Andean process of subduction or by the Himalayan-style collision of continents. However, recent studies show that many ranges were formed by another mechanism: the slow accretion, or buildup, of blocks of crust known as terranes.

However diverse it may be in its component parts and origins, a terrane is a single geologic entity. It may be a fragment of crust wrenched from a continent's side; a giant sedimentary fan deposited at the mouth of a river system; a volcanic arc; or a seamount or oceanic plateau.

Tectonic processes are constantly generating such terranes, and the spreading sea floor eventually conveys them to the edges of continents. It packs them against coastlines, compresses them, then shunts in new material so that the first heap of flotsam and jetsam may end up forming a mountain range far inland.

The Coastal Range comprises a patchwork of such terranes, including Stikine, Yukon-Tanana, Cache Creek, Chulitna, and Wrangellia. Scientists believe that Wrangellia was originally a volcanic island arc that emerged just south of the equator some 300 million years ago and traveled 3,700 miles (6,000 km) northward as the Pacific Ocean crust spread. About 90 million years ago it collided with the western coastline of North America. Bits of Wrangellia, broken off by continued faulting, were then carried even farther north. As a result, the terrane was extended and its basalt fragments are now found scattered like the unstrung beads of a necklace from Oregon into the Wrangell mountains of southern Alaska.

Later, more terranes packed the coast, leaving Wrangellia stranded. Terranes are still arriving, further complicating the land's patchwork quilt.

- ▨ Stikine (a volcanic island arc that collided with North America 160 million years ago)
- ▮ Yukon-Tanana (metamorphic rocks that accreted against the edge of North America about 190 million years ago)
- ▨ Wrangellia (an island arc that formed south of the equator 300 million years ago and collided with North America 90 million years ago)
- ▨ Cache Creek (oceanic crust that formed in the western Pacific about 350 million years ago and docked in British Columbia 180 million years ago)
- ▮ Chulitna (oceanic crust that formed as early as 390 million years ago and reached Alaska some 90 million years ago)

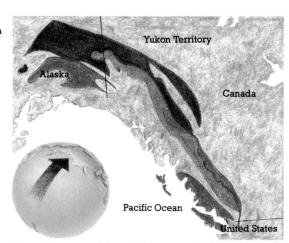

MASS TRANSPORT. Many of the mountains in western North America consist of blocks of crust that have migrated thousands of miles across the Pacific.

THE ANDES – CONTINENTAL OVERRIDE

The mountain chain of the Andes, the longest and second-highest in the world, stretches along the entire western edge of South America. It has emerged as the oceanic crust of the Nazca plate has pushed below the continental crust of the South American plate.

The coming together of these two plates does not fold and heap the layers of rock one on top of the other, as in the case of the Himalayas. Instead, the sea floor dives down beneath the more buoyant continental crust, to be devoured at a deep ocean trench in a process known as subduction.

As the sea floor has been carried down into the asthenosphere, the friction of the sliding plates and the heat and pressure of the earth's interior have caused the rocks to melt. Some of the hot volcanic rock has then risen to the surface, building the chain of volcanoes that fringes the continent. Much of it, however, has come to rest a few miles beneath the surface, where it has solidified in vast subterranean seepages known as batholiths.

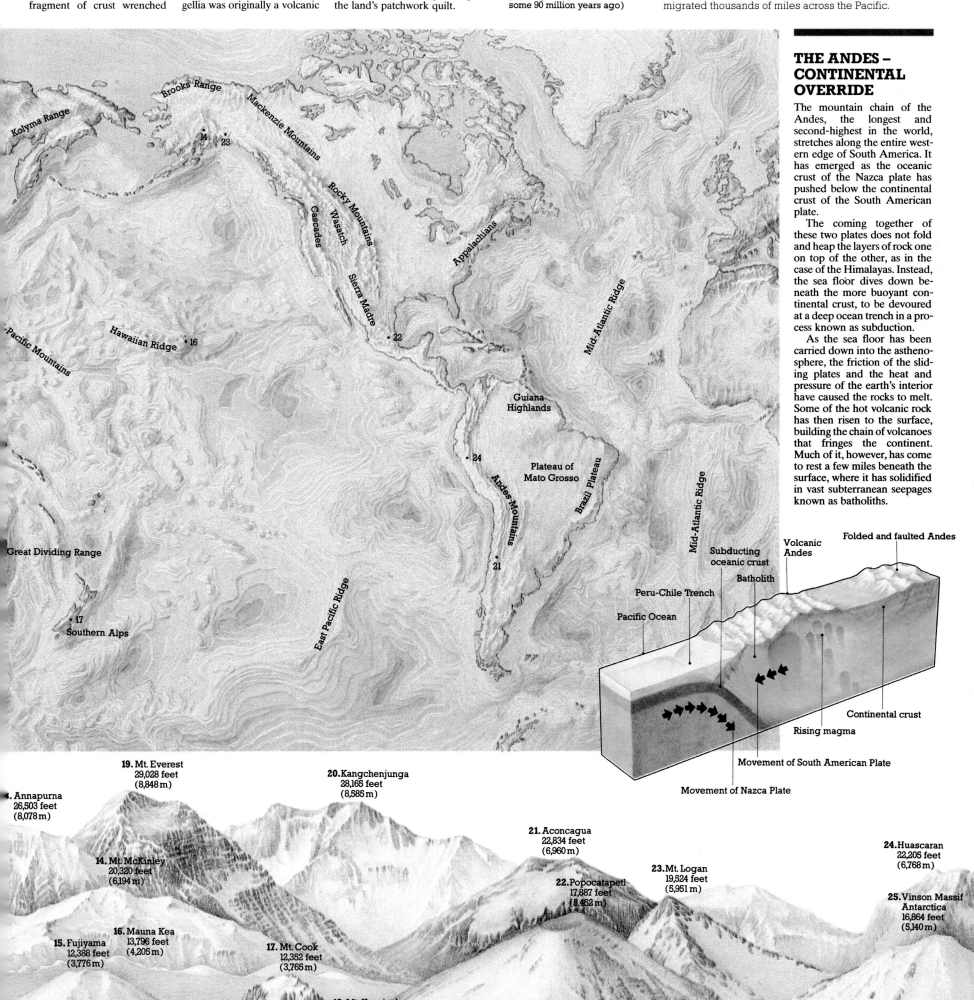

19. Mt. Everest 29,028 feet (8,848 m)

20. Kangchenjunga 28,165 feet (8,585 m)

. Annapurna 26,503 feet (8,078 m)

14. Mt. McKinley 20,320 feet (6,194 m)

21. Aconcagua 22,834 feet (6,960 m)

23. Mt. Logan 19,524 feet (5,951 m)

24. Huascaran 22,205 feet (6,768 m)

22. Popocatapetl 17,887 feet (5,452 m)

15. Fujiyama 12,388 feet (3,776 m)

16. Mauna Kea 13,796 feet (4,205 m)

17. Mt. Cook 12,352 feet (3,765 m)

25. Vinson Massif Antarctica 16,864 feet (5,140 m)

18. Mt. Kosciusko 7,316 feet (2,230 m)

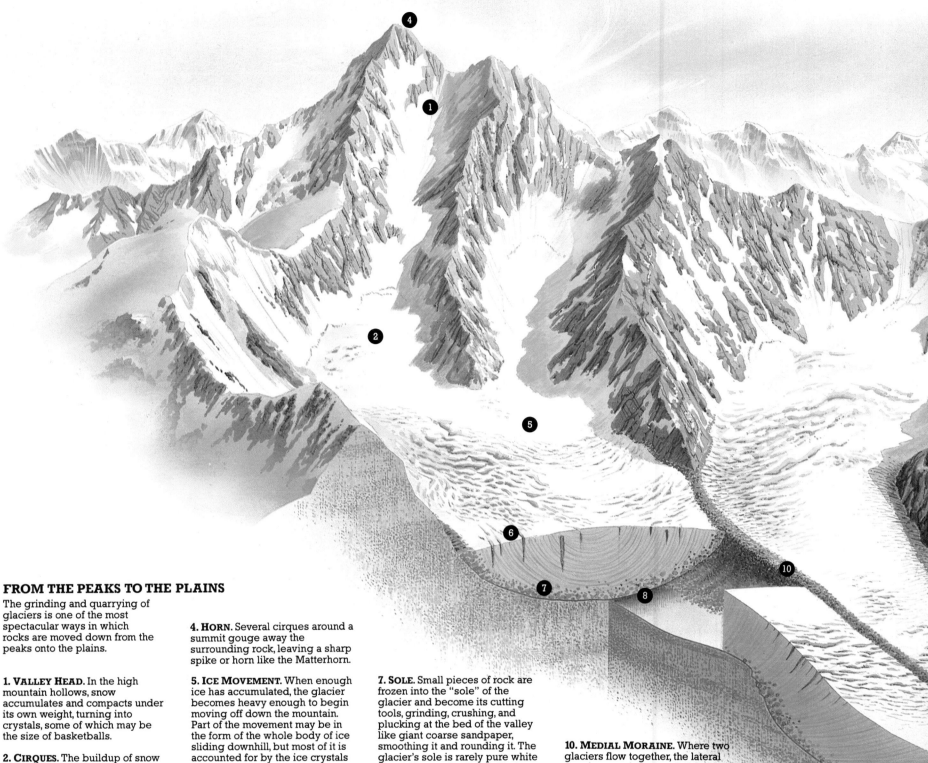

FROM THE PEAKS TO THE PLAINS

The grinding and quarrying of glaciers is one of the most spectacular ways in which rocks are moved down from the peaks onto the plains.

1. VALLEY HEAD. In the high mountain hollows, snow accumulates and compacts under its own weight, turning into crystals, some of which may be the size of basketballs.

2. CIRQUES. The buildup of snow and ice in small bowls on the mountainside leads to the creation of deep, armchair-shaped hollows called cirques. As snow accumulates near the top and melts toward the bottom of the hollow, the whole block of ice becomes unstable and revolves, as if slumping down into the chair, cutting away and deepening the cirque as it does so.

3. ARÊTE. Two cirques on either side of a ridge create a knife edge called an arête.

4. HORN. Several cirques around a summit gouge away the surrounding rock, leaving a sharp spike or horn like the Matterhorn.

5. ICE MOVEMENT. When enough ice has accumulated, the glacier becomes heavy enough to begin moving off down the mountain. Part of the movement may be in the form of the whole body of ice sliding downhill, but most of it is accounted for by the ice crystals slipping over each other as the whole glacier becomes deformed under its own weight.

6. CREVASSES. The fastest flow in the glacier is down the middle. The flanks are slowed by friction against the valley sides. If the flow is fast enough, stretch marks appear on the glacier surface in the form of thin vertical cracks called crevasses. Where the glacier flows over a rock step, the ice breaks up into the beautiful chaos of an ice-fall.

7. SOLE. Small pieces of rock are frozen into the "sole" of the glacier and become its cutting tools, grinding, crushing, and plucking at the bed of the valley like giant coarse sandpaper, smoothing it and rounding it. The glacier's sole is rarely pure white ice and is usually dirty with the material it has collected.

8. WATER LAYER. A thin layer of water, thawed by the vast pressures of the ice above it, may line the sole of the glacier. This lubrication makes it easier for the glacier to flow.

9. LATERAL MORAINES. As the glacier grinds against the walls of the valley, it picks up and carries bands of rock fragments known as lateral moraines.

10. MEDIAL MORAINE. Where two glaciers flow together, the lateral moraines are incorporated in the main glacier as a medial moraine, striping it along the flow line.

11. TRUNCATED SPUR. As the glacier bites downward, turning the valley into a U-shaped trough, it cuts off the spurs that used to project into the valley.

12. HANGING VALLEY. When the glacier melts, it leaves the side valleys hanging above the main valley, with their streams dropping in waterfalls or rapids.

13. GLACIAL MOULIN. A stream of meltwater cuts into the glacier, creating a moulin — a vertical tube that plunges deep into the body of the ice.

Mountain Sculpture: Landscapes of Erosion

Mountains are built by the collision of segments of the earth's crust, some of them carrying entire continents. These segments move across the globe at a rate a little slower than the speed at which a fingernail grows — about an inch a year — traveling distances that are staggering over tens of millions of years. The mountains produced by the titanic collisions of continents are sculpted and eventually ground down by the vast forces of erosion — water, wind, ice, and the sea. Finally, they are moved down, as fine grains of sand and dust, to the ocean floor and the deepest parts of the earth's surface, the ocean trenches.

The mountains now towering above the valleys will all, in time, be leveled. Their memory will be preserved only in the twisted and folded rocks that

are now buried beneath them. The ways in which rocks are broken down range from the spectacular to the insidiously slow. Earthquakes can release devastating masses of unstable rock. Water can seep into cracks, freeze solid, and then lever rocks apart. The burrowing of plant roots and animals can loosen the surface. In the winter, as groundwater freezes and expands, earth particles are raised at right angles to the slope, where, in the springtime thaw, they fall downhill. On almost every slope the surface is creeping downhill in this way — so slowly that only the effect and not the movement itself is visible. Fences on such a creeping hillside tilt toward the valley and the trunks of trees growing there are often bent, recording the struggle between the downhill

creep and the natural inclination of the plant to grow vertically toward the light.

Gravity ensures that one hundred billion tons of rock, eroded from the earth's surface, are carried down each year into the oceans. The combination of four factors — geology, climate, vegetation, and relief — means that in different places the earth's surface is being worn away at vastly different rates. In the high mountains of the Himalayas, where the monsoon is heavy and where the steep slopes allow rock fragments to move quickly downhill, more than 7,500 tons are stripped from each square mile every year. In the Sahara or the Gibson Desert in Australia, on the other hand, virtually nothing is ever removed from the dry, barren flatness.

EROSION IN ACTION

The surface of the earth is constantly being whittled away. The forces of erosion work slowly and with stealth; on average, less than one thousandth of an inch is clipped off a mountain top each year. But the cumulative effect is enormous. As we look around, we see the landscapes of removal.

The great agents of removal are running water and the wind, but before they can get to work the rock itself must be broken up. Several forces achieve this dismantling of the landscape. In high mountains and during ice ages, the daily temperature often fluctuates around freezing. Water that percolates into cracks in the rock alternately freezes by night (when it expands by about 9 percent) and thaws by day, gradually pushing the sides of the crack apart until eventually a slab of the rock splits away. In high mountains, wide aprons of rock fragments can build up at the foot of cliffs from which they have been levered away.

Even in the absence of water, rocks may split with sudden changes in temperature, just as a glass may do when filled with hot water.

On a larger scale, the structure of a whole valley can be wrecked by massive landslides. If large amounts of water percolate into the soil, making it heavier and more mobile, and if that layer rests on top of slippery clay, the whole hillside can slide down into the valley in a few seconds, as if off a shovel. The rock walls of a valley deeply scoured by a glacier can have so much of their foundations removed that the sudden shock of an earthquake can trigger a rockslide of such enormous proportions that the whole mountainside careers down into the valley in a river of rock.

Mildly acid rain dissolves the chemical structure of rocks such as limestone. Great caverns and tunnels are eroded by the water as it percolates through the massif.

Life itself is a vast shaper of the landscape. In an average square mile (2.6 sq km), earthworms penetrating about 4 feet (1.2 m) below the surface can move 6,500 tons of soil a year. Tree roots pushing down in search of water and minerals can lever aside large boulders and even split rocks apart by widening the cracks in them. The burrows of rabbits bring soil and pebbles to the surface, where they can be easily carried away. On the smallest scale, the roots of lichens clinging to the surface of granite, for example, can weave their way between or even through the crystals of the rock, breaking them up and shattering the outer layers of the boulder.

Once the materials of the landscape are broken down, the removal agents begin to take the fragments away. The sheer weight of ice in a glacier can rub away at the valley floor, plucking boulders and scouring rock dust from its bed. Water — the single most important factor in the shaping of landscapes — provides the fluid in which huge tonnages of rock are carried away.

The winds pick up the finest particles, so that breezes are always full of little specks of rock. Only in a dry climate does wind become more significant than water. In deserts, the winds thick with dust particles can act as sandblasters, cutting strange sculptures from the rocks. Here, as in many other places, the underlying geology becomes important. The forces of erosion pick and choose, eating away at soft or broken rocks, but no more than nibbling at the harder ones.

SHERMAN GLACIER. An earthquake in Alaska in 1964 triggered a massive rockslide down the Sherman Glacier.

WAVE ROCK. Winds, water, and the passage of time have sculpted the 50 feet (15 m) high Wave Rock in southwest Australia.

DELICATE ARCH. The weather has eaten away at soft layers in the sandstone in the Arches National Park, Utah, leaving the harder rock as a graceful arch.

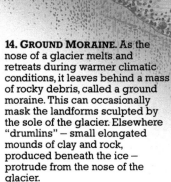

14. GROUND MORAINE. As the nose of a glacier melts and retreats during warmer climatic conditions, it leaves behind a mass of rocky debris, called a ground moraine. This can occasionally mask the landforms sculpted by the sole of the glacier. Elsewhere "drumlins" — small elongated mounds of clay and rock, produced beneath the ice — protrude from the nose of the glacier.

15. GLACIAL ERRATICS. Stones and boulders of all sizes, known as glacial erratics, which were plucked from the mountain and can be the size of a truck or a house, stand about on the glacial plain as evidence of the glacier's extraordinary power.

16. END MORAINE. At the nose or snout of the glacier, the rock it has cut from the valley is dropped by the melting ice in a long ridge across the valley called an end moraine.

17. ROCK FLOUR. At the melting nose of a glacier, "rock flour" — the tiny fragments it has rubbed away from the mountain — is carried away in the milky waters of a glacial stream.

Rivers and Lakes

Earth is the water planet, seven-tenths submerged or covered by ice. Our heads are wreathed in a thin veil of water vapor. The ground beneath our feet is continuously worn away by the flow of running water. And our lakes provide us with some of the planet's most breathtaking sites of natural beauty and most of the fresh water we use.

Gravity pulls a river downhill, giving it the power to carry a vast cargo of rock particles that have been rubbed and flaked away from the mountains by the weather. Although only 0.0001 percent of the earth's water is in its rivers, running water has a monumental

effect on the landscape. Wherever a stream encounters weakness in the land through which it passes, it cuts wide valleys, and through harder rocks it scours narrow gorges as it works its way to the sea. The river collects more material along the way, carrying it downstream in a process that constantly reshapes the landscape. But, even though rivers have the power to move mountains to the sea, earth movements cause new hills to rise up. New rivers are born and old rivers are rejuvenated. The life cycle of the landscape — a ceaseless renewal — begins again.

The rivers of the world are like great conveyor

belts, emptying over a billion cubic feet of fresh water into the oceans every second. One day's discharge from the Amazon alone, which accounts for 20 percent of the total, could supply New York with water for nine years. The weathered remains of mountain ranges are swept along by rivers, in the form of more than 10 billion tons of sediment a year. Of this, about 40 percent is discharged by the Huang He, Yangtze, Irrawaddy, Mekong, Ganges, and Indus. These six rivers rise on the rooftop of the world in the icy wastes of the Himalayas and Tibet — an area that accounts for only 4 percent of the earth's land surface.

FROM MOUNTAINS TO THE SEA
Born in the mountain snows, this idealized river runs through the varied phases of its life — from its youth in the peaks to full maturity in the valley below.

WHERE THE WATER IS

The heat of the sun evaporates water from the earth's surface into the atmosphere — a giant mixing system that recycles some 124,000 cubic miles (516,000 cu km) of water a year back to sea and land as rain or snow. Of this, about 25,000 cubic miles (104,000 cu km) falls on the land to flow as rivers toward the sea. Only 0.6 percent of the earth's water is liquid fresh, and at any one time a mere fraction of that is in its rivers and lakes. The remainder is groundwater — rain that has sunk underground and is either tapped for wells or issues as springs.

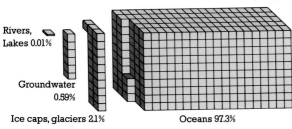

Rivers,
Lakes 0.01%

Groundwater
0.59%

Ice caps, glaciers 2.1%   Oceans 97.3%

LIQUID ASSETS. Most of the world's water is in the oceans. A small proportion is bound up in ice sheets and glaciers, while a tiny fraction — about 1/10,000 — exists in rivers and lakes.

THE LIFE OF A RIVER

The course of a river, from its first gurgle at the source to the mingling of its waters with the sea, has often been likened to a life story. During its youth in the mountains, the river plunges over waterfalls, cuts abrasively through gorges, and careers along rapids, carving its course through the landscape. By maturity, it has smoothed a path for itself; its gradient is less steep and its course more sinuous. Fed by tributaries, the river continues to expand. As it sways from side to side, the course of its meanderings cuts away at the high ground con-straining it, widening the valley and smoothing out a broad flood plain. Downstream of the early meanderings, the river continues to rework the landscape. In its lowland course, its "old age," it is still vigorous enough both to eat away at one part of the land and to build up another. Sand bars and oxbow lakes are left stranded by its shifting over time. But these are only temporary consequences of the river's constant search for an equilibrium — a course that in its steady gradient, its rounded channel, and the smoothness of its bed provides the least resistance in its long and varied journey to the sea.

1. RAINFALL AND RUNOFF. Rainwater that is not immediately evaporated into the atmosphere from vegetation reaches the ground. Some soaks into the soil to form reserves of groundwater beneath the surface. The rest, the runoff, flows toward a stream.

2. HEADWATERS. At the valley head, the runoff converges with groundwater that has seeped back to the surface in springs to make a stream.

3. WATERFALL. The river tumbles over the hard, rocky lip of a waterfall, eroding the softer rock downstream and cutting a narrow V-shaped valley below it. Eventually the back-splash of the falling water, armed with pebbles, undermines the cliff face. The overhang above collapses, and the lip of the waterfall retreats upstream.

4. RAPIDS. Streams proceed in fits and starts according to the amount of resistance they meet from the rocks over which they flow. Sometimes the erosion by a river is slowed down in one section by resistant rock, while downstream the rock is softer and more easily eroded. A rapid drop develops at the boundary between the two types of rock. Eventually erosion smooths away the rapids and the flow evens.

5. GORGE. Hard particles of sand and gravel, carried by the river from above, bombard the bedrock and banks, cutting a steep-sided gorge below the waterfall.

6. DAMMED BASIN. Man can harness the energy of a stream, as it drops under gravity from the mountains, by constructing a dam across a valley.

7. ALLUVIAL FAN. A tributary emerging from a steep hill-valley into a sloping plain slows down and deposits its load of sediment, or alluvium, in the shape of a fan. The heavier materials settle at the valley mouth; finer ones are carried farther out.

8. FLOOD PLAIN. The flood plain is new, often fertile land built of sand, silt, and clay laid down by the river. It is continuously reshaped by flooding and by changes in the river's course.

9. WETLANDS. The lowest-lying parts of a coastal flood plain — if unprotected by sea walls or embankments — can be swamped both by high tides and by floods.

10. TRIBUTARIES. The river is fed by the streams that pour into it. The extra volume of water cuts a wider and deeper channel and the flow of water in the main river speeds up.

11. SAND BAR. As the river rounds the inside of a bend, it drops its load of sand and gravel. These materials settle to form sand bars, which are left as crescent-shaped banks in midstream as the river shifts to follow a course of least resistance.

12. OXBOW LAKE. The course of the river changes over time. This oxbow lake was once the loop of a meander that has now been bypassed by a short cut in the river's route.

13. TERRACES. Benches, or terraces, cut in the rock may be the legacy of a time when the land mass was lower relative to the sea. Near the mouth of the river, these terraces may be the remains of an earlier shore, when the sea level was higher.

HOW THE EARTH WORKS TO SHAPE ITS LAKES

You can often learn the story of a lake's origins by looking at its shape. For a lake is, quite simply, a body of standing water that has collected in a depression or basin in the land. Such depressions have been formed by one or more of a variety of earth forces.

Very deep lakes, for example, may have been created by tectonic upheavals — when huge blocks in the earth's crust sank. Round, high-rimmed craters may have formed when a volcano blew its top or collapsed. Slender, finger-shaped lakes may be the remains of glacial valleys. And crescent-shaped lakes in the lower reaches of a river are usually the result of more recent changes in a river's course.

But none of these freshwater bodies is permanent. As the land formed them, so can it eradicate them. Rivers work both to drain lakes and to fill them with mud. Plant growth may entirely choke them or they may disappear in a drought.

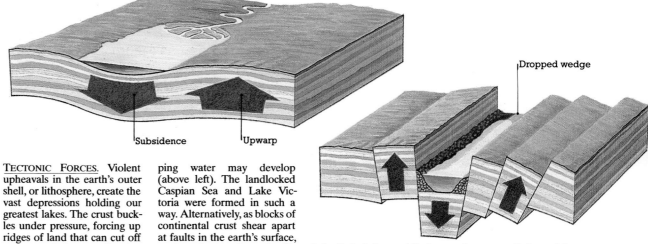

Subsidence   Upwarp

Dropped wedge

TECTONIC FORCES. Violent upheavals in the earth's outer shell, or lithosphere, create the vast depressions holding our greatest lakes. The crust buckles under pressure, forcing up ridges of land that can cut off an arm of the sea. Sagging between two ridges, a subsidence basin capable of trap-ping water may develop (above left). The landlocked Caspian Sea and Lake Victoria were formed in such a way. Alternatively, as blocks of continental crust shear apart at faults in the earth's surface, wedges drop to form the fissures that hold our deepest and oldest lakes (above right).

Lake Baikal, the world's deepest lake, Lake Tanganyika, the second deepest, and the Dead Sea were all formed by massive earth movements more than 20 million years ago.

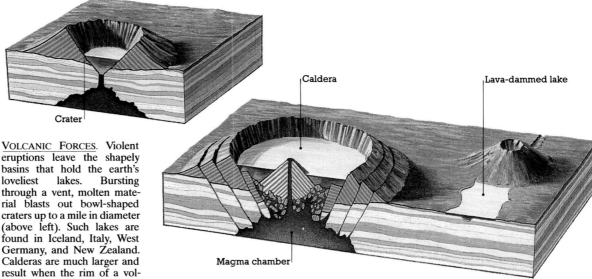

Crater

Caldera   Lava-dammed lake

Magma chamber

VOLCANIC FORCES. Violent eruptions leave the shapely basins that hold the earth's loveliest lakes. Bursting through a vent, molten material blasts out bowl-shaped craters up to a mile in diameter (above left). Such lakes are found in Iceland, Italy, West Germany, and New Zealand. Calderas are much larger and result when the rim of a volcano collapses into the vacant magma chamber below. In rampages of destruction, mud and ice-covered crater lakes break through their rims or are blown out by new eruptions (above right). Crater Lake in the United States and Lake Toba in Indonesia were created in this way when enormous volcanoes collapsed. Outpourings of volcanic material can block river valleys with lava dams; Lake Kivu on an arm of the African Rift Valley was formed in this way.

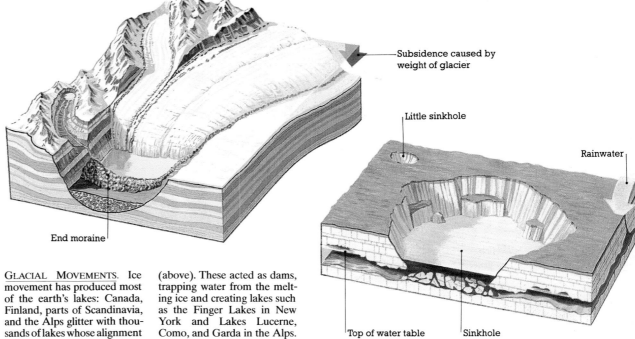

Subsidence caused by weight of glacier

Little sinkhole

Rainwater

End moraine

Top of water table   Sinkhole

GLACIAL MOVEMENTS. Ice movement has produced most of the earth's lakes: Canada, Finland, parts of Scandinavia, and the Alps glitter with thousands of lakes whose alignment often indicates the direction of the ice flow. During an ice age in areas of high latitude, depths of up to three miles (5 km) of ice depressed the crust. As the glaciers advanced and then retreated, the ice, sharp with rock particles, scoured the valley floors, gouged pockets from between jagged peaks, and deposited mounds of rocky debris called moraines (above). These acted as dams, trapping water from the melting ice and creating lakes such as the Finger Lakes in New York and Lakes Lucerne, Como, and Garda in the Alps. The five Great Lakes of North America were created in a similar way, after the final retreat of the glaciers which began about 15,000 years ago. The Baltic Sea emerged too at the end of the last ice age, as the Scandinavian ice sheet, which had once covered most of northern Europe, melted and retreated north toward the Arctic regions.

OTHER FORCES. Silt deposited by a river, or rockfalls on its banks, can block the outlet from a basin and thus cut off a tributary stream. The same forces can pinch off a loop in a river to form an oxbow lake. In addition, the acids contained in water can dissolve passages and caves in soluble rocks, such as limestone. When the roof of the cave collapses, sinkholes form and can fill with water. Such underground lakes are found in Yugoslavia and in the Yucatán Peninsula of Mexico.

Rocks: Recording the History of the Earth

Every rock is a picture of a forgotten landscape, preserving the memory of the time in which it was made: a sandstone ridge may be the remains of an ancient desert; a coal mine may cut into the great thickness of dead plants from a 300-million-year-old swamp; a limestone massif is, perhaps, the uplifted and eroded remains of the sort of seabed now to be found in the Red Sea.

The variety of rocks on earth is bewildering at first, but each conforms to one of three basic types — igneous, sedimentary, and metamorphic — depending on the way it was formed.

Igneous rocks all began as hot fluid, or magma, that rose from the earth's interior. Their name means "formed by fire," and they vary from granites, which solidify deep underground, to basalts, the hardened remains of surface lava flows. Sedimentary rocks (meaning "rocks that have settled") are formed from beds of small particles that have collected on flood plains, in river deltas, and on the sea floor. Metamorphic rocks ("those whose form has changed") are produced when rocks already in existence are subjected to heat and pressure. Mountain building can squeeze and weld existing rock beds so that they change completely in character. Marble, for example, is metamorphosed limestone, and slate is the product of heavily stressed mudstone.

IGNEOUS ROCKS: BORN IN FIRE

The hummocky surface of a granite moorland, such as Dartmoor in southwest England, began life as a large reservoir of hot, buoyant, and partly molten rock. This magma pushed its way upward from deep underneath a range of mountains as it formed a few hundred million years ago. Erosion has stripped away most of the overlying rocks to reveal the hard, crystalline granite underneath. In one part, the roof of the magma chamber has survived as a "roof pendant" of rock, metamorphosed by the heat and pressure of the rising magma. The moorland is dotted with "tors," small towers of exposed rock. Here, the weather has eaten away at the pattern of cracks and joints in the granite that were created as the original molten mass cooled and shrank. At one edge of the moor, the weathering of the granite has been so severe that its structure has rotted away. The sands and clays that result have been mined for kaolin or china clay, the mineral used in the making of paper, porcelain, toothpaste, and many other products. Mountains of white waste smother the landscape.

Magma that erupts from volcanoes as lava cools into rocks such as basalt. It is often highly resistant to erosion and

BURIED TREASURE. A diamond lies embedded in kimberlite.

HIDDEN PRESSURE. Deep beneath the Chilean Andes, magma — granite in the making — thrusts upward.

can stand out in the most dramatic forms. The solidified neck of a volcano stands up as a ragged tower long after the surrounding cone of ashes has been washed or blown away. A flow of lava that once ran down a valley will survive as a long ridge well after the valley walls that once shaped it have been eroded into valleys themselves.

One of the rarest of volcanic effects is the production of diamonds. These gems are produced only under enormous pressures and in great heat, 90 miles (145 km) down in the earth's mantle. Volcanic pipes force the diamond-bearing kimberlite up from there.

ROCK FOUNTAIN. Lava, pouring from Kilauea, Hawaii, will eventually cool into solid basalt.

1. GRANITE MOORLAND. A dome of molten magma has become a solid mass of granite.

2. GRANITE TOR. Erosion has shaped the granite into notched and isolated tors.

3. ROOF PENDANT. Part of the original roof of the magma chamber survives as a metmorphosed block.

4. CHINA CLAY QUARRY. Where the granite has rotted, it has been quarried for china clay.

5. CHINA CLAY WASTE. White mounds of sand are the leftovers from the quarrying process.

6. METAMORPHIC AUREOLE. Immediately next to the granite, the rock has been baked into dark hornfels.

7. COPPER MINE. A large copper ore body has been exploited by open-cast mining.

8. VOLCANIC DIKE. Lava pushing up through weaknesses in the rock now stands out in basalt dikes.

9. METAMORPHOSED BELT. The heat and pressure of mountain building in the distant past has contorted these layers into metamorphic rocks.

10. MARBLE QUARRY. Vast, square-edged cuts have been made into a marble mountain.

METAMORPHIC ROCKS: CONTORTED BANDS IN THE EARTH'S CRUST

Surrounding the block of granite is a wide strip of rocks that have been metamorphosed by heat and pressure. In this metamorphic "aureole," or halo, the rocks nearest the granite have been severely altered into hard hornfels, baked by contact with the mass of molten rock intruding into them. At the outer edge of the metamorphosed belt is a block of marble that is the product of limestone when it has been subjected to heat and pressure. The original sedimentary layering of the rock has been

transformed into a dense crystalline structure that, when quarried, can take finely detailed carving and a high polish. Under equivalent conditions, sedimentary mudstone behaves differently, turning into slate that can be quarried and split into fine sheets.

Shot through the metamorphic belt are a series of volcanic dikes. Here, molten magma has been pressed out through cracks in the surrounding rocks and solidified in place. This volcanic rock is often harder than the rock around it. When erosion gets to work, the dikes are left standing as narrow ridges running many miles across the landscape.

As the magma rises, hot liquids penetrate into any cracks and weakness they can find. These liquids carry metals

that have been washed out both from the magma itself and from the surrounding rocks. When they cool, they solidify as ores and vein-filling metallic minerals. Concentrations of ores formed in this way are often rich in metals and gemstones, which can be mined. The valuable deposits usually make up only 10 percent or even less of the ore. Vast quantities of rock have to be removed to recover the minerals, leaving deep pits and slag heaps that scar the surface.

MINERAL CACHE. Hot liquids carrying copper and iron solidified as crystals deep underground in Tasmania.

PRECIOUS LOAD. Emeralds, made green by tiny amounts of chromium, lie partly buried in a vein of quartz.

SEDIMENTARY ROCKS: THE LAYING DOWN OF THE LANDSCAPE

The minerals of which rocks are made are constantly being recycled by gravity, the weather, plants, and animals — all of which have an effect on the earth's surface. The great thicknesses of sediment that build up both on the land and in the oceans are, in a sense, the sump for many of these processes, the settled resting place for vast quantities of rock.

In warm, shallow seas on the continental shelves the tropical sun evaporates vast amounts of water from the surface. The calcium carbonate dissolved in the sea is precipitated into crystals, which collect on the sea floor. Over millions of years this process, together with the accumulation of the shells of dead animals, can build limestones that are thousands of feet thick. Coral reefs that had grown on the sea floor are often found in the rock.

When the sea floor is raised by the collision of continents into high mountain ranges, the percolation of rainwater through the limestone can set this process into reverse. Where the removal of water by the sun had created the rock in the first place, the addition of water now starts to eat it away, dissolving channels and caverns along the beds and faults in the rock.

Chalk is a rather soft form of limestone, which crumbles easily and produces the rounded and well-drained landscapes of downland. Unlike many mountain limestones, it is made up from the minute skeletons of algae, known as coccoliths. In a slow and steady underwater snowfall, they can build up in thick drifts over tens of millions of years, both in shelf waters and in the deep ocean.

Sandstones can originate in deserts, rivers, and deltas, in the waters of the continental shelves, and on the deep ocean floor. Shifting currents, either of the winds or of the waters, can leave their mark on the rock in the form of cross-bedding. Tens of millions of years after the wind blew or the current drifted, the layers of quartz grains in the sand remain quite visibly piled up in the once-prevailing direction of the wind or water current.

In the widespread swamps of about 300 million years ago, most of the great coal seams of the world were laid down. The waters of swamps are often poor in oxygen, and the dead vegetation that falls into them does not rot away. Bacteria attack the plant remains, releasing gases and leaving a residue of vegetable matter. The peat that is formed at first is then buried to form a soft brown coal called lignite. As the sediment is buried deeper and deeper in the earth, the higher temperatures and pressures compact it, eventually producing high-quality, hard, dark, bituminous coal. By then, the seam will only be a tenth of the thickness of the peat from which it formed.

Like coal, oil and natural gas are fossil fuels but, unlike coal, they originate in the plant and animal remains that get buried in the muds at the bottom of the sea or in lakes. After they have been buried by other sediments, chemical reactions convert them into liquids and gases. Both oil and gas are buoyant and mobile, and will tend to rise toward the surface unless blocked by an impermeable layer such as shale. Traveling through the overlying sediments, they can find their way into "reservoir rocks," such as sandstone, where they can be stored in the spaces between the sand grains. The simplest form of oil trap is an anticline, in which a cap of impermeable rock seals an oil and gas reservoir beneath it. Another effective form of oil trap occurs when a layer of salt, which is relatively light compared with the rocks around it, pushes up to form a salt dome. Here, at the boundaries of the dome, the buckling of the rock layers creates sealed pockets in which the oil and gas are caught. Holes drilled from rigs at the surface release the oil and gas. Only rarely is the natural pressure enough to make oil gush out of the hole. It usually has to be pumped out.

DUNE ROCK. The desert dunes of Saudi Arabia might one day, in the right conditions, harden into sandstone.

MOUNTAIN BUILDING. Corals in the Red Sea make their skeletons out of calcium carbonate — the stuff of a limestone massif.

UNRAVELING THE LANDSCAPE
The ground beneath our feet is only the topmost layer of a complex pattern of rock types and geological structures. By delving deep into its past, we can understand the history of a typical modern landscape.

11. SLATE QUARRY. The material for millions of roofs has been quarried from a layer of slate.

12. VOLCANIC NECK. The solidified lava in the neck of an ancient volcano stands up long after the cone has been eroded away.

13. BASALT RIDGE. Lava that once flowed at the bottom of a valley has outlived the valley walls that shaped it.

14. DIAMOND PIPE. Volcanic pipes, stretching up from many miles underground, deliver diamonds to a minable depth.

15. LIMESTONE RIDGE. A block of limestone is pitted with holes, through which water sinks underground.

16. LIMESTONE CAVES. Water running through layers in the rock erodes caves and channels.

17. CHALK DOWNLAND. The soft, permeable beds of chalk give rise to rounded, well-drained hills.

18. SANDSTONE RIDGE. The massive buildup of desert sands has now been compacted into relatively hard sandstone.

19. DEEP COAL MINE. Where coal seams lie well below the surface, shafts are driven down to extract the mineral.

20. STRIP COAL MINE. Coal near or at the surface can most easily be mined in a series of strips.

21. SALT DOME OIL TRAP. Buoyant salt pushing up from below distorts the surroundings, trapping oil in reservoir rocks.

22. ANTICLINE OIL TRAP. A simple upfold in sedimentary layers provides a cap under which oil is trapped.

31

At Ocean's Edge

The restless waters of the sea confront the apparently solid bulk of land in a shifting battle zone known as the shore. Waves take advantage of any weakness in our coastal defenses, exploiting every crack and crevice in the rocks. Under the attack, the cliffs retreat and the lines of the shore are redrawn.

The sea, however, builds almost as much as it batters. Along a typical coastline there are places where the sea has eroded the land: storm-beaten cliffs, headlands that are the tough solitary survivors of the sea's invasion, and bays where ground has been given. In other places land is constantly being reclaimed from the sea through the deposit of water-borne sediments: beaches and barrier islands, spits, and salt marshes.

The forces that sculpt the coastlines of the world range from the relentless pounding of the waves in the temperate latitudes to the flow of glaciers in the Arctic and Antarctic, and the organic growth of coral islands in the tropics. But forces even greater than these are at work.

Over long periods of time, the level of the sea changes, either drowning what had been land or exposing what had been seabed. The location of the shoreline at any one time can be divined only by following a trail of clues: drowned forests off the coasts of North America and Europe, rhinoceros bones trapped in fishermen's nets in the North Sea, the fossils of sea animals stranded on the coast, river beds sunk beneath the surface of the sea.

THE RISE AND FALL OF LAND AND SEA

The tales of catastrophic floods told in the folklore and legends of many different cultures, from the Old Testament Book of Genesis to the myths of the ancient Greeks, are corroborated by scientific evidence. The sea level of today is almost 500 feet (150 m) higher than it was 25,000 years ago. Yet, in the context of geological history, this is one episode in the ebb and flow of the shore, as the land emerges or is submerged, depending on the relative level of land and sea.

Coasts emerge when the sea level falls or the land rises, exposing terraces that marked earlier coastlines and marooning deposits, such as marine shell beds or the prehistoric fossils of sea animals, on dry land. Coasts are submerged when the sea level rises or the land sinks. Here, the topography of the land can occasionally be traced on the seabed in the form perhaps of submerged terraces, flooded forests that are exposed at low tide, and drowned river valleys known as fjords and rias.

The level of the land shifts when, for example, continents collide to hurl up great mountain chains, or when the ice sheets, which have depressed parts of the earth's crust for millennia, melt and the crust springs back to its natural position. Worldwide changes of sea level, however, may be the result of melting in the polar ice caps or changes in the capacity of the ocean basins as sediment from the land is disgorged by rivers into the sea.

SUBMERGED COAST. The sea-floor valleys of the Java Sea link up with those on land in a network of river systems. This is a legacy of the time when the sea was about 330 feet (100 m) lower and today's islands were all part of one land mass.

THE MAKING OF THE SHORE

The left half of this illustration of an idealized coastline in the temperate latitudes depicts features caused by erosion; the right half depicts features created by deposition.

1. CLIFFS. Waves, loaded with rock fragments, pound against the cliff and cut a notch at its base. As the overhanging rocks crumble into the sea, the cliff retreats, leaving behind a sloping platform littered with rock debris, which stretches from the high-tide mark to below low tide.

2. COVE. When the sea penetrates a line of weakness in a rocky limestone coast, it may scoop out a bay in the outcrops of softer rocks behind. In the cove, which is protected by the headland, the cliffs slope more gently and are sculpted as much by rainfall as by the force of the sea.

3. SEA CAVE. Cracks and joints in the rock are particularly vulnerable to erosion by the sea. At these fractures, waves surge into every crevice and scour caves in the cliff, compressing the air trapped inside. This may escape as a plume of spray and water through a blowhole – a puncture in the roof of the cave.

4. SEA ARCH. Caves on either side of a headland may meet in the middle to form a tunnel or arch.

5. STACK. When the bridge of a sea arch collapses, a stack – a solitary finger of resistant rock – is left stranded in the sea.

6. HEADLAND. Rocks that can withstand the constant battering of the waves protrude as headlands, sheltering the rest of the coast. Over many years, however, the process of refraction, which concentrates the force of the waves against the sides of the headland and disperses it in the bays, tends to smooth out any irregularities in the coast.

7. DUNES. Winds blow dried sand to the back of the beach, building a belt of dunes. Storm waves trim this back, but during calmer weather a new belt may be formed in front of it.

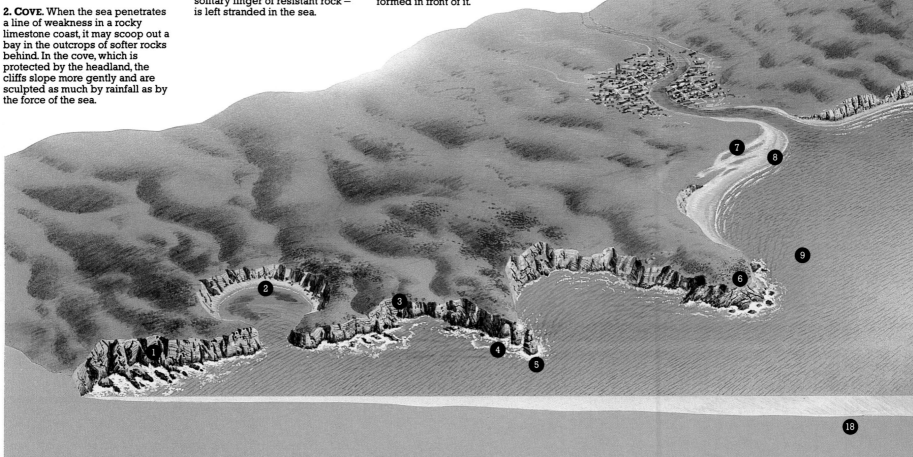

8. BEACH. Sand and pebbles that have been eroded from the cliffs behind, or transported from other stretches of the coastline, may accumulate between the low-tide mark and the landward limit of the storm waves. These sediments, worn down and sorted into well-rounded grains of a similar size, pack closely together to form the smooth surface of a beach.

9. LONGSHORE DRIFT. Waves are generated by the wind so that, like the wind, they can vary in any direction offshore. As they approach the coast, however, their crests become more nearly – but rarely completely – parallel to the shore. The backwash of the waves, on the other hand, moves straight back down the slope toward the sea. As a result, the sediment transported by the surf zigzags along the shore.

10. BAYMOUTH BAR. Where longshore drift is strong and where the flow from rivers draining the land is weak, a spit may stretch right across the bay, cutting it off from the sea.

11. TOMBOLO. A ridge of sand or pebbles links a rocky island to the mainland.

12. SPIT. Longshore drift carries sand and pebbles along the coast, where they are deposited in a ridge that extends the line of the nearby shore. Currents or refracted waves may then recurve the end of the spit landward in the shape of a hook.

13. LAGOON. A barrier protects a former inlet in the coast from the sea, creating a lagoon. Near the sea the water is salty, but to the rear, where small freshwater streams drain the land, the lagoon becomes less brackish.

WAVES AT WORK

The turbulence of the wind stirs the surface of the sea; waves are the result. When waves that have traveled hundreds of miles across the ocean encounter the coast, the steady swell of their journey is broken within a matter of yards. The impact of this collision is the single greatest factor in shaping our shores, as the waves lap gently at the beaches or pound the cliffs with a force of up to 30 tons per square yard. Stones and pebbles carried in the water are the wave's cutting edge, reputed to have shattered lighthouse windows 330 feet (100m) up, sawing and grinding at the cliff faces and gradually pushing back the line of the coast.

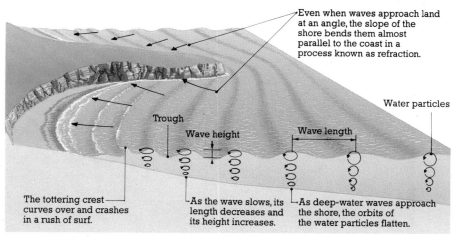

Even when waves approach land at an angle, the slope of the shore bends them almost parallel to the coast in a process known as refraction.

Water particles

Trough

Wave height

Wave length

The tottering crest curves over and crashes in a rush of surf.

As the wave slows, its length decreases and its height increases.

As deep-water waves approach the shore, the orbits of the water particles flatten.

WAVE POWER. The water particles in the sea follow an orbital movement, returning to more or less the same position from which they started. As a result, it is the energy derived from the wind, rather than the water particles themselves, that is transferred across the sea in waves.

MINERALS AND MATERIALS FROM THE SEA SHORE

The ocean is the great reservoir of global wealth. Valuable salts and minerals are washed down by the rivers and out to sea. One seventh of the world's salt is now supplied from sea water by the simple process of evaporation. And it is likely that, over the next century, man will look increasingly to the sea for other minerals and raw materials. The construction industry already uses great suction pipes on board ships to dredge aggregates, such as sand and gravel for concrete and shells for cement, from the bottom of the sea. These were deposited on the continental shelf by rivers and glaciers when the sea level was lower than it is today. The world's major sand and gravel deposits are to be found on the Atlantic coast of North America and in the North Sea.

There are yet more valuable deposits known as placers. These resilient minerals, such as gold and tin, were originally eroded from ore bodies on land and dropped on beaches or just offshore. The world's leading source of tin is from the shallow sands off Malaysia and Indonesia. Gold has been mined on the beaches of Alaska, and the volume of diamonds dredged from the sands and gravels of the West African coast now rivals that mined inland.

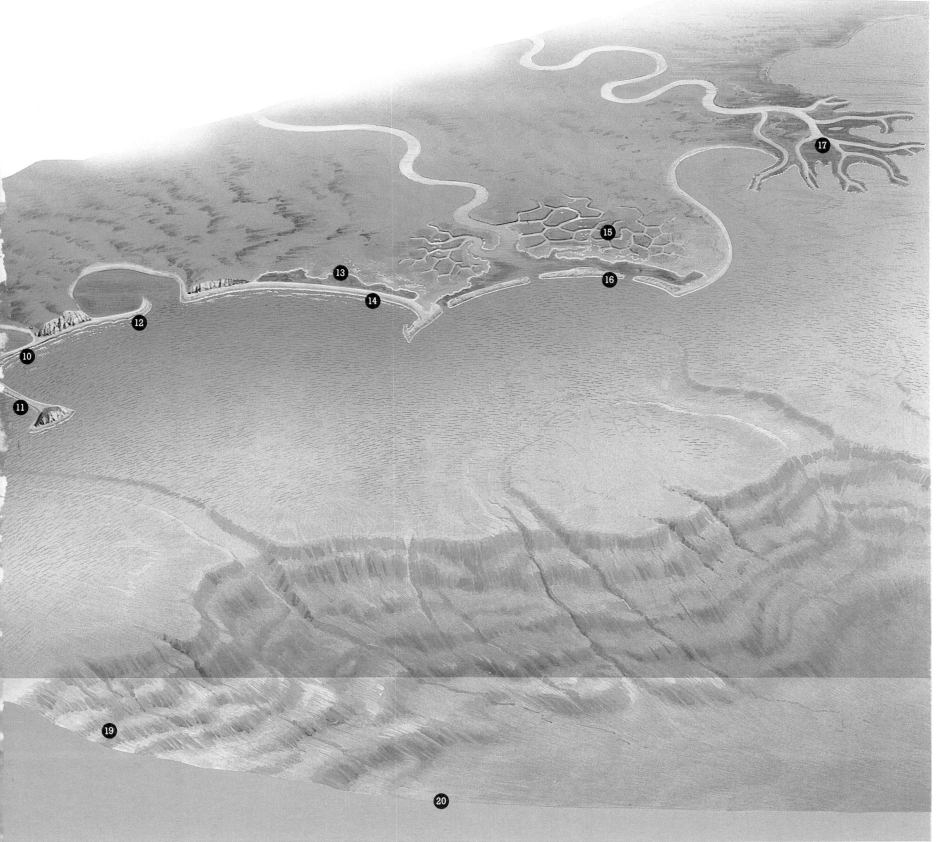

14. BARRIER. Barriers are similar in appearance to baymouth bars, although generally much bigger.

15. SALT MARSH. Plants colonize the land on the sheltered side of spits or barriers and filter out the sediment carried in by the rising tide. Gradually, the level of the mud flats rises.

16. BARRIER ISLANDS. Sometimes — for example, at estuaries — the volume of water poured into the sea by large rivers prevents a continuous barrier from forming. Here, a chain of barrier islands, covered with sand dunes and separated from each other by tidal inlets, may be found.

17. DELTA. Where a river deposits sediments more rapidly than the sea can remove them, a delta forms. Shapes of deltas range from the cone of the Nile to the bird's foot of the Mississippi.

18. CONTINENTAL SHELF. The gently sloping platform that stretches beneath sea level toward the continental slope is known as the continental shelf.

19. CONTINENTAL SLOPE. At the shelf break, the sea floor plunges downward. Turbidity currents — underwater avalanches of sediment that have slumped downhill at speeds of up to 60 miles (100km) per hour — have gouged steep valleys in the sides of the slope. These submarine canyons may be far bigger than the Grand Canyon.

20. CONTINENTAL RISE. As the slope's gradient becomes less steep, it merges into the continental rise — a gentle inclination dropping down toward the deep ocean floor.

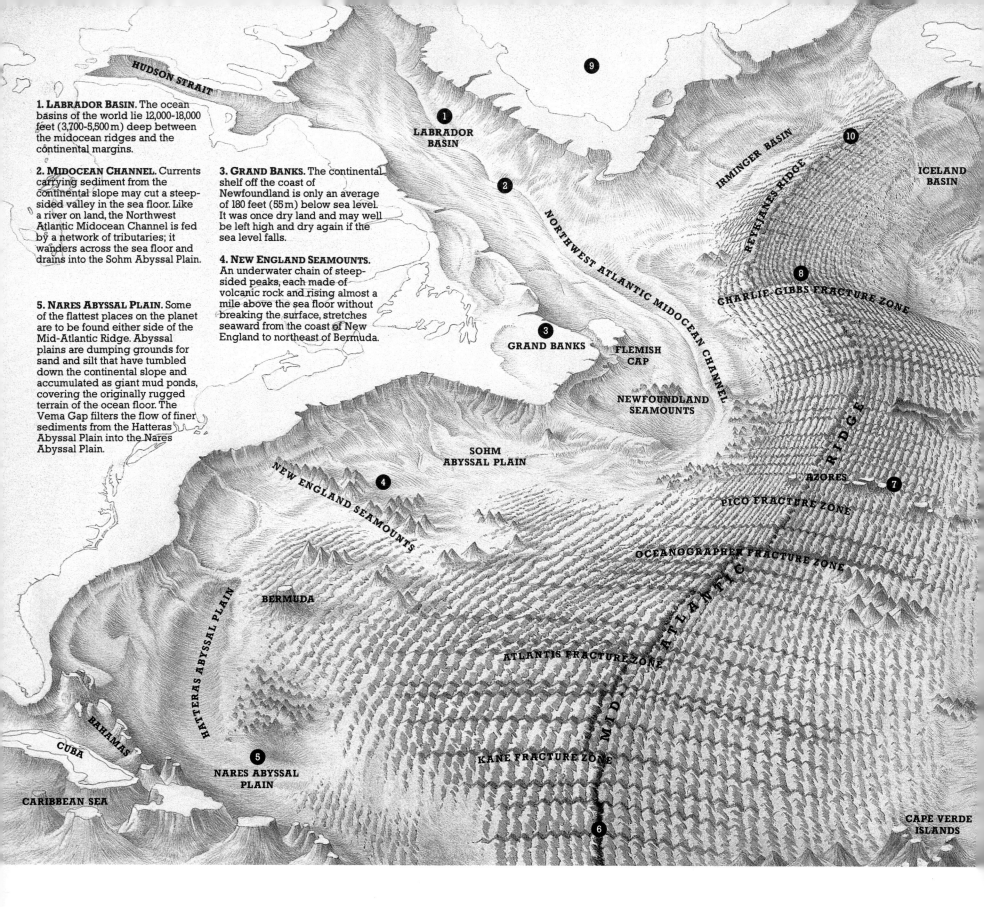

1. LABRADOR BASIN. The ocean basins of the world lie 12,000-18,000 feet (3,700-5,500 m) deep between the midocean ridges and the continental margins.

2. MIDOCEAN CHANNEL. Currents carrying sediment from the continental slope may cut a steep-sided valley in the sea floor. Like a river on land, the Northwest Atlantic Midocean Channel is fed by a network of tributaries; it wanders across the sea floor and drains into the Sohm Abyssal Plain.

3. GRAND BANKS. The continental shelf off the coast of Newfoundland is only an average of 180 feet (55 m) below sea level. It was once dry land and may well be left high and dry again if the sea level falls.

4. NEW ENGLAND SEAMOUNTS. An underwater chain of steep-sided peaks, each made of volcanic rock and rising almost a mile above the sea floor without breaking the surface, stretches seaward from the coast of New England to northeast of Bermuda.

5. NARES ABYSSAL PLAIN. Some of the flattest places on the planet are to be found either side of the Mid-Atlantic Ridge. Abyssal plains are dumping grounds for sand and silt that have tumbled down the continental slope and accumulated as giant mud ponds, covering the originally rugged terrain of the ocean floor. The Vema Gap filters the flow of finer sediments from the Hatteras Abyssal Plain into the Nares Abyssal Plain.

Atlantic: Driving Continents Apart

Drain the ocean basins of the world and you would find not a flat and featureless sea floor but a landscape as varied as that on the continents. There are hills and valleys, plains and plateaus, submarine canyons that plunge thousands of feet into the ocean bed, and volcanic islands whose peaks rear high above sea level. The midoceanic ridge, a mountain range up to 13,000 feet (4,000 m) high and 40,000 miles (65,000 km) long, is the most dramatic feature of them all; yet its existence was not known until earlier this century. It is the largest relief feature on the earth's surface, and in the Atlantic a section of it dominates the ocean bed.

Compared with the Pacific or with the Mediterranean — a remnant of an ancient sea known as Tethys — the Atlantic is a relatively young ocean. It began to form some 160 million years ago as the rifts that split the supercontinent of Pangaea widened. The process continues to this day. At the Mid-Atlantic Ridge the plates are pushed apart at the rate of about an inch (2 cm) a year, as molten rock rises from the mantle below and spreads on either side, cooling and solidifying into slivers of new oceanic crust. These are driven apart by new magma rising at the ridge.

Layers of sediment deposited on the ocean floor record the history of the Atlantic. In the late 1960's the U.S. research ship *Glomar Challenger* began to drill hundreds of feet into the deep ocean bed and to remove sediment cores. These samples have since provided some of the strongest evidence for the phenomenon of sea-floor spreading. For they show that the thickness and age of the sediment on the ocean bed increase with distance from the newly formed crust at the midoceanic ridge.

Unlike the margins of the Pacific where oceanic plates collide with continents, causing earthquakes and building volcanoes, the margins of the Atlantic are quiet or "passive." Ocean and continent ride on the same plate; there is no collision.

Some of the greatest rivers of the world, including the Saint Lawrence, the Mississippi, the Amazon, the Congo, and the Orinoco, disgorge loads of sediment from the continents into the Atlantic. These flow down into the deep abyssal plains, coating the sea floor and smoothing its originally rough topography. The mountains that ring the Pacific, on the other hand, cause many of the rivers on the surrounding continents to flow away from the Pacific, and the layer of sediment is thinner than that in the Atlantic.

MAPPING THE SEA FLOOR

During the 19th century the mapping of the deep ocean floor was a rather laborious business, which involved the lowering of lead-weighted lines from the side of a ship. The invention of the echo sounder in the 1920's was a major breakthrough. It transmitted sound waves toward the ocean floor and, by measuring the time taken for the echo to be bounced back to the device,

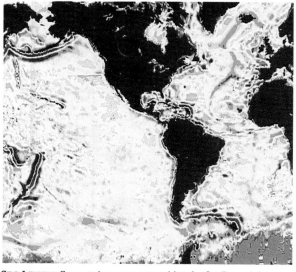

SEA LEVELS. Seasat data, processed by the Jet Propulsion Laboratory, show variations in the height of the sea surface, and hence of the sea floor. These range from depressions (deep blue) through the average (white) to rises (red).

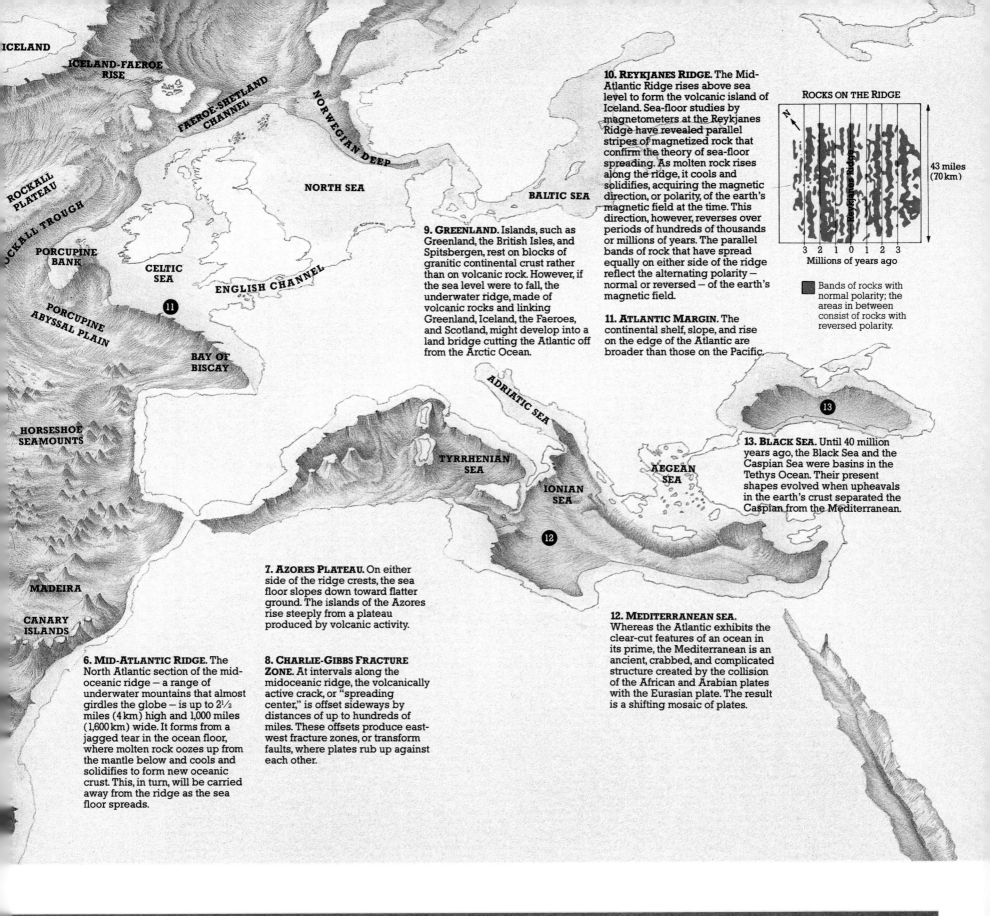

ICELAND

ICELAND-FAEROE RISE

FAEROE-SHETLAND CHANNEL

NORWEGIAN DEEP

ROCKALL PLATEAU

ROCKALL TROUGH

PORCUPINE BANK

NORTH SEA

BALTIC SEA

CELTIC SEA

ENGLISH CHANNEL

PORCUPINE ABYSSAL PLAIN

BAY OF BISCAY

HORSESHOE SEAMOUNTS

MADEIRA

CANARY ISLANDS

ADRIATIC SEA

TYRRHENIAN SEA

IONIAN SEA

AEGEAN SEA

10. REYKJANES RIDGE. The Mid-Atlantic Ridge rises above sea level to form the volcanic island of Iceland. Sea-floor studies by magnetometers at the Reykjanes Ridge have revealed parallel stripes of magnetized rock that confirm the theory of sea-floor spreading. As molten rock rises along the ridge, it cools and solidifies, acquiring the magnetic direction, or polarity, of the earth's magnetic field at the time. This direction, however, reverses over periods of hundreds of thousands or millions of years. The parallel bands of rock that have spread equally on either side of the ridge reflect the alternating polarity — normal or reversed — of the earth's magnetic field.

11. ATLANTIC MARGIN. The continental shelf, slope, and rise on the edge of the Atlantic are broader than those on the Pacific.

ROCKS ON THE RIDGE

N

43 miles (70 km)

3 2 1 0 1 2 3
Millions of years ago

Bands of rocks with normal polarity; the areas in between consist of rocks with reversed polarity.

9. GREENLAND. Islands, such as Greenland, the British Isles, and Spitsbergen, rest on blocks of granitic continental crust rather than on volcanic rock. However, if the sea level were to fall, the underwater ridge, made of volcanic rocks and linking Greenland, Iceland, the Faeroes, and Scotland, might develop into a land bridge cutting the Atlantic off from the Arctic Ocean.

13. BLACK SEA. Until 40 million years ago, the Black Sea and the Caspian Sea were basins in the Tethys Ocean. Their present shapes evolved when upheavals in the earth's crust separated the Caspian from the Mediterranean.

7. AZORES PLATEAU. On either side of the ridge crests, the sea floor slopes down toward flatter ground. The islands of the Azores rise steeply from a plateau produced by volcanic activity.

6. MID-ATLANTIC RIDGE. The North Atlantic section of the mid-oceanic ridge — a range of underwater mountains that almost girdles the globe — is up to 2½ miles (4 km) high and 1,000 miles (1,600 km) wide. It forms from a jagged tear in the ocean floor, where molten rock oozes up from the mantle below and cools and solidifies to form new oceanic crust. This, in turn, will be carried away from the ridge as the sea floor spreads.

8. CHARLIE-GIBBS FRACTURE ZONE. At intervals along the midoceanic ridge, the volcanically active crack, or "spreading center," is offset sideways by distances of up to hundreds of miles. These offsets produce east-west fracture zones, or transform faults, where plates rub up against each other.

12. MEDITERRANEAN SEA. Whereas the Atlantic exhibits the clear-cut features of an ocean in its prime, the Mediterranean is an ancient, crabbed, and complicated structure created by the collision of the African and Arabian plates with the Eurasian plate. The result is a shifting mosaic of plates.

---

enabled scientists to calculate the depth.

Echo sounders have provided much of the data from which cartographers draw maps of the seabed. The reconstructions of the Atlantic floor on these pages, for example, and of the Pacific floor on the next two pages are based on a digital echo-sounder database developed by the U.S. Navy. The information was then processed by computer to produce a three-dimensional relief map, exaggerating the contours of the ocean bed. This then formed the reference basis for the artist's rendering of the ocean above.

In the past few decades, space technology has combined with developments in oceanography to give us new insights and extra detail.

In 1978, a NASA satellite called Seasat orbited the earth for three months at a height of 500 miles (800 km). It was equipped with a radar altimeter that bounced radar pulses off the surface of the sea, measuring the distance between the satellite and the sea to within about 4 inches (10 cm). Because the orbit of the satel-

lite was known to be so dependable, any differences in this distance were interpreted as variations in the level of the sea. When mapped, these deviations were found to correspond remarkably closely with our previous knowledge of sea-floor topography.

For example, at spreading centers, such as the Mid-Atlantic Ridge, or on the continental shelves, the surface of the sea is up to 25 feet (8 m) higher than at the deep ocean trenches or the abyssal plains. This is because the shape of the sea surface is controlled by the earth's gravitational field. The anomalies in this field, such as the higher-than-average gravity at ridge crests and the lower-than-average gravity at ocean trenches, cause the sea level there to bulge or sag. Measurements from space of the height of the sea surface can therefore provide accurate information on the landscape that lies beneath.

Whereas Seasat portrays large swaths of the sea floor, the sidescan sonar Gloria creates more detailed snapshots. Unlike the echo sounder, which simply beams sound

waves vertically down to the seabed, it emits pulses of sound that spread out in a fan up to 19 miles (30 km) on either side of the device. The first sound waves to be reflected back off objects in their path are those almost vertically beneath the device, followed by sound waves progressively farther to port and starboard.

As Gloria is towed along by a research vessel at speeds of up to 11 miles (18 km) an hour, acoustic pictures that look like photographs of the sea floor are built up line by line. Gloria can give information about the texture as well as the topography of the seabed because some materials, such as rough lava, reflect the pulses of sound much more efficiently than beds of smooth sea-floor sediment, for example.

Since the 1960's, Gloria has answered many of the riddles of the deep. It has mapped stretches of the plate boundaries — midocean ridges, fracture zones, and deep sea trenches. It has traced the paths of submarine canyons and followed the flow over hundreds of miles of underwater rivers of muddy sediment.

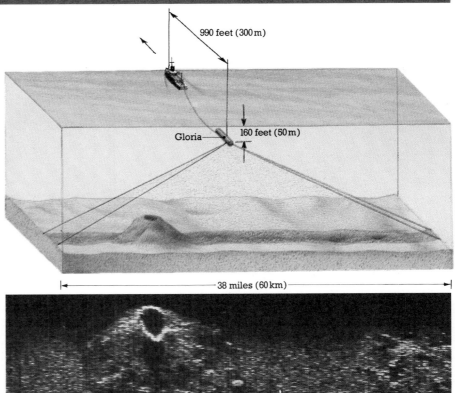

990 feet (300 m)

Gloria

160 feet (50 m)

38 miles (60 km)

SOUNDING THE SEABED. Sound waves emitted by Gloria (above) fan out before hitting the seabed. Some are scattered by the slope of a volcano rising 5,000 feet (1,500 m) above the sea floor. Echoes detected by Gloria create the acoustic image (below).

1. ALEUTIAN ISLAND ARC. Near the trench where two plates meet, the rock that has been pushed back down into the earth begins to melt under intense heat and pressure. Over millions of years, dry land has emerged from the ocean depths as the rising magma has solidified into an arc or chain of about 70 islands.

2. GREAT BARRIER REEF. Most shorelines between 30°N and 30°S are fringed by coral reefs. The most breathtaking of all is the Great Barrier Reef, which is about 60 miles (100 km) wide and stretches for 1,250 miles (2,000 km) off the northeast coast of Australia. It is the most colossal monument ever built by living creatures. For its building blocks are the skeletal remains of tiny organisms known as coral polyps, which thrive in the clear, warm, sunlit ocean waters of this zone.

3. MARIANA TRENCH. Parts of the Mariana Trench are more than 36,000 feet (11,000 m) below sea level — plunging almost 25 percent farther toward the bowels of the earth than Mount Everest soars toward the heavens.

Pacific: The Vanishing Ocean

Whereas the Atlantic is still growing, the Pacific is in decline. The giant among oceans is about half the size of its ancestor, Panthalassa, which surrounded the supercontinent of Pangaea some 190 million years ago. According to most projections, the Pacific will grow smaller still. At its edges, old oceanic crust is disappearing beneath the overriding continental plates on either side. This is happening faster than the rate at which new sea floor is being created at the Pacific section of the midoceanic ridge. Like the Atlantic, the Pacific is divided by a submarine mountain range, where molten rock rises through a rift in the sea floor to form new oceanic crust. The East Pacific Rise is the portion of this ridge that runs southward from the Gulf of California.

Over the last 160 million years, the collision of plates carrying oceanic and continental crust has shaped the borders of the Pacific Ocean. On the eastern edge, it has caused the earth's crust to buckle, creating the almost unbroken mountain chains that stretch from Alaska in the north to Tierra del Fuego in the south. From the mountain ranges, a narrow continental shelf, 12-24 miles (20-40 km) wide, plunges down a steep slope toward the ocean floor.

On the western edge, the devouring, or subduction, of one plate beneath another has caused deep ocean trenches to develop. These stretch from the Kuril Trench in the north to the Tonga Trench in the south. A festoon of island arcs, ranging from the Aleutians to the Philippines and enclosing a network of small seas, has risen behind the trenches. Subduction occurs all around the Pacific, causing earthquakes and volcanoes, and threatening to transform its edges into geological trouble spots. But very little subduction — and hence seismic activity — takes place around the Atlantic.

THE GIANT AMONG OCEANS

The Pacific is an ocean of superlatives. It is double the size of the Atlantic and bigger than the whole land surface of the globe. With an area of 64 million square miles (165 million sq km), it covers almost a third of the earth's surface. And its long, V-shaped trenches are the deepest places on the earth's surface.

SEA FROM SPACE. The Pacific covers almost an entire hemisphere in this view from 70,000 miles (110,000 km) in space.

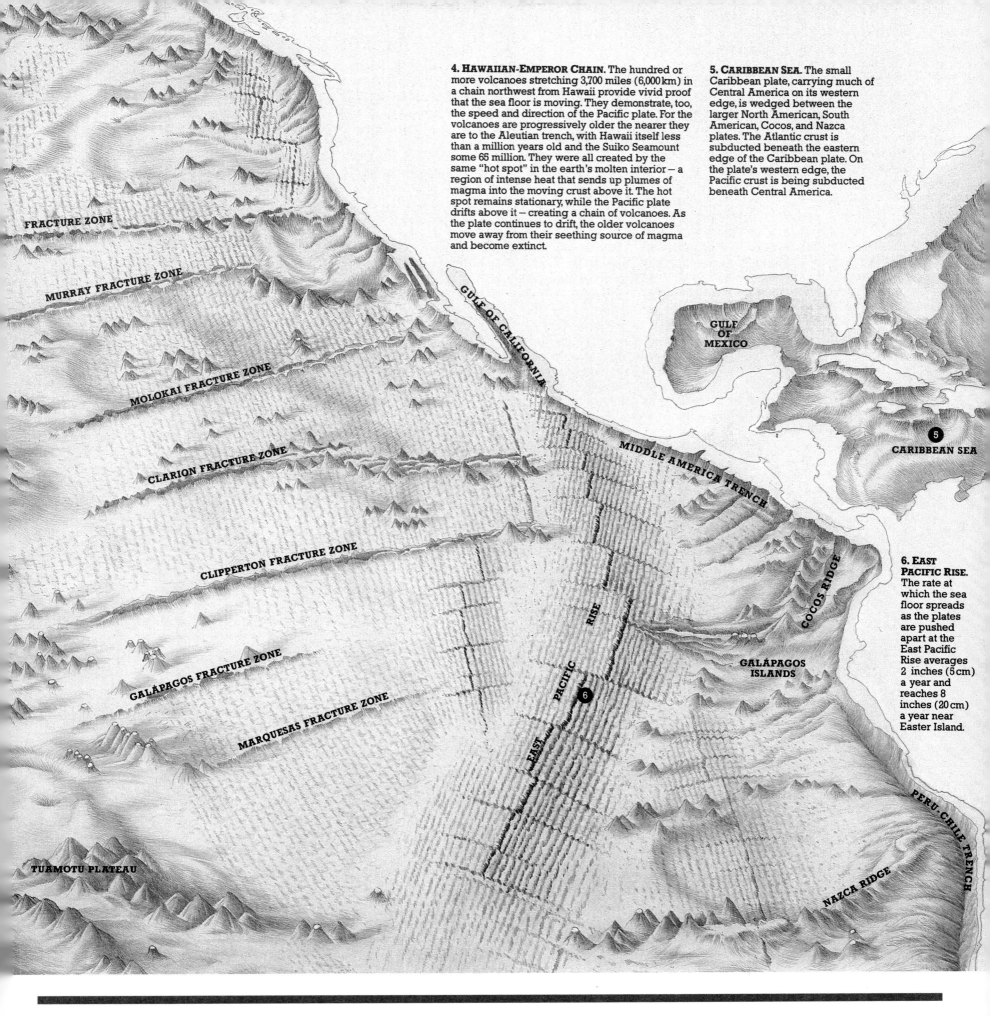

4. HAWAIIAN-EMPEROR CHAIN. The hundred or more volcanoes stretching 3,700 miles (6,000 km) in a chain northwest from Hawaii provide vivid proof that the sea floor is moving. They demonstrate, too, the speed and direction of the Pacific plate. For the volcanoes are progressively older the nearer they are to the Aleutian trench, with Hawaii itself less than a million years old and the Suiko Seamount some 65 million. They were all created by the same "hot spot" in the earth's molten interior – a region of intense heat that sends up plumes of magma into the moving crust above it. The hot spot remains stationary, while the Pacific plate drifts above it – creating a chain of volcanoes. As the plate continues to drift, the older volcanoes move away from their seething source of magma and become extinct.

5. CARIBBEAN SEA. The small Caribbean plate, carrying much of Central America on its western edge, is wedged between the larger North American, South American, Cocos, and Nazca plates. The Atlantic crust is subducted beneath the eastern edge of the Caribbean plate. On the plate's western edge, the Pacific crust is being subducted beneath Central America.

6. EAST PACIFIC RISE. The rate at which the sea floor spreads as the plates are pushed apart at the East Pacific Rise averages 2 inches (5 cm) a year and reaches 8 inches (20 cm) a year near Easter Island.

FRACTURE ZONE
MURRAY FRACTURE ZONE
MOLOKAI FRACTURE ZONE
CLARION FRACTURE ZONE
CLIPPERTON FRACTURE ZONE
GALÁPAGOS FRACTURE ZONE
MARQUESAS FRACTURE ZONE
TUAMOTU PLATEAU
GULF OF CALIFORNIA
MIDDLE AMERICA TRENCH
GULF OF MEXICO
CARIBBEAN SEA
COCOS RIDGE
GALÁPAGOS ISLANDS
EAST PACIFIC RISE
NAZCA RIDGE
PERU-CHILE TRENCH

THE METAL-RICH SEDIMENTS OF THE SEABED

Scientists classify the thick layer of muddy sediment that has settled on the ocean floor according to its origin. *Terrigenous* sediment is washed off the land before being carried in the water toward the ocean bed. Some settles to form reserves of minerals and raw materials on the sea shore. *Biogenous* sediment consists of the remains of tiny marine organisms that have died and sunk to their mass burial ground at the bottom of the sea. *Hydrogenous* sediment is made up of minerals that were originally leached from solid rocks, usually on land, and dissolved in sea water.

The hydrogenous sediments with the greatest economic potential are probably the blackish potato-sized lumps known as manganese nodules. These consist of minerals that have been dissolved in water and carried away by the ocean currents before crystallizing around objects on the sea bed, such as sharks' teeth or pebbles. Although the nodules grow at rates of up to only a few inches every million years, many million tons of them are produced every year. They may already cover up to 20 percent of the Pacific floor, with particular concentrations in the southwest Pacific, off the coast of southern California, and off South America.

In addition to manganese, the nodules are composed of more valuable elements such as iron, copper, cobalt, and nickel. Extraction, however, is costly and the feasibility of mining the metals of the sea floor will depend on the development of submarine robots.

Another source of metal-rich sediments, particularly in the Pacific, are the vents in the oceanic crust known as "black smokers." During the late 1970's scientists on board the deep-diving U.S. submersible *Alvin* studied portions of the East Pacific Rise near the Galápagos Islands, where smoke appeared to belch from the ocean bed.

In fact, the cloudy solution consists not of smoke but of sea water that has seeped into the cracks where new oceanic crust is being formed. At temperatures of up to 300°C, the sea water has combined chemically with the minerals within the hot rock. When the hot solution is spewed into the cold sea water above, it cools and oxidizes, and deposits sulfur, copper, iron, zinc, and manganese on the sea floor. The deposits coat the vents, eventually forming chimneys up to 33 feet (10 m) tall.

One day these hot-water vents could be of some economic importance. But, in the meantime, they have answered a question that has perplexed geochemists. As the rivers disgorge their loads of sediment into the sea, the chemical composition of the oceans might be expected to change continuously. The fact that it does not is due, in large part, to the chemical transformations that take place at the vents.

MANGANESE NODULE. Most of the manganese nodules that carpet large areas of the Pacific are only a few inches in diameter (left). As the X-ray photograph of a nodule's layered cross section suggests (right), they accumulate gradually, around an object on the sea floor.

BLACK SMOKER. Clouds of hot sea water, carrying metals in solution, gush from vents in the oceanic crust.

Currents and Tides: The Energy Balance of the Oceans

The currents in the world's oceans are the veins and arteries of a living earth. As part of our planet's system of heat exchange, they bring vast amounts of warmth from the tropics into colder latitudes that without them would be almost uninhabitable. Along with the winds, by which they are largely driven, the currents maintain the steady, balanced temperatures we experience on earth. Without them, the tropics would grow gradually hotter and the higher latitudes more and more frozen.

The scale on which the currents work is enormous. The Gulf Stream alone carries 50 to 70 times as much water as all the world's rivers put together. The great Antarctic Circumpolar Current, which girdles the earth deep in the southern latitudes, can at times be a stream well over a mile in depth and with the flow of 2,000 Mississippis. These interconnecting ocean currents are so effective at smoothing out the differences in the temperature of the oceans that 90 percent of all sea water varies by no more than 18°F.

The global pattern is one of extraordinary symmetry. In each hemisphere of the world's three great oceans — the Pacific, the Atlantic, and the Indian — there are rotating whorls of surface currents called gyres. In each of these giant whirlpools, thousands of miles across, warm water moves up the western side of the ocean, cools in the higher latitudes, and is then brought back in a wide stream down the eastern side of the ocean toward the equator. Strong westward-flowing equatorial currents complete the cycle.

TIDES: THE BULGING OF THE OCEANS

Tides are caused mainly by the gravitational pull of the moon on the waters of the ocean. The attraction of the moon is strongest on the side of the earth which is facing it. Here the above-average pull causes the waters to bulge out toward the moon in a high tide. At the same time, on the far side of the earth, the moon's attraction is at its weakest and the waters on that side bulge away from the moon in an equal and opposite high tide.

In the course of just over 24 hours, the rotating earth passes through both of these liquid bulges, producing two high tides, with two low tides in between them.

The sun, too, has a gravitational effect on the earth. Although its mass is far greater than the moon's, the effect of the sun's gravity on the tides is approximately half that of the moon because it is so much farther away. When, every other week, the sun and the moon are both in line with the earth, at new and full moon, the two gravitational forces are added together, and exceptionally strong tides called springs are produced. In the intervening weeks, when the sun and the

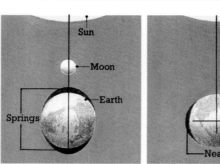

SPRINGS AND NEAPS. When sun and moon are in line with earth (left), severe tides called springs occur; when they are at 90° (right), the result is lesser tides called neaps.

moon are at 90° to each other, at the first and third quarters of the moon, the pull of the sun cancels out half of the moon's gravitational effect, and weak tides called neaps result.

This theoretical pattern does not operate in every part of the world ocean. The shape of the continents prevents water from flowing uninterrupted across the surface of the planet, and this has complex effects on the regularity and number of tides. In some places, such as Southampton Water in southern England, there are four high tides in the space of 24 hours, while on the southwestern coast of Australia there is only one high tide and one low tide a day. At a few places on the ocean's surface, all the tidal forces cancel each other out, and at these "amphidromic points" the ocean tides are extremely small.

In restricted seas, such as the Mediterranean, the tides are almost imperceptible, while in other areas, such as the long and narrow Bay of Fundy in Canada, the range between high and low tide may be up to 49 feet (15 m) at springs.

The most spectacular tidal effect often occurs at the spring and autumn equinoxes, when the combined gravitational effect of the sun and moon is at its strongest. At these times, the sudden rush of water into an estuary at high tide creates a visible wavefront called a bore. The most spectacular is the one at the mouth of the Amazon, more than half a mile (1 km) wide, 16 feet (5 m) high, and sweeping inland at 13 miles (21 km) an hour.

WARM OCEAN CURRENTS

1. GULF STREAM. Waters from the tropics follow this trunk route north and then east into the North Atlantic.

2. NORTH ATLANTIC DRIFT. The northern extension of the Gulf Stream warms the coasts of Iceland, Norway, and Spitsbergen.

3. IRMINGER CURRENT. The northernmost arm of the Gulf Stream brings warmish waters to meet the cold of the Arctic Ocean.

4. KUROSHIO. "The black current," Pacific equivalent of the Atlantic's Gulf Stream, brings dark tropical waters up past Japan.

5. SOMALI CURRENT. In June and August, during the Southwest monsoon, the Somali current flows north, but during the winter it reverses direction.

6. AGULHAS CURRENT. The strongest north-south current in the southern hemisphere stays close to the coast of southern Africa.

7. SOUTH EQUATORIAL CURRENT. The westward current is diverted northward by the corner of Brazil, feeding the sources of the Gulf Stream.

8. NORTH PACIFIC CURRENT. The Pacific equivalent of the North Atlantic Drift brings the warm waters of the Kuroshio to the coast of America.

9. EQUATORIAL COUNTER-CURRENT. The Trade Winds build up water on the western side of the oceans; the Equatorial Countercurrent flows eastward, restoring the balance.

10. GUINEA CURRENT. The extension of the Atlantic Equatorial Countercurrent was used by Portuguese explorers sailing down the coast of Africa.

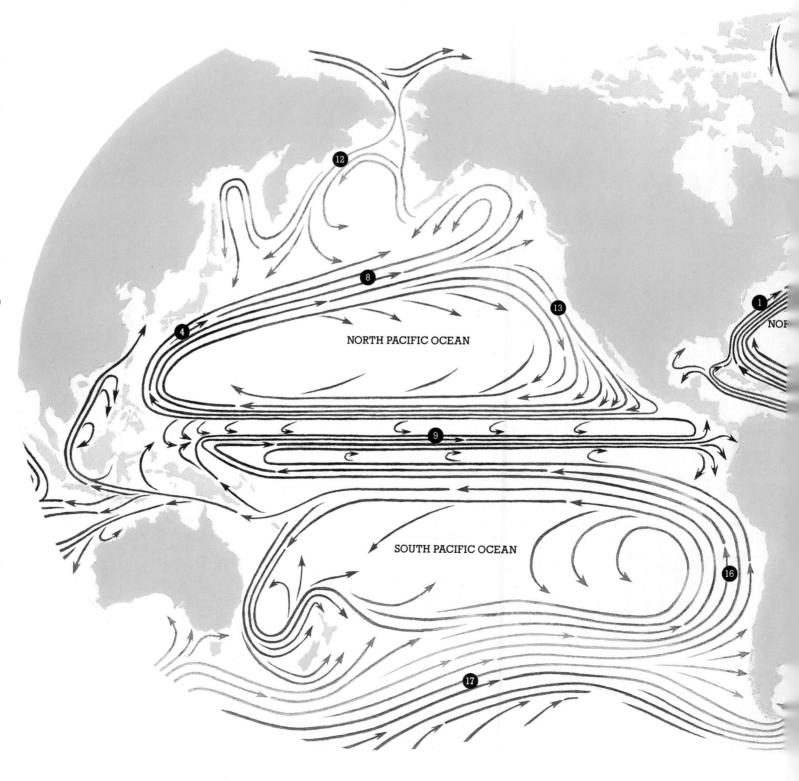

NORTH PACIFIC OCEAN

SOUTH PACIFIC OCEAN

THE DYNAMIC OCEAN

As winds blow over the surface of the sea, friction between the air and the water starts to drag the water along. This is the driving force behind most of the world's surface currents. The turning of the globe itself, however, disrupts the pattern. By a phenomenon known as the Coriolis effect, any movement in the northern hemisphere is deflected to the right and in the southern to the left, turning the currents away from the direction of the wind that produced them.

Each layer of water drags on the one below it, and at each layer the Coriolis effect continues to work. The flow turns farther and farther away from the direction of the wind until, at about 330 feet (100 m) below the surface, the flow is in the opposite direction.

The overall result of this process, which is called the Ekman spiral after its Swedish discoverer, V. W. Ekman, is that the net flow of a wind-driven current is at 90° to the wind at the surface.

In this way the currents of the world's oceans are twisted into the great circulatory systems called gyres, which move clockwise in the northern hemisphere and counterclockwise in the southern.

Below the surface, a system of deep ocean currents is driven by variations in temperature and salinity.

Heavy, salty water (1) flows out of the Mediterranean through the Strait of Gibraltar and spreads out at a depth of about 3,300 feet (1,000 m).

Very cold water from the poles is denser than water from warmer regions. Antarctic Deep Water (2), hugging the ocean bed, has been traced in the Atlantic as far north as

Cape Cod. Arctic Deep Water (3) flows southward at a slightly lesser depth, while the rather warmer Antarctic Intermediate Water (4) flows slowly northward within 6,600 feet (2,000 m) of the surface.

The Antarctic Circumpolar Current (5) is both a surface and a deep current, penetrating to a depth of 10,000 feet (3,000 m) or more. The buildup of water in the western Atlantic from the Benguela Current (6) and the Equatorial Current (7) is released by both the Gulf Stream (8) and the powerful, eastward-flowing Equatorial Undercurrent (9).

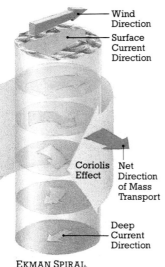

EKMAN SPIRAL. A combination of the wind and the turning of the earth directs the currents.

Labels: Wind Direction; Surface Current Direction; Coriolis Effect; Net Direction of Mass Transport; Deep Current Direction

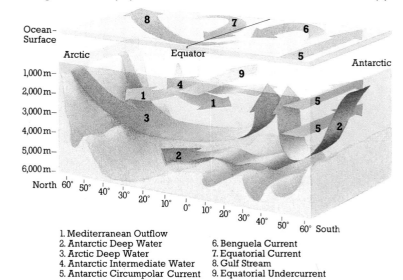

Labels: Ocean Surface; Arctic; Equator; Antarctic; 1,000 m — 6,000 m; North 60° 50° 40° 30° 20° 10° 0° 10° 20° 30° 40° 50° 60° South

1. Mediterranean Outflow
2. Antarctic Deep Water
3. Arctic Deep Water
4. Antarctic Intermediate Water
5. Antarctic Circumpolar Current
6. Benguela Current
7. Equatorial Current
8. Gulf Stream
9. Equatorial Undercurrent

ATLANTIC INTERIOR CURRENTS. In this schematic cross-section of the Atlantic Ocean, water masses from cold or salty regions move through the body of the ocean.

GULF STREAM

The Gulf Stream is one of the most powerful of all the world's currents, the warm benefactor of Europe, transporting massive amounts of heat toward the northern seas.

The current is the western and most concentrated arm of the great North Atlantic gyre, fed by the equatorial currents coming up from the Caribbean. At its peak, off the coast of Florida, the stream, running at about 6 mph (10 kph) and

about 2,950 feet (900 m) deep, carries up to 4,200 million cubic feet (120 million cu m) of water a second. It flows in a meandering jet, but its western edge, known as the Cold Wall, can sometimes be so sharp that a U.S. Coast Guard frigate once measured a temperature difference of 22°F (12°C) between bow and stern.

North of Cape Hatteras, the stream turns eastward into the Atlantic and develops large-scale loops and eddies, 100 miles (160 km) or more across.

HOT WATERS. The Gulf Stream is shown here off the east coast of America. The false colors on the satellite image represent different temperatures: white, less than 37°F (clouds); blue, 37°-55°F (coastal waters and continental shelf); beige to brown, 55°-63°F (outer Gulf Stream); violet to black, over 63°F (core of Gulf Stream and some land).

COLD OCEAN CURRENTS

11. EAST GREENLAND CURRENT. Cold Arctic waters make their way southward into the Atlantic.

12. OYASHIO. The Pacific twin of the East Greenland Current is heavy with the cold waters moving south from the Bering Sea.

13. CALIFORNIA CURRENT. A wide, cold, and sluggish current follows the west coast of the United States as far as Baja California.

14. LABRADOR CURRENT. Cold waters and icebergs are brought down from Baffin Bay and meet the warm Gulf Stream off Newfoundland, producing the fogs of the Grand Banks.

15. BENGUELA CURRENT. The Benguela Current drives water northward and westward into midocean. This produces a strong upwelling of water and nutrients from the ocean bed, supporting enormous numbers of fish.

16. HUMBOLDT (or PERU) CURRENT. A cold current brings nutrients to the sea surface, which teems with life. Every ten years or so, complex weather conditions strengthen the warm, eastward-flowing Equatorial Countercurrent. The Humboldt Current is disrupted. The nutrients no longer rise from the ocean depths, and fish starve. Peruvian fishermen have named this disastrous phenomenon El Niño ("the Child") because of its occurrence around Christmas.

17. ANTARCTIC CIRCUMPOLAR CURRENT. The greatest current of all is driven by the Westerlies. It circles the Antarctic continent, traveling at about half a mile an hour around the Southern Ocean.

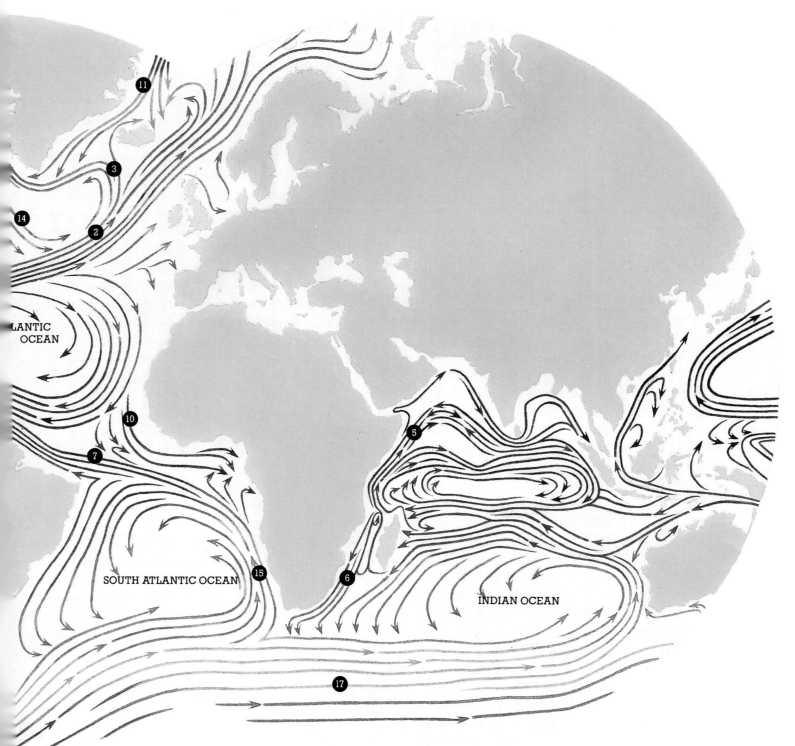

Map labels: ATLANTIC OCEAN; SOUTH ATLANTIC OCEAN; INDIAN OCEAN

Atmosphere: The Earth's Screen

Indoors or out, everyone on earth carries an invisible burden. This is the weight of the air above us, the envelope of gases (over 99 percent nitrogen and oxygen) that we call the atmosphere. These gases, upon which the lungs of the living world depend for survival, are clutched to the surface of the planet by the earth's own gravity. They are densest toward the bottom and, at sea level, the average individual carries about a quarter of a ton of air on his head. We do not feel the burden, however, because the compensating pressure of fluids within our bodies is acting outward.

Without this multilayered and protective shield, life on earth would be very different. If there were no atmosphere to absorb or reflect back many of the sun's harmful rays, the whole planet would be a desert, baked by radiation during the day, and frozen at night as the warmth escaped unimpeded into space.

About 15 percent of the incoming radiation is absorbed by the atmosphere. A further 35 percent is reflected back into space by clouds and by the surface of land and sea. The remaining 50 percent is absorbed at sea and ground level.

As we know from the warmth of a summer evening after nightfall, the earth itself radiates the heat that it has received from the sun back into the atmosphere. The earth is cooler than the sun and hence its radiation is of a longer wavelength than the sun's. As a result, much of it is unable to pass back through the atmosphere and out into space and is trapped within the relatively thin layer immediately above us known as the troposphere.

This trapped heat is the source of energy that powers the weather machine. Air near the surface is warmed up. It collects water vapor from the lakes and oceans and rises to colder levels, where the vapor condenses as clouds. This simple mechanism lies behind the pageant of the weather — our everyday experience of the atmosphere in action.

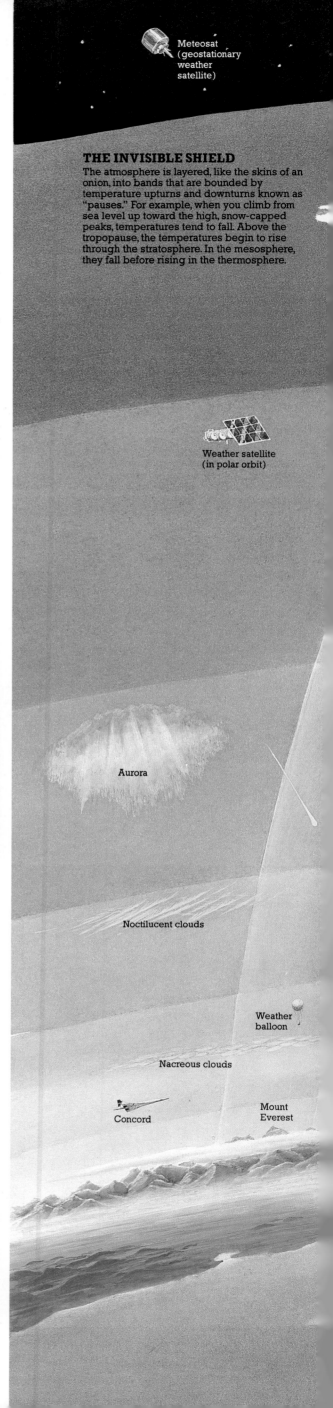

THE INVISIBLE SHIELD

The atmosphere is layered, like the skins of an onion, into bands that are bounded by temperature upturns and downturns known as "pauses." For example, when you climb from sea level up toward the high, snow-capped peaks, temperatures tend to fall. Above the tropopause, the temperatures begin to rise through the stratosphere. In the mesosphere, they fall before rising in the thermosphere.

Meteosat (geostationary weather satellite)

Weather satellite (in polar orbit)

Aurora

Noctilucent clouds

Weather balloon

Nacreous clouds

Concord

Mount Everest

TRICKS OF LIGHT

Blue skies, multicolored rainbows, sunsets that blaze like fire — these are all tricks of the earth's atmosphere, special effects in the stagelighting of the planet.

The sun's energy reaches the earth almost entirely in the form of electromagnetic radiation. Solar radiation flashes through space at a speed of about 186,000 miles (300,000 km) per second, traveling in waves of different length. The visible color spectrum lies between the two extremes of short-wave gamma rays and longer radio waves. Overall, the human eye is sensitive to about half of the sun's rays, perceiving them in the form of light.

Light ranges between short-wave, high-frequency violet through blue, green, yellow, and orange to long-wave, low-frequency red. "White" sunlight is really composed of the full range. As it enters the earth's atmosphere, this white light is refracted, or bent, by different angles according to its component wavelengths. Objects then appear in different colors according to which wavelengths they reflect. Green grass, for example, reflects only medium-frequency green wavelengths, absorbing the high and low frequencies.

The English scientist Sir Isaac Newton (1643–1727) demonstrated how light can be refracted and separated into its various wavelengths by passing sunlight through a clear glass prism to produce the color spectrum on a blank wall.

DOUBLE RAINBOW. Raindrops, acting as natural prisms, refract and split up the sunlight, creating a double arc of color above the Cape Peninsula, South Africa.

Rainbows are created in the same way, as the natural prism of raindrops hanging in the air separates out an arc of colors. Refraction can also cause a "halo" or ring of colored light to appear around the sun or moon. This is usually caused by a veil of ice particles in the atmosphere.

When the air is clean and free of moisture, the sky appears blue overhead. This is because air molecules themselves scatter sunlight, and do so most efficiently at the high-frequency blue or violet end of the spectrum. Water droplets and specks of dust, on the other hand, scatter light in all its wavelengths, so that the sky often appears whitish. On some quiet summer evenings, as the sun sets on the horizon, its beams have to travel through a lot of atmosphere before they reach the eye. The relatively large dust particles that have accumulated in the still skies scatter the longer red wavelengths, creating a deep red glow.

Tricks of light are not confined to color alone. Perhaps the most uncanny optical phenomena are mirages. Light bends as it travels between air layers of differing temperatures and densities. Over deserts and oceans, heat may cause beams of light to bend so that images, even of objects beyond the horizon, are brought into view; this is called a superior mirage. Inferior mirages are seen below the real object, and upside down. We have all seen mirror images of the sky, shimmering above the hot surface of a road to create the illusion of a lake.

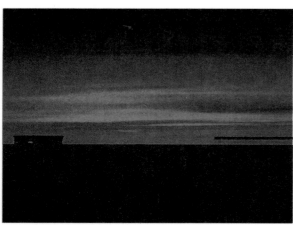

ICEBERG MIRAGE. The images of two icebergs beyond the horizon float in the layer of air above Antarctica.

HALO AT SUNSET. Ice crystals in the air above Spitsbergen refract the light, causing a halo around the setting sun.

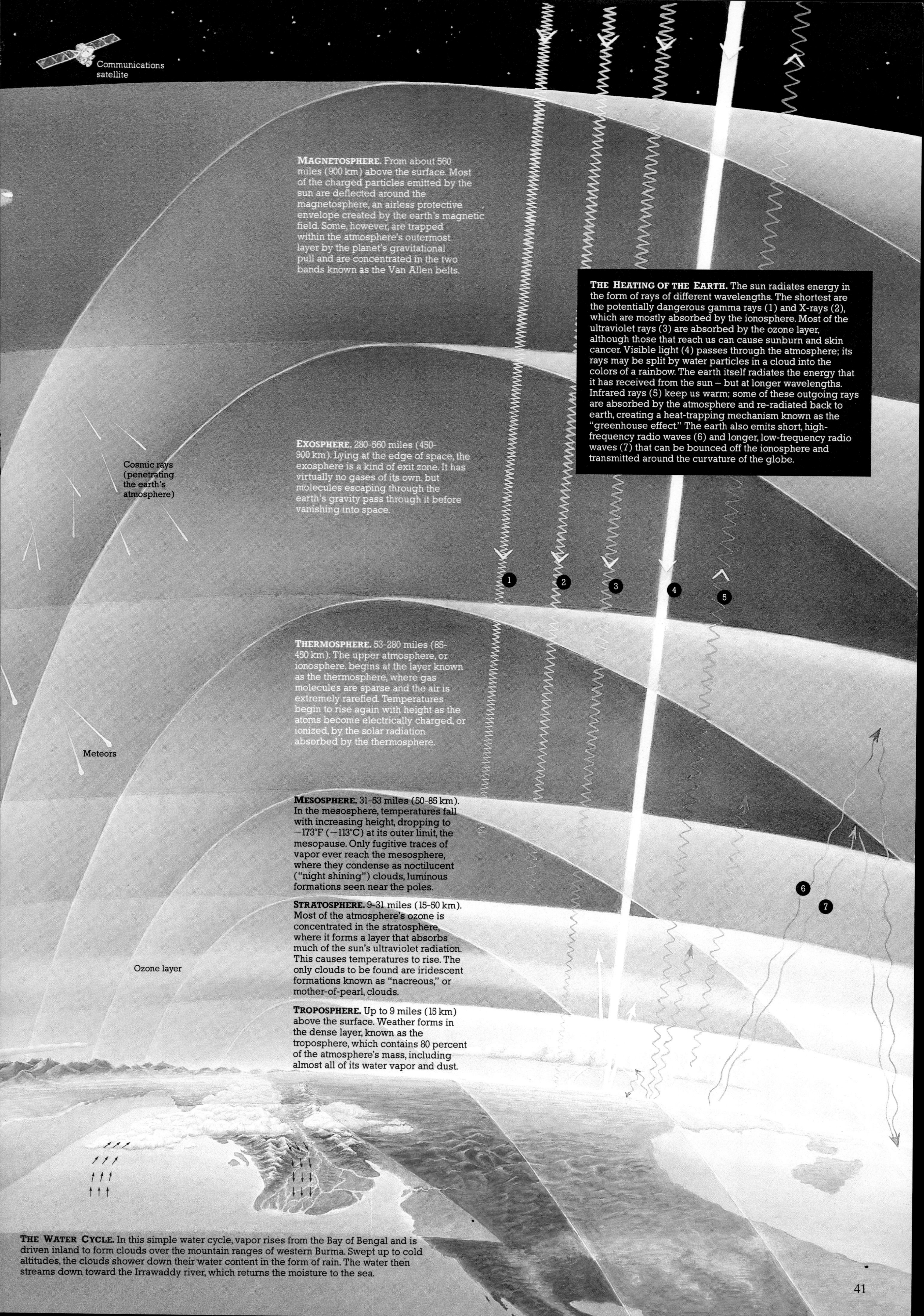

Communications
satellite

MAGNETOSPHERE. From about 560
miles (900 km) above the surface. Most
of the charged particles emitted by the
sun are deflected around the
magnetosphere, an airless protective
envelope created by the earth's magnetic
field. Some, however, are trapped
within the atmosphere's outermost
layer by the planet's gravitational
pull and are concentrated in the two
bands known as the Van Allen belts.

THE HEATING OF THE EARTH. The sun radiates energy in
the form of rays of different wavelengths. The shortest are
the potentially dangerous gamma rays (1) and X-rays (2),
which are mostly absorbed by the ionosphere. Most of the
ultraviolet rays (3) are absorbed by the ozone layer,
although those that reach us can cause sunburn and skin
cancer. Visible light (4) passes through the atmosphere; its
rays may be split by water particles in a cloud into the
colors of a rainbow. The earth itself radiates the energy that
it has received from the sun — but at longer wavelengths.
Infrared rays (5) keep us warm; some of these outgoing rays
are absorbed by the atmosphere and re-radiated back to
earth, creating a heat-trapping mechanism known as the
"greenhouse effect." The earth also emits short, high-
frequency radio waves (6) and longer, low-frequency radio
waves (7) that can be bounced off the ionosphere and
transmitted around the curvature of the globe.

Cosmic rays
(penetrating
the earth's
atmosphere)

EXOSPHERE. 280-560 miles (450-
900 km). Lying at the edge of space, the
exosphere is a kind of exit zone. It has
virtually no gases of its own, but
molecules escaping through the
earth's gravity pass through it before
vanishing into space.

Meteors

THERMOSPHERE. 53-280 miles (85-
450 km). The upper atmosphere, or
ionosphere, begins at the layer known
as the thermosphere, where gas
molecules are sparse and the air is
extremely rarefied. Temperatures
begin to rise again with height as the
atoms become electrically charged, or
ionized, by the solar radiation
absorbed by the thermosphere.

MESOSPHERE. 31-53 miles (50-85 km).
In the mesosphere, temperatures fall
with increasing height, dropping to
−173°F (−113°C) at its outer limit, the
mesopause. Only fugitive traces of
vapor ever reach the mesosphere,
where they condense as noctilucent
("night shining") clouds, luminous
formations seen near the poles.

STRATOSPHERE. 9-31 miles (15-50 km).
Most of the atmosphere's ozone is
concentrated in the stratosphere,
where it forms a layer that absorbs
much of the sun's ultraviolet radiation.
This causes temperatures to rise. The
only clouds to be found are iridescent
formations known as "nacreous," or
mother-of-pearl, clouds.

Ozone layer

TROPOSPHERE. Up to 9 miles (15 km)
above the surface. Weather forms in
the dense layer, known as the
troposphere, which contains 80 percent
of the atmosphere's mass, including
almost all of its water vapor and dust.

THE WATER CYCLE. In this simple water cycle, vapor rises from the Bay of Bengal and is
driven inland to form clouds over the mountain ranges of western Burma. Swept up to cold
altitudes, the clouds shower down their water content in the form of rain. The water then
streams down toward the Irrawaddy river, which returns the moisture to the sea.

Weather: The Restless Air

The air is an ocean, and its currents are the winds. We live on the floor of this great sea, buffeted by its streams, subject to its vast atmospheric swirling, and dependent on the life-giving rain it brings us.

Nothing is more famously capricious than the weather, but behind even its most sudden and unpredictable changes, there is a system at work. Two principles lie behind the movements of the weather machine: hot air rises because it is lighter than its surroundings, and air packed relatively tightly into a region of high pressure tends to flow out of it into stormy "lows." Air movements produced by these two principles can exist at almost every size — from a plume of air rising above the heat of an electric light bulb to a giant current girdling the entire planet.

On a global scale, this restlessness of the atmosphere takes the form of a giant heat exchange, in which hot air is moved poleward from the tropics and cold air moves from the poles toward the equator. This redistribution of the world's energy helps to maintain a balanced overall temperature for the earth. Without it, the tropics would become increasingly hot and the middle latitudes increasingly cold.

The weather is a complex system, influenced by a number of factors. Chief among them are the spinning of the planet from west to east, a movement that helps to direct the winds; the fact that the sea gains and gives up its heat more slowly than the land; the ocean currents, which both are dependent on the winds and influence the winds themselves, helping to carry heat into the colder parts of the earth; and the existence of great mountain ranges, which disturb and disrupt the worldwide movements of the air.

THE WEATHER PUMP

This composite view of planet earth on a day in September is based on satellite photographs taken 23,000 miles (37,000 km) out in space. Clouds depict the various workings of the weather pump, from the tight spiral of a hurricane to the high-altitude band of the jet stream.

1. NORTH ATLANTIC DEPRESSIONS. Stormy depressions mature as they move eastward across the Atlantic. As air flows counterclockwise around these "lows," they follow a track roughly parallel to the jet stream high above them.

2. JET STREAM. A ribbon of wispy cirrus cloud marks the broad river of midlatitude westerlies. Above them — more than 9 miles (15 km) high — the winds concentrate into narrow belts: the jet streams.

3. HURRICANE. The destructive vortex of a hurricane, some 620 miles (1,000 km) across, is the deepest of all low-pressure systems. It draws in from warm tropical seas the energy that drives it.

4. SAHARA HIGH. As air brought from the tropics sinks over North Africa, it warms up and absorbs moisture, creating clear skies — one of the conditions for earth's largest desert.

5. JUNGLE HUMIDITY. Clouds hang over the lush vegetation of the Amazon Basin. The rain forest is both the product of heavy rainfall and, because vegetation retains more water than bare soil, a massive source of moisture itself.

6. BETWEEN THE TROPICS. The weather has its own equator — the Intertropical Convergence Zone. Here, above the doldrums, warm, moist air rises into giant thunderheads at the powerhouse of the globe's weather system.

7. MOUNTAIN CLOUD. Water vapor from the warm Pacific rises to condense in a blanket of cloud over the great mountain barrier of the Andes.

8. SOUTH ATLANTIC DEPRESSIONS. In the southern hemisphere, air masses, flooding into a depression, spiral clockwise, influenced by the rotation of the earth.

WHERE THE WINDS BLOW

The weather machine is powered by the difference in temperature between the tropics and the poles. In the tropics, hot, moisture-laden air rises from the zone near the equator, where land and sea are at their warmest, helping to create an area of low pressure there. The risen air then spreads north and south, at a height of 9 miles (15 km), to about 30° latitude, where it begins to sink. These are the first links in the major subtropical circulation system known as a Hadley cell. The full cycle is completed by the trade winds that blow in at the surface, toward the equatorial

region of low pressure, called the Intertropical Convergence Zone. Nearer the poles than 30° latitude, the Hadley cell system breaks down, disrupted by the rotation of the earth.

Our planet spins on its axis from west to east once a day. As a result, a point on the equator moves at 1,030 miles (1,657 km) an hour; but a point nearer the pole, where the planet's girth is smaller, does not need to move as fast to make a complete rotation in the space of a day. New York is moving much more slowly than Brasilia, for example.

Imagine for a moment a block of air that begins to move northward from the equator in Brazil toward New York. It will

tend to keep some of its original momentum, moving eastward across the earth close to its equatorial speed even in the more sluggish northern latitudes. The result, when it arrives over New York, is that it appears — to observers on the ground — to be moving rapidly from west to east as a strong west wind.

The result of this phenomenon, known as the Coriolis effect, is that winds curve under the influence of the earth's rotation — to the right in the northern hemisphere, to the left in the southern.

Poleward of 30° latitude, the Coriolis effect becomes so severe that another global weather pattern takes over

GLOBAL LOGIC. World weather is one highly interrelated system.

from the Hadley cell. Long waves, moving in a broad ribbon of westerly winds, concentrate near the tropopause

into the fast-moving bands of the jet streams. These "planetary waves," measuring up to 3,100 miles (5,000 km) from

crest to crest, girdle each hemisphere of the planet and transfer large amounts of heat to earth's temperate regions.

ANATOMY OF A DEPRESSION

As the jet stream accelerates high above the earth, it draws air up away from the surface and a region of low pressure

develops beneath it. Cold polar air swings toward this new low from the north, while warm tropical air is drawn from the south. As the air masses flow into the depression, they are deflected by the rotation of the

earth. The result is that winds in depressions move counterclockwise in the northern hemisphere and clockwise in the southern.

As the depression matures, the boundaries between the air masses become quite distinct and they come to form "fronts," the hallmark of a depression and the source of much of the bad weather to be found in middle latitudes.

At the warm front, the tropical air mass climbs gradually, producing a succession of clouds whose structure changes with altitude. From the ground, the first signs of an approaching depression are the high wisps of cirrus clouds, followed by the banks of altocumulus — commonly known as mackerel sky — and altostratus, then stratus, and finally the heavy blanket of nimbostratus, which drops the light and widespread rain that is typical of a warm front.

At the cold front of the depression, the warm air climbs steeply above the wedge of cold air pushing in below it. The rapid ascent of the relatively warm air cools it, and

the water vapor condenses. Cumulonimbus clouds are produced which may tower as far as the tropopause — 9 miles (15 km) above the earth — where they will spread out in the shape of an anvil.

It is in these buoyant clouds that the great thunderstorms of the cold front occur. The rapidly cooled air releases large amounts of rain, which drops through the cloud, creating a downdraught of cold air that fans out from the base of the storm in a gusty squall.

Under certain conditions,

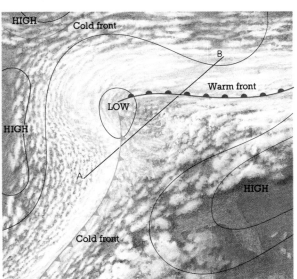

CHARTING THE WEATHER. The cold (blue) and warm (red) fronts of a depression converge above the United States. Section A-B is shown in the illustration below.

currents within the storm can carry droplets up and down inside it. At high altitudes the droplets freeze to become ice pellets. Each time around, the pellets acquire another skin of ice until eventually they become too heavy and fall from the storm as hail.

At other times, the energies of a thunderstorm, derived from the meeting of cold and warm air masses, can be concentrated into the extraordinary destructiveness of a tornado, a narrow funnel of extreme low pressure.

VICIOUS TWISTER. The long limb of a tornado reaches down to farmland in the American Midwest.

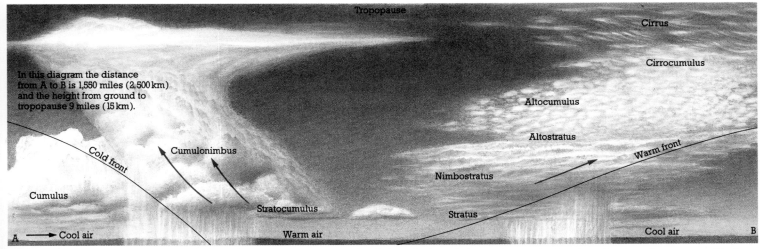

WEATHER SLICE. The movements of air masses within a depression are quite distinct. On the left, the cold nose of polar air pushes in under a warmer block that rises steeply above it, creating the violence of a thunderstorm. On the right, at the warm front, the ascent is far more gradual and the weather gentler.

In this diagram the distance from A to B is 1,550 miles (2,500 km) and the height from ground to tropopause 9 miles (15 km).

HURRICANES AND THEIR BREEDING GROUNDS

Only near the Intertropical Convergence Zone do conditions occur in which a ripple of instability in the air can become a storm strong enough to devastate whole cities. The sea there has a surface temperature of over 80°F (27°C), above which an intense area of low pressure can develop into a storm. It is also far enough from the equator for the earth's spin to make the young storm rotate.

Water vapor from the warm

sea is drawn into the areas of low pressure. It rises and condenses into banks of clouds — intensifying the inward flow of air. Energy is released in torrential downpours and in winds that have been measured at up to 190 miles (300 km) an hour. In the central "eye" of the

storm, however, the skies are still and clear.

A hurricane cuts a great curving swath across sea and sometimes, devastatingly, land, spending its force after six days or so when it runs out of fuel — the energy provided by the warm tropical water.

NURSERIES OF DESTRUCTION. The tropical cyclone — called a hurricane in the Atlantic, a typhoon in the Pacific, and a cyclone in the Indian Ocean — breeds in a worldwide belt.

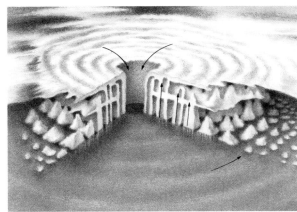

HURRICANE FORCE. Banks of cumulonimbus clouds spiral around the eye of the hurricane. The violent updraughts created within the storm draw in more warm, humid air.

Climate: Clothing the Landscape

Weather can change from day to day. Climate, however, is much slower to shift, for it is the average of a region's weather pattern: its seasonal temperatures and rainfall over many years. It influences all aspects of our lives, determining everything from the sort of roofs we put on our houses to worldwide patterns of human settlement.

Animal life has evolved in response to the demands of climate and its effect on vegetation. Fresh water is essential to human survival, and the most densely populated areas of the world are, in general, well served by water. Fertile river valleys cradled the first civilizations of Mesopotamia, the Indus valley, Egypt, and China.

These were warm, lowland cultures that arose in areas with rich, alluvial soils produced by annual floods. However, their settled populations lived close to nomadic tribes from the harsher climates of desert,

mountain, and steppe. Conflicts between town and tent-dweller occurred again and again in the ancient world. When civilization spread to the Mediterranean, Greeks and Romans came to dread the restless horsemen who surged in waves from the cool, dry immensities of the Asian steppes. Indeed, some of the mightiest Old World encounters between civilization and "barbarism" can be seen as clashes of climate, shaping the course of modern history.

Scientists classify different types of climate, ranging from the polar to the tropical. But the distribution of these types is based on much more than latitude alone. For example, the desert wilderness of Sinai, the snow-capped summit of Mount Everest, and the junglelike forests of Florida all lie roughly 28°N of the equator. The marked differences between these places illustrate something of the complexity of climate on earth.

SHAPING THE WORLD WE LIVE IN

Vegetation provides so reliable a guide to a region's climate that it is often used, in conjunction with average temperature and rainfall, to define climate. This slice of the earth's surface from the Arctic to South America cuts through nine different types of climate – from the polar regions, where the sun's rays are dispersed, to the tropical regions, where they strike most directly.

MONSOON: CLIMATIC GEAR CHANGE

The word "monsoon" derives from the Arabic *mausim*, meaning season, and describes any noticeably seasonal wind which blows over a large climatic region. More specifically, however, the word refers to the wind system of India and southern Asia, which produces two seasons a year. One is dry and the other is wet. If the latter delivers too much or too little of its vital moisture load, the results can be catastrophic.

In June, during the northern hemisphere summer, hot air rises in immense volumes from the Asian land mass, helping to create an area of low pressure. Moist monsoon winds then blow in from the Indian Ocean toward the low-pressure area and shed their water content in torrents over the thirsty earth. Some sites on the slopes of the Himalayas, for example, routinely receive over 400 inches (10 m) of rain a year.

In January, during the northern hemisphere winter, the winds perform their seasonal gear change and go into reverse. Cool, dry air sinks over Asia and spills south to create the winds that produce the dry season.

Rice is a crop that requires hot sun and heavy rain in suc-

PROMISED RAIN. Life-giving rain clouds gather over the Gulf of Thailand. Without them, southeast Asia would starve.

cession. It is grown in vast quantities throughout the monsoon zone, on swampy paddy fields and on terraces that are flooded ankle-deep during the rainy season. Millions of people rely for sustenance upon the coming of the rains, but their times of arrival and quantities can be unpredictable. Too little, too late, can cause widespread drought and famine. Too much can cause devastating floods.

MICROCLIMATE: POCKET WEATHER

Inverewe, on the northwest coast of Scotland, lies at a latitude farther north than Moscow or Labrador City. Yet it boasts gardens where palm, bamboo, eucalyptus, and other subtropical plants flourish in the open air. The paradox is not hard to explain, for Britain has a maritime climate which protects it from great extremes of hot and cold. Inverewe's shores, moreover, are caressed

by the great Gulf Stream, a warm ocean current originating off Florida.

A map of world climates can show only the general characteristics of a region. In reality, local climates vary significantly according to such modest topographical features as the slope of a hillside or the nearness of a wood. Any dip in terrain may, for example, become a "frost hollow," where heavy, freezing air is prone to accumulate. Woodlands, on the other hand, screen off winds, moderating temperatures and raising humidity.

SUBTROPICAL SCOTLAND. The subtropical gardens at Inverewe are free from the frosts of similar latitudes.

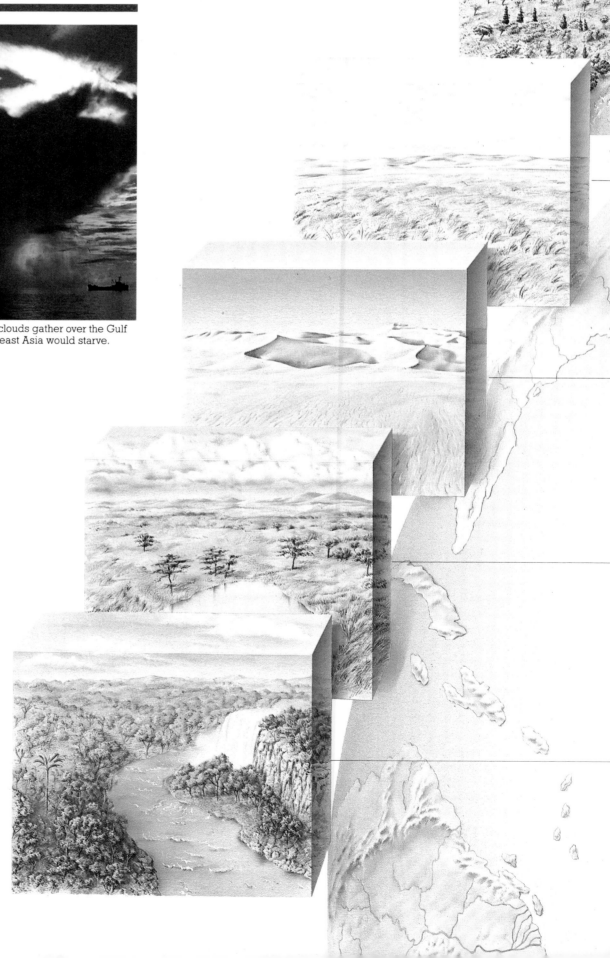

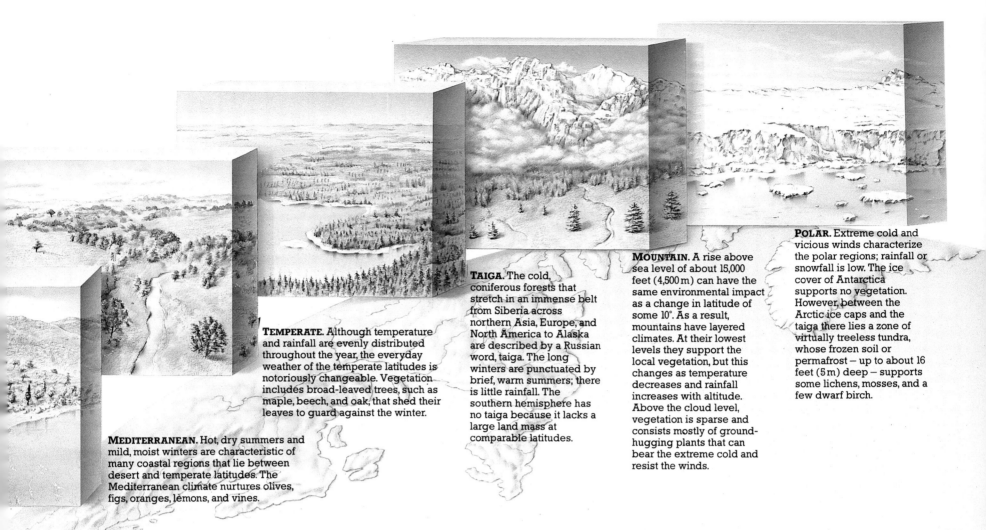

TEMPERATE. Although temperature and rainfall are evenly distributed throughout the year, the everyday weather of the temperate latitudes is notoriously changeable. Vegetation includes broad-leaved trees, such as maple, beech, and oak, that shed their leaves to guard against the winter.

MEDITERRANEAN. Hot, dry summers and mild, moist winters are characteristic of many coastal regions that lie between desert and temperate latitudes. The Mediterranean climate nurtures olives, figs, oranges, lemons, and vines.

TAIGA. The cold, coniferous forests that stretch in an immense belt from Siberia across northern Asia, Europe, and North America to Alaska are described by a Russian word, taiga. The long winters are punctuated by brief, warm summers; there is little rainfall. The southern hemisphere has no taiga because it lacks a large land mass at comparable latitudes.

MOUNTAIN. A rise above sea level of about 15,000 feet (4,500 m) can have the same environmental impact as a change in latitude of some 10°. As a result, mountains have layered climates. At their lowest levels they support the local vegetation, but this changes as temperature decreases and rainfall increases with altitude. Above the cloud level, vegetation is sparse and consists mostly of ground-hugging plants that can bear the extreme cold and resist the winds.

POLAR. Extreme cold and vicious winds characterize the polar regions; rainfall or snowfall is low. The ice cover of Antarctica supports no vegetation. However, between the Arctic ice caps and the taiga there lies a zone of virtually treeless tundra, whose frozen soil or permafrost – up to about 16 feet (5 m) deep – supports some lichens, mosses, and a few dwarf birch.

DRY GRASSLAND. The prairies of North America and the pampas of Argentina, the veld of South Africa, and the steppes of Asia are all screened from the moisture-laden ocean air either by mountains or by the distances they lie inland. These are the traditional lands of cattle and maize.

HOT DESERT. Daytime temperatures of more than 100°F (38°C) and annual rainfall of less than 10 inches (25 cm) characterize most of the world's hot deserts. Moisture is so scarce that only the most efficient water-storing plants, such as thick-skinned cacti, can easily survive.

SUBTROPICAL. Although temperatures are high throughout the year, there are marked seasonal variations in rainfall – especially in the monsoon lands of India and its neighbors. Vegetation ranges from cultivated rice in southern Asia to the tall, straw-colored grasses of the East African savanna.

TROPICAL. The climate in the tropics is one of high temperatures and heavy rainfall throughout the year. These conditions create the canopy of luxuriant evergreen vegetation that is found in the rain forests of the Amazon, the Zaire Basin, and southeast Asia.

THE GEOGRAPHY OF CLIMATE

At first glance, a world map of climates may appear to be a very intricate jigsaw. However, four basic climatic bands underlie the picture: tropical, desert, temperate, and polar. Tropical climates occur at and near the equator, where the air is always hot and moist. Deserts occur in belts to either side of the equator, where the air, depleted of its moisture, sinks to linger in dry areas of high pressure. In the temperate midlatitudes, warm air meets cold polar winds, and the weather is mild and changeable. Closer to the poles themselves, the air is cold and dry.

In addition to the four basic bands are four intermediate zones: subtropical, dry grassland, taiga, and "Mediterranean." This last term describes a type of warm coastal climate experienced not only around the Mediterranean Sea but also at similar latitudes both north and south of the equator: in northern California, parts of South Africa, and southern Australia.

Finally, mountains present a special case. Mount Kenya, for example, rises from subtropical savanna. But at 6,890 feet (2,100 m) that vegetation gives way to tropical rain forest and bamboo thickets. Little rainfall occurs above the general cloud level at about 9,850 feet (3,000 m). Here, sparse mountain vegetation has colonized the upper slopes before giving way to the permanent snow cap of the summit.

Climate classifications are based on more than latitude and annual statistics of temperature and rainfall. Warmth and moisture vary greatly with the seasons, height above sea level, proximity to the ocean, and prevailing air currents. For example, in a single year, temperate Boston and monsoon-drenched Madras may receive the same amount of rainfall. But Boston receives its share throughout the year, while Madras gets most of it between June and December.

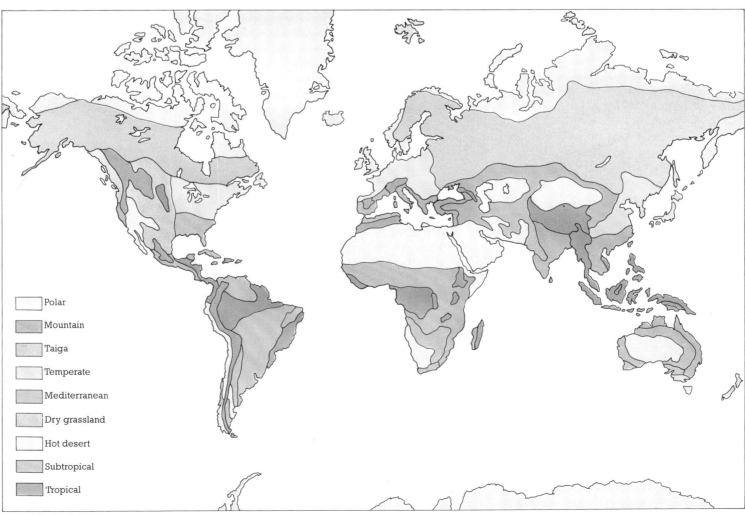

Polar
Mountain
Taiga
Temperate
Mediterranean
Dry grassland
Hot desert
Subtropical
Tropical

PATTERNED EARTH. The mosaic of world climates is a record of the many ways in which the earth and its atmosphere can interact.

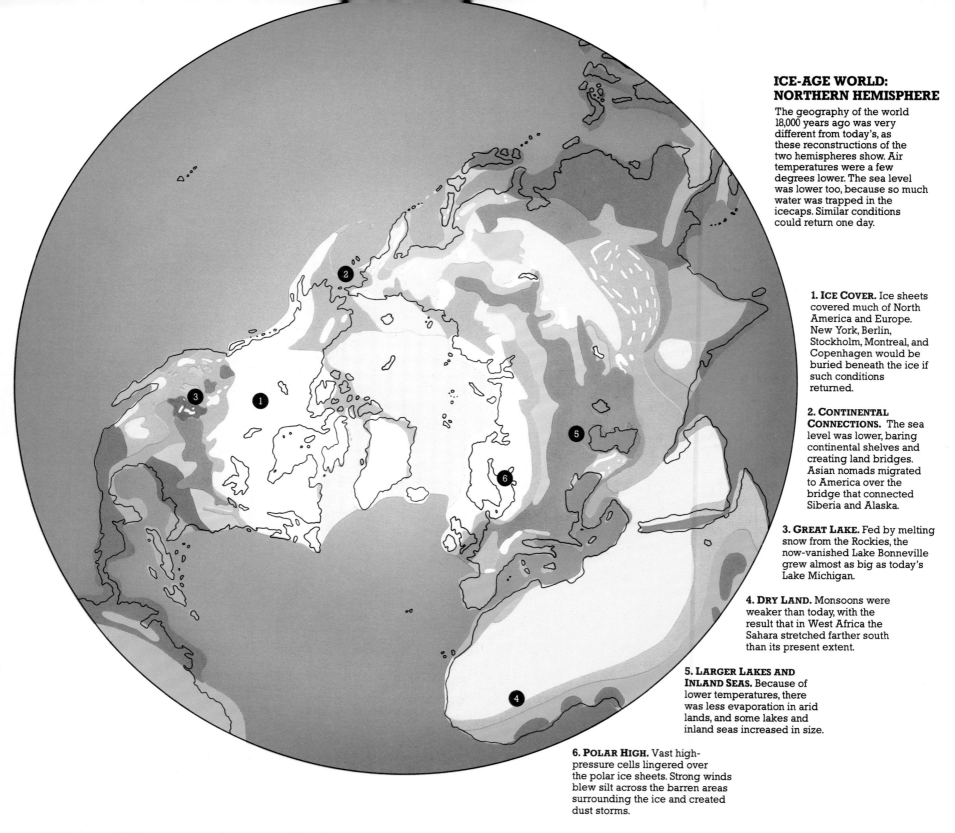

The geography of the world 18,000 years ago was very different from today's, as these reconstructions of the two hemispheres show. Air temperatures were a few degrees lower. The sea level was lower too, because so much water was trapped in the icecaps. Similar conditions could return one day.

1. ICE COVER. Ice sheets covered much of North America and Europe. New York, Berlin, Stockholm, Montreal, and Copenhagen would be buried beneath the ice if such conditions returned.

2. CONTINENTAL CONNECTIONS. The sea level was lower, baring continental shelves and creating land bridges. Asian nomads migrated to America over the bridge that connected Siberia and Alaska.

3. GREAT LAKE. Fed by melting snow from the Rockies, the now-vanished Lake Bonneville grew almost as big as today's Lake Michigan.

4. DRY LAND. Monsoons were weaker than today, with the result that in West Africa the Sahara stretched farther south than its present extent.

5. LARGER LAKES AND INLAND SEAS. Because of lower temperatures, there was less evaporation in arid lands, and some lakes and inland seas increased in size.

6. POLAR HIGH. Vast high-pressure cells lingered over the polar ice sheets. Strong winds blew silt across the barren areas surrounding the ice and created dust storms.

The Changing Climate

We inhabit a thin, damp tissue of the atmosphere, where hospitable warmth and moisture are maintained in a critical balance. What we think of as the planet's "normal" weather patterns are typical only of the period in which we live.

Clues to the climate of the future lie in the facts of the past. There is every likelihood that the climatic conditions that gripped the earth at the height of the last ice age 18,000 years ago will return one day. A drop in global average temperature of only 4°F

(2°C) could initiate a new ice age. The advancing glaciers would imprison so much of the world's water that the oceans would shrink, stripping the seas from the continental shelves. New York City would lie under an ice sheet thick enough to bury the Empire State Building twice over. Montreal, Detroit, and Chicago would be entombed in snow, and the Midwestern prairies would survive only as wind-whipped steppe. Japan would become a peninsula of Asia, and you would be able to walk from

England to France. On the other hand, some scientists believe that a rise of only a few degrees in global temperature would start a meltdown of the polar ice sheets and flood low-lying cities worldwide.

Many forces interact to create changes in the earth's climate. These include tilts in the planet's axis and changes in its orbital path, sunspots that swell the stream of radiation emitted by the sun, and spasms of volcanic activity that hurl veils of dust into the atmosphere.

A CHRONOLOGY OF CLIMATE

Since the height of the last ice age, some 18,000 years ago, the earth has experienced a series of radical changes in its climate.

Many of the clues to these climates past come from the human record and range from cave paintings to harvest statistics. Others come from the annual growth of tree rings. In a mild, wet year the ring will grow thicker than in a harsh, dry one. In addition, the age of fossils trapped in the seabed and in glacial sediment, or of pollen grains embedded in the mud at the bottom of lakes, can help to define the climate of an era.

One of the most accurate

means of reconstructing temperature changes, however, is by examining the oxygen content of water trapped in deep-sea sediments and polar icecaps. The atmosphere contains two types of oxygen which react in different ways to warmth. Oxygen 16 is light, and water molecules that incorporate it evaporate more easily from the surface of the oceans than molecules containing the heavier oxygen 18. During an ice age, the snow that falls at the poles tends to contain more oxygen 16 because its heavier counterpart — oxygen 18 — tends to sink to the ocean floor. Examination of the ratio between the two types, strata by strata, therefore reveals temperature trends era by era.

20000 - 15000 B.C. The height of the last great ice age.	14000 B.C. Major melting of the ice sheets. Sea level starts to rise; glaciers recede, and the Great Lakes appear.	9000 - 8000 B.C. Final cold snap of the great ice age. The Gulf Stream retreats south, and Europe freezes. 5000 B.C. Warmer, wetter weather begins.	4000 B.C. Flooding in Mesopotamia. Cave paintings from this date show cattle grazing in the Sahara. 3000 B.C. Rise in sea level almost complete.	900 B.C. Iron Age people experience a spell of severe weather.	A.D. 986. Ice-free waters enable Norsemen to colonize Greenland. A.D. 1196. Locusts are sighted as far north as Hungary and Austria.	A.D. 1350. Another period of cold weather begins to affect the northern hemisphere. The old Norse colony in Greenland declines.	A.D. 1450. The Little Ice Age lasts for the next 400 years.	A.D. 1683-4. The biggest of many Frost Fairs is held on the River Thames, which is frozen for two months of the year.	A.D. 1800. Cold weather brings a series of white Christmases to England. A.D. 1883. Krakatoa erupts and causes a reduction in the sun's intensity.	A.D. 1900. A 50-year period of warmer weather begins, which peaks in 1940. A.D. 1980. Mount St. Helens erupts, creating a dust pall across North America.

Warmer ⟶ Colder

| 20,000 B.C. | 15,000 B.C. | 10,000 B.C. | 5000 B.C. | 4000 B.C. | 3000 B.C. | 2000 B.C. | 1000 B.C. | 0 | 1000 A.D. | 1100 A.D. | 1200 A.D. | 1300 A.D. | 1400 A.D. | 1500 A.D. | 1600 A.D. | 1700 A.D. | 1800 A.D. | 1900 A.D. | Today |

CLIMATE IN HISTORY. This model of global temperature change over the past 22 millennia is based on variations in the oxygen content of water in the ice cores of Greenland.

SECRET RHYTHMS OF HEAT AND ICE

The planet has throbbed hot and cold, according to a pattern. We live at the end of an interglacial — a warm spell, lasting about 10,000 years. It is sandwiched between recurring ice ages, each lasting about 100,000 years. If the pattern continues, the next big freeze might begin within a few hundred years.

Rhythms of sunshine — in the form of three long-term oscillations — affect the way in which the sun's rays strike the earth. Cycles in the earth's spin, tilt, and orbit — of 22,000 years, 41,000 years, and 100,000 years respectively — are known after Milutin Milankovich, the Yugoslavian scientist who proposed their climatic effect in the 1920's.

Together, these cycles influence the way in which heat is distributed around the globe at different times of the year, disturbing the nature of our seasons. When a summer is cool and new ice fails to melt, the icecap grows. Since snow and ice are brilliant mirrors which reflect much of the sun's radiation back into space, the earth grows colder still. The next summer is likely to be even colder, as the earth plunges into a new ice age.

The first of the Milankovich cycles is governed by the irre-gularities in the shape of the earth. It is not a perfect sphere because it bulges at the equator. The gravitational pull of sun and moon tugs at this bulge and causes the earth to wobble as it spins about its axis. Over a period of 22,000 years, the earth's axis gyrates in space so that the seasons occur at different points of the earth's elliptical orbit. When the northern hemisphere is tilted toward the sun, causing summer, the earth is at the farthest point of its orbit. Some 11,000 years ago, however, summer in the northern hemisphere occurred when the earth was closest to the sun.

The second cycle operates over a 41,000-year period. The degree of tilt in the earth's axis varies between 21.8° and 24.4°. Today's tilt of 23.4° is gradually decreasing, with the result that the difference between the seasons will become less marked. Summers will become cooler.

Finally, over a 100,000-year period, the earth's orbit changes from an ellipse, along which the sun is farther from the earth during certain months than in others, to a near-perfect circle, when the earth is the same distance from the sun throughout the year. If the earth's orbit is very elliptical, and summer in the northern hemisphere occurs at the farthest point, the winter snow will not melt.

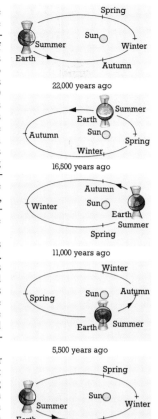

22,000 years ago

16,500 years ago

11,000 years ago

5,500 years ago

Today

GLOBAL WOBBLE. Over 22,000 years, each of the earth's poles traces a cone in space. As a result, seasons occur at different points in the earth's ellipse.

FROM SNOW BLITZ TO SUPERHEAT

Man is caught between two opposing trends. There is a long-term drift toward glaciation, but the planet is also heating up, as carbon dioxide accumulates in the air.

In a process known as the greenhouse effect, carbon dioxide keeps the earth warm by preventing infrared radiation from escaping into space. Plants and animals all absorb the gas during their lifetimes, and when they die a quantity is stored with them. When we burn logs or use fossil fuels, such as coal and oil, we unlock the deposit box and return carbon dioxide to the atmosphere. Levels of carbon dioxide are expected to rise by 75 percent before the middle of the next century.

Computer models suggest that this would cause an average rise of up to 8°F (4.5°C) in world temperature, making climates warmer than at any time in the past 100,000 years.

NOT WAVING BUT DROWNING. The Statue of Liberty rises above the meltwater ocean.

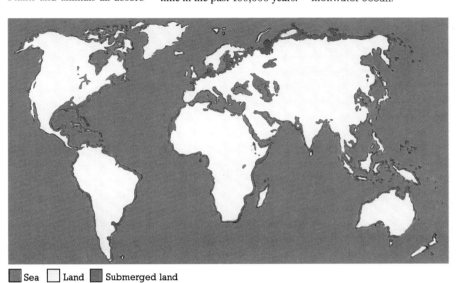

☐ Sea   ☐ Land   ☐ Submerged land

GLOBAL MELTDOWN. A rise in temperature, sufficient to melt all of the world's ice sheets, could raise the sea level by 230 feet (70 m), drowning the world's coastlines.

ICE-AGE WORLD: SOUTHERN HEMISPHERE

7. COLD SEAS. Ocean temperatures were, on global average, some 4°F (2°C) lower than today.

8. DEFORESTATION. The tropical rain forests of South America virtually disappeared — to be replaced by savanna and semi-desert, with extensive sand dunes in places.

9. ICE CONTINENT. Unlike the North Pole, which was covered with sea ice, the continental land mass of Antarctica carried an extensive ice sheet fringed by a rim of sea ice.

10. DESERT LAND. Central Australia was much more arid. Many of today's sand dunes, particularly around Ayers Rock and in the Simpson Desert, are remnants of this period.

☐ Ice sheet

☐ Sea ice

☐ Tundra

☐ Desert (cold or hot)

☐ Semi-desert and steppe

☐ Loess terrains (or wind-blown silt)

☐ Forest steppe

☐ Grassland savanna

☐ Forest

☐ Lakes and seas

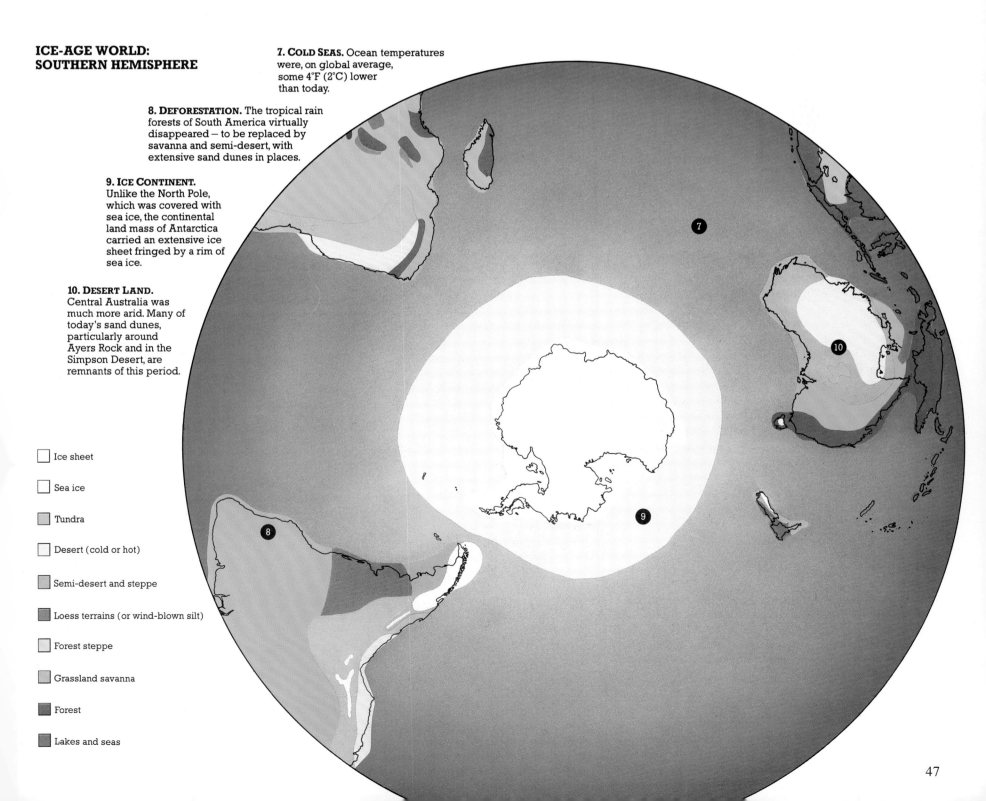

The Story of Life on Earth

When life began, 3.5 billion years ago, the first oceans were still only a few degrees below boiling point. There, in waters bombarded by ultraviolet light from space and played on by lightning from massive thunderstorms, the first amino and nucleic acids, the building blocks for life, were formed. It has happened many times and in many places in the universe — astronomers have detected amino acids floating between the stars — but on earth it gave rise to a history of life which may be unique in its extraordinary variety and abundance.

There are between 3 million and 10 million different kinds of plants and animals alive today, and possibly twice as many were once alive but are now extinct. Every one has been built from those first basic materials, and yet every one is unique. That is the double miracle of evolution: the flow of genetic information across the ages and the editing of that information into almost countless separate categories. The editor is the environment. It selects those organisms for survival that are best suited to life in each particular environmental niche, and ruthlessly destroys those that cannot make use of the resources around them.

An astonishing variety has been created in the genetic pool. It has allowed life to flourish in almost every corner of the world, so that there are organisms alive today that can live and proliferate in blocks of ice, while others exist and breed in bubbling pools of natural petroleum.

TONGUES AND CLAWS

Anteaters from very different evolutionary lines now occupy parts of every continent except Europe. Despite their different ancestries, each, under pressure from the environment, has developed the equipment that is necessary for an ant-eating life: protection from predators, claws to dig into the anthills, and a long tongue with which to extract the prey.

The Australian spiny anteater is a primitive, egg-laying marsupial. On its back are sharp protective spines, and on its front legs equally sharp claws for excavating ant nests. In its long tubelike jaws is the tongue which it flicks into the ant nests. The Asian and North African pangolin's long tongue can penetrate 16 inches (40 cm) beyond its nose. When threatened, the animal rolls up into a tight ball inside its scaly armor. The aardvark in Africa south of the Sahara, by contrast, uses its heavily muscled front legs for digging and for parrying large predators such as lions. The aardvark's tongue, sticky like those of the other anteaters, can dive a foot (30 cm) into an ant nest. The ant bear, wandering the pampas of South America, is 6 feet 6 inches (2 m) long and is equipped with such long claws for opening termite hills that it must walk on the side of its feet. Its snout — in effect the tongue-case — is actually longer than its legs.

Ant bear
(South America)

Pangolin
(Central Africa; Asia)

Aardvark
(Southern Africa)

Spiny anteater
(Australia)

THE ORIGIN OF SPECIES

It is impossible for a cow to give birth to anything but a calf or for a salmon to breed with anything but another salmon. Nevertheless, both animals have, without doubt, emerged from the same distant ancestor. Scientists are still unsure exactly how the process of speciation occurs, but there are many clues in the world about us. The beautiful songbird called the golden whistler is to be found on the tropical archipelago of the Solomon Islands in the Pacific Ocean. Although the birds on each island are still recognizably part of the same species, there are distinct differences in the

Nissan Island   Malaita Island

MOVING APART. Golden whistlers from separate islands of the Solomon archipelago in the Pacific have different markings.

colors of their markings from island to island. Over the many generations in which the birds of each island have been separated from the others, slight distortions in the genetic information passed from parent to offspring have begun to push them apart. Eventually the change in appearance may become so extreme that, even when birds from different islands are brought together, they will not recognize each other as potential mates. Then the two lines will go their separate ways. This sort of isolation may be one way in which species originate.

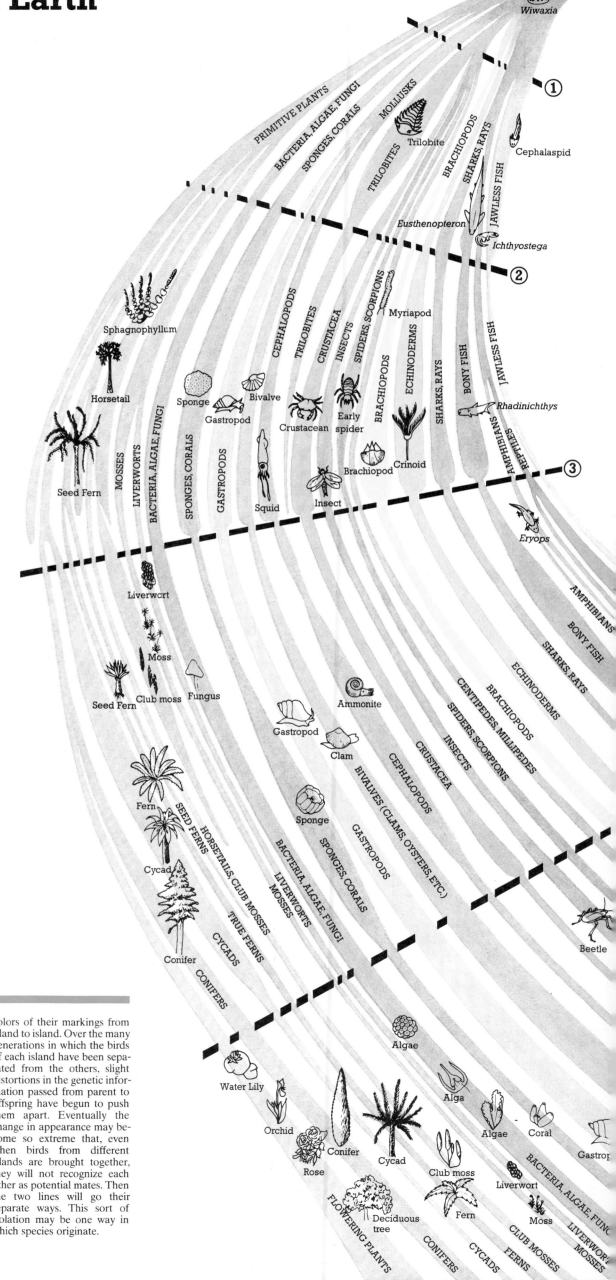

48

1. THE FIRST ABUNDANCE

About 570 million years ago, the continents moved apart, and the climate of the world became more congenial. The polar ice caps melted, and warm shallow seas came to cover wide stretches of the continental margins. Here, on a sea floor rich with nutrients washed down from the land, was the signal for a sudden new abundance. At that immensely distant time, the sea was filled with many strange forms, such as *Wiwaxia* (1) and *Opabinia* (2), which have no known relatives, but fossils of other creatures have been found whose descendants still thrive in the tropical seas of today. Simple sponges, such as *Vauxia* (3) and *Eiffelia* (4), constructed their delicate skeletons. Soft corals called sea pens (5), with long feathery bodies, grew fixed to the mud of the sea floor. Segmented worms (6) burrowed in the mud, and some primitive jellyfish floated above it.

It may have been a change in the chemistry of the sea that allowed the building of hard bodies for the first time. There were many shelled animals, the ancestors of the mollusks, and tall, symmetrical creatures with stalks called crinoids (7).

The kings of the Cambrian seas, however, were the trilobites (8), armored for protection with a mixture of lime and chitin. Some species of trilobite could roll up for protection like woodlice. Others floated upside down, scanning the sea floor for food. The trilobites flourished for more than 200 million years, after which they eventually all but died out and their role was taken over by the crabs and the lobsters.

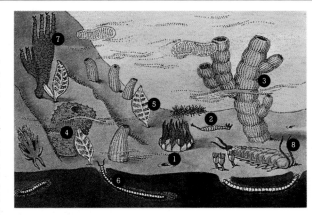

CAMBRIAN DIVERSITY. The seas of 570 million years ago were bright and various with new forms of life.

2. MOVING ON TO LAND

Plants made the first move onto the land. Algae and then club mosses (1) and primitive ferns (2) crept up from the edges of estuaries and rivers in low, damp, tangled mats of green. These were the necessary pioneers. Without the shelter, the food, the shade, and above all, the wetness which they provided, no animal could have survived on land. Among the first creatures to make use of them, about 400 million years ago, were giant millipedes (3), some small spiders and early, flightless insects flourishing among the tree ferns (4). About 350 million years ago, our own ancestors lumbered out of the teeming waters. Animals such as the lungfish (5) could use their bony front fins to haul themselves onto the mud. In time, the first amphibians, such as *Ichthyostega* (6), developed, still returning occasionally to the water to breed.

In the following 100 million years, life on land developed explosively. Great tropical forests flourished. Crocodile-like amphibians ate scaly fish, and the earliest reptiles laid the first shelled eggs.

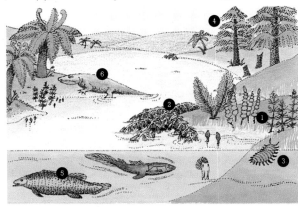

FIRST STEPS. With four bony limbs — our own pattern — the amphibians came onto land 350 million years ago.

3. MASS DISAPPEARANCE

About 225 million years ago, the two supercontinents, Laurasia in the north and Gondwanaland in the south, came together to form one global land mass, Pangaea. The pattern of ocean currents changed; the polar ice caps expanded; the seasons became more severe, and the global food supply fluctuated wildly. Most important of all, the area of the continental shelves — the richest of all environments on earth — was halved. This combination of effects brought about the greatest catastrophe ever experienced by life on earth. About half of all the species alive at the time disappeared. Three-quarters of the amphibians and four-fifths of the reptiles became extinct. The creatures that died out included *Rhinesuchus* (1), a crocodilelike fish-eating amphibian; the first plant-eating reptiles, such as *Dicynodon* (2), living on the mud-banks of river deltas; and the small insect-eating reptile, *Millerosaurus* (3). The widespread *Glossopteris* tree (4), forests of which covered large parts of the southern continents, also died away.

The earth took about 20 million years to return to its normal level of biological diversity. Some organisms, such as the mammal-like reptile *Galechirus* (5), survived, perhaps to become the ancestor of the first true mammals. Plants such as horsetails (6) have persevered until today.

Many new families of shelled animals appeared, including snails, periwinkles, and oysters. The great spirals of the ammonites began to jet-propel their way around the oceans. On the land, the first snakes and early dinosaurs appeared in the forests. At night, our new tiny shrew-like ancestors, the first true mammals, crept about unseen.

EVE OF DISASTER. The animals of 225 million years ago browse at the water's edge before the catastrophe.

4. END OF THE DINOSAURS

About 65 million years ago, something strange happened to the earth. Many existing animal families disappeared. All the marine reptiles, all the flying reptiles (1), and any land animal with a body weight of more than about 22 lb (10 kg) died out. The dinosaurs were the principal victims. They had diversified into hundreds of different ecological niches. Some were meat-eaters; others, such as the heavily armored *Triceratops* (2), grazed on the early grasses; and the hadrosaur (3) fed off trees, such as the monkey puzzle (4) or the conifers (5).

The impact from a large meteorite may have disrupted the entire life-system of the planet. Another theory suggests, however, that the sudden disappearance of the dinosaurs is illusory. It may have happened over about 2 million years, and could have been the result of a cooling of the earth.

Birds (6) took over the air. Flowering and seed-bearing plants, such as early magnolia bushes (7), now conquered the world, and mammals, such as the insect-eating *Triconodon* (8), began to flourish.

ALL CHANGE. As the dinosaurs' dominance comes to an end, their successor, the tiny mammal, crouches in the grass.

FLOWERINGS AND EXTINCTIONS

Like a mountain stream, the flow of life seems to have gone through a series of long and relatively quiet periods, interrupted by moments of sudden and dramatic change. At each of these "gates" up to half of all living organisms, both in the oceans and on the land, have quite rapidly disappeared. Those that survived emerged into a world of opportunity, rich with ecological niches left empty by the death of their predecessors. At these moments, organisms have suddenly radiated into a proliferation of new forms.

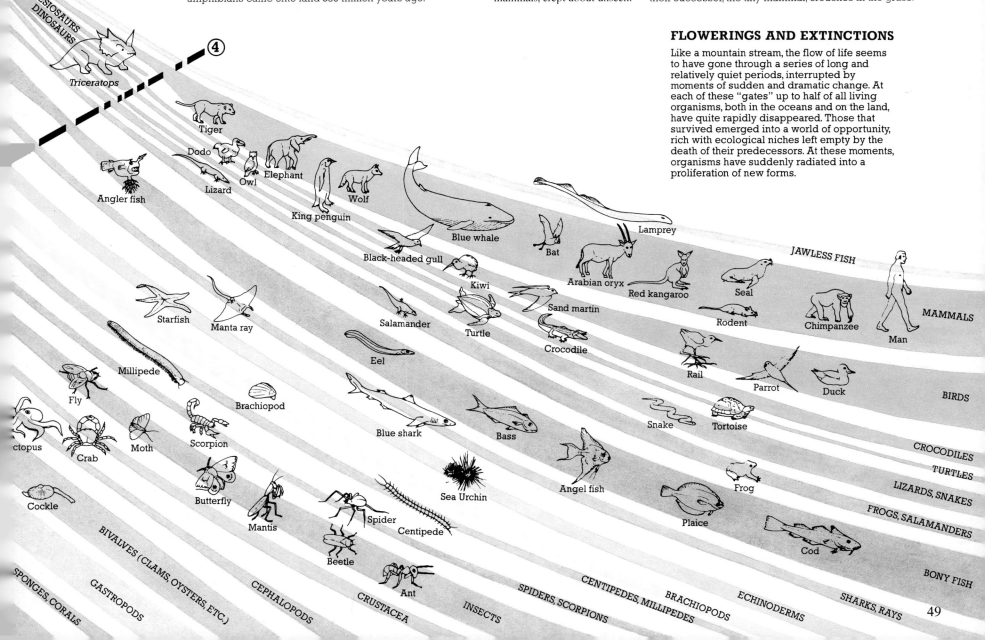

The Emergence of Man

The story of mankind begins in the tropical forests of at least 65 million years ago. By then the first primates, the order of mammals to which man belongs, had appeared. These tiny creatures of the night had gradually developed hands for gripping branches, preying upon insects and testing fruit for ripeness. Since complex hand-to-brain nerve "wiring" was required for these tasks, the capacity to explore with the hand may have contributed to an inquiring and expanding brain.

Many of the characteristics that we share with other primates then began to develop: sensitive finger pads; binocular vision that enables us to see in three dimensions; a large brain; and an "opposable" thumb that is capable of touching the fingers on the same hand, providing both a powerful and a precise, manipulative grip.

Man's closest relatives are the apes, the next most intelligent primates. The gorilla, the chimpanzee, and the manlike hominids may have shared a common ancestor until as recently as 5 million years ago.

Since then the various hominid types have not evolved in easy succession. At times different types have existed side by side, like separate branches bursting simultaneously from one tree. Consequently, not all of the "fossil men" discovered by scientists are our direct ancestors. There are gaps in the fossil record too, and many things that fossilized bones simply cannot tell us. Our bodies may still, as Charles Darwin once said, bear the indelible stamp of our lowly origin, but the exact route by which we have arrived at our present state is still something of a mystery.

1. THE FIRST STEPS

The time when the hominids rose onto their hindlegs and took their first faltering steps was as exciting, in evolutionary terms, as the thrill every parent feels when a child learns to walk.

During a great drop in global temperature between 7 and 5 million years ago, Africa's tropical forests succumbed to the encroaching grassland. Our vegetarian ancestors, it is thought, came down from the trees and gradually adapted to the open country. At first, perhaps, they sheltered in clumps of trees overnight and foraged on foot in the grasslands during the day. It has even been suggested that since the first hominids were small, they had to rear on their hindlegs to see over the grasses.

The earliest known hominids were the *australopithecines* (southern apes). They lived between at least 4 million and 1.5 million years ago, and their fossils have been found along the East African Rift Valley and in several South African caves.

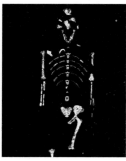

WALKING TALL. The skeleton of a female from Hadar in Ethiopia, more than 3 million years old, has been named Lucy. The hip and thigh bone suggest that she walked upright, and probably stood a little over 3 feet (1 m) tall.

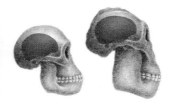

DISTANT RELATIVES. Remains of a creature known as *Australopithecus africanus* have been found in South Africa. This hominid, which is sometimes known as the "gracile" or slender australopithecine (left), lived 3-2 million years ago and may have been our ancestor. Its later, more robust relative, *Australopithecus boisei,* or "Nutcracker Man" (right), was more thick-set and was not a direct human ancestor.

OLDEST FOOTPRINTS. This trail of footprints, belonging perhaps to two adults and a child, was found preserved in a bed of volcanic ash at Laetoli in Tanzania. It proves that hominids were walking upright some 3.75 million years ago.

2. THE HANDYMAN

About 2 million years ago, the brains of one hominid line started to expand, and their bodies developed sufficiently manlike attributes for scientists to have dignified them with the name of *Homo* ("man"). Specifically, this creature is known as *Homo habilis* — the Handyman."

These habilines had powerful hands that were also capable of precision working. They made efficient implements and even engineered tools that were designed for making other tools — hammerstones, for instance.

The habilines probably hunted live game only rarely. On most occasions, they may have used their tools to cut and scrape meat from dead animals that were brought back to communal campsites.

EARLY MAN. A skull recovered from Koobi Fora shows that the habilines had a larger and more rounded cranium than the australopithecines, with less of an apelike muzzle.

THE PREHISTORIC WORLD

The map locates the major sites where evidence of early man has been found; the numbers beside each of the locations relate the find to the appropriate stage in man's evolution — to be found in sequence around the edge of the globe. All the skulls — and the brains inside them — are to the same scale. The map also charts the major surges in which our ancestors colonized the earth. About 1.6 million years ago, groups of them came out of Africa; within the past 40,000 years, modern man reached the Americas and Australasia.

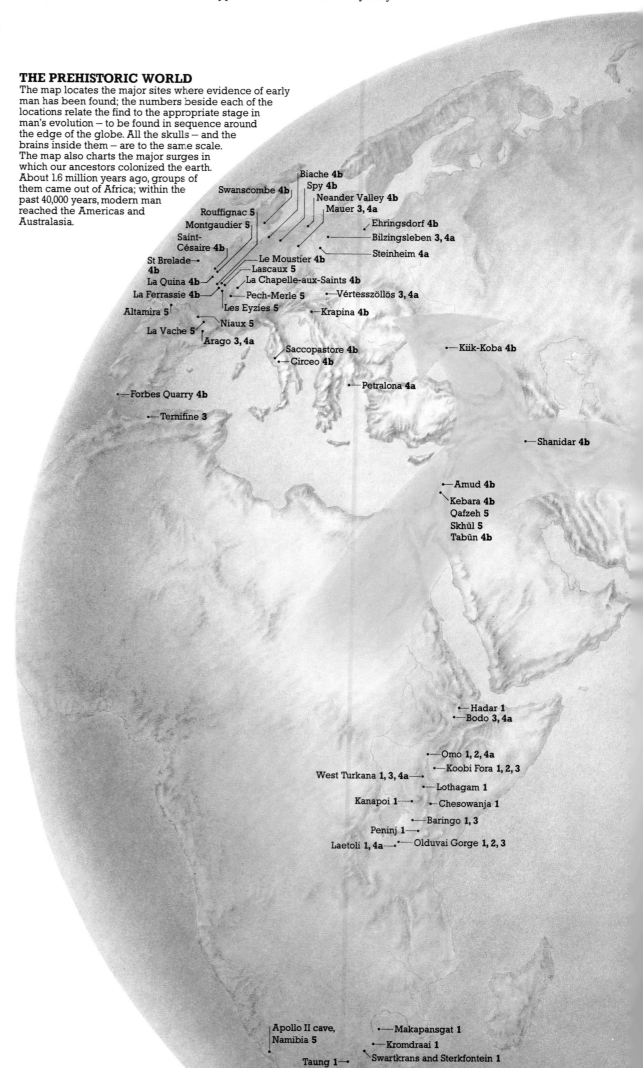

Biache **4b**
Swanscombe **4b**
Spy **4b**
Neander Valley **4b**
Mauer **3, 4a**
Rouffignac **5**
Montgaudier **5**
Ehringsdorf **4b**
Saint-Césaire **4b**
Bilzingsleben **3, 4a**
Steinheim **4a**
St Brelade **4b**
Le Moustier **4b**
Lascaux **5**
La Quina **4b**
La Chapelle-aux-Saints **4b**
La Ferrassie **4b**
Pech-Merle **5**
Vértesszöllös **3, 4a**
Altamira **5**
Les Eyzies **5**
Krapina **4b**
La Vache **5**
Niaux **5**
Arago **3, 4a**
Saccopastore **4b**
Kiik-Koba **4b**
Circeo **4b**
Forbes Quarry **4b**
Petralona **4a**
Ternifine **3**
Shanidar **4b**
Amud **4b**
Kebara **4b**
Qafzeh **5**
Skhūl **5**
Tabūn **4b**
Hadar **1**
Bodo **3, 4a**
Omo **1, 2, 4a**
West Turkana **1, 3, 4a**
Koobi Fora **1, 2, 3**
Lothagam **1**
Kanapoi **1**
Chesowanja **1**
Baringo **1, 3**
Peninj **1**
Laetoli **1, 4a**
Olduvai Gorge **1, 2, 3**
Apollo II cave, Namibia **5**
Makapansgat **1**
Kromdraai **1**
Taung **1**
Swartkrans and Sterkfontein **1**

3. OUT OF AFRICA

The fossil record suggests that *Homo habilis* and the earlier hominids were confined to Africa until about 1.6 million years ago. From then on, a new species of hominid known as *Homo erectus*, or upright man, existed not only in Africa but also across Asia and possibly Europe. *Homo erectus* had a larger brain than the habilines and, as well as greater skill at toolmaking, at least one major technological breakthrough to his name: the making of fire.

Fire provided a natural focus for social life. *Homo erectus* may have been a regu-

PEKING MAN. Remains of *Homo erectus*, dating from between 600,000 and 200,000 years ago, and evidence of fire were found at Zhoukoudian, near Beijing (Peking) in China.

TOOL TECHNOLOGY. The chipping of tear-drop axes, from 1.5 million years ago, is witness to the finely honed skills of *Homo erectus*.

lar hunter who brought back slaughtered game to the communal hearth for cooking and distribution. Carnivores need much more territory per head than vegetarians, and there-

fore it is the hunting habit that may explain the sudden migratory surge out of Africa. Upright man pursued game into terrains too harsh for a tropical vegetarian.

4. NEANDERTHAL MAN

Homo erectus evolved into a more advanced kind of human called archaic *Homo sapiens* (4a). In Africa and perhaps in Asia, these people eventually evolved into modern man, but in Europe, the Near East, and Central Asia they became *Homo sapiens neanderthalensis* (4b), or Neanderthal man.

Because of his low brow and lantern jaw, Neanderthal man fits the brutish cartoon image of a caveman. But such a picture is wrong. For these remarkable people were capable of sensitivity and great spiritual feeling.

They lived from more than 100,000 to 35,000 years ago, making tools, using fire, fashioning clothes, and probably holding ceremonies. Archeologists have, for example, found Neanderthal graves in the Zagros mountains of Iraq. In one, a 40-year-old man with a withered arm may have been laid to rest on a bed of woody horsetail. In another, the body was possibly garlanded with cornflowers, hollyhocks, and hyacinths.

The Neanderthals — an offshoot of the main hominid line — died out about 35,000 years ago during the last ice age.

LAID TO REST. The graves at Shanidar in northern Iraq are testament both to the spirituality and humanity of Neanderthal people.

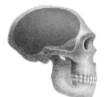

HALFWAY MAN. Archaic *Homo sapiens* is a stage between *Homo erectus* and both Neanderthals and modern man.

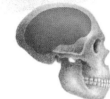

HEAVY-BROWED. The Neanderthal skull is distinguished by a heavy brow ridge and a large projecting nose.

5. THE COMMUNICATOR

Some 35,000 years ago, human beings physically just like ourselves were living in Europe, Africa, and Asia. And by 30,000 years ago — during the last ice age when a land bridge connected Siberia with Alaska and people could walk most of the way from the Asian mainland to Java — large parts of the Americas and Australasia had probably been colonized by our own subspecies, *Homo sapiens sapiens*. He is called "the wise, wise man" to distinguish him from the Neanderthals and to celebrate his crowning characteristic — intelligence.

What identifies the Ice Age hunting peoples more than anything else is their use of symbols to represent things. They carved female figures

MODERN MAN. Modern man's rounded cranium encloses a brain of about 80 cubic inches (1,350 cu cm).

out of bone and stone, and they decorated cave walls with magnificent images of animals. The high point of their culture comes with the harshest period of the ice age, around 18,000 years ago. It was soon after then that the beautiful cave paintings of Lascaux in southern France and at Altamira in northern Spain were created. Man had clearly become a very skilled communicator and artist.

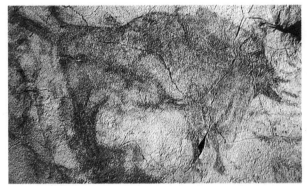

STONE AGE STYLE. This bison from the caves at Altamira in Spain, painted between 15,000 and 12,000 B.C., illustrates the exquisite naturalism of Stone Age art.

ICE AGE FOOD. The horses on the cave walls at Lascaux in France, painted about 15,000 B.C., may represent prey.

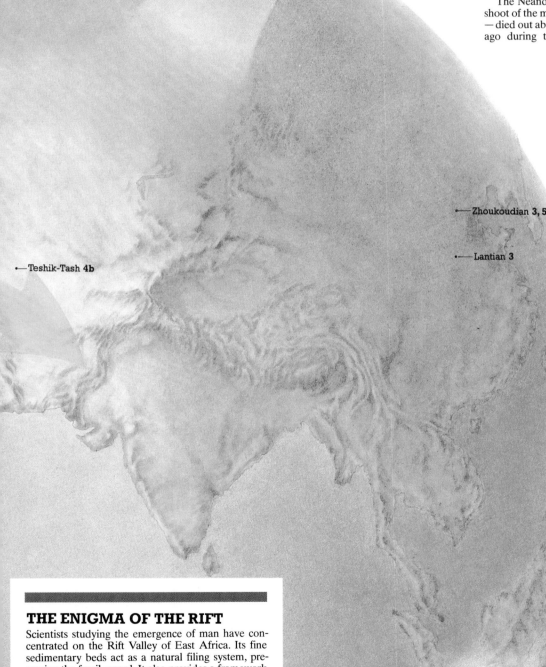

— Teshik-Tash 4b

— Zhoukoudian 3, 5

— Lantian 3

Sangiran 3
Modjokerto 3
Trinil 3—
Ngandong 3

Kenniff Cave 5 —

Lake Mungo 5—

THE ENIGMA OF THE RIFT

Scientists studying the emergence of man have concentrated on the Rift Valley of East Africa. Its fine sedimentary beds act as a natural filing system, preserving the fossil record. It also provides a framework for understanding our own origins.

The Rift started to form some 20-15 million years ago as the continents drifted and an extended strip of East Africa began to tug away from the East African plate, leaving a long geological fault enclosing a system of stream-fed lake basins. To the east, huge outflows of volcanic rock created the great mountains of the Kenyan and Ethiopian highlands, which acted as a cloud barrier and deprived the valley of its rainfall. As a result, patchy woodland and savanna replaced humid equatorial forests. In conditions like these, it is not hard to see how communities of our apelike ancestors might have become isolated from the apestock of the deep forests. With every climatic dry spell, they would have been forced to adapt to life in the open country. It was a case not so much of our ancestors leaving the trees as of the trees deserting them.

The Settling of Man: Farming and the City

Although the ways of the farmer and the city dweller may seem poles apart, their history is intimately related. Over the first 2 million years of human history, our ancestors were entirely dependent upon nature's whims for food. It is only within the last 10,000 years that they have settled down to farm the land and control their own food supply.

The earliest settlements were farming villages — ancient Jericho was little more than such. But, as crop surpluses grew and trade and industry thrived, the village became the organized city, crowded with specialist craftsmen — builders, carriers, sculptors, physicians, bureaucrats, and priests.

The great thaw at the end of the last Ice Age, some 10,000 years ago, may have started this process on its way. For it brought milder weather and the spread of the wild grass ancestors of modern cereal crops.

What happened next has been seen, in part, as a revolution in containers. Pots, vats, cattle pens, granaries, water cisterns, and the walled town itself were all storage devices designed to shelter and protect. Farming and city life depended not only on the new skills of organization and technology. They also required the home base and nurturing skills traditionally connected with womanhood. In Egyptian hieroglyphs, for example, the symbols for "house" and "town" also stand for "mother." And our own concept of civilized living implies, as well as the use of cunning gadgetry, the comfort and security of a settled life.

MESOAMERICA: MONUMENTS OF A VANISHED CIVILIZATION

The construction of huge, immovable objects is one of the hallmarks of a settled people. The Olmecs, who created the first major civilization in the Americas, built vast pyramid-shaped temples as well as some of the most colossal statuary seen in the ancient world.

From about 5000 B.C., a form of maize was being cultivated in Mesoamerica — Mexico and the isthmus to the south. By 2000 B.C., farming villages were well established, and the skills of pottery and weaving were being practiced.

The Olmec swamplands lie on the east coast of Mexico. The discovery here of artificially raised platforms and

OLMEC HEAD. A huge helmeted head, carved from basalt and erected by the Olmecs between 500 and 100 B.C., demonstrates the power and organization of their culture.

drainage works implies the communal mobilization of manpower. From 1200–600 B.C., the Olmecs built a series of ceremonial centers, the greatest of which was La Venta.

For sheer grandeur, nothing could rival the colossal heads which the Olmecs set up there. They were carved from giant blocks of basalt, sometimes weighing as much as 34 tons, which had to be brought from a quarry many miles away.

PERU: FARMING BY STAGES

The sky-raking peaks of the Central Andes have never tempted human settlement, but cupped among them are cultivable valleys and plains long grazed by native llamas. Soil erosion is a constant threat on the steep slopes and, to deal with this, the Andeans had begun to terrace their hillsides by 1000 B.C.

By the 16th century A.D., when Andean society reached its zenith under the Incas, agricultural terraces contoured even the most tortuous mountain slopes. Maize, beans, potatoes, cucumber, and peppers burgeoned from the stepped hillsides. The terraces were often faced with stone, and the soil was constantly revitalized with human and animal fertilizer.

The cities often needed terracing too. In Machu Picchu, perched 9,000 feet (2,743 m) above sea level, tiers for buildings were cut out of the living rock and connected by steep flights of stone stairs. Communications in this mountainous country were problematic, but the Incas built a marvelous road system to serve imperial messengers who ran in relay from the capital at Cuzco. The routes often followed high ridges rather than swooping into the switchback valleys.

The state was strictly hierarchical, utterly dependent on the figure of the emperor. When the Spaniards under Francisco Pizarro invaded in 1532 and usurped the emperor, they were able to inherit the whole stepped edifice of Inca civilization.

TERRACED SOPHISTICATION. Machu Picchu, high in the Peruvian Andes, embodies the terraced style of Inca cities.

MESOPOTAMIA: WHERE HISTORY BEGINS

The skill of writing divides history from prehistory. And the earliest evidence of writing — and of the wheel and monumental architecture — comes from Mesopotamia, the region between the rivers Tigris and Euphrates, in modern Iraq.

In ancient times, the rivers' floods washed down fertile alluvial soils but rainfall was uncertain and, without manipulating the river waters, no crops could have been grown. Irrigation works were essential, and the maintenance of such a system both required cooperation and put power in

CLAY LEDGER. Field areas were noted down on a tablet in southern Mesopotamia, about 2900 B.C.

the hands of the communities that controlled the canals. The rewards were bumper crops, enough to support a wealth of specialist craftsmen who never needed to work in the fields.

Cities arose in Mesopotamia around 4000 B.C. In places such as Ur, Uruk, Eridu, and Susa, huge temples and palaces were built. Workshops turned out mass-produced pottery for export, in exchange for materials scarce on the silty plain: stone, timber, and metal ore. Masted cargo vessels and wheeled carts developed in response to the needs of trade during the 4th millennium B.C.

Writing first appeared in southern Mesopotamia in about 3100 B.C. It evolved from stylized picture images and was not at first used to list dynasties or record epic adventures. The first texts, pressed into wet clay tablets, merely totted up heads of cattle or sacks of grain.

THE RISE OF CIVILIZATION

Writing or town planning, monumental architecture or a legal code, sophisticated farming or the working of metals – each of the eight ancient cultures presented here is remarkable for one of these key features of civilization. They all arose in a broad climatic band that favored the growth of crops.

La Venta

Machu Picchu • • Cuzco

BABYLON: THE RULE OF LAW

Without the framework of law, the complex structures of urban civilization would soon break down. Among the great powers that rose and fell in the Near East during the 2nd and 3rd millennia B.C., Babylon was outstanding for its legal system. Prominent among the lawmakers was King Hammurabi (1792–1750 B.C.), who gathered together the common laws of Babylon and Sumer to create a single legal code.

Like other monarchs of his day, Hammurabi was absolute ruler of a slave-owning society. Records from the archives of the palace at Mari, which he sacked, show him to be a cynical diplomat, skilled in international power play. Nevertheless, his great law code, collated for use in courts throughout his empire, marks a milestone in the story of civilization.

Here, in 282 articles, were gathered together guidelines for coping with the myriad disputes likely to arise in the teeming cities of his time.

LAWMAKER. The law code of Hammurabi was carved on upright stone tablets, or stele. It covers loans, bequests, wages, medical fees, divorce, adoption, and real estate. It is often humane. For example, if a nobleman divorces his wife because she is infertile, he must pay back her dowry. But the articles can be severe too. A man who permits an irrigation dike to be breached shall be sold as a slave, the proceeds going to those who have suffered by his negligence.

EGYPT: KINGDOM OF THE GODS

Like the many separate city states of Mesopotamia, ancient Egypt grew up around a regimen of river flooding and water management. But the solitary ribbon of the Nile gave a special cohesion to its society. From about 3100 B.C., upper and lower Egypt were joined under a single pharaoh, Menes. Thereafter, Egyptian civilization evolved continuously, under successive dynasties of kings, for 2,500 years.

The key to Egypt's unique sense of national identity lies in the dual role of the sovereign. The pharaoh was both king and god, throned at the apex of a rigidly hierarchical society in which state and religion were one. Supported by an extremely efficient bureaucracy of scribes, Egypt's god-kings could undertake massive projects, from pyramid building to imperial conquest.

But the Egyptians delighted in earthly pleasures also. The ruling classes invented the free-standing suburban villa, distanced from the hubbub of the

GOD-KING. Blessed by the sun, Tutankhamun's queen spreads perfumed oil on the Pharaoh's collar (1358-1351 B.C.).

city center. And they benefited from the best medical science then known. There were practical textbooks on diagnosis and treatment.

There were doctors who specialized in different forms of ailment: eye specialists, for example, and dentists. Splints, casts, and sutures were available for injury, and physicians used a wide range of medicinal plants. Castor oil was prescribed as a laxative, and opium was used to pacify babies. Egyptian doctors even devised sophisticated methods of birth control.

CHINA: FOOD FROM THE FLOOD PLAIN

Farming began independently in China, based on quite different crops from those grown in Mesopotamia, Egypt, and India. The cultivation of rice (in the south), of millet (in the north), and of soy beans and yams from about 7000 B.C. spawned an increase in rural population. Not until much later, about 2000 B.C., after some contact across central Asia with the Near East, did real urban settlement begin.

The fertile flood plain of the Huang He, or Yellow River, cradled the seeds of the earliest civilization in China. Surplus food encouraged a booming population, urban growth, and the development of fine bronze casting based on massive deposits of copper and tin in southeast Asia.

Under the Shang dynasty of the 18th–11th centuries B.C., a fully fledged Chinese civilization emerged. Horse-drawn chariots, probably introduced from western Asia, plied the streets of An Yang, the royal capital. It was a rigidly stratified society, in which power radiated from the divine monarch, spread out through the aristocracy, and was eventually imposed on the subject masses. This radical difference between the value of the lives of those at the top and at the bottom of Chinese society is symbolized by the large and glorious royal tombs. Not only the monarch but hundreds of slaughtered retainers are buried there, a massive provision of soldiers and servants for the king's afterlife.

China's unique script was also developed under the Shang. It does not seem to have been a tool of commerce. Most of the early examples are found on oracle bones that were used by priests for prophecies.

BRONZE ARTISTRY. This Shang dynasty ritual vessel — a tiger protecting a man — was made in the 14th-12th centuries B.C. It is covered in the animal motifs of a fertility cult.

(map with labels:)
Mycenae
CRETE — Knossos
Mari
Jericho
Euphrates River
Eridu
Ur
Nile River
Tigris River
Babylon
Uruk
Susa
Persian Gulf
Harappa
Mohenjo-Daro
Indus River
An Yang
Huang He (Yellow River)

MINOAN CRETE: CITADEL OF THE SEA

The Island of Crete, in the eastern Mediterranean, was near enough to the great Bronze Age power sources in Egypt and Mesopotamia to be influenced by them, as a network of trading links reached out from the shore. But, unlike their nearer neighbors, it was far enough away not to be swamped by them. Crete, dependent on the sea and protected by it, developed a bright and powerful culture of its own, which reached its height between 2000 and 1450 B.C., before being conquered from the north by Mycenaeans sailing over from mainland Greece.

Mariners had been plying sea routes through the Aegean almost from the end of the Ice Age, and the many islands and long coastlines of the Aegean fostered a tradition of maritime skill and enterprise. Cretan workshops exported exquisite products, including vases, figurines, rings, and seals to Cyprus, Egypt, and the Near East. It was from the proceeds of such trade that the great palaces of Knossos, Mallia, Phaistos, and Zakros were built. Such sophisticated and painted palaces were the centers of small towns.

Minoan art is marked by an extraordinary gaiety. No solemn, bearded patriarch is seen among the bull-leaping youths and bare-breasted women. Minoan images give the impression of a fearless society. The palaces are unique among ancient examples in lacking defensive walls: the sea itself was Crete's rampart.

SEA KINGDOM. A fresco from the Cretan palace on Thera (Santorini), until recently concealed by volcanic dust, reveals all the brilliance of Minoan civilization

THE INDUS: ANCIENT TOWN PLANNING

From about 3000 B.C., scores of settlements grew up on the flood plain of the Indus valley, in the area of modern Pakistan. The largest, Mohenjo-Daro and Harappa, each contained about 30,000 inhabitants at their peak. They were, essentially, farming people whose crops included wheat, barley, sesame, peas, and cotton. They manufactured cotton cloth for export, and, from the evidence of artifacts found at their sites, clearly traded a long way by sea, up the Persian Gulf as far as Mesopotamia.

The Indus culture had its own script and its own religion, with ascetic practices and fire rituals akin to those of later Hinduism. Religion alone seems to have played the dominant role in this tightly organized society, with its well-planned settlements. For — quite unlike Egypt or Mesopotamia — there are no traces of the palaces of kings or aristocrats.

A standardized system of weights and measures applied throughout the Indus civilization. And its towns were planned according to a rigorous, rectangular grid system — even the bricks were made to uniform size. Particular care was taken over the water supply and the drainage and washing facilities. Houses in Mohenjo-Daro, which were often built two stories high, included bathrooms served by earthenware pipes. In some cases, sit-down toilets were built, with sloping channels to drains in the street.

GREAT BATH. The brick-walled public bath at Mohenjo-Daro (foreground) has survived four millennia of neglect.

The Wanderings of Man and the Making of History

Throughout history, people have moved across the planet's surface, sometimes in trickles of individual families and sometimes in mass population surges. Famine, overpopulation, the search for a better life, or flight from an enemy may set a people in motion. And the results can be complex as one initial surge puts pressure on neighboring communities, who in turn displace neighbors of their own. In such a way, throughout antiquity, stirrings among steppeland nomads in the heart of Asia brought ripples of catas-trophe to the civilizations of Rome to the west and China to the east.

Religious faith may motivate a migration: it spurred the Islamic conquerors and the Pilgrim Fathers alike. Sometimes, too, peoples have been forcibly transported, as happened to the black victims of the Atlantic slave trade, which reached its peak in the 18th century. The great Diaspora, or dispersion, of Jewish people can similarly be traced to one episode of history. It started in the 6th century B.C., when the Jews were deported from ancient Israel into captivity in Babylon. Successive persecutions later drove their communities to disperse over much of the world.

The story of man's wanderings encompasses epics of exploration and adventure, ranging from the voyages of the Stone Age Polynesians to the expeditions of Magellan and Captain Cook. Whether thought of as pilgrims or vagabonds, we remain, after ten millennia of settled living, a species with wanderlust.

THE DORIANS: THE SETTLING OF A TRIBE

The rise of classical civilization in Europe can be traced back to the wanderings of a few barbarian tribes late in the second millennium B.C. Initially, the influx of Dorians from the north plunged Greece into a dark age in which society fell apart and the skill of literacy was lost. However, the new-comers possessed one technology which their precursors did not have: the use of iron. This gave them the ability to make more effective weapons and superior farming implements, such as sickle blades and stronger plowshares — capable of breaking up heavy soils that had never been exploited before. By 800 B.C., improved agriculture had started a popu-lation explosion — and the rise of a vibrant new Greek culture.

Farming stimulated the growth of self-contained city states, each consisting of a town with its surrounding countryside. The busy Greek *polis* — from which we get the term "politics" — was the basic unit of civilization.

The boom in population and the need to trade prompt-ed overseas emigration. Greek colonies were founded as far afield as North Africa, Sicily, southern Italy, and southern France and, with the conquests of Alexander the Great (356-323 B.C.), territories as far east as India were opened to Greek influence. Where settlers went, so too did the splendors of Greek art, architecture, and philosophy.

THE VIKINGS: VISITATIONS OF TERROR

Toward the end of the 8th cen-tury A.D., the pagan Vikings first appeared on the horizons of western Christendom. And, for the next 200 years, the prayer which rang out from the churches of Europe echoed the terror inspired by the early Danes, Swedes, and Norwe-gians. "From the fury of the Northman, O Lord, deliver us."

The Vikings were coastal farmers whose adventure was triggered by the pressure of a booming population on lim-ited farming land in Scandi-navia. This was aggravated by the practice of primogeniture,

VIKING LONGSHIP. The approach of this longship, which dates from before A.D. 800 and is now in the Viking Ship Museum in Oslo, would once have signaled orgies of blood-shed, smoke, and plunder.

whereby a chieftain's domain passed to his oldest son, leav-ing the younger sons to form a volatile class of land-hungry warriors. The development of the longship gave Scandinavia the means to export its quarrel-some surplus manpower.

The migratory surge was over by about A.D. 1000, but it left its legacy around Europe. The Rus, who gave their name to Russia, were a band of 9th-century Vikings who made their capital at Kiev. And the Normans who settled in France, Britain, and Sicily were descendants of the Vikings.

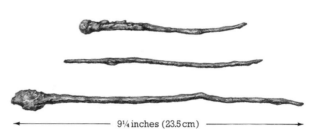

9¼ inches (23.5 cm)

CURRENCY INSTRUMENTS. Iron-working spread to Greece with the Dorians. By the 8th century B.C., iron spits were being used for currency in the city of Sparta.

THE HUNS: HORSE-RIDING NOMADS OF THE STEPPE

"A hideous dwarf" is how one Roman chronicler described Attila, the squat and sparsely bearded leader of the Huns; yet this 5th-century warrior straddled the two worlds of barbarism and high civilization like a colossus and can even lay claim to being one of the founders of modern Europe.

The Huns were a confedera-tion of tribal groups which formed in outer Mongolia in the 4th century A.D. After the death of Attila in 453, their empire crumbled.

But their invasion of Europe had already triggered mass migrations that would have a lasting effect on the peopling of the continent. Germanic tribes had been swept westward by the Hunnish advance: the Franks, for example, overran much of Gaul, creating the embryo of modern France; the Angles and Saxons invaded Britain, eventually creating a unified kingdom of England. Meanwhile, the Slavs, who originated in Asia, shifted westward from the steppes of eastern Europe to occupy territories once held by the Germanic tribes.

MAN ON THE MOVE
Six of the great migrations, illustrated by arrows on the maps, are epics in themselves. Their legacies include the shaping of modern Europe and the spread of classical civilization.

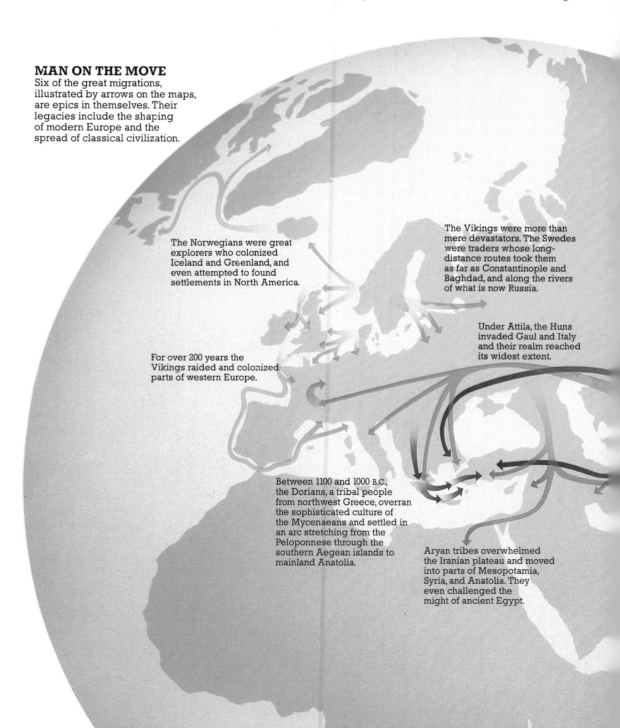

The Norwegians were great explorers who colonized Iceland and Greenland, and even attempted to found settlements in North America.

The Vikings were more than mere devastators. The Swedes were traders whose long-distance routes took them as far as Constantinople and Baghdad, and along the rivers of what is now Russia.

For over 200 years the Vikings raided and colonized parts of western Europe.

Under Attila, the Huns invaded Gaul and Italy and their realm reached its widest extent.

Between 1100 and 1000 B.C., the Dorians, a tribal people from northwest Greece, overran the sophisticated culture of the Mycenaeans and settled in an arc stretching from the Peloponnese through the southern Aegean islands to mainland Anatolia.

Aryan tribes overwhelmed the Iranian plateau and moved into parts of Mesopotamia, Syria, and Anatolia. They even challenged the might of ancient Egypt.

SCOURGE OF GOD. Although Pope Leo I persuaded Attila the Hun not to ransack Rome in A.D. 452, this Italian plaque commemorates the barbarian leader as "The Scourge of God."

THE TURKS: FROM HERDSMAN TO EMPEROR

The Turks did not originate in Turkey but in the foothills of the Altai mountains of central Asia, thousands of miles to the east. In the 6th century A.D., the pastoral Turkic tribes emerged as leaders of a nomad confederation. Over the next few centuries, they spread onto the central Asian steppe before settling on the Anatolian plateau that now bears their name. And it was here that, under the Ottomans, they built an empire which was later to become the equal of any European power, covering much of Eastern Europe, North Africa, and the Middle East.

Paradoxically, the Ottomans' very strength dealt a trump card to Europe. Because the Turks blocked the overland trade routes to the east, European explorers were forced to look for sea passages to the fabled lands of silks and spices. In their lonely voyages across the ocean, these explorers gave Europe global interests that the mighty Ottomans never quite attained.

TURK TERROR. In this contemporary painting by a French artist, the Turks led by the Ottoman sultan, Mehmet II, lay siege to Constantinople (now Istanbul) in 1453. The city, the last bastion of the Byzantine Empire, fell to the Turks after a siege of six weeks.

THE ARYANS: BARBARIAN BEARERS OF A GLOBAL LANGUAGE

In the second millennium B.C. waves of herdsmen started to flow southward from the steppes of central Asia and the Ukraine. These barbarian peoples shared a common family of languages known today as Indo-European. They drove horse-drawn, spoke-wheeled chariots, which gave them mobility and strength in war.

One group invaded India from the northwest, probably contributing to the sudden fall of the Indus Valley civilization. With the Aryans came closely related tribes, such as the Kassites, the Mittani, and the Hittites. These peoples were Indo-European speakers; their rulers sometimes had pure Aryan names; and many of them worshiped Aryan gods.

The language family and the charioteering practice traveled northward and westward too. In Europe, vigorous new tribes, such as Dorian Greeks, Latins, Celts, Germans, and Slavs, started to emerge. The English word "brother" is *"Bruder"* in German, *bhrátar* in Sanskrit, and *frater* in Latin. The Indo-European language family is the largest on earth today—its tongues are spoken by half the people in the world.

THE POLYNESIANS: STONE AGE SAILORS

Oceania is an island-spangled expanse of the Pacific Ocean that stretches for thousands of miles between Asia and the Americas. The colonization of this vast sea is a tribute to the seafaring skills of its Stone Age settlers, the ancestors of today's Melanesians, Micronesians, and Polynesians.

The great period of expansion probably began in about 1500 B.C. when the Lapita people, the ancestors of the Polynesians, moved across Oceania's blue vastness, carrying with them their food plants and domestic animals. They knew wind and wave patterns well, and navigated by the sun and stars. To discover lands beyond the horizon, they probably employed skills that are still in use today, such as studying the flight of birds toward landfall, the drift of vegetation, and even the pattern and coloring of distant cloud masses, which change in character as they pass over an island.

OCEANGOING CANOE. The traditional craft of the Polynesians are double canoes and single outriggers, equipped with matting sails.

Mounted on horseback, the Huns surged from their heartland in the steppes of outer Mongolia and, thundering westward through Persia, reached the Roman Empire.

The early Turkic tribes spilled down from their mountain fastnesses onto the central Asian steppe.

Known as the Aryans, the invaders of India brought with them the Indo-European language known as Sanskrit as well as a wealth of hymns, spells, and rituals which later made up the Vedas (India's first literature).

During the 11th century, the Turks swarmed south and west, crushing a Byzantine army in 1071 and establishing themselves on the Anatolian plateau.

In 1453, Turkish armies, led by a group called the Ottomans, captured Constantinople and ended the 1,000-year-old Byzantine empire.

Although New Guinea was inhabited at least 40,000 years ago, the peopling of the most remote Polynesian islands was not completed until about A.D. 1000.

The settlement of New Zealand in about A.D. 750, probably from eastern Polynesia, was among the last and greatest achievements of the Polynesian navigators.

← Dorians   ← Huns   ← Vikings   ← Turks   ← Aryans   ← Polynesians

Discovery, Empire, and Independence

In the Middle Ages the earth was thought to be a flat plain surrounded by waters, with Jerusalem at its center and Paradise somewhere in the Far East. Then, in the late 15th and early 16th centuries, Europe's conquest of the sea revolutionized man's knowledge of his planet and helped to give Europe a new supremacy in world affairs.

Explorers such as Columbus, Vasco da Gama, and Magellan enmeshed the world with a cat's cradle of communication routes. Soldiers, traders, missionaries, and administrators soon followed in their wake, tightening the strings of European control.

In trickles at first and then in a human flood, Europeans overwhelmed the new lands. They settled especially in temperate zones suited to their crops and flocks. The whole bio-luggage of Europe was freighted abroad. European pests, weeds, and diseases — sparrows, dandelions, and measles were among the most invasive — wreaked havoc among the plant and animal species of the new worlds.

By the standards of ancient Rome, China, and Egypt, the colonial empires of Europe were short-lived. But the pageant of empire had left the planet with a wholly new geography of life and culture.

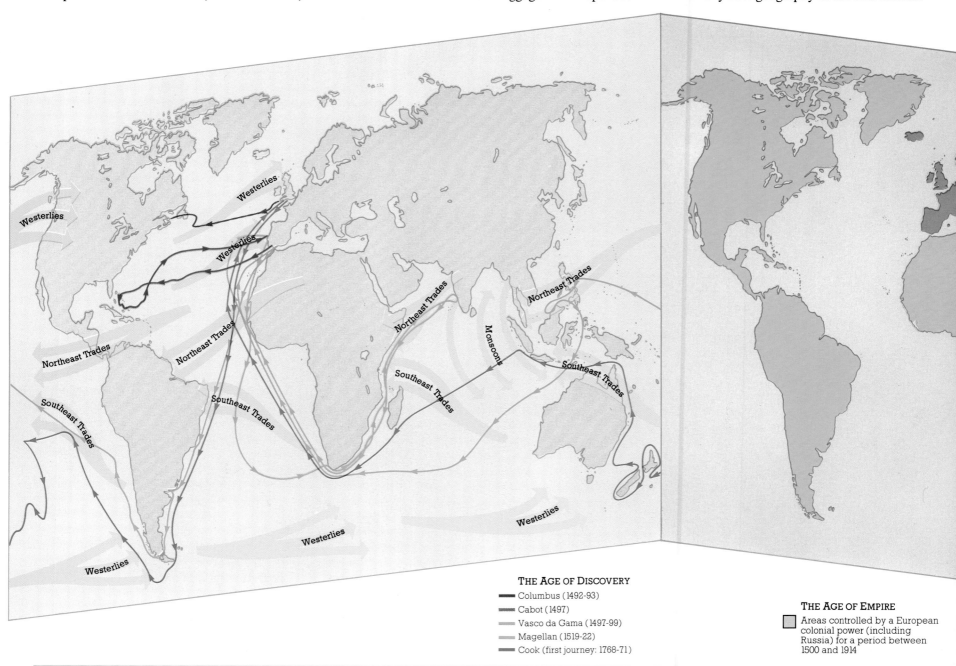

THE AGE OF DISCOVERY
- Columbus (1492-93)
- Cabot (1497)
- Vasco da Gama (1497-99)
- Magellan (1519-22)
- Cook (first journey: 1768-71)

THE AGE OF EMPIRE
- Areas controlled by a European colonial power (including Russia) for a period between 1500 and 1914

1. THE WORLDFINDERS

The great age of exploration began in the mid-14th century, when European sailors ventured out into the Atlantic. Mariners rediscovered the Canary Islands, which the Romans had known as the "Fortunate Isles." As Spain settled the archipelago and as Portugal settled the neighboring Madeiras and Azores, Europe acquired Atlantic outstations — springboards for the oceanic leaps to come.

It was from the Canaries that Christopher Columbus weighed anchor on August 3, 1492. The great Genoese navigator, financed by the king and queen of Spain, went on to discover the Americas by mistake: he was sailing westward in the hope of reaching the silks and spices of Asia. In the following decades, the legendary wealth of the Orient continued to act as a great magnet for explorers and their patrons, whether they were looking for easterly or westerly routes.

FLAGSHIP. The *Santa Maria* had two square sails with a lateen sail at the stern.

Portuguese navigators, such as Vasco da Gama, who completed the first trip to India and back in 1499, sailed south and east. Spanish navigators, such as Ferdinand Magellan, whose expedition was the first to circumnavigate the globe, in 1519-22, sailed south and west. English, French, and Dutch navigators generally looked for passages in the northern hemisphere. John Cabot, for example, was authorized to travel westward to Asia by Henry VII, king of England — but instead he discovered Newfoundland in 1497.

The ship that first opened the seas was the three-masted Portuguese caravel, rigged with triangular lateen sails and designed for working around gusty coasts. The lateen (an Arab invention) allowed mariners to sail much closer to the wind. But for long oceanic voyages, square sails were required to catch the full force of a fair wind behind the ship. The result was a craft like Columbus's flagship *Santa Maria*: square-sailed but with a lateen at the stern.

The planet's winds were the seafarers' great energy resource. Particularly important were the great rotating cogwheels of the weather machine which spin north and south of the equator. These revolving air masses create the Trade Winds, which drove Columbus to the Americas and Magellan across the Pacific.

Prevailing westerlies in the northern hemisphere provided an airstream in which ships could return to Europe from America. The same winds in the southern hemisphere powered ships around the southern oceans. The monsoon pattern, blowing from the north in winter and the south in summer, helped the passage to and fro across the Indian Ocean.

Apart from storms, the mariners' great enemy was the doldrums, the equatorial belt of pitiless calms in which many a seaman learned terror of a flat sea's indifference.

By the 18th century, mapmakers were already producing a reasonable picture of the world we know today. The first successful marine chronometer — developed in 1761 by the British horologist John Harrison — offered a reliable means of measuring longitude. People still believed, however, that some vast southern continent must exist to balance the mass of Asia in the north. The British Captain Cook, on his first voyage of 1768-1771, that Australia could not be this continent. He later disproved the theory of a weighty southern continent altogether.

2. GLOBAL LANDLORDS

By 1914, the habitable earth was almost entirely controlled by Europeans or people of European descent. Africa was carved up in a late-19th-century scramble for possessions that left only Liberia and Ethiopia as lonely pockets of self-rule. And India had become a British imperial possession in 1858.

Other countries were more subtly exploited. While merchant companies tapped their economic resources, power was exercised more by manipulating local rulers than by formal conquest. Nevertheless, Europe's military hardware — from musket to Maxim gun — was the ultimate arbiter in any disputes. In 1900, for example, the Chinese who had risen against the foreigners in the Boxer Rebellion were crushed by force of arms.

Conquests were most spectacular in the new worlds. No sooner were America and Australasia discovered than they were completely overrun, their often sparse native populations being replaced by Europeans as the dominant ethnic groups.

The empire-builders' conquests were biological as much as military. European diseases such as influenza, whooping cough, and measles proved lethal to native populations that had no immunity to European infection. Smallpox, for example, accompanied the conquistadores through Latin America, exterminating vastly more Aztecs and Incas than gunpowder ever did. Settlers' cattle, horses, rabbits, rats, and weeds escaped and ran wild, bursting onto virgin lands with the same intrusive self-assurance as the human pioneers.

The new worlds sprouted new versions of Europe as vast numbers of Europeans emigrated. Between the mid-19th century and 1914, one person in ten left the mother continent to seek opportunities elsewhere. English, Scots, Irish, Russians, Germans, Italians, Swedes, Slovaks, Magyars,

THE PEOPLE BUSINESS

Between the 16th and the mid-19th centuries, black Africa lost almost 10 million of her inhabitants to the Americas. The Africans did not go willingly; they were victims of the Atlantic slave trade and the thinly populated New World's voracious needs for labor.

Ships bearing captives from Africa started crossing the Atlantic in 1530, destined for the Spanish and Portuguese sugar plantations. Profits were so great that the English, the French, and the Dutch soon joined in. By the end of the 18th century, millions of men, women, and children had been exported in the slavers' holds.

A three-cornered traffic evolved, slickly keyed to the Atlantic pattern of winds and currents. Ships laden with European merchandise sailed for West Africa, where the goods were swapped for slaves. The ships were off-loaded in the New World, and the same ships returned to Europe, reloaded with the produce of the American plantations: sugar, tobacco, rum, coffee, cotton, and other goods.

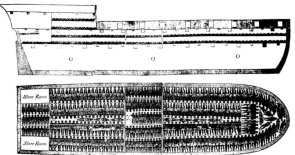

SLAVE STOWAGE. At least one-fifth of the 609 slaves crammed on board the *Brooks* died on their journey to the Americas.

Ample evidence has survived of the human cruelties. Slaves were crammed between decks like herds of human cattle or even (in the words of one captain) "like books on a shelf."

Those who survived the journey to the Americas might simply be worked to death on arrival — new shipments of slaves were sometimes required every few years in order to repeople entire plantations.

It was not until the middle of the 19th century that the slave trade was eradicated. However, the new worlds still needed workers and, by then, European expansion had triggered some major population movements among non-European peoples. Masses of Chinese emigrants moved to work in southeast Asia and California. This was the era when "Chinatowns" started to spring up in cities as far apart as San Francisco, Havana, and London. Meanwhile, Indian emigrants moved in great numbers to East and South Africa and to the Caribbean, to take advantage of the new opportunities there.

Many of the unskilled Asian laborers, widely known as "coolies," went under long-term, enforceable contracts. Working on railroads, plantations, and mines, they lived in conditions of virtual serfdom. This indenture system, though much criticized, was not abolished until the 1920's.

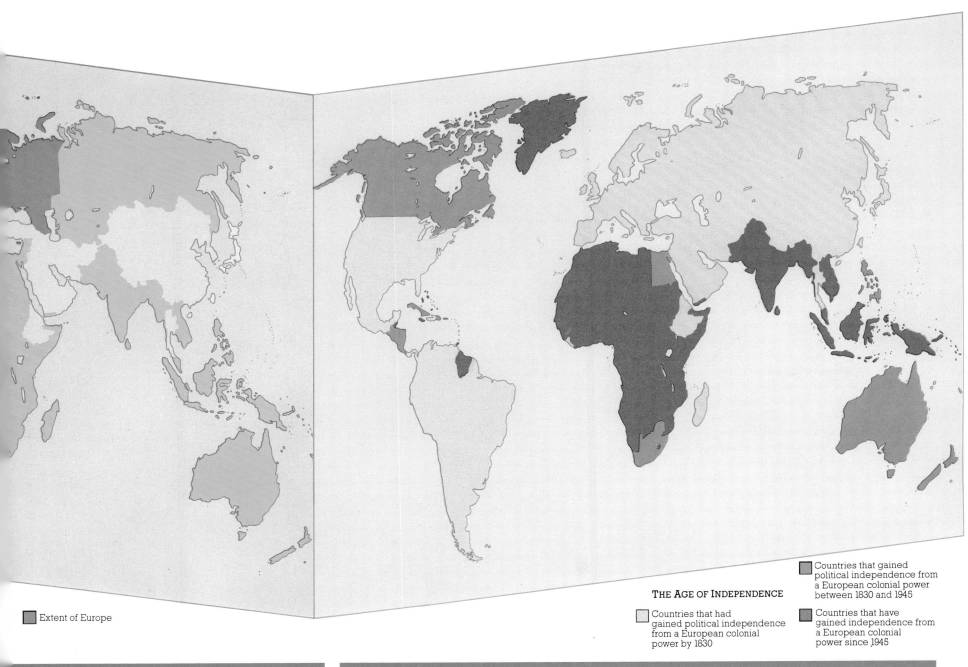

THE AGE OF INDEPENDENCE

Extent of Europe

Countries that had gained political independence from a European colonial power by 1830

Countries that gained political independence from a European colonial power between 1830 and 1945

Countries that have gained independence from a European colonial power since 1945

BRITISH RULE. This 18th-century painting of an officer on his elephant is evidence of British power in the subcontinent — long before India officially became a British possession.

Greeks — they all crowded the new steamships and settled wherever climates were favorable, to farm the land, start workshops, build railways, and found businesses. America was the big magnet, the United States alone absorbing 30 million new inhabitants. But there were other important destinations, such as New Zealand and the coasts of Australia. Within the Russian empire, 7 million peasant colonists crossed over from European Russia into the arable belt of Asiatic Siberia. In total, the European exodus involved 50 million people — the biggest population movement ever.

3. THE END OF EMPIRES?

Two world wars in the 20th century broke Europe's grip on the globe. And the new superpowers, the United States and the Soviet Union, both proclaimed themselves hostile to the principles of direct political imperialism.

The process of decolonization, however, had begun long before the carnage of the world wars. Soon after their establishment, many New World settlements had started to develop a sense of their own interests and identity. Inevitably, they sought political independence. Thirteen of Britain's colonies in North America were first to cut themselves adrift, winning independence as the United States in the American Revolution (1775-83). Between 1810 and 1830, virtually all of Latin America was liberated too.

A second great wave of emancipations occurred within the cloak of the British Empire. The "white dominions" of Canada, Newfoundland, Australia, New Zealand, and South Africa were granted increasing responsibility for their own affairs, achieving autonomy as the British Commonwealth of Nations in 1931.

The third great wave began after 1945, and was accompanied by huge upheavals. One milestone was passed when India was granted independence from Britain in 1947, following Mahatma Gandhi's long campaigns of civil disobedience. Ghana's independence in 1957 initiated a sequence of generally peaceful handovers in Africa and the Caribbean. But there were traumas too. Vietnam (1954) and Algeria (1962) both won freedom from France after periods of violent conflict. The armed struggle for independence in Portugal's African colonies of Angola and Mozambique did not end until 1975.

Flag-waving jingoists at the turn of the century described the "civilizing mission" of empire. Businessmen, on the other hand, believed that empires existed to provide industrial Europe with markets, commodities, and living space for her surplus populations. The age of empires created a global economy, connecting distant continents through bonds of trade. The fact that political control was not always essential to ensure profitable commerce explains the Victorian statesman Benjamin Disraeli's shrewd remark that "colonies do not cease to be colonies because they are independent." This remains the paradox of many new nations today: although politically emancipated, they remain the clients of an industrial world that still governs ghost empires of influence.

REMOVING THE TRACES OF EMPIRE.
Workmen remove a bust of the Belgian king from a plinth in Stanleyville (now Kisangani) during a drive to erase all traces of the Belgian administration. The Belgian Congo (now Zaire) gained independence on June 30, 1960.

Earth's People: Health and Wealth

About 5 billion people are alive today. Every second, three more are added to the total, a growth of more than 10,000 an hour, and over 80 million in the space of a year. The world population has doubled since 1950; and even though the rate at which it is growing has slowed from its peak of 2.4 percent a year in 1965, it will have risen to over 6 billion by the turn of the century. This massive expansion has been fueled not by an increasing birth rate but by a gradual extension of life expectancy and by a huge reduction in the number of children who die when young. More than half the people now living are under 25. In Africa, almost half are under 14.

In Europe, Japan, and North America, however, the number of births has already dropped so as to be almost in balance with the number of deaths, and the population there is now virtually stable. For the world as a whole, this balance will not come, according to United Nations predictions, until about the year 2110, when there might be 10.5 billion people striving for living space.

Population is concentrated now, as it always has been, in those tolerable climatic belts where people can live most comfortably and where enough food can be grown to support them. These areas have given birth to the great cities that are the hallmark of modern industrial society. Nearly half of the world's population — over 2.27 billion people — are now urbanized, half of them in cities of more than 500,000 people. This increasing concentration of the species in great urban patches is true of both the developed and the developing world. By the turn of the century, twice the number of people will be living in the cities of the Third World, where the great bulk of population growth is occurring, as in those of the relatively stable north.

THE SPAN OF LIFE

Three-quarters of the world's people cannot expect to reach their sixtieth birthday. Poverty, an inadequate diet, the widespread absence of a safe water supply, and ignorance of even the simplest rules of hygiene all help to lower the average life expectancy in the less developed countries to 57 years.

That figure is an average for men and women taken together. In fact, in most countries, women tend to live slightly longer than men. However, the opposite is true in the Indian subcontinent and Iran. The low status of women and the wear of giving birth to many children may contribute

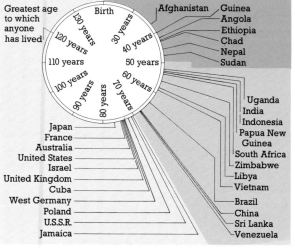

LIFE CLOCK. The chart shows life expectancy at birth for selected countries in 1980-1985.

POPULATION STATISTICS

The following statistics show the number of millions of people in countries with 1985 populations of 300,000 or more. Predictions for the year 2000 are from estimates prepared by the United Nations.

	1985	2000
Afghanistan	15.6	24.2
Albania	3.0	4.1
Algeria	22.0	35.2
Angola	8.8	13.2
Argentina	30.6	37.2
Australia	15.7	18.7
Austria	7.5	7.5
Bahrain	0.4	0.7
Bangladesh	101.1	145.8
Belgium	9.9	9.9
Benin	4.0	6.4
Bhutan	1.4	1.9
Bolivia	6.4	9.7
Botswana	1.0	1.9
Brazil	135.6	179.5
Bulgaria	9.2	9.7
Burkina Faso	6.9	10.5
Burma	39.5	55.2
Burundi	4.6	7.0
Cameroon	9.7	14.4
Canada	25.6	29.4
Cape Verde	0.3	n.a
Central African Republic	2.6	3.7
Chad	5.0	7.3
Chile	12.1	14.9
China	1,063.1	1,255.7
Colombia	28.7	38.0
Comoros	0.4	n.a.
Congo	1.7	2.6
Costa Rica	2.6	3.6
Cuba	10.0	11.7
Cyprus	0.7	n.a.
Czechoslovakia	15.6	16.8
Denmark	5.1	5.1
Djibouti	0.3	n.a.
Dominican Republic	6.2	8.4
Ecuador	9.4	14.6
Egypt	46.8	65.2
El Salvador	5.5	8.7
Equatorial Guinea	0.4	0.6
Ethiopia	36.5	58.4
Fiji	0.7	0.8
Finland	4.9	5.0
France	54.6	57.1
Gabon	1.2	1.6
Gambia	0.6	0.9
Germany, East	16.6	16.6
Germany, West	61.1	59.8
Ghana	13.5	21.9
Greece	9.9	10.7
Guatemala	8.4	12.7
Guinea	5.4	7.9
Guinea-Bissau	0.9	1.2
Guyana	1.0	1.2
Haiti	6.6	9.9
Honduras	4.4	7.0
Hungary	10.8	10.9
India	761.2	961.5
Indonesia	164.9	204.5
Iran	45.1	65.6
Iraq	15.7	24.9
Ireland	3.6	4.2
Israel	4.3	5.4
Italy	56.9	58.2
Ivory Coast	9.8	15.6
Jamaica	2.3	2.8
Japan	120.1	127.7
Jordan	3.5	6.4
Kampuchea	7.4	9.9
Kenya	20.6	38.5
Korea, North	20.1	27.3
Korea, South	40.9	49.5
Kuwait	1.8	3.0
Laos	4.4	6.2
Lebanon	2.7	3.6
Lesotho	1.5	2.3
Liberia	2.2	3.6
Libya	3.6	6.1
Luxembourg	0.4	0.4
Madagascar	10.0	15.6
Malawi	7.0	11.7
Malaysia	15.6	20.6
Mali	8.1	12.4
Malta	0.4	0.4
Mauritania	1.9	3.0
Mauritius	1.0	1.3
Mexico	79.0	109.2
Mongolia	1.9	2.7
Morocco	23.6	36.3
Mozambique	14.1	21.8
Namibia	1.1	n.a.
Nepal	16.5	23.0
Netherlands	14.5	15.0
New Zealand	3.3	3.7
Nicaragua	3.3	5.3
Niger	6.1	9.8
Nigeria	95.2	161.9
Norway	4.1	4.2
Oman	1.2	1.9
Pakistan	101.7	142.6
Panama	2.2	2.9
Papua New Guinea	3.7	5.3
Paraguay	3.7	5.4
Peru	19.7	28.0
Philippines	54.7	74.8
Poland	37.6	41.4
Portugal	10.1	11.0
Puerto Rico	3.3	n.a.
Qatar	0.3	0.5
Romania	23.1	25.6
Rwanda	6.1	10.6
Saudi Arabia	11.2	18.9
Senegal	6.5	10.0
Sierra Leone	3.6	4.9
Singapore	2.6	3.0
Somalia	5.6	7.1
South Africa	32.4	47.0
South Yemen	2.1	3.3
Spain	39.0	43.4
Sri Lanka	16.4	20.8
Sudan	21.6	32.9
Suriname	0.4	0.4
Swaziland	0.6	1.0
Sweden	8.3	8.1
Switzerland	6.3	5.9
Syria	10.6	18.1
Tanzania	22.5	39.1
Thailand	51.6	66.1
Togo	2.9	4.6
Trinidad and Tobago	1.1	1.3
Tunisia	7.2	9.7
Turkey	50.0	68.5
Uganda	15.7	26.8
U.S.S.R.	278.4	314.8
United Arab Emirates	1.3	1.9
United Kingdom	55.6	56.2
United States	237.7	268.1
Uruguay	3.0	3.4
Venezuela	18.4	27.2
Vietnam	59.5	78.1
Yemen	6.5	9.9
Yugoslavia	23.2	25.2
Zaire	33.1	52.4
Zambia	6.7	11.2
Zimbabwe	8.8	15.1

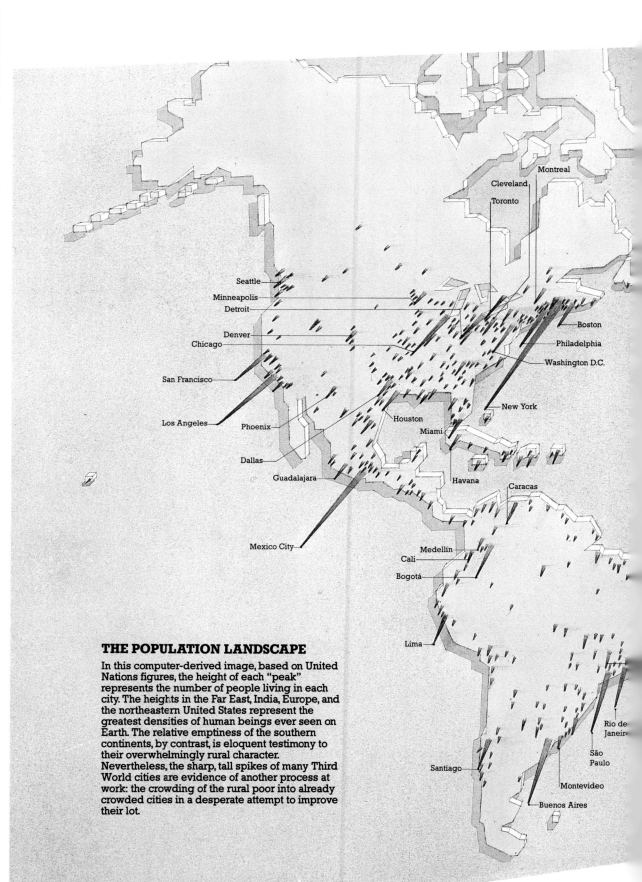

THE POPULATION LANDSCAPE

In this computer-derived image, based on United Nations figures, the height of each "peak" represents the number of people living in each city. The heights in the Far East, India, Europe, and the northeastern United States represent the greatest densities of human beings ever seen on Earth. The relative emptiness of the southern continents, by contrast, is eloquent testimony to their overwhelmingly rural character. Nevertheless, the sharp, tall spikes of many Third World cities are evidence of another process at work: the crowding of the rural poor into already crowded cities in a desperate attempt to improve their lot.

to their relatively early death in these countries.

In the developed world, the general provision of health care, good food, and, above all, an appreciation of cleanliness have raised the average life expectancy for men to 73 years and for women to 79.

In parts of the developing world, educational programs have started to improve the prospects. The average life expectancy in less developed countries in 1955 was more than 16 years lower than it is today. In China, to take the outstanding instance of progress, the expectation of life was raised, between 1962 and 1982, from 39 to 69 years. Elsewhere, in Afghanistan and Sub-Saharan Africa, for example, the average age at death still hovers around 40.

Meanwhile, in Japan, North America, and western Europe, the benefits of universal health care and education have extended life into the late 70's. These benefits have, however, produced the problems of an aging population in cultures where the aged are sometimes considered an expensive and unproductive burden.

THE WORLD'S WEALTH

In this distorted map, the area occupied by each country has been enlarged or reduced in proportion to its share of the wealth created each year in the world. In the shriveling of Africa and the great fattening of Europe and North America, the map reveals the great divide between the more developed industrialized nations of the "north," where 80 percent of the world's wealth is created by 28 percent of the world's population, and the predominantly agricultural "south," where nearly three-quarters of the world's people must subsist on a fifth of the world's goods. As a measure of relative wealth and poverty, each of the countries is colored — in broad categories — according to the average income of the people who live there. This is calculated by first adding up the annual output of each country's trade, services, and industry to give a total known as the Gross National Product (GNP). To calculate a rough idea of average income, the GNP is then divided by the population.

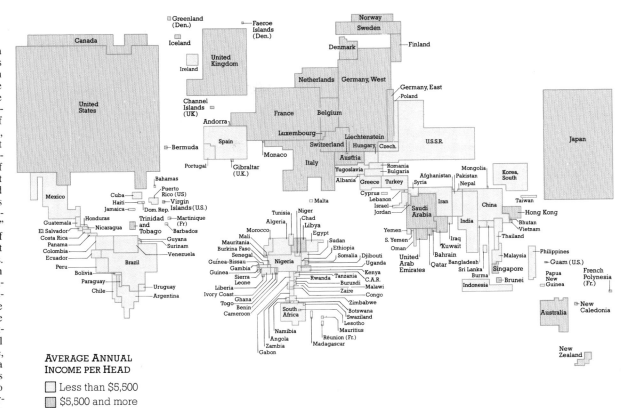

AVERAGE ANNUAL INCOME PER HEAD

☐ Less than $5,500
▨ $5,500 and more

RICH AND POOR. The wealth of industrialized countries sets them apart from the poverty of those in the developing "south."

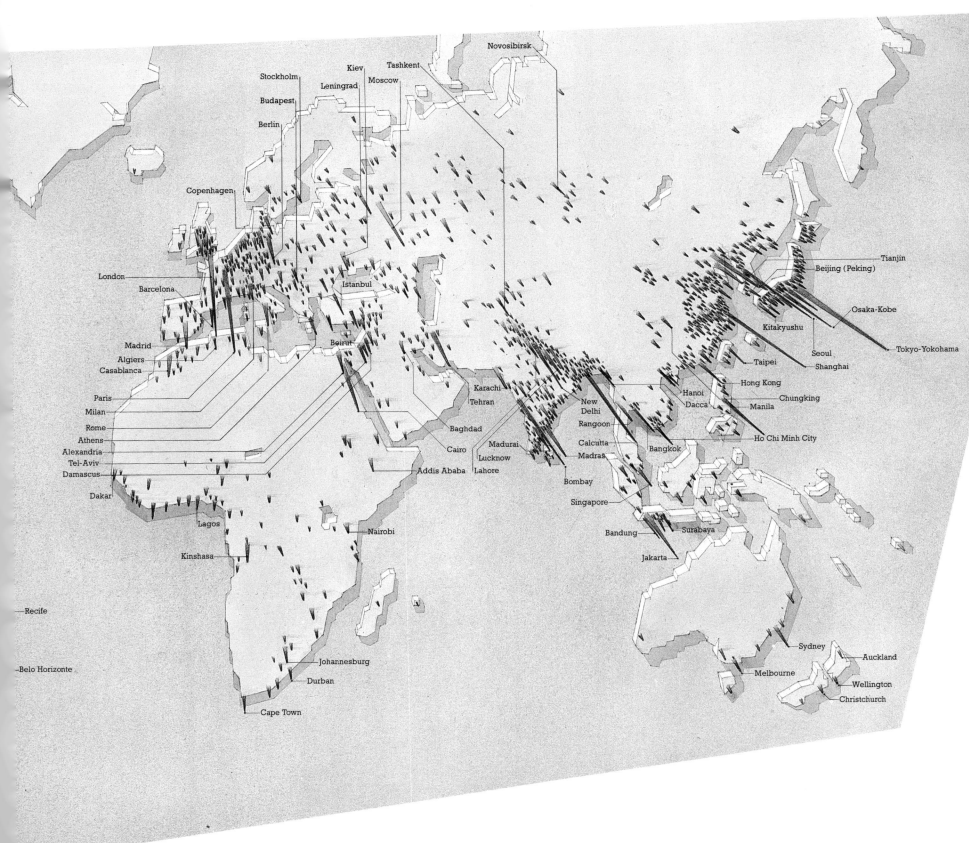

A Global Harvest

Food is mankind's raw energy resource—the fuel that fires the human boiler — and maintaining supplies constitutes man's biggest single concern.

Agricultural efficiency has increased at a staggering pace: in 1980 the world's farms produced twice as much food as they did in 1950. As a result, the earth today grows enough food to support its population, with plenty to spare. But the pattern of production is uneven, and many areas still go short.

Thousands of different types of plants are consumed by man, but just three — wheat, corn, and rice — account for about half of the world's harvest. By no means every niche of the planet's surface can be exploited for crop farming, however, for a combination of three basic factors — sunshine, moisture, and soil — determines where the global harvest can be gathered in. At present only 11 percent of the earth's land surface is farmed for crops, while a further 20 percent is thought to be cultivable.

BEYOND THE GREEN REVOLUTION

One major factor in the recent boom in food production has been the development of new, high-yielding strains of wheat, corn, and rice. Cultivated with modern fertilizers, herbicides, pesticides, and irrigation techniques, these grains have generated what is known as the Green Revolution. The term was first coined to describe the transformation of farming in India but is now used wherever high-technology agriculture is applied in the developing world.

RICE BOWL. Traditional farming techniques are still practiced in the terraced rice fields of central Java.

Bumper harvests have been the result. But the techniques, modeled on the practices of U.S. agriculture, have had their critics too. The chemicals required by high-yield strains are derived chiefly from fossil fuels, which have become increasingly costly since the oil crisis of 1973. Mechanized farming, too, guzzles our energy resources — about 25 gallons of gasoline are required to produce an acre of corn in the United States. Such farming tends to benefit the large farmer with capital to invest at the expense of the small farmer.

In the coming decades the world may well see some adjustment toward the kind of organic farming practiced in China. Here, crop waste is recycled to provide fertilizer, so that less synthetic matter is required. In addition, mixed cropping is practiced: grains are planted with legumes, such as peas and beans, which produce their own nitrogen for fertilizer through the bacteria

in their roots. One legume — the soybean — is already a post-World War II success story in the developing world. It is grown increasingly for its high-protein content and adaptability, and its oil is used for making paints and chemicals, as well as margarines and cooking oils.

Perhaps the greatest hopes for feeding future generations lie in plant breeding and genetics. Resistance to pests and diseases can be bred into crops so that spraying with hazardous chemicals becomes increasingly obsolete. Strains may be developed to cope with the harsh climates of desert or tundra. Modern techniques of gene transfer offer possibilities for cultivating radically improved species. Tens of thousands of potentially edible species have been identified, and it may yet prove possible to carpet the world's most barren wastes with new forms of nutritious vegetation.

MIXED CROPPING. Farm laborers in Guangdong province, southern China, tend a mixed crop of corn and beans.

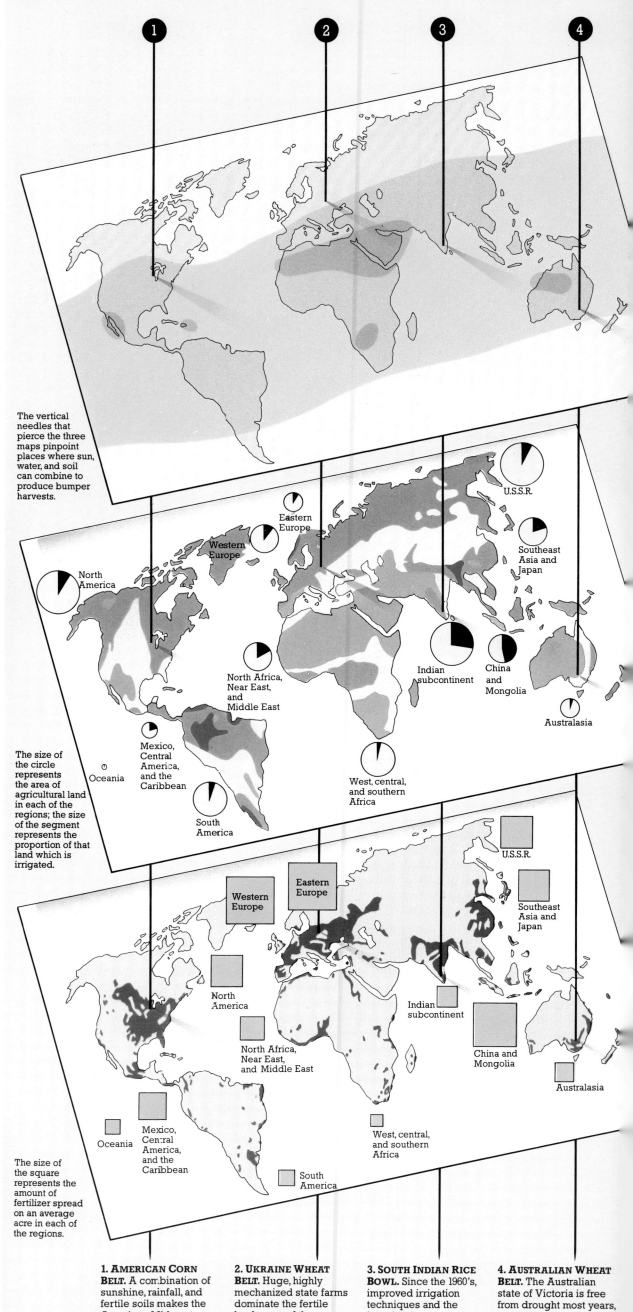

The vertical needles that pierce the three maps pinpoint places where sun, water, and soil can combine to produce bumper harvests.

The size of the circle represents the area of agricultural land in each of the regions; the size of the segment represents the proportion of that land which is irrigated.

U.S.S.R.
Eastern Europe
Western Europe
North America
Southeast Asia and Japan
Indian subcontinent
China and Mongolia
North Africa, Near East, and Middle East
Australasia
Mexico, Central America, and the Caribbean
Oceania
West, central, and southern Africa
South America

The size of the square represents the amount of fertilizer spread on an average acre in each of the regions.

U.S.S.R.
Eastern Europe
Western Europe
North America
Southeast Asia and Japan
Indian subcontinent
North Africa, Near East, and Middle East
China and Mongolia
Australasia
Mexico, Central America, and the Caribbean
Oceania
West, central, and southern Africa
South America

1. AMERICAN CORN BELT. A combination of sunshine, rainfall, and fertile soils makes the American Midwest almost perfect for arable farms. Modern methods have quadrupled output since the 1930's.

2. UKRAINE WHEAT BELT. Huge, highly mechanized state farms dominate the fertile landscape of the Ukraine. High yields of wheat and corn are achieved unless there is a severe winter frost.

3. SOUTH INDIAN RICE BOWL. Since the 1960's, improved irrigation techniques and the introduction of high-yielding varieties have trebled rice production in the Indian state of Tamil Nadu.

4. AUSTRALIAN WHEAT BELT. The Australian state of Victoria is free from drought most years, and high yields — between those of the American Midwest and the Ukraine — are usually achieved.

HOW THE PLANET PROVIDES

Climate and environment are the world's great chefs, giving Mexico its tortillas, Greece its goatsmilk cheese, China its pork spareribs, and Japan its seafood dishes. And it is regional variations in these two factors that·strongly influence what is raised where.

The world's three main cereals are wheat, corn, and rice, each of which has its special needs. Wheat is a crop of the temperate prairies and will tolerate very cold winters. Corn is vulnerable to frost and is therefore confined to a warmer climate band. And rice favors the special combination of warmth and copious rainfall that is found especially in monsoon zones.

Grain constitutes about half of the world's food production by weight, but similar factors associate other crops with particular environments: for example, grapes with Mediterranean climates, and the potato with dull, cloudy skies and clammy soils.

There are vast expanses of desert and bleak uplands whose lean and rocky soils support little more than coarse grasses. Since the human stomach cannot digest grass, it is the livestock here — in particular,

STRIP CROPPING. In this aerial view of a farm in Ohio, strips of corn, following the contour lines, have been planted alongside strips of grass mixed with legumes.

WHEAT BELT. In this aerial view of a farm in Washington State, wheat has been harvested from the light strips, while the darker strips have been left fallow for a season.

the sheep and the goats — that act as our food converters, yielding meat, milk, and cheese.

Cattle can be raised in a temperature band stretching from the edge of the Sahara to the margins of the Arctic circle. But cattle, like sheep, are ruminants whose digestives system calls for a diet chiefly of grass, and which require a wide grazing area. They are an inefficient food resource for the world's overpopulated regions and, due to their vulnerability to the tsetse fly, are especially scarce in the humid tropics. Pigs provide the world's main source of meat. A pig's diet is adaptable, and the creatures can be farmed in fairly confined spaces. China is the main producer of pork, yielding nearly 40 percent of the global total.

Fish, like all other food-stuffs, display preferences for habitat. Cod favors the cold waters of the North Atlantic, while tuna prefer warmer seas; flatfish, such as halibut, feed on the seabed, while herring cruise close to the surface. The principal fishing grounds are all in coastal zones where nutrients, leached from the land, mix with the rich sediment that is swept up from the sea floor by ocean currents and offshore winds. These waters comprise our teeming marine meadowlands, thick with tiny plankton supporting larger organisms that are, in turn, consumed by shoaling fish.

In total, the earth's fishing fleets bring in some 68 million tons a year. Japan, with its intricate network of islands, has an ancient fishing tradition and remains the largest single harvester of the sea.

FEAST AND FAMINE

If the global harvest were shared out equally, each person could receive 5 lb (2.3 kg) of food per day. Hunger need never be with us.

The reason why famines still take their terrible toll has more to do with the complexities of politics, economics, storage, and distribution than with the physical capacity of the earth itself. The planet is fertile. Science has opened up new possibilities. And, in the opinion of many experts, the age-old scourge of hunger could, with global cooperation, be eradicated by the year 2000.

To meet future needs, we can colonize the world's inhospitable areas. The earth's total cultivable land is some 7.9 billion acres (3.2 billion hectares), of which less than half is currently being farmed. Although the remainder may be harsh or inaccessible terrain, we have the means to drain swamps, plant hillsides, and bring deserts into bloom.

One short-term response to starvation in the Third World is to transport surplus food from where it is stockpiled to where it is needed. The biggest grain exporters are the United States, Canada, Australia, and Argentina. Thanks to the Green Revolution, India, Thailand, Burma, and Suriname can now be added to the list of the smaller net exporters. Many others, for example Mexico and the U.S.S.R., would be net grain exporters but for the demands of livestock, which now consume more grain than grass.

In the long term, however, this does nothing to help farmers in poor countries to produce more. Indeed, pouring cheap food into the Third World can lower prices there so much that local farmers are put out of business. Except in emergencies, perhaps what poor countries need most is appropriate technology, transport facilities, education, and better administration.

One global measure of food production is provided by the average numbers of calories supplied by the agriculture of different countries. How many calories an individual actually needs depends on his or her body weight, type of activity, and the environmental temperature. Accounting for these variables, the Food and Agriculture Organization of the United Nations estimates the average daily needs of a person in Finland, where a relatively old population lives in a cold climate, at 2,710 calories per day. In Indonesia, where a youthful population lives in a tropical climate, the average is 2,160 calories per day.

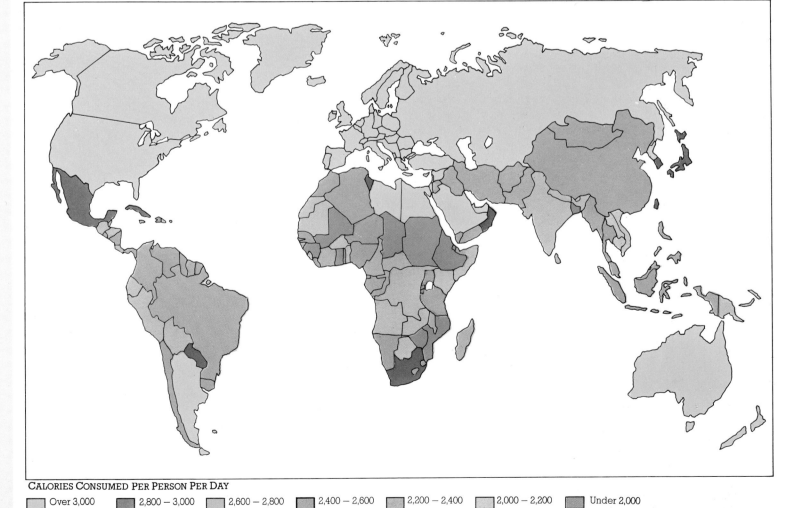

CALORIES CONSUMED PER PERSON PER DAY

| Over 3,000 | 2,800 – 3,000 | 2,600 – 2,800 | 2,400 – 2,600 | 2,200 – 2,400 | 2,000 – 2,200 | Under 2,000 |

CALORIE COUNT. The map charts the average numbers of calories consumed per person per day in different countries of the world. In countries where each person receives less than 2,000 calories per day on average, it is inevitable that quite a high proportion of the population is sometimes hungry. War or drought, for example, can easily tip the balance between tenuous supply and growing demand. The result can be mass starvation, as in Ethiopia in 1984-85.

Managing the Planet's Future

Photographs taken by the first astronauts gave mankind a new vision of the world, as a fragile oasis in the sterile darkness of space. This image, above all others, crystallized a new understanding of the earth. From being a place that could be exploited and used at will, the world became a global environment to be managed and sustained. Scientists began to voice fears over continued indifference to the health of such global systems as the atmosphere, the tropical forests, and the world genetic pool, in which diversity — the only final guarantee of survival — was being ignorantly and widely reduced.

Like an oil tanker at sea, the course the world is following cannot be changed in an instant. The dauntingly difficult task that now confronts the human race is to reconcile two equally urgent and, in some ways, contradictory imperatives: first, to reduce the terrible poverty and hunger in the Third World; and, second, to lessen the strains on the biological systems of the planet.

LOOKING AFTER LIFE

We still do not know, even approximately, the total number of species that live on the planet. New plants and animals are discovered each year, especially in the tropics. Meanwhile, the relentless growth both in human population and in the intensity of land use results in a steady encroachment on remaining wilderness areas. At least 34 species of mammals and 94 species of birds have been lost since the early 18th century. Uncounted numbers of insects, plants, fungi, and microorganisms have certainly disappeared without scientists ever having recognized their existence.

A Convention on International Trade in Endangered Species (CITES) now prohibits trade in 600 rare species of plants and animals, and a few of the rare species maintain a precarious existence in zoos and botanical gardens. But for most life-forms this is not the answer. The only secure way to prevent the destruction of our wildlife heritage is to preserve whole habitats in which a group of mutually dependent species of plants and animals coexist. A network of 261 Biosphere Reserves has now been established by the United Nations Educational, Scientific, and Cultural Organization (UNESCO). They include the Great Barrier Reef off Australia, the Bialowieza National Park in Poland, and several of the U.S. national parks such as Yellowstone and Everglades, which were among the pioneer achievements of the modern conservation movement.

PROTECTED COUNTRY. A herd of bison graze at Yellowstone, which was established in 1872 and is the oldest national park in the world.

MAINTAINING THE TROPICAL FORESTS

The dense, multilayered canopy of the tropical forests is one of the miracles of life on earth. It covers only about 8 percent of the earth's surface but may harbor more than 40 percent of all species of plants and animals. This massive biological resource not only provides fuel and building materials but is a crucial regulator of the world environment, protecting the topsoil, governing the even flow of rivers, and, on a global scale, helping to maintain a balanced climate.

But the forests are under pressure. As many as 100 acres (40 hectares) of tropical forest are being destroyed every minute — a total of over 83,000 square miles (210,000 sq km) a year. Perhaps twice that area is being seriously degraded. Timber harvesting and cattle ranching play their part in the destruction, but just as significant are the slash-and-burn techniques of the 150 million forest farmers in the world today. Most of the nutrients in the forest are bound up not in the soil but in the living plants. When an area is cleared by burning, most of its worth is dispersed in the wind. Farming on the cleared ground is possible only for one or two seasons before the land is either exhausted or eroded away.

Some places, such as westernmost Amazonia and parts of the Zaire Basin, where the population pressure is not so intense, can be sure to survive at least partly intact. But in west Africa, southeast Asia, and the Himalayan watershed, most of the unique and irreplaceable forest will soon have gone forever.

The only real solutions to the destruction of tropical rain forest lie in the control of population growth; increasing yields on good land; planting alternative sources of timber and fuelwood; and ecological sensitivity in development projects.

KEEPING THE DESERT AT BAY

About one-third of the earth's surface, fringing the great deserts, is arid, often subject to prolonged drought. Natural ecosystems here are adapted to long dry spells and can take them in their stride. But when such areas are put under pressure by rising populations and the demand for food, their ability to spring back to productiveness after drought is severely reduced. The rains, when they come, rather than soaking into and feeding the land, can wash away the soil, extending the limits of the desert. Every year about 47,000 square miles (122,000 sq km) of agricultural land are made worthless in this way.

This process of "desertification" is probably worsened by the increasing levels of carbon dioxide and other gases in the atmosphere, produced by the burning of fossil fuels, which are likely to raise global temperatures within the next century by up to 8°F (4.5°C).

Unchecked, desertification tends to be self-sustaining. The destruction of vegetation by overuse of the land makes the surface of the soil more reflective and less absorbent. Both evaporation and rainfall decrease, and regrowth becomes less likely.

A problem of such vast proportions is not easily dealt with. A reduction in carbon dioxide emissions from the industrial countries will help.

Keeping animals and vehicles off certain areas can reestablish vegetation. The deliberate planting of forest and shrub stands — in the Soviet Union, India, and China — reduces erosion on a local scale.

PINNING THE DUNES. Sand that threatens to encroach on farmland in Tunisia is stabilized with palm seedlings.

HARNESSING CLEAN ENERGY

The environmental impact of fossil fuels — coal, oil, and gas — and their limited supplies have led to the search for renewable sources of energy.

Hydroelectric power at the moment supplies 7 percent of the world's energy needs. It is cheap, clean, and efficient, and by the 21st century, world hydroelectric output might be three times what it is today.

If only a tiny fraction of the solar radiation intercepted by our planet could be put into harness, it would supply all of humanity's energy needs. The problem is that solar energy is thinly spread over a vast area and needs to be collected, concentrated, and stored. Different regions, moreover, have very different potentials. Ethiopia may be a sunshine millionaire, but the United Kingdom is a pauper. The first solar power station, linked to an electricity grid and using computer-directed mirrors to focus the sun onto boilers, was opened in Sicily in 1981.

Three tidal power stations now operate in the world, in the Bay of Fundy in Canada, the Rance estuary in northern France, and Kislaya Bay in the Soviet Union. In each case, the incoming and outgoing waters pass through turbines at the dammed mouth of an inlet. There are, however, few sites in the world where the mouth is narrow enough and the tidal reach great enough to make such energy economical.

In the long term, the ocean's greatest asset may be the temperature difference between the surface and the depths. In the tropics, this may be as much as 40°F (22°C). By a process known as Ocean Thermal Energy Conversion (OTEC), floating offshore power stations can exploit the differential to condense and evaporate a fluid, driving turbine generators.

The wind has been explored with renewed interest since the

Yellowstone National Park (Elk, grizzly bear)

Galápagos Islands (Tortoises, iguanas, Darwin's finches)

La Amistad Talamanca (Lowland and montane rain forests)

Sangay Volcano National Park (Tropical rain forest up to snowline)

Everglades National Park (Wetlands, waterfowl, alligators)

Bialowieza National Park (Largest undisturbed forest in Europe)

Brazil (The building of the Transamazonian Highway encourages slash-and-burn farmers to move into ecologically fragile and irreplaceable forest)

ALTERNATIVE ENERGY SOURCES
- ■ Hydroelectric
- ▲ Solar
- ■ Tidal
- Ocean Thermal Energy Conversion Experiments
- ✳ Wind
- ○ Geothermal

DEFORESTATION AREAS
- Tropical Moist Forests

DESERTIFICATION AREAS
- Existing desert
- Zones in need of protection from desertification

NATURE RESERVES
- ✳ UNESCO Reserves

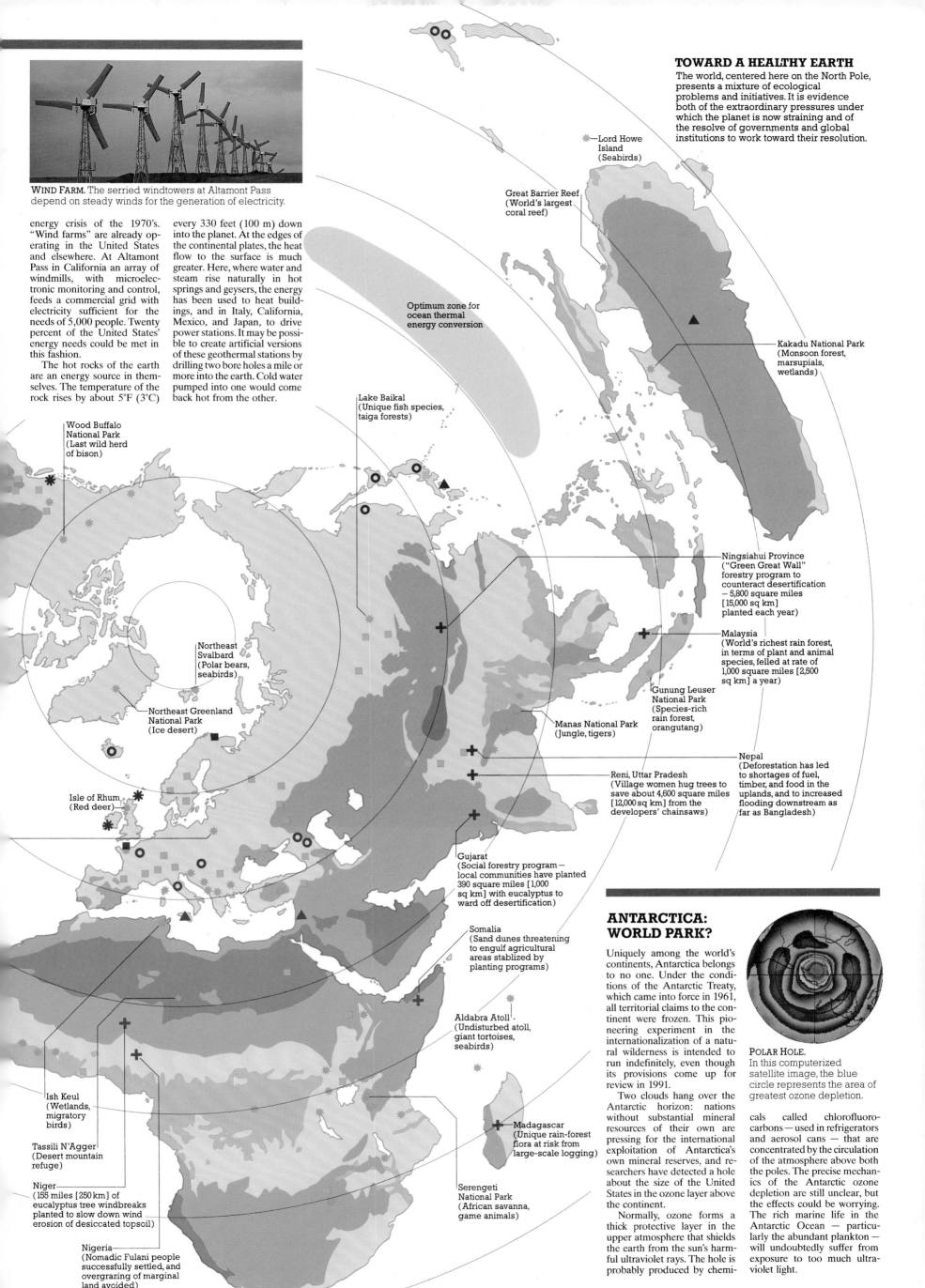

WIND FARM. The serried windtowers at Altamont Pass depend on steady winds for the generation of electricity.

energy crisis of the 1970's. "Wind farms" are already operating in the United States and elsewhere. At Altamont Pass in California an array of windmills, with microelectronic monitoring and control, feeds a commercial grid with electricity sufficient for the needs of 5,000 people. Twenty percent of the United States' energy needs could be met in this fashion.

The hot rocks of the earth are an energy source in themselves. The temperature of the rock rises by about 5°F (3°C)

every 330 feet (100 m) down into the planet. At the edges of the continental plates, the heat flow to the surface is much greater. Here, where water and steam rise naturally in hot springs and geysers, the energy has been used to heat buildings, and in Italy, California, Mexico, and Japan, to drive power stations. It may be possible to create artificial versions of these geothermal stations by drilling two bore holes a mile or more into the earth. Cold water pumped into one would come back hot from the other.

TOWARD A HEALTHY EARTH

The world, centered here on the North Pole, presents a mixture of ecological problems and initiatives. It is evidence both of the extraordinary pressures under which the planet is now straining and of the resolve of governments and global institutions to work toward their resolution.

Lord Howe Island (Seabirds)

Great Barrier Reef (World's largest coral reef)

Kakadu National Park (Monsoon forest, marsupials, wetlands)

Optimum zone for ocean thermal energy conversion

Wood Buffalo National Park (Last wild herd of bison)

Lake Baikal (Unique fish species, taiga forests)

Northeast Svalbard (Polar bears, seabirds)

Northeast Greenland National Park (Ice desert)

Ningsiahui Province ("Green Great Wall" forestry program to counteract desertification — 5,800 square miles [15,000 sq km] planted each year)

Malaysia (World's richest rain forest, in terms of plant and animal species, felled at rate of 1,000 square miles [2,500 sq km] a year)

Gunung Leuser National Park (Species-rich rain forest, orangutang)

Manas National Park (Jungle, tigers)

Nepal (Deforestation has led to shortages of fuel, timber, and food in the uplands, and to increased flooding downstream as far as Bangladesh)

Reni, Uttar Pradesh (Village women hug trees to save about 4,600 square miles [12,000 sq km] from the developers' chainsaws)

Isle of Rhum (Red deer)

Gujarat (Social forestry program — local communities have planted 390 square miles [1,000 sq km] with eucalyptus to ward off desertification)

Somalia (Sand dunes threatening to engulf agricultural areas stabilized by planting programs)

ANTARCTICA: WORLD PARK?

Uniquely among the world's continents, Antarctica belongs to no one. Under the conditions of the Antarctic Treaty, which came into force in 1961, all territorial claims to the continent were frozen. This pioneering experiment in the internationalization of a natural wilderness is intended to run indefinitely, even though its provisions come up for review in 1991.

Two clouds hang over the Antarctic horizon: nations without substantial mineral resources of their own are pressing for the international exploitation of Antarctica's own mineral reserves, and researchers have detected a hole about the size of the United States in the ozone layer above the continent.

Normally, ozone forms a thick protective layer in the upper atmosphere that shields the earth from the sun's harmful ultraviolet rays. The hole is probably produced by chemi-

POLAR HOLE.
In this computerized satellite image, the blue circle represents the area of greatest ozone depletion.

cals called chlorofluorocarbons — used in refrigerators and aerosol cans — that are concentrated by the circulation of the atmosphere above both the poles. The precise mechanics of the Antarctic ozone depletion are still unclear, but the effects could be worrying. The rich marine life in the Antarctic Ocean — particularly the abundant plankton — will undoubtedly suffer from exposure to too much ultraviolet light.

Aldabra Atoll (Undisturbed atoll, giant tortoises, seabirds)

Ish Keul (Wetlands, migratory birds)

Tassili N'Agger (Desert mountain refuge)

Niger (155 miles [250 km] of eucalyptus tree windbreaks planted to slow down wind erosion of desiccated topsoil)

Nigeria (Nomadic Fulani people successfully settled, and overgrazing of marginal land avoided)

Madagascar (Unique rain-forest flora at risk from large-scale logging)

Serengeti National Park (African savanna, game animals)

The Challenge to Mapmakers

The globe is the only way to show geographic locations in true relationship to one another, a fact recognized as long ago as the second century A.D. by the Greek scholar Claudius Ptolemy. However, to be useful, a globe would have to be impractically large. The challenge to cartographers is to project the three-dimensional reality of our planet on a flat surface—a process that leads, inevitably, to distortion.

Even though his world was limited largely to the Mediterranean area, Ptolemy knew that the earth was round, and he had a solution to the problem of representing it as flat. His map, as reconstructed below, is recognizable today—even though he exaggerated the Eurasian landmass to occupy half the globe. The perpetuation of this error led Columbus to underestimate the distance to Asia as he set out across the Atlantic, and thus he failed to realize that he had discovered the intervening New World.

Martin Waldseemüller's 1507 map (opposite, top right) peeled the globe like an orange, spread it flat, and called Columbus's discovery America, showing two continents separated from Asia by a sea. The first circumnavigator of the globe, Ferdinand Magellan, named it the Pacific Ocean.

The foremost cartographer of the age of discovery, Gerardus Mercator, produced his first world map in 1538 (bottom), which effectively shows a polar view of a round earth. This map was found pasted inside his copy of a Ptolemy atlas. Mercator eventually arrived at a solution to the puzzle of accurately representing the globe on a flat surface: the cylindrical projection bearing his name, which guided generations of lonely navigators to safe landfalls and is still in use today.

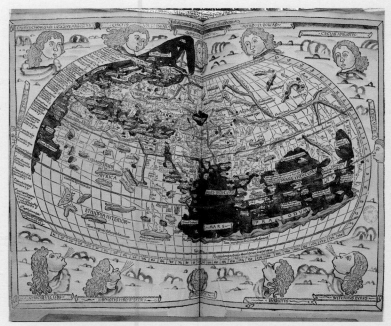

Ptolemy's second-century A.D. map of the world, as reproduced in 1486

Northern Hemisphere of Mercator's first world map, 1538

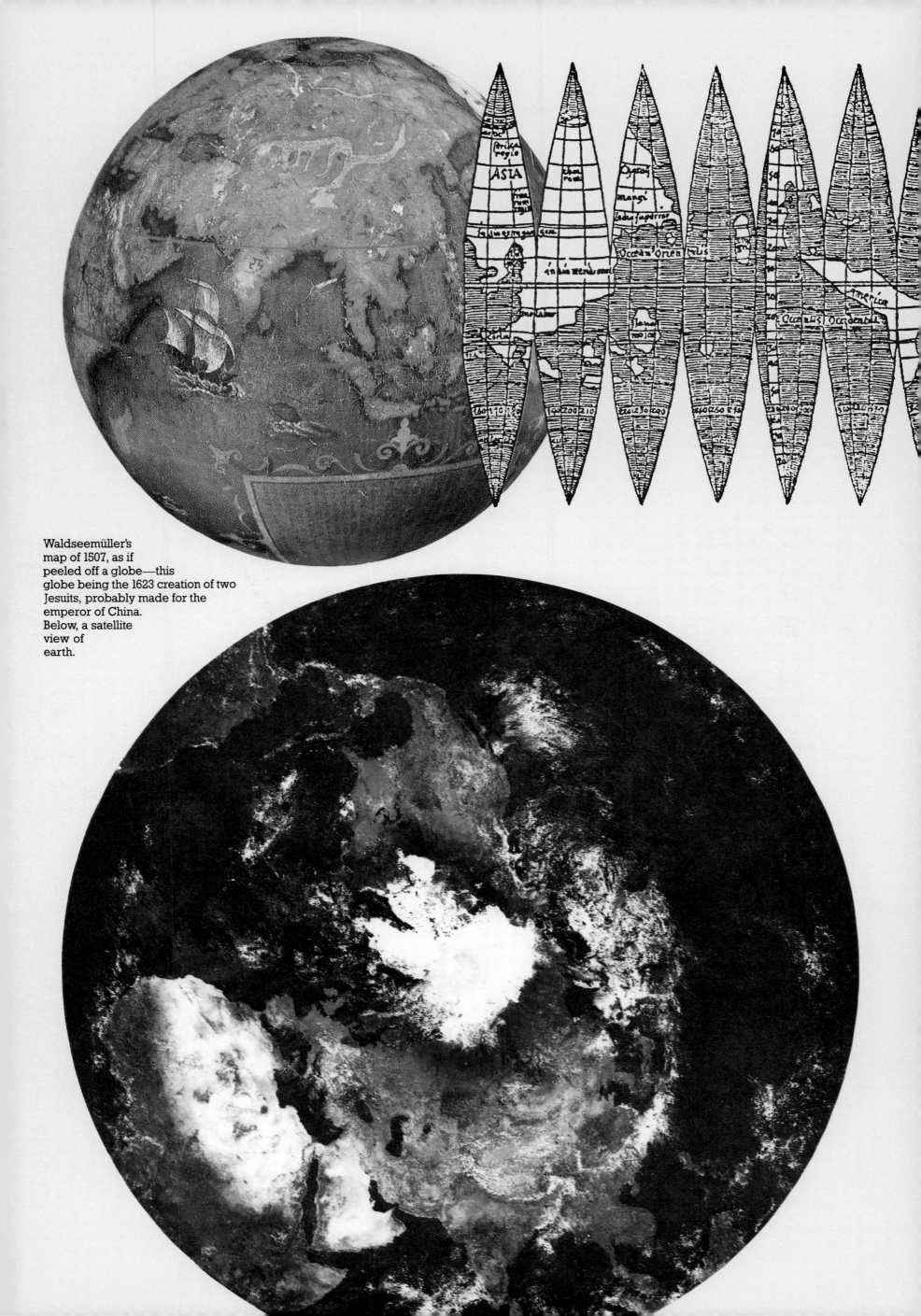

Waldseemüller's
map of 1507, as if
peeled off a globe—this
globe being the 1623 creation of two
Jesuits, probably made for the
emperor of China.
Below, a satellite
view of
earth.

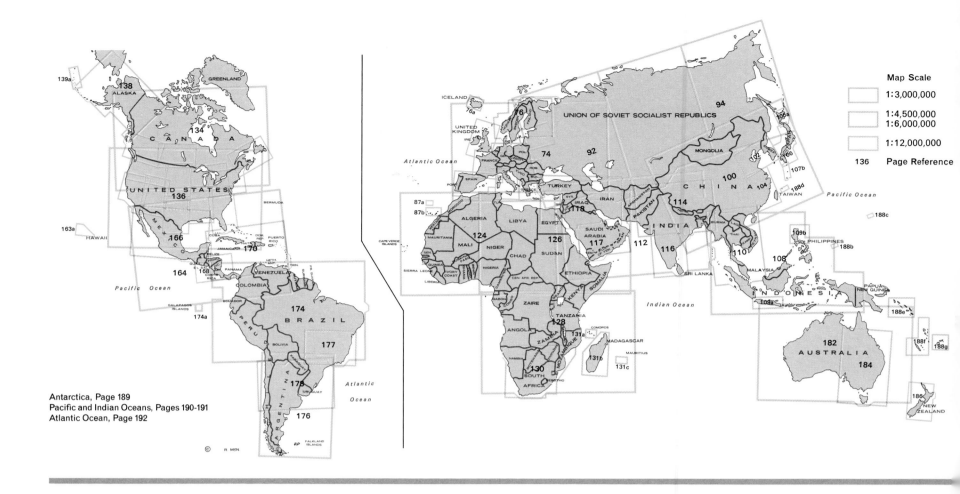

Antarctica, Page 189
Pacific and Indian Oceans, Pages 190-191
Atlantic Ocean, Page 192

Map Scale

1:3,000,000

1:4,500,000
1:6,000,000

1:12,000,000

136   Page Reference

Legend to Maps

This legend applies to all the maps referred to in the index maps above and to the World Political Map. Special legends for the Environment maps accompany each map and a legend for the Physical maps is on pages 70-71.

Inhabited Localities

The symbol represents the number of inhabitants within the locality

Maps at 1:12,000,000 scale		Maps at other scales	
·	Less than 50,000	·	Less than 10,000
⊚	50,000-100,000	○	10,000-25,000
⊡	100,000-250,000	⊙	25,000-100,000
⊠	250,000-1,000,000	⊡	100,000-250,000
■	Over 1,000,000	⊠	250,000-1,000,000
		■	Over 1,000,000

Urban Area (area of continuous industrial, commercial, and residential development)

The size of type indicates the relative economic and political importance of the locality

| Écommoy | Lisieux | **Rouen** |
| Trouville | **Orléans** | **PARIS** |

Bi'r Safâjah ○   **Oasis**

Capitals of Political Units

BUDAPEST   Independent Nation

Cayenne   Dependency (Colony, protectorate, etc.)

Villarica   State, Province, County, Oblast, etc.

Alternative Names

| **Basel** Bâle | **MOSKVA** MOSCOW | English or second official language names are shown in smaller type |
| **Harare** (Salisbury) | **Volgograd** (Stalingrad) | Historical or other alternative names are shown in parentheses |

Political Boundaries

International (First-order political unit)

Demarcated, Undemarcated, and Administrative

Indefinite or Undefined

Disputed de facto

Disputed de jure

Demarcation Line

Internal

State, Province, etc. (Second-order political unit)
GUAIRA

County, Oblast, etc. (Third-order political unit)
WESTCHESTER

GALAPAGOS (Ecuador)   Administering Country

ANDALUCIA   Historical Region (No boundaries indicated)

Miscellaneous Features

PARQUE NACIONAL CANAIMA ▲	National or State Park, Monument or Reservation	*AMISTAD DAM*	Dam
FORT DIX ▪	Military Installation	⟨⟩	Lock
		STEINHAUSEN	Church, Monastery
▲ *TANGLEWOOD*	Point of Interest (battlefield, cave, historical site, monument, etc.)	*UXMAL*	Ruins
		WINDSOR CASTLE	Castle

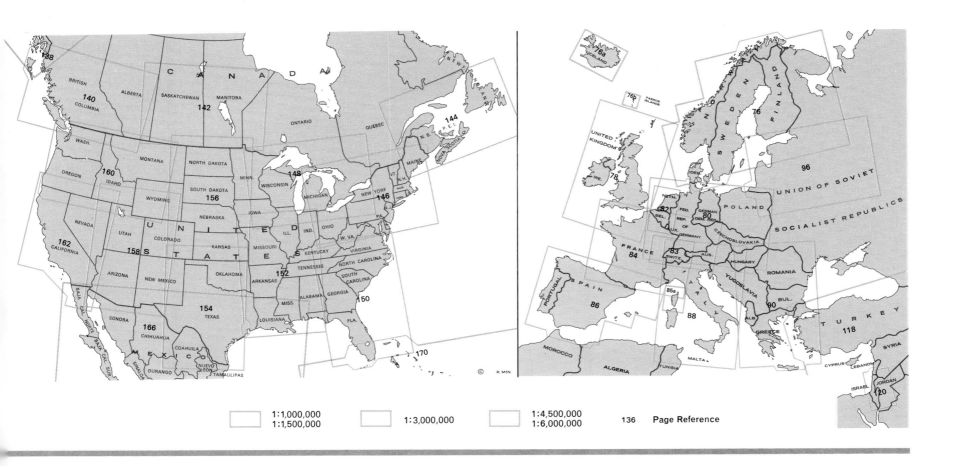

1:1,000,000 1:1,500,000	1:3,000,000	1:4,500,000 1:6,000,000	136 Page Reference

Transportation

Maps at scale of:

1:12,000,000	1:3,000,000 1:4,500,000 1:6,000,000	1:1,000,000 1:1,500,000	
			Primary Road
			Secondary Road
			Tertiary Road
			Minor Road, Trail
			Primary Railway
			Other Railway

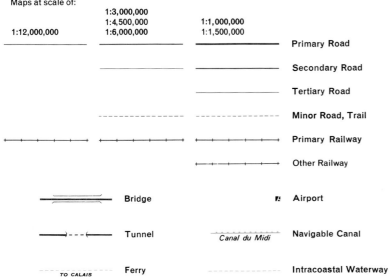

Bridge	Airport
Tunnel	Navigable Canal — Canal du Midi
Ferry — TO CALAIS	Intracoastal Waterway

Key to Elevation and Depth Tints

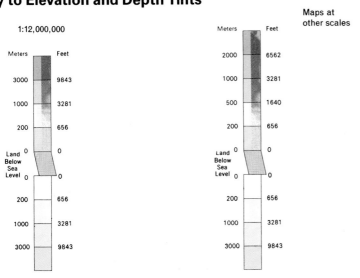

1:12,000,000

Meters	Feet
3000	9843
1000	3281
200	656
0	0
Land Below Sea Level 0	0
200	656
1000	3281
3000	9843

Maps at other scales

Meters	Feet
2000	6562
1000	3281
500	1640
200	656
0	0
Land Below Sea Level 0	0
200	656
1000	3281
3000	9843

Hydrographic Features

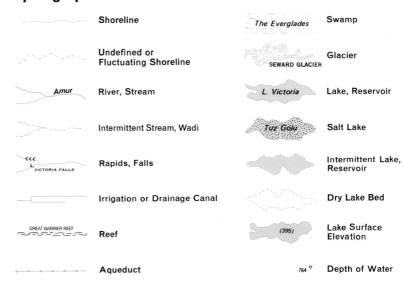

Shoreline		The Everglades	Swamp
Undefined or Fluctuating Shoreline		SEWARD GLACIER	Glacier
Amur	River, Stream	L. Victoria	Lake, Reservoir
	Intermittent Stream, Wadi	Tuz Golu	Salt Lake
VICTORIA FALLS	Rapids, Falls		Intermittent Lake, Reservoir
	Irrigation or Drainage Canal		Dry Lake Bed
GREAT BARRIER REEF	Reef	(395)	Lake Surface Elevation
	Aqueduct	764 ▽	Depth of Water

Topographic Features

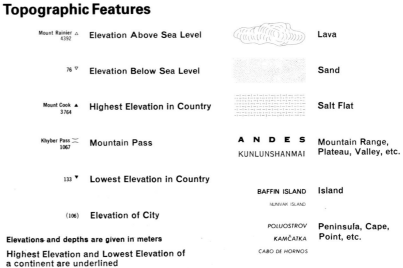

Mount Rainier △ 4392	Elevation Above Sea Level		Lava
76 ▽	Elevation Below Sea Level		Sand
Mount Cook ▲ 3764	Highest Elevation in Country		Salt Flat
Khyber Pass ⚊ 1067	Mountain Pass	A N D E S KUNLUNSHANMAI	Mountain Range, Plateau, Valley, etc.
133 ▼	Lowest Elevation in Country	BAFFIN ISLAND NUNIVAK ISLAND	Island
(106)	Elevation of City	POLUOSTROV KAMČATKA CABO DE HORNOS	Peninsula, Cape, Point, etc.

Elevations and depths are given in meters

Highest Elevation and Lowest Elevation of a continent are underlined

ARCTIC OCEAN

Beaufort Sea

GREENLAND (Den.)

Thule

Baffin Bay

VICTORIA ISLAND

BAFFIN ISLAND

Godhavn

Norwe

Godthåb

Angmagssalik

ICELAND

FAEROE ISLANDS (Den.)

Reykjavik

U.S.S.R.

UNITED STATES

Arctic Circle

Bering Strait

Nome

Inuvik

Yukon

Mackenzie

Yellowknife

Anchorage

Fairbanks

Mount McKinley

Gulf of Alaska

Bering Sea

CANADA

Edmonton

Churchill

Hudson Bay

Goose Bay

NEWFOUNDLAND

Glasgow

Dublin

IRELAND

UNI KING LON

ALEUTIAN ISLANDS

ROCKY MOUNTAINS

Vancouver

Calgary

Winnipeg

Lake Superior

St. Lawrence

Québec

St. John's

Halifax

ATLANTIC OCEAN

PACIFIC

Seattle

Portland

Minneapolis

Lake Huron

Ottawa

Montréal

L. Ontario

Toronto

L. Erie

Boston

NEW YORK

PHILADELPHIA

Washington

PORTO

PORTUGAL

Lisboa

SPA

NORTH AMERICA

UNITED STATES

San Francisco

Salt Lake City

Denver

CHICAGO

Lake Michigan

St. Louis

DETROIT

APPALACHIAN MOUNTAINS

Atlanta

AÇORES AZORES (Port.)

ARQUIPÉLAGO DA MADEIRA (Port.)

GIBRALTAR (U.K.)

W

OCEAN

LOS ANGELES

San Diego

Phoenix

El Paso

Dallas

Houston

New Orleans

Mississippi

Rio Grande

Miami

BERMUDA (U.K.)

Rabat

Casablanca

MOROCCO

A

MIDWAY ISLANDS (U.S.)

Tropic of Cancer

CABO SAN LUCAS

Gulf of Mexico

BAHAMAS

WESTERN SAHARA

S

HAWAIIAN ISLANDS (U.S.)

Honolulu

Monterrey

Guadalajara

MEXICO

CIUDAD DE MÉXICO

MEXICO CITY

La Habana

CUBA

HAITI

DOMINICAN REPUBLIC

Port-au-Prince

PUERTO RICO (U.S.)

San Juan

GUADELOUPE (Fr.)

Nouakchott

MAURI-TANIA

CAPE VERDE

JOHNSTON ATOLL (U.S.)

GUATEMALA

BELIZE

Guatemala

JAMAICA

Kingston

Santo Domingo

MARTINIQUE (Fr.)

BARBADOS

SENEGAL

Dakar

GAMBIA

Banjul

Tombouctou

Bamako

BU

POLYNESIA

San Salvador

HONDURAS

Tegucigalpa

EL SALVADOR

Managua

NICARAGUA

Caribbean Sea

TRINIDAD AND TOBAGO

Port of Spain

GUINEA-BISSAU

GUINEA

Ouga

ÎLE CLIPPERTON (Fr.)

COSTA RICA

PANAMA

San José

Panamá

Caracas

VENEZUELA

Maracaibo

GUYANA

Georgetown

SURI-NAME

Paramaribo

FRENCH GUIANA

Conakry

SIERRA LEONE

Freetown

Yamoussou

IVORY COAST

LINE ISLANDS

Equator

Bogotá

Medellín

COLOMBIA

Cali

Monrovia

LIBERIA

Abidja

Equator

PHOENIX ISLANDS

ECUADOR

Quito

ARCHIPIÉLAGO DE COLÓN GALÁPAGOS ISLANDS (Ec.)

Guayaquil

Iquitos

Manaus

Amazon

Belém

Fortaleza

CABO DE SÃO ROQUE

Natal

TOKELAU (N.Z.)

ÎLES MARQUISES

Madeira

B R A Z I L

Recife

ATLANTIC OCEAN

WALLIS AND FUTUNA (Fr.)

W. SAMOA

AM. SAMOA

Trujillo

Lima

SOUTH AMERICA

Salvador

FIJI

Apia

ÎLES TUAMOTU

ANDES

La Paz

BOLIVIA

Sucre

Goiânia

Brasília

Belo Horizonte

NIUE (N.Z.)

COOK ISLANDS (N.Z.)

ÎLES DE LA SOCIÉTÉ SOCIETY ISLANDS

FRENCH POLYNESIA

Arequipa

SÃO PAULO

RIO DE JANEIRO

TONGA

Tropic of Capricorn

PITCAIRN (U.K.)

ISLA SAN AMBROSIO (Chile)

Antofagasta

PARAGUAY

Asunción

Santos

Curitiba

CHILE

ISLA DE PASCUA EASTER ISLAND (Chile)

Co. Aconcagua 6959

Córdoba

Paraná

Porto Alegre

Valparaíso

Santiago

Rosario

URUGUAY

PACIFIC

ARCHIPIÉLAGO JUAN FERNÁNDEZ (Chile)

Concepción

BUENOS AIRES

ARGENTINA

Montevideo

Mar del Plata

Bahía Blanca

OCEAN

International Date Line

CHATHAM ISLANDS (N.Z.)

FALKLAND ISLANDS (U.K.)

SOUTH GEORGIA (U.K.)

Punta Arenas

CABO DE HORNOS CAPE HORN

Drake Passage

SOUTH ORKNEY ISLANDS (B.A.T.)

Antarctic Circle

ANTARCTIC PENINSULA

Ross Sea

Bellingshausen Sea

Weddell Sea

ROSS ICE SHELF

MARIE BYRD LAND

Vinson Massif 4897

A N T A R R

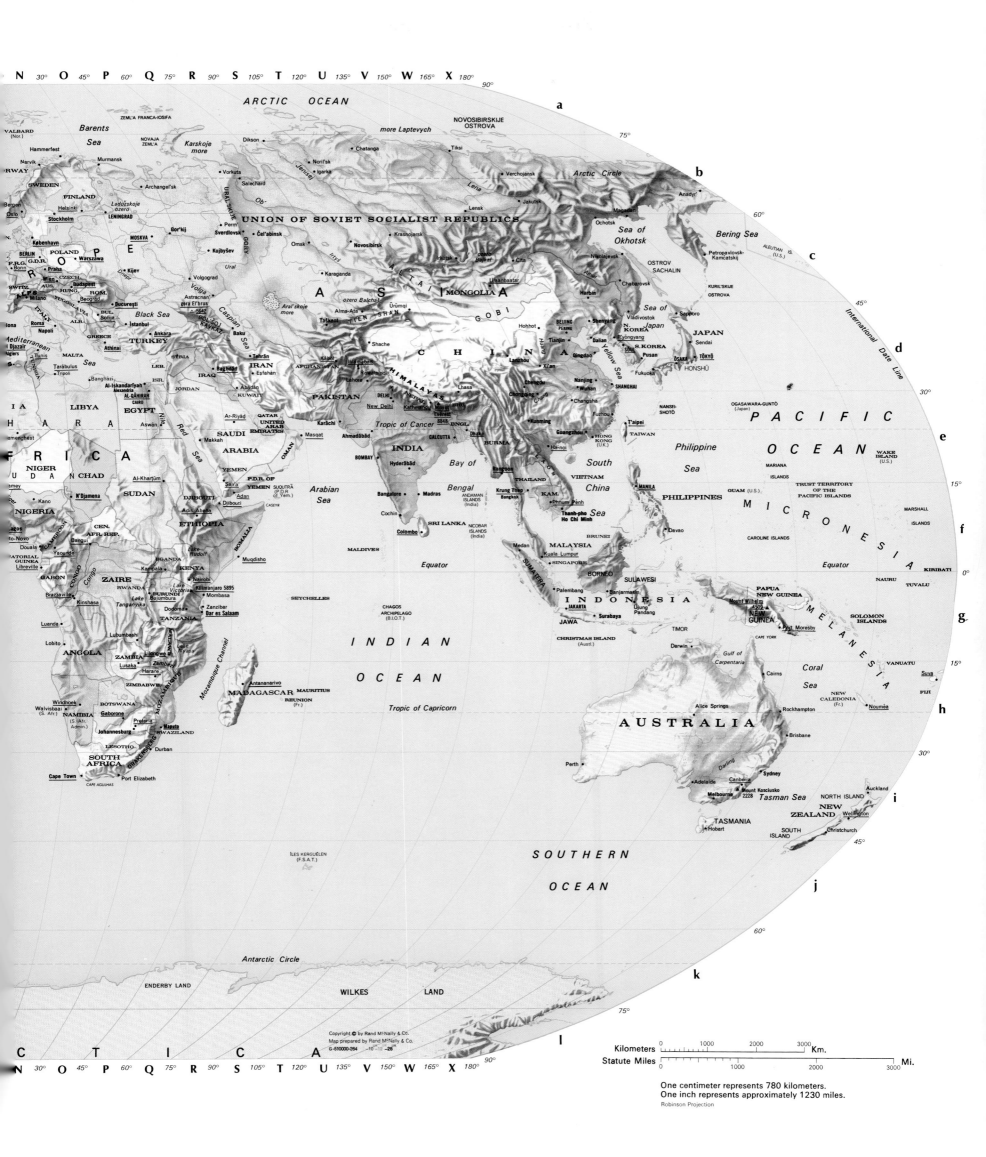

ARCTIC OCEAN

VALBARD (Nor.)
Barents Sea
ZEML'A FRANCA-IOSIFA
NOVOSIBIRSKIJE OSTROVA
a
Hammerfest
NOVAJA ZEML'A
Karskoje more
Dikson
more Laptevych
75°
Murmansk
Narvik
Archangel'sk
Vorkuta
Jenisej
Igarka
Chatanga
Tiksi
NORWAY
SWEDEN
FINLAND
Noril'sk
Verchojansk
Arctic Circle
b
Anadyr'
Bergen
Oslo
Helsinki
Ladožskoje ozero
LENINGRAD
URAL SKIJE
Salechard
Ob'
Lena
Jakutsk
Magadan
60°
Petropavlovsk-Kamčatskij
c
Kobenhavn
Stockholm
MOSKVA
Gor'kij
Perm'
Sverdlovsk
Omsk
Novosibirsk
Krasnojarsk
Irkutsk
ozero Bajkal
Čita
Ochotsk
Nikolajevsk
Chabarovsk
OSTROV SACHALIN
ALEUTIAN IS. (U.S.)
BERLIN
POLAND
G.D.R.
Warszawa
EUROPE
Kijev
Volgograd
Kujbyšev
Čel'abinsk
Karaganda
UNION OF SOVIET SOCIALIST REPUBLICS
Ulaanbaatar
Sea of Okhotsk
Bering Sea
KURIL'SKIJE OSTROVA
Vladivostok
Sea of Japan
Sapporo
JAPAN
45°
International Date Line
d

ENDERBY LAND
WILKES LAND
75°
l

Copyright © by Rand McNally & Co.
Map prepared by Rand McNally & Co.
G-610000-264 -10-12 -26

Kilometers 0 1000 2000 3000 Km.
Statute Miles 0 1000 2000 3000 Mi.

One centimeter represents 780 kilometers.
One inch represents approximately 1230 miles.
Robinson Projection

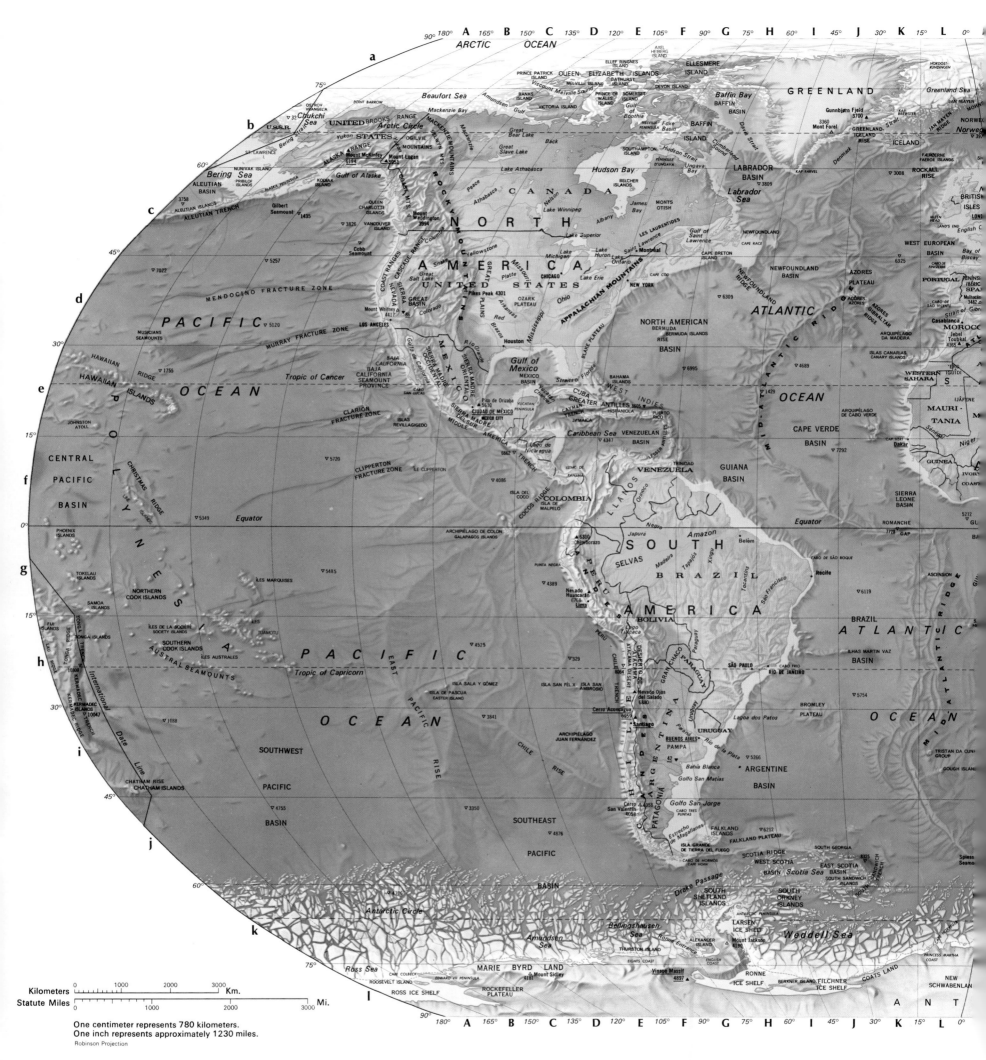

One centimeter represents 780 kilometers.
One inch represents approximately 1230 miles.
Robinson Projection

The legend below also relates to the maps on pages 189, 190-191, and 192.

Land Features

Ice and Snow

High Barren Areas

Tundra and Alpine

Needleleaf Trees (Taiga)

Broadleaf Trees

Tropical Rainforest

Grassland

Dry Scrub

Desert

Submarine Features

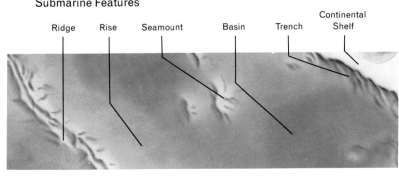

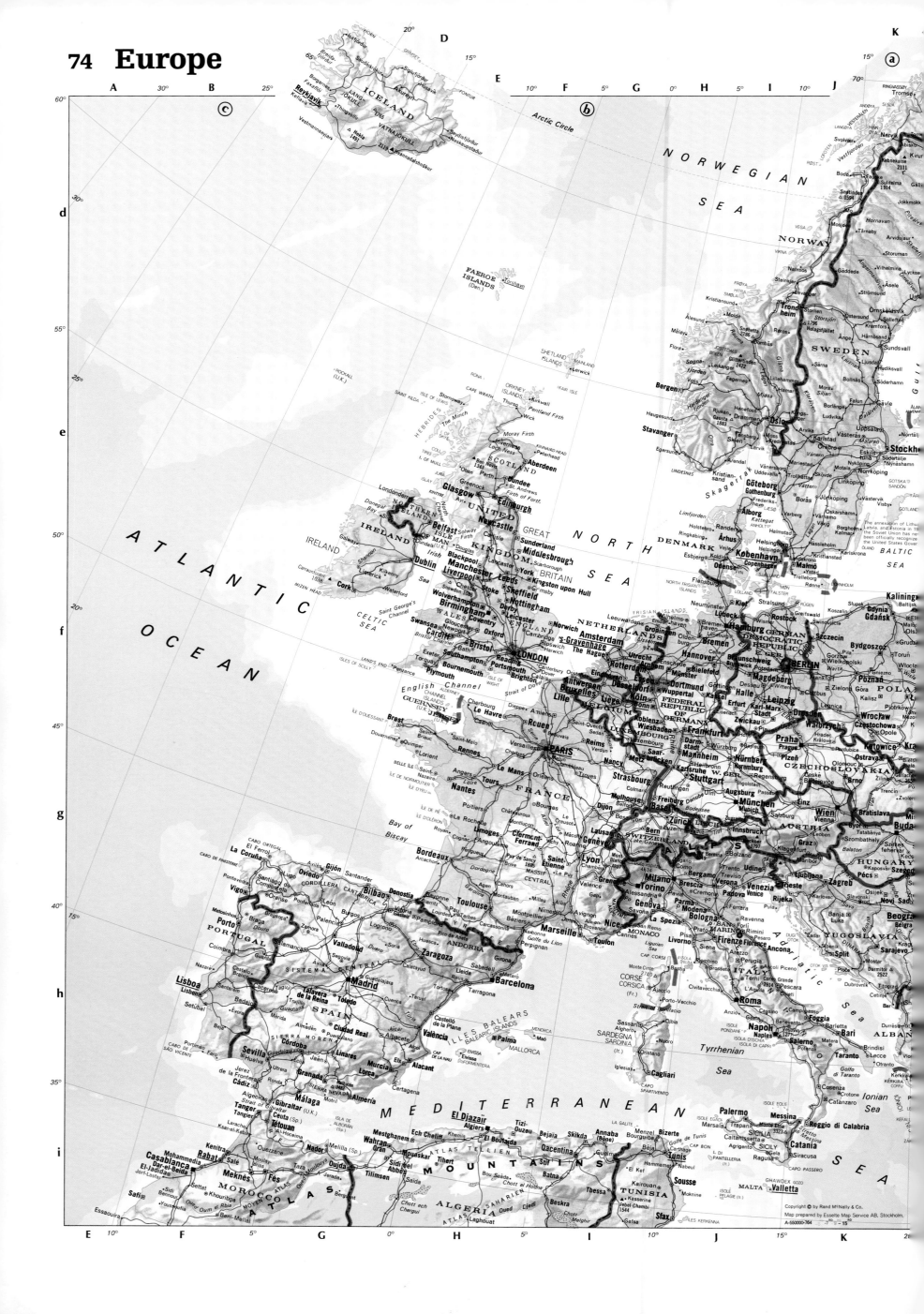

One centimeter represents 120 kilometers.
One inch represents approximately 190 miles.

Scale 1:12,000,000
Miller Oblated Stereographic Projection

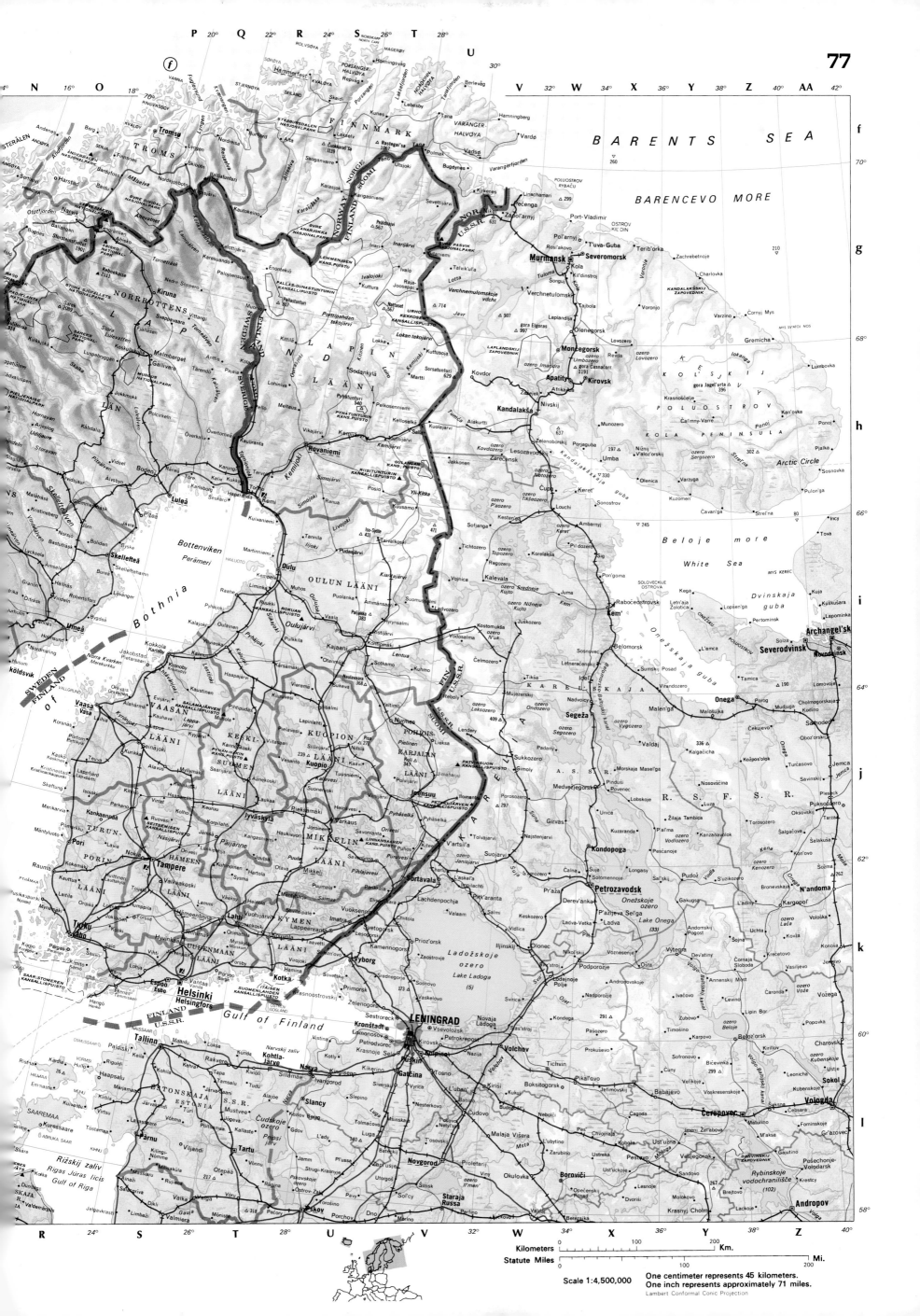

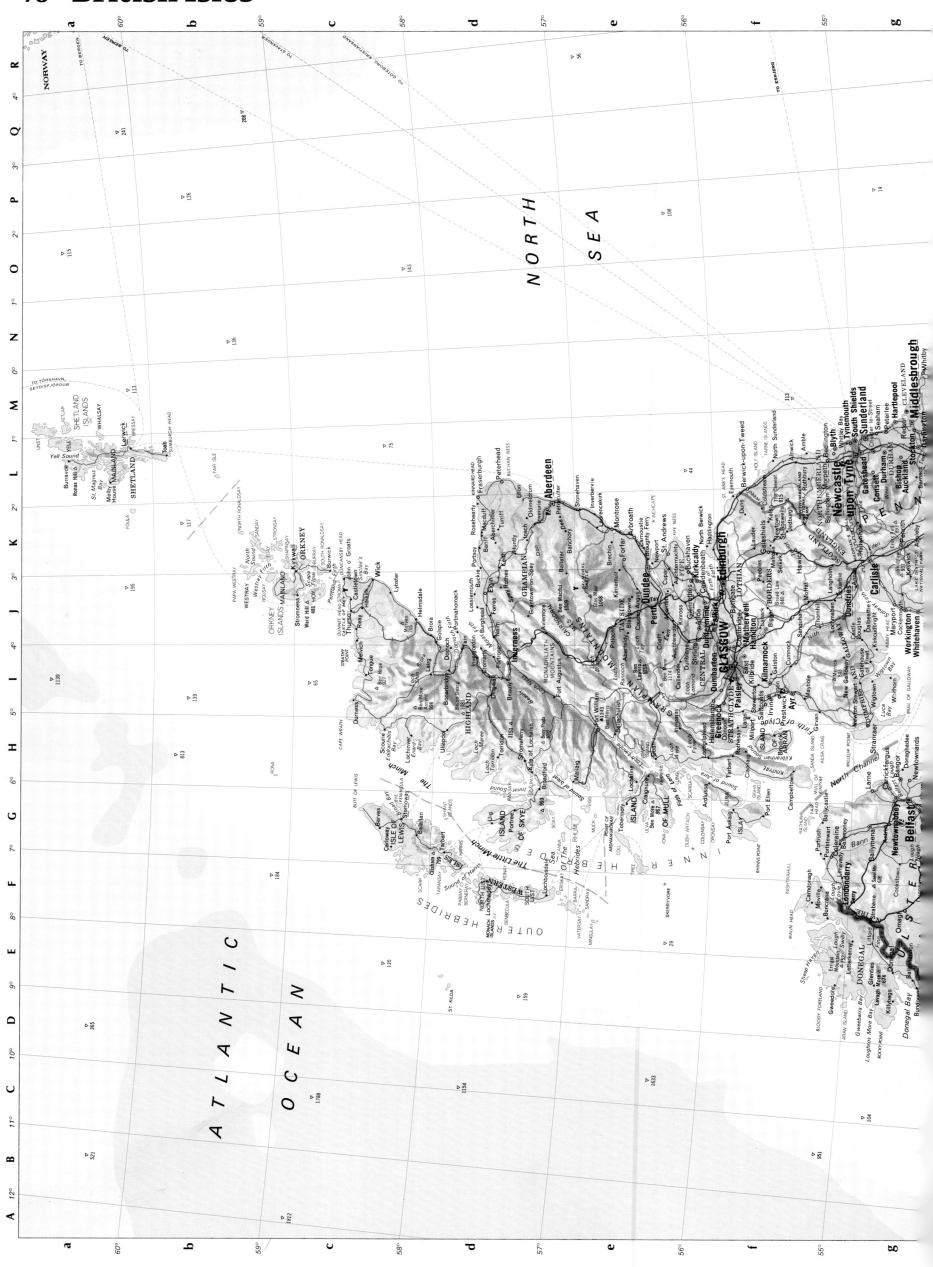

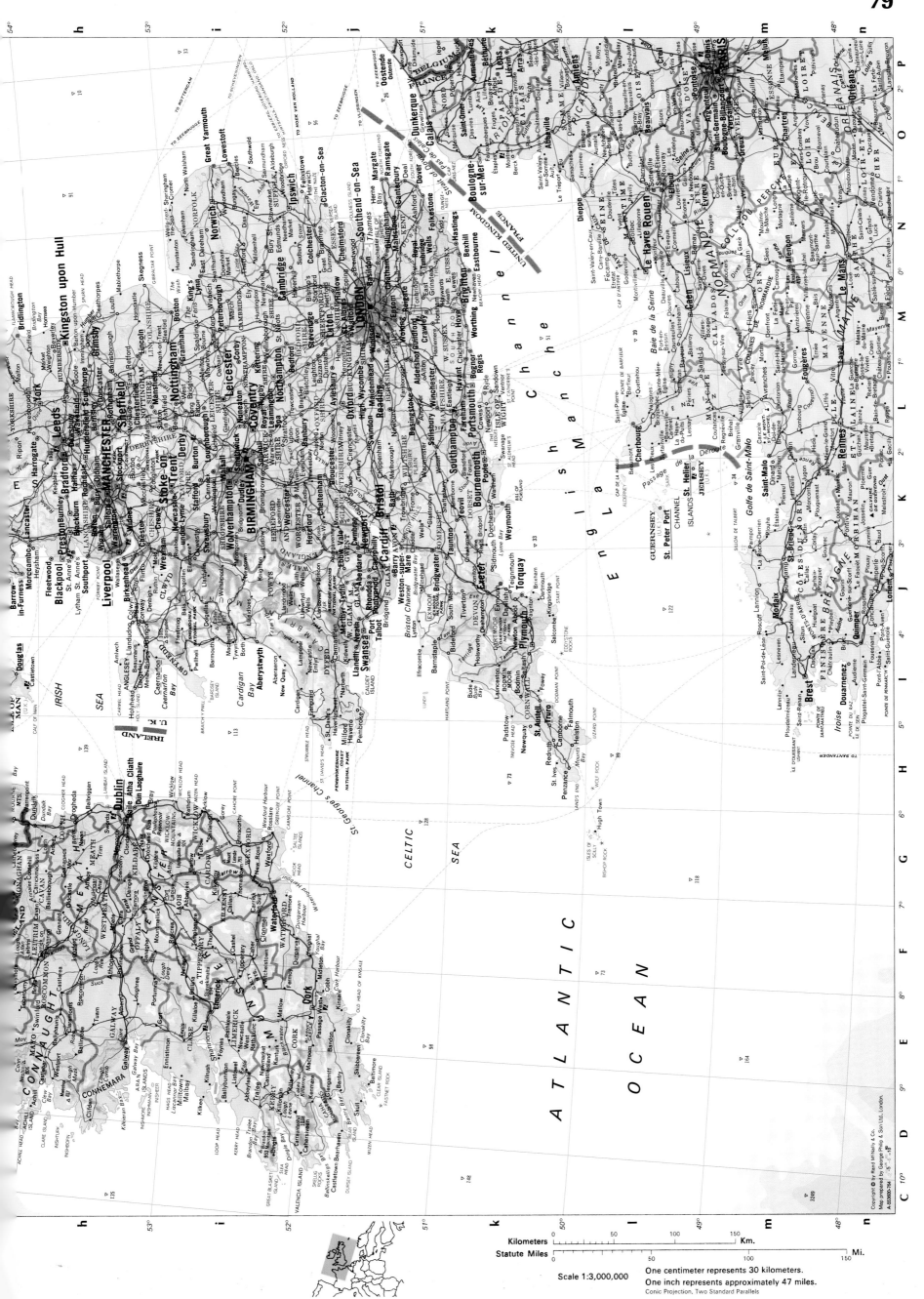

Kilometers
Statute Miles

One centimeter represents 30 kilometers.
One inch represents approximately 47 miles.

Scale 1:3,000,000

Conic Projection, Two Standard Parallels

NORTH SEA

Scale 1:3,000,000

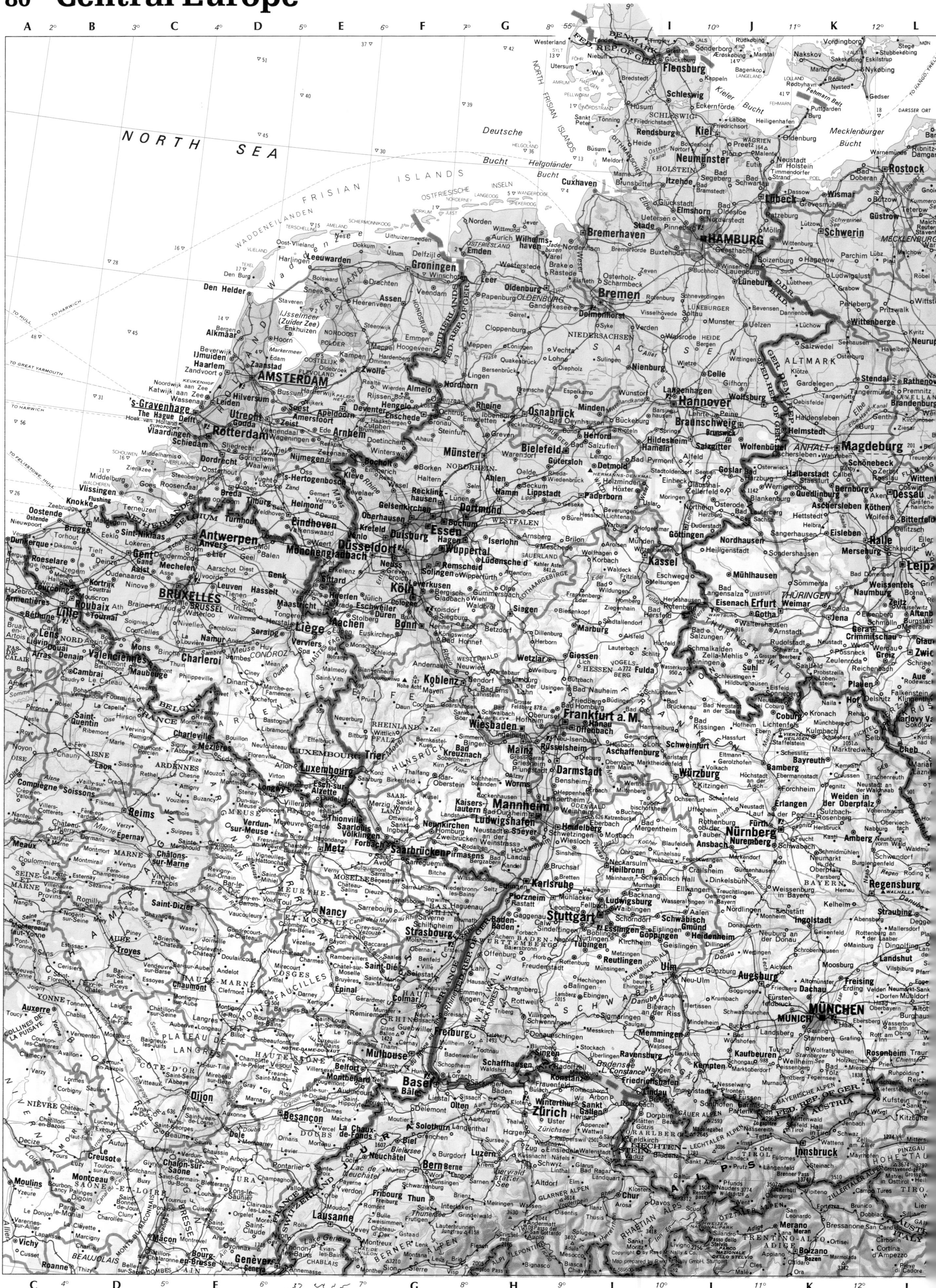

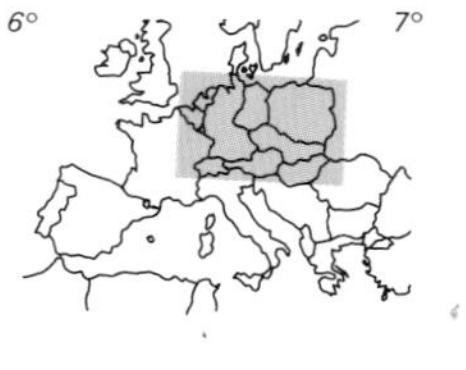

One centimeter represents 30 kilometers.
One inch represents approximately 47 miles.
Conic Projection, Two Standard Parallels.

Kilometers

Statute Miles

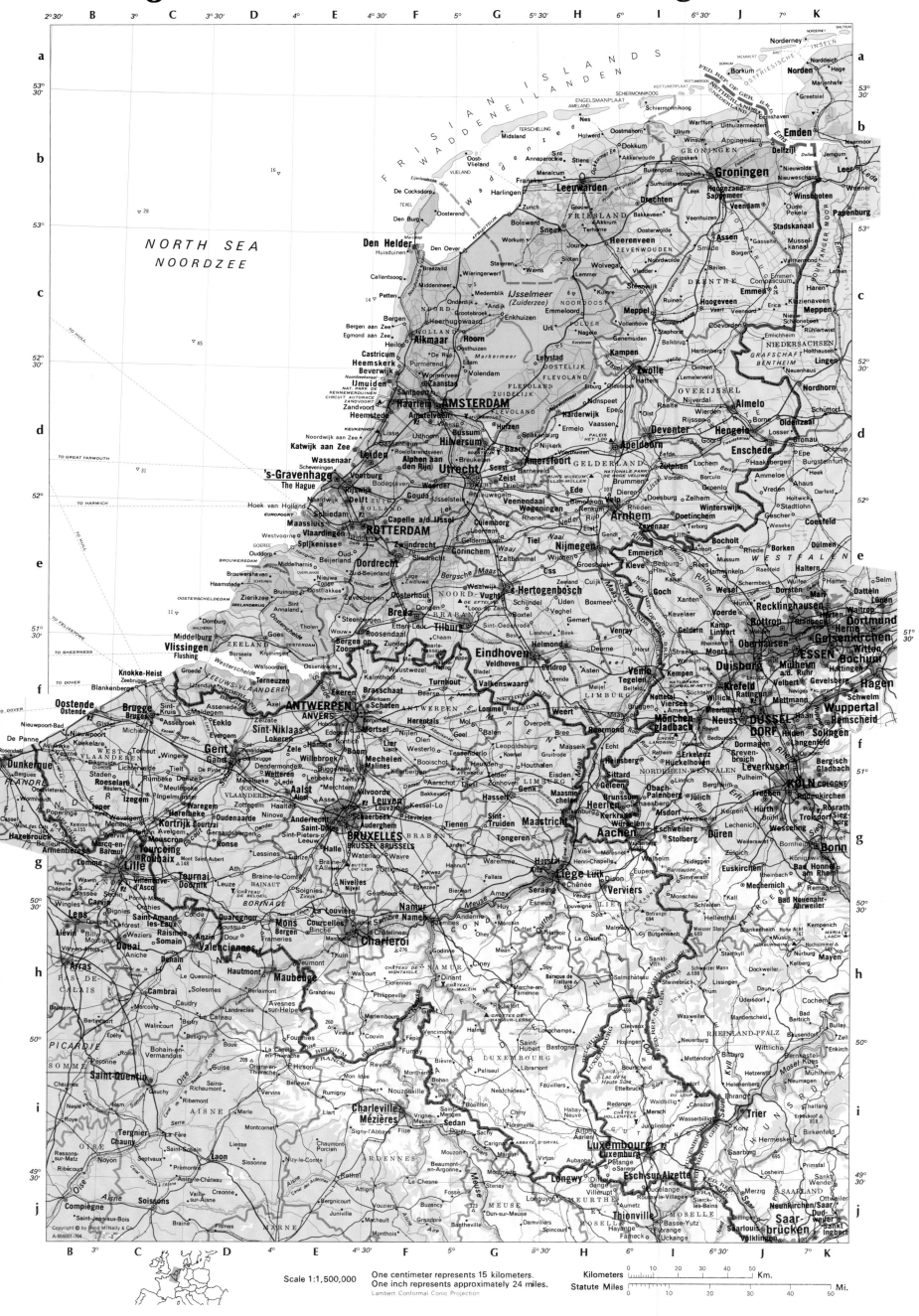

Scale 1:1,500,000
One centimeter represents 15 kilometers.
One inch represents approximately 24 miles.
Lambert Conformal Conic Projection

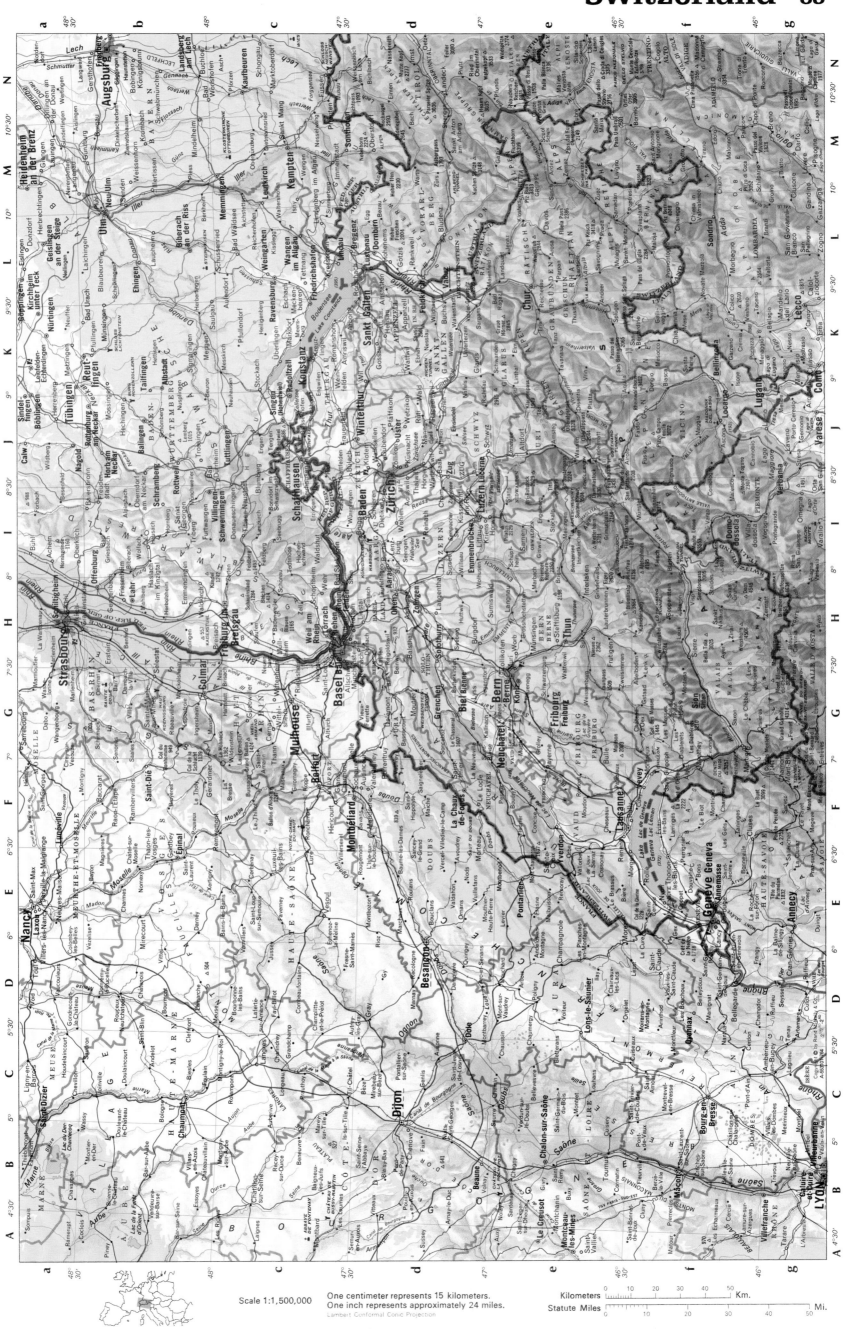

Scale 1:1,500,000

One centimeter represents 15 kilometers.
One inch represents approximately 24 miles.

Lambert Conformal Conic Projection

Kilometers
0 10 20 30 40 50 Km.

Statute Miles
0 10 20 30 40 50 Mi.

Kilometers
Statute Miles

Scale 1:3,000,000
One centimeter represents 30 kilometers.
One inch represents approximately 47 miles.
Lambert Conformal Conic Projection

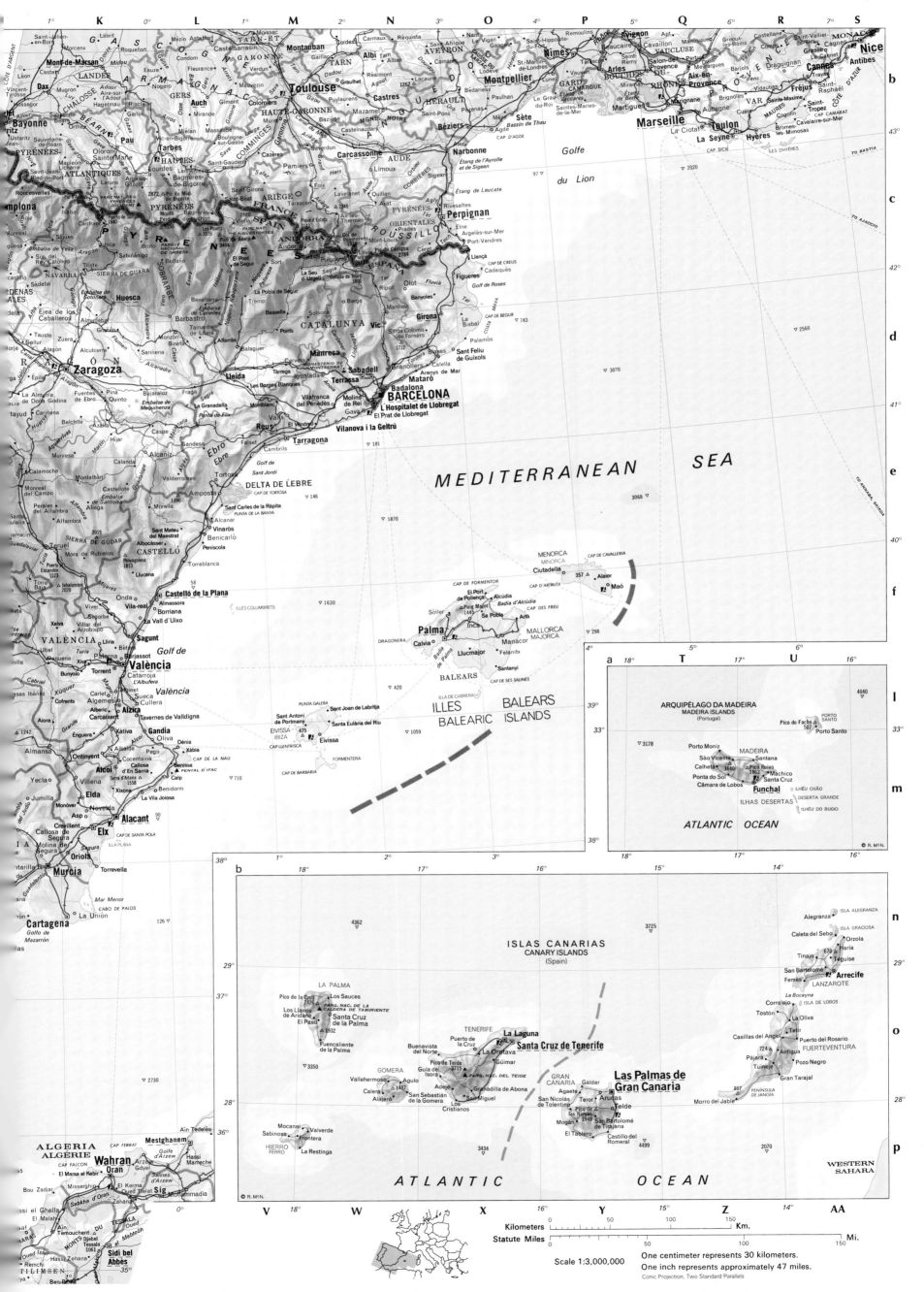

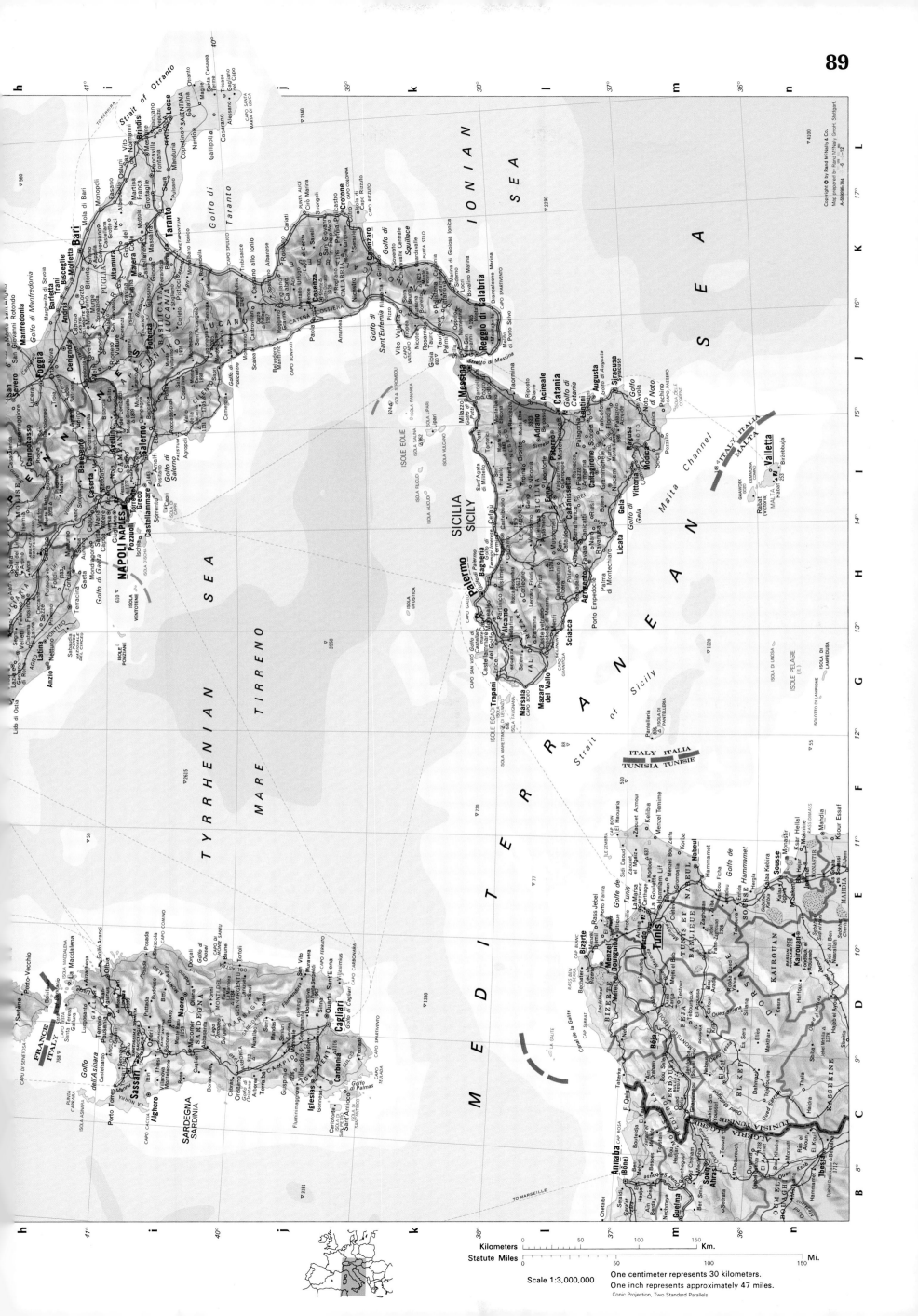

Kilometers
Statute Miles

Scale 1:3,000,000

One centimeter represents 30 kilometers.
One inch represents approximately 47 miles.
Conic Projection, Two Standard Parallels

Kilometers

Statute Miles

Scale 1:3,000,000

One centimeter represents 30 kilometers.
One inch represents approximately 47 miles.
Conic Projection. Two Standard Parallels

Copyright © by Rand McNally & Co.
Map prepared by Rand McNally GmbH, Stuttgart.
A-550000-764

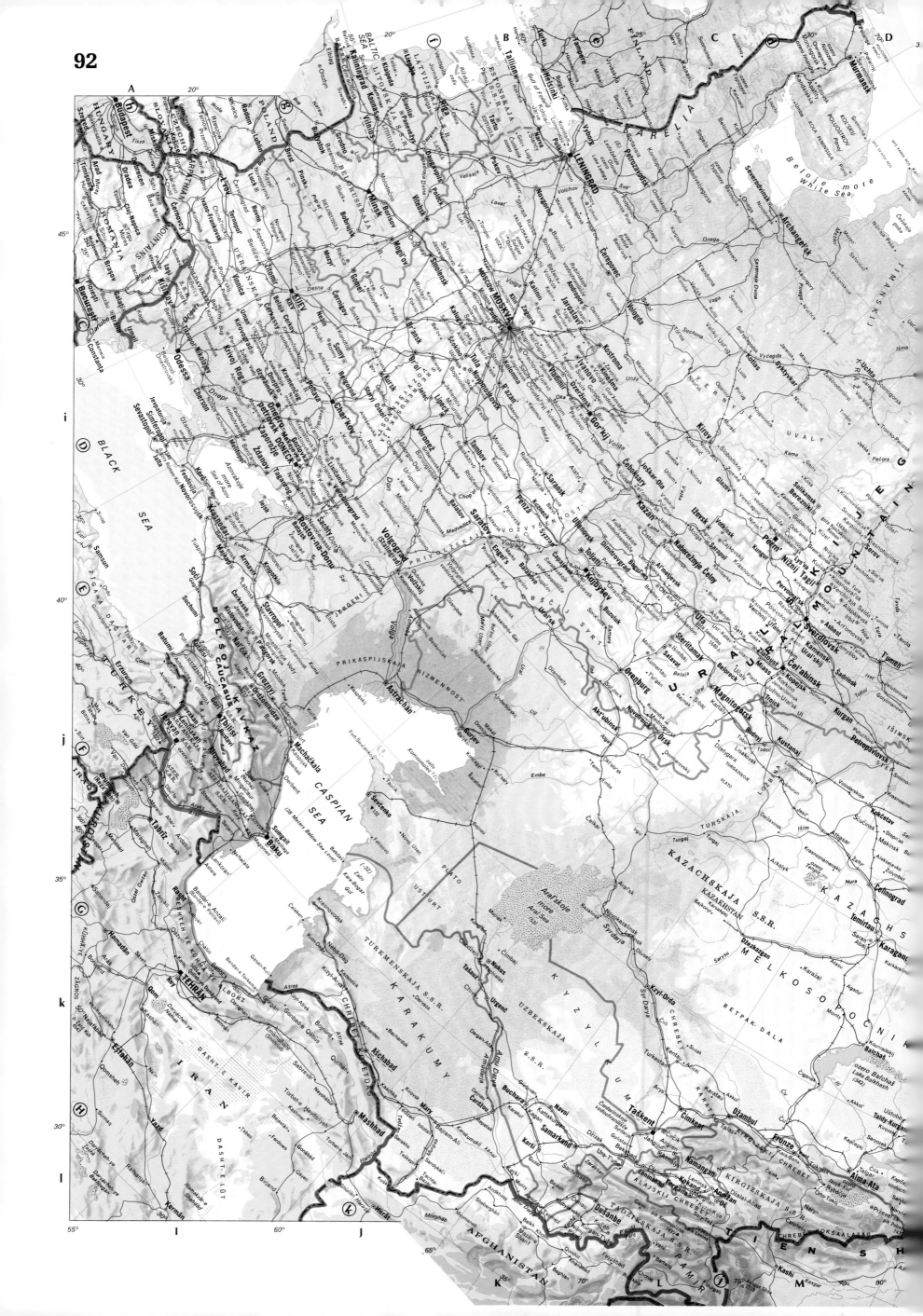

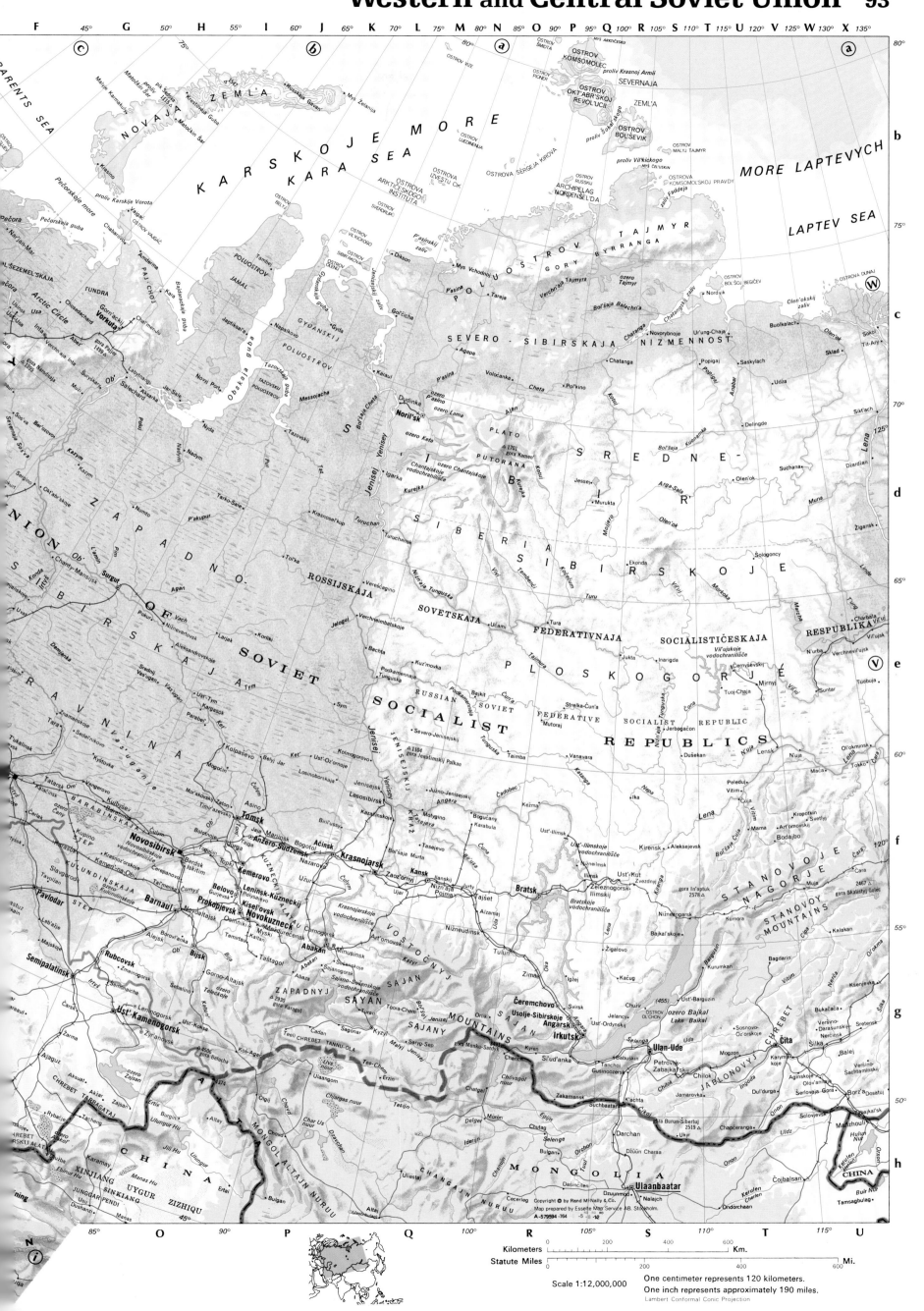

Scale 1:12,000,000

One centimeter represents 120 kilometers.
One inch represents approximately 190 miles.
Lambert Conformal Conic Projection

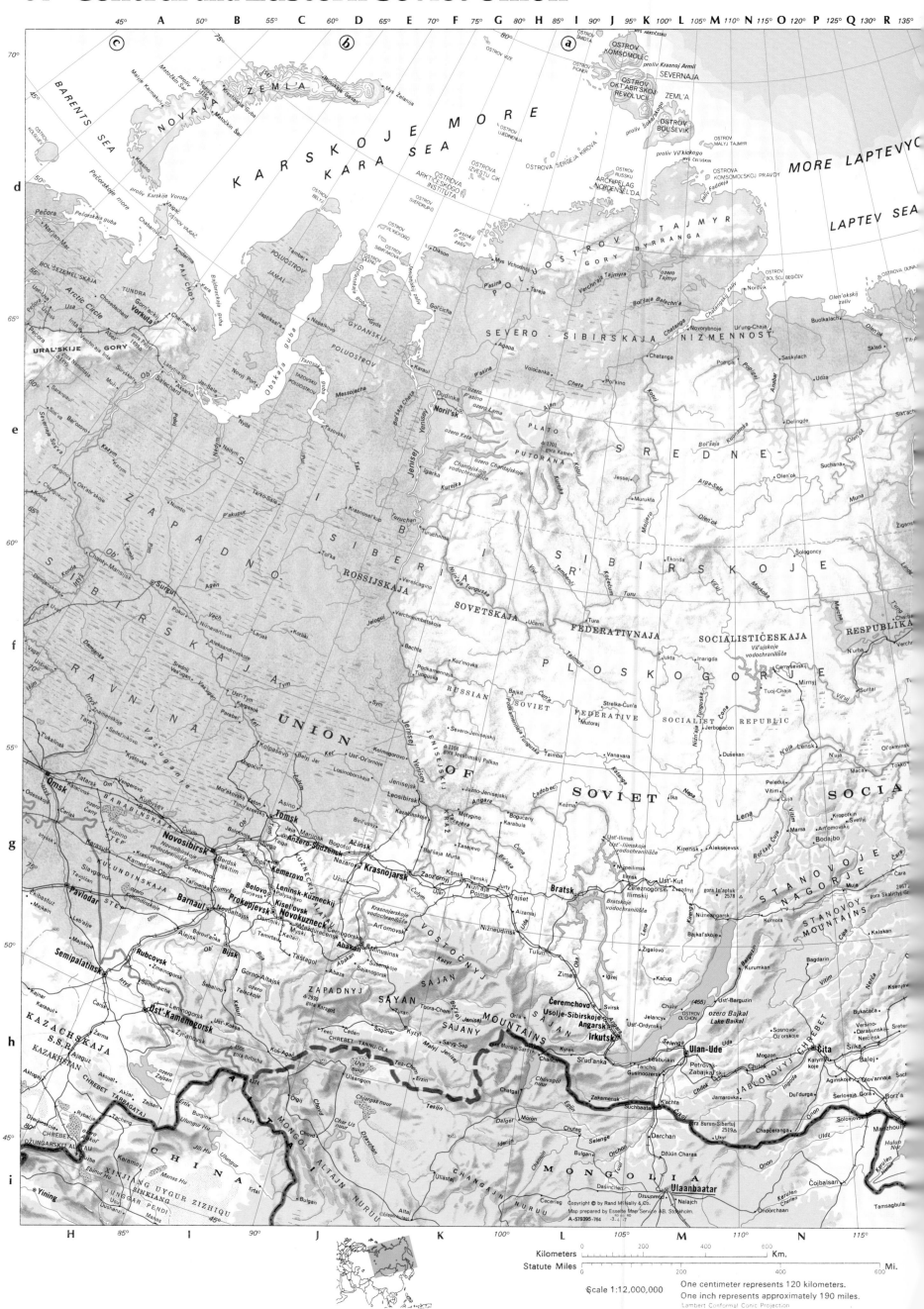

Scale 1:12,000,000
One centimeter represents 120 kilometers.
One inch represents approximately 190 miles.
Lambert Conformal Conic Projection

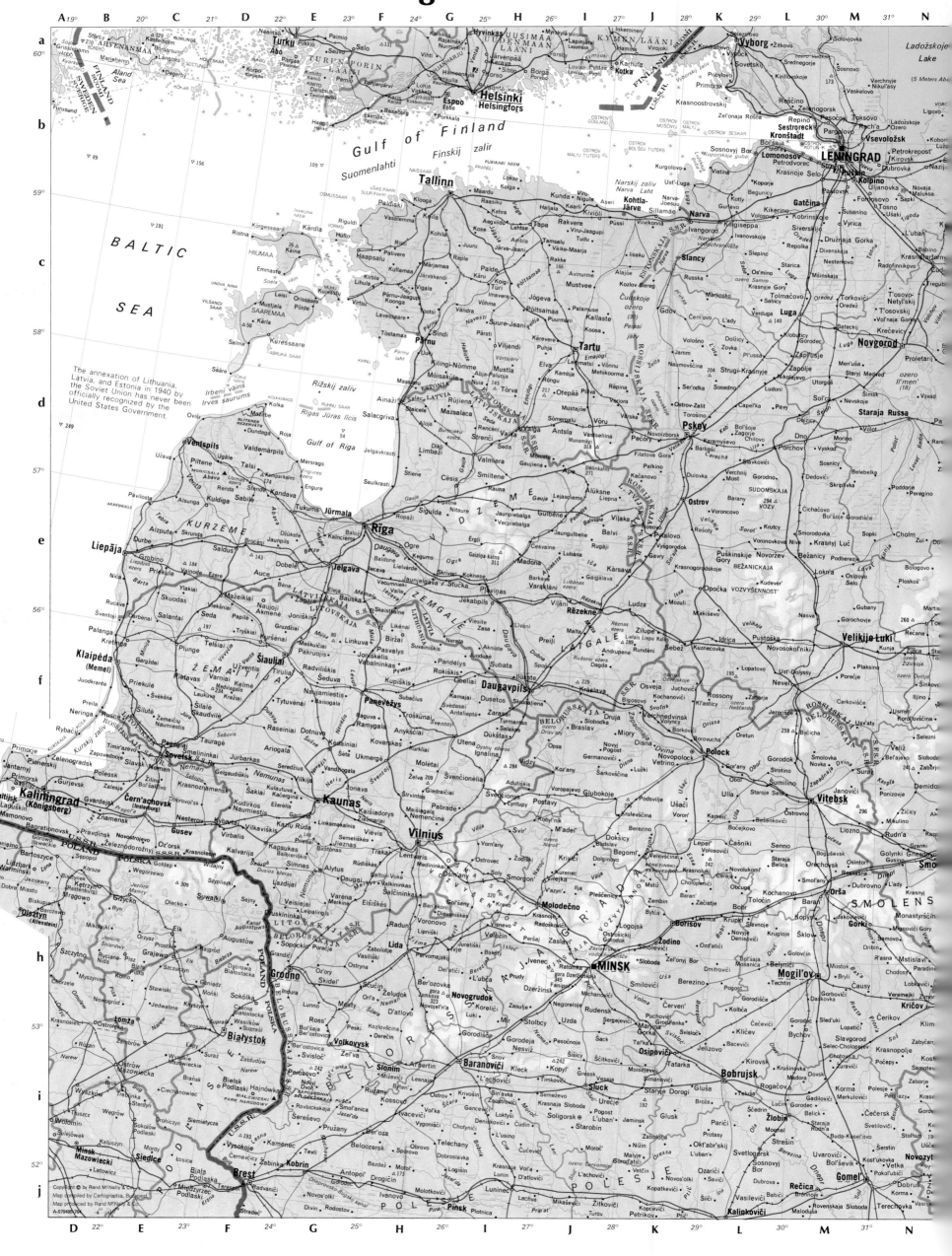

The annexation of Lithuania, Latvia, and Estonia in 1940 by the Soviet Union has never been officially recognized by the United States Government.

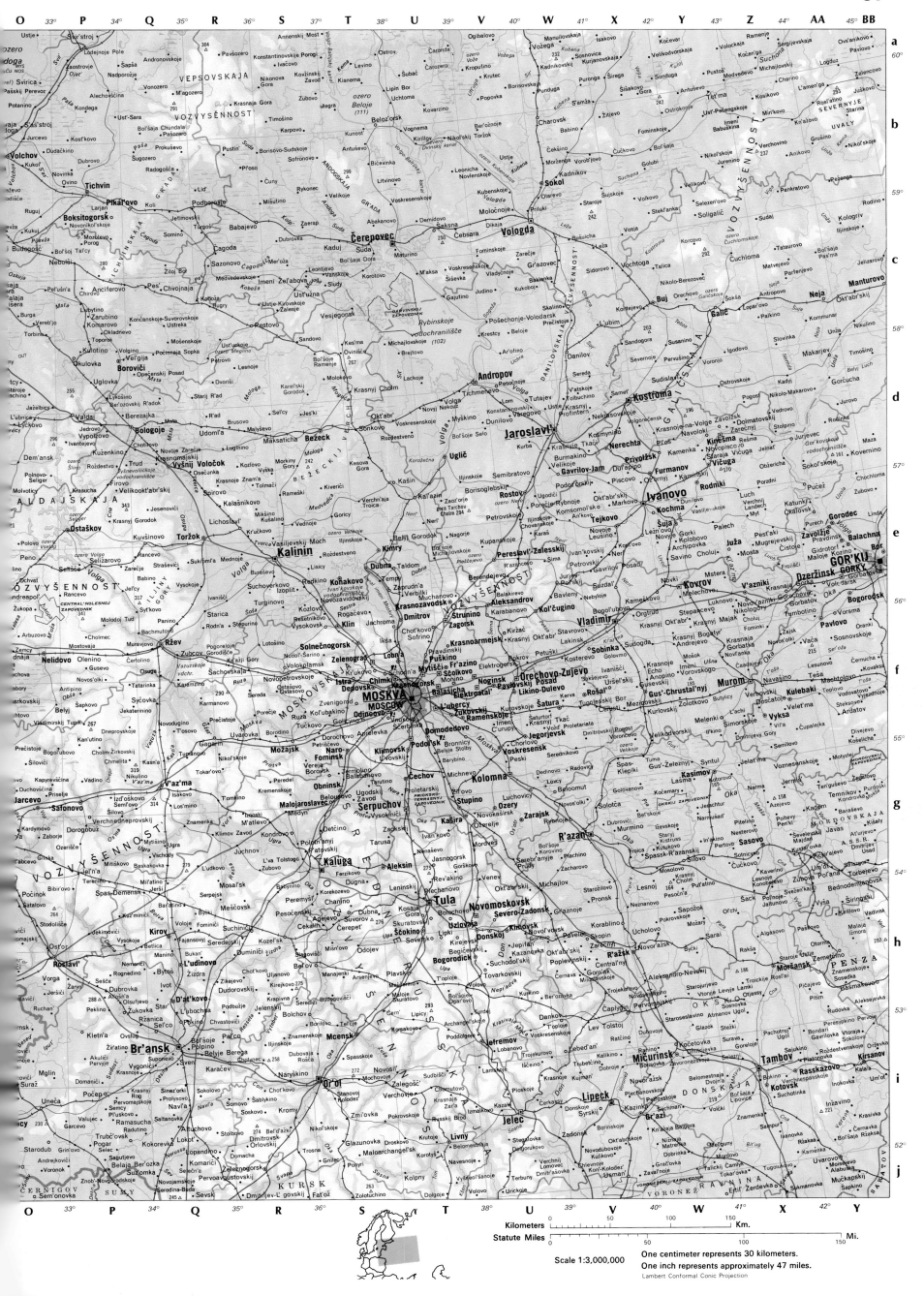

One centimeter represents 30 kilometers.
One inch represents approximately 47 miles.

Scale 1:3,000,000

Lambert Conformal Conic Projection

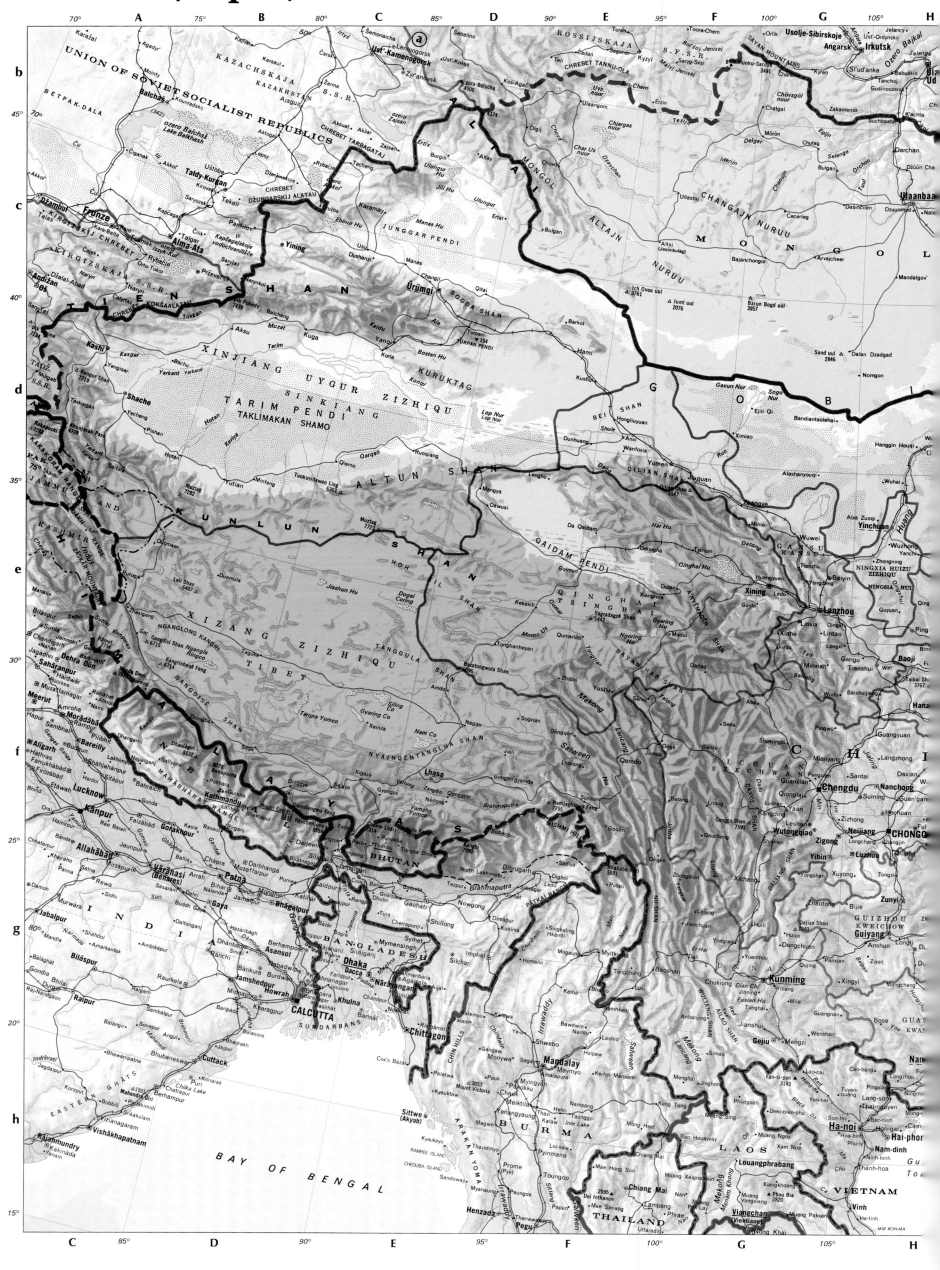

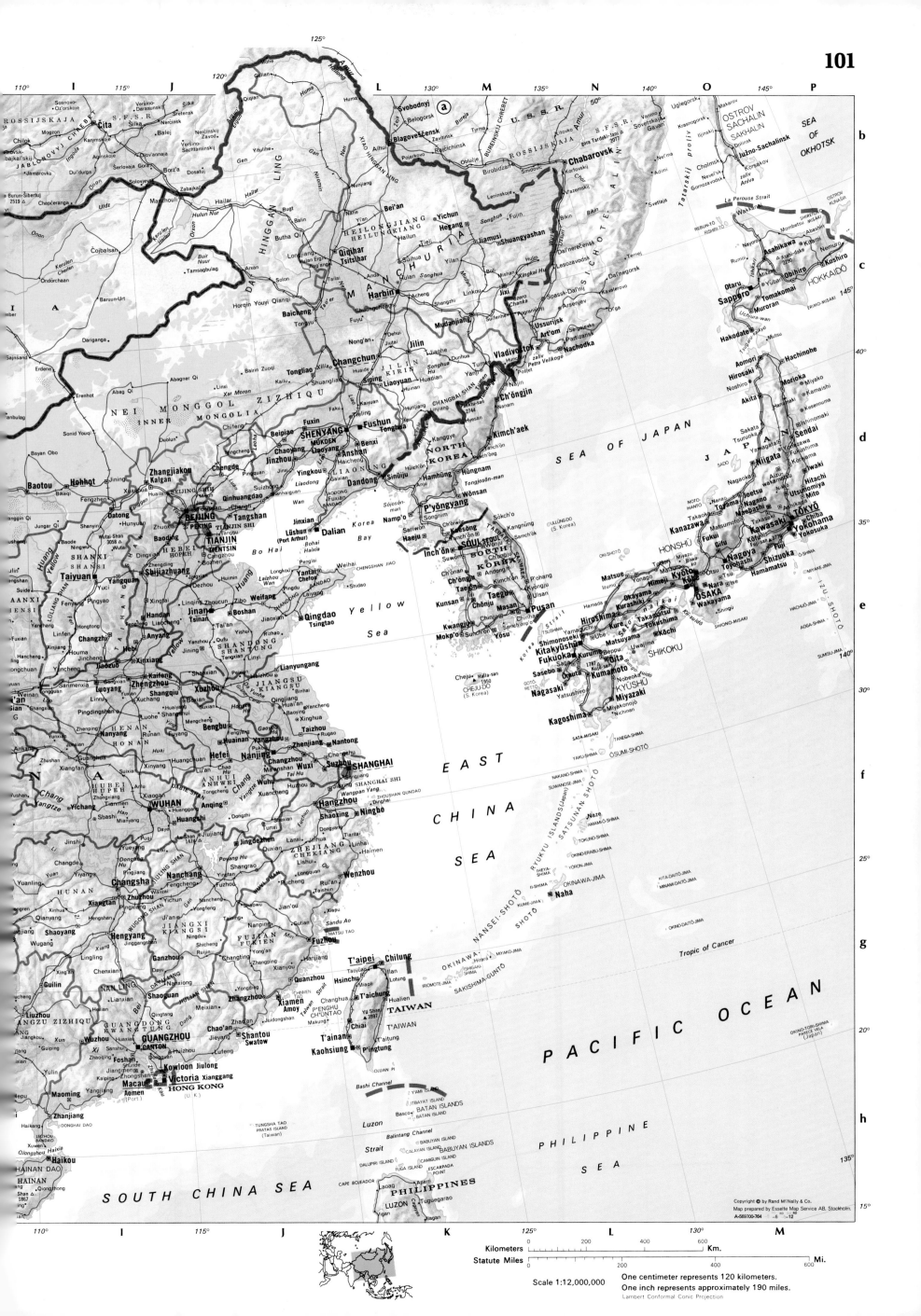

SEA OF OKHOTSK

U.S.S.R.

SEA OF JAPAN

MANCHURIA

HEILONGJIANG
HEILUNGKIANG

NEI MONGGOL ZIZHIQU
INNER MONGOLIA

JILIN KIRIN

NORTH KOREA

JAPAN

HONSHU

HOKKAIDO

LIAONING

HEBEI HOPEH

SHANXI SHANSI

SHANDONG SHANTUNG

SOUTH KOREA

Yellow Sea

Korea Bay

Bo Hai

HONAN

JIANGSU KIANGSU

ANHUI ANHWEI

Yangtze

SHIKOKU

KYŪSHŪ

EAST CHINA SEA

ZHEJIANG CHEKIANG

HUBEI HUPEH

HUNAN

JIANGXI KIANGSI

FUJIAN FUKIEN

RYUKYU ISLANDS (Japan)

SATSUNAN SHOTŌ

NANSEI-SHOTŌ

Tropic of Cancer

GUANGDONG KWANGTUNG

GUANGZU ZIZHIQU

TAIWAN T'AIWAN

PACIFIC OCEAN

HONG KONG (U.K.)

Bashi Channel

Luzon Strait

PHILIPPINE SEA

HAINAN

SOUTH CHINA SEA

PHILIPPINES

LUZON

Scale 1:12,000,000

Kilometers
0   200   400   600 Km.

Statute Miles
0   200   400   600 Mi.

One centimeter represents 120 kilometers.
One inch represents approximately 190 miles.
Lambert Conformal Conic Projection

Copyright © by Rand McNally & Co.
Map prepared by Esselte Map Service AB, Stockholm.
A-569700-764   -6   -6 -12

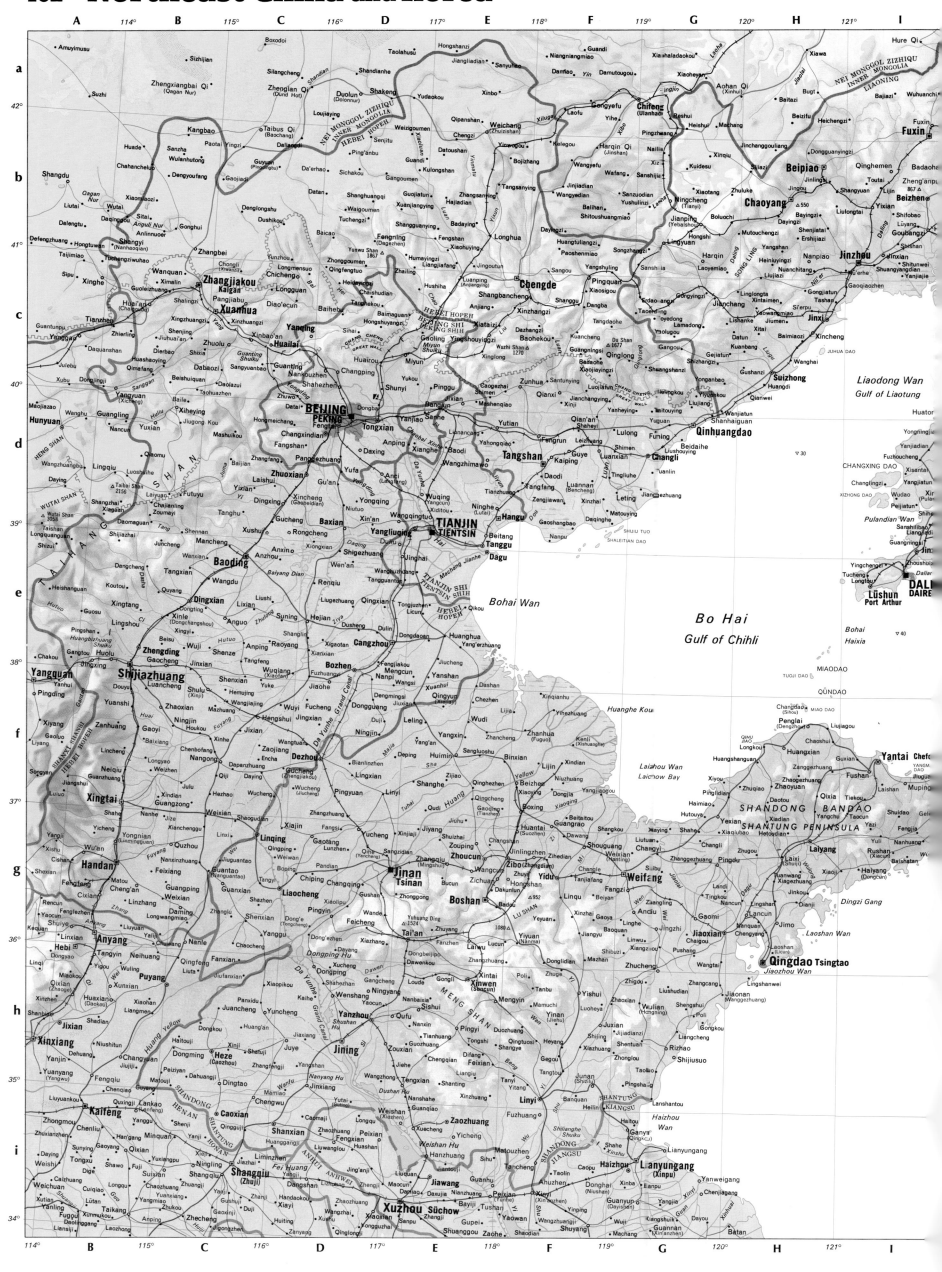

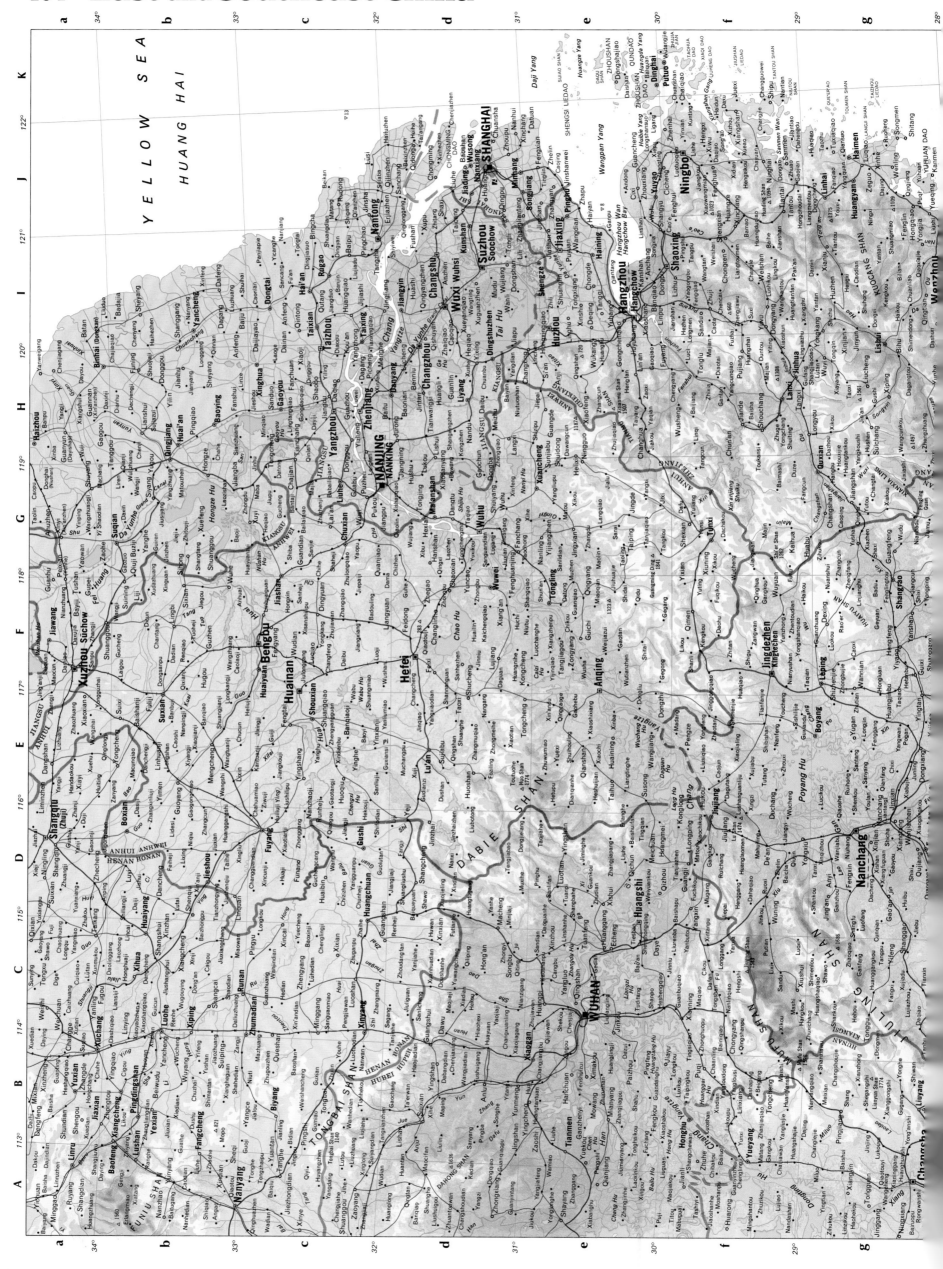

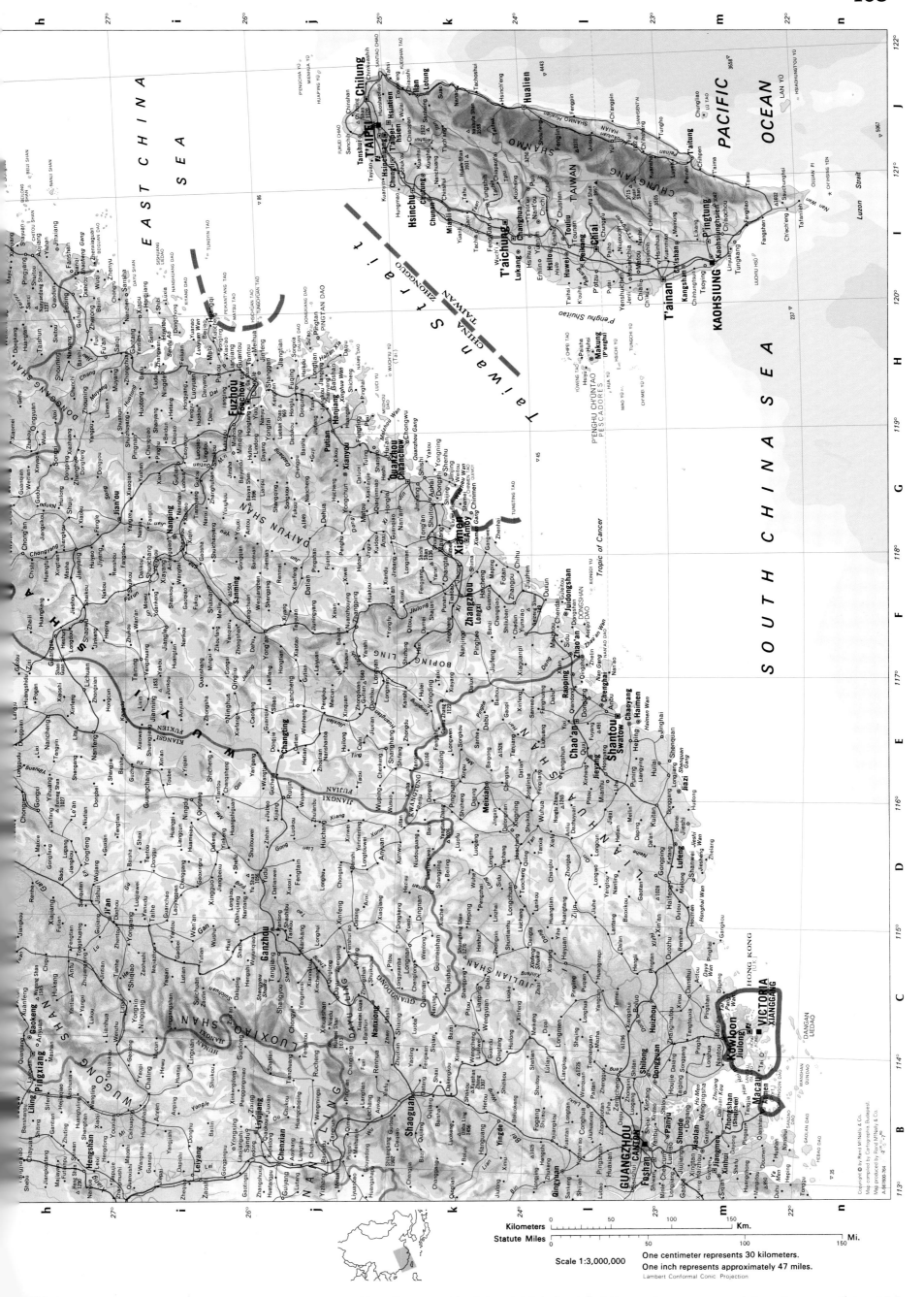

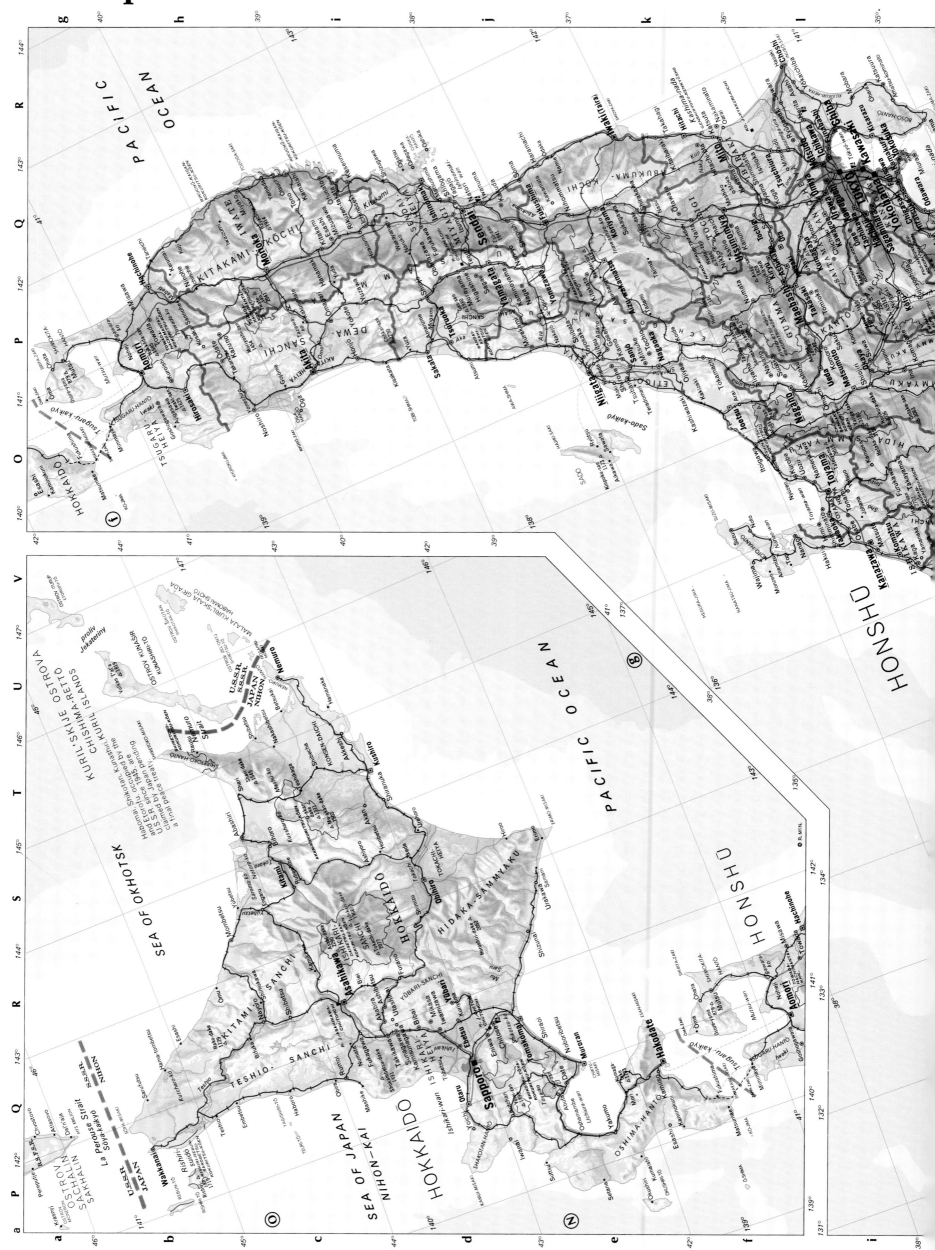

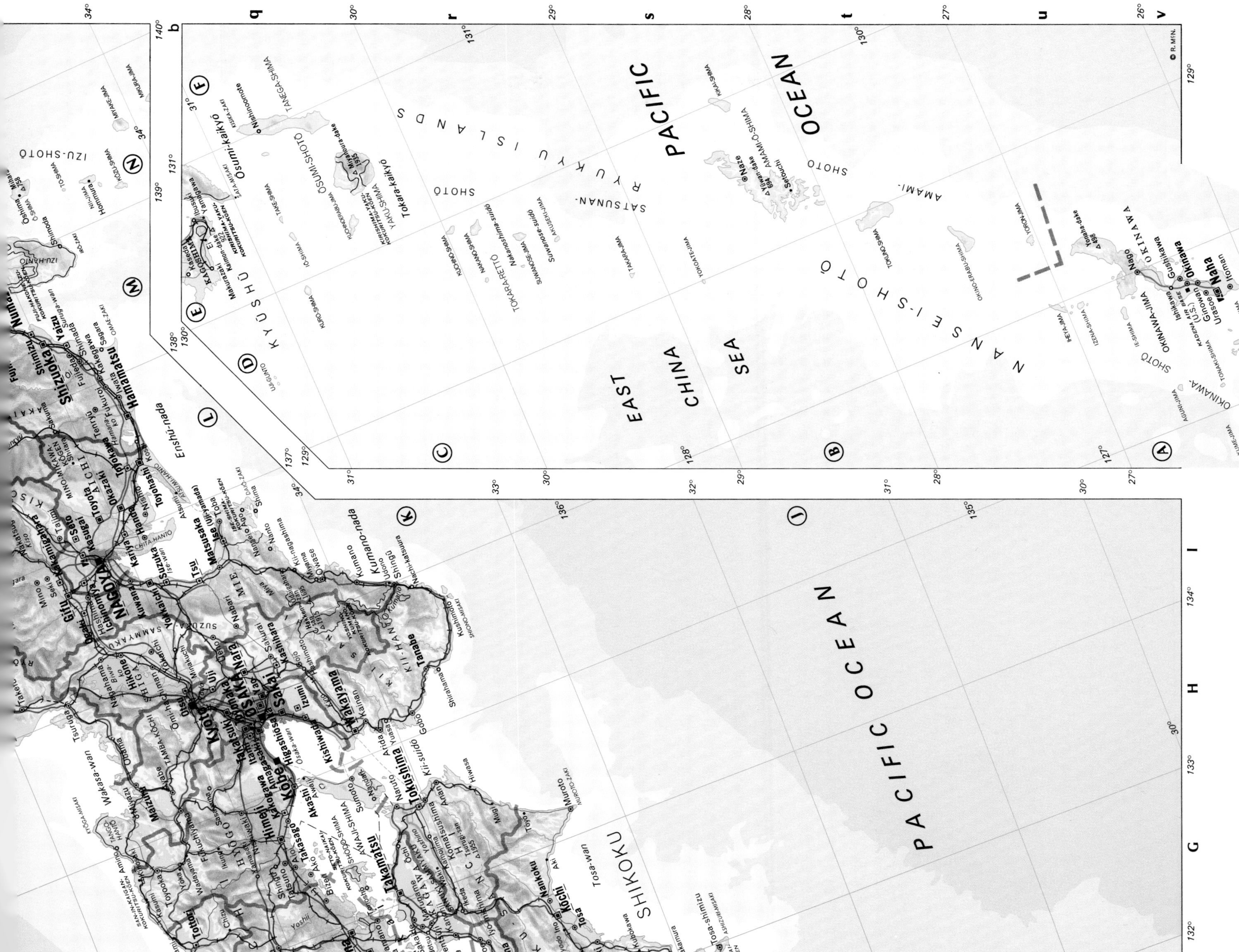

PACIFIC OCEAN

RYUKYU ISLANDS

EAST CHINA SEA

NANSEI-SHOTO

SATSUNAN SHOTO

AMAMI-SHOTO

OKINAWA

Naha

OKINAWA-JIMA

KYUSHU

OSUMI-SHOTO

TANEGA-SHIMA

YAKU-SHIMA

TOKARA-RETTO

Osumi-kaikyo

Tokara-kaikyo

IZU-SHOTO

SEA OF JAPAN

NIHON-KAI

OKI-SHOTO

DOGO

DOZEN

Shimonoseki

Kitakyushu

Fukuoka

Nagasaki

Sasebo

Kagoshima

Miyazaki

Kumamoto

Yatsushiro

Beppu

Oita

Nobeoka

Hyuga-nada

SHIKOKU

Matsuyama

Kochi

Takamatsu

Tokushima

Uwajima

Tosa-wan

NAGOYA

KYOTO

OSAKA

Kobe

Himeji

Okayama

Kurashiki

Fukuyama

Onomichi

Kure

Hiroshima

Iwakuni

Yamaguchi

Ube

Matsue

Tottori

Shizuoka

Hamamatsu

Suzuka

Tsu

Wakayama

Tanabe

Kii-Hanto

Kumano-nada

Enshu-nada

KII-SUIDO

Bungo-suido

Korea Strait

TSUSHIMA

GOTO-RETTO

FUKUE-JIMA

Scale 1:3,000,000

One centimeter represents 30 kilometers.

One inch represents approximately 47 miles.

Lambert Conformal Conic Projection

Kilometers
0   50   100   150   Km.

Statute Miles
0   50   100   150   Mi.

Copyright © by Rand McNally & Co.

Map prepared by Teikoku-Shoin Co., Ltd., Tokyo.

A-661900-764

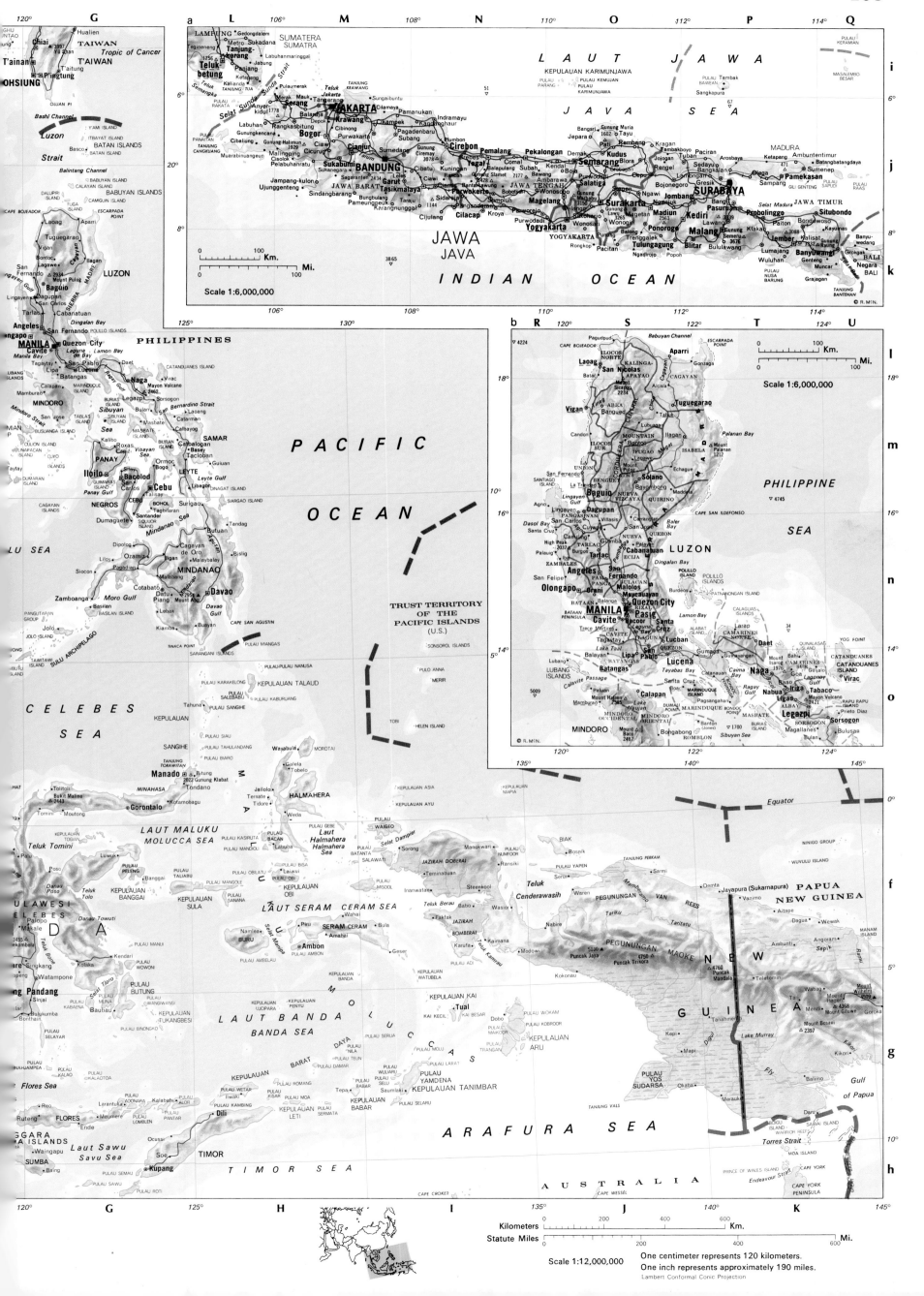

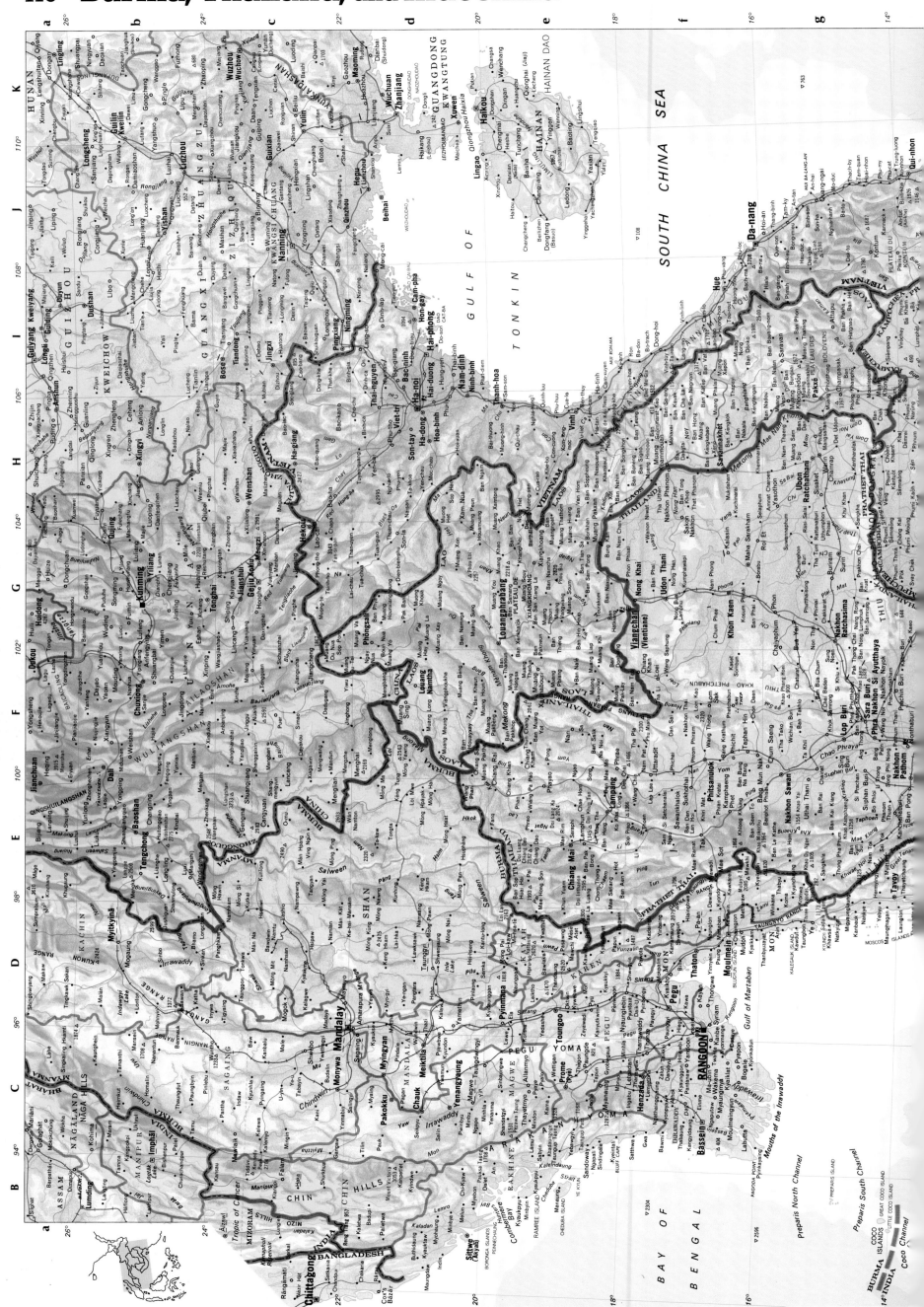

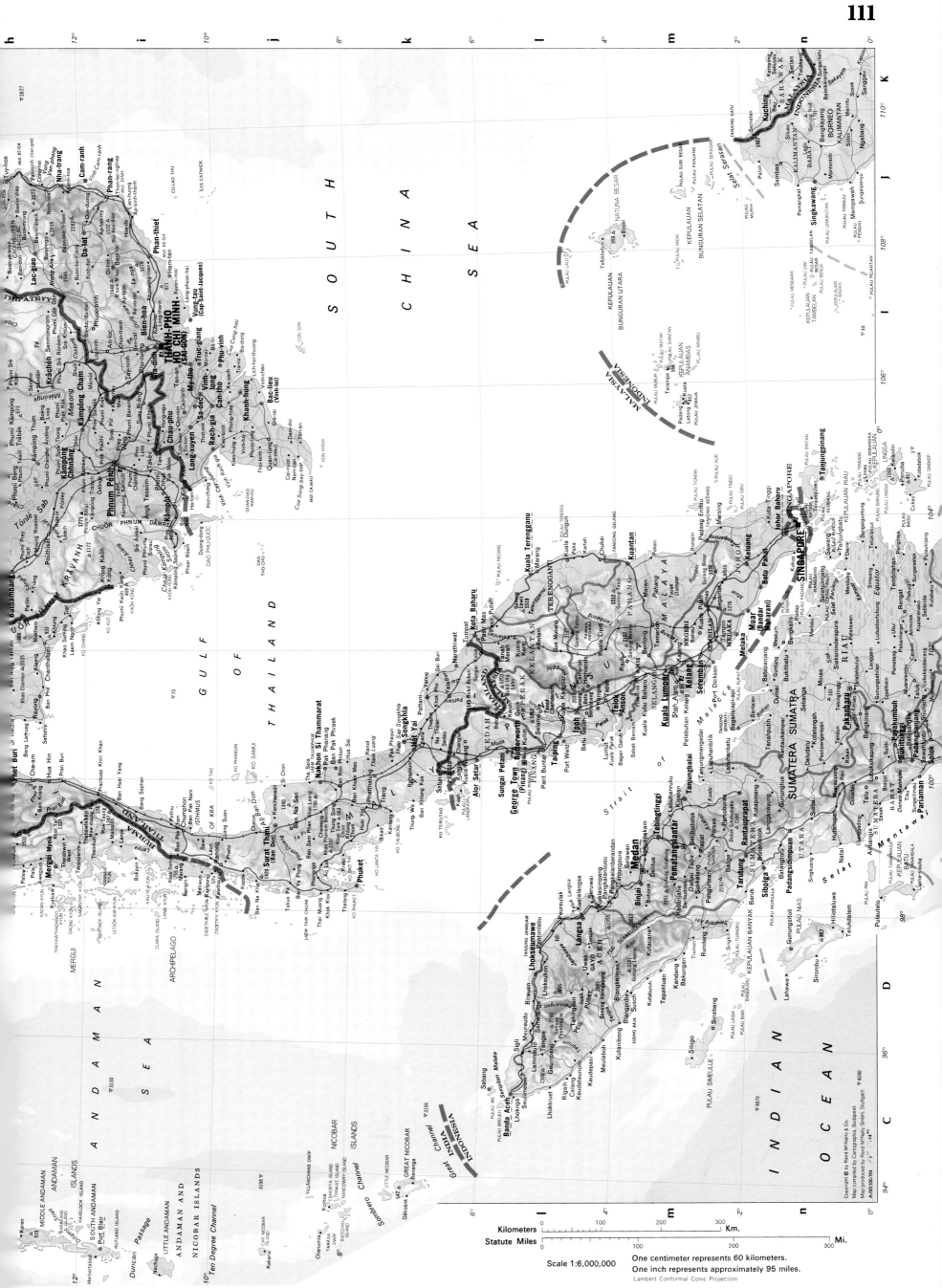

SOUTH CHINA SEA

GULF OF THAILAND

THAILAND

BURMA

ANDAMAN SEA

ANDAMAN ISLANDS

NICOBAR ISLANDS

INDIAN OCEAN

BORNEO

KALIMANTAN

SARAWAK

MALAYSIA

INDONESIA

MALAYA

SUMATERA

SINGAPORE

Kilometers 0 100 200 300 Km.
Statute Miles 0 100 200 300 Mi.

Scale 1:6,000,000

One centimeter represents 60 kilometers.
One inch represents approximately 95 miles.

Lambert Conformal Conic Projection

Copyright © by Rand McNally & Co.
Map compiled by Cartographia, Budapest.
Map produced by Rand McNally GmbH, Stuttgart.
A-561100-764

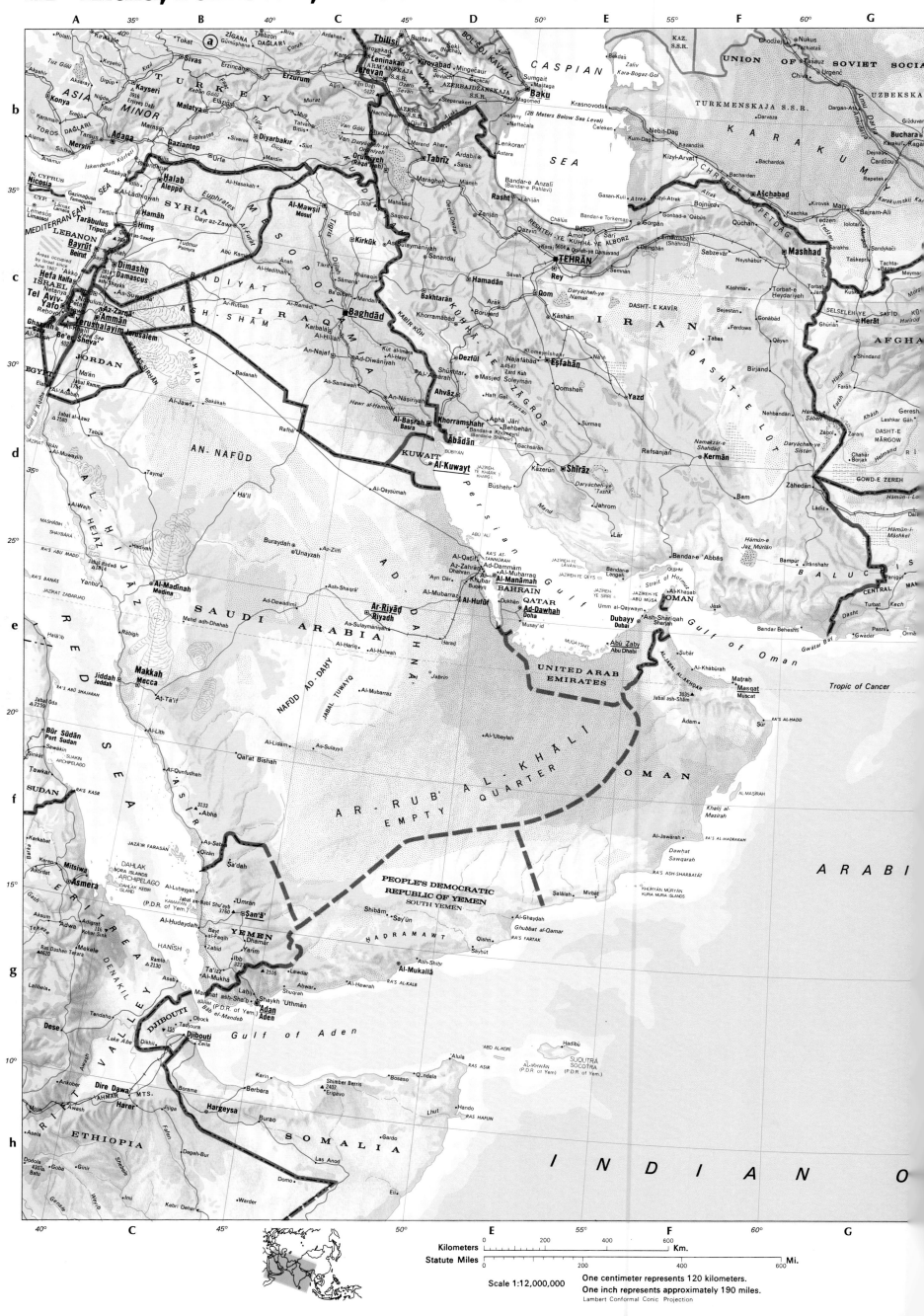

Kilometers

Statute Miles

Scale 1:12,000,000

One centimeter represents 120 kilometers.
One inch represents approximately 190 miles.

Lambert Conformal Conic Projection

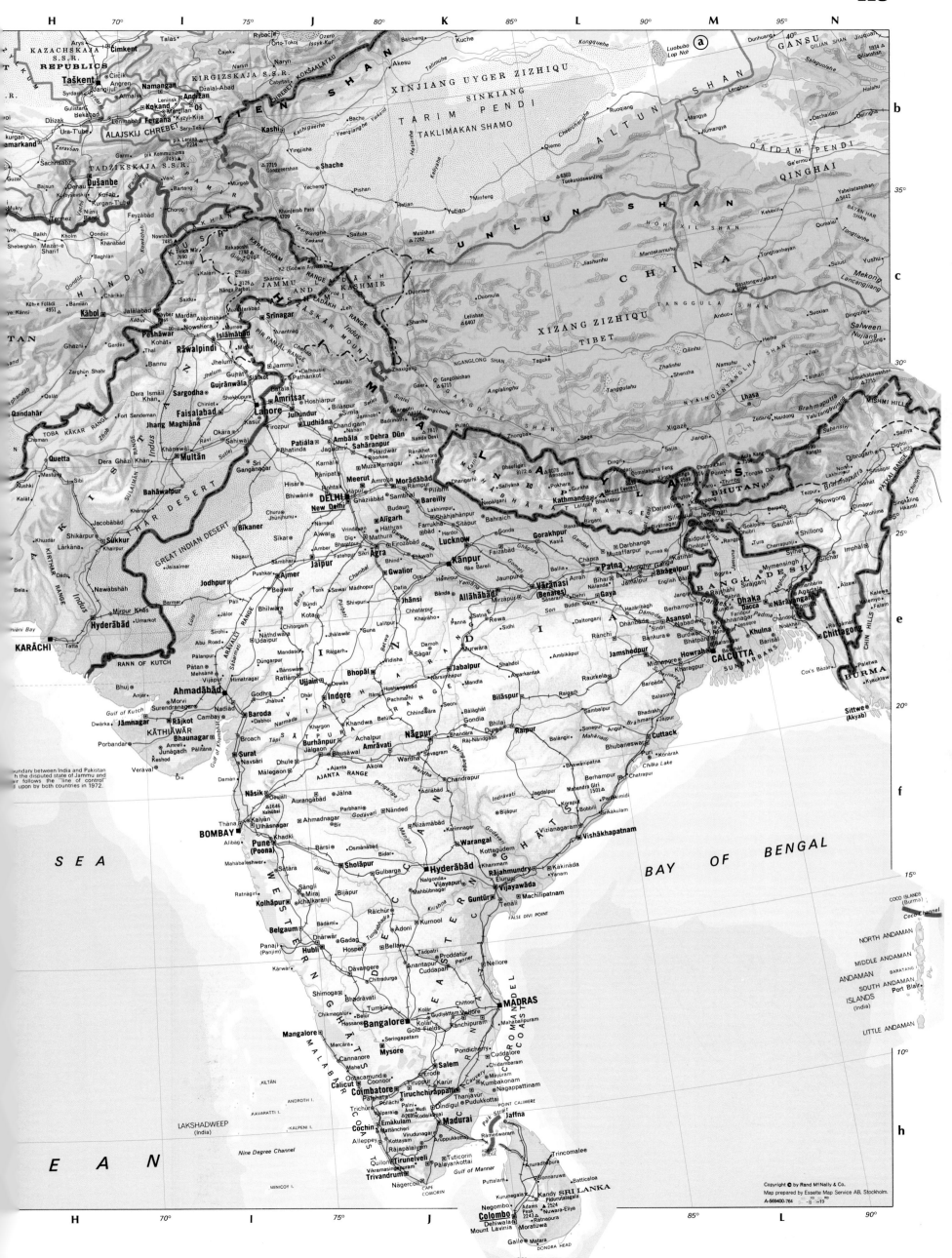

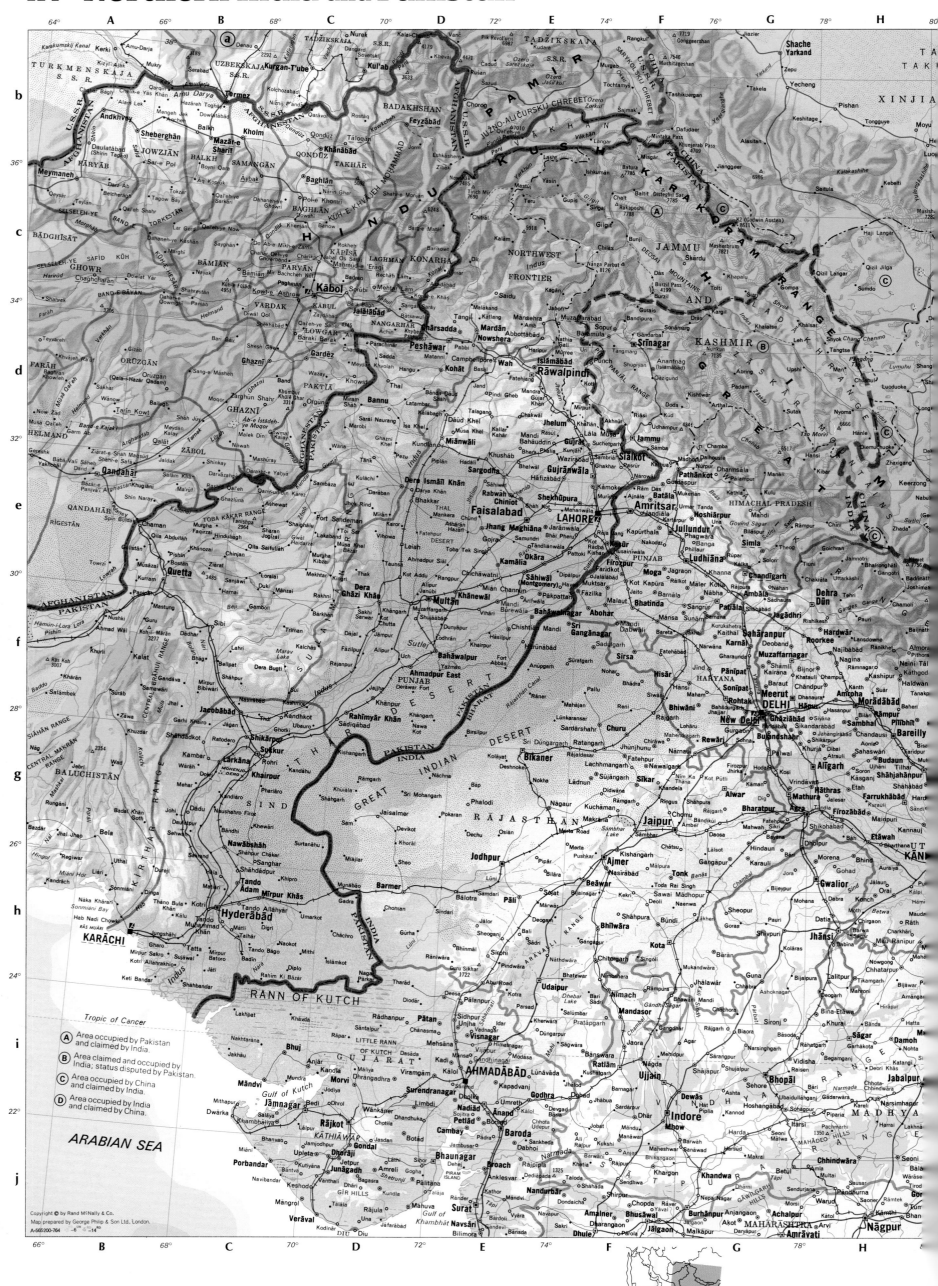

ARABIAN SEA

RANN OF KUTCH

Tropic of Cancer

(A) Area occupied by Pakistan and claimed by India.
(B) Area claimed and occupied by India; status disputed by Pakistan.
(C) Area occupied by China and claimed by India.
(D) Area occupied by India and claimed by China.

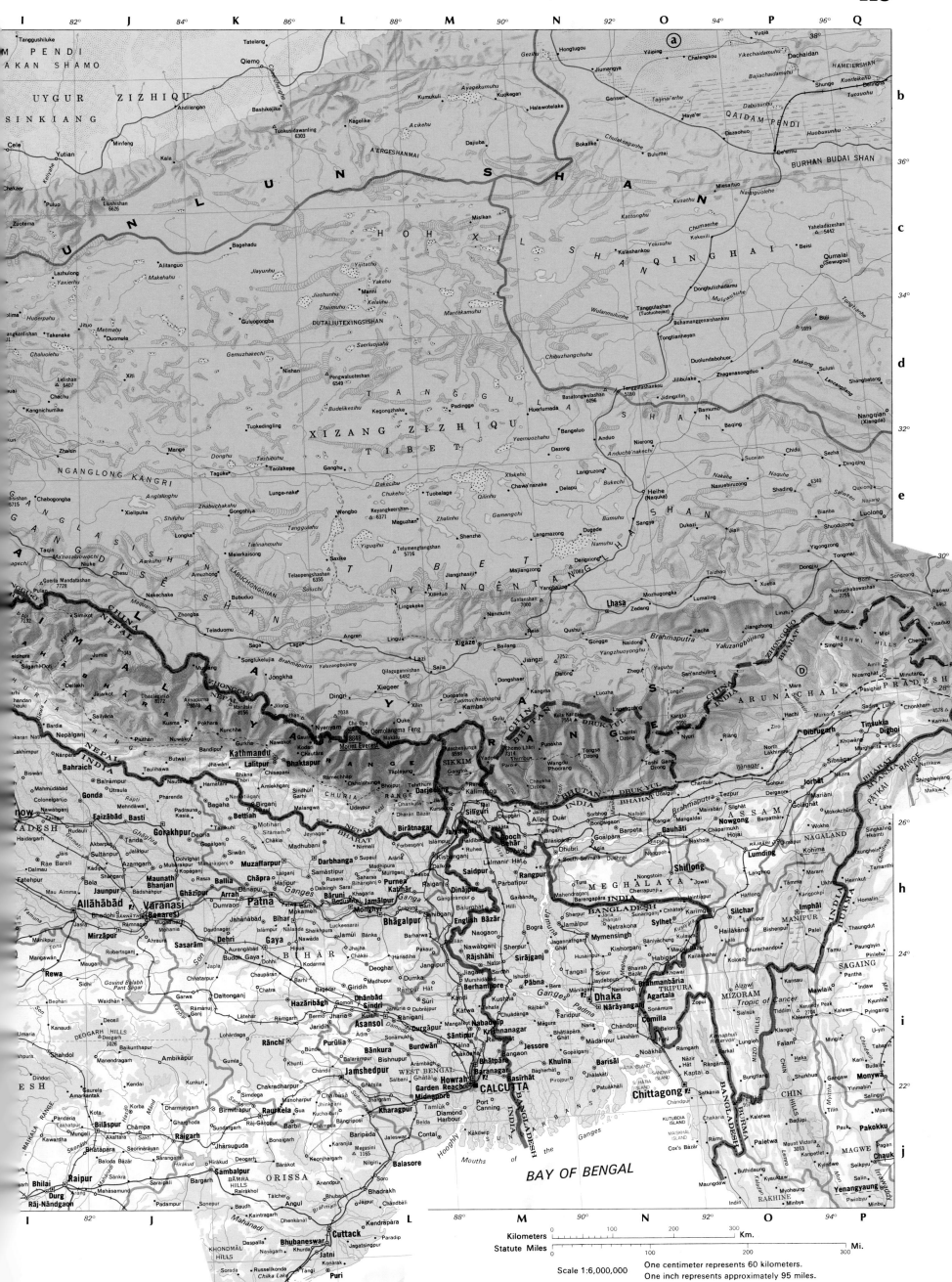

BAY OF BENGAL

Kilometers
0   100   200   300   Km.

Statute Miles
0   100   200   300   Mi.

Scale 1:6,000,000

One centimeter represents 60 kilometers.
One inch represents approximately 95 miles.
Lambert Conformal Conic Projection

Scale 1:6,000,000
One centimeter represents 60 kilometers.
One inch represents approximately 95 miles.
Lambert Conformal Conic Projection

Copyright © by Rand McNally & Co.
Map prepared by George Philip & Son Ltd. London.
A-565300-764

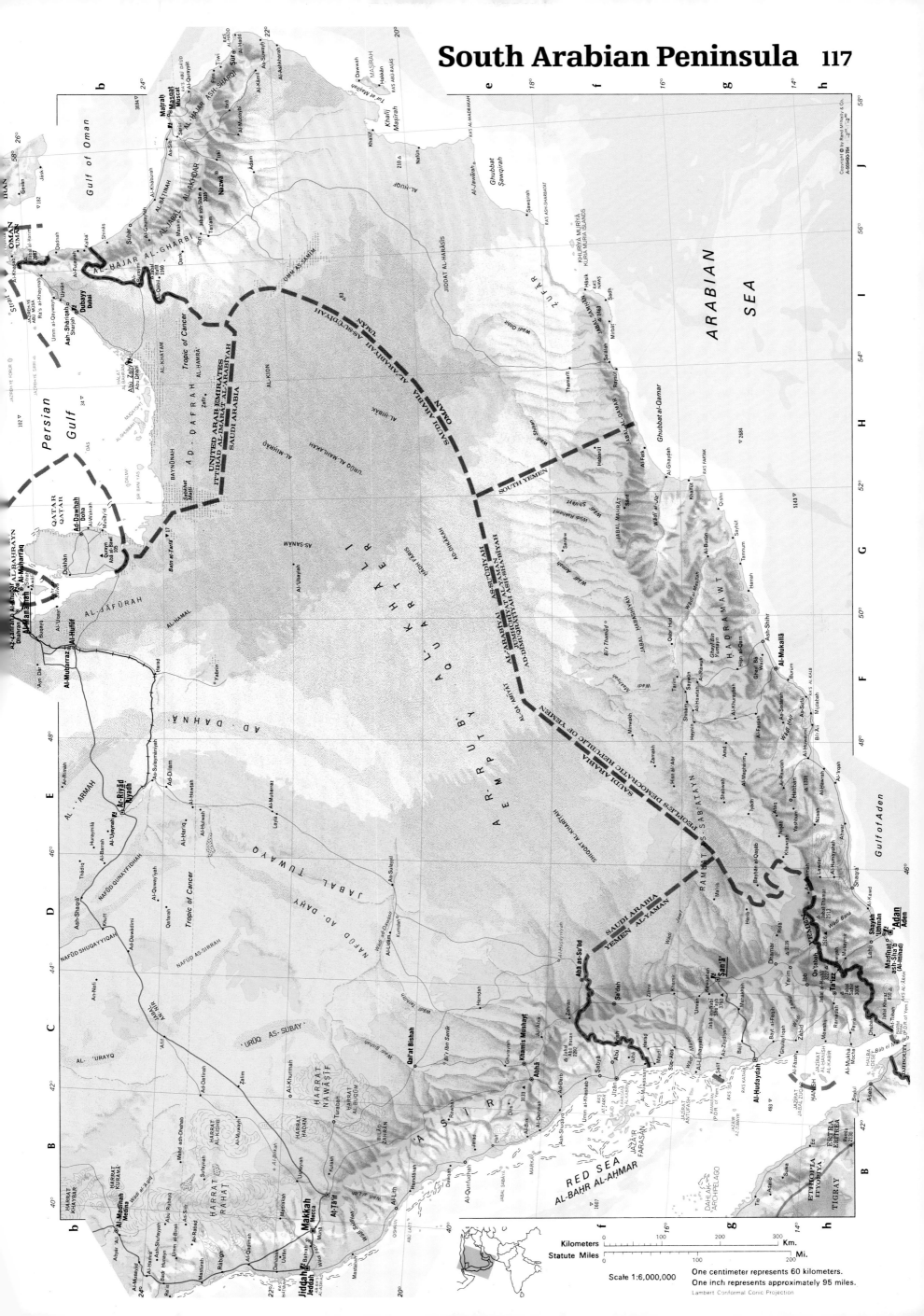

ARABIAN SEA

Gulf of Oman

Persian Gulf

Gulf of Aden

RED SEA
AL-BAHR AL-AHMAR

R U B '   A L   K H A L I

A D - D A H N A

A S I R

HADRAMAWT

ZUFAR

OMAN

SAUDI ARABIA
AL-'ARABIYAH AS-SU'UDIYAH

UNITED ARAB EMIRATES
ITTIHAD AL-IMARAT AL-'ARABIYAH

QATAR

AL-BAHRAYN

SOUTH YEMEN
PEOPLE'S DEMOCRATIC REPUBLIC OF YEMEN

YEMEN
YEMEN AL-YAMAN

IRAN

ETHIOPIA
ITIYOPYA

ERITREA
ERTRA

TIGRAY

Maskat
Muscat

Makkah
Mecca

Al-Madinah
Medina

Ar-Riyad
Riyadh

San'a

Aden
Adan

Al-Hudaydah

Ta'izz

Jiddah
Jeddah

At-Ta'if

Scale 1:6,000,000

One centimeter represents 60 kilometers.
One inch represents approximately 95 miles.

Lambert Conformal Conic Projection

Kilometers
Statute Miles

0   100   200   300 Km.
0   100   200 Mi.

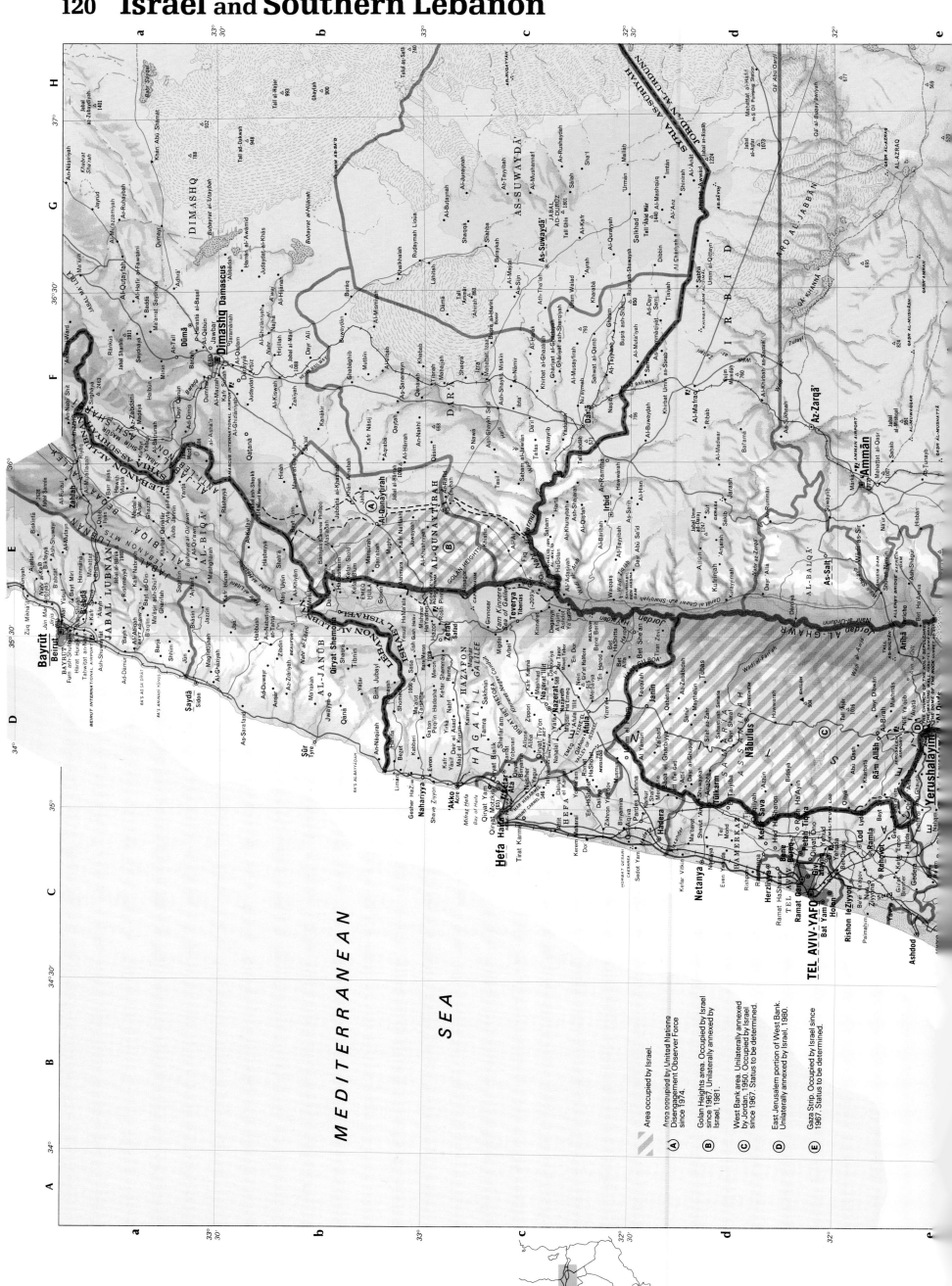

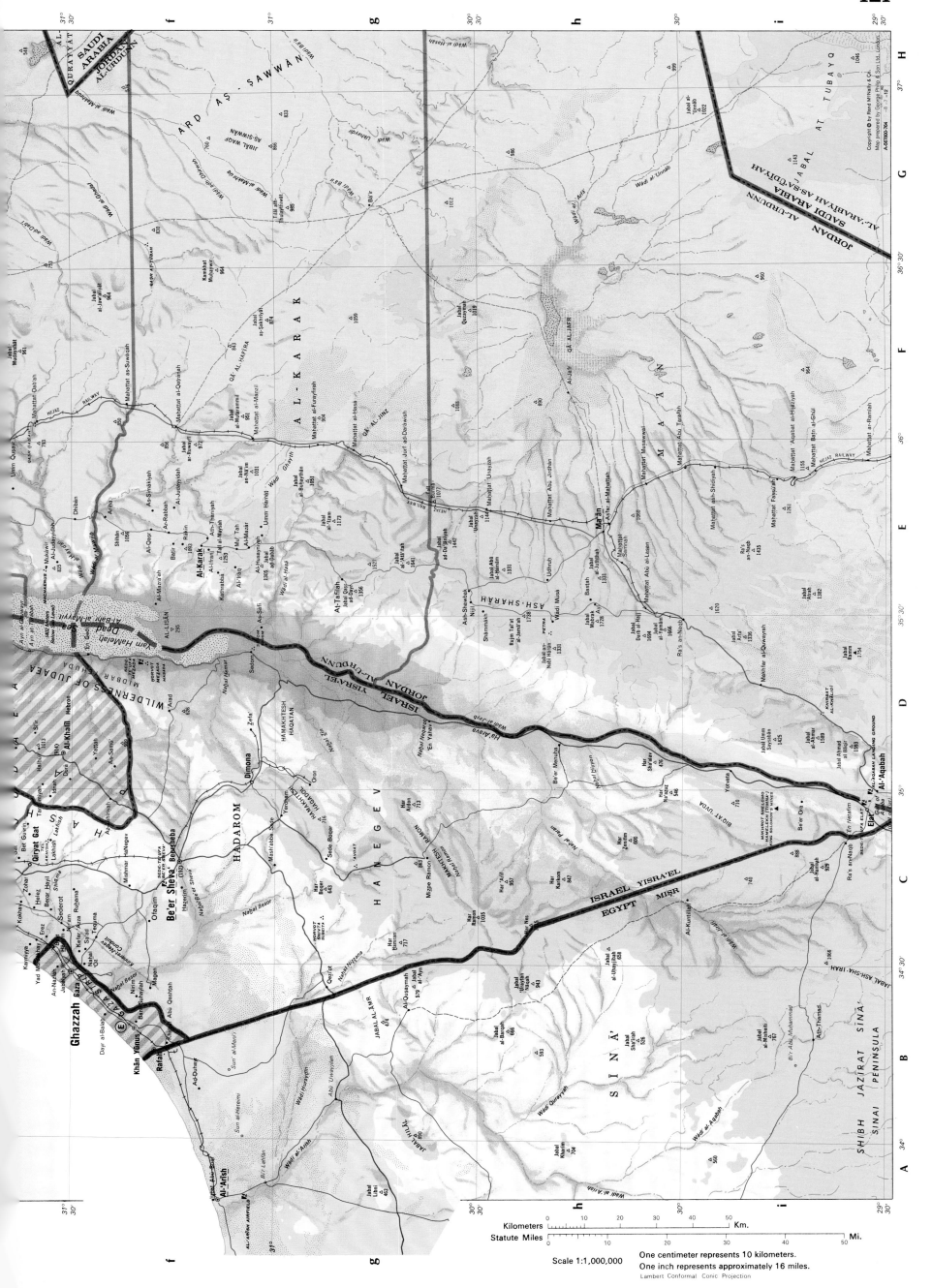

Kilometers

Statute Miles

One centimeter represents 10 kilometers.
One inch represents approximately 16 miles.

Scale 1:1,000,000

Lambert Conformal Conic Projection

123

AFRICA • Environments

Major Urban Areas
Symbol indicates importance

Cropland
Cropland & Woodland
Cropland & Grazing Land
Grassland, Grazing Land

Forest, Woodland
Swamp, Marshland
Tundra
Shrub, Sparse Grass; Wasteland (pattern)
Barren Land

One centimeter represents 240 kilometers.
One inch represents approximately 380 miles.

Scale 1:24,000,000

Lambert Azimuthal Equal-Area Projection

Kilometers
Statute Miles

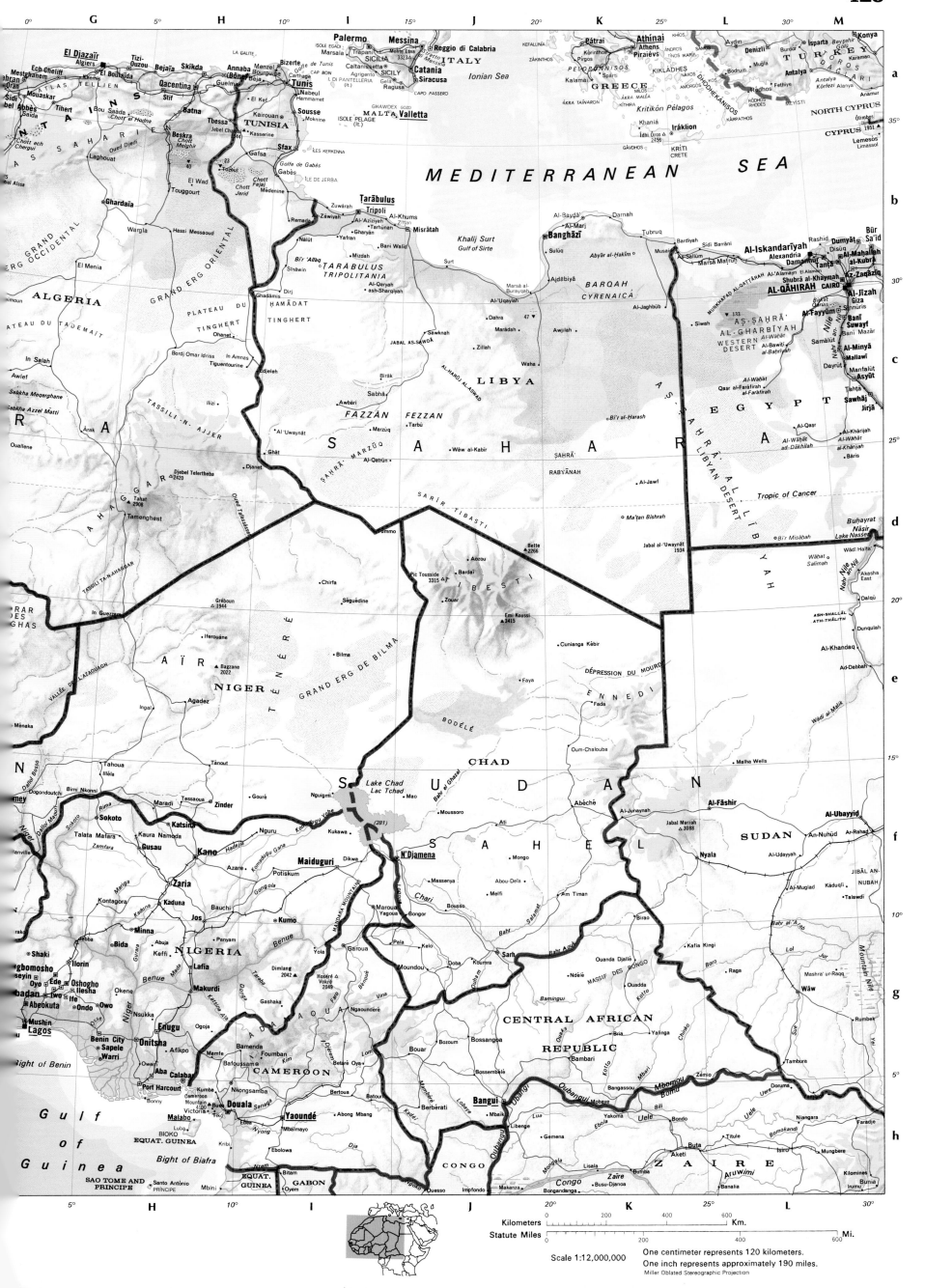

MEDITERRANEAN SEA

ALGERIA

LIBYA

EGYPT

TUNISIA

NIGER

CHAD

SUDAN

NIGERIA

CAMEROON

CENTRAL AFRICAN REPUBLIC

ZAIRE

CONGO

GABON

EQUAT. GUINEA

Gulf of Guinea

Scale 1:12,000,000
One centimeter represents 120 kilometers.
One inch represents approximately 190 miles.
Miller Oblated Stereographic Projection

Kilometers
Statute Miles

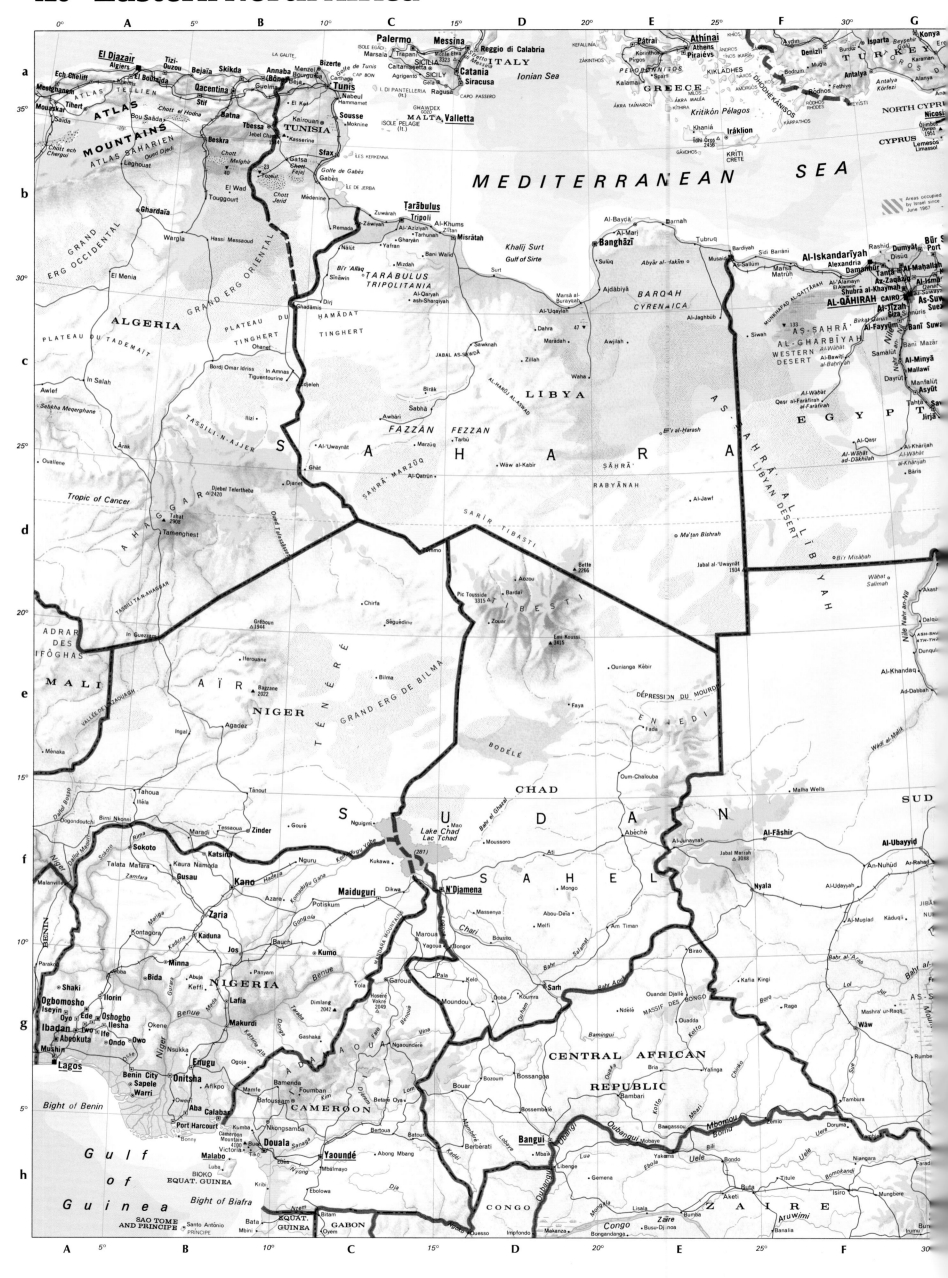

Copyright © by Rand McNally & Co.
Map prepared by Esselte Map Service AB, Stockholm.
A-589391-764 -6-8-18

Kilometers
Statute Miles

Km.
Mi.

Scale 1:12,000,000
One centimeter represents 120 kilometers.
One inch represents approximately 190 miles.
Miller Oblated Stereographic Projection

35°   G   40°   H   45°   I   50°   J   55°   K

0°

INDIAN   OCEAN
Equator

b

SOMALIA

KENYA
Nairobi
Machakos
Arusha
Mombasa

SEYCHELLES
Victoria

5°

TANZANIA
MASAI
STEPPE
Tanga
Zanzibar
Dar es Salaam

AMIRANTE ISLANDS
(Sey.)
ÎLE DESROCHES
(Sey.)
PLATTE ISLAND (Sey.)

COETIVY ISLAND
(Sey.)

c
ALPHONSE ISLAND (Sey.)

MAFIA ISLAND

ALDABRA ISLAND
(Sey.)
COSMOLEDO I.
(Sey.)
SAINT PIERRE ISLAND
(Sey.)
PROVIDENCE ISLAND
(Sey.)
CERF ISLAND
(Sey.)

ASSUMPTION ISLAND
(Sey.)
ASTOVE ISLAND
(Sey.)
FARQUHAR GROUP
(Sey.)

10°

AGALEGA ISLANDS
(Mauritius)

Lindi
Mwara
CABO DELGADO

COMOROS
Moroni

LES GLORIEUSES
(Reunion)
CAP D'AMBRE
Antsiranana

Lake
Nyasa
Lake Malawi
MALAWI
Lilongwe

ARCHIPEL   DES   COMOROS

MAYOTTE
(Fr.)
Dzaoudzi

NOSY BE
Hell-Ville

d

Nacala
Nampula

MASSIF DU
MAROMOKOTRO 2876
TSARATANANA

Antalaha

Moçambique

Mahajanga
Marovoay

ÎLE TROMELIN
(Reunion)

15°

Blantyre
MOZAMBIQUE
Quelimane

ÎLE JUAN DE NOVA
(Reunion)

PRESQU'ÎLE
DE MASOALA

NOSY BORAHA
Ambodifototra

e

Beira

NOSY BARREN

MADAGASCAR

Toamasina
Antananarivo
Antsirabe

Port Louis
Curepipe   Mahébourg
Saint-Denis   MAURITIUS
Le Port
Saint-Paul
Saint-Pierre   REUNION
(Fr.)

20°

Morondava

Fianarantsoa

MASCARENE
ISLANDS

BASSAS DA INDIA
(Reunion)

ÎLE EUROPA
(Reunion)

Toliara

Tropic of Capricorn

f

INHACA
Xai-Xai

CAP SAINTE-MARIE

25°

INDIAN   OCEAN

g

30°

35°   G   40°   H   I   50°   J   55°   K   60°

Kilometers   0   200   400   600   Km.
Statute Miles   0   200   400   600   Mi.

Scale 1:12,000,000
One centimeter represents 120 kilometers.
One inch represents approximately 190 miles.
Miller Oblated Stereographic Projection

The United Nations declared an end to the mandate of South Africa over Namibia in October, 1966. Administration of the territory by South Africa is not recognized by the United Nations.

ATLANTIC OCEAN

Copyright © by Rand McNally & Co.
Map prepared by George Philip & Son Ltd., London.
A-589292-764

Kilometers
Statute Miles

Scale 1:6,000,000
One centimeter represents 60 kilometers.
One inch represents approximately 95 miles.
Lambert Azimuthal Equal-Area Projection

Kilometers
Statute Miles

Scale 1:12,000,000
One centimeter represents 120 kilometers.
One inch represents approximately 190 miles.
Lambert Conformal Conic Projection

Kilometers
Statute Miles
Scale 1:12,000,000
One centimeter represents 120 kilometers.
One inch represents approximately 190 miles.
Albers Conical Equal-Area Projection

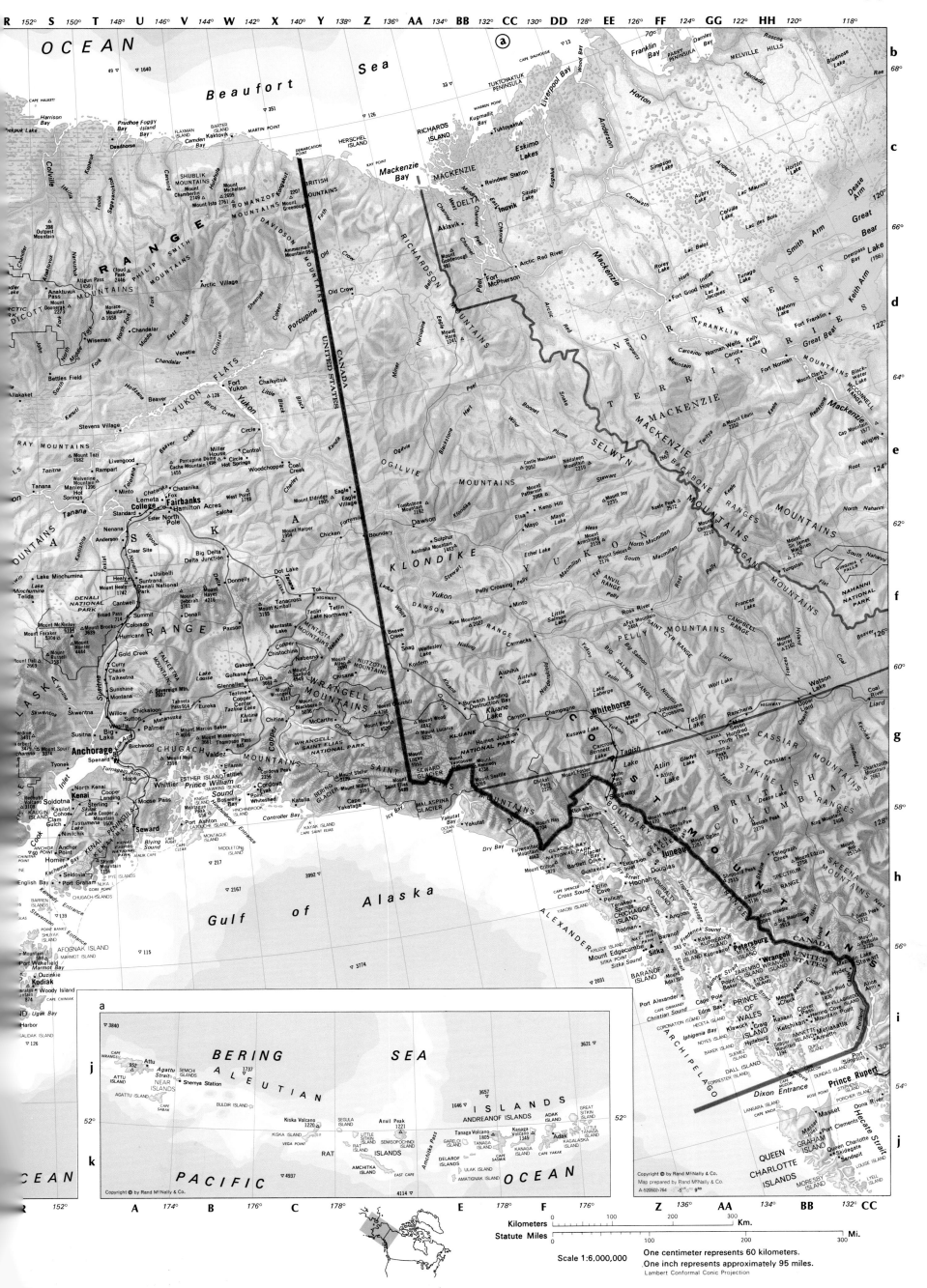

Kilometers 0   50   100   150 Km.
Statute Miles 0   50   100   150 Mi.

Scale 1:3,000,000

One centimeter represents 30 kilometers.
One inch represents approximately 47 miles.
Lambert Conformal Conic Projection

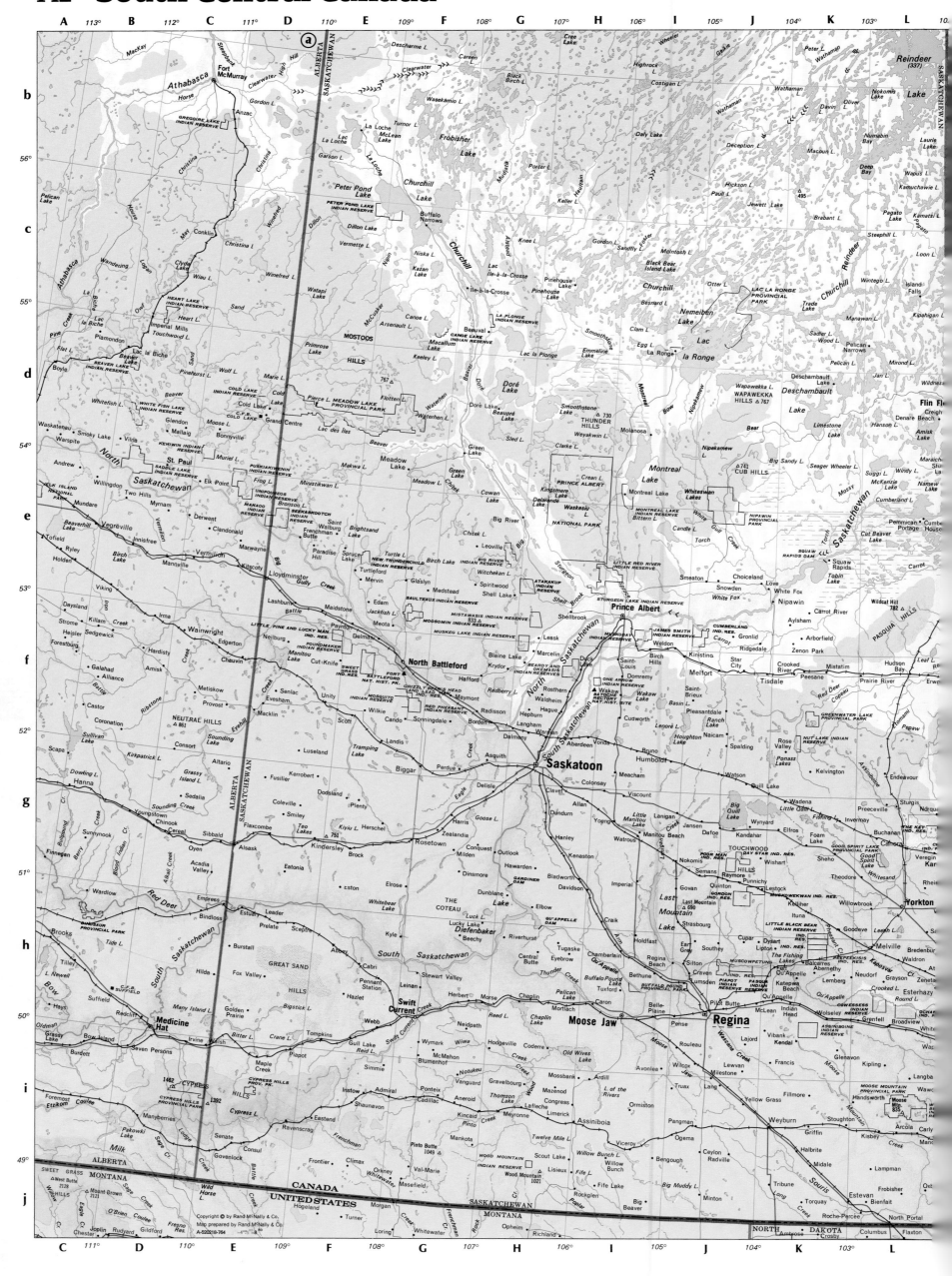

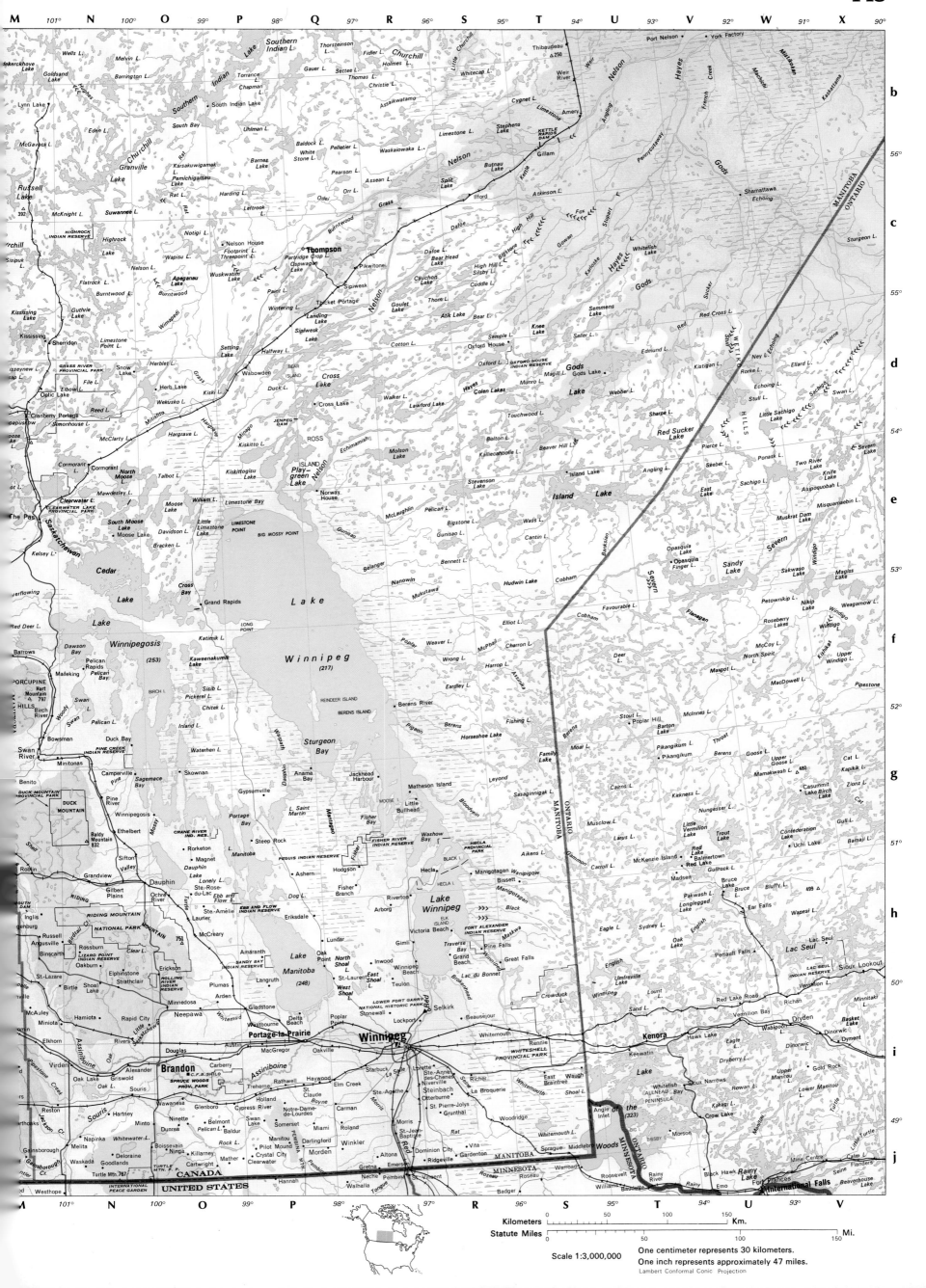

Kilometers 0 50 150 Km.

Statute Miles 0 50 100 150 Mi.

Scale 1:3,000,000

One centimeter represents 30 kilometers.
One inch represents approximately 47 miles.

Lambert Conformal Conic Projection

LABRADOR SEA

Gulf of Lawrence

NEWFOUNDLAND

SAINT PIERRE AND MIQUELON
(France)
SAINT-PIERRE-ET-MIQUELON

Corner Brook

St. John's

Sydney
Glace Bay
North Sydney

CAPE BRETON ISLAND

ATLANTIC OCEAN

Kilometers
Statute Miles
0   50   100   150

One centimeter represents 30 kilometers.
One inch represents approximately 47 miles.
Scale 1:3,000,000
Lambert Conformal Conic Projection

Copyright © by Rand McNally & Co.
Map prepared by Rand McNally & Co.
A-520219-764

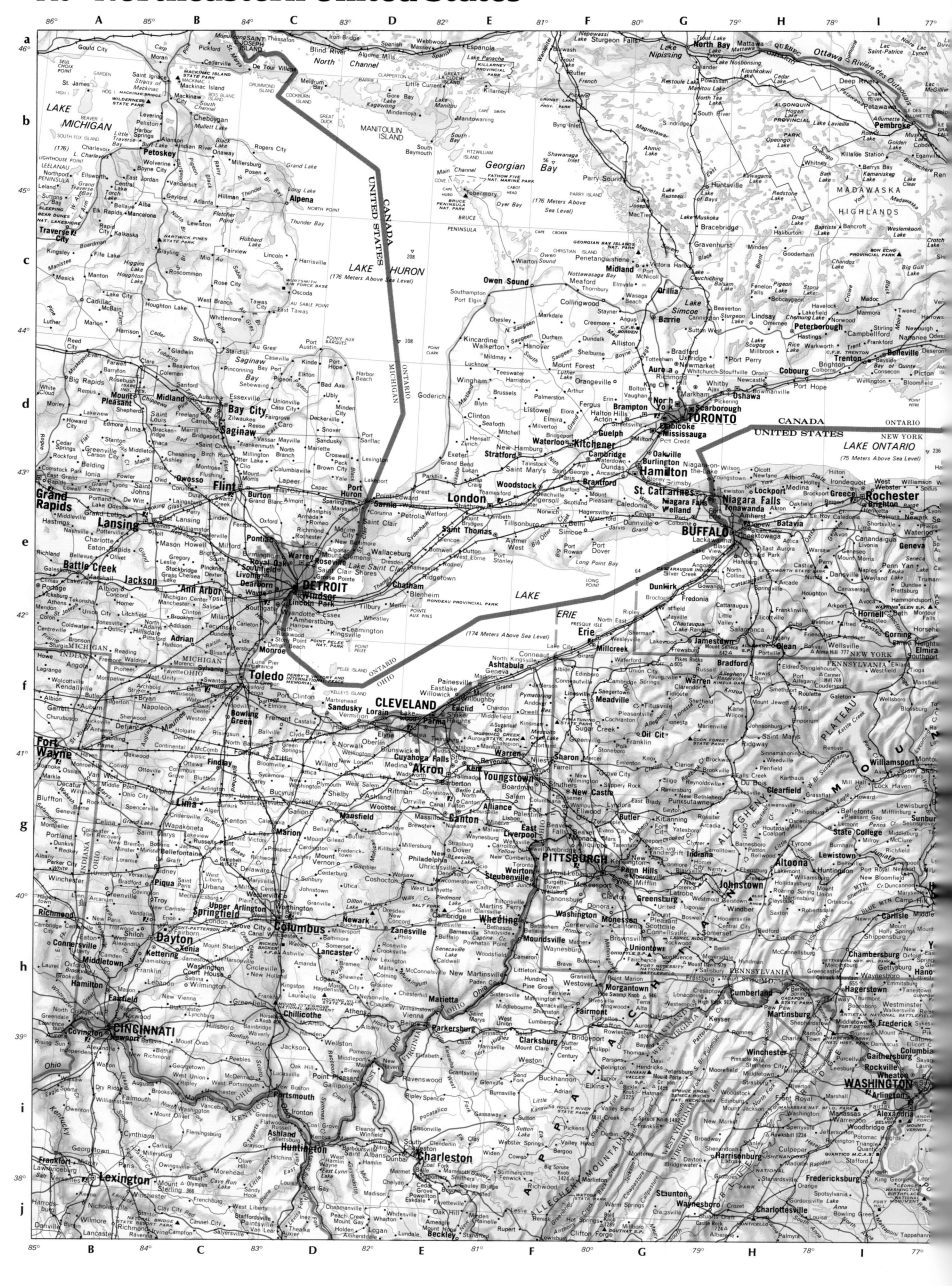

Kilometers

Statute Miles

Scale 1:3,000,000

One centimeter represents 30 kilometers.
One inch represents approximately 47 miles.
Albers Conical Equal-Area Projection

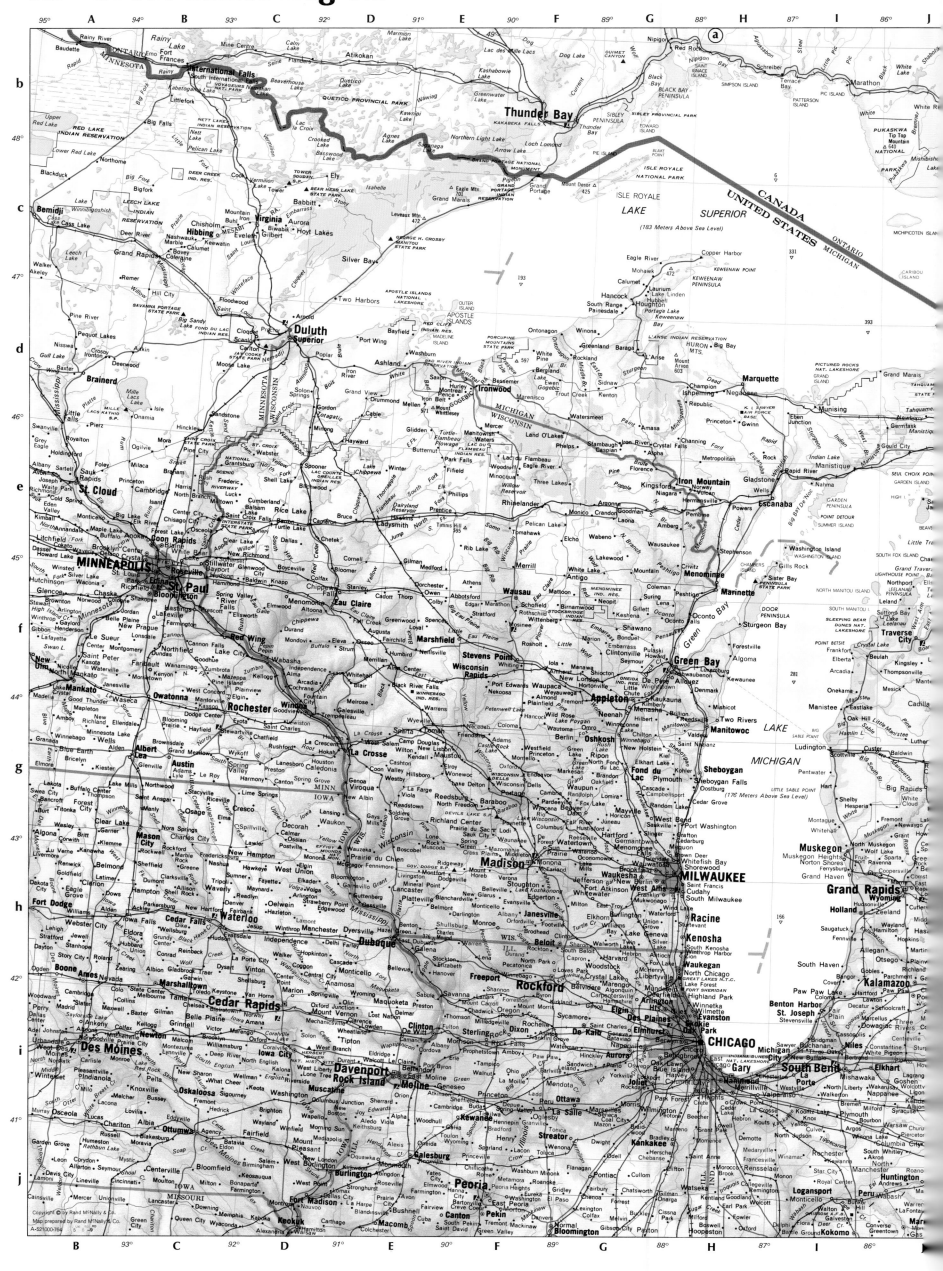

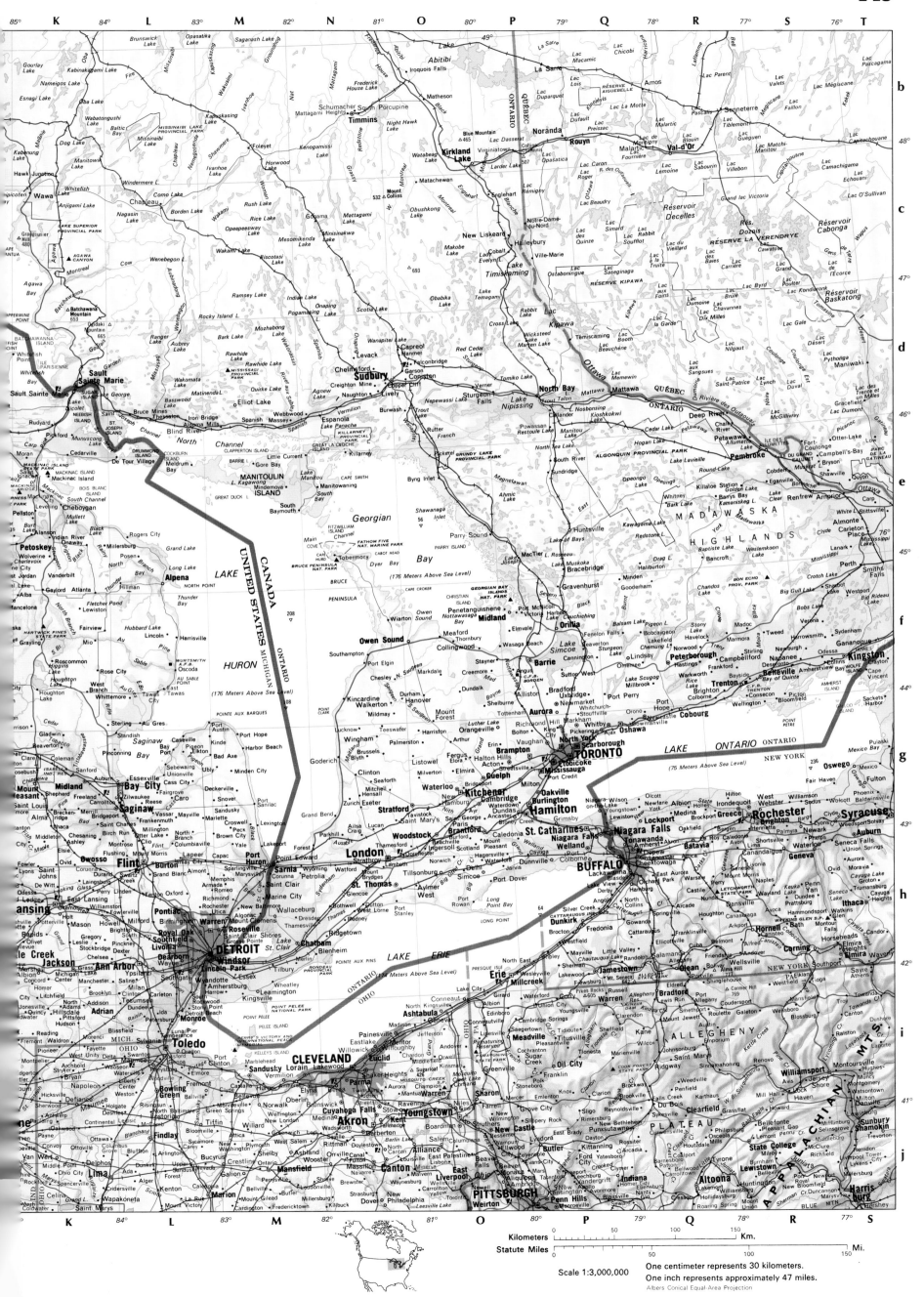

Kilometers
Statute Miles

Scale 1:3,000,000

One centimeter represents 30 kilometers.
One inch represents approximately 47 miles.
Albers Conical Equal-Area Projection

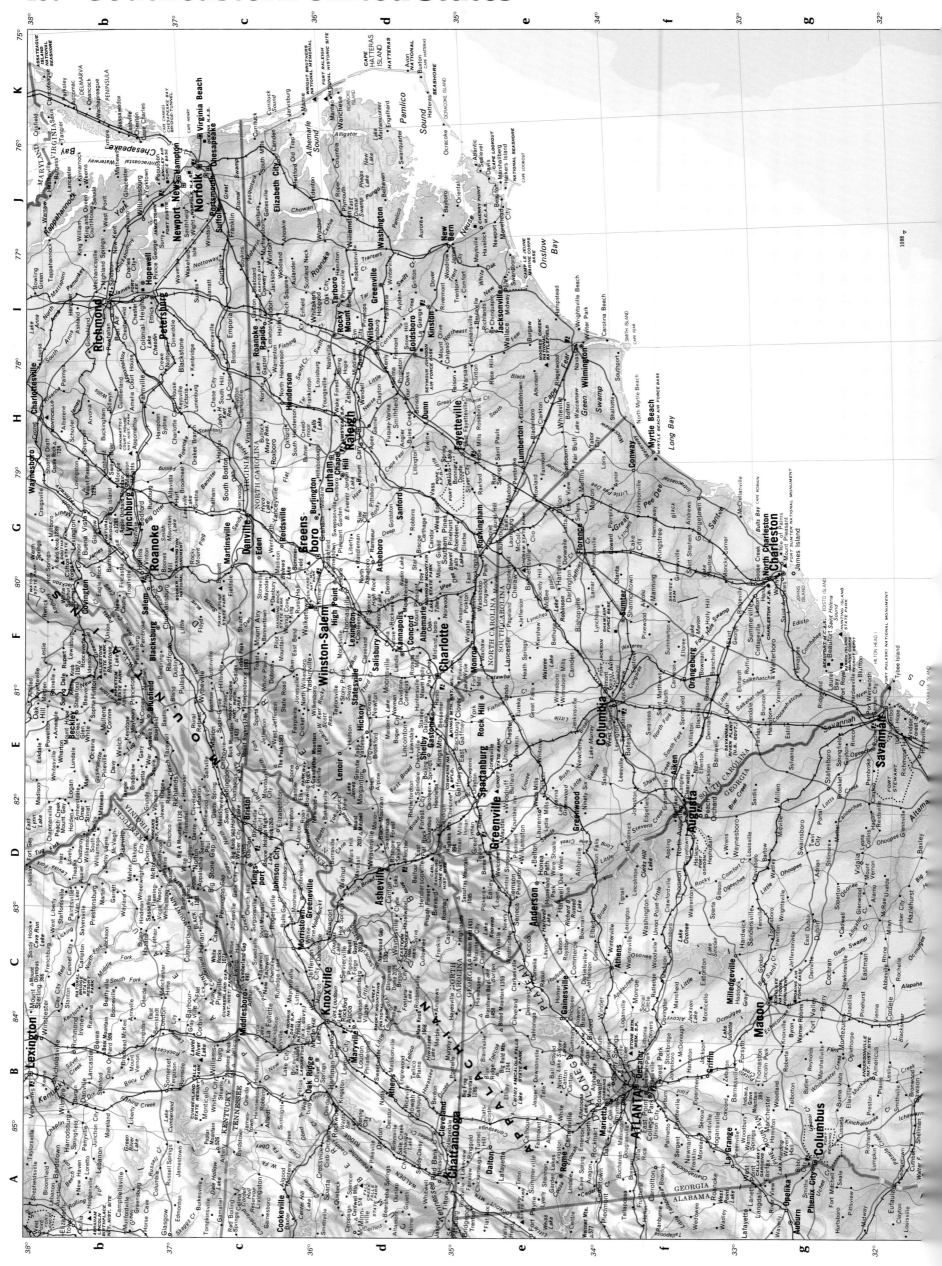

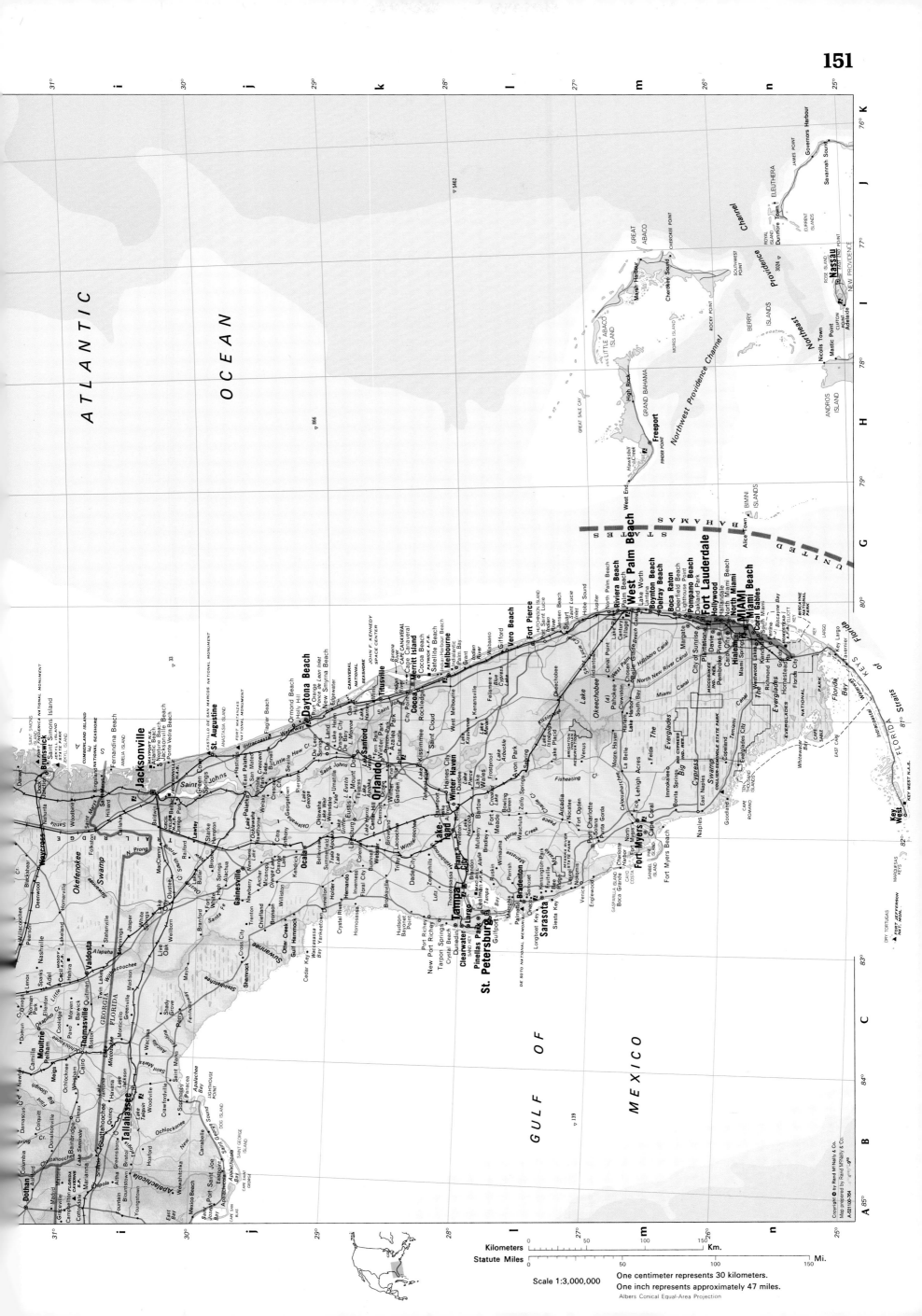

Kilometers
Statute Miles

Scale 1:3,000,000

One centimeter represents 30 kilometers.
One inch represents approximately 47 miles.

Albers Conical Equal-Area Projection

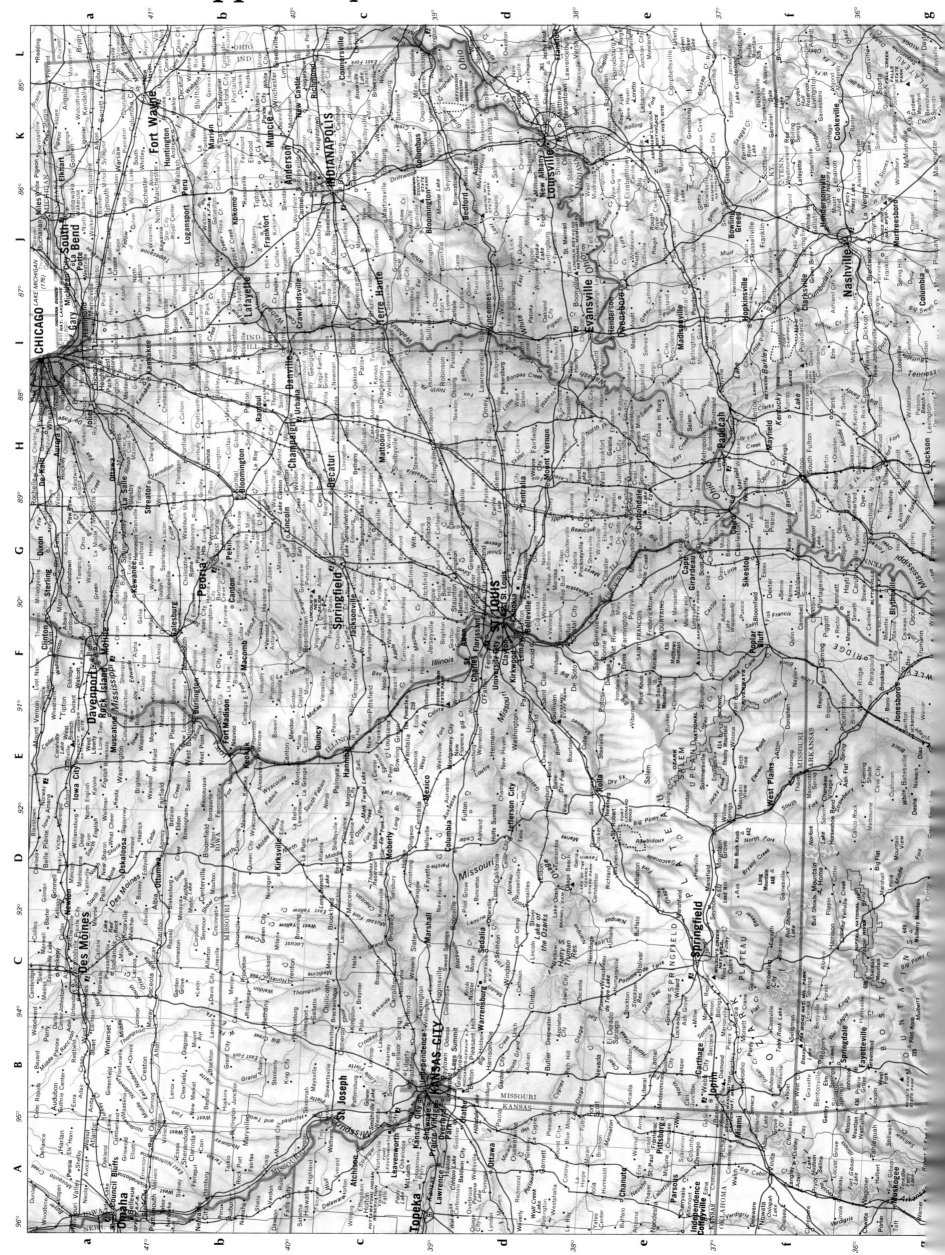

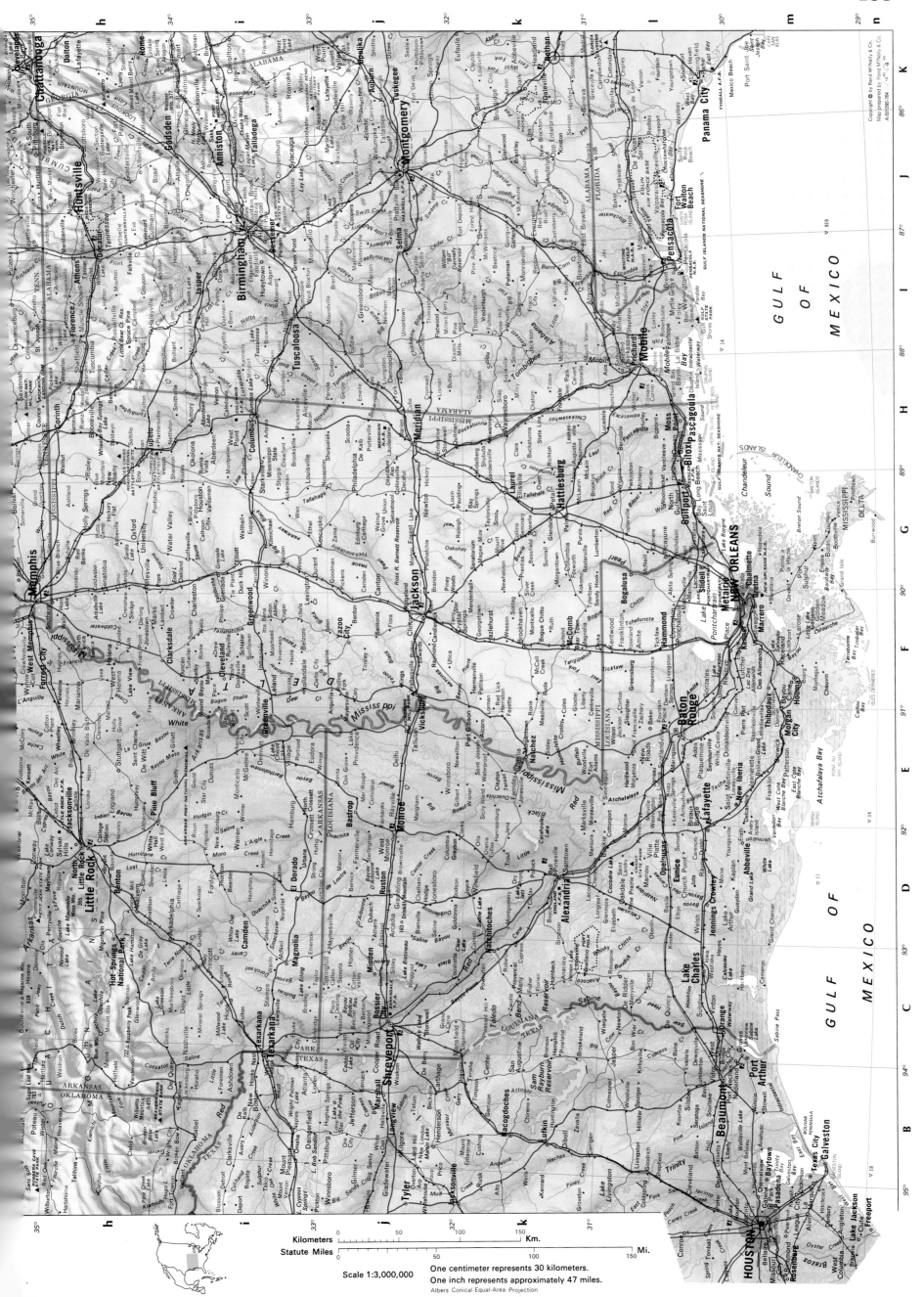

Kilometers

Statute Miles

Km.

Mi.

Scale 1:3,000,000
One centimeter represents 30 kilometers.
One inch represents approximately 47 miles.
Albers Conical Equal-Area Projection

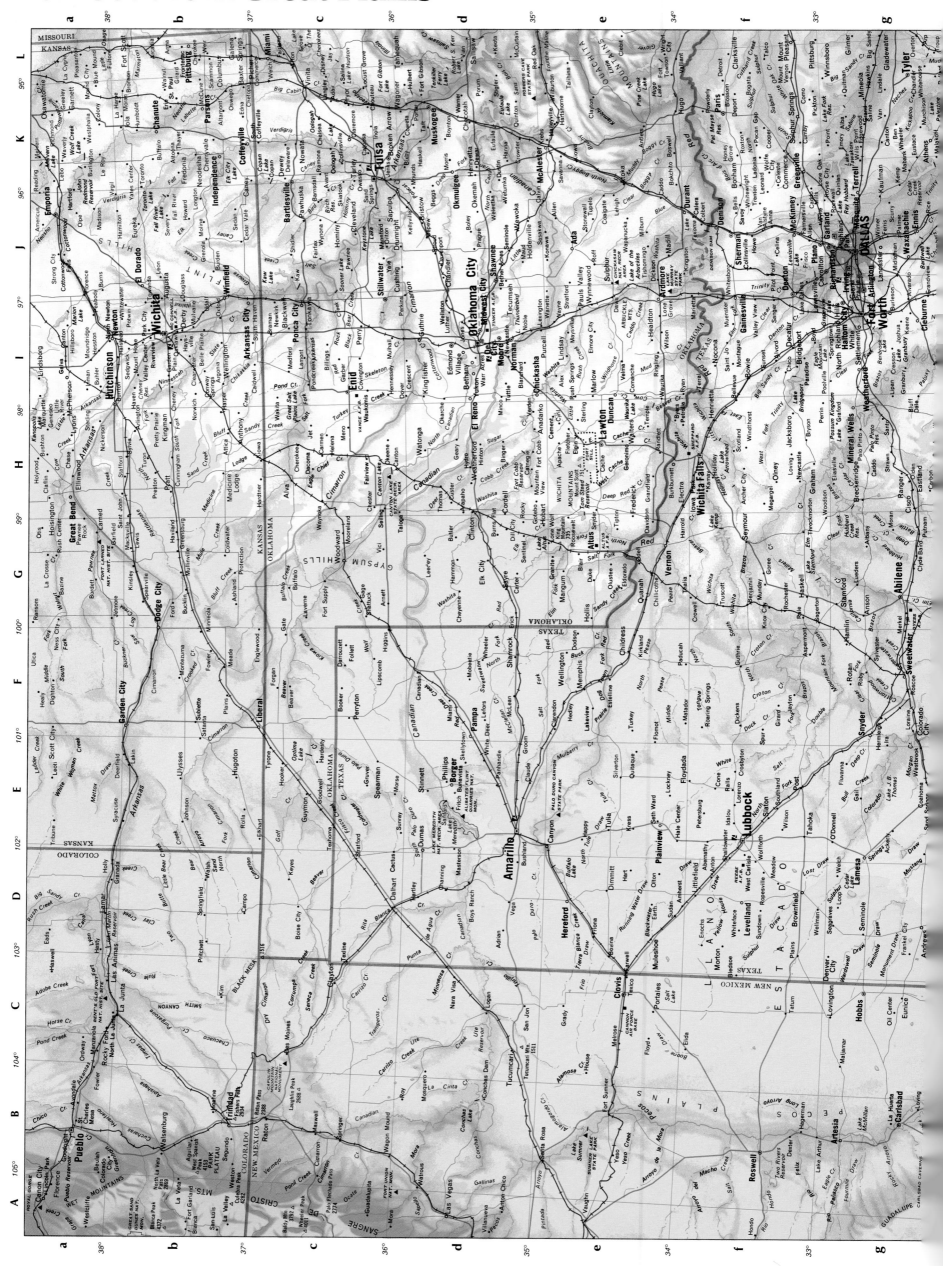

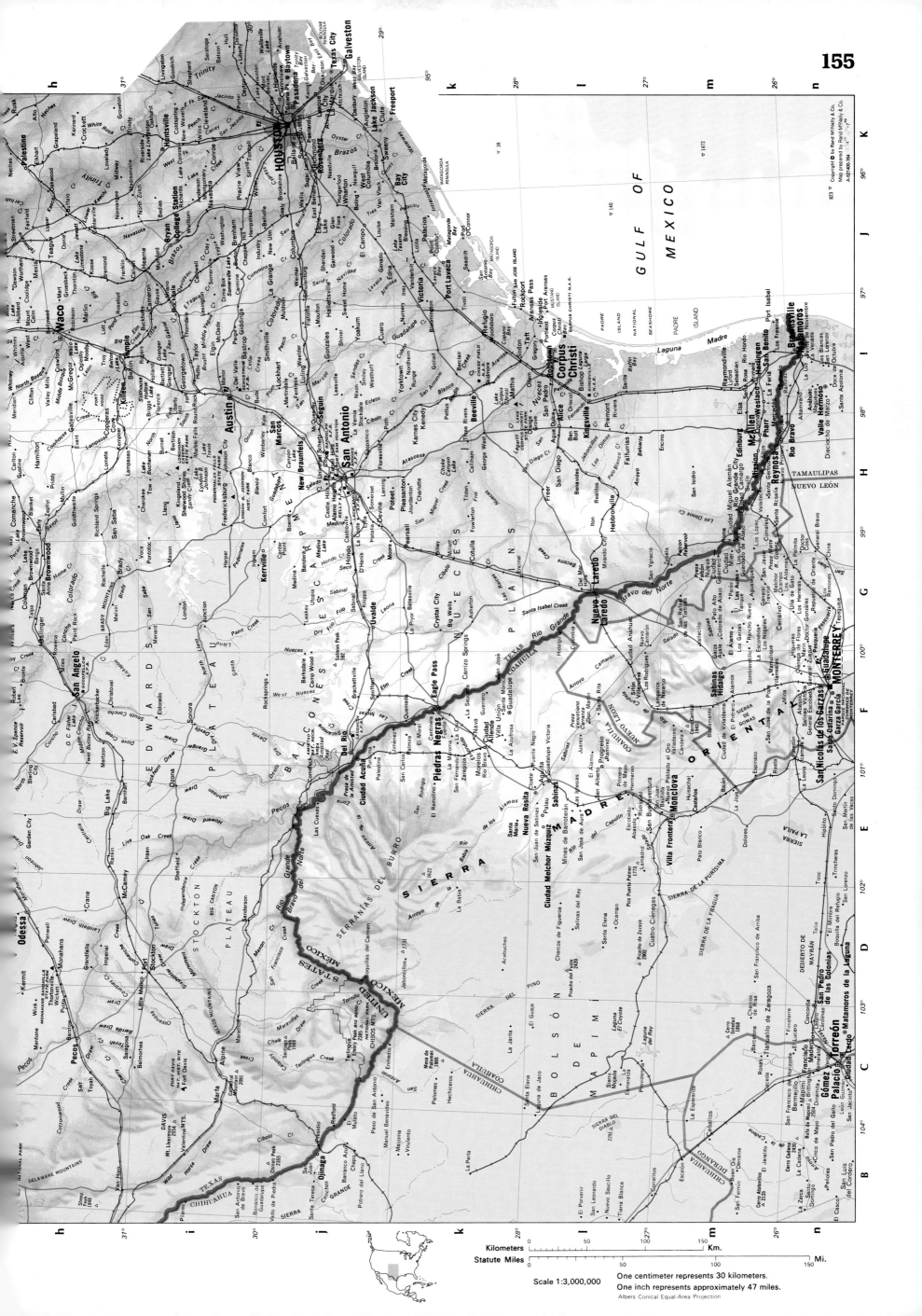

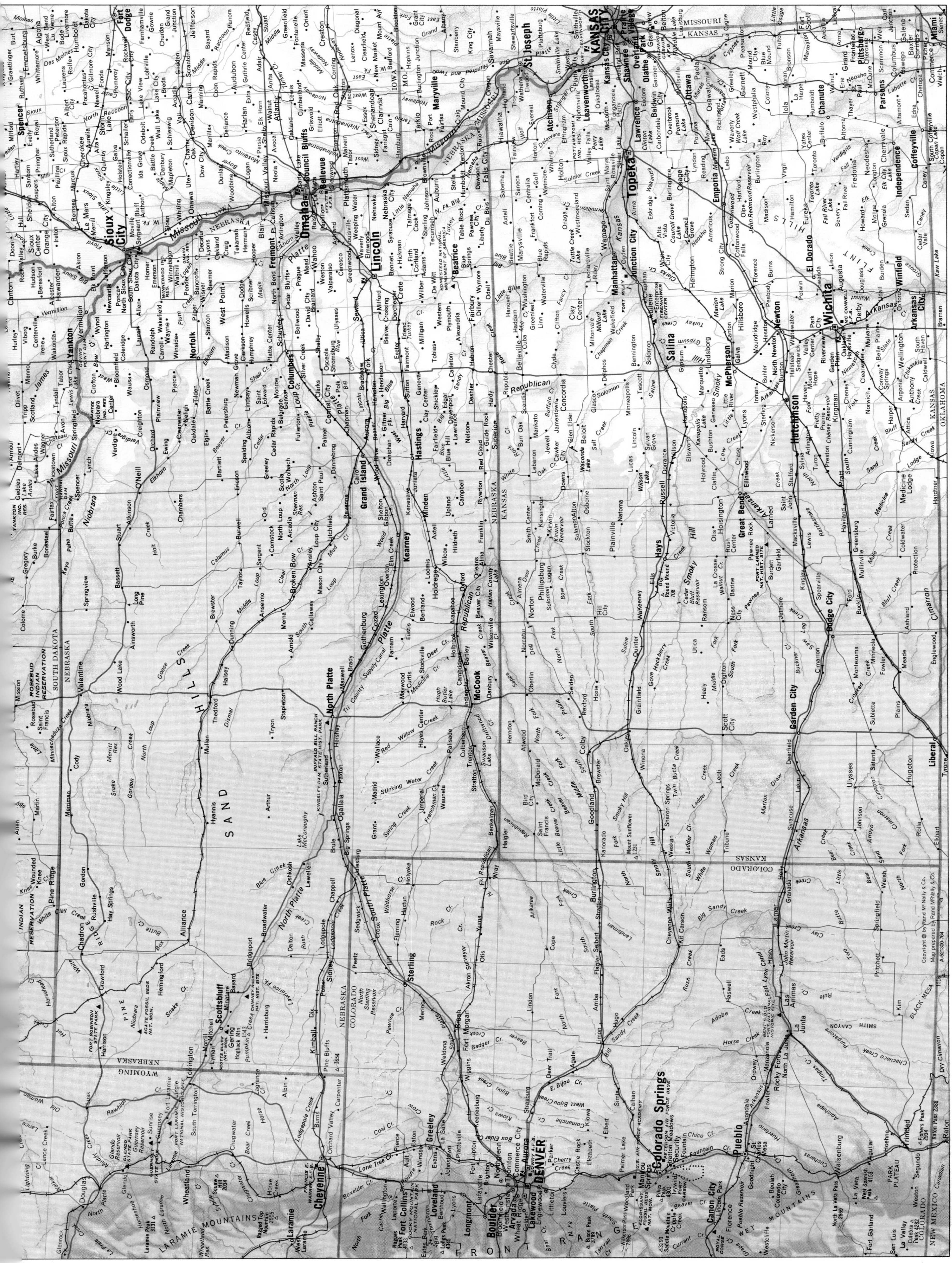
SOUTH DAKOTA
NEBRASKA
IOWA
MISSOURI
KANSAS
WYOMING
COLORADO
OKLAHOMA
NEW MEXICO
SAND HILLS
FLINT HILLS
LARAMIE MOUNTAINS
FRONT RANGE
WET MOUNTAINS
Cheyenne
Denver
Boulder
Colorado Springs
Pueblo
North Platte
Grand Island
Lincoln
Omaha
Sioux City
Kansas City
St. Joseph
Topeka
Wichita
Salina
Hutchinson
Dodge City
Garden City
Liberal
Scottsbluff
Copyright © by Rand McNally & Co.
Made in U.S.A.

Kilometers 0 50 100 150 Km.
Statute Miles 0 50 100 150 Mi.

Scale 1:3,000,000

One centimeter represents 30 kilometers.

One inch represents approximately 47 miles.

Albers Conical Equal-Area Projection

Kilometers

Statute Miles

Scale 1:3,000,000

One centimeter represents 30 kilometers.
One inch represents approximately 47 miles.
Albers Conical Equal-Area Projection

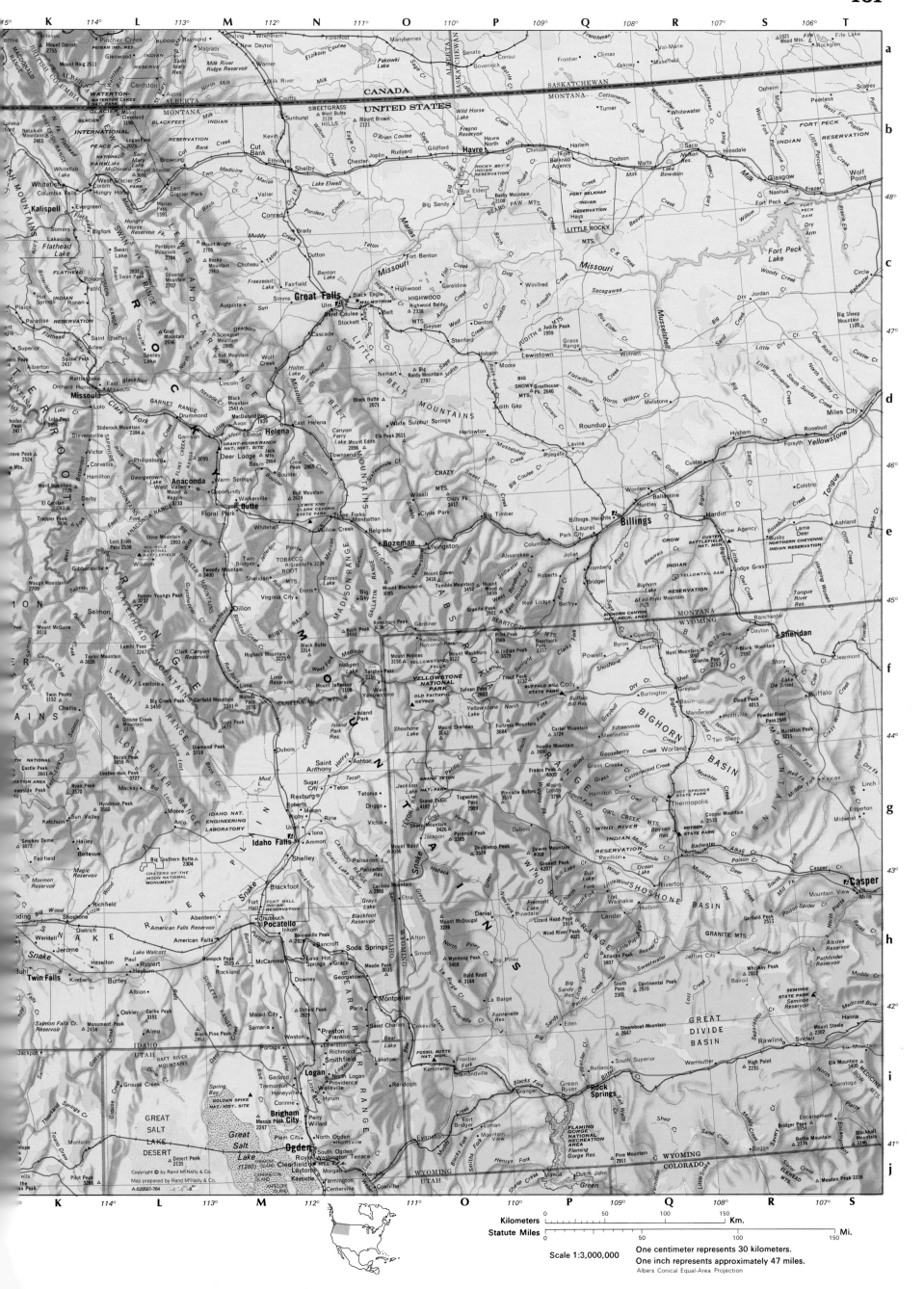

Scale 1:3,000,000

One centimeter represents 30 kilometers.
One inch represents approximately 47 miles.

Albers Conical Equal-Area Projection

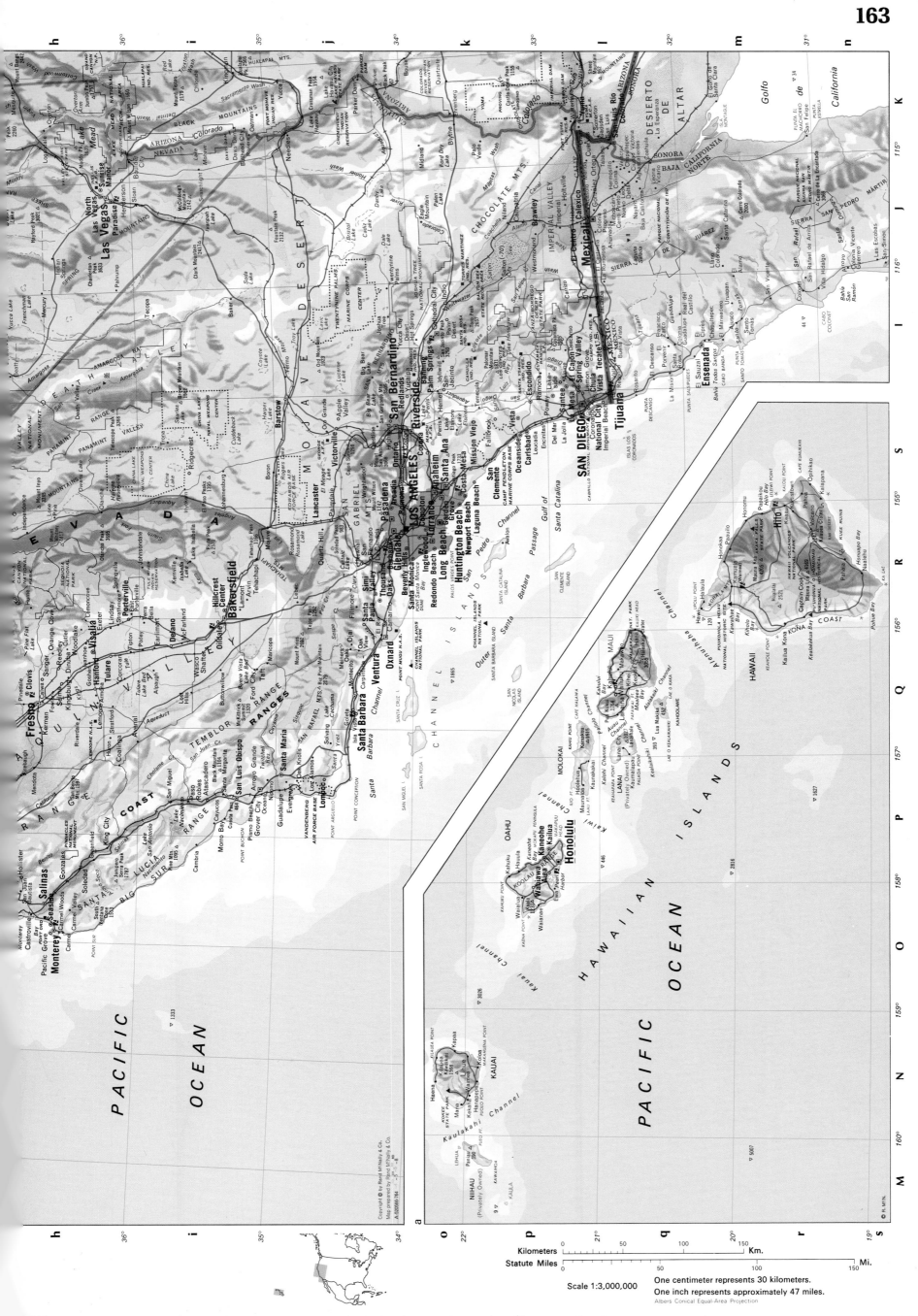

Scale 1:3,000,000

Kilometers
Statute Miles

One centimeter represents 30 kilometers.
One inch represents approximately 47 miles.
Albers Conical Equal-Area Projection

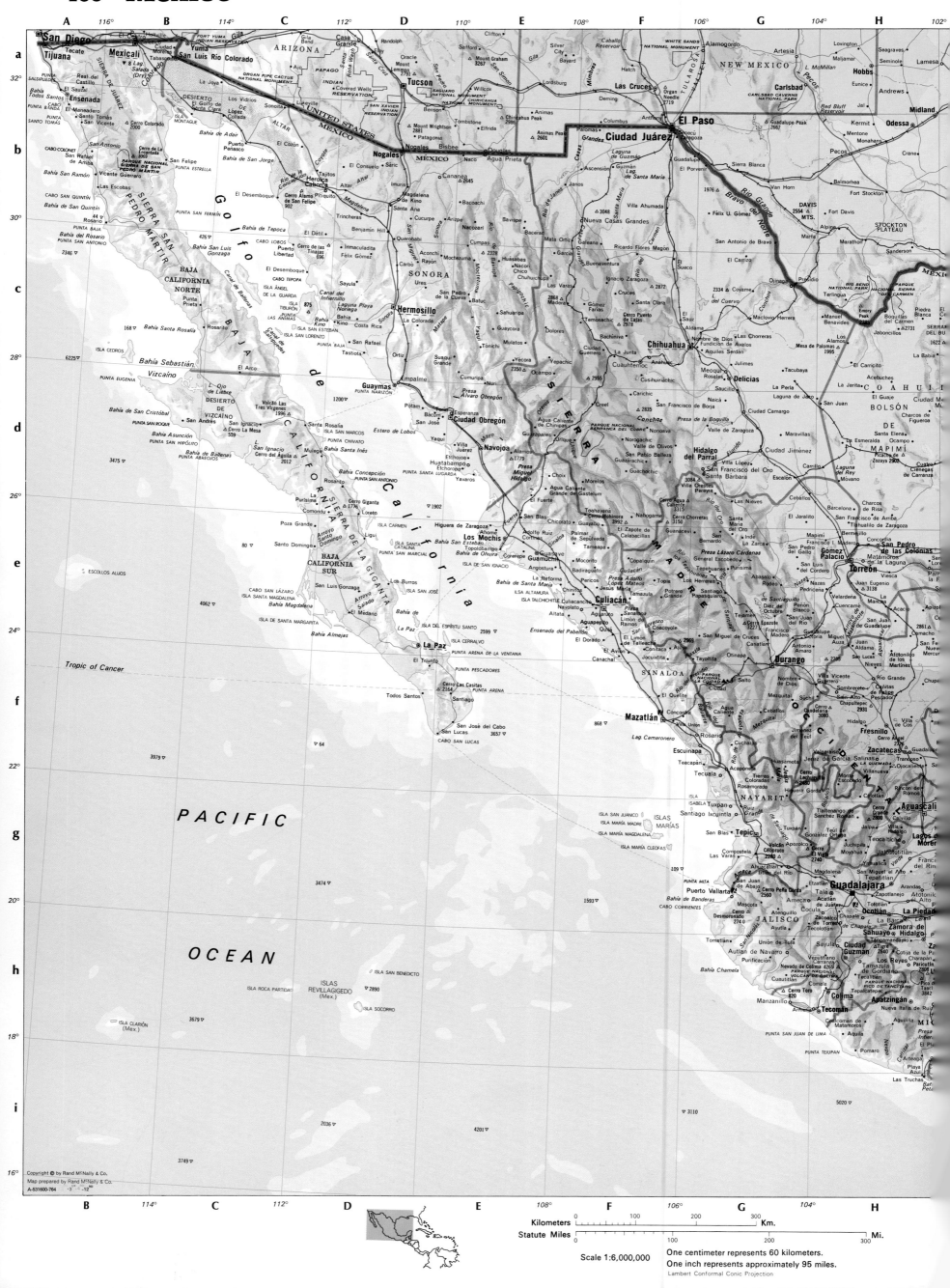

Copyright © by Rand McNally & Co.
Map prepared by Rand McNally & Co.
A-531600-764

Scale 1:6,000,000
One centimeter represents 60 kilometers.
One inch represents approximately 95 miles.
Lambert Conformal Conic Projection

Kilometers
Statute Miles

Km.
Mi.

0   100   200   300

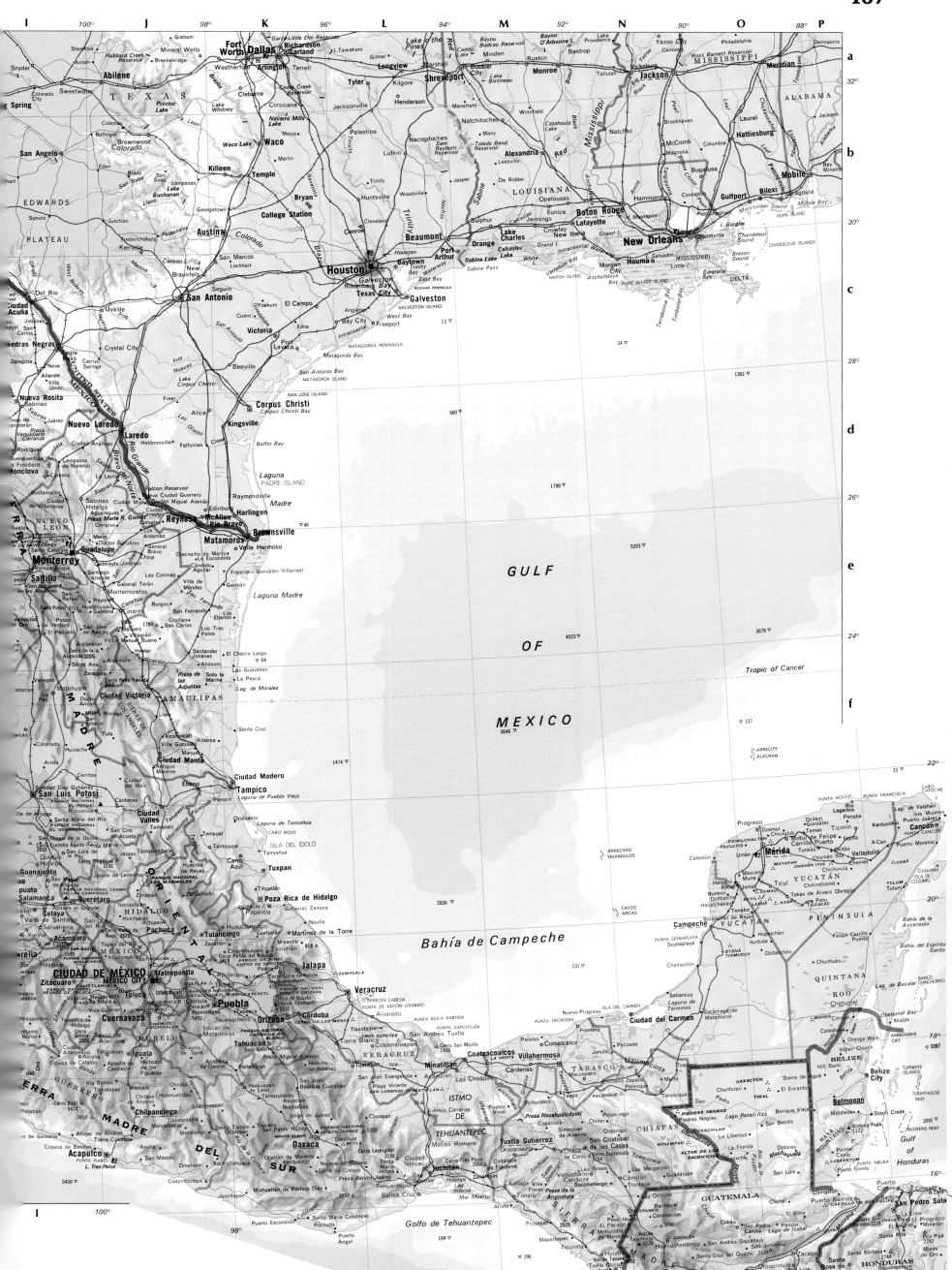

GULF OF MEXICO

88° A 86° B 84° C 26°

United States
FLORIDA

West Palm Beach
Fort Myers
Belle Glade
Lake Okeechobee
Lake Worth
Palm Beach
Delray Beach
Boca Raton
Pompano Beach
Fort Lauderdale
Hollywood
Naples
Everglades
MIAMI
Miami Beach
Coral Gables
Hialeah
Homestead
Everglades National Park
TEN THOUSAND ISLANDS
CAPE SABLE
EVERGLADES NATIONAL PARK
Florida Bay
Key Largo
Key West
FLORIDA KEYS
DRY TORTUGAS
Marquesas Keys
SANIBEL ISLAND
PINE ISLAND
Charlotte Harbor
BISCAYNE NATIONAL PARK
KEY LARGO

Straits of Florida

West End
GRAND BAHAMA
Freeport
LITTLE ABACO ISLAND
GREAT ABACO
Marsh Harbour
Cherokee Sound
Dunmore Town
BERRY ISLANDS
BIMINI ISLANDS
Alice Town
Nassau
NEW PROVIDENCE
Rock Sound
ELEUTHERA
Governors Harbour
Nicolls Town
Adelaide
ANDROS ISLAND
Andros Town
Kemps Bay
BAHAMAS
Arthurs Town
CAT ISLAND
Mount Alvernia 63
Old Bight
Columbus Point
SAN SALVADOR (WATLING I.)
EXUMA
Clarence Town
LONG ISLAND
Deadmans Cay
RUM CAY
RAGGED ISLAND RANGE
CROOKED ISLAND
The Bight of Acklins
ACKLINS ISLAND
SAMANA CAY
MAYAGUANA

WEST

GREAT BAHAMA BANK

La Habana
HAVANA
Marianao
Guanabacoa
Matanzas
Guanajay
San José de las Lajas
Artemisa
Cárdenas
Jovellanos
Güira de Melena
Güines
Colón
Pinar del Río
Santa Clara
Sagua la Grande
Placetas
Cienfuegos
Sancti Spíritus
Ciego de Ávila
Florida
Camagüey
Trinidad
Nuevitas
Holguín
Banes
Bayamo
Manzanillo
Palma Soriano
Guantánamo
Santiago de Cuba
Baracoa
SIERRA MAESTRA

CUBA

GREATER

ISLA DE LA JUVENTUD (ISLA DE PINOS)
Nueva Gerona
CAYMAN ISLANDS (U.K.)
Georgetown
GRAND CAYMAN
LITTLE CAYMAN
CAYMAN BRAC

YUCATAN CHANNEL
Cancún
MÉXICO
Puerto Morelos
Cozumel
ISLA DE COZUMEL
YUCATAN PENINSULA
QUINTANA ROO
Tulum
Bahía de la Ascensión
Bahía del Espíritu Santo
BANCO CHINCHORRO

JAMAICA
Montego Bay
Falmouth
Ocho Rios
Port Maria
Port Antonio
Savanna-la-Mar
Mandeville
Spanish Town
Kingston
May Pen
Blue Mountain Peak 2256
MORANT POINT
PORTLAND POINT

Jérémie
NAVASSA ISLAND (U.S.)
Pic de Macaya 2347
Coteaux
Anse-d'Hainault
POINTE L'ABACOU

CARIBBEAN

Gulf of Honduras
ISLAS DE LA BAHÍA
Guanaja
ISLA DE GUANAJA
Roatán
ISLA DE ROATÁN
Utila
La Ceiba
Pico Bonito 2435
Trujillo
Tela
Limón
CABO CAMARÓN
LA MOSQUITIA
CABO GRACIAS A DIOS
Puerto Lempira
HONDURAS
Tegucigalpa
Juticalpa
Catacamas
Danlí
NICARAGUA
Pico Mogotón 2107
Puerto Cabezas
COSTA DE MOSQUITOS
Matagalpa
León
Managua
Lago de Managua
Masaya
Granada
Lago de Nicaragua
Bluefields
El Bluff
ISLA DE OMETEPE
COSTA RICA
Liberia
San José
Limón
Cartago
PENÍNSULA DE NICOYA
Golfo de Nicoya
PANAMÁ
Colón
Panamá
ISTMO DE PANAMÁ
Bocas del Toro
Golfo de los Mosquitos

SAN ANDRÉS Y PROVIDENCIA (Col.)
ISLA DE SAN ANDRÉS
San Andrés
ISLA DE PROVIDENCIA
RONCADOR BANK (Col.)
SERRANA BANK (Col.)
SERRANILLA BANK (Col.)
QUITA SUEÑO BANK (Col.)
ROSALIND BANK
PEDRO CAYS (Jam.)
MORANT CAYS (Jam.)

PACIFIC OCEAN

Santa Marta
Ciénaga
Barranquilla
Soledad
Cartagena
Sincelejo
Magangué
MAGDALENA
BOLÍVAR
SUCRE
CÓRDOBA
ATLÁNTICO
Golfo de Morrosquillo
ISLAS DE ROSARIO

Copyright by Rand McNally & Co.
Map prepared by Rand McNally & Co.
A-530100-764

Kilometers
Statute Miles

Scale 1:6,000,000
One centimeter represents 60 kilometers.
One inch represents approximately 95 miles.
Lambert Conformal Conic Projection

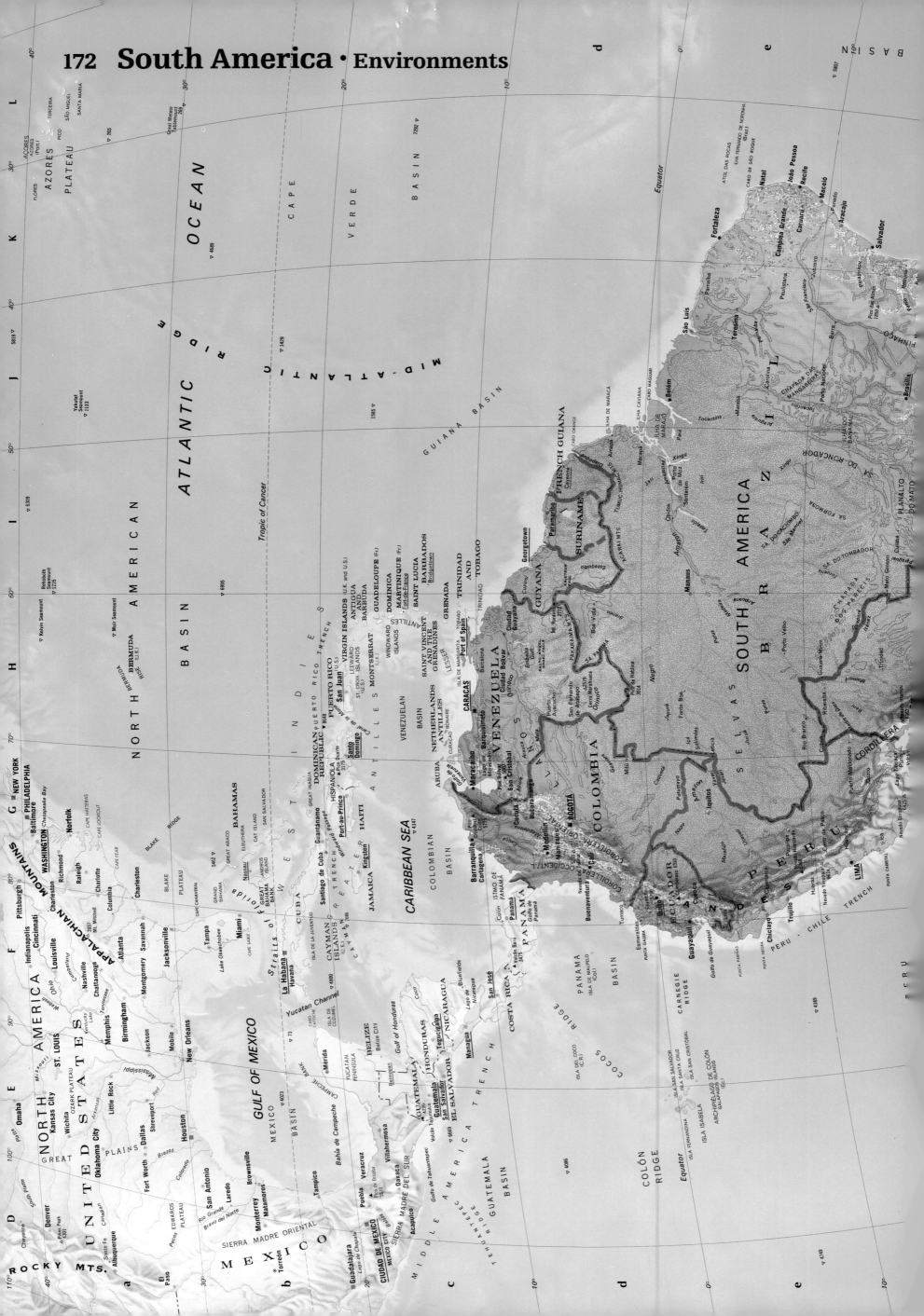

Scale 1:12,000,000
One centimeter represents 120 kilometers.
One inch represents approximately 190 miles.
Oblique Conic Conformal Projection

FALKLAND
ISLANDS
ISLAS MALVINAS
(U.K.)

JASON ISLANDS

WEST
FALKLAND

•Stanley

EAST
FALKLAND

ATLANTIC

OCEAN

PACIFIC

OCEAN

CHILE

BOLIVIA

PARAGUAY

BRAZIL

ARGENTINA

URUGUAY

Tropic of Capricorn

Copyright © by Rand McNally & Co.
Map prepared by Esselte Map Service AB, Stockholm
A-549200-764

Kilometers

Statute Miles

Scale 1:12,000,000

One centimeter represents 120 kilometers.
One inch represents approximately 190 miles.
Oblique Conic Conformal Projection

Kilometers 0   100   200   300   Km.

Statute Miles 0   100   200   300   Mi.

Scale 1:6,000,000

One centimeter represents 60 kilometers.
One inch represents approximately 95 miles.

Oblique Conic Conformal Projection

a

b

c

d

e

f

g

h

Scale 1:12,000,000

Kilometers
Statute Miles

One centimeter represents 120 kilometers.
One inch represents approximately 190 miles.

Lambert Conformal Conic Projection

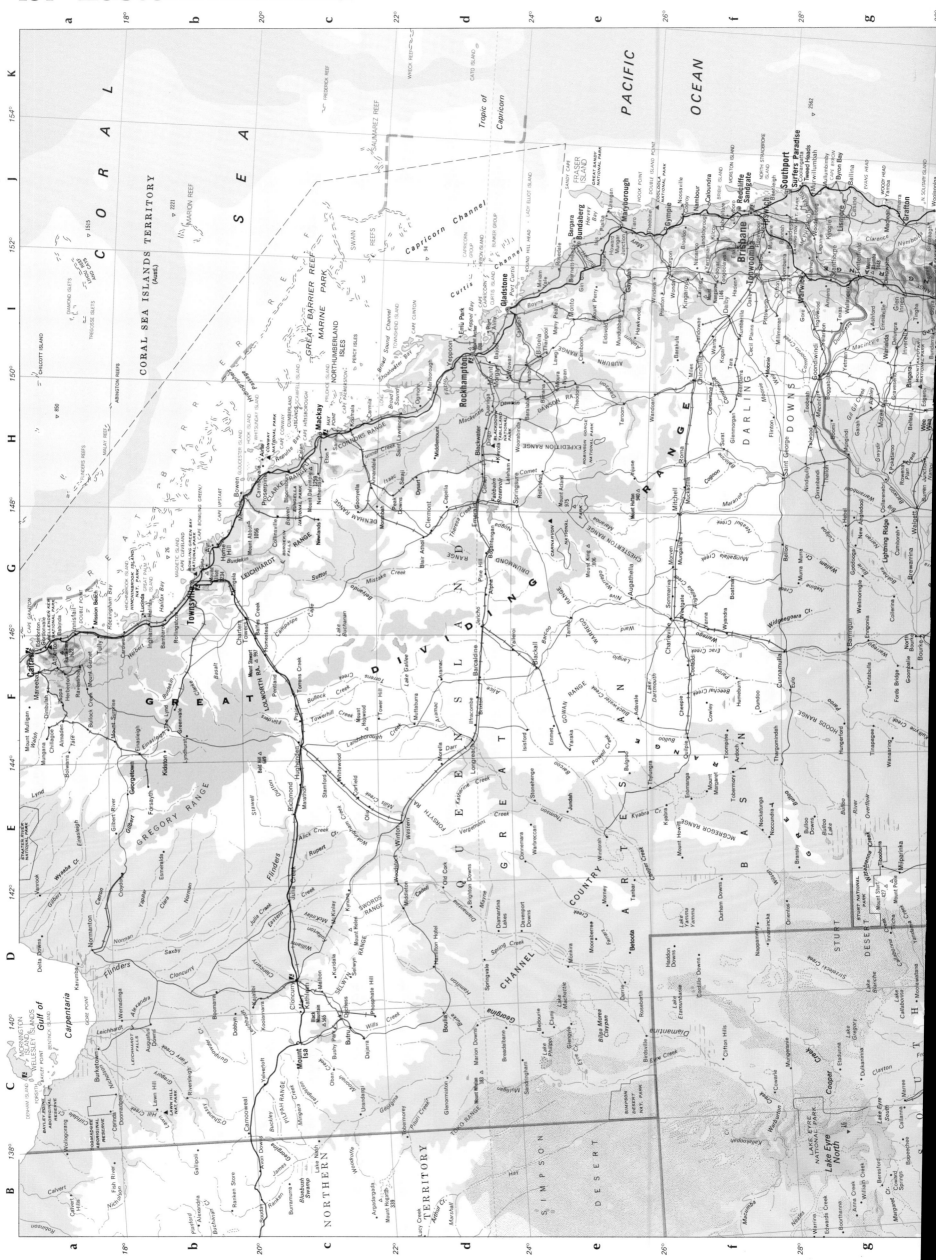

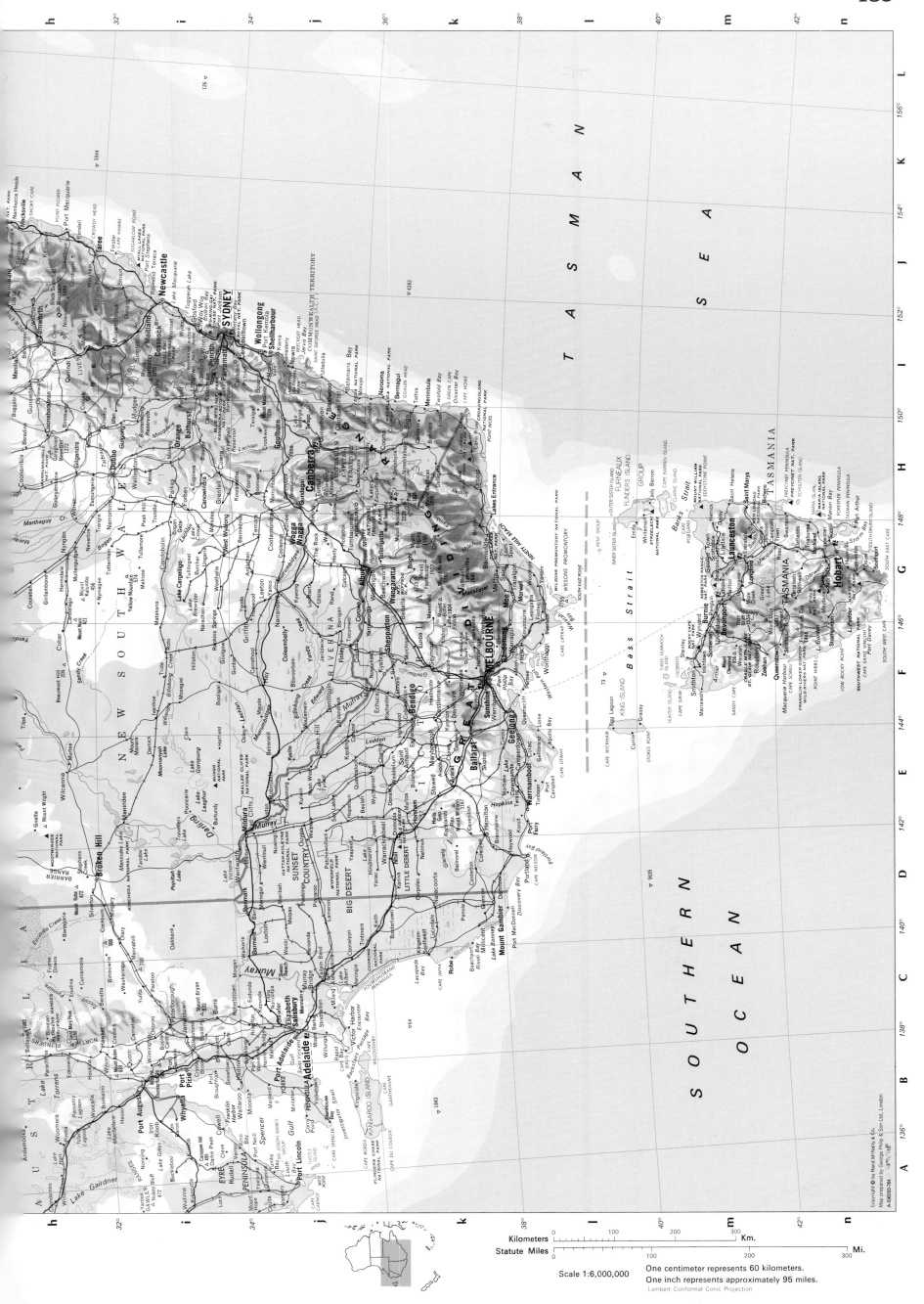

Kilometers 0   100   200   300 Km.

Statute Miles 0   100   200   300 Mi.

Scale 1:6,000,000

One centimeter represents 60 kilometers.
One inch represents approximately 95 miles.
Lambert Conformal Conic Projection

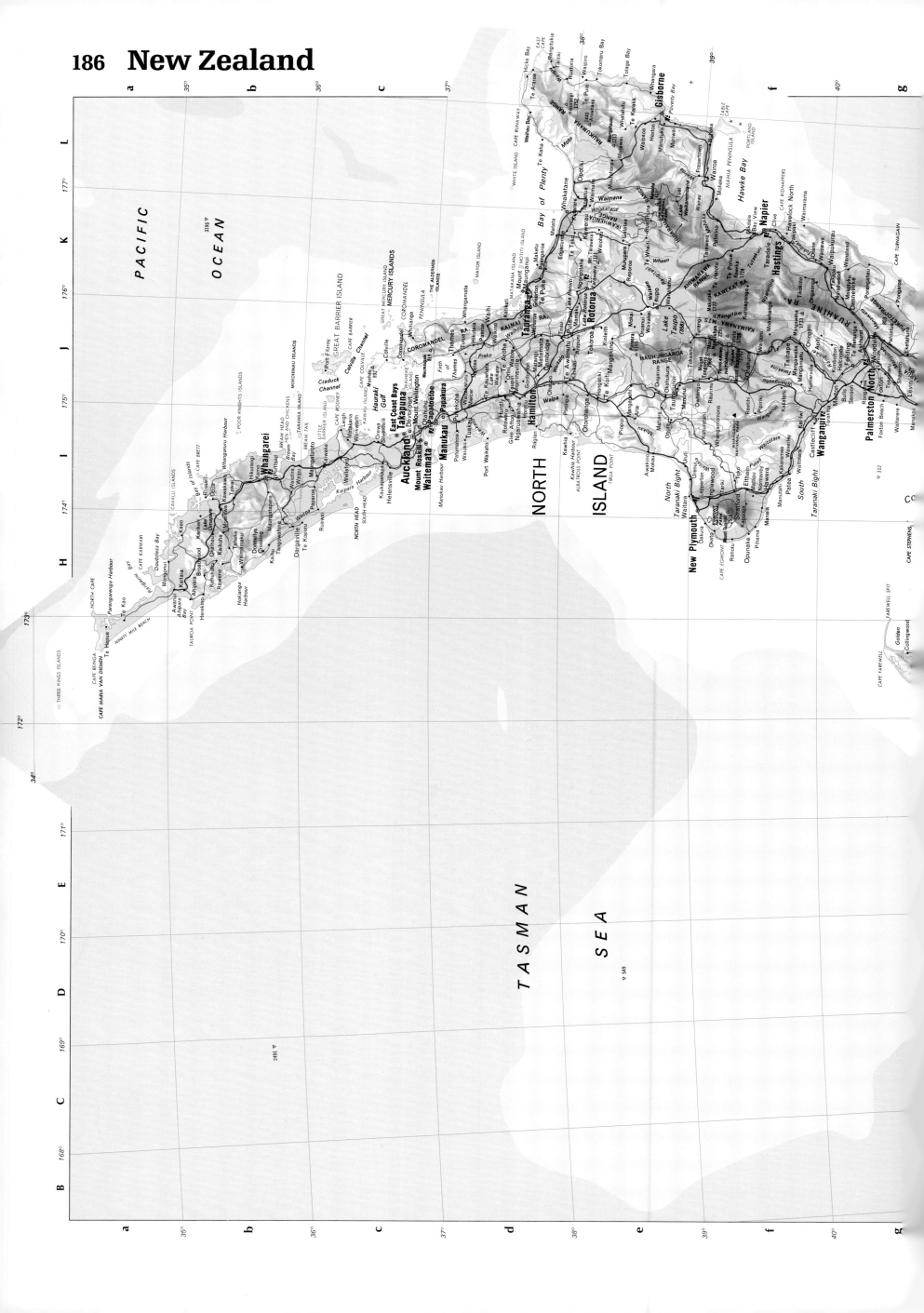

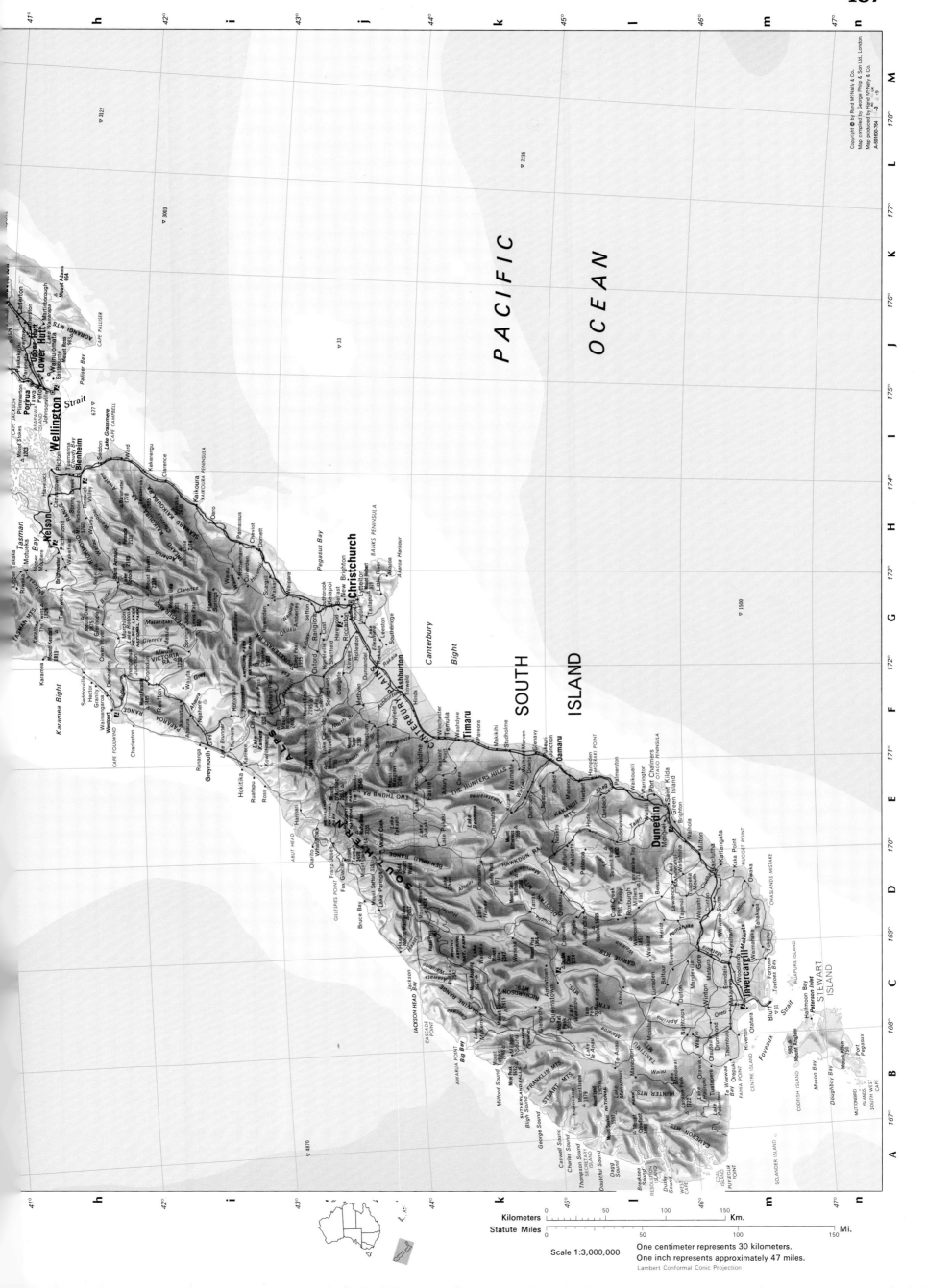

Kilometers
Statute Miles

Scale 1:3,000,000

One centimeter represents 30 kilometers.
One inch represents approximately 47 miles.
Lambert Conformal Conic Projection

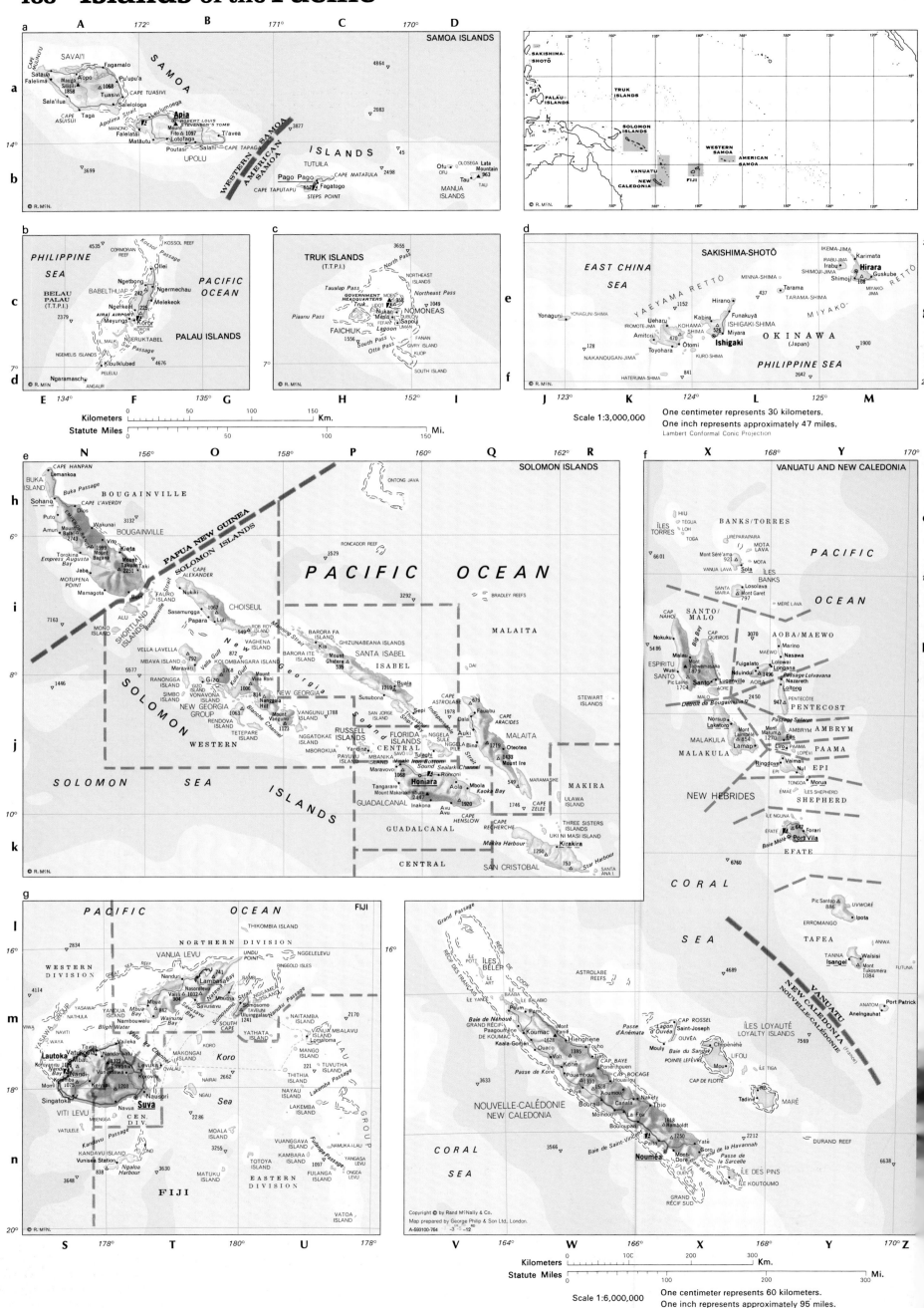

SAMOA ISLANDS

SAVAI'I

Fagamalo
Pu'upu'a
'Aopo
Maugā 1068
Silisili 1858
Tuasivi
CAPE TUASIVI
CAPE MAUNU'U
Sataua
Falelima
Sala'ilua
CAPE TAGA
Taga
Salelologa
Apolima Strait
MANONO
Faleatai
Matautu
Poutasi
Salani
CAPE TAPAGA
Apia
ROBERT LOUIS STEVENSON'S TOMB
Mount Fito 1097
Lotofaga
Ti'avea
UPOLU
3877
4864
2083
45
2498
Ofu
OLOSEGA
OFU
Lata Mountain
Tau
963

TUTUILA
CAPE MATATULA
Pago Pago
Fagatogo
CAPE TAPUTAPU
STEPS POINT
MANUA ISLANDS

WESTERN SAMOA
AMERICAN SAMOA
SAMOA
ISLANDS

3699
172°
171°
170°
14°

PHILIPPINE SEA

BELAU PALAU (T.T.P.I.)

KOSSOL REEF
4535
CORMORAN REEF
Ngetbong
Ollei
BABELTHUAP
Ngermechau
Ngerkeai
Melekeok
225
PACIFIC OCEAN
Ngerkeel
Meyungs
Koror
EL MALK
NGERUKTABEL
Kloulklubed
4676
PELELIU
Ngaramasch
ANGAUR
2379
NGEMELIS ISLANDS
Sar Passage
AIRAI AIRPORT
134°
135°
7°

TRUK ISLANDS (T.T.P.I.)

3655
North Pass
NORTHEAST REEF
Northeast Pass
GOVERNMENT HEADQUARTERS
Tauolap Pass
Truk MOEN
UDOT
DUBLON
1049
NOMONEAS
Nukan
Masa
FEFAN
Sapou
UMAN
Piaanu Pass
1556
FAICHUK
South Pass
Otta Pass
FANAN
GWRY ISLAND
KUOP
SOUTH ISLAND
152°
7°

SAKISHIMA-SHOTŌ

EAST CHINA SEA

IKEMA-JIMA
IRABU-JIMA
Karimata
SHIMOJI-JIMA
Hirara
526
Guskube
108
MINNA-SHIMA
Tarama
TARAMA-SHIMA
437
MIYAKO-JIMA
Hirano
1152
YAEYAMA RETTŌ
Yonaguni
YONAGUNI-SHIMA
IROMOTE-JIMA
Ueharu
Kabira
Funakyu
KOHAMA-SHIMA
ISHIGAKI-SHIMA
Miyara
OKINAWA (Japan)
1900
Amitori
470
Ishigaki
128
Ōtomi
Toyohara
KURO-SHIMA
NAKANOUGAN-JIMA
HATERUMA-SHIMA
841
2642
PHILIPPINE SEA
123°
124°
125°

Scale 1:3,000,000
One centimeter represents 30 kilometers.
One inch represents approximately 47 miles.
Lambert Conformal Conic Projection

Kilometers 0 50 100 150 Km.
Statute Miles 0 50 100 150 Mi.

SOLOMON ISLANDS

BUKA ISLAND
CAPE HANPAN
Lemanoa
Sohano
Buka Passage
BOUGAINVILLE
Amun
Puto
Mount Balbi 2743
Dios
Wakunai
3132
Vito
Torokina
Empress Augusta Bay
Mount Bagana 1999
Taki
Mount Takuan 2251
Jaba
MOTUPENA POINT
Mamagota
7163
Boin
FAURO ISLAND
ALU
Nukiki
SHORTLAND ISLANDS
MONO ISLAND
VELLA LAVELLA
CHOISEUL
1067
Sasamungga
Papara
Luti
549
Mount Vita Roni
VAGHENA ISLAND
792
872
MBAVA ISLAND
RANONGGA ISLAND
Maravari
Gizo
1006
1446
5577
SIMBO ISLAND
814
VONAVONA ISLAND
Nangzala Hill
1063
1123
NEW GEORGIA GROUP
RENDOVA ISLAND
TETEPARE ISLAND
WESTERN
Vangunu
VANGUNU ISLAND
1788
NGGATOKAE ISLAND
SOLOMON SEA
MBOROKUA
ISLANDS

PAPUA NEW GUINEA
SOLOMON ISLANDS

PACIFIC OCEAN

ONTONG JAVA

RONCADOR REEF
3529
3292
BRADLEY REEFS
MALAITA
BORARA FA ISLAND
GHIZUNABEANA ISLANDS
Kia
BORARA ITE ISLAND
Mount Ghatere 539
SANTA ISABEL
ISABEL
1219
Buala
Susubona
CAPE ASTROLABE
679
DAI
Dala
Fauabu
Auki
1978
SAN JORGE ISLAND
CAPE ARACIDES
Sepi
FLORIDA ISLANDS
CENTRAL
1219
MALAITA
NGGELA PILE
Oteotea
NGGELA SULE
1433
Tulaghi
Mount Ire
PAVUU ISLAND
SEALARK CHANNEL
Yandina
MARAMASIKE
MBANIKA
SAVO ISLAND
Iron Bottom Sound
MAKIRA
Maravovo
1068
Ronsoni
STEWART ISLANDS
Honiara
Aola
Mbola
549
ULAWA ISLAND
Tangarare
Mount Makarakomburu 2446
Kaoka Bay
1920
1746
CAPE ZELEE
Inakona
Avu
Avu
THREE SISTERS ISLANDS
GUADALCANAL
CAPE HENSLOW
UKI NI MASI ISLAND
CAPE RECHERCHE
1250
Kirakira
Makira Harbour
753
Star Harbour
SANTA ANA I.
CENTRAL
SAN CRISTOBAL

SOLOMON
SEA
ISLANDS

156°
158°
160°
162°
6°
8°
10°

VANUATU AND NEW CALEDONIA

HIU
ÎLES TORRES
TEGUA
LOH
TOGA
BANKS/TORRES
UREPARAPARA
MOTA LAVA
Mont Séré'ama 921
6601
VANUA LAVA
MOTA
Sola
MÉRÉ LAVA
ÎLES BANKS
PACIFIC OCEAN
SANTA MARIA
Losolava
797
Mont Garet
SANTO/MALO
CAP QUEIROS
3070
AOBA/MAEWO
PIC NAHOI
Nokuru
5486
MAEWO
Marino
Nasawa
ESPIRITU SANTO
Malau
Mont Tabwemasana 1879
Wusi
Ndundul
Fuigalato
Loiowai
1496
LONGANA
Passage Lolvavana
Pic Laini 1704
Santo
Luganville
AOBA
Nazareth
Loltong
MALO
2450
947
PENTECOTE
Detroit de Bougainville
Nérsup
Passage Selwyn
MALAKULA
Lakatoro
Mont Lambele 1270
AMBRYM
Eas
Mount Marum 1279
Liro
LOPEVI
Lamap
Vaimali
Nul
EPI
MALAKULA
Ringdove
TONGOA
Morua
PAAMA
EMAÉ
ÎLES SHEPHERD
NEW HEBRIDES
SHEPHERD
ÎLE NGUNA
EFATE
Baie Mele
Port Vila
647
Forari
6760
EFATE
CORAL
Pic Santop 886
UVWORÉ
Ipota
ERROMANGO
SEA
TAFEA
4689
TANNA
Isangel
Waisisi
Mont Tukosméra 1084
ANWA
FUTUNA
ANATOM
Port Patrick
Aneingauhat
VANUATU
NOUVELLE-CALÉDONIE
NEW CALEDONIA (France)
168°
170°

FIJI

PACIFIC OCEAN
THIKOMBIA ISLAND
NORTHERN DIVISION
VANUA LEVU
741
Nanduri
Lambasa
RAMBI
NGGELELEVU
UNDU POINT
RINGGOLD ISLES
WESTERN DIVISION
1032
Nasorelevu
Mbua
904
842
1241
Savusavu
Nambouwalu
Somosomo
TAVEUNI
2170
YANDUA ISLAND
SOUTH CAPE
YASAWA
Mbua Bay
Wainunu Bay
NAITAMBA ISLAND
NAMBOUWALU
Ulanggalau Mountain
VANUA MBALAVU
4114
NATHULA
YANDUA
Bligh Water
YATHATA ISLAND
Lomaloma
MAKONGAI ISLAND
2662
Koro
MANGO ISLAND
TUVUTHA ISLAND
WAYA
WAYA
VITI LEVU
Tavua
1123
OVALAU
Levuka
THITHIA ISLAND
LAKEMBA PASSAGE
Lautoka
Vatukoula
NAIRAI
NAYAU ISLAND
Vunindawa
1075
Korovou
LAKEMBA ISLAND
Mba
Nandi
Nandarivatu
Koro Sea
MBENGA
CEN. DIV.
22.86
MOALA ISLAND
NAMUKA-I-LAU
Singatoka
Navua
Suva
VATULELE
Nausori
VUANGGAVA ISLAND
KAMBARA ISLAND
FULANGA PASSAGE
ONGEA LEVU
KANDAVU ISLAND
3255
1097
YANGASA LEVU
3648
838
Ngaloa Harbour
3630
MATUKU ISLAND
TOTOYA ISLAND
FULANGA ISLAND
Vunisea Station
VIWA
NAVITI
FIJI
EASTERN DIVISION
VATOA ISLAND
178°
180°
178°
16°
18°
20°

Grand Passage
RÉCIF DE COOK
ÎLES BÉLEP
ÎLE ART
ÎLE POTT
RÉCIF DES FRANÇAIS
Grand Passage
ÎLE YANDE
Baie de Néhoué
GRAND RÉCIF DE KOUMAC
Poum
Arama
ASTROLABE REEFS
BAABA
Balabio
4689
Koumac
Mont Panié 1628
Kaala-Gomén
Voh
Koné
Mont 1385
Hienghène
Touho
Passe d'Anémata
Lagon d'Ouvéa
OUVÉA
Saint-Joseph
CAP ROSSEL
Mouly
LIFOU
Poya
3633
CAP BAYE
Pouembout
Poindimié
CAP BOCAGE
Ponérihouen
POINTE LEFÈVRE
Mou
ÎLE TIGA
Kouaoua
Bourail
1818
Moindou
Houaïlou
La Foa
Thio
1508
MARÉ
ÎLES LOYAUTÉ
LOYALTY ISLANDS
7569
CAP DE FLOTTE
Tadine
1250
Boulouparis
Hambolt
NOUVELLE-CALÉDONIE
NEW CALEDONIA
2212
DURAND REEF
3566
Païta
Goro
Col de la Havannah
6638
Baie de Saint-Vincent
Nouméa
Mont Dore
Yaté
Passe de la Sarcelle
CORAL SEA
QUEN
ÎLE DES PINS
GRAND RÉCIF SUD
ÎLE KOUTOUMO
164°
166°
168°
170°

Copyright © by Rand McNally & Co.
Map prepared by George Philip & Son Ltd., London.
A-593100-764   -3   -12

Kilometers 0 100 200 300 Km.
Statute Miles 0 100 200 300 Mi.
Scale 1:6,000,000
One centimeter represents 60 kilometers.
One inch represents approximately 95 miles.
Lambert Conformal Conic Projection

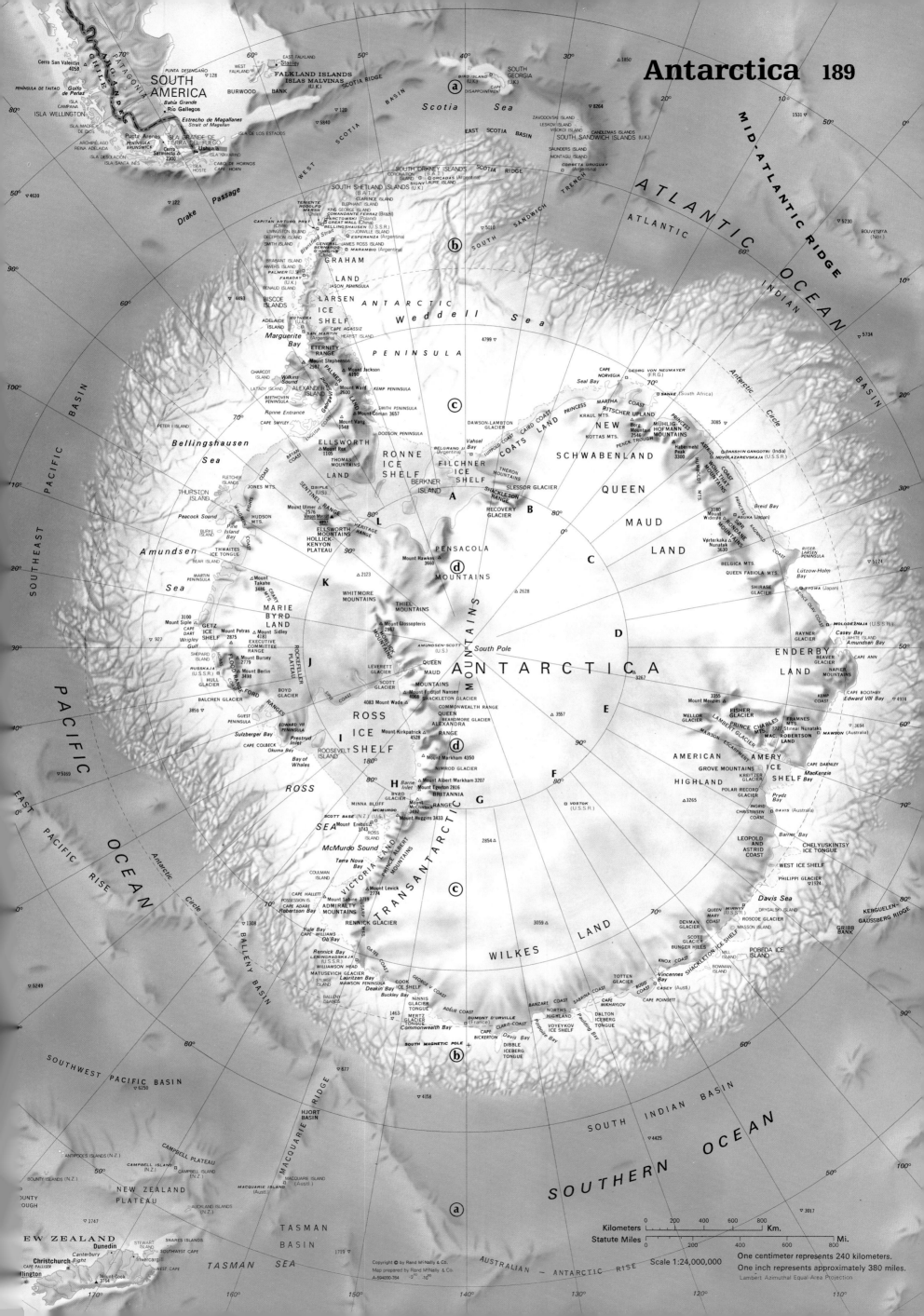

SOUTHERN OCEAN

INDIAN OCEAN

ARABIAN SEA

Bay of Bengal

South China Sea

Philippine Sea

MEDITERRANEAN SEA

UNION OF SOVIET SOCIALIST REPUBLICS

CHINA

INDIA

AUSTRALIA

ANTARCTICA

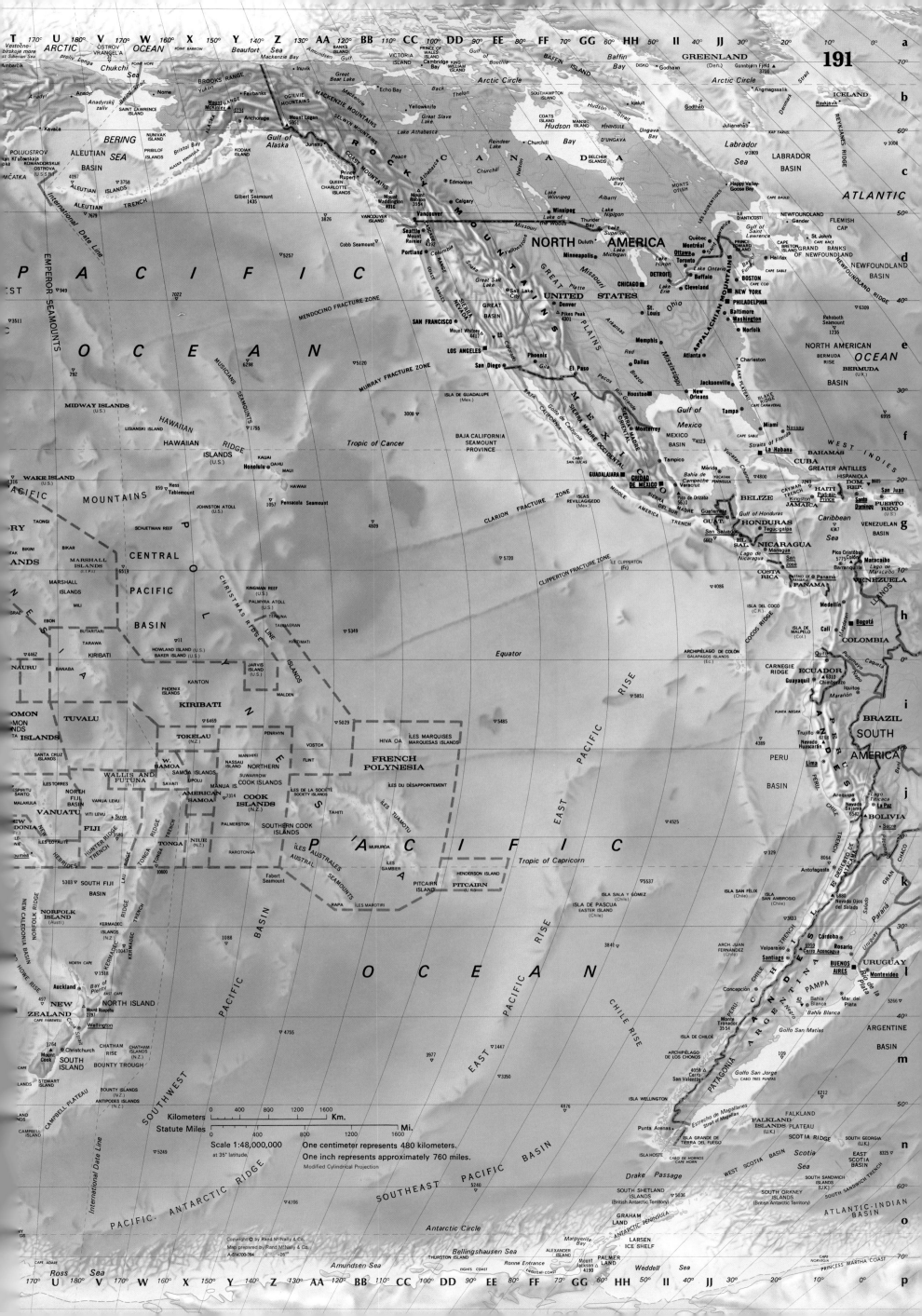

World Information Table

This table gives the area, population, population density, capital, and political status of every country in the world. The political units listed are categorized by political status in the last column of the table, as follows: A—independent countries; B—internally independent political entities which are under the protection of another country in matters of defense and foreign affairs; C—colonies and other dependent political units; and D—the major administrative subdivisions of Australia, Canada, China, the Soviet Union, the United Kingdom, and the United States. For comparison, the table also includes the continents and the world. For units categorized B, the protecting countries are identified in the political status column. For units categorized C, the names of administering countries are given in parentheses in the first column. A key to abbreviations of country names appears on page 197. All footnotes to this table appear on page 196.

The populations are estimates for January 1, 1989, made by Rand McNally & Company on the basis of the latest available official data, United Nations and U.S. Census Bureau estimates, and other information. Area figures include inland water.

English Name	Local Name	Area in sq. mi.	Area in sq. km.	Population	Pop. per sq. mi.	Pop. per sq. km.	Capital	Political Status
†Afghanistan	Afghānestān	251,826	652,225	14,655,000	58	22	Kābol	A
Africa	. . .	11,700,000	30,300,000	642,100,000	55	21	. . .	. . .
Alabama, U.S.	Alabama	51,704	133,913	4,125,000	80	31	Montgomery	D
Alaska, U.S.	Alaska	591,004	1,530,693	558,000	0.9	0.4	Juneau	D
†Albania	Shqipëri	11,100	28,748	3,181,000	287	111	Tiranë	A
Alberta, Can.	Alberta	255,287	661,190	2,450,000	9.6	3.7	Edmonton	D
†Algeria	Algérie (French) / Djazaïr (Arabic)	919,595	2,381,741	24,215,000	26	10	El Djazaïr (Algiers)	A
American Samoa (U.S.)	American Samoa (English) / Amerika Samoa (Samoan)	77	199	40,000	519	201	Pago Pago	C
Andorra	Andorra	175	453	51,000	291	113	Andorra	B(Sp., Fr.)
†Angola	Angola	481,354	1,246,700	8,385,000	17	6.7	Luanda	A
Anguilla (U.K.)	Anguilla	35	91	7,000	200	77	The Valley	B(U.K.)
Anhwei, China	Anhui	54,054	140,000	53,970,000	998	386	Hefei	D
Antarctica	. . .	5,400,000	14,000,000	. . .	. . .	. . .	. . .	. . .
†Antigua and Barbuda	Antigua and Barbuda	171	443	84,000	491	190	St. John's	A
†Argentina	Argentina	1,073,400	2,780,092	32,205,000	30	12	Buenos Aires	A
Arizona, U.S.	Arizona	114,002	295,264	3,558,000	31	12	Phoenix	D
Arkansas, U.S.	Arkansas	53,191	137,764	2,410,000	45	17	Little Rock	D
Armenian S.S.R., U.S.S.R.	Arm'anskaja S.S.R.	11,506	29,800	3,505,000	305	118	Jerevan	D
Aruba	Aruba	75	193	66,000	880	342	Oranjestad	B(Neth.)
Asia	. . .	17,400,000	45,000,000	3,130,600,000	180	70	. . .	. . .
†Australia	Australia	2,966,155	7,682,300	16,955,000	5.7	2.2	Canberra	A
Australian Capital Territory, Austl.	Australian Capital Territory	927	2,400	281,000	303	117	Canberra	D
†Austria	Österreich	32,377	83,855	7,584,000	234	90	Wien (Vienna)	A
Azerbaijan S.S.R., U.S.S.R.	Azerbajdžanskaja S.S.R.	33,436	86,600	7,020,000	210	81	Baku	D
†Bahamas	Bahamas	5,382	13,939	243,000	45	17	Nassau	A
†Bahrain	Al-Bahrayn	256	662	458,000	1,789	692	Al-Manāmah	A
†Bangladesh	Bangladesh	55,598	143,998	111,390,000	2,003	774	Dhaka (Dacca)	A
†Barbados	Barbados	166	430	255,000	1,536	593	Bridgetown	A
†Belgium	Belgique (French) / België (Flemish)	11,783	30,518	9,862,000	837	323	Bruxelles (Brussels)	A
†Belize	Belize	8,866	22,963	184,000	21	8.0	Belmopan	A
†Benin	Bénin	43,484	112,622	4,725,000	109	42	Porto-Novo and Cotonou [5]	A
Bermuda (U.K.)	Bermuda	21	54	56,000	2,667	1,037	Hamilton	C
†Bhutan	Druk-Yul	17,954	46,500	1,519,000	85	33	Thimbu	B(India)
†Bolivia	Bolivia	424,165	1,098,581	7,184,000	17	6.5	La Paz and Sucre	A
Bophuthatswana [2]	Bophuthatswana	15,641	40,509	2,202,000	141	54	Mmabatho	B(S. Afr.)
†Botswana	Botswana	224,711	582,000	1,230,000	5.5	2.1	Gaborone	A
†Brazil	Brasil	3,286,488	8,511,965	145,930,000	44	17	Brasília	A
British Columbia, Can.	British Columbia (English) / Colombie-Britannique (French)	365,948	947,800	2,965,000	8.1	3.1	Victoria	D
British Indian Ocean Territory (U.K.)	British Indian Ocean Territory	23	60	. . .	. . .	. . .	. . .	C
†Brunei	Brunei	2,226	5,765	247,000	111	43	Bandar Seri Begawan	A
†Bulgaria	Bålgarija	42,823	110,912	8,997,000	210	81	Sofija (Sofia)	A
†Burkina Faso	Burkina Faso	105,869	274,200	8,596,000	81	31	Ouagadougou	A
†Burma	Myanmā	261,228	676,577	41,860,000	160	62	Rangoon	A
†Burundi	Burundi	10,745	27,830	5,200,000	484	187	Bujumbura	A
†Byelorussia, U.S.S.R.	Belorusskaja S.S.R.	80,155	207,600	10,215,000	127	49	Minsk	D
California, U.S.	California	158,704	411,041	28,630,000	180	70	Sacramento	D
†Cameroon	Cameroun (French) / Cameroon (English)	183,569	475,442	11,495,000	63	24	Yaoundé	A
†Canada	Canada	3,849,674	9,970,610	25,895,000	6.7	2.6	Ottawa	A
†Cape Verde	Cabo Verde	1,557	4,033	359,000	231	89	Praia	A
Cayman Islands (U.K.)	Cayman Islands	100	259	25,000	250	97	Georgetown	C
†Central African Republic	République centrafricaine	240,535	622,984	3,089,000	13	5.0	Bangui	A
†Chad	Tchad	495,755	1,284,000	4,845,000	9.8	3.8	N'Djamena	A
Chekiang, China	Zhejiang	39,382	102,000	42,255,000	1,073	414	Hangzhou	D
†Chile	Chile	292,135	756,626	12,925,000	44	17	Santiago	A
†China (excl. Taiwan)	Zhongguo	3,718,782	9,631,600	1,094,700,000	294	114	Beijing (Peking)	A
Christmas Island (Austl.)	Christmas Island	52	135	2,000	38	15	. . .	C
Ciskei [2]	Ciskei	3,008	7,790	1,006,000	334	129	Bisho	B(S. Afr.)
Cocos (Keeling) Islands (Austl.)	Cocos (Keeling) Islands	5.4	14	600	111	43	. . .	C
†Colombia	Colombia	440,831	1,141,748	30,465,000	69	27	Bogotá	A
Colorado, U.S.	Colorado	104,094	269,602	3,392,000	33	13	Denver	D
†Comoros	Comores (French) / Al-Qumur (Arabic)	838	2,171	436,000	520	201	Moroni	A
†Congo	Congo	132,047	342,000	2,191,000	17	6.4	Brazzaville	A
Connecticut, U.S.	Connecticut	5,019	12,999	3,233,000	644	249	Hartford	D
Cook Islands	Cook Islands	91	236	17,000	187	72	Avarua	B(N.Z.)
†Costa Rica	Costa Rica	19,730	51,100	2,990,000	152	59	San José	A
†Cuba	Cuba	42,804	110,861	10,440,000	244	94	La Habana (Havana)	A
†Cyprus	Kípros (Greek) / Kıbrıs (Turkish)	2,276	5,896	573,000	252	97	Nicosia (Levkosía)	A
Cyprus, North	Kuzey Kıbrıs	1,295	3,355	172,000	133	51	Nicosia (Lefkoşa)	A
†Czechoslovakia	Československo	49,384	127,905	15,605,000	316	122	Praha (Prague)	A
Delaware, U.S.	Delaware	2,045	5,297	655,000	320	124	Dover	D
†Denmark	Danmark	16,638	43,092	5,135,000	309	119	København (Copenhagen)	A
District of Columbia, U.S.	District of Columbia	69	179	619,000	8,971	3,458	Washington	D
†Djibouti	Djibouti	8,958	23,200	324,000	36	14	Djibouti	A
†Dominica	Dominica	290	752	100,000	345	133	Roseau	A
†Dominican Republic	República Dominicana	18,704	48,442	7,069,000	378	146	Santo Domingo	A
†Ecuador	Ecuador	109,484	283,561	10,345,000	94	36	Quito	A
†Egypt	Misr	386,662	1,001,450	52,490,000	136	52	Al-Qāhirah (Cairo)	A
†El Salvador	El Salvador	8,124	21,041	5,122,000	630	243	San Salvador	A
England, U.K.	England	50,363	130,439	47,510,000	943	364	London	D
†Equatorial Guinea	Guinea Ecuatorial	10,831	28,051	438,000	40	16	Malabo	A
Estonia, U.S.S.R.	Estonskaja S.S.R.	17,413	45,100	1,585,000	91	35	Tallinn	D
†Ethiopia	Ityopiya	483,123	1,251,282	48,470,000	100	39	Adis Abeba	A
Europe	. . .	3,800,000	9,900,000	685,400,000	180	69	. . .	. . .
Faeroe Islands	Føroyar	540	1,399	48,000	89	34	Tórshavn	B(Den.)
Falkland Islands (U.K.) [3]	Falkland Islands (English) / Islas Malvinas (Spanish)	4,700	12,173	2,000	0.4	0.2	Stanley	C
†Fiji	Fiji	7,078	18,333	749,000	106	41	Suva	A
†Finland	Suomi (Finnish) / Finland (Swedish)	130,559	338,145	4,949,000	38	15	Helsinki (Helsingfors)	A
Florida, U.S.	Florida	58,668	151,949	12,605,000	215	83	Tallahassee	D
†France (excl. Overseas Departments)	France	211,208	547,026	55,970,000	265	102	Paris	A
French Guiana (Fr.)	Guyane française	35,135	91,000	93,000	2.6	1.0	Cayenne	C

World Information Table

English Name	Local Name	Area in sq. mi.	Area in sq. km.	Population	Pop. per sq. mi.	Pop. per sq. km.	Capital	Political Status
French Polynesia (Fr.)	Polynésie française	1,544	4,000	194,000	126	49	Papeete	C
Fukien, China	Fujian	47,491	123,000	28,355,000	597	231	Fuzhou	D
†Gabon	Gabon	103,347	267,667	1,056,000	10	3.9	Libreville	A
†Gambia	Gambia	4,361	11,295	789,000	181	70	Banjul	A
Georgia, U.S.	Georgia	58,914	152,587	6,401,000	109	42	Atlanta	D
Georgia, U.S.S.R.	Gruzinskaja S.S.R.	26,911	69,700	5,330,000	198	76	Tbilisi	D
†German Democratic Republic	Deutsche Demokratische Republik	41,828	108,333	16,582,000	396	153	Berlin, Ost- (East Berlin)	A
†Germany, Federal Republic of	Bundesrepublik Deutschland	96,027	248,707	61,380,000	639	247	Bonn	A
†Ghana	Ghana	92,098	238,533	14,575,000	158	61	Accra	A
Gibraltar (U.K.)	Gibraltar	2.3	6.0	31,000	13,478	5,167	Gibraltar	C
†Greece	Ellás	50,944	131,944	10,030,000	197	76	Athínai (Athens)	A
Greenland	Kalaallit Nunaat (Eskimo) / Grønland (Danish)	840,004	2,175,600	55,000	0.1	. . .	Godthåb	B(Den.)
†Grenada	Grenada	133	344	95,000	714	276	St. George's	A
Guadeloupe (incl. Dependencies) (Fr.)	Guadeloupe	687	1,780	340,000	495	191	Basse-Terre	C
Guam (U.S.)	Guam	209	541	137,000	656	253	Agana	C
†Guatemala	Guatemala	42,042	108,889	8,818,000	210	81	Guatemala	A
Guernsey (incl. Dependencies) (U.K.)	Guernsey	30	78	56,000	1,867	718	St. Peter Port	C
†Guinea	Guinée	94,926	245,857	6,999,000	74	28	Conakry	A
†Guinea-Bissau	Guiné-Bissau	13,948	36,125	962,000	69	27	Bissau	A
†Guyana	Guyana	83,000	214,969	765,000	9.2	3.6	Georgetown	A
Hainan, China	Hainan	13,127	34,000	6,520,000	497	192	Haikou	D
†Haiti	Haïti	10,714	27,750	6,346,000	592	229	Port-au-Prince	A
Hawaii, U.S.	Hawaii	6,473	16,765	1,110,000	171	66	Honolulu	D
Heilungkiang, China	Heilongjiang	177,607	460,000	34,810,000	196	76	Harbin	D
Honan, China	Henan	64,479	167,000	80,900,000	1,255	484	Zhengzhou	D
†Honduras	Honduras	43,277	112,088	5,047,000	117	45	Tegucigalpa	A
Hong Kong (U.K.)	Hong Kong	412	1,068	5,731,000	13,910	5,366	Hong Kong (Victoria)	C
Hopeh, China	Hebei	78,379	203,000	58,020,000	740	286	Shijiazhuang	D
Hunan, China	Hunan	81,468	211,000	58,790,000	722	279	Changsha	D
†Hungary	Magyarország	35,920	93,033	10,580,000	295	114	Budapest	A
Hupeh, China	Hubei	72,587	188,000	51,560,000	710	274	Wuhan	D
†Iceland	Ísland	39,769	103,000	248,000	6.2	2.4	Reykjavík	A
Idaho, U.S.	Idaho	83,566	216,435	1,010,000	12	4.7	Boise	D
Illinois, U.S.	Illinois	57,872	149,888	11,615,000	201	77	Springfield	D
†India (incl. part of Jammu and Kashmir)	India (English) / Bharat (Hindi)	1,237,062	3,203,975	825,000,000	667	257	New Delhi	A
Indiana, U.S.	Indiana	36,417	94,320	5,539,000	152	59	Indianapolis	D
†Indonesia	Indonesia	741,101	1,919,443	185,860,000	251	97	Jakarta	A
Inner Mongolia, China	Nei Monggol	463,323	1,200,000	20,020,000	43	17	Hohhot	D
Iowa, U.S.	Iowa	56,275	145,752	2,818,000	50	19	Des Moines	D
†Iran	Īrān	636,296	1,648,000	52,760,000	83	32	Tehrān	A
†Iraq	Al-'Irāq	169,235	438,317	17,900,000	106	41	Baghdād	A
†Ireland	Ireland (English) / Éire (Gaelic)	27,136	70,283	3,524,000	130	50	Dublin (Baile Átha Cliath)	A
Isle of Man	Isle of Man	221	572	62,000	281	108	Douglas	B(U.K.)
†Israel	Yisra'el (Hebrew) / Isrā'īl (Arabic)	8,019	20,770	4,374,000	545	211	Yerushalayim (Jerusalem)	A
Israeli Occupied Areas [4]	. . .	2,947	7,632	1,728,000	586	226	. . .	. . .
†Italy	Italia	116,320	301,268	57,500,000	494	191	Roma (Rome)	A
†Ivory Coast	Côte d'Ivoire	123,847	320,763	11,400,000	92	36	Abidjan and Yamoussoukro [5]	A
†Jamaica	Jamaica	4,244	10,991	2,470,000	582	225	Kingston	A
†Japan	Nihon	145,870	377,801	123,010,000	843	326	Tōkyō	A
Jersey (U.K.)	Jersey	45	116	81,000	1,800	698	St. Helier	C
†Jordan	Al-Urdunn	35,135	91,000	2,904,000	83	32	'Ammān	A
†Kampuchea (Cambodia)	Kâmpúchéa Prâchéathipâtéyy	69,898	181,035	6,760,000	97	37	Phnum Pénh (Phnom Penh)	A
Kansas, U.S.	Kansas	82,282	213,109	2,500,000	30	12	Topeka	D
Kansu, China	Gansu	150,580	390,000	21,345,000	142	55	Lanzhou	D
Kazakhstan, U.S.S.R.	Kazachskaja S.S.R.	1,049,156	2,717,300	16,680,000	16	6.1	Alma-Ata	D
Kentucky, U.S.	Kentucky	40,414	104,672	3,741,000	93	36	Frankfort	D
†Kenya	Kenya	224,961	582,646	25,825,000	115	44	Nairobi	A
Kiangsi, China	Jiangxi	63,707	165,000	36,235,000	569	220	Nanchang	D
Kiangsu, China	Jiangsu	39,382	102,000	65,240,000	1,657	640	Nanjing (Nanking)	D
Kirghiz S.S.R., U.S.S.R.	Kirgizskaja S.S.R.	76,641	198,500	4,330,000	56	22	Frunze	D
Kiribati	Kiribati	280	726	69,000	246	95	Bairiki	A
Kirin, China	Jilin	72,201	187,000	24,195,000	335	129	Changchun	D
Korea, North	Chosŏn-minjujuŭi-inmīn-konghwaguk	46,540	120,538	22,250,000	478	185	P'yŏngyang	A
Korea, South	Taehan-min'guk	38,025	98,484	42,840,000	1,127	435	Sŏul (Seoul)	A
†Kuwait	Al-Kuwayt	6,880	17,818	2,002,000	291	112	Al-Kuwayt (Kuwait)	A
Kwangsi Chuang, China	Guangxi Zhuangzu	91,506	237,000	40,285,000	440	170	Nanning	D
Kwangtung, China	Guangdong	76,062	197,000	58,730,000	772	298	Guangzhou (Canton)	D
Kweichow, China	Guizhou	67,182	174,000	30,980,000	461	178	Guiyang	D
†Laos	Lao	91,429	236,800	3,892,000	43	16	Viangchan (Vientiane)	A
Latvia, U.S.S.R.	Latvijskaja S.S.R.	24,595	63,700	2,695,000	110	42	Rīga	D
†Lebanon	Al-Lubnān	4,015	10,400	3,351,000	835	322	Bayrūt (Beirut)	A
†Lesotho	Lesotho	11,720	30,355	1,689,000	144	56	Maseru	A
Liaoning, China	Liaoning	58,301	151,000	38,645,000	663	256	Shenyang (Mukden)	D
†Liberia	Liberia	38,250	99,067	2,553,000	67	26	Monrovia	A
†Libya	Lībiyā	679,362	1,759,540	4,019,000	5.9	2.3	Tarābulus (Tripoli)	A
Liechtenstein	Liechtenstein	62	160	29,000	468	181	Vaduz	A
Lithuania, U.S.S.R.	Litovskaja S.S.R.	25,174	65,200	3,715,000	148	57	Vilnius	D
Louisiana, U.S.	Louisiana	47,750	123,672	4,517,000	95	37	Baton Rouge	D
†Luxembourg	Luxembourg	998	2,586	368,000	369	142	Luxembourg	A
Macau (Port.)	Macau	6.6	17	432,000	65,455	25,412	Macau	C
†Madagascar	Madagasikara (Malagasy) / Madagascar (French)	226,658	587,041	11,250,000	50	19	Antananarivo	A
Maine, U.S.	Maine	33,265	86,156	1,205,000	36	14	Augusta	D
†Malawi	Malaŵi	45,747	118,484	8,440,000	184	71	Lilongwe	A
†Malaysia	Malaysia	127,502	330,224	17,255,000	135	52	Kuala Lumpur	A
†Maldives	Maldives	115	298	209,000	1,817	701	Male	A
†Mali	Mali	478,767	1,240,000	9,039,000	19	7.3	Bamako	A
†Malta	Malta	122	316	370,000	3,033	1,171	Valletta	A
Manitoba, Can.	Manitoba	250,947	649,950	1,095,000	4.4	1.7	Winnipeg	D
Marshall Islands (Trust Territory)	Marshall Islands	70	181	40,000	571	221	Majuro (island)	B(U.S.)
Martinique (Fr.)	Martinique	425	1,100	338,000	795	307	Fort-de-France	C
Maryland, U.S.	Maryland	10,461	27,094	4,605,000	440	170	Annapolis	D
Massachusetts, U.S.	Massachusetts	8,286	21,461	5,880,000	710	274	Boston	D
†Mauritania	Mauritanie (French) / Mūrītāniyā (Arabic)	397,956	1,030,700	1,948,000	4.9	1.9	Nouakchott	A
†Mauritius (incl. Dependencies)	Mauritius	788	2,040	1,057,000	1,341	518	Port Louis	A
Mayotte (Fr.) [6]	Mayotte	144	373	79,000	549	212	Dzaoudzi and Mamoudzou [5]	C
†Mexico	México	761,605	1,972,547	85,300,000	112	43	Ciudad de México (Mexico City)	A

English Name	Local Name	Area in sq. mi.	Area in sq. km.	Population	Pop. per sq. mi.	Pop. per sq. km.	Capital	Political Status
Michigan, U.S.	Michigan	97,107	251,506	9,186,000	95	37	Lansing	D
Micronesia, Federated States of (Trust Territory)	Federated States of Micronesia	271	702	108,000	399	154	Kolonia	B(U.S.)
Midway Islands (U.S.)	Midway Islands	2.0	5.2	500	250	96	. . .	C
Minnesota, U.S.	Minnesota	86,614	224,329	4,283,000	49	19	St. Paul	D
Mississippi, U.S.	Mississippi	47,691	123,519	2,647,000	56	21	Jackson	D
Missouri, U.S.	Missouri	69,697	180,514	5,145,000	74	29	Jefferson City	D
Moldavia, U.S.S.R.	Moldavskaja S.S.R.	13,012	33,700	4,260,000	327	126	Kišin'ov (Kishinev)	D
Monaco	Monaco	0.7	1.9	29,000	41,429	15,263	Monaco	A
†Mongolia	Mongol Ard Uls	604,250	1,565,000	2,097,000	3.5	1.3	Ulaanbaatar (Ulan Bator)	A
Montana, U.S.	Montana	147,045	380,845	814,000	5.5	2.1	Helena	D
Montserrat (U.K.)	Montserrat	40	103	12,000	300	117	Plymouth	C
†Morocco (excl. Western Sahara)	Al-Magrib	172,414	446,550	25,600,000	148	57	Rabat	A
†Mozambique	Moçambique	308,642	799,379	17,660,000	57	22	Maputo	A
Namibia (excl. Walvis Bay)(S. Afr.) (7)	Namibia	317,818	823,144	1,337,000	4.2	1.6	Windhoek	C
Nauru	Nauru (English) / Naoero (Nauruan)	8.1	21	9,000	1,111	429	Yaren District	A
Nebraska, U.S.	Nebraska	77,350	200,336	1,599,000	21	8.0	Lincoln	D
†Nepal	Nepāl	56,827	147,181	18,415,000	324	125	Kathmandu	A
†Netherlands	Nederland	16,133	41,785	14,815,000	918	355	Amsterdam and 's-Gravenhage (The Hague)	A
Netherlands Antilles	Nederlandse Antillen	309	800	194,000	628	243	Willemstad	B(Neth.)
Nevada, U.S.	Nevada	110,562	286,354	1,061,000	9.6	3.7	Carson City	D
New Brunswick, Can.	New Brunswick (English) / Nouveau-Brunswick (French)	28,355	73,440	718,000	25	9.8	Fredericton	D
New Caledonia (Fr.)	Nouvelle-Calédonie	7,366	19,079	161,000	22	8.4	Nouméa	C
Newfoundland, Can.	Newfoundland (English) / Terre-Neuve (French)	156,649	405,720	571,000	3.6	1.4	St. John's	D
New Hampshire, U.S.	New Hampshire	9,278	24,030	1,089,000	117	45	Concord	D
New Jersey, U.S.	New Jersey	7,787	20,168	7,739,000	994	384	Trenton	D
New Mexico, U.S.	New Mexico	121,594	314,927	1,547,000	13	4.9	Santa Fe	D
New South Wales, Austl.	New South Wales	309,500	801,600	5,820,000	19	7.3	Sydney	D
New York, U.S.	New York	52,737	136,588	17,880,000	339	131	Albany	D
†New Zealand	New Zealand	103,519	268,112	3,391,000	33	13	Wellington	A
†Nicaragua	Nicaragua	50,193	130,000	3,689,000	73	28	Managua	A
†Niger	Niger	489,191	1,267,000	7,329,000	15	5.8	Niamey	A
†Nigeria	Nigeria	356,669	923,768	113,580,000	318	123	Lagos and Abuja (5)	A
Ningsia Hui, China	Ningxia Huizu	25,483	66,000	4,270,000	168	65	Yinchuan	D
Niue	Niue	102	263	2,400	24	9.1	Alofi	B(N.Z.)
Norfolk Island (Austl.)	Norfolk Island	14	36	2,000	143	56	Kingston	C
North America	. . .	9,400,000	24,400,000	420,100,000	45	17	. . .	. . .
North Carolina, U.S.	North Carolina	52,669	136,412	6,532,000	124	48	Raleigh	D
North Dakota, U.S.	North Dakota	70,702	183,117	676,000	9.6	3.7	Bismarck	D
Northern Ireland, U.K.	Northern Ireland	5,453	14,122	1,575,000	289	112	Belfast	D
Northern Mariana Islands (Trust Territory)	Northern Mariana Islands	184	477	22,000	120	46	Saipan (island)	B(U.S.)
Northern Territory, Austl.	Northern Territory	519,771	1,346,200	168,000	0.3	0.1	Darwin	D
Northwest Territories, Can.	Northwest Territories (English) / Territoires du Nord-Ouest (French)	1,322,910	3,426,320	56,000	. . .	. . .	Yellowknife	D
†Norway (incl. Svalbard and Jan Mayen)	Norge	149,412	386,975	4,221,000	28	11	Oslo	A
Nova Scotia, Can.	Nova Scotia (English) / Nouvelle-Écosse (French)	21,425	55,490	886,000	41	16	Halifax	D
Oceania (incl. Australia)	. . .	3,300,000	8,500,000	26,300,000	8.0	3.1	. . .	. . .
Ohio, U.S.	Ohio	44,786	115,995	10,780,000	241	93	Columbus	D
Oklahoma, U.S.	Oklahoma	69,957	181,188	3,327,000	48	18	Oklahoma City	D
†Oman	'Umān	82,030	212,457	1,284,000	16	6.0	Masqat (Muscat)	A
Ontario, Can.	Ontario	412,581	1,068,580	9,375,000	23	8.8	Toronto	D
Oregon, U.S.	Oregon	97,076	251,426	2,743,000	28	11	Salem	D
Pacific Islands, Trust Territory of the	Trust Territory of the Pacific Islands	721	1,868	185,000	257	99	Saipan (island)	B(U.S.)
†Pakistan (incl. part of Jammu and Kashmir)	Pākistān	339,732	879,902	108,990,000	321	124	Islāmābād	A
Palau (Trust Territory)	Palau (English) / Belau (Palauan)	196	508	15,000	77	30	Koror	B(U.S.)
†Panama	Panamá	29,762	77,082	2,346,000	79	30	Panamá	A
†Papua New Guinea	Papua New Guinea	178,704	462,840	3,639,000	20	7.9	Port Moresby	A
†Paraguay	Paraguay	157,048	406,752	4,210,000	27	10	Asunción	A
Peking, China	Beijing	6,487	16,800	10,070,000	1,552	599	Beijing (Peking)	D
Pennsylvania, U.S.	Pennsylvania	46,047	119,261	11,950,000	260	100	Harrisburg	D
†Peru	Perú	496,225	1,285,216	21,535,000	43	17	Lima	A
†Philippines	Pilipinas	115,831	300,000	60,110,000	519	200	Manila	A
Pitcairn (incl. Dependencies) (U.K.)	Pitcairn	19	49	70	3.7	1.4	Adamstown	C
†Poland	Polska	120,728	312,683	37,955,000	314	121	Warszawa (Warsaw)	A
†Portugal	Portugal	35,516	91,985	10,445,000	294	114	Lisboa (Lisbon)	A
Prince Edward Island, Can.	Prince Edward Island (English) / Île-du Prince-Édouard (French)	2,185	5,660	130,000	59	23	Charlottetown	D
Puerto Rico	Puerto Rico	3,515	9,104	3,301,000	939	363	San Juan	B(U.S.)
†Qatar	Qatar	4,416	11,437	400,000	91	35	Ad-Dawhah (Doha)	A
Quebec, Can.	Québec	594,860	1,540,680	6,595,000	11	4.3	Québec	D
Queensland, Austl.	Queensland	666,876	1,727,200	2,849,000	4.3	1.6	Brisbane	D
Reunion (Fr.)	Réunion	967	2,504	580,000	600	232	Saint-Denis	C
Rhode Island, U.S.	Rhode Island	1,212	3,139	994,000	820	317	Providence	D
†Romania	România	91,699	237,500	23,085,000	252	97	Bucureşti (Bucharest)	A
Russian Soviet Federative Socialist Republic, U.S.S.R.	Rossijskaja S.F.S.R.	6,592,849	17,075,400	147,780,000	22	8.7	Moskva (Moscow)	D
†Rwanda	Rwanda	10,169	26,338	7,192,000	707	273	Kigali	A
†St. Christopher-Nevis	St. Christopher-Nevis	104	269	47,000	452	175	Basseterre	A
St. Helena (incl. Dependencies) (U.K.)	St. Helena	162	419	7,800	48	19	Jamestown	C
†St. Lucia	St. Lucia	238	616	148,000	622	240	Castries	A
St. Pierre and Miquelon (Fr.)	Saint-Pierre-et-Miquelon	93	242	6,500	70	27	Saint-Pierre	C
†St. Vincent and the Grenadines	St. Vincent and the Grenadines	150	388	125,000	833	322	Kingstown	A
San Marino	San Marino	24	61	24,000	1,000	393	San Marino	A
†Sao Tome and Principe	São Tomé e Príncipe	372	964	119,000	320	123	São Tomé	A
Saskatchewan, Can.	Saskatchewan	251,866	652,330	1,030,000	4.1	1.6	Regina	D
†Saudi Arabia	Al-'Arabīyah as-Su'ūdīyah	864,869	2,240,000	15,775,000	18	7.0	Ar-Riyāḍ (Riyadh)	A
Scotland, U.K.	Scotland	29,794	77,167	5,150,000	173	67	Edinburgh	D
†Senegal	Sénégal	75,955	196,722	7,394,000	97	38	Dakar	A
†Seychelles	Seychelles	175	453	70,000	400	155	Victoria	A
Shanghai, China	Shanghai	2,239	5,800	12,700,000	5,672	2,190	Shanghai	D
Shansi, China	Shanxi	60,618	157,000	27,475,000	453	175	Taiyuan	D
Shantung, China	Shandong	59,074	153,000	80,790,000	1,368	528	Jinan	D
Shensi, China	Shaanxi	75,676	196,000	31,420,000	415	160	Xi'an (Sian)	D
†Sierra Leone	Sierra Leone	27,925	72,325	4,015,000	144	56	Freetown	A

World Information Table

English Name	Local Name	Area in sq. mi.	Area in sq. km.	Population	Pop. per sq. mi.	Pop. per sq. km.	Capital	Political Status
†Singapore	Singapore	239	620	2,663,000	11,142	4,295	Singapore	A
Sinkiang Uighur, China	Xinjiang Uygur	635,910	1,647,000	14,230,000	22	8.6	Ürümqi	D
†Solomon Islands	Solomon Islands	10,954	28,370	295,000	27	10	Honiara	A
†Somalia	Somaliya	246,201	637,657	8,118,000	33	13	Muqdisho (Mogadishu)	A
†South Africa (incl. Walvis Bay)	South Africa (English) / Suid-Afrika (Afrikaans)	433,680	1,123,226	35,480,000	82	32	Pretoria, Cape Town, and Bloemfontein	A
South America	. . .	6,900,000	17,800,000	287,500,000	42	16	. . .	. . .
South Australia, Austl.	South Australia	379,925	984,000	1,435,000	3.8	1.5	Adelaide	D
South Carolina, U.S.	South Carolina	31,116	80,590	3,494,000	112	43	Columbia	D
South Dakota, U.S.	South Dakota	77,120	199,740	713,000	9.2	3.6	Pierre	D
South Georgia and the South Sandwich Islands (U.K.)	South Georgia and the South Sandwich Islands (U.K.)	1,450	3,755	. . .	. . .	. . .	. . .	C
†Spain	España	194,885	504,750	39,330,000	202	78	Madrid	A
Spanish North Africa (Sp.) (8)	Plazas de Soberanía en el Norte de África	12	32	100,000	8,333	3,125	. . .	C
†Sri Lanka	Sri Lanka	24,962	64,652	16,730,000	670	259	Colombo and Sri Jayawardenapura (5)	A
†Sudan	As-Sūdān	967,500	2,505,813	24,255,000	25	9.7	Al-Khartūm (Khartoum)	A
†Suriname	Suriname	63,251	163,820	398,000	6.3	2.4	Paramaribo	A
†Swaziland	Swaziland	6,704	17,364	727,000	108	42	Mbabane and Lobamba (5)	A
†Sweden	Sverige	173,732	449,964	8,444,000	49	19	Stockholm	A
Switzerland	Schweiz (German) / Suisse (French) / Svizzera (Italian)	15,943	41,293	6,590,000	413	160	Bern (Berne)	A
†Syria	As-Sūrīyah	71,498	185,180	11,530,000	161	62	Dimashq (Damascus)	A
Szechwan, China	Sichuan	219,692	569,000	106,950,000	487	188	Chengdu	D
Taiwan	T'aiwan	13,900	36,002	20,125,000	1,448	559	T'aipei	A
Tajik S.S.R., U.S.S.R.	Tajikskaja S.S.R.	55,251	143,100	5,135,000	93	36	Dušanbe	D
†Tanzania	Tanzania	364,900	945,087	24,055,000	66	25	Dar es Salaam and Dodoma (5)	A
Tasmania, Austl.	Tasmania	26,178	67,800	452,000	17	6.7	Hobart	D
Tennessee, U.S.	Tennessee	42,143	109,150	4,913,000	117	45	Nashville	D
Texas, U.S.	Texas	266,805	691,022	17,415,000	65	25	Austin	D
†Thailand	Prathet Thai	198,115	513,115	55,375,000	280	108	Krung Thep (Bangkok)	A
Tibet, China	Xizang	471,817	1,222,000	2,080,000	4.4	1.7	Lhasa	D
Tientsin, China	Tianjin	4,247	11,000	8,430,000	1,985	766	Tianjin (Tientsin)	D
†Togo	Togo	21,925	56,785	3,393,000	155	60	Lomé	A
Tokelau (N.Z.)	Tokelau	4.6	12	1,700	370	142	. . .	C
Tonga	Tonga	270	699	100,000	370	143	Nuku'alofa	A
Transkei (2)	Transkei	16,216	42,000	3,900,000	241	93	Umtata	B(S. Afr.)
†Trinidad and Tobago	Trinidad and Tobago	1,980	5,128	1,295,000	654	253	Port of Spain	A
Tsinghai, China	Qinghai	278,380	721,000	4,270,000	15	5.9	Xining	D
†Tunisia	Tunisie (French) / Tunis (Arabic)	63,170	163,610	7,876,000	125	48	Tunis	A
†Turkey	Türkiye	300,948	779,452	51,970,000	173	67	Ankara	A
Turkmen S.S.R., U.S.S.R.	Turkmenskaja S.S.R.	188,456	488,100	3,545,000	19	7.3	Ašchabad	D
Turks and Caicos Islands (U.K.)	Turks and Caicos Islands	166	430	10,000	60	23	Grand Turk	C
Tuvalu	Tuvalu	10	26	8,700	870	335	Funafuti	A
†Uganda	Uganda	93,104	241,139	16,725,000	180	69	Kampala	A
†Ukraine, U.S.S.R.	Ukrainskaja S.S.R.	233,090	603,700	51,620,000	221	86	Kijev (Kiev)	D
†Union of Soviet Socialist Republics	Sojuz Sovetskich Socialističeskich Respublik	8,600,387	22,274,900	287,550,000	33	13	Moskva (Moscow)	A
†United Arab Emirates	Ittiḥād al-Imārāt al-ʿArabīyah	32,278	83,600	2,047,000	63	24	Abū Zaby (Abu Dhabi)	A
†United Kingdom	United Kingdom	93,629	242,496	57,090,000	610	235	London	A
†United States	United States	3,679,245	9,529,202	247,410,000	67	26	Washington	A
†Uruguay	Uruguay	67,574	175,016	3,184,000	47	18	Montevideo	A
Utah, U.S.	Utah	84,902	219,895	1,732,000	20	7.9	Salt Lake City	D
Uzbek S.S.R., U.S.S.R.	Uzbekskaja S.S.R.	172,742	447,400	20,135,000	117	45	Taškent	D
†Vanuatu	Vanuatu	4,706	12,189	155,000	33	13	Port-Vila	A
Vatican City	Città del Vaticano	0.2	0.4	800	4,000	2,000	Città del Vaticano (Vatican City)	A
Venda (2)	Venda	2,654	6,875	556,000	209	81	Thohoyandou	B(S. Afr.)
†Venezuela	Venezuela	352,145	912,050	19,010,000	54	21	Caracas	A
Vermont, U.S.	Vermont	9,614	24,900	556,000	58	22	Montpelier	D
Victoria, Austl.	Victoria	87,877	227,600	4,325,000	49	19	Melbourne	D
Vietnam	Viet Nam	127,242	329,556	66,030,000	519	200	Ha-noi	A
Virginia, U.S.	Virginia	40,763	105,576	6,031,000	148	57	Richmond	D
Virgin Islands (U.S.)	Virgin Islands (U.S.)	133	344	106,000	797	308	Charlotte Amalie	C
Virgin Islands, British (U.K.)	British Virgin Islands	59	153	13,000	220	85	Road Town	C
Wake Island (U.S.)	Wake Island	3.0	7.8	300	100	38	. . .	C
Wales, U.K.	Wales	8,019	20,768	2,855,000	356	137	Cardiff	D
Wallis and Futuna (Fr.)	Wallis et Futuna	98	255	15,000	153	59	Mata-Utu	C
Washington, U.S.	Washington	68,139	176,479	4,630,000	68	26	Olympia	D
Western Australia, Austl.	Western Australia	975,101	2,525,500	1,625,000	1.7	0.6	Perth	D
Western Sahara	. . .	102,703	266,000	97,000	0.9	0.4	El Aaiún (Laayone)	. . .
†Western Samoa	Western Samoa (English) / Samoa i Sisifo (Samoan)	1,097	2,842	180,000	164	63	Apia	A
West Virginia, U.S.	West Virginia	24,236	62,771	1,886,000	78	30	Charleston	D
Wisconsin, U.S.	Wisconsin	66,213	171,491	4,828,000	73	28	Madison	D
Wyoming, U.S.	Wyoming	97,808	253,322	494,000	5.1	2.0	Cheyenne	D
†Yemen	Al-Yaman	75,290	195,000	10,110,000	134	52	San'a	A
†Yemen, People's Democratic Republic of	Jumhūrīyat al-Yaman ad-Dīmuqrāṭīyah ash-Sha'bīyah	130,066	336,369	2,551,000	20	7.6	'Adan (Aden)	A
†Yugoslavia	Jugoslavija	98,766	255,804	23,970,000	243	94	Beograd (Belgrade)	A
Yukon Territory, Can.	Yukon Territory	186,661	483,450	24,000	0.1	0.1	Whitehorse	D
Yunnan, China	Yunnan	168,341	436,000	35,580,000	211	82	Kunming	D
†Zaire	Zaïre	905,568	2,345,409	33,795,000	37	14	Kinshasa	A
†Zambia	Zambia	290,586	752,614	7,682,000	26	10	Lusaka	A
†Zimbabwe	Zimbabwe	150,873	390,759	9,003,000	60	23	Harare (Salisbury)	A
WORLD	. . .	57,900,000	149,900,000	5,192,000,000	90	35	. . .	. . .

† Member of the United Nations (1988).
. . . None, or not applicable.
(1) No permanent population.
(2) Bophuthatswana, Ciskei, Transkei, and Venda are not recognized by the United Nations.
(3) Claimed by Argentina.
(4) Includes West Bank, Golan Heights, and Gaza Strip.
(5) Future capital.
(6) Claimed by Comoros.
(7) In October 1966 the United Nations terminated the South African mandate over Namibia, a decision which South Africa did not accept.
(8) Comprises Ceuta, Melilla, and several small islands.

Introduction to the Index

This universal index includes in a single alphabetical list more than 40,000 names of features that appear on the reference maps. Each name is followed by a map-reference key and a page reference.

Names Local official names are used on the maps and in the index. The names are shown in full, including diacritical marks. Features that extend beyond the boundaries of one country and have no single official name are usually named in English. Many conventional English names and former names are cross-referenced to the official names. Names that appear in shortened versions on the maps due to space limitations are spelled out in full in the index. The portions of these names omitted from the maps are enclosed in brackets – for example, Acapulco [de Juárez].

Transliteration For names in languages not written in the Roman alphabet, the locally official transliteration system has been used where one exists. Thus, names in the Soviet Union and Bulgaria have been transliterated according to the systems adopted by the academies of science of these countries. Similarly, the transliteration for mainland Chinese names follows the Pinyin system, which has been officially adopted in mainland China. For languages with no one locally accepted system, notably Arabic, transliteration closely follows a system adopted by the United States Board on Geographic Names.

Abbreviation and Capitalization Abbreviations of names on the maps have been standardized as much as possible. Names that are abbreviated on the maps are generally spelled out in full in the index. Periods are used after all abbreviations regardless of local practice. The abbreviation 'St.' is used only for 'Saint' where it occurs in the British Isles. 'Sankt' and other forms of this term are spelled out.

Most initial letters of names are capitalized, except for generic terms in the Soviet Union and a few Dutch names, such as ''s-Gravenhage'. Capitalization of noninitial words in a name generally follows local practice.

Alphabetization Names are alphabetized in the order of the letters of the English alphabet. Spanish *ll* and *ch*, for example, are not treated as distinct letters. Furthermore, diacritical marks are disregarded in alphabetization–German or Scandinavian *ä* or *ö* are treated as *a* or *o*.

The names of physical features may appear inverted, since they are always alphabetized under the proper, not the generic, part of the name, thus: 'Gibraltar, Strait of ⊔'. Otherwise every entry, whether consisting of one word or more, is alphabetized as a single continuous entity. 'Lakeland,' for example, appears after 'La Crosse' and before 'La Salle.' Names beginning with articles other than 'The' (Le Havre, Den Helder, Al-Qāhirah, As-Suways) are not inverted. Names beginning 'Mc' are alphabetized as though spelled 'Mac,' and names beginning 'St.', 'Ste.' and 'Sainte' as though spelled 'Saint.'

In the case of identical names, towns are listed first, then political divisions, then physical features. Entries that are completely identical (including symbols, discussed below) are distinguished by abbreviations of their official country names. The country abbreviations used for places in the United States, Canada and United Kingdom indicate the state, province or political division in which the feature is located. (See List of Abbreviations below.)

Symbols City and town names are not followed by symbols. The names of all other features are followed by symbols that graphically represent broad categories of features, for example, ∧ for mountain (Everest, Mount ∧). Superior numbers indicate finer distinctions, for example, $\wedge^{1}$ for volcano (Fuji-san $\wedge^{1}$). A complete list of symbols, including those with superior numbers, follows the List of Abbreviations.

All cross-references are indicated by the symbol →.

Map-Reference Keys and Page References The map-reference keys and page references are found in the last two columns of each entry.

Each map-reference key consists of a lowercase letter followed by one or two uppercase letters. Corresponding lowercase letters appear along the sides of the maps. Uppercase letters appear across the top and bottom of the maps.

Map-reference keys for point features, such as towns, cities and mountain peaks, indicate the locations of the symbols. For extensive features, such as countries or mountain ranges, locations are given for the approximate center of the feature. Those for linear features, such as canals and rivers, are given for the position of the name.

The page number generally refers to the map that shows the feature at the best scale. Countries, mountain ranges and other extensive features are usually indexed to maps that both show the features completely and also show them in their relationship to broad areas. Page references to two-page maps always refer to the left-hand page. If a page contains several maps or insets, a lowercase letter identifies the specific map or inset.

List of Abbreviations

	LOCAL NAME	ENGLISH
Ab., Can.	Alberta	Alberta
Afg.	Afghānestān	Afghanistan
Afr.		Africa
Ak., U.S.	Alaska	Alaska
Al., U.S.	Alabama	Alabama
Alg.	Algérie / Djazaïr	Algeria
Am. Sam.	American Samoa / Amerika Samoa	American Samoa
And.	Andorra	Andorra
Ang.	Angola	Angola
Anguilla	Anguilla	Anguilla
Ant.		Antarctica
Antig.	Antigua and Barbuda	Antigua and Barbuda
Ar., U.S.	Arkansas	Arkansas
Arc. O.		Arctic Ocean
Arg.	Argentina	Argentina
Ar. Su.	Al-ʿArabīyah as-Suʿūdīyah	Saudi Arabia
Aruba	Aruba	Aruba
Asia		Asia
Atl. O.		Atlantic Ocean
Austl.	Australia	Australia
Az., U.S.	Arizona	Arizona
Ba.	Bahamas	Bahamas
Bahr.	Al-Baḥrayn	Bahrain
Barb.	Barbados	Barbados
B.A.T.	British Antarctic Territory	British Antarctic Territory
B.C., Can.	British Columbia / Colombie-Britannique	British Columbia
Bdi.	Burundi	Burundi
Bel.	Belgique / België	Belgium
Belize	Belize	Belize
Bénin	Bénin	Benin
Ber.	Bermuda	Bermuda
Ber. S.		Bering Sea
B.I.O.T.	British Indian Ocean Territory	British Indian Ocean Territory
Blg.	Bâlgarija	Bulgaria
Bngl.	Bangladesh	Bangladesh
Bol.	Bolivia	Bolivia
Boph.	Bophuthatswana	Bophuthatswana
Bots.	Botswana	Botswana
Bra.	Brasil	Brazil
B.R.D.	Bundesrepublik Deutschland	Federal Republic of Germany
Bru.	Brunei	Brunei
Br. Vir. Is.	British Virgin Islands	British Virgin Islands
Burkina	Burkina Faso	Burkina Faso
Ca., U.S.	California	California
Cam.	Cameroun / Cameroon	Cameroon
Can.	Canada	Canada
Carib. S.		Caribbean Sea
Cay. Is.	Cayman Islands	Cayman Islands
Centraf.	République centrafricaine	Central African Republic
Česko.	Československo	Czechoslovakia
Chile	Chile	Chile
Christ. I.	Christmas Island	Christmas Island
Ciskei	Ciskei	Ciskei
C. Iv.	Côte d'Ivoire	Ivory Coast
C.M.I.K.	Chosŏn-minjujuŭi-inmīn-konghwaguk	North Korea
Co., U.S.	Colorado	Colorado
Cocos Is.	Cocos (Keeling) Islands	Cocos (Keeling) Islands
Col.	Colombia	Colombia
Comores	Comores / Al-Qumur	Comoros
Congo	Congo	Congo
Cook Is.	Cook Islands	Cook Islands
C.R.	Costa Rica	Costa Rica
Ct., U.S.	Connecticut	Connecticut
Cuba	Cuba	Cuba
C.V.	Cabo Verde	Cape Verde
Dan.	Danmark	Denmark
D.C., U.S.	District of Columbia	District of Columbia
D.D.R.	Deutsche Demokratische Republik	German Democratic Republic
De., U.S.	Delaware	Delaware
Dji.	Djibouti	Djibouti
Dom.	Dominica	Dominica
D.Y.	Druk-Yul	Bhutan
Ec.	Ecuador	Ecuador
Ellás	Ellás	Greece

El Sal.	El Salvador	El Salvador
Eng., U.K.	England	England
Esp.	España	Spain
Europe		Europe
Falk. Is.	Falkland Islands / Islas Malvinas	Falkland Islands
Fiji	Fiji	Fiji
Fl., U.S.	Florida	Florida
Før.	Føroyar	Faeroe Islands
Fr.	France	France
Ga., U.S.	Georgia	Georgia
Gabon	Gabon	Gabon
Gam.	Gambia	Gambia
Ghana	Ghana	Ghana
Gib.	Gibraltar	Gibraltar
Gren.	Grenada	Grenada
Guad.	Guadeloupe	Guadeloupe
Guam	Guam	Guam
Guat.	Guatemala	Guatemala
Guernsey	Guernsey	Guernsey
Gui.-B.	Guiné-Bissau	Guinea-Bissau
Gui. Ecu.	Guinea Ecuatorial	Equatorial Guinea
Guinée	Guinée	Guinea
Guy.	Guyana	Guyana
Guy. fr.	Guyane française	French Guiana
Haï.	Haïti	Haiti
Hi., U.S.	Hawaii	Hawaii
H.K.	Hong Kong	Hong Kong
Hond.	Honduras	Honduras
Ia., U.S.	Iowa	Iowa
Id., U.S.	Idaho	Idaho
I.I.A.	Ittiḥād al-Imārāt al-ʿArabīyah	United Arab Emirates
Il., U.S.	Illinois	Illinois
In., U.S.	Indiana	Indiana
India	India / Bharat	India
Ind. O.		Indian Ocean
Indon.	Indonesia	Indonesia
I. of Man	Isle of Man	Isle of Man
Īrān	Īrān	Iran
ʿIrāq	Al-ʿĪrāq	Iraq
Ire.	Ireland / Éire	Ireland
Ísland	Ísland	Iceland
Isr. Occ.		Israeli Occupied Areas
It.	Italia	Italy
Ityo.	Ityopiya	Ethiopia
Jam.	Jamaica	Jamaica
Jersey	Jersey	Jersey
Jugo.	Jugoslavija	Yugoslavia
J.Y.D.S.	Jumhūrīyat al-Yaman ad-Dīmuqrāṭīyah ash-Shaʿbīyah	People's Democratic Republic of Yemen
Kal. Nun.	Kalaallit Nunaat / Grønland	Greenland
Kam.	Kâmpŭchéa Prâchéathĭpâtéyy	Kampuchea (Cambodia)
Kenya	Kenya	Kenya
Kıbrıs	Kuzey Kıbrıs	North Cyprus
Kípros	Kípros / Kıbrıs	Cyprus
Kiribati	Kiribati	Kiribati
Ks., U.S.	Kansas	Kansas
Kuwayt	Al-Kuwayt	Kuwait
Ky., U.S.	Kentucky	Kentucky
La., U.S.	Louisiana	Louisiana
Lao	Lao	Laos
Leso.	Lesotho	Lesotho
Liber.	Liberia	Liberia
Lībiyā	Lībiyā	Libya
Liech.	Liechtenstein	Liechtenstein
Lubnān	Al-Lubnān	Lebanon
Lux.	Luxembourg	Luxembourg
Ma., U.S.	Massachusetts	Massachusetts
Macau	Macau	Macau
Madag.	Madagasikara / Madagascar	Madagascar
Magreb	Al-Magreb	Morocco
Magy.	Magyarország	Hungary
Malaŵi	Malaŵi	Malawi
Malay.	Malaysia	Malaysia
Mald.	Maldives	Maldives
Mali	Mali	Mali
Malta	Malta	Malta
Mart.	Martinique	Martinique
Maur.	Mauritanie / Mūrītāniyā	Mauritania
Maus.	Mauritius	Mauritius
Mayotte	Mayotte	Mayotte

Mb., Can.	Manitoba	Manitoba
Md., U.S.	Maryland	Maryland
Me., U.S.	Maine	Maine
Medit. S.		Mediterranean Sea
Méx.	México	Mexico
Mi., U.S.	Michigan	Michigan
Mid. Is.	Midway Islands	Midway Islands
Miṣr	Miṣr	Egypt
Mn., U.S.	Minnesota	Minnesota
Mo., U.S.	Missouri	Missouri
Moç.	Moçambique	Mozambique
Monaco	Monaco	Monaco
Mong.	Mongol Ard Uls	Mongolia
Monts.	Montserrat	Montserrat
Ms., U.S.	Mississippi	Mississippi
Mt., U.S.	Montana	Montana
Mya.	Myanmā	Burma
N.A.		North America
Namibia	Namibia	Namibia
Nauru	Nauru / Naoero	Nauru
N.B., Can.	New Brunswick / Nouveau-Brunswick	New Brunswick
N.C., U.S.	North Carolina	North Carolina
N. Cal.	Nouvelle-Calédonie	New Caledonia
N.D., U.S.	North Dakota	North Dakota
Ne., U.S.	Nebraska	Nebraska
Ned.	Nederland	Netherlands
Ned. Ant.	Nederlandse Antillen	Netherlands Antilles
Nepāl	Nepāl	Nepal
Nf., Can.	Newfoundland / Terre-Neuve	Newfoundland
N.H., U.S.	New Hampshire	New Hampshire
Nic.	Nicaragua	Nicaragua
Nig.	Nigeria	Nigeria
Niger	Niger	Niger
Nihon	Nihon	Japan
N. Ire., U.K.	Northern Ireland	Northern Ireland
Niue	Niue	Niue
N.J., U.S.	New Jersey	New Jersey
N.M., U.S.	New Mexico	New Mexico
Nor.	Norge	Norway
Norf. I.	Norfolk Island	Norfolk Island
N.S., Can.	Nova Scotia / Nouvelle-Écosse	Nova Scotia
N.T., Can.	Northwest Territories / Territoires du Nord-Ouest	Northwest Territories
Nv., U.S.	Nevada	Nevada
N.Y., U.S.	New York	New York
N.Z.	New Zealand	New Zealand
Oc.		Oceania
Oh., U.S.	Ohio	Ohio
Ok., U.S.	Oklahoma	Oklahoma
On., Can.	Ontario	Ontario
Or., U.S.	Oregon	Oregon
Öst.	Österreich	Austria
Pa., U.S.	Pennsylvania	Pennsylvania
Pac. O.		Pacific Ocean
Pāk.	Pākistān	Pakistan
Pan.	Panamá	Panama
Pap. N. Gui.	Papua New Guinea	Papua New Guinea
Para.	Paraguay	Paraguay
P.E., Can.	Prince Edward Island / Île-du Prince-Édouard	Prince Edward Island
Perú	Perú	Peru
Pil.	Pilipinas	Philippines
Pit.	Pitcairn	Pitcairn
Pol.	Polska	Poland
Poly. fr.	Polynésie française	French Polynesia
Port.	Portugal	Portugal
P.Q., Can.	Québec	Quebec
P.R.	Puerto Rico	Puerto Rico
P.S.N.Á.	Plazas de Soberanía en el Norte de África	Spanish North Africa
Qaṭar	Qaṭar	Qatar
Rep. Dom.	República Dominicana	Dominican Republic
Réu.	Réunion	Reunion
R.I., U.S.	Rhode Island	Rhode Island
Rom.	România	Romania
Rw.	Rwanda	Rwanda
S.A.		South America
S. Afr.	South Africa / Suid-Afrika	South Africa
S.C., U.S.	South Carolina	South Carolina

S. Ch. S.		South China Sea
Schw.	Schweiz / Suisse / Svizzera	Switzerland
Scot., U.K.	Scotland	Scotland
S.D., U.S.	South Dakota	South Dakota
Sén.	Sénégal	Senegal
Sey.	Seychelles	Seychelles
Shq.	Shqīpëri	Albania
Sing.	Singapore	Singapore
Sk., Can.	Saskatchewan	Saskatchewan
S.L.	Sierra Leone	Sierra Leone
S. Lan.	Sri Lanka	Sri Lanka
S. Mar.	San Marino	San Marino
Sol. Is.	Solomon Islands	Solomon Islands
Som.	Somaliya	Somalia
S.S.S.R.	Sojuz Sovetskich Socialističeskich Respublik	Union of Soviet Socialist Republics
St. C.-N.	St. Christopher and Nevis	St. Christopher and Nevis
St. Hel.	St. Helena	St. Helena
St. Luc.	St. Lucia	St. Lucia
S. Tom./P.	São Tomé e Príncipe	Sao Tome and Principe
St. P./M.	Saint-Pierre-et-Miquelon	St. Pierre and Miquelon
St. Vin.	St. Vincent and the Grenadines	St. Vincent and the Grenadines
Sūd.	As-Sūdān	Sudan
Suomi	Suomi / Finland	Finland
Sur.	Suriname	Surinam
Sūrīy.	As-Sūrīyah	Syria
Sve.	Sverige	Sweden
Swaz.	Swaziland	Swaziland
T.a.a.f.	Terres australes et antarctiques françaises	French Southern and Antarctic Territories
Taehan	Taehan-min'guk	South Korea
T'aiwan	T'aiwan	Taiwan
Tan.	Tanzania	Tanzania
Tchad	Tchad	Chad
T./C. Is.	Turks and Caicos Islands	Turks and Caicos Islands
Thai	Prathet Thai	Thailand
Tn., U.S.	Tennessee	Tennessee
Togo	Togo	Togo
Tok.	Tokelau	Tokelau
Tonga	Tonga	Tonga
Transkei	Transkei	Transkei
Trin.	Trinidad and Tobago	Trinidad and Tobago
T.T.P.I.	Trust Territory of the Pacific Islands	Trust Territory of the Pacific Islands
Tun.	Tunisie / Tunis	Tunisia
Tür.	Türkiye	Turkey
Tuvalu	Tuvalu	Tuvalu
Tx., U.S.	Texas	Texas
Ug.	Uganda	Uganda
U.K.	United Kingdom	United Kingdom
ʿUmān	ʿUmān	Oman
Ur.	Uruguay	Uruguay
Urd.	Al-Urdunn	Jordan
U.S.	United States	United States
Ut., U.S.	Utah	Utah
Va., U.S.	Virginia	Virginia
Vanuatu	Vanuatu	Vanuatu
Vat.	Città del Vaticano	Vatican City
Ven.	Venezuela	Venezuela
Venda	Venda	Venda
Viet.	Viet Nam	Vietnam
Vir. Is., U.S.	Virgin Islands (U.S.)	Virgin Islands (U.S.)
Vt., U.S.	Vermont	Vermont
Wa., U.S.	Washington	Washington
Wake I.	Wake Island	Wake Island
Wales, U.K.	Wales	Wales
Wal./F.	Wallis et Futuna	Wallis and Futuna
Wi., U.S.	Wisconsin	Wisconsin
W. Sah.		Western Sahara
W. Sam.	Western Samoa / Samoa i Sisifo	Western Samoa
W.V., U.S.	West Virginia	West Virginia
Wy., U.S.	Wyoming	Wyoming
Yaman	Al-Yaman	Yemen
Yis.	Yisra'el / Isrā'īl	Israel
Yk., Can.	Yukon Territory	Yukon Territory
Zaïre	Zaïre	Zaire
Zam.	Zambia	Zambia
Zhg.	Zhongguo	China
Zimb.	Zimbabwe	Zimbabwe

Key to Symbols

Λ Mountain	⊁ Cape	±⁴ Cliff	c Bay, Gulf	⊤³ Anchorage	□⁴ Province, Region, Oblast	⊥ Historical Site
Λ¹ Volcano	⊁¹ Peninsula	±⁵ Cave, Caves	c¹ Estuary	⊤⁴ Oasis, Well, Spring	□⁵ Department, District, Prefecture	✦ Recreational Site
Λ² Hill	⊁² Spit, Sand Bar	±⁶ Crater	c² Fjord			⊠ Airport
⊀ Mountains	I Island	±⁷ Depression	c³ Bight	✦ Submarine Features	□⁶ County	✦ Military Installation
⊀¹ Plateau	I¹ Atoll	±⁸ Dunes	⌀ Lake, Lakes	✦¹ Depression	□⁷ City, Municipality	
⊀² Hills	I² Rock	±⁹ Lava Flow	⌀¹ Reservoir	✦² Reef, Shoal	□⁸ Miscellaneous	✦ Miscellaneous
)(Pass	II Islands	≃ River	⊞ Swamp	✦³ Mountain, Mountains	□⁹ Historical	✦¹ Region
	II¹ Rocks	≃¹ River Channel		✦⁴ Slope, Shelf		✦² Desert
V Valley, Canyon	⊥ Other Topographic Features	≊ Canal	⊠ Ice Features, Glacier		Political Unit	✦³ Forest, Moor
≃ Plain	⊥¹ Continent	≊¹ Aqueduct	⊤ Other Hydrographic Features	□ Independent Nation	℣ Cultural Institution	✦⁴ Reserve, Reservation
≃¹ Basin	⊥² Coast, Beach	L Waterfall, Rapids	⊤¹ Ocean	□¹ Dependency	℣¹ Religious Institution	✦⁵ Transportation
≃² Delta	⊥³ Isthmus	ц Strait	⊤² Sea	□² State, Canton, Republic	℣² Educational Institution	✦⁶ Dam
				□³	℣³ Scientific, Industrial Facility	✦⁷ Mine, Quarry
						✦⁸ Neighborhood

Index

Name | Map Ref. | Page

Allenstein → Olsztyn b T 80
Allentown g K 146
Allentsteig g O 80
Alleppey h D 116
Aller ≃ c I 80
Allerton j B 148
Allgäu ◆¹ h J 80
Allgäuer Alpen ⋏ e Q 84
Alliance, Ne., U.S. i E 156
Alliance, Oh., U.S. g E 146
Al-Lidām d D 117
Allier □⁵ f I 84
Allier ≃ f J 84
Alligator ≃ d J 150
Allinge n N 76
Al-Lisān >¹ f D 120
Allison h C 148
Alliston f P 148
Al-Līth d B 117
Alloa e J 78
Allora g I 184
Allouez f G 148
Al-Luḥayyah g C 117
Allumette Lake ⊜ e R 148
Allyn c C 160
Alma, N.B., Can. g I 144
Alma, P.Q., Can. d B 144
Alma, Ar., U.S. g B 152
Alma, Ga., U.S. h D 150
Alma, Ks., U.S. I K 156
Alma, Mi., U.S. g K 148
Alma, Ne., U.S. k H 156
Alma, Wi., U.S. f D 148
Alma-Ata i M 92
Alma Center f E 148
Almada g B 86
Almadén g G 86
Al-Madīnah (Medina) b A 117
Al-Mafraq d F 120
Al-Maḥallah al-Kubrā g D 118
Almalyk i K 92
Al-Manāmah a G 117
Almansa g J 86
Al-Manshāh i D 118
Al-Manṣūrah g D 118
Al-Manzilah g D 118
Almanzor ∧ e F 86
Al-Marāghah i D 118
Al-Marj b E 126
Almas, Pico das ∧ b H 177
Al-Maṭarīyah g E 118
Al-Mawṣil (Mosul) d J 118
Al-Mayādīn e I 118
Almeida e E 86
Almeirim f C 86
Almelo d J 82
Almena I H 156
Almenara d H 177
Almendralejo g E 86
Almería i I 86
Almería, Golfo de c i I 86
Al'metjevsk g H 92
Al-Minyā h D 118
Almira c G 160
Almirante h L 168
Al-Mismīyah b F 120
Almo h L 160
Almodôvar h C 86
Almond f F 148
Almont h L 148
Almonte, On., Can. e S 148
Almonte, Esp. h E 86
Almora f H 114
Al-Mubarraz j M 118
Al-Muglad f F 126
Al-Muḥarraq a G 117
Al-Mukallā g F 117
Al-Mukhā (Mocha) h C 117
Al-Muwayliḥ i F 118
Alnwick f L 78
Alor, Pulau I g G 108
Alor Setar k F 110
Alosno h D 86
Alost (Aalst) g E 82
Alpaugh i F 162
Alpena, Ar., U.S. f C 152
Alpena, Mi., U.S. e L 148
Alpena, S.D., U.S. g I 156
Alpes-de-Haute-Provence □⁵ h M 84
Alpes Maritimes □⁵ i N 84
Alpha, Austl. d G 184
Alpha, Il., U.S. i E 148
Alpha, Mi., U.S. d G 148
Alpharetta e B 150
Alphen aan den Rijn d F 82
Alpiarça f C 86
Alpine, Az., U.S. k G 158
Alpine, Ca., U.S. I I 162
Alpine, Tx., U.S. i C 154
Alps ⋏ f J 74
Al-Qaḍārif f H 126
Al-Qāhirah (Cairo) g D 118
Al-Qāmishlī d I 118
Al-Qaryah ash-Sharqīyah b C 126
Al-Qaryatayn e G 118
Al-Qaṣr j C 118
Al-Qaṭīf i N 118
Al-Qaṭrūn d C 126
Al-Qayṣūmah h L 118
Al-Qunayṭirah b E 120
Al-Qunayṭirah □⁸ c E 120
Al-Qunfudhah e B 117
Al-Qurnah g L 118
Al-Quṣayr i F 118
Al-Qūṣīyah i D 118
Al-Quṭayfah a G 120
Alsace □⁹ d N 84
Alsea f B 160
Alsea ≃ f B 160
Alsen c I 156
Alsfeld e I 80
Alta, Nor. g R 76
Alta, Ia., U.S. i L 156
Alta Gracia, Arg. f F 178
Altagracia, Ven. i I 170
Altai ⋏ b D 100
Altaj (Jesönbulag) b F 100
Altamaha ≃ h E 150
Altamira, Bra. d H 174
Altamira, Chile c D 178
Altamont, Il., U.S. c H 152
Altamont, Ks., U.S. n L 156
Altamont, Or., U.S. h D 160
Altamont, Tn., U.S. g K 152
Altamura i K 88
Altar b D 166
Altar, Desierto de ◆² b C 166
Altata e F 166
Alta Verapaz □⁵ b D 168
Alta Vista, Ks., U.S. m K 156
Altavista, Va., U.S. b G 150
Altay b D 100
Altdorf e J 83
Altenburg e L 80
Altentreptow b M 80
Alter do Chão f D 86
Altha i A 150
Altheimer h E 152
Althofen i N 80
Altiplano ⋏¹ g E 174
Altkirch e N 84
Altmark □⁹ c K 80
Altmühl ≃ f J 80
Alto h K 154
Alto Araguaia d B 177
Altomünster g K 80
Alton, Eng., U.K. j M 78
Alton, Il., U.S. d F 152
Alton, Ia., U.S. i K 156
Alton, Ks., U.S. I I 156
Alton, Mo., U.S. f E 152
Alton, N.H., U.S. d O 146
Altona i Q 142
Altoona, Al., U.S. h J 152
Altoona, Ia., U.S. i B 148
Altoona, Ks., U.S. n L 156
Altoona, Pa., U.S. g H 146
Altoona, Wi., U.S. f D 148
Alto Parnaíba e I 174
Alto Río Senguerr f B 176
Altötting g L 80
Altstätten, Öst. b D 88
Altstätten, Schw. d L 83
Altuchovo i Q 96
Altun Shan ⋏ d D 100
Alturas c E 162
Altus, Ar., U.S. g C 152
Altus, Ok., U.S. e G 154
Al-'Ubaylah d G 117
Al-Ubayyiḍ f G 126
Al-Uḍayyah f F 126
Alūksne d J 96
Alum Rock g D 162
Alunda k P 76
Al-'Uqaylah b D 126
Al-Uqṣur (Luxor) j E 118
Al-'Uwaynāt c C 126
Alva c H 154
Alvaiázere f C 86
Älvängen m M 76
Alvarado, Méx. h L 166
Alvarado, Tx., U.S. g I 154
Álvaro Obregón, Presa ⊜¹ d E 166
Alvdal j L 76
Älvdalen k N 76
Alvear e J 178
Alverca g B 86
Alvesta m N 76
Alvin j K 154
Alvito g D 86
Älvkarleby k O 76
Alvord f I 154
Älvros j N 76
Älvsborgs Län □⁶ I M 76
Älvsbyn i Q 76
Al-Wajh i G 118
Alwar g G 114
Al-Wāsiṭah h D 118
Alxa Zuoqi d H 100
Alytus g G 96
Alzamaj f K 94
Alzey f H 80
Alzira (Alcira) f K 86
Amadeus, Lake ⊜ d F 182
Amadjuak Lake ⊜ c R 134
Amagansett g N 146
Amagasaki m J 106
Amagi n E 106
Amakusa-nada ⊤² o D 106
Amakusa-shotō II o E 106
Amakuso-Shimo-shima I o E 106
Åmål I M 76
Amalāpuram d G 116
Amalfi, Col. b C 174
Amalfi, It. i I 88
Amaliás I E 90
Amalner j F 114
Amambaí b K 178
Amambay, Cordillera de ⋏ b K 178
Amami-Ō-shima I s D 107b
Amami-shotō II t C 107b
Amana i D 148
Amanda h D 146
Amapá c H 174
Amarante e J 174
Amarapura d D 110
Amareleja g D 86
Amares d C 86
Amargosa ≃ h I 162
Amargosa Range ⋏ h I 162
Amarillo d E 154
Amarkantak g C 100
Amasa d G 148
Amasya b F 118
Amatikulu g J 130
Amatique, Bahía de c b F 168
Amay g G 82
Amazon (Solimões) (Amazonas) ≃ d G 174
Ambāla e G 114
Ambalavao r V 131b
Ambanja n W 131b
Ambarčik d X 94
Ambargasta, Salinas de ≚ e F 178
Ambarnāth c B 116
Ambāsamudram h D 116
Ambato d C 174
Ambatolampy q V 131b
Ambatondrazaka p W 131b
Amber g F 114
Amberg, B.R.D. f K 80
Amberg, Wi., U.S. e H 148
Ambérieu-en-Bugey g L 84
Ambikāpur i J 114
Ambilobe n W 131b
Amble f O 78
Ambodifototra p W 131b
Amboina → Ambon f H 108
Amboise e G 84
Ambon f H 108
Ambositra r V 131b
Ambovombe t V 131b
Amboy, Il., U.S. i F 148
Amboy, Mn., U.S. g A 148
Ambre, Cap d' > m W 131b
Ambridge g F 146
Ambrières d F 84
Ambriz c B 128
Ambrose c D 156
Ambrosia Lake i I 158
Ambrym I q Y 188f
Ambunti f K 108
Āmbūr f E 116
Amchitka Island I k D 139a
Amderma d J 92
Amdo e E 100
Ameagle b E 150
Ameca g G 166
Amecameca [de Juárez] h J 166
Ameland I b H 82
Amelia g G 88
Amelia Court House b I 150
Amelia Island I i E 150
Americana g E 177
American Falls h M 160
American Falls Reservoir ⊜¹ h M 160
American Fork d E 158
American Highland ⋏¹ c E 189
American Samoa □² e J 180
Americus, Ga., U.S. g B 150
Americus, Ks., U.S. m K 156
Amersfoort, Ned. d G 82
Amersfoort, S. Afr. f I 130
Amery e C 148
Amery Ice Shelf ⌓ b E 189
Ames h B 148
Amesbury e P 146
Ámfissa k F 90
Amga ≃ e R 94
Amgun' ≃ g S 94
Amherst, N.S., Can. g I 144
Amherst, Ma., U.S. e N 146
Amherst, N.Y., U.S. e H 146
Amherst, Oh., U.S. f D 146
Amherst, Tx., U.S. e D 154
Amherst, Va., U.S. b G 150
Amherst, Wi., U.S. f F 148
Amherstburg h L 148
Amherstdale j E 146
Amherstview f S 148
Amidon e D 156
Amiens c I 84
Amīndīvi Islands II g B 116
Amirante Islands II c J 128
Amistad Reservoir (Presa de la Amistad) ⊜¹ j E 154
Amite I F 152
Amite ≃ I F 152
Amity, Ar., U.S. h C 152
Amity, Or., U.S. e B 160
Åmli I K 76
Amlwch h I 78
'Ammān e E 120
Ämmänsaari i U 76
Ammarnäs i O 76
Ammon g N 160
Ammonoosuc ≃ c O 146
Amne Machin Shan → A'nyêmaqên Shan ⋏ d F 100
Amnicon ≃ d D 148
Amnok-kang (Yalu) ≃ c M 102
Amo ≃ g M 114
Āmol d O 118
Amorgós I m I 90
Amory i H 152
Amos b Q 148
Åmot I K 76
Amoy → Xiamen k G 104
Ampanihy t U 131b
Amparo g E 177
Amposta e L 86
Amqui d F 144
Amrāvati j G 114
Amreli j D 114
Amriswil c K 83
Amritsar e F 114
Amroha f H 114
Åmsele i P 76
Amsteg e J 83
Amstelveen d F 82
Amsterdam, Ned. d F 82
Amsterdam, S. Afr. f J 130
Amsterdam, N.Y., U.S. e L 146
Amsterdam, Île I I K 190
Amsterdam-Rijnkanaal ≅ e G 82
Amstetten g N 80
Am Timan f E 126
Amu Darya (Amudarja) ≃ i J 92
Amundsen Gulf c b H 134
Amundsen-Scott ʋ³ d J 189
Amundsen Sea ⊤² c K 189
Amuntai f F 108
Amur (Heilong) ≃ g S 94
Anabar ≃ c N 94
'Anabtā d D 120
Anacoco k C 152
Anaconda d M 160
Anacortes b C 160
Anadarko d H 154
Anadyr' e AA 94
Anadyr' ≃ e Z 94
Anadyrskij zaliv c e BB 94
Anadyrskoje ploskogorje ⋏¹ d Z 94
Anagni h H 88
'Ānah e I 118
Anaheim k H 162
Anáhuac, Méx. c F 166
Anahuac, Tx., U.S. j L 154
Ānai Mudi ∧ g D 116
Anakāpalle d G 116
Analalava o V 131b
Ana María, Golfo de c d E 170
Anambas, Kepulauan II m I 110
Anamoose d G 156
Anamosa h D 148
Anamur d E 118
Anamur Burnu > d E 118
Anan n I 106
Ānand i E 114
Anantapur e D 116
Anantnāg (Islāmābād) d F 114
Anápolis d D 177
Anastasia Island I j E 150
Anatolia □⁹ c F 118
Anatom I s Y 188f
Añatuya e G 178
Anauá ≃ c F 174
Anawalt b E 150
Anbanjing c F 110
Anbu I E 104
Anbyŏn d O 102
Ancaster g O 148
Anchang e I 104
Anchorage f T 138
Anchor Point g S 138
Anci (Langfang) d D 102
Anciferovo c Q 96
Ancona f H 88
Ancud e B 176
Ancud, Golfo de c e B 176
Anda b L 100
Andalgalá d E 178
Åndalsnes j J 76
Andalucía □⁴ h G 86
Andalucía □⁹ h G 86
Andalusia k J 152
Andaman Islands II h B 110
Andaman Sea ⊤² i C 110
Andamooka h B 184
Andapa o W 131b
Andeer e K 83
Andelot d L 84
Andenes g O 76
Andenne h G 82
Anderlecht g E 82
Andermatt e J 83
Andernach e G 80
Anderson, Al., U.S. h I 152
Anderson, Ca., U.S. d C 162
Anderson, In., U.S. b K 152
Anderson, Mo., U.S. f B 152
Anderson, S.C., U.S. e D 150
Anderson, Tx., U.S. i K 154
Anderson ≃ b DD 138
Anderson Dam g J 160
Andes ⋏ g H 172
Andhra Pradesh □³ d E 116
Andijk c G 82
Andikíthira I n G 90
Andimákhia m K 90
Andīmeshk f M 118
Ándissa j I 90
Andižan i L 92
Andkhvoy b A 114
Andong g P 102
Andorra c M 86
Andorra □¹ g H 74
Andover, Eng., U.K. j L 78
Andover, Me., U.S. c P 146
Andover, Ma., U.S. e O 146
Andover, N.Y., U.S. e I 146
Andover, Oh., U.S. f F 146
Andover, S.D., U.S. f J 156
Andøya I g N 76
Andradina f C 177
Andreanof Islands II j F 138
Andreapol' e O 96
Andrejevo f X 96
Andrew d V 140
Andrews, In., U.S. b K 152
Andrews, N.C., U.S. d C 150
Andrews, S.C., U.S. f G 150
Andrews, Tx., U.S. g D 154
Andria h K 88
Andriamena p V 131b
Androka t U 131b
Andropov (Rybinsk) c U 96
Ándros I I H 90
Androscoggin ≃ c P 146
Andros Island I b F 170
Androth Island I g B 116
Andrychów f S 80
Andújar g G 86
Anécho g G 124
Anegada I e L 170
Anegada Passage ʊ e M 170
Anegam I D 158
Aneta d J 156
Aneto, Pico de ∧ c L 86
Anfeng, Zhg. b I 104
Anfeng, Zhg. c I 104
Anfu h C 104
Angamos, Punta > b C 178
Ang'angxi b K 100
Angara ≃ f Q 92
Angarsk g L 94
Ånge j N 76
Ángel, Salto (Angel Falls) ʟ b F 174
Ángel de la Guarda, Isla I c C 166
Angeles n S 109b
Angel Falls → Ángel, Salto ʟ b F 174
Ängelholm m M 76
Angelina ≃ k B 152
Angels Camp f E 162
Ångermanälven ≃ j O 76
Angermünde b N 80
Angers e F 84
Angerville d I 84
Angicos e K 174
Angier d H 150
Angkor, Ruines d' ⊥ h G 110
Ângk Tasaôm i H 110
Anglalinghu ⊜ e J 114
Angle Inlet b L 156
Anglesey I h I 78
Angleton j K 154
Angmagssalik c Y 134
Angoche e G 128
Angoche, Ilha I e G 128
Angol i B 178
Angola, In., U.S. a L 152
Angola, N.Y., U.S. e G 146
Angola □¹ d C 128
Angola Basin ⊹¹ j G 122
Angoon h AA 138
Angora → Ankara c E 118
Angoram f K 108
Angostura e E 166
Angostura, Presa de la ⊜¹ i M 166
Angoulême g G 84
Angoumois □⁹ g F 84
Angra dos Reis g F 177
Angren i L 92
Anguilla j F 152
Anguilla □² e M 170
Angul b H 116
Anguo e C 102
Angus f P 148
Angwin f C 162
Anhai k G 104
Anholt I m L 76
Anhui (Anhwei) □⁴ e J 100
Aniak f O 138
Animas m H 158
Animas ≃ h I 158
Animas Peak ∧ m H 158
Anina d E 90
Anita j M 156
Anjan j M 76
Anjangaon b D 116
Anjār i D 114
Anji e H 104
Anjou □⁹ e F 84
Anju d M 102
Ankang e H 100
Ankara c E 118
Ankaratra ⋏ q V 131b
Ankarsrum m O 76
Ankavandra q U 131b
Ankazoabo s U 131b
Ankazobe q V 131b
Ankeny i B 148
Anklam b M 80
Anklesvar b B 116
Ankober g H 126
An-loc i I 110
Anlu d B 104
Anmyŏn-do I g N 102
Ann, Cape > b D 189
Anna, Il., U.S. e G 152
Anna, Tx., U.S. f J 154
Anna, Lake ⊜¹ a I 150
Annaba (Bône) a H 124
Annaberg-Buchholz e M 80
An-Nabk e G 118
An-Nafūd ◆² h I 118
An-Najaf g K 118
Annamitique, Chaîne ⋏ f I 110
Annan g J 78
Annandale, Austl. c H 184
Annandale, Mn., U.S. e A 148
Annapolis i J 146
Annapolis Royal h H 144
Annapurna ∧ f J 114
Ann Arbor h L 148
An-Nāṣirīyah g L 118
An-Nazlah e B 120
Annecy g M 84
Annemasse f M 84
Annette i CC 138
An-nhon h J 110
Anniston i K 152
Annobón I b A 128
Annonay g K 84
An-Nuhūd f F 126
Annville, Ky., U.S. b C 150
Annville, Pa., U.S. g J 146
Anoka e B 148
Anopino f W 96
Anori d F 174
Anping d D 102
Anqing e F 104
Anqiu g G 102
Ans g H 82
Ansbach f J 80
Anselmo j H 156
Anshan b J 102
Anshun a H 110
Ansley j H 156
Anson g G 154
Ansŏng f O 102
Ansongo e G 124
Ansonville d F 150
Ansted i E 146
Antakya (Antioch) d G 118
Antalaha o X 131b
Antalya d D 118
Antalya Körfezi (Gulf of Antalya) c d D 118
Antananarivo q V 131b
Antarctica ⊥¹ d E 189
Antarctic Peninsula >¹ b L 189
Antelope Island I d D 158
Antelope Peak ∧ c K 162
Antequera h G 86
Anthon i L 156
Anthony, Fl., U.S. j D 150
Anthony, Ks., U.S. n I 156
Anthony, N.M., U.S. I J 158
Anthony, Tx., U.S. m J 158
Anti-Atlas ⋏ b E 124
Antibes i N 84
Anticosti, Île d' I c J 144
Antigo e F 148
Antigonish g L 144
Antigua and Barbuda □¹ f N 170
Antiguo Morelos f J 166
Anti-Lebanon → Sharqī, Al-Jabal ash- ⋏ a F 120
Antilla d G 170
Antimony f E 158
Antioch → Antakya, Tür. d G 118
Antioch, Il., U.S. h G 148
Antioquia b C 174
Antipodes Islands II h I 180
Antlers e K 154
Antofagasta b C 178
Antofagasta □⁴ b D 178
Antofalla, Salar de ≚ c E 178
Antofalla, Volcán ∧¹ c E 178
Anton f D 154
Anton Chico i K 158
Antongila, Helodrano c o W 131b
Antonina c N 178
Antonio Amaro e G 166
Antonito g J 158
Antopol' i G 96
Antrain d E 84
Antrim g G 78
Antrodoco g H 88
Antsirabe, Madag. o W 131b
Antsirabe, Madag. q V 131b
Antsiranana n W 131b
Anttis h R 76
Antwerp → Antwerpen f E 82
Antwerp f B 146
Antwerpen (Anvers) f E 82
Antwerpen □⁴ f F 82
An Uaimh h G 78
Anuradhapura h F 116
Anvers (Antwerpen) f E 82
Anvers Island I b L 189
Anvik e N 138
Anxi, Zhg. c F 100
Anxi, Zhg. j G 104
Anxin e C 102
Anyang, Taehan f N 102
Anyang, Zhg. g B 102
A'nyêmaqên Shan ⋏ d F 100
Anyi g D 104
Anykščiai f H 96
Anyuan h B 104
Anžero-Sudžensk f O 92
Anzhen d I 104
Anzhou e C 102
Anzin b J 84
Anzio h G 88
Aoba I p X 188f
Aoga-shima I e N 100
Aohan Qi (Xinhui) a G 102
Aoji a R 102
Aojiang h I 104
Aomori g O 106
Aóös (Vijosë) ≃ j D 90
A'opo a A 188a
Aôral, Phnum ∧ h H 110
Aosta d B 88
Aouk, Bahr ≃ g E 126
Aoukâr ◆¹ e E 124
Aozou d D 126
Apa ≃ b J 178
Apache e H 154
Apache Junction k E 158
Apache Peak ∧ m F 158
Apalachicola j B 150
Apalachicola ≃ i A 150
Apalachicola Bay c j A 150
Apaporis ≃ d D 174
Aparri I S 109b
Apaseo el Grande g I 166
Apatin d B 90
Apatity d D 92
Apatzingán [de la Constitución] h H 166
Apaxtla de Castrejón h J 166
Apeldoorn d H 82
Apex d H 150
Api ∧ f I 114
Apia a B 188a
Apiacás, Serra dos ⋏¹ f G 174
Apizaco h J 166
Apizolaya e H 166
Apo, Mount ∧ d H 108
Apolakkiá m K 90
Apolda d K 80
Apolima Strait ʊ a A 188a
Apollo g G 146
Apolo f E 174
Aporé ≃ g H 174
Apostle Islands II d E 148
Apóstoles d K 178
Apozolco g G 166
Appalachia c D 150
Appalachian Mountains ⋏ c K 136
Äppelbo k N 76
Appennino (Apennines) ⋏ f G 88
Appenzell d K 83
Appenzell-Ausser Rhoden □³ d K 83
Appingedam b J 82
Apple ≃, U.S. h E 148
Apple ≃, Wi., U.S. e C 148
Appleby g K 78
Applegate ≃ b B 162
Appleton, Mn., U.S. f K 156
Appleton, Wi., U.S. f G 148
Appleton City d B 152
Apple Valley j H 162
Appling f D 150
Appomattox b H 150
Appomattox ≃ b H 150
Aprelevka f T 96
Apt i L 84
Apucarana b M 178
Apure ≃ b E 174
Apurímac ≃ f D 174
Aqaba, Gulf of c h F 118
Aquidauana h G 174
Aquila, Méx. h H 166
Aquila, Schw. e J 83
Aquiles Serdán c G 166
Aquilla h I 154
Arab h J 152
'Arab, Baḥr al- ≃ g F 126
Arab, Shatt al- ≃ g M 118
Arabako □⁴ c I 86
Arabi m F 152
Arabian Basin ⊹¹ h G 98
Arabian Desert → Sharqīyah, Aṣ-Ṣaḥrā' ash- ◆² c G 126
Arabian Peninsula >¹ g E 98
Arabian Sea ⊤² f H 112
Araçá ≃ c F 174
Aracaju f K 174
Aracati d K 174
Araçatuba f C 177
Aracena h E 86
Aracruz e H 177
Araçuaí d G 177
Arad c E 90
Arad □⁶ c E 90
Arafura Sea ⊤² d E 180
Aragarças c B 177
Aragon e A 150
Aragón □⁴ d H 86
Aragón ≃ c J 86
Araguacema e I 174
Aragua de Barcelona j L 170
Araguaia ≃ e I 174
Araguari e D 177
Araguari ≃ c I 174
Araguatins e I 174
Ârak, Alg. c G 124
Arāk, Īrān e M 118
Arakan Yoma ⋏ e C 110
Aral Sea → Aral'skoje more ⊤² h J 92
Aral'sk h J 92
Aral'skoje more (Aral Sea) ⊤² h J 92
Aramac d F 184
Aramac ≃ d F 184
Aramberri e J 166
Ārān e N 118
Aranda de Duero d H 86
Arandas g H 166
Aranđelovac e D 90
Ārani f E 116
Aran Islands II h D 78
Aranjuez e H 86
Aransas ≃ k I 154
Aransas Pass I I 154
Aranyaprathet h G 110
Arao o E 106
Araouane e F 124
Arapaho d H 154
Arapahoe k H 156
Arapawa Island I h I 186
Arapiraca e K 174
Arapongas b M 178
'Ar'ar g I 118
Araranguá e N 178
Araraquara f D 177
Araras b O 178
Ararat k E 184
Ararat, Mount → Ağrı Dağı ∧ c K 118
Áratos h I 90
Aratuípe b I 177
Arauca b D 174
Arauca ≃ b E 174
Arauco i B 178
Arauco, Golfo de c i B 178
Arauquita b D 174
Arāvalli Range ⋏ h E 114
Araxá e E 177
Arba Minch g H 126
Arboga I N 76
Arbois f L 84
Arbon c K 83
Arborg h Q 142
Arbroath e K 78
Arbuckle e C 162
Arc, Bayou des ≃ g E 152
Arcachon h E 84
Arcade, Ca., U.S. j G 162
Arcade, N.Y., U.S. e H 146
Arcadia, Ca., U.S. j G 162
Arcadia, Fl., U.S. I E 150
Arcadia, In., U.S. b J 152
Arcadia, Ia., U.S. i L 156
Arcadia, Ks., U.S. n M 156
Arcadia, La., U.S. j D 152
Arcadia, Mi., U.S. f I 148
Arcadia, Mo., U.S. e F 152
Arcadia, Ne., U.S. j H 156
Arcadia, Pa., U.S. g H 146
Arcadia, S.C., U.S. e E 150
Arcadia, Wi., U.S. f D 148
Arcanum h B 146
Arcata d A 162
Arc Dome ∧ f H 162
Arcelia h I 166
Archangel'sk e F 92
Archbold f B 146
Archdale d G 150
Archer j D 150
Archer City f H 154
Archipovka e X 96
Arcidosso g F 88
Arco g L 160
Arco de Baúlhe d D 86
Arcola, Il., U.S. c H 152
Arcola, Ms., U.S. i F 152
Arcos de la Frontera i F 86
Arcot f E 116
Arcoverde e K 174
Arctic Bay b O 134
Arctic Ocean ⊤¹ a A 132
Arctic Red ≃ c BB 138
Arctic Village b V 138
Arḍ, Ra's al- > h M 118
Arda ≃ h I 90
Ardabīl c M 118
Ardahan b J 118
Ardakān f O 118
Årdalstangen k J 76
Ardatov f Z 96
Ardèche □⁵ h K 84
Ardee h G 78
Arden f D 162
Arden, Mount ∧ i B 184
Ardennes □⁵ c K 84
Ardennes ◆¹ e E 80
Ardez e M 83
Ardila ≃ g D 86
Ardlethan j G 184
Ardlussa e H 78
Ardmore, Al., U.S. h J 152
Ardmore, Ok., U.S. e I 154
Ardmore, Pa., U.S. g K 146
Ardoch f F 184
Åre j M 76
Arecibo e K 170
Areia Branca d K 174
Arena, Punta > f E 166
Arena de la Ventana, Punta > e E 166
Arendal I K 76
Arendonk f G 82
Arequipa g D 174
Arezzo f F 88
Argadargada c B 184
Arganda e H 86
Argelès-Gazost i G 84
Argelès-sur-Mer j J 84
Argenta, It. e F 88
Argenta, Il., U.S. c H 152
Argentan d F 84
Argentat g H 84
Argentera ∧ e B 88
Argentina □¹ c D 176
Argentine Basin ⊹¹ i J 172
Argentino, Lago ⊜ g B 176
Argeș □⁶ e H 90
Argeș ≃ e I 90
Arghandāb ≃ d B 114
Argonia n J 156
Argonne e G 148
Argonne ◆¹ c L 84
Árgos, Ellás I F 90
Argos, In., U.S. a J 152
Argostólion k D 90
Argun' (Ergun) ≃ g P 94
Argyle c K 156
Argyle, Lake ⊜¹ c E 182
Århus m L 76
Ariano Irpino h J 88
Arica, Chile g D 174
Arica, Col. d D 174
Arichat g L 144
Arid, Cape > f D 182
Arida m J 106
Ariège □⁵ j H 84
Arīḥā (Jericho) e D 120
Arikaree ≃ I E 156
Arima i N 170
Arinos ≃ f G 174
Arinthod f L 84
Ario de Rosales h I 166
Ariogala f F 96
Aripuanã ≃ e F 174
Ariquemes e F 174
'Arīsh, Wādī al- V g E 118
Arista, Méx. j M 166
Arista, Méx. f I 166
Ariton k K 152
Arizaro, Salar de ≚ c E 178
Arizgoiti b I 86
Arizona h F 178
Arizona □³ e D 136
Arizpe b D 166
Årjäng I M 76
Arjay c C 150
Arjeplog h O 76
Arkadelphia h C 152
Arkalyk g K 92
Arkansas □³ d H 136
Arkansas ≃ d H 136
Arkansas City, Ar., U.S. i E 152
Arkansas City, Ks., U.S. n J 156
Arklow i G 78
Arkoma g B 152
Arkona, Kap > a M 80
Arkonam f E 116
Arkport e I 146
Arktičeskij, mys > a K 94
Arktičeskogo Instituta, ostrova II b N 92
Arlbergpass)(d M 83
Arlberg-Tunnel ◆⁵ d M 83
Arlee c K 160
Arles i K 84
Arlington, S. Afr. g H 130
Arlington, Ga., U.S. h B 150
Arlington, Ia., U.S. h D 148
Arlington, Ks., U.S. n I 156
Arlington, Ky., U.S. f G 152
Arlington, Mn., U.S. f A 148
Arlington, Ne., U.S. j K 156
Arlington, Oh., U.S. g C 146
Arlington, Or., U.S. e E 160
Arlington, S.D., U.S. g J 156
Arlington, Tn., U.S. g G 152
Arlington, Tx., U.S. g I 154
Arlington, Vt., U.S. d M 146
Arlington, Va., U.S. i I 146
Arlington, Wa., U.S. b C 160
Arlington Heights h H 148
Arlon (Aarlen) i H 82
Arma n M 156
Armada h M 148
Armageddon → Tel Megiddo ⊥ c D 120
Armagh g G 78
Armagnac □⁹ i G 84
Arm'anskaja Sovetskaja Socialističeskaja Respublika □³ i F 92
Armant j E 118
Armavir h F 92
Armenia c C 174
Armenia → Arm'anskaja Sovetskaja Socialističeskaja Respublika □³ i F 92
Armentières b I 84
Armería h H 166
Armidale h I 184
Armijo i J 158
Armona h F 162
Armour h I 156
Armstrong, B.C., Can. g O 140
Armstrong, Ia., U.S. h M 156
Armstrong, Mo., U.S. c D 152
Armstrong, Mount ∧ e BB 138
Armstrong Station f O 134
Arnaud ≃ e R 134
Arnaudville I E 152
Arnay-le-Duc e K 84
Årnes k L 76
Arnett c G 154
Arnhem e H 82
Arnhem, Cape > b G 182
Arnhem Land ◆¹ b F 182
Árnissa i E 90
Arno ≃ f E 88
Arno Bay i B 184
Arnold, Ca., U.S. f E 162
Arnold, Mn., U.S. d C 148
Arnold, Mo., U.S. d F 152
Arnold, Ne., U.S. j G 156
Arnolds Park h L 156
Arnoldstein i M 80
Arnprior e S 148
Arnsberg d H 80
Arnstadt e J 80
Aroab f D 130
Arolsen d I 80

Symbols in the index are identified on page 198.

Symbols in the index are identified on page 198.

Name	Map Ref.	Page

Symbols in the index are identified on page 198.

Name	Map Ref.	Page
Boydton	c H	150
Boyer ≃	j L	156
Boyertown	g K	146
Boykins	c I	150
Boyle, Ire.	h E	78
Boyle, Ms., U.S.	i F	152
Boylston	j J	152
Boyne ≃, Austl.	e I	184
Boyne ≃, Ire.	h G	78
Boyne City	e J	148
Boynton	d K	154
Boynton Beach	e F	150
Boysen Reservoir ⊜[1]	g Q	160
Boys Ranch	d D	154
Bozel	g M	84
Bozeman	e N	160
Bozen → Bolzano	c F	88
Bozhen	e D	102
Bozoum	b D	126
Bra	g F	82
Brabant □[4]	g F	82
Brabant Island I	b L	189
Brač, Otok I	f K	88
Bracciano	g G	88
Bracciano, Lago di ≃	g G	88
Bracebridge	e P	148
Bräcke	j N	76
Brackendale	h K	140
Brackettville	j F	154
Brackley	i L	78
Brad	c F	90
Bradenton	I D	150
Bradford, On., Can.	f P	148
Bradford, Eng., U.K.	h L	78
Bradford, Ar., U.S.	g E	152
Bradford, Il., U.S.	i F	148
Bradford, Oh., U.S.	g B	146
Bradford, Pa., U.S.	f H	146
Bradford, Tn., U.S.	f H	152
Bradford, Vt., U.S.	d N	146
Bradley, Ar., U.S.	i C	152
Bradley, Fl., U.S.	I E	150
Bradley, Il., U.S.	i H	148
Bradley, S.D., U.S.	k J	156
Bradshaw, Ne., U.S.	k J	156
Bradshaw, W.V., U.S.	b E	150
Brady, Mt., U.S.	b N	160
Brady, Ne., U.S.	j G	156
Brady, Tx., U.S.	h G	154
Braga	d C	86
Bragado	h H	178
Bragança, Bra.	d I	174
Bragança, Port.	d E	86
Bragança Paulista	b O	178
Braham	B	148
Brähmanbāria	i N	114
Brähmani ≃	j K	114
Brahmaputra (Yaluzangbujiang) ≃	g O	114
Braich y Pwll ⊁	i I	78
Braidwood, Austl.	j H	184
Braidwood, Il., U.S.	i G	148
Bräila	d K	90
Bräila □[6]	d K	90
Brainard	j J	156
Braine-l'Alleud (Eigenbrakel)	g E	82
Braine-le-Comte ('s-Gravenbrakel)	g E	82
Brainerd	d A	148
Braintree	j N	78
Brake	b H	80
Braman	c I	154
Brampton	g P	148
Bramsche	c G	80
Branchville	f F	150
Branco ≃	e B	174
Brandberg ʌ	c B	130
Brandbu	k L	76
Brandenburg, D.D.R.	c L	80
Brandenburg, Ky., U.S.	d J	152
Brandenburg □[9]	c M	80
Brand-Erbisdorf	e M	80
Brandfort	g H	130
Brandon, Mb., Can.	I O	142
Brandon, Fl., U.S.	I D	150
Brandon, Ms., U.S.	j G	152
Brandon, S.D., U.S.	h K	156
Brandon, Vt., U.S.	d M	146
Brandon, Wi., U.S.	h E	148
Brandvlei	h E	130
Brandýs nad Labem	e N	80
Branford	d J	150
Braniewo	a S	80
Bransby	g E	184
Bransfield Strait ⌣	b L	189
Brańsk, Pol.	c V	80
Br'ansk, S.S.S.R.	h Q	96
Branson	g O	152
Brantford	g O	148
Brant Lake	d M	146
Brantley	k J	152
Brantville	e I	144
Branxholme	k D	184
Bras d'Or Lake ⊜	g M	144
Brasília	f E	174
Brasília	c E	177
Braşov	d I	90
Braşov □[6]	d H	90
Brasschaat	f E	82
Brasstown Bald ʌ	e C	150
Bratislava	g Q	80
Bratsk	f L	94
Bratskoje vodochranilišče ⊜[1]	f R	92
Brattleboro	e N	146
Braunau [am Inn]	g M	80
Braunlage	d J	80
Braunschweig (Brunswick)	c J	80
Brava I	f B	124
Brava, Costa ≃[2]	d O	86
Brave	f F	150
Bravo del Norte (Rio Grande) ≃	f F	136
Brawley	i J	162
Brawley Peaks ⚹	f G	162
Bray	h G	78
Braymer	c C	152
Brazeau	e R	140
Brazeau, Mount ʌ	e Q	140
Brazil	c I	152
Brazil (Brasil) □[1]	f H	174
Brazil Basin ⚹[1]	j K	192
Brazoria	j K	154
Brazos ≃	j H	154
Brazzaville	b C	128
Brčko	e B	90
Brea	k H	162
Breadalbane	d C	184
Breaux Bridge	d E	150
Brécey	e K	84
Brechin	e K	78
Breckenridge, Co., U.S.	e J	158
Breckenridge, Mi., U.S.	g K	148
Breckenridge, Mn., U.S.	e K	156
Breckenridge, Mo., U.S.	c C	152
Breckenridge, Tx., U.S.	g H	154
Břeclav	g P	80
Brecon	j J	78
Brecon Beacons National Park ◆	j J	78
Breda, Ned.	e F	82
Breda, Ia., U.S.	i M	156
Bredasdorp	j E	130
Bredstedt	a H	80
Bree	f H	82
Breë ≃	j E	130
Breese	d G	152
Breezand	c F	82
Bregenz	h I	80
Breguzzo	c E	88
Bréhal	d E	84
Breidafjördur c	b B	76a
Breisach	g G	80
Brejo	d J	174
Brekken	j L	76
Brekstad	j K	76
Bremen, B.R.D.	b H	80
Bremen, Ga., U.S.	f A	150
Bremen, In., U.S.	a J	152
Bremen, Oh., U.S.	h D	146
Bremerhaven	b H	80
Bremerton	c C	160
Bremervörde	b I	80
Bremond	h J	154
Brenham	i J	154
Brenner Pass ⋊	h K	80
Brent, Al., U.S.	j I	152
Brent, Fl., U.S.	I I	152
Brentwood, Eng., U.K.	j N	78
Brentwood, N.Y., U.S.	g M	146
Brentwood, Tn., U.S.	g I	152
Brescia	c J	88
Breslau → Wrocław	d Q	80
Bressanone	c F	88
Bresse ≃[1]	f L	84
Brest, Fr.	d B	84
Brest, S.S.S.R.	c W	80
Bretagne (Brittany) □[9]	d C	84
Breteuil	c I	84
Breteuil-sur-Iton	d G	84
Breton Islands II	m G	152
Breton Sound ⌣	m G	152
Brett, Cape ⊁	b I	186
Bretten	f H	80
Breukelen	d G	82
Brevard	d D	150
Breves	d H	174
Brewarrina	g A	184
Brewer	c R	146
Brewster, Ks., U.S.	I F	156
Brewster, Mn., U.S.	h L	156
Brewster, Ne., U.S.	j H	156
Brewster, Oh., U.S.	g G	146
Brewster, Wa., U.S.	b Q	132
Brewster, Kap ⊁	b Q	132
Brewster, Lake ⊜	g I	184
Brewton	k I	152
Breyten	f J	130
Brežice	d J	88
Brezno	g S	80
Bria	g E	126
Briançon	h M	84
Brian Head ʌ	g D	158
Bricelyn	g B	148
Briceville	c B	150
Bricquebec	c E	84
Bridge City	I C	152
Bridgend	j J	78
Bridgeport, On., Can.	g O	148
Bridgeport, Al., U.S.	h K	152
Bridgeport, Ca., U.S.	f F	162
Bridgeport, Ct., U.S.	f M	146
Bridgeport, Il., U.S.	d I	152
Bridgeport, Ne., U.S.	j D	156
Bridgeport, Tx., U.S.	g H	154
Bridgeport, Wa., U.S.	b Q	132
Bridgeport, W.V., U.S.	h F	146
Bridgeport, Lake ⊜[1]	f I	154
Bridger	e Q	160
Bridgeton	h K	146
Bridgetown, Austl.	f C	182
Bridgetown, Barb.	I O	170
Bridgetown, N.S., Can.	h H	144
Bridgeville	i K	146
Bridgewater, Austl.	n G	184
Bridgewater, N.S., Can.	h I	144
Bridgewater, Me., U.S.	f F	144
Bridgewater, Ma., U.S.	f P	146
Bridgewater, S.D., U.S.	h J	156
Bridgewater, Va., U.S.	i H	146
Bridgman	i I	148
Bridgnorth	c P	146
Bridgton	c D	146
Bridgwater	j J	78
Bridlington	g M	78
Bridport	k K	78
Brie ≃	d J	84
Briec	d B	84
Brienne-le-Château	d K	84
Brienz	e I	83
Brienzersee ≃	c L	83
Briey	c L	84
Brig	i I	83
Briggs	i I	154
Brigham City	c D	158
Bright	k G	184
Brighton, On., Can.	f R	148
Brighton, Eng., U.K.	k M	78
Brighton, Co., U.S.	e L	158
Brighton, Il., U.S.	c F	152
Brighton, Ia., U.S.	i D	156
Brighton, Mi., U.S.	h L	148
Brighton, N.Y., U.S.	d I	146
Brighton Downs	d D	184
Brightwater	d H	186
Brignoles	e T	84
Brigus	e T	144
Brikama	h I	152
Brilliant	h I	152
Brillion	d H	148
Brilon	c H	80
Brindisi	h E	88
Brinkley	h E	152
Briouze	d F	84
Brisbane	f J	184
Bristol, Eng., U.K.	I G	152
Bristol, Ct., U.S.	f N	146
Bristol, Fl., U.S.	i O	150
Bristol, N.H., U.S.	d D	146
Bristol, Pa., U.S.	g L	146
Bristol, R.I., U.S.	f O	146
Bristol, S.D., U.S.	f J	156
Bristol, Tn., U.S.	c D	150
Bristol, Vt., U.S.	d M	146
Bristol Bay c	c C	138
Bristol Channel ⌣	j I	78
Bristol Lake ⊜	i J	162
Bristow	c C	154
Britânia	c C	177
Britannia Range ⚹	d H	189
British Antarctic Territory ⊡	I	192
British Columbia □[4]	f G	134
British Honduras → Belize □[1]	i O	166
British Indian Ocean Territory	i K	190
British Isles II	c L	70
Brits	e H	130
Britstown	h F	130
Britt	f B	148
Brittany → Bretagne □[9]	d C	84
Britton	f J	156
Brive-la-Gaillarde	g H	84
Brixham	g H	78
Brixton	d F	184
Brno	f P	80
Broach	j E	114
Broad ≃	e E	150
Broadalbin	d L	146
Broadback ≃	f Q	134
Broadford	d H	78
Broad Sound ⌣	d H	184
Broadus	f B	156
Broadview	h L	142
Broadwater	j E	156
Broadway	i H	146
Brochet	e L	134
Brockport	d I	146
Brockton, Ma., U.S.	e O	146
Brockton, Mt., U.S.	c C	156
Brockville	c K	146
Brockway	f E	146
Brocton	e G	146
Brodeur Peninsula ⊁[1]	b O	134
Brodhead, Ky., U.S.	b B	150
Brodhead, Wi., U.S.	h F	148
Brodick	f H	78
Brodnax	c H	150
Brodnica	b S	80
Brogan	f H	160
Broglie	c G	84
Broken Arrow	c K	154
Broken Bay c	i I	184
Broken Bow, Ne., U.S.	j H	156
Broken Bow, Ok., U.S.	i K	156
Broken Bow Lake ⊜[1]	h B	152
Broken Hill, Austl.	h D	184
Broken Hill → Kabwe, Zam.	b H	174
Brokopondo	b O	174
Bromptonville	b O	146
Bromsgrove	i K	78
Brønderslev	m K	76
Bronkhorstspruit	e I	130
Bronnicy	f U	96
Brønnøysund	i M	76
Bronson, Fl., U.S.	j D	150
Bronson, Ks., U.S.	n L	156
Bronson, Mi., U.S.	i J	148
Bronson, Tx., U.S.	k B	152
Bronte, It.	l I	88
Bronte, Tx., U.S.	h F	154
Bronwood	h B	150
Brook	b I	152
Brookeland	k B	152
Brooker	j D	150
Brookfield, N.S., Can.	h I	144
Brookfield, Mo., U.S.	c C	152
Brookfield, Wi., U.S.	g G	148
Brookford	d E	150
Brookhaven	k F	152
Brookings, Or., U.S.	h A	160
Brookings, S.D., U.S.	f J	156
Brookland	d Q	144
Brooklet	g E	150
Brooklyn, N.S., Can.	h I	144
Brooklyn, Ia., U.S.	i C	148
Brooklyn, Mi., U.S.	h K	148
Brooklyn, Ms., U.S.	k G	152
Brooklyn Center	e B	148
Brooklyn Park	e B	148
Brookneal	b H	150
Brookport	e H	152
Brooks, Ab., Can.	g W	140
Brooks, Me., U.S.	c Q	146
Brooks, Mount ʌ	e S	138
Brookshire	j K	154
Brooks Range ⚹	c P	138
Brooksville, Fl., U.S.	k D	150
Brooksville, Ky., U.S.	i B	146
Brooksville, Ms., U.S.	i I	152
Brookton	f C	182
Brookville, In., U.S.	b B	150
Brookville, Pa., U.S.	f G	146
Brookville Lake ⊜[1]	b B	150
Broome	e K	158
Broomfield	d D	184
Brooms	d D	184
Brooten	f L	156
Brora	c J	78
Broughty Ferry	e K	78
Brouwersdam ⫩[6]	e D	82
Brouwershaven	e D	82
Browerville	e M	156
Brown City	g M	148
Brown Deer	g G	148
Brownfield	f D	154
Browning, Mo., U.S.	b C	152
Browning, Mt., U.S.	b L	160
Brownlee Reservoir ⊜[1]	h F	160
Brownsburg, P.Q., Can.	b L	146
Brownsburg, In., U.S.	c J	152
Brownsdale	g G	148
Brownstown, Il., U.S.	d G	152
Brownstown, In., U.S.	d K	152
Browns Valley	f K	156
Brownsville, Ky., U.S.	s J	152
Brownsville, Or., U.S.	f C	160
Brownsville, Tn., U.S.	g G	152
Brownsville, Tx., U.S.	m I	154
Brownton	f A	148
Brownville, Al., U.S.	i H	152
Brownville, Me., U.S.	b Q	146
Brownville, Ne., U.S.	k L	156
Brownville Junction	b Q	146
Brownwood	h H	154
Browse Island I	b D	182
Bruay-en-Artois	b I	84
Bruce, Ms., U.S.	i G	152
Bruce, S.D., U.S.	g K	156
Bruce, Wi., U.S.	e E	148
Bruce, Mount ʌ	h U	142
Bruce Mines	i C	148
Bruce Peninsula ⊁[1]	e N	148
Bruce Peninsula National Park ◆	e N	148
Bruchsal	f H	80
Bruck [an der Grossglocknerstrasse]	h L	80
Bruck an der Leitha	h O	80
Bruck an der Mur	h O	80
Brückeberg	d V	140
Bruderheim	f C	83
Bruges (Brugge)	f C	82
Brugg	c K	83
Brugge (Bruges)	f C	82
Brugge-Gent, Kanaal	f C	82
Brühl	e F	80
Bruinisse	e E	82
Bruin Point ʌ	e F	158
Brule	j F	156
Brule ≃	e G	148
Brûlé, Lac ⊜	f T	134
Brumado	c H	177
Brumath	d N	84
Brummen	d I	82
Brumunddal	k L	76
Brundidge	k K	152
Bruneau	h J	160
Bruneau ≃	h J	160
Brunei ≃	e B	108
Brunei □[1]	e B	108
Brunflo	j N	76
Brunkeberg	I K	76
Bruno	f I	142
Brunsbüttel	b I	80
Brunson	g E	150
Brunssum	g H	82
Brunswick → Braunschweig, B.R.D.	c J	80
Brunswick, Ga., U.S.	h E	150
Brunswick, Me., U.S.	d Q	146
Brunswick, Md., U.S.	h I	146
Brunswick, Mo., U.S.	c C	152
Brunswick, Oh., U.S.	f E	146
Brunswick, Peninsula ⊁[1]	g B	176
Bruntál	f Q	80
Brus, Laguna de c	b J	168
Brush	k D	156
Brus Laguna	b J	168
Brusque	d N	178
Brussels → Bruxelles	g E	82
Brussels	g N	148
Bruthen	k G	184
Bruxelles (Brussel) (Brussels)	g E	82
Bruyères	d M	84
Bryan, Oh., U.S.	f B	146
Bryan, Tx., U.S.	i J	154
Bryansk → Br'ansk	h Q	96
Bryant, Ar., U.S.	h D	152
Bryant, S.D., U.S.	g J	156
Bryce Canyon National Park ◆	g D	158
Bryson, P.Q., Can.	b J	146
Bryson City	f H	150
Bryson City	d C	150
Brzeg	e Q	80
Brzesko	f T	80
Brzeziny	d S	80
Bua Yai	g G	110
Buayan	f O	108
Bubaque	f C	124
Bübüyän I	h M	118
Bublitz → Bobolice	b P	80
Bubus, Bukit ʌ	k F	110
Bucaramanga	b D	174
Buccaneer Archipelago II	c D	182
Buccino	i J	88
Buchanan, Liber.	g D	124
Buchanan, Ga., U.S.	f A	150
Buchanan, Mi., U.S.	i I	148
Buchanan, Va., U.S.	b G	150
Buchanan, Lake c	f F	184
Buchanan, Lake ⊜[1]	i H	154
Buchans	d Q	144
Bucharest → Bucureşti	e J	90
Buchen	f I	80
Buchholz	b I	80
Buchloe	g J	80
Buchs, Schw.	d I	83
Buchs, Schw.	d K	83
Buchy	c H	84
Buckatunna	k H	152
Bückeburg	c I	80
Buckeye	k D	158
Buckeye Lake	h D	146
Buckhannon	i F	146
Buckhaven	e J	78
Buckholts	i I	154
Buckingham, P.Q., Can.	b K	146
Buckingham, Va., U.S.	b H	150
Buckingham Bay c	b G	182
Buckinghamshire □[6]	j M	78
Buckland	d N	138
Bucklands	d H	184
Buckley, Il., U.S.	j G	148
Buckley, Wa., U.S.	c C	160
Buckley ≃	c H	184
Bucklin, Ks., U.S.	n H	156
Bucklin, Mo., U.S.	c C	152
Bucksport	c R	146
Buctouche	f I	144
Bucureşti (Bucharest)	e J	90
Bucyrus	g D	146
Bud	j J	76
Buda, Il., U.S.	i F	148
Buda, Tx., U.S.	i I	154
Budapest	h S	80
Búdardalur	b C	76a
Budaun	f H	114
Buddh Gaya	e K	112
Bude, Eng., U.K.	k I	78
Bude, Ms., U.S.	k F	152
Büdingen	e I	80
Budir	b G	76a
Budogošč'	b O	96
Buea	i H	124
Buena Esperanza	g G	178
Buenaventura, Col.	c F	174
Buenaventura, Méx.	c F	166
Buena Vista, Bol.	g F	177
Buena Vista, Co., U.S.	f J	158
Buena Vista, Ga., U.S.	g B	150
Buena Vista, Ms., U.S.	i H	152
Buena Vista, Va., U.S.	b G	150
Buenavista	h F	108
Buena Vista Lake Bed ≃[1]	i E	162
Buenos Aires, Arg.	h K	174
Buenos Aires, C.R.	h K	168
Buenos Aires □[5]	h J	174
Buenos Aires, Lago (Lago General Carrera) ≃	f B	176
Buffalo, Ks., U.S.	n L	156
Buffalo, Mn., U.S.	e B	148
Buffalo, Mo., U.S.	d D	152
Buffalo, N.Y., U.S.	d H	146
Buffalo, Oh., U.S.	h E	146
Buffalo, Ok., U.S.	c E	154
Buffalo, S.C., U.S.	e E	150
Buffalo, S.D., U.S.	d D	156
Buffalo, Tx., U.S.	h J	154
Buffalo, Wy., U.S.	g U	160
Buffalo ≃, Can.	d H	134
Buffalo ≃, Mn., U.S.	d K	156
Buffalo ≃, Ms., U.S.	k E	152
Buffalo ≃, Tn., U.S.	f D	152
Buffalo ≃, Wi., U.S.	f D	148
Buffalo Center	g B	148
Buffalo Lake	g M	156
Buffalo Narrows	c F	142
Buford	e B	150
Bug ≃	e L	74
Buga	c C	174
Buggenhout	f E	82
Bugojno	e L	88
Bugøynes	g U	76
Bugt	b K	100
Bugul'ma	g H	92
Buguruslan	g H	92
Buhl, Id., U.S.	h K	160
Buhl, Mn., U.S.	c C	148
Buhler	m J	156
Buhuşi	c J	90
Builth Wells	i J	78
Buin, Chile	g E	150
Buin, Pap. N. Gui.	i N	188e
Buir Nuur ≃	b J	100
Buitenpost	b I	82
Buj	c X	96
Bujalance	h G	86
Bujnaksk	i G	92
Bujumbura	b E	128
Buka Island I	h N	188e
Bukama	c E	128
Bukavu	b E	128
Bukittinggi	o F	110
Bükkoba	b F	128
Bukovina □[9]	b I	90
Bukoba	b F	128
Bukittinggi	g B	176
Bulacan ≃	n S	109b
Bülach	c J	83
Bulan, Pil.	o F	109b
Bulan, Ky., U.S.	c C	150
Bulandshahr	f G	114
Bulawayo	c I	130
Bulgan, Mong.	b E	100
Bulgan, Mong.	b G	100
Bulgaria (Bãlgarija) □[1]	g M	74
Bulkley ≃	c G	140
Bullard	g J	154
Bullas	g J	86
Buller, Mount ʌ	k G	184
Bullfinch	f C	182
Bullhead	f F	156
Bullhead City	i B	158
Bullion	a F	184
Bulloo ≃	g E	184
Bulls	e Q	80
Bulls Gap	c C	150
Bull Shoals	f D	152
Bull Shoals Lake ⊜[1]	f D	152
Bulsär	j E	114
Bultfontein	g H	130
Bulukumba	g H	108
Bulusan	o U	109b
Bumba	a D	128
Buna	I C	154
Bunavista	d D	152
Bunbury	f C	182
Bunceton	d D	152
Buncrana	f F	78
Bundaberg	e J	184
Bünde	c H	80
Bundi	e I	114
Bundoran	g F	78
Bungay	i O	78
Bungo-suidö c	g F	106
Bungo-takada	n F	106
Bunguran Utara, Kepulauan II	I J	110
Bunia	a E	128
Bunker	e E	152
Bunker Group II	d J	184
Bunker Hill, Il., U.S.	c G	152
Bunker Hill, Or., U.S.	b J	152
Bunker Hill ʌ	I D	162
Bunkie	I D	152
Bunnell	j E	150
Buntok	f F	108
Bura	b G	128
Burang	e C	114
Buras	n G	152
Buraydah	i I	118
Burbank, Ca., U.S.	j G	162
Burbank, Wa., U.S.	b D	160
Burco	g I	126
Burdekin ≃	c G	184
Burden	n K	156
Burdett	m H	156
Burdur	d D	118
Burdwän	j K	114
Bureå	c M	76
Bureinskij chrebet ⚹	i O	94
Büren	d H	80
Burfjord	d O	76
Burford	g O	148
Burg	c K	80
Burg [auf Fehmarn]	a K	80
Burg [bei Magdeburg]	c L	80
Burgaw	e I	150
Burgdorf, B.R.D.	c J	80
Burgdorf, Schw.	b L	83
Burgenland □[3]	h P	80
Burgeo	g P	144
Burgersdorp	h H	130
Burgess	b I	150
Burgettstown	g F	146
Burghausen	g L	80
Burghead	d J	78
Burghüth, Sabkhat al-	e I	118
Burgin, Ky., U.S.	m J	152
Burgin, S.D., U.S.	b D	100
Burglengenfeld	f L	80
Burgos, Esp.	c I	86
Burgos, Méx.	e J	166
Burgos □[4]	c I	86
Burgstädt	e L	80
Burgsvik	m P	76
Burgundy → Bourgogne □[9]	e K	84
Burhänpur	j G	114
Burias Island I	o T	109b
Burien	b E	160
Burin	g R	144
Burin Peninsula ⊁[1]	g R	144
Buriram	f F	110
Burjassot	e K	86
Burkburnett	f K	154
Burke	g G	160
Burke ≃	b D	184
Burke Channel ⌣	f G	140
Burkesville	m K	152
Burketown	b D	184
Burkina Faso □[1]	f K	124
Burleson	g K	154
Burley	h L	160
Burlingame, Ca., U.S.	g H	162
Burlingame, Ks., U.S.	m L	156
Burlington, On., Can.	g P	148
Burlington, Co., U.S.	e M	158
Burlington, Ia., U.S.	j D	156
Burlington, Ks., U.S.	m L	156
Burlington, N.J., U.S.	g L	146
Burlington, N.C., U.S.	c G	150
Burlington, N.D., U.S.	c F	156
Burlington, Vt., U.S.	c M	146
Burlington, Wa., U.S.	b C	160
Burlington, Wy., U.S.	f Q	160
Burlington Junction	b A	152
Burma □[1]	a B	108
Burmakino	d W	96
Burnaby	h L	140
Burnet	i H	154
Burnett ≃	e J	184
Burney	d D	162
Burnham	m F	184
Burnley	h K	78
Burns, Ks., U.S.	m K	156
Burns, Or., U.S.	g F	160
Burns, Tn., U.S.	f I	152
Burns, Wy., U.S.	j C	156
Burns Flat	d G	154
Burnside	c E	150
Burnsville, Fl., U.S.	j J	152
Burnsville, Ms., U.S.	h H	152
Burnsville, N.C., U.S.	d D	150
Burnsville, W.V., U.S.	i F	146
Burnt ≃	f H	160
Burnt Island	e O	144
Burntwood ≃	c Q	142
Burra	i C	184
Burragorang, Lake ⊜[1]	c B	184
Burramurra	c B	184
Burravoe	e B	184
Burrel	h D	90
Burrendong Reservoir ⊜[1]	i H	184
Burrinjuck Reservoir ⊜[1]	j H	184
Burr Oak	I I	156
Burro Peak ʌ	I H	158
Burrton	m J	156
Burrwood	n G	152
Burruyacú	d F	178
Bursa	i C	118
Bür Safäjah	j E	118
Bür Sa'íd (Port Said)	f C	118
Bür Südän (Port Sudan)	e H	126
Burt	h M	156
Burt Lake	e K	148
Burton, Eng., U.K.	i L	78
Burton, Mi., U.S.	g L	148
Burton, Tx., U.S.	i I	154
Burtundy	i E	184
Buru I	f H	108
Burundi □[1]	b F	128
Burwash	d O	148
Burwell	j H	156
Burwick	c K	78
Bury	h K	78
Bury Saint Edmunds	i N	78
Busalla	e C	88
Busanga Island I	g J	142
Busayrah	e I	118
Busby	e B	160
Büsehr	h N	118
Bushimaie ≃	c D	128
Bushland	d D	154
Bushman Land □[9]	g D	130
Bushnell, Fl., U.S.	k D	150
Bushnell, Il., U.S.	j E	148
Bushton	m I	156
Busko Zdrój	e T	80
Busra ash-Shäm	c F	120
Busselton	f C	182
Bussey	i C	148
Bussum	d G	82
Bustamante	d I	166
Busto Arsizio	c C	88
Busu-Djanoa	a D	128
Büsum	a H	80
Buta	a D	128
Butare	b E	128
Bute Inlet c	g J	140
Butera	l I	88
Butha Buthe	g I	130
Butha Qi	b K	100
Butler, Al., U.S.	j H	152
Butler, Ga., U.S.	g B	150
Butler, In., U.S.	a L	152
Butler, Mo., U.S.	d B	152
Butler, Oh., U.S.	g D	146
Butler, Pa., U.S.	g G	146
Butte, Mt., U.S.	e M	160
Butte, Ne., U.S.	e H	156
Butte du Lion ⌂	h C	160
Butte Creek ≃	e D	162
Butternut	d E	148
Butterworth, Malay.	I F	110
Butterworth, Transkei	i H	130
Buttonwillow	i F	162
Butuan	e H	108
Butung, Pulau I	g G	108
Butzbach	e I	80
Bützow	b K	80
Buukle	g D	108
Buurgplaatz ʌ	h I	82
Buxtehude	b I	80
Buxton, Eng., U.K.	h L	78
Buxton, N.C., U.S.	e K	150
Buxton, Or., U.S.	d I	148
Buzancy	c K	84
Buzău	e J	90
Buzău □[6]	e J	90
Buzău ≃	d K	90
Buzen	n F	106
Buzuluk	g H	92
Byam Martin Island I	B	134
Bychov	h O	96
Bydgoszcz	b R	80
Byers	h R	154
Byesville	h E	146
Bygdeå	c M	76
Byglandsfjord	I Q	76
Byhalia	h G	152
Bylas	k F	158
Bylot Island I	a O	134
Byng Inlet	e O	148
Byrdstown	c B	150
Byron, Il., U.S.	h F	148
Byron, Wy., U.S.	f Q	160
Byron, Cape ⊁	g J	176
Byron Bay	g J	184
Byrranga, gory ⚹	b L	94
Byske	c M	76
Bystrzyca Kłodzka	e P	80
Bytom (Beuthen)	e R	80
Bytoš'	h Q	96
Bytów	a Q	80
Byxelkrok	m O	76

C

Name	Map Ref.	Page
Ca ≃	e H	110
Caacupé	c J	178
Caaguazú □[5]	c K	178
Caála	d C	128
Caazapá	d J	178
Caazapá □[5]	d J	178
Cabaiguán	e D	170
Caballo Reservoir ⊜[1]	l I	158
Cabanatuan	n S	109b
Cabano	e E	144
Cabedelo	e G	174
Cabeza del Buey	g F	86
Cabimas	a D	174
Cabinda	b C	128
Cabinda □[5]	b C	128
Cable	d D	148
Cabo	d J	174
Cabo Blanco	f C	176
Cabonga, Réservoir ⊜[1]	c S	148
Caboolture	f J	184
Cabora Bassa Dam ◆	e F	128
Cabot	h D	152
Cabot Strait ⌣	g N	144
Cabra	h G	86
Cabramurra	j H	184
Cabrobó	e K	174
Çabuçar	d M	178
Caçador	d M	178
Čačak	f D	90
Caçapava	b P	178
Cacapon ≃	h H	146
Caccamo	l H	88
Cáceres, Bra.	g G	174
Cáceres, Esp.	f E	86
Cache ≃	e H	154
Cache ≃	e G	152
Cache Creek	g M	140
Cache la Poudre ≃	d K	158
Cache Peak ʌ	h L	160
Cachimbo, Serra do ≫	b I	177
Cachoeira	b I	177
Cachoeira do Sul	f L	178
Cachoeira Paulista	g F	177
Cachoeiro de Itapemirim	f H	177
Cacólo	c C	128
Caconda	d C	128
Cactus	c D	154
Cactus Peak ʌ	g I	162
Caçumba, Ilha I	h I	177
Caddo, Ok., U.S.	e J	154
Caddo, Tx., U.S.	g H	154
Caddo ≃	h C	152
Caddo Lake ⊜[1]	j B	152
Caddo Mills	f J	166
Cadereyta Jiménez	e J	166
Cader Idris ʌ	i J	78
Cadillac, Fr.	f J	84
Cadillac, Mi., U.S.	f K	148
Cadiz, Esp.	i E	86
Cadiz, Ky., U.S.	f I	152
Cadiz, Oh., U.S.	g F	146
Cádiz, Golfo de c	i D	86
Cadobeč ≃	f K	94
Cadott	f D	148
Cadwell	h K	150
Caen	c F	84
Caernarfon	h I	78
Caernarfon Bay c	h I	78
Caerphilly	j J	78
Cæsarea → Qesari, Horbat ⌂	c C	118
Caeté	e G	177
Caetité	g G	177
Cafayate	e F	178
Cagayan ≃[4]	I S	109b
Cagayan de Oro	d G	108
Cagayan Islands II	d G	108
Cagli	f G	88
Cagliari	j C	88
Cagliari, Golfo di c	j D	88
Cagnes	j D	84
Çagoda	b R	96
Cagua	a K	170
Caguas	e K	170
Cahaba ≃	j I	152
Caher	i F	78
Cahersiveen	j C	78
Cahokia	c F	152
Cahors	h H	84
Caia ≃	e G	128
Caiabis, Serra dos ≫[1]	b B	177
Caiapó, Serra do ≫	d B	177
Caiapônia	d B	177
Caibarién	c E	170
Cai-bau, Dao I	c D	110
Caicara	d E	174
Caicó	e K	174
Caicos Islands II	d I	170
Caicos Passage ⌣	c I	170
Caimanera	d J	170
Cainsville	b C	152
Caird Coast ≃[2]	b C	192
Cairngorm Mountains ⚹	d J	78
Cairns	a F	184
Cairo → Al-Qāhirah, Mişr	d D	118
Cairo, Ga., U.S.	i B	150
Cairo, Il., U.S.	e G	152
Cairo, Ne., U.S.	j I	156
Cairo, W.V., U.S.	h E	146
Cairo Montenotte	e C	88
Caiundo	d C	128
Cajamarca	c C	174
Cajàzeiras	e K	174
Cajon Summit ⋊	i I	162
Čakovec	c K	88
Cakovice	f K	80
Calabar	h G	124
Calabozo	b E	174
Calabria □[4]	j K	88
Calacoaste	i F	178
Calacuccia	j D	88
Calafat	f E	90
Calahorra	c J	86
Calais, Fr.	b H	84
Calais, Me., U.S.	b S	146
Calais, Pas de (Strait of Dover) ⌣	I O	78
Calama	a D	178
Calamar	b D	174
Calamian Group II	c F	108
Calamus ≃	j H	156
Calañas	h E	86
Calang	l O	109b
Calapan	n S	109b
Calarasi	s O	90
Calatafimi	l G	88
Calatayud	d J	86
Calau	d M	80
Calavite Passage ⌣	n S	109b
Calbayog	c H	108
Calbe	d K	80
Calcasieu ≃	l D	152
Calcasieu Lake ⌣	m C	152
Calchaquí	e H	178

Symbols in the index are identified on page 198.

Name	Map Ref.	Page
Calçoene	c H	174
Calcutta	i M	114
Caldaro	c F	88
Caldas da Rainha	f B	86
Caldera	d C	178
Caldwell, Id., U.S.	g I	160
Caldwell, Ks., U.S.	n J	156
Caldwell, Oh., U.S.	h E	146
Caldwell, Tx., U.S.	i J	154
Caledon ≃	h H	130
Caledonia, N.S., Can.	h H	144
Caledonia, On., Can.	g P	148
Caledonia, Mn., U.S.	g D	148
Caledonia, Ms., U.S.	i H	152
Caledonia, N.Y., U.S.	e I	146
Caledonia, Oh., U.S.	g D	146
Calella	d N	86
Calera, Esp.	o W	87b
Calera, Al., U.S.	i J	152
Calera, Ok., U.S.	f J	154
Caleta del Sebo	n AA	87b
Calexico	l J	162
Calfkiller ≃	f K	152
Calf of Man I	g I	78
Calfpasture ≃	i G	146
Calgary	f T	140
Calhan	l C	156
Calheta	m T	87a
Calhoun, Al., U.S.	j J	152
Calhoun, Ga., U.S.	e B	150
Calhoun, Ky., U.S.	e I	152
Calhoun, Mo., U.S.	d C	152
Calhoun, Tn., U.S.	d B	150
Calhoun City	i G	152
Calhoun Falls	e D	150
Cali	c C	174
Calico Rock	f D	152
Calicut	g C	116
Caliente	g K	162
California, Mo., U.S.	d D	152
California, Pa., U.S.	g G	146
California □³	d B	136
California, Golfo de ⊂	d D	166
California Aqueduct ≃¹	h E	162
Calimere, Point >	g E	116
Calion	i D	152
Calipatria	k J	162
Calispell Peak ∧	b H	160
Calistoga	f C	162
Calitri	i J	88
Calitzdorp	i E	130
Callabonna, Lake ⊜	g D	184
Callac	d C	84
Callaghan, Mount ∧	e I	162
Callahan	i E	150
Callan	i F	78
Callander, On., Can.	d P	148
Callander, Scot., U.K.	e I	78
Callanna	g B	184
Callantsoog	c F	82
Callao	f C	174
Callaway	j H	156
Calliham	k H	154
Callosa de Segura	g K	86
Calmar, Ab., Can.	d U	140
Calmar, Ia., U.S.	g D	148
Caloosahatchee ≃	m E	150
Caloundra	f J	184
Calp	g L	86
Caltagirone	l I	88
Caltanissetta	l I	88
Calumet, Mi., U.S.	c G	148
Calumet, Mn., U.S.	c B	148
Calumet City	a I	152
Calunda	d D	128
Caluula	f K	126
Calvados □⁵	c F	84
Calvert, Al., U.S.	k H	152
Calvert, Tx., U.S.	i J	154
Calvi	l W	85a
Calvia	f N	86
Calvillo	g H	166
Calvin	e I	154
Calvinia	h D	130
Calw	g H	80
Calwa	h F	162
Calypso	d H	150
Camabatela	c B	128
Camacho	e H	166
Camacupa	d C	128
Camagüey	d F	170
Camaiore	f E	88
Camaná	g D	174
Camanche	i E	148
Camaquã	f M	178
Camará	d F	174
Camargue ✦¹	i K	84
Camarillo	j F	162
Camarines Norte □⁴	n T	109b
Camarines Sur □⁴	o T	109b
Camarón, Cabo >	a I	168
Camarones	e C	176
Camas	h E	86
Ca-mau → Quan-long	j H	110
Cambay	i E	114
Cambodia → Kampuchea □¹	c D	108
Camboon	e I	184
Camborne	k H	78
Cambrai	b J	84
Cambria, Ca., U.S.	i D	162
Cambria, Wi., U.S.	g F	148
Cambrian Mountains ↗	i J	78
Cambridge, On., Can.	g O	148
Cambridge, N.Z.	d J	186
Cambridge, Eng., U.K.	i N	78
Cambridge, Id., U.S.	f I	160
Cambridge, Il., U.S.	i E	148
Cambridge, Ia., U.S.	i B	148
Cambridge, Md., U.S.	i J	146
Cambridge, Ma., U.S.	e O	146
Cambridge, Mn., U.S.	e B	148
Cambridge, Ne., U.S.	k G	156
Cambridge, N.Y., U.S.	d M	146
Cambridge, Oh., U.S.	g E	146
Cambridge Bay	c K	134
Cambridge City	c K	152
Cambridgeshire □⁶	i M	78
Cambridge Springs	f F	146
Cambundi-Catembo	d C	128
Camden, Austl.	j I	184
Camden, Al., U.S.	k I	152
Camden, Ar., U.S.	i D	152
Camden, De., U.S.	h K	146
Camden, Me., U.S.	c G	146
Camden, Ms., U.S.	j G	152
Camden, N.J., U.S.	h K	146
Camden, N.Y., U.S.	d K	146
Camden, N.C., U.S.	c J	150
Camden, Oh., U.S.	h B	146
Camden, S.C., U.S.	e F	150
Camden, Tn., U.S.	f H	152
Camdenton	d D	152
Cameron, La., U.S.	m C	152
Cameron, Mo., U.S.	c B	152
Cameron, S.C., U.S.	f F	150
Cameron, Tx., U.S.	i J	154
Cameron, W.V., U.S.	h F	146
Cameron, Wi., U.S.	e D	148
Cameron Highlands	l F	110
Cameron Hills ↗²	e I	134
Cameroon (Cameroun) □¹	g I	124
Cameroon Mountain ∧	h H	124
Camerota	i J	88
Cametá	d I	174
Camiguin Island I	b G	108
Camiling	n S	109b
Camilla	h B	150
Caminha	d C	86
Camino	f E	162
Camiranga	d I	174
Camiri	h F	174
Camissombo	c D	128
Camocim	d J	174
Camooweal	b C	184
Camorta Island I	j B	110
Campaign	g K	152
Campana	h I	178
Campana, Isla I	f A	176
Campanario	g F	86
Campania □⁴	i I	88
Campbell, S. Afr.	g F	130
Campbell, Ca., U.S.	g D	162
Campbell, Mn., U.S.	e K	156
Campbell, Mo., U.S.	f F	152
Campbell, Ne., U.S.	k I	156
Campbell, Cape >	h I	186
Campbellford	f R	148
Campbell Hill ∧²	g C	146
Campbell Island I	a H	189
Campbellpore	d E	114
Campbell River	g I	140
Campbell's-Bay	d J	146
Campbellsport	g G	148
Campbellsville	e K	152
Campbellton, N.B., Can.	d G	144
Campbellton, Nf., Can.	c S	144
Campbellton, P.E., Can.	f I	144
Campbellton, Fl., U.S.	i A	150
Campbelltown, Austl.	j I	184
Campbell Town, Austl.	m G	184
Campbeltown	f H	78
Camp Douglas	g E	148
Campeche	h N	166
Campeche, Bahía de ⊂	g M	166
Campeche Bank ✦⁴	g J	132
Camperdown	l E	184
Cam-pha	d I	110
Camp Hill, Al., U.S.	j K	152
Camp Hill, Pa., U.S.	g J	146
Campina Grande	e K	174
Campinas	b O	178
Campo	n E	156
Campoalegre	c C	174
Campo Alegre de Goiás	d E	177
Campobasso	h I	88
Campobello Island I	h G	144
Campo Belo	f F	177
Campo de Criptana	f H	86
Campo Gallo	d G	178
Campo Grande	f A	177
Campo Largo	c N	178
Campo Maior, Bra.	d J	174
Campo Maior, Port.	f D	86
Campo Mourão	c L	178
Campos	f H	177
Campos do Jordão	b P	178
Camp Point	b E	152
Campti	k C	152
Campton	b C	150
Camp Verde	j E	158
Camp Wood	j F	154
Cam-ranh	i J	110
Camrose	d V	140
Canaan, Ct., U.S.	e M	146
Canaan, Vt., U.S.	c O	146
Canachal	e F	166
Canada □¹	d M	134
Cañada de Gómez	g H	178
Cañada Honda	f D	178
Canadian	d F	154
Canadian ≃, U.S.	d J	154
Canadian ≃, Co., U.S.	d J	158
Canajoharie	e L	146
Çanakkale	b B	118
Çanakkale Boğazı (Dardanelles) ꓘ	b B	118
Canal Flats	g S	140
Canal Fulton	g E	146
Canal Point	m F	150
Canal Winchester	h D	146
Canandaigua	e I	146
Cananea	b D	166
Canápolis	e D	177
Canarias, Islas (Canary Islands) II	o Y	87b
Canarreos, Archipiélago de los II	d D	170
Canary Islands → Canarias, Islas II	c C	124
Cañas	g I	168
Canaseraga	e I	146
Canastota	d K	146
Canastra, Serra da ↗²	j A	177
Canatlán	e G	166
Canaveral, Cape >	k F	150
Canavieiras	c I	177
Canberra	j H	184
Canby, Ca., U.S.	c E	162
Canby, Mn., U.S.	g K	156
Canby, Or., U.S.	e C	160
Cancale	d E	84
Cancún	g P	166
Cancún, Punta >	g P	166
Candeias	b I	177
Candela	d I	166
Candelária	e L	178
Candia → Iráklion	n I	90
Cándido Aguilar	e J	166
Candle	d N	138
Candlestick	j F	152
Candlewood, Lake ⊜	f M	146
Cando	c H	156
Candor, N.Y., U.S.	e J	146
Candor, N.C., U.S.	d G	150
Candover	f J	130
Cane ≃	k D	152
Canea → Khaniá	n H	90
Canelli	c D	88
Canelones	h J	178
Cañete	h E	176
Caney	n L	156
Caney ≃	c K	154
Cangkuang, Tanjung >	j L	109a
Cangombe	d C	128
Canguçu	f L	178
Cangzhou	e D	102
Caniapiscau ≃	e S	134
Caniapiscau, Lac ⊜	f S	134
Canicatti	l H	88
Canisteo	e I	146
Canisteo ≃	e I	146
Canistota	h J	156
Cañitas de Felipe Pescador	f H	166
Çankırı	b E	118
Canmore	f S	140
Cannanore	g C	116
Cannel City	b C	150
Cannelton	e J	152
Cannes	i N	84
Canning	g I	144
Cannington	f P	148
Cannock	i K	78
Cannon ≃	f B	148
Cannon Ball	e G	156
Cannonball ≃	e G	156
Cannon Beach	e B	160
Cannon Falls	f C	148
Cann River	k H	184
Canoas ≃	d M	178
Canoinhas	d M	178
Canon	e C	150
Canon City	f K	158
Canonsburg	g F	146
Canoochee ≃	g E	150
Canora	g L	142
Canosa [di Puglia]	h K	88
Canossa ⊥	e E	88
Canouan I	h N	170
Canova	h J	156
Canova Beach	k F	150
Canowindra	i H	184
Canso	g L	144
Cantabria □⁴	b G	86
Cantábrica, Cordillera ↗	b F	86
Cantal □⁵	g I	84
Cantanhede	e C	86
Cantaura	j L	170
Canterbury, N.B., Can.	g F	144
Canterbury, Eng., U.K.	j O	78
Canterbury Bight ⊂³	k G	186
Canterbury Plains ≃	k F	186
Can-tho	i H	110
Canton, Ga., U.S.	e B	150
Canton, Il., U.S.	j E	148
Canton, Ks., U.S.	m J	156
Canton, Mn., U.S.	g D	148
Canton, Ms., U.S.	j F	152
Canton, Mo., U.S.	b E	152
Canton, N.Y., U.S.	c K	146
Canton, N.C., U.S.	d D	150
Canton, Oh., U.S.	g E	146
Canton, Ok., U.S.	c H	154
Canton, Pa., U.S.	f J	146
Canton, S.D., U.S.	h K	156
Canton, Tx., U.S.	g K	154
Canton → Guangzhou, Zhg.	l B	104
Canton → Kanton I	d J	180
Canton Lake ⊜¹	c H	154
Cantonment	l I	152
Cantù	d D	88
Cantwell	e T	138
Cañuelas	h I	178
Canutama	e F	174
Canutillo	m J	158
Čany, ozero ⊜	g M	92
Cany-Barville	c G	84
Canyon	e E	154
Canyon City	f G	160
Canyon Ferry Lake ⊜¹	d N	160
Canyonlands National Park ♦	f G	158
Canyonville	h B	160
Cao-bang	c I	110
Cao Nguyen Dac-lac ↗¹	h J	110
Caoxian	i C	102
Çapac	g M	148
Čapajevsk	g G	92
Capanaparo ≃	b E	174
Capanema	c L	178
Capão Bonito	c N	178
Cap-aux-Meules (Grindstone Island)	e L	144
Cap-Chat	c G	144
Cape (Kaap) □⁴	h F	130
Cape ≃	c G	184
Cape Arid National Park ♦	f D	182
Cape Barren Island I	m H	184
Cape Basin ✦¹	l G	122
Cape Breton Highlands National Park ♦	f M	144
Cape Breton Island I	f M	144
Cape Canaveral	k F	150
Cape Charles	b J	150
Cape Coast	g F	124
Cape Cod Bay ⊂	f P	146
Cape Coral	m E	150
Cape Dorset	d Q	134
Cape Elizabeth	d P	146
Cape Fear ≃	e H	150
Cape Girardeau	e G	152
Cape Lisburne	b K	138
Capelle [aan den IJssel]	e F	82
Capelongo	d C	128
Cape May	i L	146
Cape May Court House	h L	146
Cape Pole	i BB	138
Cape Porpoise	d P	146
Capernaum ⊥	c E	120
Cape Romanzof	f L	138
Capesterre	f N	170
Cape Tormentine	f J	144
Cape Town (Kaapstad)	i D	130
Cape Verde (Cabo Verde) □¹	e B	124
Cape Verde Basin ✦¹	c E	122
Cape Vincent	c J	146
Cape Yakataga	f W	138
Cape York Peninsula >¹	b H	182
Cap-Haïtien	e H	170
Capim ≃	d I	174
Capitan	k K	158
Capitan Peak ∧	k K	158
Capitola	h D	162
Capitol Peak ∧	c H	162
Capitol Reef National Park ♦	f E	158
Capitol View	f F	150
Capivari	g E	177
Čaplygin	h V	96
Cap-Pelé	f I	144
Capreol	d O	148
Capri, Isola di I	i I	88
Capricorn, Cape >	d J	184
Capricorn Channel ꓘ	d J	184
Capricorn Group II	d J	184
Caprivi Zipfel (Caprivi Strip) □⁹	a F	130
Capron	h G	148
Captain Cook	r R	163a
Captains Flat	j H	184
Capua	h I	88
Caquetá (Japurá) ≃	d D	174
Čara ≃	e P	94
Caracal	e H	90
Caracaraí	c F	174
Caracas	i K	170
Caraguatatuba	g F	177
Carajás, Serra dos ↗	e H	174
Carangola	f G	177
Caransebeș	d F	90
Carapó	b K	178
Caraquet	e I	144
Caraș-Severin □⁶	d E	90
Caratasca, Laguna de ⊂	b K	168
Caratinga	e G	177
Carauari	d E	174
Caravaca	g J	86
Caravaggio	d D	88
Caravelas	d I	177
Caraway	g F	152
Caràzinho	e L	178
Carazo □⁵	f H	168
Carballiño	c C	86
Carberry	i O	142
Carbó	c D	166
Carbon	g H	154
Carbon ≃	c D	160
Carbondale, Co., U.S.	e I	158
Carbondale, Il., U.S.	e G	152
Carbondale, Ks., U.S.	m L	156
Carbondale, Pa., U.S.	f K	146
Carbonear	e T	144
Carbon Hill	i I	152
Carbonia	j C	88
Carcaixent	f K	86
Carcassonne	i I	84
Carcross	f AA	138
Cárdenas, Cuba	c D	170
Cárdenas, Méx.	f J	166
Cárdenas, Méx.	i M	166
Cardiel, Lago ⊜	f B	176
Cardiff	j J	78
Cardigan, P.E., Can.	f K	144
Cardigan, Wales, U.K.	i I	78
Cardigan Bay ⊂	i I	78
Cardinal	c K	146
Cardington	g D	146
Cardston	h U	140
Cardwell, Austl.	b G	184
Cardwell, Mo., U.S.	f F	152
Čardžou	j J	92
Carei	b F	90
Careiro	d G	174
Carencro	l D	152
Carentan	c E	84
Cares ≃	b G	86
Caretta	b E	150
Carey	g C	146
Carey, Lake ⊜	e D	182
Cargados Carajos Shoals II	k F	98
Carhaix-Plouguer	d C	84
Cariaco, Golfo de ⊂	i L	170
Cariati	j K	88
Caribbean Sea ⊤²	f J	164
Cariboo Mountains ↗	d M	140
Caribou, N.S., Can.	g K	144
Caribou, Me., U.S.	f E	144
Caribou ≃	e M	134
Caribou Mountain ∧	g N	160
Caribou Mountains ↗	e I	134
Carichic	d F	166
Carignan	c L	84
Carinhanha	c G	177
Carini	k H	88
Caripito	i M	170
Carleton, Mi., U.S.	h L	148
Carleton, Ne., U.S.	k J	156
Carleton, Mount ∧	e G	144
Carleton Place	e S	148
Carletonville	f H	130
Carlin	d I	162
Carlinville	c G	152
Carlisle, Eng., U.K.	g K	78
Carlisle, Ar., U.S.	h E	152
Carlisle, In., U.S.	d I	152
Carlisle, Ia., U.S.	i B	148
Carlisle, Ky., U.S.	i B	148
Carlisle, Pa., U.S.	g I	146
Carl Junction	e B	152
Carlópolis	g D	177
Carlos Casares	h H	178
Carlow	i G	78
Carlow □⁶	i G	78
Carloway	c G	78
Carlsbad, Ca., U.S.	k H	162
Carlsbad, N.M., U.S.	g B	154
Carlsbad, Tx., U.S.	h F	154
Carlsbad Caverns National Park ♦	g B	154
Carlton, Mn., U.S.	d C	148
Carlton, Or., U.S.	e B	160
Carlton, Tx., U.S.	h H	154
Carlyle, Sk., Can.	i L	142
Carlyle, Il., U.S.	d G	152
Carlyle Lake ⊜¹	d G	152
Carmacks	e Z	138
Carmagnola	e B	88
Carman	i P	142
Carmanville	c S	144
Carmarthen	j I	78
Carmaux	h I	84
Carmel, Ca., U.S.	h D	162
Carmel, In., U.S.	c I	152
Carmel, N.Y., U.S.	f M	146
Carmel, Mount → HaKarmel, Har ∧	c D	120
Carmel Head >	h I	78
Carmelo	h I	178
Carmel Valley	h D	162
Carmel Woods	h D	162
Carmen	c H	154
Carmen, Isla I	e D	166
Carmen de Patagones	e D	176
Carmi	d H	152
Carmichael	f D	162
Carmine	i J	154
Carmona	h F	86
Carnarvon, Austl.	d B	182
Carnarvon, S. Afr.	h F	130
Carnatic ✦¹	g J	112
Carndonagh	f F	78
Carnduff	i M	142
Carnegie	d H	154
Carnegie, Lake ⊜	e D	182
Carniche, Alpi ↗	c H	88
Car Nicobar Island I	j B	110
Carnot, Cape >	j A	184
Carnoustie	e K	78
Carnsore Point >	i G	78
Caro	g L	148
Carol City	n F	150
Caroleen	d E	150
Carolina, Bra.	e I	174
Carolina, S. Afr.	f J	130
Carolina Beach	e I	150
Caroline Islands II	c F	180
Caroní ≃	b F	174
Carora	i I	170
Carouge	f E	83
Carp	e S	148
Carp ≃	d K	148
Carpathian Mountains ↗	f L	74
Carpații Meridionali ↗	d H	90
Carpentaria, Gulf of ⊂	b G	182
Carpenter	j C	156
Carpentersville	h G	148
Carpentras	h L	84
Carpi	e E	88
Carpinteria	j F	162
Carpio	c F	156
Carpolac	k D	184
Carrabelle	j B	150
Carranza, Cabo >	b B	178
Carrara	e E	88
Carrauntoohil ∧	j D	78
Carrboro	d G	150
Carreria	a I	178
Carretas, Punta >	f C	174
Carriacou I	h N	170
Carrickfergus	g H	78
Carrickmacross	h G	78
Carrick on Shannon	h E	78
Carrick on Suir	i F	78
Carriere	l G	152
Carriers Mills	e H	152
Carrillo	d H	166
Carrington	d H	156
Carrión de los Condes	c G	86
Carrizal Bajo	e C	178
Carrizo Mountain ∧	k K	158
Carrizo Springs	k G	154
Carrizozo	k K	158
Carroll, Ia., U.S.	i M	156
Carroll, Ne., U.S.	i J	156
Carrollton, Al., U.S.	i H	152
Carrollton, Ga., U.S.	f A	150
Carrollton, Il., U.S.	c F	152
Carrollton, Ky., U.S.	d K	152
Carrollton, Mi., U.S.	g L	148
Carrollton, Ms., U.S.	i G	152
Carrollton, Mo., U.S.	c C	152
Carrollton, Oh., U.S.	g E	146
Carrollton, Tx., U.S.	g J	154
Carrolltown	g H	146
Carrot ≃	f L	134
Carrot River	e K	142
Carrville	j K	152
Carson, N.D., U.S.	e F	156
Carson, Wa., U.S.	e D	160
Carson ≃	e F	162
Carson City, Mi., U.S.	g K	148
Carson City, Nv., U.S.	e F	162
Carson Range ↗	e E	162
Carson Sink ⊜	e G	162
Carstairs	f U	140
Cartagena, Col.	i G	170
Cartagena, Esp.	h K	86
Cartago, Col.	c C	174
Cartago, C.R.	h K	168
Cartago □⁴	h K	168
Cartaxo	f C	86
Carter	d G	154
Carter Lake	j B	148
Carter Mountain ∧	f P	160
Cartersville	e B	150
Carterton	h J	186
Carterville	e G	152
Carthage, Tun.	a I	124
Carthage, Ar., U.S.	h D	152
Carthage, Il., U.S.	j D	148
Carthage, In., U.S.	c K	152
Carthage, Ms., U.S.	j G	152
Carthage, Mo., U.S.	e B	152
Carthage, N.Y., U.S.	d K	146
Carthage, N.C., U.S.	d G	150
Carthage, S.D., U.S.	g J	156
Carthage, Tn., U.S.	f K	152
Carthage, Tx., U.S.	j B	152
Cartier Islands II	b D	182
Cartwright	f U	134
Caruaru	e K	174
Carúpano	i M	170
Carutapera	d I	174
Caruthersville	f G	152
Carvin	b I	84
Carvoeiro	d F	174
Cary, Ms., U.S.	j F	152
Cary, N.C., U.S.	d H	150
Caryville, Fl., U.S.	l K	152
Caryville, Tn., U.S.	c B	150
Casablanca (Dar-el-Beida)	b E	124
Casa Branca	a O	178
Casa Grande	l E	158
Casale Monferrato	d C	88
Casanare ≃	b D	174
Casarano	i M	88
Casas Adobes	l F	158
Casas Grandes ≃	b F	166
Casas Ibáñez	f J	86
Casasimarro	f I	86
Casavieja	e G	86
Cascade, Id., U.S.	f I	160
Cascade, Ia., U.S.	h D	148
Cascade, Mt., U.S.	c N	160
Cascade, Wi., U.S.	g G	148
Cascade Locks	e D	160
Cascade Range ↗	c B	136
Cascade Reservoir ⊜¹	f I	160
Cascais	g B	86
Cascavel	c L	178
Cascina	f E	88
Casco Bay ⊂	d P	146
Caserta	h I	88
Caseville	g L	148
Casey, Il., U.S.	c I	152
Casey, Ia., U.S.	j M	156
Caseyr >	f K	126
Cashel	i F	78
Cashiers	d C	150
Cashmere	c E	160
Cashton	g E	148
Casilda	g H	178
Casillas del Angel	o AA	87b
Casino	g J	184
Çasiquiare ≃	c E	174
Čáslav	f O	80
Čašniki	g L	96
Casper	b J	158
Caspian	d G	148
Caspian Sea ⊤²	i H	92
Cass ≃	g L	148
Cassai (Kasai) ≃	c D	128
Cassano allo Ionio	j K	88
Cass City	g L	148
Casselman	b K	146
Casselton	e J	156
Cassiar	g DD	138
Cassiar Mountains ↗	e G	134
Cassinga	e C	128
Cassino	h H	88
Cass Lake	c A	148
Cassopolis	i I	148
Cassville, Mo., U.S.	f C	152
Cassville, Wi., U.S.	h E	148
Castalia	f D	146
Castanheira de Pêra	e C	86
Castelbuono	l I	88
Castelfiorentino	f E	88
Castelfranco Veneto	d F	88
Castellammare del Golfo	k G	88
Castellammare [di Stabia]	i I	88
Castellane	i M	84
Castellaneta	i K	88
Castelló □⁴	e K	86
Castelló de la Plana	f K	86
Castelmassa	d F	88
Castelnaudary	i H	84
Castelo Branco	f D	86
Castelsarrasin	h H	84
Castelvetrano	l G	88
Castets	i E	84
Castile	e H	146
Castilla	h B	174
Castilla-La Mancha □⁴	f H	86
Castilla la Nueva □⁹	f I	86
Castilla la Vieja □⁹	d G	86
Castilla-León □⁴	d F	86
Castillo del Romeral	p Y	87b
Castillos	h L	178
Castine	c R	146
Castlebar	h D	78
Castleberry	k I	152
Castleblayney	g G	78
Castlecliff	f I	186
Castle Dale	e F	158
Castle Douglas	g J	78
Castlegar	h Q	140
Castle Hills	j H	154
Castleisland	i D	78
Castlemaine	k F	184
Castle Mountain ∧	d AA	138
Castle Peak ∧, Co., U.S.	e J	158
Castle Peak ∧, Id., U.S.	f K	160
Castlerea	h E	78
Castlereagh ≃	h H	184
Castle Rock, Co., U.S.	e L	158
Castle Rock, Wa., U.S.	d C	160
Castle Rock ∧	f G	160
Castle Rock Lake ⊜¹	g F	148
Castleton	d M	146
Castletown, I. of Man	g I	78
Castletown, Scot., U.K.	c J	78
Castletown Bearhaven	j D	78
Castlewood, S.D., U.S.	g J	156
Castlewood, Va., U.S.	c D	150
Castor	e W	140
Castor ≃	e F	152
Castres	i I	84
Castricum	c F	82
Castries	g N	170
Castro, Bra.	c M	178
Castro, Chile	e B	176
Castro Daire	e D	86
Castro del Río	h G	86
Castro Marim	h D	86
Castro Verde	h C	86
Castroville, Ca., U.S.	h D	162
Castroville, Tx., U.S.	j H	154
Castuera	g F	86
Casummit Lake	g V	142
Catacamas	c I	168
Catacaos	e B	174
Catahoula Lake ⊜	k D	152
Catalão	e E	177
Catalina, Nf., Can.	d T	144
Catalina, Chile	c D	178
Catalonia → Catalunya □⁴	d M	86
Catalunya □⁴	d M	86
Catamarca	b C	176
Catamarca □⁴	d E	178
Catanduanes Island I	c G	108
Catanduva	f D	177
Catania	l J	88
Catania, Golfo di ⊂	l J	88
Catanzaro	k K	88
Catarman	c G	108
Catarroja	f K	86
Catawba ≃	e F	150
Catawissa	g J	146
Cat-ba, Dao I	d I	110
Catbalogan	c G	108
Catete	c B	128
Cathcart	i H	130
Cathedral City	k I	162
Cathlamet	d B	160
Ca' Tiepolo	e G	88
Cat Island I, Ba.	b G	170
Cat Island I, Ms., U.S.	l G	152
Catlettsburg	i D	146
Catlin	b I	152
Catnip Mountain ∧	c F	162
Catoche, Cabo >	g P	166
Cato Island I	d K	184
Catonsville	h J	146
Catoosa	c K	154
Catorce	f I	166
Catriló	i G	178
Catrimani ≃	c F	174
Catskill	e M	146
Catskill Mountains ↗	e L	146
Cattaraugus	e H	146
Cattolica	f G	88
Catwick, Îles II	i J	110
Caubvick, Mount (Mont d'Iberville) ∧	e T	134
Cauca ≃	b C	174
Caucasus → Bol'šoj Kavkaz ↗	i F	92
Caucete	f D	178
Caudry	b J	84
Caulonia	k K	88
Caúngula	c C	128
Cauquenes	h B	178
Caura ≃	b F	174
Çausapscal	d F	144
Čausy	h M	96
Cauvery ≃	g E	116
Cauvery Falls ↘	f D	116
Caux, Pays de ✦¹	c G	84
Cavaillon	i L	84
Cavalaire-sur-Mer	i M	84
Cavalcante	b E	177
Cavalier	c J	156
Cavalla (Cavally) ≃	g E	124
Cavalli Islands II	b H	186
Cavan	g F	78
Cavan □⁶	h F	78
Cavarzere	d G	88
Cave City, Ar., U.S.	g E	152
Cave City, Ky., U.S.	e K	152
Cave In Rock	e H	152
Cavendish	k E	184
Cave Run Lake ⊜¹	i C	146
Cave Spring	e A	150
Caviana, Ilha I	c H	174
Cavite	n S	109b
Cavite □⁴	n S	109b
Cawker City	l I	156
Cawood	c C	150
Cawston	h O	140
Caxias	d J	174
Caxias do Sul	e M	178
Caxito	c B	128
Cayambe	c C	174
Cayambe ∧¹	c C	174
Cayce	f E	150
Cayenne	c H	174
Cayey	e K	170
Cayman Brac I	e E	170
Cayman Islands □²	e D	170
Cayman Trench ✦¹	h K	132
Cay Sal Bank ✦²	c D	170
Cayucos	i E	162
Cayuga, On., Can.	h P	148
Cayuga, In., U.S.	c I	152
Cayuga, N.D., U.S.	e J	156
Cayuga, Tx., U.S.	h K	154
Cayuga Heights	e J	146
Cayuga Lake ⊜	e J	146
Cazenovia	e K	146
Cazères	i H	84
Cazombo	d D	128
Ceanannus Mór	h G	78
Ceará-Mirim	e K	174
Ceballos, Méx.	d G	166
Ceballos, Méx.	f G	166
Cebollar	e E	178
Cebollatí ≃	g K	178
Cebollita Peak ∧	j I	158
Čebsara	b U	96
Cebu	c G	108
Cebu I	c G	108
Ceccano	h H	88
Čecerleg	b G	100
Čečersk	i M	96
Čechov	f T	96
Čechy □⁹	f N	80
Cecil	h C	150
Cecilia	e K	152
Cecina	f E	88
Cedar ≃, U.S.	i D	148
Cedar ≃, Mi., U.S.	f K	148
Cedar ≃, Ne., U.S.	j I	156
Cedar ≃, N.Y., U.S.	d L	146
Cedar Bluff Reservoir ⊜¹	m H	156
Cedar Bluffs	j K	156
Cedarburg	g H	148
Cedar City, Mo., U.S.	d D	152
Cedar City, Ut., U.S.	g C	158
Cedar Creek Reservoir ⊜¹	g J	154
Cedaredge	f I	158
Cedar Falls	h C	148
Cedar Grove, W.V., U.S.	i E	146
Cedar Grove, Wi., U.S.	g H	148
Cedar Hill	f J	152
Cedar Key	j C	150
Cedar Lake	a I	152
Cedar Lake ⊜¹	e N	142
Cedar Mountain ∧	c E	162
Cedar Rapids, Ia., U.S.	i D	148
Cedar Rapids, Ne., U.S.	j I	156
Cedar Springs	g J	148
Cedartown	e A	150
Cedar Vale	n K	156
Cedarville, S. Afr.	h I	130
Cedarville, Ca., U.S.	c E	162
Cedarville, Mi., U.S.	d K	148
Cedarville, N.J., U.S.	h K	146
Cedillo, Embalse de ⊜¹	f D	86
Cedros	e I	166
Cedros, Isla I	c B	166
Ceerigaabo	f J	126
Cefalù	k I	88
Cegléd	h S	80
Çehegin	g J	86
Čekalin	g S	96
Čel'abinsk	f J	92
Celano	g H	88
Celaya	g I	166
Celebes → Sulawesi I	f G	108
Celebes Sea ⊤²	e G	108
Celeste	f J	154
Celestún	g N	166
Celina, Oh., U.S.	g B	146
Celina, Tn., U.S.	f K	152
Celina, Tx., U.S.	f J	154
Celinograd	g L	92
Čelje	c J	88
Čelkar	h I	92
Celldömölk	h Q	80
Celle	c J	80
Celorico da Beira	e D	86
Celtic Sea ⊤²	j G	78
Čel'uskin, mys >	b R	92
Çement	e H	154
Čemerno	f M	88
Cenderawasih, Teluk ⊂	f J	108
Centennial Mountains ↗	f N	160
Center, Co., U.S.	g J	158
Center, Mo., U.S.	c E	152
Center, Ne., U.S.	i J	156
Center, N.D., U.S.	d F	156
Center, Tx., U.S.	k B	152
Centerburg	g D	146
Center City	e C	148
Center Hill	k E	150
Center Hill Lake ⊜¹	f K	152
Center Moriches	g N	146
Center Mountain ∧	e J	160
Center Point, Al., U.S.	i J	152
Center Point, Ia., U.S.	h D	148
Center Point, Tx., U.S.	j G	154
Centerville, In., U.S.	c L	152
Centerville, Ia., U.S.	j C	148
Centerville, Mo., U.S.	e F	152
Centerville, Pa., U.S.	g G	146
Centerville, S.D., U.S.	h K	156
Centerville, Tn., U.S.	g I	152
Centerville, Tx., U.S.	h K	154
Centerville, Ut., U.S.	c E	158
Cento	e F	88
Central, Az., U.S.	l G	158
Central, N.M., U.S.	l H	158
Central, S.C., U.S.	e D	150
Central □⁴	e I	78
Central □⁵	c J	178
Central, Cordillera ↗, Col.	b C	174
Central, Cordillera ↗, C.R.	g J	168
Central, Cordillera ↗, Perú	e C	174
Central, Cordillera ↗, P.R.	e K	170
Central, Massif ↗	g J	84
Central, Planalto ↗¹	g J	174
Central, Sistema ↗	e F	86
Central African Republic □¹	g E	126
Central City, Il., U.S.	d G	152
Central City, Ia., U.S.	h D	148
Central City, Ky., U.S.	e I	152
Central City, Ne., U.S.	j I	156
Central City, Pa., U.S.	g H	146
Central Heights	k F	158
Centralia, Il., U.S.	d G	152
Centralia, Ks., U.S.	l K	156
Centralia, Mo., U.S.	c D	152
Centralia, Wa., U.S.	d C	160
Central Lake	e J	148
Central Makrān Range ↗	d G	112
Central'nyj	h V	96
Central Pacific Basin ✦¹	c J	180
Central Point	h C	160
Central Range ↗	g I	130
Central Square	d J	146
Central Valley	d C	162
Centre	h K	152
Centre, Canal du ≍	f K	84
Centreville, Al., U.S.	j I	152
Centreville, Md., U.S.	h J	146
Centreville, Mi., U.S.	i J	148

Symbols in the index are identified on page 198.

Name	Map Ref.	Page

Symbols in the index are identified on page 198.

Symbols in the index are identified on page 198.

Name	Map Ref.	Page

Name	Map Ref.	Page
Diksmuide (Dixmude)	f B	82
Dikson	c H	94
Dikwa	f I	124
Dill City	d G	154
Dillenburg	e H	80
Diller	k K	156
Dilley	k G	154
Dillingen	f F	80
Dillingen [an der Donau]	g J	80
Dillingham	g O	138
Dillon, Co., U.S.	e J	158
Dillon, Mt., U.S.	e M	160
Dillon, S.C., U.S.	e G	150
Dillon ≃	c E	142
Dillon Lake ⊜[1]	g D	146
Dillon Mountain ∧	k H	158
Dillwyn	b H	150
Dilolo	d D	128
Dilworth	e K	156
Dimāpur	h O	114
Dimashq (Damascus)	a F	120
Dimashq □[8]	a G	120
Dimboola	k E	184
Dîmbovița □[6]	e I	90
Dîmbovița ≃	e I	90
Dime Box	i J	154
Dimitrovgrad, Blg.	g I	90
Dimitrovgrad, S.S.S.R.	g G	92
Dimlang ∧	g I	124
Dimmitt	e D	154
Dimona	f D	120
Dinājpur	h M	114
Dinan	d D	84
Dinant	h F	82
Dinara ⋏	f K	88
Dinard	d D	84
Dinaric Alps → Dinara ⋏	f K	88
Dindigul	g D	116
Dingalan Bay ⊂	n S	109b
Dinggyê	f D	100
Dinghai	e K	104
Dingle	i C	78
Dingle Bay ⊂	i C	78
Dingolfing	g L	80
Dingqing	e P	114
Dingri	f L	114
Dingshuzhen	d H	104
Dingwall, N.S., Can.	f M	144
Dingwall, Scot., U.K.	d I	78
Dingxi	d G	100
Dingxian	e B	102
Dinh-lap	d I	110
Dinkelsbühl	f J	80
Dinorwic	i V	142
Dinosaur	d G	158
Dinuba	h F	162
Dinwiddie	b I	150
Diomede	d J	138
Diourbel	f C	124
Dipolog	d G	108
Dippoldiswalde	e M	80
Dīr	c D	114
Dire Dawa	g I	126
Diriamba	f H	168
Dirico	e D	128
Dirj	b C	126
Dirk Hartog Island I	e B	182
Dirranbandi	g H	184
Dirty Devil ≃	f F	158
Disappointment, Cape ≻	d A	160
Disappointment, Lake ⊜	d D	182
Disaster Bay ⊂	k I	184
Discovery Bay ⊂	l D	184
Disentis	e J	83
Dishman	c H	160
Dishnā	i E	118
Disko I	c V	134
Disko Bugt ⊂	c V	134
Dismal ≃	j G	156
Disna	f K	96
Disney	c K	154
Dison	g H	82
Disraeli	b O	146
Disūq	g D	118
Diu	j D	114
Divernon	c G	152
Divinópolis	f F	177
Divisões, Serra das ⋏[2]	d C	177
Divisor, Serra do ⋏[1]	e D	174
Dix	j D	156
Dix ≃	b B	150
Dixfield	c P	146
Dixie Valley V	d G	162
Dixmude (Diksmuide)	f B	82
Dixon, Ca., U.S.	f D	162
Dixon, Il., U.S.	i F	148
Dixon, Ky., U.S.	e I	152
Dixon, Mo., U.S.	e D	152
Dixon, N.M., U.S.	h K	158
Dixon Entrance ʊ	c B	140
Dixons Mills	j I	152
Diyarbakır	d I	118
Dja ≃	h I	124
Djakarta → Jakarta	j M	109a
Djambala	b B	128
Djanet	d H	124
Djedi, Oued V	b G	124
Djénné	f F	124
Djérem ≃	g I	124
Djibouti	f I	126
Djibouti □[1]	f I	126
Djokupunda	c D	128
Djougou	g G	124
Djúpivogur	b F	76a
Djurås	k N	76
Dmitrija Lapteva, proliv ʊ	c T	94
Dmitrijev-L'govskij	i R	96
Dmitrov	e T	96
Dnepr ≃	h D	92
Dneprodzeržinsk	h D	92
Dnepropetrovsk	h D	92
Dnestr ≃	h C	92
Dnieper → Dnepr ≃	h D	92
Dniester → Dnestr ≃	h C	92
Dno	d L	96
Doaktown	f G	144
Doany	o W	131b
Doba	e D	126
Dobbiaco	c G	88
Dobbyn	b D	184
Dobele	e F	96
Döbeln	d M	80
Doberai, Jazirah ≻[1]	f I	108
Doboj	e B	90
Dobruja ◆[1]	e L	90
Dobruš	i N	96
Dobson	c F	150
Doce ≃	e H	177
Dock Junction	h E	150
Doctor Arroyo	f I	166
Doctor González	e J	166
Dod Ballāpur	f D	116
Doddridge	i C	152
Doddsville	i F	152
Dodecanese → Dhodhekánisos II	m J	90
Dodge	j K	156
Dodge Center	f C	148
Dodge City	n G	156
Dodgeville	h E	148
Dodola	g H	126
Dodoma	c G	128
Dodson, La., U.S.	j D	152
Dodson, Mt., U.S.	b Q	160
Dodson, Tx., U.S.	e F	154
Doerun	h C	150
Doesburg	d I	82
Doetinchem	e I	82
Dogai Coring ⊜	e D	100
Dōgo I	k H	106
Dogondoutchi	f G	124
Doha → Ad-Dawḥah	b G	117
Dohad	i F	114
Doiran, Lake ⊜	h F	90
Dokka	k L	76
Dokkum	b I	82
Dokšicy	g J	96
Doland	g I	156
Dolbeau	g R	134
Dol-de-Bretagne	d E	84
Dole	e L	84
Dolgellau	i J	78
Dolgeville	d L	146
Dolisie	b B	128
Dolj □[6]	e G	90
Dolmatovskij	d Y	96
Dolomites → Dolomiti ⋏	c F	88
Dolomiti ⋏	c F	88
Dolores, Arg.	i J	178
Dolores, Méx.	c E	166
Dolores, Co., U.S.	g H	158
Dolores, Ur.	g I	178
Dolores ≃	f H	158
Dolores Hidalgo	g I	166
Dolphin and Union Strait ʊ	c I	134
Dom Aquino	c A	177
Dombås	j K	76
Dombóvár	i R	80
Dombrád	g U	80
Domburg	e D	82
Domeyko	e C	178
Domeyko, Cordillera ⋏	b D	178
Dominica □[1]	g N	170
Dominica Channel ʊ	g N	170
Dominican Republic (República Dominicana) □[1]	e I	170
Dominion	f M	144
Dominion, Cape ≻	c R	134
Domo	g J	126
Domodedovo	f T	96
Domodossola	c C	88
Dom Pedrito	f K	178
Domuyo, Volcán ∧[1]	i C	178
Don ≃, S.S.S.R.	h F	92
Don ≃, Scot., U.K.	d K	78
Dona Ana	l J	158
Donaghadee	g H	78
Donald	k E	184
Donaldson	h D	152
Donaldsonville	l F	152
Donalsonville	h B	150
Doñana, Parque Nacional de ♠	h E	86
Donaueschingen	h H	80
Donauwörth	g J	80
Don Benito	g F	86
Doncaster	h L	78
Dondo, Ang.	c B	128
Dondo, Moç.	b L	130
Dondra Head ≻	j F	116
Doneck	h E	92
Donegal	g E	78
Donegal □[6]	g E	78
Donegal Bay ⊂	g E	78
Doneraile	e G	150
Donetsk → Doneck	h E	92
Dong ≃	l F	104
Donga ≃	g I	124
Dongara	e B	182
Dongchuan	a G	110
Dongen	e F	82
Dongfang (Basuo)	e J	110
Dongfeng	a M	102
Dongguan	l B	104
Donghaidao I	d K	110
Dong-hoi	f I	110
Dongio	f J	83
Dong-nai ≃	i I	110
Dongtai	c I	104
Dongting Hu ⊜	g A	104
Dongyang	f I	104
Dongzhi	e E	104
Donie	h J	154
Doniphan, Mo., U.S.	f F	152
Doniphan, Ne., U.S.	k I	156
Donjek ≃	f Y	138
Donji Vakuf	e L	88
Donna	m H	154
Donnelly	f I	160
Donner	m F	152
Donner Pass)(	e E	162
Donner und Blitzen ≃	g G	160
Donnybrook	h I	130
Donora	g G	146
Donostia (San Sebastián)	b J	86
Donskoj	h U	96
Doolow	h I	126
Doomadgee	a C	184
Doon	h K	156
Doornik (Tournai)	g C	82
Door Peninsula ≻[1]	f H	148
Dora	i I	152
Doraville	f B	150
Dorcheat, Bayou ≃	i C	152
Dorchester, N.B., Can.	g I	144
Dorchester, On., Can.	h N	148
Dorchester, Eng., U.K.	k K	78
Dorchester, Ne., U.S.	k J	156
Dorchester, Wi., U.S.	e E	148
Dorchester, Cape ≻	c Q	134
Dorchester Crossing	f I	144
Dordogne □[5]	g G	84
Dordogne ≃	h H	84
Dordrecht, Ned.	e F	82
Dordrecht, S. Afr.	h H	130
Doré Lake ⊜	d G	142
Dorena	g C	160
Dores do Indaiá	e F	177
Dorfen	g L	80
Dornach	d H	83
Dornbirn	h I	80
Dornoch	d I	78
Dorochovo	f S	96
Dorog	h R	80
Dorogobuž	g P	96
Dorohoi	b J	90
Dorotea	i O	76
Dorrance	m I	156
Dorre Island I	e B	182
Dorrigo	h J	184
Dorris	c D	162
Dorset □[6]	k K	78
Dortmund	d G	80
Dorton	b D	150
Doruma	h F	126
Dos Bahías, Cabo ≻	e C	176
Dosčatoje	f Y	96
Dos Hermanas	h F	86
Dos Palos	h E	162
Dothan	k K	152
Dotnuva	f F	96
Douai	b J	84
Douala	h H	124
Douarnenez	d B	84
Double Island Point ≻	e J	184
Double Point ≻	a G	184
Double Springs	h I	152
Doubletop Peak ∧	g O	160
Doubs □[5]	e M	84
Doubs ≃	e L	84
Doubtful Sound ʊ	l A	186
Doudeville	c G	84
Douentza	e F	124
Douglas, I. of Man	g I	78
Douglas, S. Afr.	g F	130
Douglas, Ak., U.S.	g AA	138
Douglas, Az., U.S.	m G	158
Douglas, Ga., U.S.	h D	150
Douglas, N.D., U.S.	d F	156
Douglas, Wy., U.S.	b K	158
Douglas, Cape ≻	g R	138
Douglas, Mount ∧	g R	138
Douglas Channel ʊ	d E	140
Douglas Lake ⊜[1]	c C	150
Douglass	n J	156
Douglasville	f B	150
Doulaincourt	d L	84
Doulevant-le-Château	d K	84
Doullens	b I	84
Dour	h D	82
Dourada, Serra ⋏[1]	f I	174
Dourados	b K	178
Dourdan	d I	84
Douro (Duero) ≃	d D	86
Dove Creek	g H	158
Dover, Austl.	n G	184
Dover, Eng., U.K.	j O	78
Dover, Ar., U.S.	g C	152
Dover, De., U.S.	h K	146
Dover, Id., U.S.	b I	160
Dover, N.H., U.S.	d P	146
Dover, N.J., U.S.	g L	146
Dover, N.C., U.S.	d I	150
Dover, Oh., U.S.	g E	146
Dover, Ok., U.S.	d I	154
Dover, Tn., U.S.	f I	152
Dover, Strait of (Pas de Calais) ʊ	j O	78
Dover-Foxcroft	b Q	146
Dovre	k K	76
Dovrefjell Nasjonalpark ♠	j K	76
Dowagiac	i I	148
Dowagiac ≃	h I	148
Dow City	j L	156
Downey	h M	160
Downham Market	i N	78
Downieville	e E	162
Downing	b D	152
Downingtown	g K	146
Downpatrick	g H	78
Downs	l I	156
Downs Mountain ∧	g P	160
Downsville	e L	146
Dow Rūd	f M	118
Dows	h B	148
Doyle	d E	162
Doylestown, Oh., U.S.	g E	146
Doylestown, Pa., U.S.	g K	146
Doyline	j C	152
Dōzen II	k H	106
Dozier	k J	152
Dra'a, Hamada du ◆[2]	c E	124
Drâa, Oued V	c E	124
Dracena	f C	177
Drachten	b I	82
Dracut	e O	146
Drăgășani	e H	90
Dragons Mouth ʊ	i N	170
Dragoon	l F	158
Draguignan	i M	84
Drain	g B	160
Drake	d G	156
Drakensberg ⋏	f I	130
Drake Passage ʊ	j H	172
Drake Peak ∧	h E	160
Drakesboro	e I	152
Drakes Branch	c H	150
Dráma	h H	90
Drammen	l L	76
Draper, N.C., U.S.	c G	150
Draper, Ut,. U.S.	d E	158
Drau (Drava) (Dráva) ≃	c H	88
Drava (Drau) (Dráva) ≃	d M	88
Drawno	b O	80
Drayton, N.D., U.S.	c J	156
Drayton, S.C., U.S.	e E	150
Drayton Valley	d T	140
Drenthe □[4]	c J	82
Dresden, On., Can.	h M	148
Dresden, D.D.R.	d M	80
Dresden, Oh., U.S.	g D	146
Dresden, Tn., U.S.	f H	152
Dresden □[5]	d N	80
Dreux	d H	84
Drew	i F	152
Driebergen	d G	82
Driffield	g M	78
Driftwood ≃	c J	152
Driggs	g N	160
Drin ≃	h C	90
Drina ≃	e C	90
Drinit, Gjiri i ⊂	h C	90
Driscoll	l I	154
Driskill Mountain ∧[2]	j D	152
Drobeta-Turnu Severin	e F	90
Drogheda	h G	78
Drohiczyn	c V	80
Droichead Nua	h G	78
Drôme □[5]	h L	84
Druja	f J	96
Drumheller	f V	140
Drummond, Mt., U.S.	d L	160
Drummond, Wi., U.S.	d D	148
Drummond Island I	d L	148
Drummond Range ⋏	e G	184
Drummondville	b N	146
Drumright	d J	154
Druskininkai	g F	96
Dry Bay ⊂	g Y	138
Dry Cimarron ≃	c C	154
Dry Creek Mountain ∧	c I	162
Dryden	i V	142
Dry Devils ≃	j F	154
Dry Fork ≃	e E	152
Dry Prong	k D	152
Dry Ridge	i B	146
Drysdale ≃	c E	182
Drysdale River National Park ♠	b E	182
Dry Tortugas II	o D	150
Duarte, Pico ∧	e I	170
Dubach	j D	152
Dubai → Dubayy	b I	117
Dubawnt Lake ⊜	d L	134
Dubayy (Dubai)	b I	117
Dubbo	i H	184
Dübendorf	d J	83
Dublin (Baile Átha Cliath), Ire.	h G	78
Dublin, Ga., U.S.	g D	150
Dublin, Tx., U.S.	g H	154
Dublin, Va., U.S.	b F	150
Dublin □[6]	h G	78
Dubna	e T	96
Dubois, Id., U.S.	f M	160
Dubois, In., U.S.	d J	152
Du Bois, Ne., U.S.	k K	156
Du Bois, Pa., U.S.	f H	146
Dubois, Wy., U.S.	a G	158
Dubréka	g D	124
Dubrovka, S.S.S.R.	h P	96
Dubrovka, S.S.S.R.	b M	96
Dubrovnik	g B	90
Dubrovno	g M	96
Dubuque	h E	148
Duchesne	d F	158
Duchesne ≃	d F	158
Duchess	c C	184
Duck ≃	g I	152
Duck Hill	i G	152
Du Couedic, Cape ≻	k B	184
Dudelange	j I	82
Duderstadt	d J	80
Dudinka	d I	94
Dudley	i K	78
Dudleyville	l F	158
Dudorovskij	h R	96
Duerna ≃	c E	86
Duero (Douro) ≃	d E	86
Due West	e D	150
Duffer Peak ∧	c G	162
Dufourspitze ∧	g N	84
Dufur	e D	160
Dugdemona ≃	j D	152
Dugger	c I	152
Dugi Otok I	e J	88
Du Gué ≃	e R	134
Duisburg	d F	80
Duitama	b D	174
Duiwelskloof	d J	130
Duke	e G	154
Duke of York Bay ⊂	c P	134
Duk Fadiat	g G	126
Dukhān	b G	117
Dulan	d F	100
Dul'apino	d W	96
Dulce	h J	158
Dulce ≃	f G	178
Dulce, Golfo ⊂	i K	168
Dulkaninna	g C	184
Dullstroom	e J	130
Dülmen	d G	80
Duluth, Ga., U.S.	e B	150
Duluth, Mn., U.S.	d C	148
Dūmā	a F	120
Dumaguete	d G	108
Dumaran Island I	c F	108
Dumaresq ≃	g I	184
Dumaring	e F	108
Dumas, Ar., U.S.	i E	152
Dumas, Tx., U.S.	d E	154
Dumbarton	f I	78
Dumfries	f J	78
Dumfries and Galloway □[4]	f I	78
Duminiči	h R	96
Dumka	h L	114
Dumont	h C	148
Dumraon	h K	114
Dumyāṭ	g D	118
Dunaföldvár	i R	80
Dunaharaszti	h S	80
Dunajec ≃	e T	80
Dunakeszi	h S	80
Dunaújváros	i R	80
Dunbar	i E	146
Dunblane	e J	78
Duncan, B.C., Can.	i K	140
Duncan, Az., U.S.	l G	158
Duncan, Ms., U.S.	h F	152
Duncan, Ok., U.S.	e I	154
Duncannon	g I	146
Duncan Passage ʊ	i B	110
Duncansby Head ≻	c J	78
Dundalk, On., Can.	f O	148
Dundalk, Ire.	g G	78
Dundalk, Md., U.S.	h J	146
Dundas, On., Can.	g P	148
Dundas, Mn., U.S.	f B	148
Dundee, S. Afr.	g J	130
Dundee, Scot., U.K.	e K	78
Dundee, Fl., U.S.	k E	150
Dundee, Mi., U.S.	i L	148
Dundee, Ms., U.S.	h F	152
Dundee, N.Y., U.S.	e J	146
Dunedin, N.Z.	l E	186
Dunedin, Fl., U.S.	k D	150
Dunedoo	i H	184
Dunfermline	e J	78
Dungannon, N. Ire., U.K.	g G	78
Dungannon, Va., U.S.	c D	150
Dungarvan	i F	78
Dungeness ≻	k N	78
Dungog	i I	184
Dunhua	c L	100
Dunhuang	c E	100
Dunilovo	d U	96
Dunkerque	a I	84
Dunkirk → Dunkerque, Fr.	a I	84
Dunkirk, In., U.S.	b K	152
Dunkirk, N.Y., U.S.	e G	146
Dunkirk, Oh., U.S.	g C	146
Dunkwa	g F	124
Dún Laoghaire	h G	78
Dunlap, Ia., U.S.	j L	156
Dunlap, Tn., U.S.	g K	152
Dunleary → Dún Laoghaire	h G	78
Dunmore	f K	146
Dunn	d H	150
Dunnellon	j D	150
Dunning	j G	156
Dunnville	h P	148
Dunoon	f I	78
Dunqulah	e G	126
Duns	f K	78
Dunseith	c G	156
Dunsmuir	c C	162
Dunstable	j M	78
Dun-sur-Meuse	c L	84
Dunville	e T	144
Duolun (Dolonnur)	a D	102
Duomaer	e B	100
Duomula	e C	100
Du Page ≃	i G	148
Dupree	f F	156
Duque de Caxias	g G	177
Duque de York, Isla I	g A	176
DuQuoin	e G	152
Durack Ranges ⋏	c E	182
Duran	j K	158
Durance ≃	i L	84
Durand, Il., U.S.	h F	148
Durand, Mi., U.S.	h L	148
Durand, Wi., U.S.	f D	148
Durango, Esp.	b I	86
Durango, Méx.	e G	166
Durango, Co., U.S.	g I	158
Durango □[3]	e G	166
Durant, Ia., U.S.	i E	148
Durant, Ms., U.S.	i G	152
Durant, Ok., U.S.	f J	154
Durazno	g J	178
Durban	g J	130
Durbin	i G	146
Đurđevac	c L	88
Düren	e F	80
Durg	j I	114
Durgāpur	i L	114
Durham, On., Can.	f O	148
Durham, Eng., U.K.	g L	78
Durham, Ca., U.S.	e D	162
Durham, N.H., U.S.	d P	146
Durham, N.C., U.S.	d H	150
Durham □[6]	g L	78
Durmitor ∧	f C	90
Durness	c I	78
Dürnkrut	g P	80
Durrell	c S	144
Durrës	h C	90
D'Urville Island I	g H	186
Dušanbe	j K	92
Dusetos	f H	96
Dushan	b I	110
Dushanzi	c C	100
Dushore	f J	146
Dusky Sound ʊ	l A	186
Duson	l D	152
Düsseldorf	d F	80
Dustin	d J	154
Dutch Harbor	j K	138
Dutch John	d G	158
Dutton, On., Can.	h N	148
Dutton, Mt., U.S.	c N	160
Dutton ≃	c E	184
Dutton, Mount ∧	f D	158
Duyun	a I	110
Dvůr Králové [nad Labem]	e O	80
Dwārka	i C	114
Dwight	i G	148
Dworshak Reservoir ⊜[1]	d J	160
Dwyka	i E	130
Dyer	f H	152
Dyer, Cape ≻	c T	134
Dyersburg	f G	152
Dyersville	h D	148
Dyfed □[6]	j I	78
Dyje (Thaya) ≃	g P	80
Dyment	i V	142
Dysart	h C	148
Dysselsdorp	i F	130
Džalal-Abad	i L	92
Džambul	i L	92
Džankoj	h D	92
Dzaoudzi	l P	131a
Dzavchan ≃	b E	100
Dzemul	g O	166
Dzeržinsk	e Z	96
Džetygara	g J	92
Džezkazgan	h K	92
Dzibalchén	h O	166
Dzierżoniów (Reichenbach)	e P	80
Dzilam González	g O	166
Dzitás	g O	166
Dzitbalché	g N	166
Džizak	i K	92
Džugdžur, chrebet ⋏	f S	94
Dzungarian Basin → Junggar Pendi ⊻[1]	b D	100
Džungarskij Alatau, chrebet ⋏	h N	92
Džüün Charaa	b H	100
Dzuunmod	b H	100

E

Name	Map Ref.	Page
Eads	m E	156
Eagar	j G	158
Eagle, Ak., U.S.	d X	138
Eagle, Co., U.S.	e J	158
Eagle ≃, Nf., Can.	f U	134
Eagle ≃, Co., U.S.	e J	158
Eagle Bend	e L	156
Eagle Butte	f F	156
Eagle Grove	h B	148
Eaglehawk	k F	184
Eagle Lake, Me., U.S.	e E	144
Eagle Lake, Tx., U.S.	j J	154
Eagle Lake ⊜	d E	162
Eagle Mountain	k J	162
Eagle Mountain ∧	d J	160
Eagle Mountain ∧[2]	c E	148
Eagle Pass	k F	154
Eagle Peak ∧	c E	162
Eagle River, Mi., U.S.	c G	148
Eagle River, Wi., U.S.	e F	148
Eagle Rock	b G	150
Eagleton Village	d C	150
Eagletown	h B	152
Eagle Village	d X	138
Ear Falls	h U	142
Earle	g F	152
Earlham	a B	152
Earlimart	i F	162
Earlington	e I	152
Earl Park	b I	152
Earlville, Il., U.S.	i G	148
Earlville, N.Y., U.S.	e K	146
Early, Ia., U.S.	i L	156
Early, Tx., U.S.	h H	154
Earth	e D	154
Easley	e D	150
East Alton	d F	152
East-Angus	b O	146
East Aurora	e H	146
East Bay ⊂	j L	154
East Bend	c F	150
East-Berlin → Berlin (Ost), D.D.R.	c M	80
East Berlin, Pa., U.S.	h J	146
East Bernard	j J	154
East Bernstadt	b B	150
Eastbourne, N.Z.	h I	186
Eastbourne, Eng., U.K.	k N	78
East Brady	g G	146
East Brewton	k I	152
East Cape ≻	d M	186
East Carbon	e F	158
East Chicago	a I	152
East China Sea ▾[2]	e L	100
East Coast Bays	c I	186
East Dereham	i N	78
East Dublin	g D	150
East Dubuque	h E	148
East Ely	e K	162
Eastend	i F	142
Easter Island → Pascua, Isla de I	g D	172
Eastern Ghāts ⋏	f E	116
East Falkland I	g E	176
East Fayetteville	d H	150
East Flat Rock	d D	150
East Frisian Islands → Ostfriesische Inseln II	b G	80
East Gaffney	d E	150
East Gallatin ≃	e N	160
East Ghor Canal → Ghawr ash-Sharqīyah, Qanāt al- ≋	d E	120
East Glacier Park	b L	160
East Grand Forks	d J	156
East Grand Rapids	h J	148
East Greenwich	f O	146
East Grinstead	j M	78
Easthampton	e N	146
East Helena	d N	160
East Jordan	e J	148
East Kilbride	f I	78
Eastlake, Mi., U.S.	f I	148
Eastlake, Oh., U.S.	f E	146
Eastland	g H	154
East Lansing	h K	148
East Laurinburg	e G	150
Eastleigh	k L	78
East Liverpool	g F	146
East London (Oos-Londen)	i H	130
East Lynn Lake ⊜[1]	i D	146
Eastmain	f Q	134
Eastmain ≃	f Q	134
Eastman	g C	150
East Millinocket	b R	146
East Missoula	d L	160
East Moline	i E	148
East Naples	m E	150
East Nishnabotna ≃	k L	156
East Olympia	d C	160
Easton, Md., U.S.	i J	146
Easton, Pa., U.S.	g K	146
Eastover	f F	150
East Palatka	j E	150
East Palestine	g F	146
East Pecos	i K	158
East Peoria	j F	148
Eastpoint, Fl., U.S.	j B	150
East Point, Ga., U.S.	f B	150
Eastport, Id., U.S.	a I	160
Eastport, Me., U.S.	c T	146
East Porterville	h G	162
East Prairie	f G	152
East Retford	h M	78
East Rockingham	e G	150
East Saint Louis	d F	152
East Siberian Sea → Vostočno-Sibirskoje more ▾[2]	c W	94
East Spencer	d F	150
East Stroudsburg	g K	146
East Tawas	f L	148
East Troy	h G	148
Eastville	b K	150
East Wenatchee	c E	160
East Wilmington	e I	150
Eaton, Co., U.S.	d L	158
Eaton, In., U.S.	b K	152
Eaton, Oh., U.S.	h B	146
Eaton Rapids	h K	148
Eatonton	f C	150
Eatonville	d C	160
Eau Claire	f D	148
Eau Claire ≃	f D	148
Eau Claire, Lac à l' ⊜	e R	134
Eau Galle ≃	f C	148
Eauze	i G	84
Ebano	f J	166
Ebbw Vale	j J	78
Eben Junction	d I	148
Ebensburg	g H	146
Ebensee	h M	80
Eberbach	f H	80
Ebermannstadt	f K	80
Ebern	e J	80
Eberndorf	i N	80
Ebersbach	d N	80
Ebersberg	g K	80
Eberstein	i N	80
Eberswalde	c M	80
Ebetsu	d P	106a
Ebingen	g I	80
Ebino	o E	106
Ebinur Hu ⊜	c C	100
Ebnat	d K	83
Ebola ≃	h E	126
Eboli	i J	88
Ebolowa	h I	124
Ebro (Ebre) ≃	e L	86
Ebro, Embalse del ⊜[1]	b H	86
Eccles	b E	150
Echague	m S	109b
Ech Cheliff	a G	124
Echo	g L	156
Echo Bay	c I	134
Echoing ≃	c W	142
Echt	f H	82
Echuca	k F	184
Écija	h F	86
Eckernförde	a I	80
Eckville	e T	140
Eclectic	j J	152
Écrins, Barre des ∧	h M	84
Ecru	h G	152
Ecuador □[1]	d C	174
Ecum Secum	h K	144
Ed	l L	76
Edam	c G	82
Eddystone Point ≻	m H	184
Eddystone Rocks II[1]	k I	78
Eddyville, Ia., U.S.	i C	148
Eddyville, Ky., U.S.	e H	152
Ede, Ned.	d H	82
Ede, Nig.	g G	124
Edéa	h I	124
Edegem	f E	82
Edelény	g T	80
Eden, Austl.	k H	184
Eden, Ms., U.S.	j F	152
Eden, Tx., U.S.	h G	154
Eden, Wy., U.S.	b G	158
Edenburg	g G	130
Edendale	g J	130
Edenderry	h F	78
Edenton	c J	150
Eden Valley	e A	148
Edenville	f H	130
Edeowie	h C	184
Eder ≃	d H	80
Edgar, Ne., U.S.	k J	156
Edgar, Wi., U.S.	f F	148
Edgard	l F	152
Edgartown	f P	146
Edgefield	f E	150
Edgeley	e I	156
Edgemont	h D	156
Edgeøya I	b C	98
Edgerton, Mn., U.S.	h K	156
Edgerton, Oh., U.S.	f B	146
Edgerton, Wi., U.S.	h F	148
Edgerton, Wy., U.S.	a J	158
Edgewater, Al., U.S.	i J	152
Edgewater, Fl., U.S.	k F	150
Edgewood, Il., U.S.	d H	152
Edgewood, Ia., U.S.	h D	148
Edgewood, Md., U.S.	h J	146
Edgewood, Tx., U.S.	g K	154
Édhessa	i F	90
Edina, Mn., U.S.	f B	148
Edina, Mo., U.S.	b D	152
Edinboro	f F	146
Edinburg, Il., U.S.	c G	152
Edinburg, In., U.S.	c K	152
Edinburg, Ms., U.S.	j G	152
Edinburg, N.D., U.S.	c J	156
Edinburg, Tx., U.S.	m H	154
Edinburg, Va., U.S.	i H	146
Edinburgh	f J	78
Edirne	b B	118
Edison	h B	150
Edisto ≃	g F	150
Edisto Island I	g F	150
Edjeleh	c H	124
Edmond	d I	154
Edmonds	c C	160
Edmonton, Austl.	a F	184
Edmonton, Ab., Can.	d U	140
Edmonton, Ky., U.S.	f K	152
Edmore, Mi., U.S.	g J	148
Edmore, N.D., U.S.	c I	156
Edmundston	e E	144
Edna, Ks., U.S.	n L	156
Edna, Tx., U.S.	k J	154
Edna Bay	i BB	138
Edolo	c E	88
Edremit	c B	118
Edsbro	l P	76
Edsbruk	l O	76
Edsbyn	k N	76
Edson	d R	140
Eduardo Castex	h F	178
Eduni, Mount ∧	d DD	138
Edward, Lake ⊜	b E	128
Edwards, Ms., U.S.	j F	152
Edwards, N.Y., U.S.	c K	146
Edwards ≃	i E	148
Edwards Plateau ⋏[1]	i F	154
Edwardsville	d G	152
Edward VII Peninsula ≻[1]	c I	189
Eefde	d I	82
Eek	f M	138
Eeklo	f D	82
Eel ≃, Ca., U.S.	d A	162
Eel ≃, In., U.S.	b J	152
Eel ≃, In., U.S.	c I	152
Eemshaven	b J	82
Éfaté I	q Y	188f
Eferding	g N	80
Effingham, Il., U.S.	c H	152
Effingham, Ks., U.S.	l L	156
Ega ≃	c I	86
Egadi, Isole II	l G	88
Egan Range ⋏	e K	162
Eganville	e R	148
Egegik	g P	138
Eger	h T	80
Egersund	l J	76
Eggenburg	g O	80
Eggenfelden	g L	80
Egg Harbor City	h L	146
Éghezée	g F	82
Egijn ≃	b G	100
Egilsstaðir	b F	76a
Egmond aan Zee	c F	82
Egmont, Cape ≻	f H	186
Eğridir Gölü ⊜	c D	118
Egypt (Miṣr) □[1]	c G	126
Ehime □[5]	n G	106
Ehingen	g I	80
Ehrenberg	k B	158
Ehrhardt	f E	150
Eibar	b I	86
Eibiswald	i O	80
Eichstätt	g K	80
Eidfjord	k J	76
Eidsvåg	j K	76
Eidsvoll	k L	76
Eifel ⋏	e F	80
Eiger ∧	e I	83
Eights Coast ⁎[2]	c K	189
Eighty Mile Beach ⁎[2]	c D	182
Eildon	k F	184
Eildon, Lake ⊜[1]	k F	184
Eilenburg	d L	80
Eina	k L	76
Einasleigh	b F	184
Einasleigh ≃	a E	184
Einbeck	d I	80
Eindhoven	f G	82
Einsiedeln	d J	83
Eirunepé	e E	174
Eisden	g H	82
Eisenach	e J	80
Eisenberg	e K	80
Eisenerz	h N	80
Eisenhüttenstadt	c N	80
Eisenkappel	i N	80
Eisenstadt	h P	80
Eisfeld	e J	80
Eisleben	d K	80
Eislingen	g I	80
Eitorf	e G	80
Eivissa	g M	86
Eivissa (Ibiza) I	f M	86
Ejea de los Caballeros	c J	86
Ejin Qi	c G	100
Ejutla de Crespo	i K	166
Ekalaka	f C	156
Ekenäs (Taamisaari)	l R	76
Ekeren	f E	82
Ekibastuz	g G	94
Eksjö, Sve.	m N	76
Eksjö, Sve.	m N	76
Ekwan ≃	f P	134
Ekwok	g P	138
El Aaiún	c D	124
Elaine	h F	152
El Alamein → Al-'Alamayn	g C	118
Elands ≃	e I	130
Elandsvlei	i D	130
El Arahal	h F	86
El Arco	c C	166
Elat	i C	120
Elat, Gulf of → Aqaba, Gulf of ⊂	h F	118
El Avión	e F	166
Elâzığ	c H	118
Elba	k J	152
Elba, Isola d' I	g E	88
El Banco	j H	170
Elbasan	h D	90
Elbe (Labe) ≃	b I	80
Elbert	l C	156
Elbert, Mount ∧	e J	158
Elberta	f I	148
Elberton	e D	150
Elbeuf	c H	84
Elbląg (Elbing)	a S	80
El Bluff	f K	168
El Boulaïda	a G	124
Elbow Lake	f L	156
El'brus, gora ∧	i F	92
Elburg	d H	82
Elburz Mountains → Alborz, Reshteh-ye Kūhhā-ye ⋏	d O	118
El Cajon	l I	162
El Campo	j J	154
El Capitan ∧	d K	160
El Carmen	c F	178
El Carmen de Bolívar	j G	170
El Carricito	c H	166
El Carrizo	c G	166
El Castillo	f J	168

Symbols in the index are identified on page 198.

Name	Map Ref.	Page

Symbols in the index are identified on page 198.

Name	Map Ref.	Page

Symbols in the index are identified on page 198.

Name	Ref.	Page
Gran Sasso d'Italia ⩘	g H	88
Gransee	b M	80
Grant, Fl., U.S.	I F	150
Grant, Mi., U.S.	g J	148
Grant, Ne., U.S.	k F	156
Grant ⩙	h E	148
Gran Tarajal	o Z	87b
Grant City	b B	152
Grantham	i M	78
Grantown-on-Spey	d J	78
Grant Park	i H	148
Grants	i I	158
Grantsburg	e C	148
Grants Pass	h B	160
Grantsville, Ut., U.S.	d D	158
Grantsville, W.V., U.S.	i E	146
Grantville	f B	150
Granville, Fr.	d E	84
Granville, Il., U.S.	i F	148
Granville, N.Y., U.S.	d M	146
Granville, N.D., U.S.	c G	156
Granville, Oh., U.S.	g D	146
Granville, W.V., U.S.	h G	146
Granville Lake ⊜	h N	142
Granvin	k J	76
Grão Mogol	d G	177
Grapeland	h K	154
Grapevine Lake ⊜[1]	e J	130
Graskop	e J	130
Grasmere	f H	130
Grasonville	i J	146
Grass ⩙, Mb., Can.	b R	142
Grass ⩙, N.Y., U.S.	c K	146
Grass Creek	g Q	160
Grasse	i M	84
Grassflat	f H	146
Grass Lake	h K	148
Grass Range	c Q	160
Grass Valley	e D	162
Grassy	m F	184
Graubünden (Grischun) □[3]	e K	83
Gravatá	e K	174
Gravelbourg	i H	142
Gravelines	b I	84
Gravelotte	d J	130
Gravenhurst	f P	148
Grave Peak ⩘	d K	160
Gravette	f B	152
Gravina in Puglia	i K	88
Gray, Fr.	e L	84
Gray, Ga., U.S.	f C	150
Gray, Ky., U.S.	b C	150
Grayback Mountain ⩘	h B	160
Grayling, Ak., U.S.	e N	138
Grayling, Mi., U.S.	f K	148
Grays Harbor c	d A	160
Grayson, Al., U.S.	h I	152
Grayson, Ky., U.S.	i D	146
Grayson, La., U.S.	j D	152
Grays Peak ⩘	e K	158
Graysville	g K	152
Grayville	e H	152
Graz	h O	80
Grazalema	i F	86
Gr'azi	i V	96
Gr'aznoje	g V	96
Gr'azovec	c W	96
Great Abaco I	a F	170
Great Artesian Basin ⩙[1]	e E	184
Great Australian Bight c[3]	f E	182
Great Bahama Bank ⩘[4]	e C	170
Great Barrier Island I	c J	186
Great Barrier Reef ⩙[2]	c l	182
Great Barrier Reef Marine Park ♦	c l	182
Great Barrington	e M	146
Great Basin ⩙[1]	e K	162
Great Basin National Park ♦	e K	162
Great Bear ⩙	d FF	138
Great Bear Lake ⊜	c H	134
Great Bend	m l	156
Great Britain I	e E	74
Great Channel ⩙	k C	110
Great Dismal Swamp ⩙	i J	150
Great Divide Basin ⩙[1]	h Q	160
Great Dividing Range ⩘	e l	182
Great Dunmow	j N	78
Greater Antilles II	d G	170
Greater Khingan Range → Da Hinggan Ling ⩘	b K	100
Greater Sunda Islands II		
Great Exuma I	c G	170
Great Falls, Mt., U.S.	c E	160
Great Falls, S.C., U.S.	e F	150
Great Himalaya Range ⩘	f J	114
Great Inagua I	d H	170
Great Indian Desert (Thar Desert) ⩙[2]	g D	114
Great Karroo ⩙[1]	i F	130
Great Lake ⊜	m G	184
Great Malvern	i K	78
Great Mercury Island I	c J	186
Great Miami ⩙	h B	146
Great Namaqualand ⩙[3]	e C	130
Great Nicobar I	k B	110
Great Palm Island I	b G	184
Great Pee Dee ⩙	f G	150
Great Plains ⩙	e l	132
Great Ruaha ⩙	c G	128
Great Sacandaga Lake ⊜	d L	146
Great Salt Lake ⊜	c D	158
Great Salt Lake Desert ⩙[2]	d C	158
Great Sandy Desert ⩙	d D	182
Great Slave Lake ⊜	d J	134
Great Smoky Mountains ⩘	d C	150
Great Smoky Mountains National Park ♦	d C	150
Great Victoria Desert ⩙[2]	e E	182
Great Wall ⫶[3]		
Great Wall → Chang Cheng ⫶	c D	102
Great Yarmouth	i O	78
Great Zab (Büyükzap) (Az-Zāb al-Kabīr) ⩙	d J	118
Gréboun ⩘	h H	124
Grecia	d I	168
Greece (Ellás) □[1]	h L	74
Greeley, Co., U.S.	k L	158
Greeley, Ks., U.S.	m L	156
Greeley, Ne., U.S.	k F	156
Greeleyville	f G	150
Green ⩙, Il., U.S.	i F	148
Green ⩙, Ky., U.S.	e E	152
Green ⩙, N.D., U.S.	c D	156
Green ⩙, Wa., U.S.	c C	160
Greenacres	c H	160
Green Bay	f G	148
Green Bay c	f H	148
Greenbrier, Ar., U.S.	g D	152
Green Brier, Tn., U.S.	f J	152
Greenbrier ⩙	i F	146
Greenburg	l F	152
Greenbush	c K	156
Greencastle, In., U.S.	c J	152
Greencastle, Pa., U.S.	h l	146
Green City	b D	152
Green Cove Springs	j E	150
Greendale	c L	152
Greene, Ia., U.S.	h C	148
Greene, N.Y., U.S.	e K	146
Greeneville	c D	150
Greenfield, Ca., U.S.	h D	162
Greenfield, Il., U.S.	c F	152
Greenfield, In., U.S.	j M	156
Greenfield, Ma., U.S.	e N	146
Greenfield, Mo., U.S.	e C	152
Greenfield, Oh., U.S.	h D	146
Greenfield, Tn., U.S.	f H	152
Green Forest	f C	152
Green Head ⫸	f B	182
Green Island	l E	186
Green Lake	g G	148
Greenland, Ar., U.S.	g B	152
Greenland (Kalaallit Nunaat) □[2]	b O	132
Greenland, Mi., U.S.	d F	148
Greenland Sea ⩙[2]	b T	132
Greenleaf	l K	156
Green Mountains ⩘	d N	146
Greenock	f l	78
Green Peter Lake ⊜[1]	f C	160
Green Pond	i l	152
Greenport	f B	150
Green River, Ut., U.S.	f F	158
Green River, Wy., U.S.	c G	158
Green River Lake ⊜[1]	e K	152
Greensboro, Al., U.S.	j l	152
Greensboro, Fl., U.S.	b B	150
Greensboro, Ga., U.S.	f C	150
Greensboro, Md., U.S.	i K	146
Greensboro, N.C., U.S.	c G	150
Greensburg, In., U.S.	c K	152
Greensburg, Ks., U.S.	n H	156
Greensburg, Ky., U.S.	e K	152
Greensburg, Pa., U.S.	g G	146
Greens Peak ⩘	j G	158
Green Springs	f C	146
Green Swamp ⩙	e H	150
Greentown	b K	152
Greenup, Il., U.S.	c H	152
Greenup, Ky., U.S.	i D	146
Greenvale	b F	184
Green Valley, Az., U.S.	m F	158
Green Valley, Il., U.S.	j F	148
Greenview	b G	152
Greenville, Liber.	g E	124
Greenville, Al., U.S.	k J	152
Greenville, Ca., U.S.	d E	162
Greenville, Fl., U.S.	i C	150
Greenville, Ga., U.S.	f B	150
Greenville, Il., U.S.	d G	152
Greenville, Ky., U.S.	e l	152
Greenville, Me., U.S.	b Q	146
Greenville, Mi., U.S.	g J	148
Greenville, Ms., U.S.	i E	152
Greenville, Mo., U.S.	e F	152
Greenville, N.H., U.S.	e O	146
Greenville, N.C., U.S.	d l	150
Greenville, Oh., U.S.	g B	146
Greenville, Pa., U.S.	f F	146
Greenville, S.C., U.S.	e D	150
Greenville, Tx., U.S.	f J	154
Greenwich, Ct., U.S.	f M	146
Greenwich, N.Y., U.S.	d M	146
Greenwich, Oh., U.S.	f D	146
Gruzinskaja Sovetskaja Socialističeskaja Respublika (Georgia) □[3]	i F	92
Grybów	f T	80
Gryfice	b O	80
Gstaad	f G	83
Guacanayabo, Golfo de c	d F	170
Guacara	c l	170
Gu Achi	l D	158
Guachochic	e G	166
Guadalajara, Esp.	e H	86
Guadalajara, Méx.	g H	166
Guadalcanal I	j Q	188e
Guadalén ⩙	g H	86
Guadalhe, Embalse de ⊜[1]	g H	86
Guadalmena ⩙	h F	86
Guadalquivir ⩙	i N	166
Guadalupe, Méx.	e l	166
Guadalupe, Méx.	e l	166
Guadalupe, Ca., U.S.	j C	162
Guadalupe, Isla I	k l	164
Guadalupe [Bravos]	f C	166
Guadalupe Garzarón ⩙	e l	166
Guadalupe Mountains National Park ♦	h B	154
Guadalupe Peak ⩘	h B	154
Guadalupe Victoria	e G	166
Guadalupita	h K	158
Guadarrama, Sierra de ⩘	e G	86
Guadeloupe □[2]	f N	170
Guadeloupe Passage ⩙	f N	170
Guadiana ⩙	h D	86
Guadix	h H	86
Guafo, Isla I	e B	176
Guaíba	f M	178
Guaimaca	e C	168
Guainía ⩙	c E	174
Guaíra, Bra.	h H	177
Guaira, Bra.	c K	178
Guajará ⩙[5]	c H	174
Guajará Mirim	f E	174
Gualala	e B	162
Gualdo Tadino	g l	88
Gualeguay	g l	178
Gualeguaychú	g l	178
Gualicho, Salina del ⩦	e c	176
Guam □[4]	b F	180
Guamini	h l	178
Guamúchil	e F	166
Guanabacoa	c C	170
Guanacaste, Cordillera de ⩘	h D	168
Guanacastes, Golfo de c	c B	170
Guanaceví	e G	166
Guanaja	b C	168
Guanaja, Isla de I	a D	168
Guanajay	c C	170
Guanajuato	g H	166
Guanambi	c l	177
Guanare	c D	170
Guandacol	e c	178
Guane	c B	170
Guang'an	e H	100
Guangdong (Kwangtung) □[4]	g l	100
Guanghua	e l	100
Guangnan	g H	100
Guangnan Zhuangzu Zizhiqu (Kwangsi Chuang) □[4]	g H	100
Guangyuan	e H	100
Guangzhou (Canton)	I B	104
Guanhães	e G	177
Guanpata	b l	168
Guanxian	e G	100
Guapí	c C	174
Guápiles	g K	168
Guaporé (Iténez) ⩙	f F	174
Guaqui	g E	174
Guarabira	e K	174
Guaranda	d C	174
Guarani de Goiás	b E	177
Guarapari	f H	177
Guarapuava	c M	178
Guaratinguetá	g F	177
Guarda	e F	86
Guardafui, Cape → Caseyr ⫸	f K	126
Guardavalle	k K	88
Guardiagrele	g l	88
Guareim (Quaraí) ⩙	e l	170
Guarenas	i K	170
Guarulhos	g E	166
Guasave	e E	166
Guasdualito	b D	174
Guasipati	b F	174
Guastalla	e E	88
Guatemala	c D	168
Guatemala □[1]	c D	168
Guatemala □[1]	e F	164
Guatire	e C	174
Guaviare ⩙	c E	174
Guaxupé	a O	178
Guayabo	d F	166
Guayama	f K	170
Guayape ⩙	c l	168
Guayaquil	d B	174
Guayaquil, Golfo de c	d A	174
Guaycora ⩙	c E	166
Guaymas	d E	166
Guazapares	d E	166
Guazárachic	d F	166
Gubacha	f l	92
Gubbio	f G	88
Gubin	d N	80
Güdalür	g E	116
Gudermes	h D	116
Gudvangen	k J	76
Guebwiller	e N	84
Guékédou	g O	148
Guelma	b G	122
Guelph	g O	148
Guémené-sur-Scorff	e l	84
Guéret	f H	84
Guernica → Gernika-Lumo	b l	86
Guernsey	b L	158
Guernsey □[2]	f G	74
Guerrero □[3]	i l	166
Gueydan	I D	152
Guge ⩘	q H	126
Guguan I	b F	180
Guía de Isora	o X	87b
Guiana Basin ⩙[1]	c l	172
Guibes	f C	130
Guichen	e E	84
Guide	d G	100
Guide Rock	k l	156
Guiding	a l	110
Guildford	j M	78
Guilford	b R	146
Guilin (Kweilin)	b K	110
Guillaume-Delisle, Lac ⊜	e Q	134
Guillaumes	h M	84
Guimarães	d C	86
Guimba	n O	106
Guin	i l	152
Guinea (Guinée) □[1]	f C	124
Guinea, Gulf of c	h G	122
Guinea Basin ⩙[1]	h F	122
Guinea-Bissau (Guiné-Bissau) □[1]	f C	124
Güines, Cuba	c C	170
Güines, Fr.	b H	84
Guingamp	d C	84
Güira de Melena	c C	170
Guiratinga	g H	177
Güiria	i M	170
Güires	c J	84
Guiuan	o P	106
Guixian	c J	110
Guiyang (Kweiyang)	a l	110
Guizhou (Kweichow) □[4]	a l	110
Gujarat □[1]	i D	114
Gujrānwāla	d F	114
Gujrāt	d F	114
Gulbarga	d D	116
Gulbene	d l	116
Guledagudda	d C	116
Gulf Hammock	i D	150
Gulfport, Fl., U.S.	l D	150
Gulfport, Ms., U.S.	l l	152
Gulf Shores	l l	152
Gulgong	i H	184
Gulistān	e B	114
Gull Lake	h F	142
Gullspång	I N	76
Gulsvik	k K	76
Gulu	h G	126
Gumaca	o T	109b
Gumal (Gowmal) ⩙	e B	114
Gumma ⩙[5]	k M	106
Gümüşhane	b H	114
Guna	g H	114
Gundagai	g l	184
Gungu	c C	128
Gunnar	e K	134
Gunnedah	i H	184
Gunnison, Co., U.S.	f J	158
Gunnison, Ut., U.S.	e H	158
Gunnison ⩙	f H	158
Guntakal	e D	116
Guntersville	h J	152
Guntersville Lake ⊜[1]	h J	152
Güntür	d E	116
Gunungsitoli	f B	110
Günzburg	g J	80
Gunzenhausen	f J	80
Gupei	c K	102
Gura Humorului	b l	90
Gurdon	i D	152
Gurguéia ⩙	e J	174
Guri, Embalse de ⊜[1]	b F	174
Gurjev	h F	92
Gurjevsk	g C	96
Gurkha	f K	114
Gurupá	d H	174
Gurupi	f l	174
Gurupi ⩙	d l	174
Gusau	f H	124
Gus'-Chrustal'nyj	f W	96
Gusev	g E	96
Gusevskij	f W	96
Gushi	c D	104
Gushikawa	u B	107b
Guspini	j C	88
Güssing	h P	80
Gustavus	g AA	138
Güstrow	b L	80
Gustine, Ca., U.S.	g E	162
Gustine, Tx., U.S.	h H	154
Guthrie, Ky., U.S.	f l	152
Guthrie, Ok., U.S.	d l	154
Guthrie, Tx., U.S.	f F	154
Guthrie Center	j M	156
Gutian	i G	104
Gutiérrez Zamora	g K	166
Guttenberg	h D	148
Guyana □[1]	b G	174
Guyandotte ⩙	i D	146
Guymon	c E	154
Guyot, Mount ⩘	d C	150
Guyra	h l	184
Guysborough	g L	144
Guyton	g E	150
Guyuan	d H	100
Güzelyurt	b F	118
Guzmán	b F	166
Gvardejsk	g D	96
Gwai	b H	130
Gwalior	g H	114
Gwanda	c l	130
Gweedore	f E	78
Gwent □[6]	j K	78
Gweru	b l	130
Gwinn	d H	148
Gwinner	f J	156
Gwynedd □[6]	h l	78
Gy	e L	84
Gyangzê	f D	100
Gyaring Co ⊜	e D	100
Gyaring Hu ⊜	e F	100
Gydanskaja guba c	c M	92
Gym Peak ⩘	l C	158
Gympie	f J	184
Gyoma	i T	80
Gyömrö	h S	80
Gyöngyös	h S	80
Györ	h Q	80
Györ-Sopron □[6]	h Q	80
Gypsum, Co., U.S.	e J	158
Gypsum, Ks., U.S.	m J	156
Gyula	i U	80

H

Name	Ref.	Page
Haag	g N	80
Haag in Oberbayern	g L	80
Haaksbergen	d J	82
Haaltert	g E	82
Haamstede	d E	82
Haapajärvi	j S	76
Haapamäki	i S	76
Haapsalu	c F	96
Haar	g K	80
Ha'Arava (Wādī al-Jayb) V	h D	120
Haarlem	D F	82
Haast	e J	186
Haast Pass ⤭	f H	117
Habarūt	f H	117
Habay-la-Neuve	i H	82
Habbān	g E	117
Habermehl Peak ⩘	c C	189
Habiganj	h N	114
Hachijō-jima I	e N	106
Hachinohe	g P	106
Hachiōji	n E	106
Hackås	j N	76
Hackberry, Az., U.S.	i C	158
Hackberry, La., U.S.	m C	152
Hackensack	g B	152
Hackett	g B	152
Hackettstown	g L	146
Hackleburg	h l	152
HaDarom □[1]	f C	120
Haddam	c K	117
Haddington	f K	78
Haddock	f C	150
Hadejia	g H	124
Hadera	n K	76
Haderslev	g C	124
Hadīyah	j H	118
Hadlock	c B	160
Hadong, Taehan	e O	100
Ha-dong, Viet.	c H	110
Hadramawt ⫸[1]	g F	117
Hadsund	l L	76
Haeju	e M	102
Haenam	e O	100
Hafik, Jabal ⩘	b l	117
Hafīzābād	d E	114
Hafnarfjördur	b C	76a
Haft Gel	d G	118
Hafun, Ras ⫸	f K	126
HaGalil (Galilee) □[9]	c D	120
Hagan	i H	184
Hagen	d E	82
Hagerman, Id., U.S.	h K	160
Hagerman, N.M., U.S.	f B	154
Hagerstown, In., U.S.	c K	152
Hagerstown, Md., U.S.	h l	146
Hagersville	h O	148
Hagetmau	f E	84
Haggin, Mount ⩘	d F	160
Hagi	m F	106
Ha-giang	b H	100
Hagondange	c M	84
Hague	i A	156
Hague, Cap de la ⫸	c E	84
Haguenau	d M	84
Hagues Peak ⩘	d K	158
Hague, The → 's-Gravenhage	e E	82
Hahajima-rettō I	a F	180
Hahira	i C	150
Haian Shanmo ⩘	l J	104
Haicheng	c K	102
Hai-dương	d H	110
Haifa → Hefa	c D	124
Haifa, Bay of → Hefa, Mifraz c	c D	120
Haig	f E	182
Haigler	k C	156
Haikang (Leizhou)	m H	100
Haiku	q Q	163a
Hā'il	b E	117
Hailākāndi	h O	114
Hailar ⩙	b H	92
Hailey	g K	160
Haileybury	c P	148
Haileyville	k E	154
Hailong (Meihekou)	a M	102
Hailun	b H	100
Haimen, Zhg.	I E	104
Haimen, Zhg.	I E	104
Hainan Dao I	d l	110
Hainaut □[4]	g D	82
Haines, Ak., U.S.	g AA	138
Haines, Or., U.S.	f H	160
Haines City	k E	150
Haines Junction	f Z	138
Hainfeld	g O	80
Hai-phong	d l	110
Haiti (Haïti) □[1]	e H	170
Haizhou	a H	104
Hajdú-Bihar □[6]	h U	80
Hajdúböszörmény	h U	80
Hajdúnánás	h U	80
Hajdúszoboszló	h U	80
Haji Langar	c H	114
Hājīpur	h K	114
Hajnówka	c W	80
HaKarmel, Har (Mount Carmel) ⩘	c D	120
Hakim, Abyār al- ⩙[4]	b E	126
Hakkâri	d J	118
Hakodate	f O	106a
Hakui	k K	106
Haku-san ⩘	k K	106
Halab (Aleppo)	b F	118
Halachó	g N	166
Halā'ib	b H	126
Halalua	p Q	163a
Halawa, Cape ⫸	q R	163a
Halbā	d K	118
Halberstadt	d K	80
Halcon, Mount ⩘	o S	109b
Halden	I l	76
Haldensleben	c K	80
Haldwāni	k H	114
Hale	c C	152
Haleakala Crater ⫶[6]	c C	163a
Haleakala National Park ♦	q Q	163a
Hale Center	e E	154
Haleyville	h l	152
Halfmoon Bay	o C	186
Halfway, Md., U.S.	h l	146
Halfway, Or., U.S.	f l	160
Halfway ⩙	n C	134
Haliburton	e Q	148
Halifax, Austl.	b G	184
Halifax, N.S., Can.	h J	144
Halifax, Eng., U.K.	h L	78
Halifax, N.C., U.S.	c l	150
Halifax Bay c	b G	184
Hall	c H	150
Halkirk	c J	78
Hall Islands II	c G	180
Halladale ⩙	i P	76
Hällnäs	k P	76
Hallock	c K	156
Hallowell	c K	146
Hall Peninsula ⫸[1]	f H	117
Halls	s C	152
Hallsberg	I N	76
Halls Creek	c E	182
Hallstahammar	k P	76
Hallstatt	g l	80
Hallstead	m J	146
Hallsville, Mo., U.S.	c D	152
Hallsville, Tx., U.S.	j B	152
Halma	h M	80
Halmahera I	c l	108
Halmahera, Laut (Halmahera Sea) ⩙[2]	f H	108
Halmstad	m M	76
Halsey, Ne., U.S.	j l	156
Halsey, Or., U.S.	f B	160
Hälsingborg → Helsingborg	m M	76
Halstad	c K	156
Halstead	m J	156
Haltern	d J	82
Haltom City	g l	154
Halton Hills	g l	148
Haltwhistle	f K	78
Hamada	m F	106
Hamadān	e M	118
Hamāh	b F	118
Hamamatsu	m L	106
Haman	k L	76
Hamar	k L	76
Hamburg, B.R.D.	b l	80
Hamburg, Ar., U.S.	i E	152
Hamburg, Ia., U.S.	l M	156
Hamburg, N.J., U.S.	f L	146
Hamburg, N.Y., U.S.	e H	146
Hamburg, Pa., U.S.	g K	146
Hamden, Ct., U.S.	f M	146
Hamden, Oh., U.S.	h D	146
Hämeen lääni □[5]	k S	76
Hämeenlinna	k S	76
Hamelin	d D	182
HaMerkaz □[5]	c D	120
Hamersley Range ⩘	d C	182
Hamersley Range National Park ♦	d C	182
Hamgyŏng-sanmaek ⩘	c P	102
Hamhŭng	d M	102
Hamilton, Austl.	k K	184
Hamilton, Ber.	b l	80
Hamilton, On., Can.	g P	148
Hamilton, N.Z.	c J	186
Hamilton, Scot., U.K.	f l	78
Hamilton, Al., U.S.	h l	152
Hamilton, Il., U.S.	b C	152
Hamilton, Mi., U.S.	g l	148
Hamilton, Mt., U.S.	d E	160
Hamilton, N.Y., U.S.	e K	146
Hamilton, Oh., U.S.	h B	146
Hamilton, Tx., U.S.	h H	154
Hamilton, Mount ⩘	e J	162
Hamilton City	e D	162
Hamilton Dome	f l	160
Hamilton Hotel	d H	184
Hamilton Inlet c	h T	134
Hamina	k T	76
Hamiota	h l	142
Hamīrpur	i H	114
Hamlet	e C	150
Hamlin, Tx., U.S.	g F	154
Hamlin, W.V., U.S.	i D	146
Hamm	d G	80
Hammamet	a l	124
Hammār, Hawr al- ⊜	e l	118
Hamme	f E	82
Hammelburg	e l	80
Hammerdal	j N	76
Hammerfest	f R	76
Hammon	d G	154
Hammond, In., U.S.	I F	152
Hammond, La., U.S.	I F	152
Hammond, Wi., U.S.	f C	148
Hammondsport	e l	146
Hammonton	h L	146
Hampden, Nf., Can.	c Q	144
Hampden, N.Z.	I E	186
Hampden, Me., U.S.	c R	146
Hampden, N.D., U.S.	c R	156
Hampden Sydney	b H	150
Hampshire	h G	148
Hampshire □[6]	j L	78
Hampstead	d D	144
Hampton, N.B., Can.	g l	144
Hampton, Ar., U.S.	i D	152
Hampton, Fl., U.S.	j D	150
Hampton, Ia., U.S.	h B	148
Hampton, Ne., U.S.	k J	156
Hampton, N.H., U.S.	e P	146
Hampton, S.C., U.S.	g E	150
Hampton, Tn., U.S.	c D	150
Hampton, Va., U.S.	b J	150
Hampton Bays	g l	146
Hampton Butte ⩘	g E	160
Hamp'yŏng	e N	102
Hamra	k N	76
Hamra, As Saquia al ⩙	c D	124
Hams Fork ⩙	c F	158
Hamyang	h O	102
Hana	q R	163a
Hanahan	e F	150
Hanamaki	g P	106
Hanapepe	p N	163a
Hanceville	h J	152
Hancheng	d l	100
Hancock, Md., U.S.	h l	146
Hancock, Mi., U.S.	c G	148
Hancock, Mn., U.S.	f L	156
Hancock, N.Y., U.S.	f K	146
Hancock, Wi., U.S.	f F	148
Handa, Nihon	m K	106
Handa, Som.	f K	126
Handan	g B	102
Handlová	g R	80
HaNegev ⤭[2]	g C	120
Haney	h F	162
Hanford	h F	162
Han-gang ⩙	f N	102
Hangchow → Hangzhou	e l	104
Hangchow Bay → Hangzhou Wan c	e j	104
Hanggin Houqi	c H	100
Hanggin Qi	d H	100
Hangö (Hanko)	I R	76
Hangu	d E	102
Hangzhou (Hangchow)	e l	104
Hangzhou Wan (Hangchow Bay) c	e l	104
Hanish II	h C	117
Hanjiang	i H	104
Hankinson	e K	156
Hanko → Hangö	d L	74
Hankow → Wuhan	e C	104
Hanmer	d O	148
Hanna, Ab., Can.	f W	140
Hanna, Ok., U.S.	d K	154
Hanna, Wy., U.S.	c J	158
Hanna City	j F	148
Hannaford	d l	156
Hannibal	c E	152
Hannover → Hannover, B.R.D.	c l	80
Hannover, On., Can.	h l	148
Hanover, Il., U.S.	h E	148
Hanover, In., U.S.	d K	152
Hanover, Ks., U.S.	l K	156
Hanover, N.H., U.S.	d N	146
Hanover, N.M., U.S.	l H	158
Hanover, Pa., U.S.	h l	146
Hanover, Va., U.S.	b l	150
Hänsi	g M	156
Hanska	g M	156
Hanstholm	k L	76
Hantsport	g l	144
Hanwood	i G	184
Hanzhong	e G	100
Haparanda	i S	76
Happy	e E	154
Happy Camp	b C	162
Happy Jack	j E	158
Happy Valley-Goose Bay	f T	134
Hāpur	f G	114
Harad	b F	117
Haramachi	j P	106
Harare (Salisbury)	a J	130
Harasīs, Bi'r ar- ⩙[4]	c D	126
Harbin	b L	100
Harbor Beach	g M	148
Harbor Springs	e K	148
Harbour Breton	e R	144
Harbour Grace	e T	144
Harcourt	d C	144
Harcuvar Mountains ⩘	k C	158
Hardangerfjorden c[2]	k J	76
Hardenberg	c J	82
Harderwijk	d G	82
Hardesty	c F	154
Hardin, Il., U.S.	c E	152
Hardin, Mt., U.S.	e R	160
Hardinsburg	d J	152
Hardtner	n H	156
Hardwar	k H	114
Hardwick, Ga., U.S.	f C	150
Hardwick, Vt., U.S.	c N	146
Hardwood	f E	152
Hardy, Ar., U.S.	f E	152
Hardy, Ne., U.S.	b S	148
Hare Bay	d S	144
Hare Bay c	a R	144
Harelbeke	g C	82
Hargeysa	g l	126

Symbols in the index are identified on page 198.

Harg-Hove

Name | Map Ref. | Page

Harghita □6 c I 90
Har Hu ⊜ d F 100
Haria n AA 87b
Harihar e C 116
Haringvliet ⊻ e E 82
Harīrūd (Tedžen) ≃ b G 112
Harkers Island e J 150
Harlan, Ia., U.S. j L 156
Harlan, Ky., U.S. c C 150
Harlan County Lake ⊜1 k H 156
Harlem, Fl., U.S. m F 150
Harlem, Ga., U.S. f D 150
Harlem, Mt., U.S. b Q 160
Harlingen, Ned. b G 82
Harlingen, Tx., U.S. m I 154
Harlow j N 78
Harlowton d P 160
Harman i G 146
Harmånger k O 76
Harmanli h I 90
Harmony, In., U.S. c I 152
Harmony, Mn., U.S. g C 148
Harney Peak ∧ h D 156
Härnösand j O 76
Haro c I 86
Harper, Liber. h E 124
Harper, Ks., U.S. n I 156
Harper, Tx., U.S. i G 154
Harrell i D 152
Harricana ≃ f Q 134
Harriman d B 150
Harrington, De., U.S. i K 146
Harrington, Me., U.S. c S 146
Harrington, Wa., U.S. c G 160
Harris e C 148
Harrisburg, Ar., U.S. g F 152
Harrisburg, Il., U.S. e H 152
Harrisburg, Ne., U.S. j D 156
Harrisburg, Or., U.S. f B 160
Harrisburg, Pa., U.S. g J 146
Harrismith g I 130
Harrison, Ar., U.S. f C 152
Harrison, Id., U.S. c I 160
Harrison, Mi., U.S. f K 148
Harrison, Ne., U.S. i D 156
Harrisonburg, La., U.S. k E 152
Harrisonburg, Va., U.S. i H 146
Harrison Lake ⊜ h M 140
Harrisonville d B 152
Harriston, On., Can. g O 148
Harriston, Ms., U.S. k E 152
Harrisville, Mi., U.S. f L 148
Harrisville, N.Y., U.S. c K 146
Harrisville, W.V., U.S. h E 146
Harrodsburg e L 152
Harrogate g L 78
Harrold e G 154
Harrow h M 148
Harrowsmith f S 148
Harry S. Truman Reservoir ⊜1 d C 152
Harstad g O 76
Hart, Mi., U.S. g I 148
Hart, Tx., U.S. e D 154
Hart ≃ d Z 138
Hart, Lake ⊜ h B 184
Hartberg h O 80
Hartford, Al., U.S. k K 152
Hartford, Ar., U.S. g B 152
Hartford, Ct., U.S. f N 146
Hartford, Ks., U.S. m L 156
Hartford, Ky., U.S. e J 152
Hartford, Mi., U.S. h I 148
Hartford, S.D., U.S. h K 156
Hartford, Wi., U.S. g G 148
Hartford City b K 152
Hartington i J 156
Hartland, N.B., Can. f F 144
Hartland, Me., U.S. c Q 146
Hartlepool g L 78
Hartley, Ia., U.S. h L 156
Hartley, Tx., U.S. d D 154
Hartola k T 76
Harts ≃ g G 130
Hartselle h J 152
Hartshorne e K 154
Hartsville, S.C., U.S. e F 150
Hartsville, Tn., U.S. f J 152
Hartville e D 152
Hartwell e D 150
Hartwell Lake ⊜1 e D 150
Hārūnābād f E 114
Hārūt ≃ c G 112
Harvard, Il., U.S. h G 148
Harvard, Ne., U.S. k I 156
Harvey, N.B., Can. g I 144
Harvey, Il., U.S. i H 148
Harvey, N.D., U.S. d H 156
Harwich j O 78
Haryana □3 f G 114
Hasā, Wādī al- ∨ g E 120
Hashā', Jabal al- ∧ h D 117
Hashima I K 106
Haskell, Ok., U.S. d K 154
Haskell, Tx., U.S. f G 154
Haskovo h I 90
Haslemere j M 78
Hasperos Canyon ∨ k K 158
Hassan f D 116
Hasselt g G 82
Hassfurt e J 80
Hassi Messaoud b H 124
Hässleholm m M 76
Hastings, On., Can. f R 148
Hastings, N.Z. f K 186
Hastings, Eng., U.K. k N 78
Hastings, Fl., U.S. j E 150
Hastings, Mi., U.S. h J 148
Hastings, Mn., U.S. f C 148
Hastings, Ne., U.S. k I 156
Hasty m E 156
Haswell m D 156
Hatch, N.M., U.S. I I 158
Hatch, Ut., U.S. g D 158
Hatchet Lake h J 144
Hatchie ≃ g G 152
Hatfield, Ar., U.S. h B 152
Hatfield, Ma., U.S. e N 146
Hāthras g H 114
Ha-tien i H 110
Ha-tinh e H 110
Hattem d I 82
Hatteras d K 150
Hatteras, Cape ▸ d K 150
Hatteras Island I d K 150
Hattiesburg k G 152
Hatton, Al., U.S. h I 152
Hatton, N.D., U.S. d J 156
Hatvan h S 80
Hat Yai k F 110
Haubstadt d I 152
Hauge I J 76
Haugesund I I 76
Haugsdorf g P 80
Haukeligrend I J 76
Haukivuori j T 76
Haunstetten g J 80
Hauraki Gulf ⊂ c J 186
Hauroko, Lake ⊜ m B 186
Hausach g H 80
Haut Atlas ⋏ b E 124
Haute-Corse □5 I X 85a
Haute-Garonne □5 i H 84
Haute-Loire □5 g J 84
Haute-Marne □5 d L 84
Hauterive c E 144
Hautes-Alpes □5 h M 84
Haute-Saône □5 e M 84
Haute-Savoie □5 f M 84
Hautes Fagnes ⋏ e F 80
Hautes-Pyrénées □5 i G 84
Haute-Vienne □5 g H 84
Haut-Folin ∧ e K 84
Hautmont b J 84
Haut-Rhin □5 e N 84
Hauula p P 163a
Havana → La Habana, Cuba c C 170
Havana, Ar., U.S. g C 152
Havana, Fl., U.S. i B 150
Havana, Il., U.S. b F 152
Havana, N.D., U.S. f J 156
Havant k M 78
Havasu, Lake ⊜1 j B 158
Havelberg c L 80
Havelock, On., Can. f R 148
Havelock, N.C., U.S. e J 150
Havelock North f K 186
Haven n J 156
Haverfordwest j I 78
Haverhill, Eng., U.K. i N 78
Haverhill, Ma., U.S. e O 146
Hāveri c C 116
Haviland n H 156
Havířov f R 80
Havlíčkův Brod f O 80
Havre b P 160
Havre de Grace h J 146
Havre North b P 160
Havre-Saint-Pierre b J 144
Haw ≃ d G 150
Hawaii □3 p Q 163a
Hawaii I r R 163a
Hawaiian Ridge ✢3 f V 190
Hawaii Volcanoes National Park ♦ r R 163a
Hawarden i K 156
Hawea, Lake ⊜ k D 186
Hawera f I 186
Hawesville e J 152
Hawi q R 163a
Hawick f K 78
Hawke, Cape ▸ i J 184
Hawke Bay ⊂ f L 186
Hawker i H 184
Hawkes, Mount ∧ d A 189
Hawkesbury b L 146
Hawkins, Tx., U.S. g K 154
Hawkins, Wi., U.S. e E 148
Hawkinsville g C 150
Hawk Junction b K 148
Hawk Lake i U 142
Hawksbill ∧ i H 146
Hawley, Mn., U.S. e K 156
Hawley, Pa., U.S. f K 146
Hawthorne, Fl., U.S. j D 150
Hawthorne, Nv., U.S. f G 162
Haxtun k E 156
Hay j F 184
Hay ≃, Austl. d B 184
Hay ≃, Can. e I 134
Hay ≃, Wi., U.S. e D 148
Hayange c M 84
Hayden, Az., U.S. k F 158
Hayden, Co., U.S. d I 158
Haydenville h D 146
Hayes i D 152
Hayes ≃, Mb., Can. b V 142
Hayes ≃, N.T., Can. c N 134
Hayes, Mount ∧ e U 138
Hayes Center k F 156
Hayesville, N.C., U.S. d C 150
Hayesville, Or., U.S. f C 160
Hayfield g C 148
Hayfork d B 162
Haynes h F 152
Haynesville j C 152
Hayneville j J 152
Hay River d I 134
Hays, Ks., U.S. m H 156
Hays, Mt., U.S. c Q 160
Hay Springs i E 156
Haystack Mountain ∧ c J 162
Haysville n J 156
Hayti, Mo., U.S. f G 152
Hayti, S.D., U.S. g J 156
Hayward, Ca., U.S. g C 162
Hayward, Wi., U.S. d D 148
Haywards Heath j M 78
Hazafon □5 c D 120
Hazard b C 150
Hazāribāgh i K 114
Hazebrouck b I 84
Hazel ≃ i I 146
Hazel Green h E 148
Hazelton, B.C., Can. b G 140
Hazelton, Id., U.S. h K 160
Hazelton, N.D., U.S. e G 156
Hazelwood d C 150
Hazen, Ar., U.S. h E 152
Hazen, N.D., U.S. d F 156
Hazlehurst, Ga., U.S. h D 150
Hazlehurst, Ms., U.S. k F 152
Hazleton, Ia., U.S. h D 148
Hazleton, Pa., U.S. g K 146
Hazor c E 120
Headland k K 152
Headley, Mount ∧ c J 160
Healdsburg f C 162
Healdton e I 154
Healesville k F 184
Healy, Ak., U.S. e T 138
Healy, Ks., U.S. m G 156
Heard Island I j Q 70
Hearne h J 154
Hearst g P 134
Hearst Island I b L 189
Heart ≃ f E 156
Heathcote k F 184
Heath Springs e F 150
Heathsville h G 146
Heavener h B 152
Hebbronville I H 154
Hebei (Hopeh) □4 d J 100
Heber, Az., U.S. j F 158
Heber, Ca., U.S. I J 162
Heber City d E 158
Heber Springs g D 152
Hebi h B 102
Hebrides II d F 74
Hebron, Nf., Can. e T 134
Hebron → Al-Khalīl, Ghaz. e D 120
Hebron, Il., U.S. h G 148
Hebron, In., U.S. a I 152
Hebron, Md., U.S. i K 146
Hebron, Ne., U.S. k J 156
Hebron, N.D., U.S. e E 156
Heby I O 76
Hecate Strait ⊻ d C 140
Hecelchakán g N 166
Hechi b J 110
Hechingen g H 80
Hechuan e H 100
Hecla f I 156
Hecla Provincial Park ♦ g R 142
Hectanooga h G 144
Hector g M 156
Hédé, Fr. d E 84
Hede, Sve. j M 76
Hedemora k N 76
He Devil ∧ e I 160
Hedley e F 154
Hedmark □6 k L 76
Hedrick i C 148
Heemskerk c F 82
Heemstede d F 82
Heerenveen c H 82
Heerhugowaard c F 82
Heerlen g H 82
Ḥefa (Haifa) c D 120
Ḥefa □5 c C 120
Ḥefa, Mifraz ⊂ c D 120
Hefei d F 104
Heflin i K 152
Hegang b M 100
Heho d D 110
Heide a I 80
Heidelberg, B.R.D. f H 80
Heidelberg, S. Afr. j E 130
Heidelberg, S. Afr. h F 130
Heidelberg, Ms., U.S. k H 152
Heidenheim f J 80
Heidenreichstein g O 80
Heihe (Naquka) e O 114
Heilbron f H 130
Heilbronn f I 80
Heiligenblut h L 80
Heiligenhafen a J 80
Heiligenstadt d J 80
Heilong (Amur) ≃ g Q 94
Heilongjiang (Heilungkiang) □4 b L 100
Heiloo c F 82
Heimaey I c C 76a
Heinävesi j U 76
Heinola k T 76
Heishan b J 102
Hejaz → Al-Ḥijāz ✦1 j H 118
Hekla ∧1 c D 76a
Hekou c G 110
Hel a R 80
Helbra d K 80
Helen, Mount ∧ c D 184
Helena, Ar., U.S. h F 152
Helena, Mt., U.S. d M 160
Helena, Ok., U.S. c H 154
Helensburgh e I 78
Helensville c I 186
Helenwood c B 150
Helgoland I a G 80
Helgoländer Bucht ⊂ a H 80
Hellertown g K 146
Hellesylt j J 76
Hellín g J 86
Hells Canyon ∨ e I 160
Hells Gate ∨ h M 140
Hell-Ville n W 131b
Helmand ≃ c G 112
Helmond f H 82
Helmsdale c J 78
Helmstedt c K 80
Helper e F 158
Helsingborg m M 76
Helsingfors → Helsinki k S 76
Helsingør (Elsinore) m M 76
Helsinki (Helsingfors) k S 76
Helska, Mierzeja ▸2 a R 80
Helston k H 78
Hemau f K 80
Hemel Hempstead j M 78
Hemet k H 162
Hemford h I 144
Hemingford i D 156
Hemingway f G 150
Hemphill k C 152
Hempstead i J 154
Hemse m P 76
Hemsedal k K 76
Henan (Honan) □4 e I 100
Hen and Chickens II b I 186
Henderson, Ky., U.S. e I 152
Henderson, Mn., U.S. f B 148
Henderson, Ne., U.S. k J 156
Henderson, Nv., U.S. h K 162
Henderson, N.C., U.S. c H 150
Henderson, Tn., U.S. g H 152
Henderson, Tx., U.S. j B 152
Henderson Island I k AA 190
Hendersonville, N.C., U.S. d D 150
Hendersonville, Tn., U.S. f J 152
Hendricks, Mn., U.S. g K 156
Hendricks, W.V., U.S. h G 146
Hendrik Verwoerddam ⊜1 h G 130
Hendrina f I 130
Henefer c E 158
Hengelo d I 82
Hengshan, Zhg. d H 100
Hengshan, Zhg. h A 104
Hengyang f I 100
Henlopen, Cape ▸ i K 146
Hennebont e C 84
Hennef e G 80
Hennenman f H 130
Hennepin i F 148
Hennessey c I 154
Hennigsdorf c M 80
Henniker d O 146
Henning, Mn., U.S. e L 156
Henning, Tn., U.S. g G 152
Henri-Chapelle (Hendrik-Kapelle) g H 82
Henrietta, N.Y., U.S. d I 146
Henrietta, N.C., U.S. d E 150
Henrietta, Tx., U.S. f H 154
Henrietta Maria, Cape ▸ e P 134
Henry, Il., U.S. i F 148
Henry, S.D., U.S. g J 156
Henry, Cape ▸ c J 150
Henry, Mount ∧ b J 160
Henryetta d K 154
Henry Kater, Cape ▸ c S 134
Henrys Fork ≃ c F 158
Hensall g N 148
Hensley h D 152
Henty j G 184
Henzada f C 110
Hephzibah f D 150
Heppenheim f H 80
Heppner e F 160
Hepu (Lianzhou) d J 110
Herāt c G 112
Hérault □5 i J 84
Herbert h G 142
Herbert ≃ b F 184
Herberton a F 184
Herbertsdale j E 130
Herborn e H 80
Herceg-Novi g B 90
Herculaneum d F 152
Heredia g J 168
Heredia □4 g J 168
Hereford, Eng., U.K. i K 78
Hereford, Az., U.S. m F 158
Hereford, Tx., U.S. e D 154
Hereford and Worcester □6 i K 78
Herentals f F 82
Herford c H 80
Herington m K 156
Herisau d K 83
Herkimer d L 146
Herleshausen d J 80
Herlong d E 162
Hermagor i M 80
Herman, Mn., U.S. f K 156
Herman, Ne., U.S. j K 156
Hermann d E 152
Hermansville e H 148
Hermanus j D 130
Hermanville k F 152
Hermiston e F 160
Hermitage, Nf., Can. e R 144
Hermitage, Ar., U.S. i D 152
Hermitage, Mo., U.S. e C 152
Hermleigh g F 154
Hermon, Mount → Shaykh, Jabal ash- ∧ b E 120
Hermosillo c D 166
Hernád ≃ g U 80
Hernandarias c K 178
Hernando, Fl., U.S. k D 150
Hernando, Ms., U.S. h G 152
Herndon, Ks., U.S. I G 156
Herndon, Pa., U.S. g J 146
Herne d G 80
Herne Bay j O 78
Herning m K 76
Heroica Caborca b C 166
Heron Lake h L 156
Herreid f G 156
Herrera □4 i N 168
Herrin e G 152
Herring Cove, N.S., Can. h J 144
Herring Cove, Ak., U.S. i CC 138
Hersbruck f K 80
Herschel Island I b Y 138
Herscher i G 148
Hershey, Ne., U.S. j F 156
Hershey, Pa., U.S. g J 146
Herstal g H 82
Hertford, Eng., U.K. j M 78
Hertford, N.C., U.S. c J 150
Hertfordshire □6 j M 78
Hertzogville g G 130
Herval d'Oeste d M 178
Hervey Bay ⊂ e J 184
Herzberg d M 80
Herzberg [am Harz] d J 80
Herzliyya d C 120
Herzogenburg g O 80
Hesdin b I 84
Hesperia j H 162
Hesperus Mountain ∧ g H 158
Hess ≃ e BB 138
Hessen □3 e I 80
Hessisch Lichtenau d I 80
Hesston m J 156
Hetch Hetchy Aqueduct ≊1 g D 162
Hettinger e E 156
Hettstedt d K 80
Heusden f G 82
Heuvelton c K 146
Heverlee g F 82
Heves h T 80
Heves □6 h T 80
Hexian g I 100
Heyburn h L 160
Heysham g K 78
Heywood I D 184
Heyworth b H 152
Heze (Caozhou) h C 102
Hialeah n F 150
Hiawassee e C 150
Hiawatha, Ks., U.S. I L 156
Hiawatha, Ut., U.S. e E 158
Hibbing c C 148
Hibbs, Point ▸ n F 184
Hibernia Reef ✢2 b D 182
Hickman, Ky., U.S. f G 152
Hickman, Ne., U.S. k K 156
Hickory, Ms., U.S. j G 152
Hickory, N.C., U.S. d E 150
Hickory Flat h G 152
Hicks, Point ▸ k H 184
Hicksville f B 146
Hico h H 154
Hidaka-sammyaku ⋏ e Q 106a
Hidalgo, Méx. d J 166
Hidalgo, Méx. e I 166
Hidalgo, Méx. e J 166
Hidalgo, Méx. f H 166
Hidalgo □3 g J 166
Hidalgo del Parral d G 166
Hida-sammyaku ⋏ k L 106
Hieflau h N 80
Hienghène s W 188f
Hierro (Ferro) I p V 87b
Higashihiroshima m G 106
Higashiichiki p E 106
Higashine i O 106
Higashiōsaka m J 106
Higbee c D 152
Higgins c F 154
Higginsville c C 152
High Hill ≃ b D 142
Highland, Ca., U.S. j H 162
Highland, Il., U.S. d G 152
Highland, In., U.S. a I 152
Highland, Ks., U.S. I L 156
Highland □4 d H 78
Highland Home k J 152
Highland Park, Il., U.S. h H 148
Highland Park, Tx., U.S. g J 154
Highlands, N.J., U.S. g M 146
Highlands, N.C., U.S. d C 150
Highlands, Tx., U.S. j K 154
Highland Springs b I 150
Highmore g H 156
High Point d F 150
High Point ∧ f L 146
High Prairie b R 140
High River g U 140
High Rock Lake ⊜1 d F 150
High Springs j D 150
Hightstown g L 146
Highwood c O 160
High Wycombe j M 78
Higuera de Zaragoza e E 166
Higuera Gorda f G 166
Higüero, Punta ▸ e K 170
Hiiumaa I c E 96
Hikari n F 106
Hikone I K 106
Hilbert f G 148
Hildburghausen e J 80
Hilden d F 80
Hildesheim c I 80
Hildreth k H 156
Hillaby, Mount ∧ h O 170
Hill City, Ks., U.S. I H 156
Hill City, Mn., U.S. d B 148
Hill City, S.D., U.S. h D 156
Hillcrest Center i G 162
Hillerød n M 76
Hilliard i E 150
Hillister I B 152
Hillman e L 148
Hills h K 156
Hillsboro, Il., U.S. c G 152
Hillsboro, Ks., U.S. m J 156
Hillsboro, Mo., U.S. d F 152
Hillsboro, N.H., U.S. d O 146
Hillsboro, N.M., U.S. I I 158
Hillsboro, N.D., U.S. d J 156
Hillsboro, Oh., U.S. h C 146
Hillsboro, Or., U.S. e C 160
Hillsboro, Tx., U.S. g I 154
Hillsboro, Wi., U.S. g E 148
Hillsboro Canal ≊ m F 150
Hillsborough, N.B., Can. g I 144
Hillsborough, N.C., U.S. c G 150
Hillsborough ≃ k D 150
Hillsborough, Cape ▸ c H 184
Hillsdale i K 148
Hillsdale Lake ⊜1 m M 156
Hillston i F 184
Hillsville c F 150
Hilo r R 163a
Hilton d I 146
Hilton Head Island I g F 150
Hilversum d G 82
Hima b C 150
Himachal Pradesh □8 e G 114
Himalayas ⋏ f K 114
Himarë i C 90
Himeji m I 106
Himi k K 106
Ḥimṣ (Homs) e G 118
Hinche e H 170
Hinchinbrook Entrance ⊻ f U 138
Hinchinbrook Island I, Austl. b G 184
Hinchinbrook Island I, Ak., U.S. f U 138
Hinckley, Il., U.S. i G 148
Hinckley, Mn., U.S. d C 148
Hinckley, Ut., U.S. e D 158
Hindaun g G 114
Hindman b D 150
Hindmarsh, Lake ⊜ k D 184
Hindu Kush ⋏ b D 114
Hindupur f D 116
Hines g F 160
Hinesville h E 150
Hinganghāt b E 116
Hingham e P 146
Hingol ≃ h A 114
Hingoli c D 116
Hinnøya I g N 76
Hinojosa del Duque g F 86
Hinsdale, Mt., U.S. b R 160
Hinsdale, N.H., U.S. e N 146
Hinterrhein ≃ e K 83
Hinton, Ab., Can. d Q 140
Hinton, Ok., U.S. d H 154
Hinton, W.V., U.S. b F 150
Hipólito e I 166
Hirado n D 106
Hīrākūd ⊜1 b G 116
Hiram d P 146
Hirara g M 188d
Hirata I G 106
Hiratsuka I N 106
Hirosaki g O 106
Hiroshima m G 106
Hirson c K 84
Hirtshals m K 76
Hisār f F 114
Hispaniola I e I 170
Hita n E 106
Hitachi k O 106
Hitachi-ōta k O 106
Hitchcock j K 154
Hitchins i D 146
Hitoyoshi o E 106
Hitra I j K 76
Hiuchi-nada ⊤2 m H 106
Hiva Oa I i Z 190
Hiwannee k H 152
Hiwassee ≃ d B 150
Hixson g K 152
Hjelmelandsvågen I J 76
Hjo I N 76
Hjørring m K 76
Hkakabo Razi ∧ f F 100
Hlatikulu f J 130
Hlobane f J 130
Hlohovec g Q 80
Hluhluwe g K 130
Ho g G 124
Hoa-binh d H 110
Hoback ≃ g O 160
Hobart, Austl. n G 184
Hobart, Ok., U.S. d G 154
Hobbs g C 154
Hobe Sound I F 150
Hobgood c I 150
Hoboken f E 82
Hobson c P 160
Hobyo g J 126
Hochalmspitze ∧ h M 80
Hochkönig ∧ h M 80
Höchstadt an der Aisch f J 80
Hockenheim f H 80
Hocking ≃ h E 146
Hodeida → Al-Ḥudaydah g C 117
Hodge j D 152
Hodgenville e K 152
Hod HaSharon d C 120
Hódmezővásárhely i T 80
Hodna, Chott el ⊜ a G 124
Hodonín g Q 80
Hoehne n C 156
Hoek van Holland e E 82
Hoeryŏng a Q 102
Hoeyang e O 102
Hof, B.R.D. e K 80
Hof, Ísland b F 76a
Höfðakaupstaður b C 76a
Hoffman f L 156
Hofgeismar d I 80
Hofheim in Unterfranken e J 80
Hofmeyr h G 130
Höfn b F 76a
Hofors k O 76
Hōfu m F 106
Hog, Tanjong ▸ d F 108
Höganäs m M 76
Hogansville f B 150
Hoggar → Ahaggar ⋏ d H 124
Högsby m O 76
Hoh ≃ c A 160
Hohenau an der March g P 80
Hohenlimburg d G 80
Hohenthurn i M 80
Hohenwald g I 152
Hoher Dachstein ∧ h M 80
Hohe Tauern ⋏ h L 80
Hohhot c I 100
Hohoe g F 124
Hoh Xil Shan ⋏ c M 114
Hoi-an g J 110
Hoisington m I 156
Hojāi g O 114
Hokah g D 148
Hokes Bluff i K 152
Hokitika i E 186
Hokkaidō □5 d Q 106a
Hokkaidō I d Q 106a
Holbrook, Austl. j G 184
Holbrook, Az., U.S. j F 158
Holbrook, Ne., U.S. k G 156
Holden, Mo., U.S. d C 152
Holden, Ut., U.S. e D 158
Holden, W.V., U.S. j D 146
Holdenville d J 154
Holder k D 150
Holdingford e A 148
Holdrege k H 156
Hole in the Mountain Peak ∧ d J 162
Holgate f B 146
Holguín d F 170
Höljes k M 76
Hollabrunn g P 80
Holladay d E 158
Holland, Mi., U.S. h I 148
Holland, Tx., U.S. i I 154
Holland → Netherlands □1 e I 74
Hollandale i F 152
Hollandia → Jayapura f K 108
Hollandsbird Island I e B 130
Hollandsch Diep ⊻ e E 82
Holley d H 146
Holliday f H 154
Hollidaysburg g H 146
Hollins b G 150
Hollis e G 154
Hollister h D 162
Hollow Rock f H 152
Holly m E 156
Holly Grove h E 152
Holly Hill, Fl., U.S. j E 150
Holly Hill, S.C., U.S. f F 150
Holly Springs h G 152
Hollywood m F 150
Holman b I 134
Hólmavík b C 76a
Holmen g D 148
Holmes, Mount ∧ f O 160
Holmestrand I L 76
Holmsund j Q 76
Holon d C 120
Holstebro m K 76
Holstein i L 156
Holston ≃ c C 150
Holston High Knob ∧ c D 150
Holsworthy k I 78
Holt, Al., U.S. i I 152
Holt, Fl., U.S. I J 152
Holt, Mi., U.S. h K 148
Holton I L 156
Holts Summit d D 152
Holtville I J 162
Holwerd b H 82
Holy Cross e O 138
Holyhead h I 78
Holy Island I, Eng., U.K. f L 78
Holy Island I, Wales, U.K. h I 78
Holyoke, Co., U.S. k E 156
Holyoke, Ma., U.S. e N 146
Holyrood m I 156
Holzkirchen h K 80
Holzminden d I 80
Homalin b C 110
Homberg d I 80
Hombori Tondo ∧ e F 124
Hombre Muerto, Salar del ⊻ c E 178
Homburg → Bad Homburg vor der Höhe, B.R.D. e H 80
Homburg, B.R.D. f G 80
Homedale g I 160
Home Hill b G 184
Homeland Park e D 150
Homer, Ak., U.S. g S 138
Homer, Ga., U.S. e C 150
Homer, La., U.S. j C 152
Homer, Mi., U.S. h K 148
Homer, Ne., U.S. i K 156
Homer, N.Y., U.S. e J 146
Homer City g G 146
Homerville h D 150
Homestead n F 150
Homewood i J 152
Hominy c J 154
Homochitto ≃ k E 152
Homosassa k D 150
Homs → Al-Khums b C 126
Homs → Ḥimṣ e G 118
Honaker b E 150
Honan → Henan □4 e I 100
Honda b D 174
Hondeklipbaai h C 130
Hondo, Nihon o E 106
Hondo, N.M., U.S. k K 158
Hondo, Tx., U.S. j G 154
Hondo ≃ h O 166
Hondo, Rio ≃ m I 158
Hondsrug ⋏2 c J 82
Honduras □1 b H 168
Honduras, Cabo de ▸ a H 168
Honduras, Gulf of ⊂ b G 164
Honea Path e D 150
Hønefoss k L 76
Honesdale f K 146
Honey Grove f K 154
Honey Lake ⊜ d E 162
Honeyville c D 158
Honfleur c G 84
Hon-gay d I 110
Hongch'ŏn f O 102
Honghu f B 104
Hongjiang f H 100
Hong Kong □2 g I 100
Hongliuyuan c F 100
Hongshuihe ≃ c J 110
Hongsŏng g N 102
Hongtong d I 100
Honguedo, Détroit d' ⊻ c J 144
Hongwŏn c O 102
Hongze Hu ⊜ b G 104
Honiara j P 188e
Honiton k J 78
Honjō h O 106
Honningsvåg f S 76
Honokaa q R 163a
Honolulu p P 163a
Honomu r R 163a
Honshū I k M 106
Hood, Mount ∧ e D 160
Hood Canal ⊂ c C 160
Hoodoo Peak ∧ b E 160
Hood Point ▸ f C 182
Hood River e D 160
Hoodsport c B 160
Hoods Range ⋏ g F 184
Hoogeveen c I 82
Hoogezand-Sappemeer b J 82
Hooghly ≃ j L 114
Hoogkerk b J 82
Hooker c E 154
Hookina h C 184
Hook Island I c H 184
Hooks i B 152
Hoolehua p P 163a
Hoonah g AA 138
Hoopa d B 162
Hooper j K 156
Hooper Bay f K 138
Hoopeston j H 148
Hoople c J 156
Hoopstad f G 130
Hoorn c G 82
Hoosick Falls e M 146
Hoover Dam ✦6 h B 158
Hooversville g H 146
Hopatcong g L 146
Hope, B.C., Can. h M 140
Hope, Ar., U.S. i C 152
Hope, In., U.S. c K 152
Hope, N.D., U.S. d J 156
Hope, Point ▸ b K 138
Hopedale, Nf., Can. e T 134
Hopedale, Il., U.S. b G 152
Hopedale, La., U.S. m G 152
Hopefield i D 130
Hopelchén h O 166
Hope Mills e H 150
Hopes Advance, Cap ▸ d S 134
Hopetoun, Austl. f D 182
Hopetoun, Austl. j E 184
Hopetown g G 130
Hope Valley f O 146
Hopewell b I 150
Hopkins, Mi., U.S. h J 148
Hopkins, Mo., U.S. b B 152
Hopkinsville f I 152
Hopkinton h D 148
Hopland f B 162
Hopwood, Mount ∧ c F 184
Hoquiam d B 160
Horatio i B 152
Horb g H 80
Hordaland □6 k J 76
Horgen d J 83
Horicon g G 148
Horlick Mountains ⋏ d J 189
Hormuz, Strait of ⊻ i Q 118
Horn g O 80
Horn ▸ a B 76a
Horn, Cape → Hornos, Cabo de ▸ h C 176
Hornavan ⊜ h O 76
Hornbeak f G 152
Hornbeck k C 152
Hornbrook c C 162
Hornby j G 186
Horncastle h M 78
Horne, Îles de II e J 180
Hornell e I 146
Hornepayne g P 134
Horn Island I I H 152
Horn Lake h F 152
Hornos, Cabo de (Cape Horn) ▸ h C 176
Horn Plateau ∧1 d I 134
Hornsea h M 78
Horqin Youyi Qianqi b K 100
Horqueta b J 178
Horse Cave e K 152
Horse Creek c K 158
Horseheads e J 146
Horsens n K 76
Horseshoe Bend, Ar., U.S. f E 152
Horseshoe Bend, Id., U.S. g I 160
Horsham, Austl. k E 184
Horsham, Eng., U.K. j M 78
Horst f I 82
Horten I L 76
Hortobágy ✦1 h T 80
Horton I L 156
Hortonville f G 148
Horw d I 83
Hosaina g H 126
Hösbach e I 80
Hosëré Vokré ∧ g I 124
Hosford i B 150
Hoshangābād i G 114
Hoshiārpur e F 114
Hosingen h I 82
Hosmer f H 156
Hospers h L 156
Hospet e D 116
Hossegor i E 84
Hosston j C 152
Hosta Butte ∧ i H 158
Hoste, Isla I h C 176
Hotagen j N 76
Hotaka-dake ∧ k L 106
Hotan d B 100
Hotan ≃ d C 100
Hotazel f F 130
Hotchkiss f I 158
Hotevilla i F 158
Hotham Inlet ⊂ c N 138
Hoting i O 76
Hot Springs, Mt., U.S. c K 160
Hot Springs → Truth or Consequences, N.M., U.S. k I 158
Hot Springs, N.C., U.S. d D 150
Hot Springs, S.D., U.S. h D 156
Hot Springs, Va., U.S. b G 150
Hot Springs National Park h C 152
Hot Sulphur Springs d J 158
Hotte, Massif de la ⋏ e H 170
Hottentotbaai ⊂ f B 130
Houdan d H 84
Houghton, Mi., U.S. c G 148
Houghton, N.Y., U.S. e H 146
Houghton Lake f K 148
Houghton Lake ⊜ f K 148
Houlka h G 152
Houlton a S 146
Houma, La., U.S. m F 152
Houma, Zhg. d I 100
Housatonic e M 146
House e C 154
Houston, B.C., Can. c H 140
Houston, Mn., U.S. g D 148
Houston, Ms., U.S. i H 152
Houston, Mo., U.S. e E 152
Houston, Tx., U.S. j K 154
Houston ≃ I C 152
Houston, Lake ⊜1 j K 154
Houthalen f G 82
Houtkraal h G 130
Houtman Abrolhos II e B 182
Houtzdale g H 146
Hove k M 78

Symbols in the index are identified on page 198.

Symbols in the index are identified on page 198.

Symbols in the index are identified on page 198.

Name	Map Ref.	Page
Lantau Island I	m B	104
Lantsch	e L	83
Lanusei	j D	88
Lanxi	f H	104
Lanzarote I	n AA	87b
Lanzhou	d G	100
Laoag	l S	109b
Laoang	c H	108
Lao-cai	c G	110
Laoha ≃	a G	100
Laois □6	i F	78
La Oliva	o AA	87b
Laon	c J	84
Laona	e G	148
La Orotava	o X	87b
La Oroya	f C	174
Laos (Lao) □1	b C	108
Lapa	c N	178
La Palma	g I	164
La Palma I	o W	87b
La Paloma	h K	178
La Pampa □4	i E	178
La Paragua	b F	174
La Paz, Arg.	g E	178
La Paz, Arg.	f I	178
La Paz, Bol.	g E	174
La Paz, Méx.	e D	166
La Paz, Méx.	f I	166
La Paz, Ur.	h J	178
La Paz □5	c D	168
La Paz Centro	e H	168
Lapeer	g L	148
La Perla	c G	166
La Perouse Strait (Sōya-kaikyō) ⋃	b Q	100b
La Pesca	f K	166
La Piedad [Cavadas]	g H	166
La Pine	g D	160
Lapin lääni □4	h T	76
Lapinlahti	j T	76
Lapland □9	h R	76
La Plata, Arg.	h J	178
La Plata, Md., U.S.	i J	146
La Plata, Mo., U.S.	b D	152
La Plata ≃	h H	158
La Plata Peak ∧	e J	158
La Pobla de Segur	c L	86
La Pocatière	e C	144
Laporte, Co., U.S.	a H	158
La Porte, In., U.S.	a J	152
Laporte, Pa., U.S.	f J	146
La Porte City	h C	148
Lappeenranta	k U	76
Lappfjärd (Lapväärtti)	j Q	76
La Pryor	k G	154
Laptev Sea → Laptevych, more ⊤2	b Q	94
Laptevych, more (Laptev Sea) ⊤2	b Q	94
Lapua	j R	76
La Purisima	d C	166
Lapwai	d I	160
L'Aquila	g H	88
Larache	a E	124
Laramie	c K	158
Laramie ≃	b L	158
Laramie Mountains ⋌	b K	158
Larap	n T	109b
L'Arbresle	g K	84
Lärbro	m P	76
Larche, Col de ⋋	h M	84
Larchwood	h K	156
L'Ardoise	g M	144
Laredo	l G	154
La Reforma	e E	166
La Réole	h F	84
La Restinga	p W	87b
Largo	l D	150
Largo, Cañon ⋎	h I	158
Largo, Cayo I	d D	170
Largs	f I	78
Larimore	d J	156
Larino	e E	88
La Rioja	e E	178
La Rioja □4, Arg.	e E	178
La Rioja □4, Esp.	c I	86
Lárisa	j F	90
Lärkäna	g C	114
Larnaca → Lárnax (Larnaca)	e E	118
Lárnax (Larnaca)	e E	118
Larne	g H	78
La Rochefoucauld	g G	84
La Rochelle	f E	84
La Roche-sur-Yon	f E	84
La Roda	g I	86
La Romana	e J	170
La Ronge	c I	142
Larose	m F	152
Larrys River	g L	144
Larsen Bay	d N	138
Larsen Ice Shelf ⋈	b L	189
La Rubia	f H	178
La Rue	g C	146
Laruns	j F	84
Larvik	l L	76
La Sal	f O	158
La Salle, Co., U.S.	d L	158
La Salle, Il., U.S.	i F	148
Las Animas	m D	158
La Sarraz	e F	83
La Sarre	b P	148
Lascano	g K	178
Lascar, Volcán ∧1	b E	178
Las Casitas, Cerro ∧1	f E	166
Lascaux, Grotte de ⋆5	g H	84
Las Choapas	i L	166
Las Chorreras	c G	166
La Scie	c R	144
Las Colimas	e I	166
Las Cruces	l J	158
Las Cuevas	c I	166
Las Delicias	j N	166
La Serena	e C	178
Las Escobas	b B	166
La Seyne	i I	84
Las Flores	g D	178
Las Guayabas	g D	178
Las Heras	g D	178
Lashio	c G	110
Lashkar Gāh	c G	112
Las Lajas	j C	178
Las Lomitas	b S	80
Lašma	g X	96
Las Margaritas	i N	166
Las Minas, Cerro ∧	e F	168
Las Nieves	e D	166
La Solana	g H	86
Las Palmas	d I	178
Las Palmas I	o Z	87b
Las Palmas de Gran Canaria	o Y	87b
La Spezia	e E	88
Las Piedras	h J	178
Las Piedras, Río de ≃	f D	174
Las Plumas	i M	178
Las Rosas	i M	166
Lassay	d F	84
Lassen Peak ∧1	d D	162
Lassen Volcanic National Park ⋆	d D	162
La Zarca	e G	166
Las Tablas	g H	164
Las Termas	b D	176
Last Mountain Lake ⊜	g I	142
Las Tórtolas, Cerro ⋏	e D	178
Lastoursville	g G	128
Las Truchas	i H	166
La Suze	e G	84
Las Varas, Méx.	c E	166
Las Varas, Méx.	g G	166
Las Varillas	f G	178
Las Vegas, Nv., U.S.	h J	162
Las Vegas, N.M., U.S.	i K	158
Latacunga	d C	174
Latady Island I	c L	189
Latakia → Al-Lādhiqīyah	e F	118
Lata Mountain ∧	b D	188a
La Teste-de-Buch	h E	84
Lathrop	c B	152
Latimer	h B	148
Latina	h G	88
Latisana	d H	88
Latorica ≃	g V	80
La Tortuga, Isla I	i L	170
Latouche Treville, Cape ⋋	c D	182
Latowicz	c U	80
La Trimouille	f H	84
La Trinidad	e H	168
Latrobe, Austl.	m G	184
Latrobe, Pa., U.S.	g G	146
Latta	e G	150
La Tuque	a G	134
Lätür	c D	116
Latvia → Latvijskaja Sovetskaja Socialističeskaja Respublika □3	d H	96
Latvijskaja Sovetskaja Socialističeskaja Respublika □3	d H	96
Lauchhammer	d M	80
Lauder	f K	78
Lauderdale	j H	152
Lauenburg	b J	80
Lauf an der Pegnitz	f K	80
Läufelfingen	e S	83
Laufen, B.R.D.	h H	80
Laufen, Schw.	d H	83
Lau Group II	m U	188g
Laukaa	j R	76
Launceston, Austl.	m G	184
Launceston, Eng., U.K.	k I	78
La Unión, Chile	j C	178
La Unión, El Sal.	d G	168
La Unión, Esp.	h K	86
La Unión, Méx.	i I	166
La Unión, N.M., U.S.	m S	109b
La Unión □4	m S	109b
Laupheim	g I	80
Laura	c H	182
Laurel, De., U.S.	i K	146
Laurel, Fl., U.S.	l D	150
Laurel, In., U.S.	c K	152
Laurel, Md., U.S.	h J	146
Laurel, Ms., U.S.	k G	152
Laurel, Mt., U.S.	e Q	160
Laurel, Ne., U.S.	i J	156
Laurel ≃	b B	150
Laurel Bay	g F	150
Laureldale	g K	146
Laurel Hill	e G	150
Laurelville	h D	146
Laurencekirk	e K	78
Laurens, Ia., U.S.	h J	156
Laurens, S.C., U.S.	e D	150
Laurentides, Les ⋆1	a I	144
Laurie Lake ⊜	i J	142
Laurière	h E	84
Laurinburg	e G	150
Laurium	c G	148
Lausanne	e F	83
Laut, Pulau I	f F	108
Lauta	d N	80
Lautaro	j B	178
Lauterbach	e I	80
Lauterbrunnen	e M	83
Lauter [Sachsen]	e L	80
Laut Kecil, Kepulauan II	f F	108
Lautoka	m S	188g
Lauzon	f B	144
Lava Hot Springs	h M	160
Laval, P.Q., Can.	b M	146
Laval, Fr.	d F	84
La Vall d'Uixo	f K	86
La Valley	h J	90
Lāvān, Jazīreh-ye I	i O	118
La Vega	e I	170
Lavelanet	j H	84
Lavello	h J	88
Lavelle	e I	146
La Vergne	g C	152
Laverne	e H	154
Laverton	e D	182
La Veta	f R	76
Lavia	i K	76
La Victoria	d E	170
Lavik	k I	76
Lavillette	e H	144
Lavina	d Q	160
La Vista	j K	156
La Volla	i H	162
Lavonia	e C	130
Lavumisa	f J	130
Lawler	h D	156
Lawley	g C	148
Lawn, Nf., Can.	c R	144
Lawn, Tx., U.S.	h I	154
Lawndale	d E	150
Lawn Hill	c B	184
Lawrence, N.Z.	l D	186
Lawrence, In., U.S.	c J	152
Lawrence, Ks., U.S.	m L	156
Lawrence, Ma., U.S.	e A	146
Lawrence, Ne., U.S.	k I	156
Lawrenceburg, In., U.S.	c L	152
Lawrenceburg, Ky., U.S.	d L	152
Lawrenceburg, Tn., U.S.	g I	152
Lawrenceville, Il., U.S.	d I	152
Lawrenceville, Ga., U.S.	g C	150
Lawrenceville, N.J., U.S.	g I	146
Lawrenceville, Va., U.S.	c I	150
Lawtey	b I	150
Lawton, Mi., U.S.	i D	148
Lawton, N.D., U.S.	d I	156
Lawton, Ok., U.S.	e H	154
Lawz, Jabal al- ∧	h F	118
Laxá	l N	76
Layton	d E	158
Laytonville	e B	162
Lazdijai	g F	96
Lazio □4	g G	88
Leachville	g F	152
Lead	g D	156
Leader	h E	142
Leadore	f L	160
Leadville	e J	158
Leaf ≃, Mn., U.S.	e L	156
Leaf ≃, Ms., U.S.	k H	152
League City	j K	154
Leakesville	k H	152
Leakey	j G	154
Leaksville	c G	150
Lealman	l D	150
Leamington	h M	148
Leary	h B	150
Leatherman Peak ∧	f L	160
Leavenworth, Ks., U.S.	l M	156
Leavenworth, Wa., U.S.	c E	160
Leawood	e B	152
Lebak	d G	108
Lebam	b J	160
Lebanon, In., U.S.	b J	152
Lebanon, Ks., U.S.	l I	156
Lebanon, Ky., U.S.	e K	152
Lebanon, Mo., U.S.	e D	152
Lebanon, N.H., U.S.	d N	146
Lebanon, Oh., U.S.	h B	146
Lebanon, Or., U.S.	f C	160
Lebanon, Pa., U.S.	g J	146
Lebanon, S.D., U.S.	f H	156
Lebanon, Tn., U.S.	f J	152
Lebanon, Va., U.S.	c D	150
Lebanon (Al-Lubnān) □1	c B	112
Lebanon Junction	e K	152
Lebanon Mountains → Lubnān, Jabal ⋋	a E	120
Lebbeke	f E	82
Lebec	j G	162
Lebed'an'	h V	96
Lebesby	f T	76
Le Blanc	f H	84
Lebo	m L	156
Lebombo Mountains ⋋2	e J	130
Lebork	a Q	80
Le Brassus	e E	83
Lebrija	i E	86
Lebu	i B	178
Le Cannet	i N	84
Le Cateau	b J	84
Lecce	i M	88
Lecco	d D	88
Le Center	f B	148
Lech	g J	80
Lech ≃	g J	80
Le Châble	f G	83
Lechtaler Alpen ⋋	h J	80
La Claire	i E	148
Lecompte	k D	152
Le Creusot	f K	84
Łęczyca	c S	80
Ledbury	i K	78
Lede	g D	82
Ledo	g G	100
Leduc	d U	140
Lee ≃	e M	146
Leechburg	g G	146
Leech Lake ⊜	c A	148
Leedey	d G	154
Leeds, Eng., U.K.	h L	78
Leeds, Al., U.S.	i J	152
Leeds, N.D., U.S.	c I	156
Leelanau Peninsula ⋋1	f E	148
Leende	f H	82
Leer	b G	80
Leerdam	e G	82
Leesburg, Fl., U.S.	k E	150
Leesburg, Ga., U.S.	h B	150
Leesburg, Va., U.S.	h I	146
Lees Summit	d B	152
Leesville, La., U.S.	k C	152
Leesville, S.C., U.S.	f E	150
Leesville, Tx., U.S.	j I	154
Leeton	j G	184
Leeudoringstad	f H	130
Leeu-Gamka	i E	130
Leeuwarden	b H	82
Leeuwin, Cape ⋋	f C	182
Lee Vining	f F	162
Leeward Islands II	f M	170
Lefors	d F	154
Legal	d U	140
Leganés	c H	86
Legazpi	o T	109b
Leggett	e B	162
Leghorn → Livorno	f E	88
Legionowo	c T	80
Legnago	d F	88
Legnano	d C	88
Legnica (Liegnitz)	d P	80
Le Grand-Lucé	e F	84
Le Grau-Du-Roi	i K	84
Leh	c G	114
Le Havre	c G	84
Lehi	d E	158
Lehigh, Ia., U.S.	h A	148
Lehigh, Ok., U.S.	e J	154
Lehigh Acres	m E	150
Lehighton	g K	146
Lehr	d H	156
Lehrte	c I	80
Lehututu	d E	130
Leibnitz	i O	80
Leicester	i L	78
Leicestershire □6	i L	78
Leichhardt ≃	a C	184
Leiden	d F	82
Leie (Lys) ≃	b J	84
Leigh Creek	h C	184
Leighton	h I	152
Leighton Buzzard	j M	78
Leikanger	k J	76
Leinfelden-Echterdingen	a K	83
Leinster □9	i I	78
Leipsic	f C	146
Leipzig	d L	80
Leipzig □5	d L	80
Leiria	f C	86
Leitchfield	e J	152
Leitha ≃	h P	80
Leitrim	g H	78
Leitrim □6	g G	78
Leivonmäki	k S	76
Leizhoubandao ⋋1	d K	110
Lek ≃	e F	82
Leksand	k N	76
Leksvik	i L	76
Leland, Fl., U.S.	l D	150
Leland, Mi., U.S.	e C	148
Leland, Ms., U.S.	i G	152
Leleque	i C	178
Lelishan ∧	d G	114
Le Locle	d G	83
Lelystad	c G	82
Le Maire, Estrecho de ⊔	g D	176
Le Mans	d G	84
Le Mars	i K	156
Lemay	f D	152
Leme	g E	177
Lemelerveld	d I	82
Lemesós (Limassol)	e E	118
Lemeta	d U	138
Lemgo	c H	80
Lemhi Pass ⋊	f L	160
Lemhi Range ⋋	f L	160
Leming	j J	154
Lemitar	j J	158
Lemmer	c H	82
Lemmon	f E	156
Lemnos → Límnos I	j l	90
Lemoncove	h F	162
Lemon Grove	l H	162
Le Mont-Saint-Michel ⋎1	d E	84
Lemoore	h F	162
Le Moule	f N	170
Lempira □5	c F	168
Lena, Il., U.S.	h F	148
Lena, Wi., U.S.	f G	148
Lena ≃	c Q	94
Lençóis	b H	177
Lenghu	e E	100
Lengua de Vaca, Punta ⋋	f C	178
Lenhovda	m N	76
Lenina, pik ∧	j l	92
Lenina ≃	i F	92
Leninakan	i F	92
Leningrad	h F	96
Leningradskaja ⊵3	b H	109b
Leninogorsk	g H	94
Leninsk, S.S.S.R.	h J	92
Leninsk, S.S.S.R.	i L	92
Leninsk-Kuzneckij	g I	94
Lenk	f G	83
Lenkoran'	j O	92
Lennox	h K	156
Lennox, Isla I	h K	176
Lennoxville	b O	146
Lenoir	d E	150
Lenoir City	d B	150
Lenox, Ga., U.S.	h C	150
Lenox, Ia., U.S.	k M	156
Lenox, Ma., U.S.	e O	146
Lenox, Tn., U.S.	f G	152
Lens	b I	84
Lensk	e N	94
Lenti	i P	80
Lentini	l J	88
Lenzburg	d l	83
Léo	f F	124
Leoben	h O	80
Leola, Ar., U.S.	h D	152
Leola, S.D., U.S.	f I	156
Leominster, Ma., U.S.	e O	146
Leominster, Eng., U.K.	i K	78
León, Esp.	c F	86
León, Fr.	i E	84
León, Nic.	e H	168
Leon, Ia., U.S.	j B	148
León, Ks., U.S.	n K	156
León □9	e H	168
Leon □9	d F	86
León [de los Aldamas]	g I	166
Leonard, N.D., U.S.	e J	156
Leonard, Tx., U.S.	f J	154
Leonardtown	i I	146
Leonardville	l K	156
Leonberg	g I	80
Leonforte	l I	88
Leongatha	l F	184
Leonora	e D	182
Leonville	e D	152
Leopold and Astrid Coast ⋆2	b E	189
Leopoldina	g H	177
Leopoldsburg (Bourg-Léopold)	f G	82
Léopoldville → Kinshasa	b C	128
Leoti	m F	156
Lepanto	g F	152
Lepe	h D	86
Lepel'	h H	96
Lezhë	h C	90
Lhokseumawe	l D	110
Lhorong	e M	114
Léros I	k D	90
Le Roy, Il., U.S.	b H	152
Le Roy, Ks., U.S.	m L	156
Le Roy, Mn., U.S.	g D	148
Le Roy, N.Y., U.S.	e I	146
Lerwick	a L	78
Les Andelys	c H	84
Lesbos → Lésvos I	j J	90
Les Cayes	e H	170
Les Diablerets	f G	83
Leshan	f G	100
Les Haudères	f G	83
Lesjaskog	j K	76
Lesjöfors	l N	76
Lesko	g V	80
Leskovac	g E	90
Leslie, Ar., U.S.	g D	152
Leslie, Mi., U.S.	h K	148
Leslie, W.V., U.S.	i F	146
Les Mosses	f F	83
Lesnoj	e N	94
Lesosibirsk	f J	94
Lesozavodsk	c E	100
Les Pieux	c E	84
Les Riceys	d K	84
Les Sables-d'Olonne	f E	84
Lessay	c E	84
Lessen (Lessines)	g D	82
Lesser Khingan Range → Xiao Hinggan Ling ⋌	b L	100
Lesser Slave Lake ⊜	b S	140
Lesser Antilles II	h N	170
Lesser Sunda Islands → Nusa Tenggara II	g G	108
Les Sueur	f B	148
Lésvos I	j J	90
Leszno	c Q	80
Letcher	h l	156
Letenye	i P	80
Leti, Kepulauan II	g H	108
Leticia	d E	174
Letjiesbos	i F	130
Letpadan	f C	110
Lichina	d G	128
Le Trayas	i M	84
Le Tréport	b H	84
Letsök-aw Kyun I	i E	110
Letterkenny	g F	78
Leucadia	l C	162
Licking ≃	i B	146
Leulumoega	a B	188a
Leuna	d L	80
Leuser, Gunung ∧	m D	110
Leutkirch	h J	80
Leuven (Louvain)	g F	82
Leuze	g D	82
Levack	d N	148
Levádhia	k F	90
Levanger	i L	76
Levanto	e D	88
Leverkusen	d F	80
Levice	h S	80
Levie	m M	84
Le Vigan	i J	84
Lévis	f B	144
Levisa Fork ≃	b K	146
Liezen	h N	80
Lifford	g F	78
Liffré	d E	84
Levittown, N.Y., U.S.	g M	146
Levittown, Pa., U.S.	g L	146
Levkás	k D	90
Levkás I	k D	90
Levroux	f H	84
Lewellen	j E	156
Lewes, Eng., U.K.	k N	78
Lewes, De., U.S.	i K	146
Lewis, Ia., U.S.	j L	156
Lewis, Ks., U.S.	n H	156
Lewis, Butt of ⋋	c G	78
Lewis, Isle of I	c G	78
Lewis, Mount ∧	d l	162
Lewis and Clark Lake ⊜1	i J	156
Lewis and Clark Range ⋌	c M	160
Lewisburg, Ky., U.S.	c J	152
Lewisburg, Pa., U.S.	g J	146
Lewisburg, Tn., U.S.	g J	152
Lewisburg, W.V., U.S.	i G	146
Lewis Pass ⋊	e J	186
Lewisport	e J	152
Lewis Range ⋌	b L	160
Lewis Run	g H	146
Lewis Smith Lake ⊜1	h l	152
Lewiston, Ar., U.S.	h D	152
Lewiston, Id., U.S.	d H	160
Lewiston, Me., U.S.	d N	146
Lewiston, Mi., U.S.	f K	148
Lewiston, Mn., U.S.	g D	148
Lewiston, N.Y., U.S.	d G	146
Lewiston, Ut., U.S.	c E	158
Lewiston Orchards	d I	160
Lewistown, Il., U.S.	b E	152
Lewistown, Mo., U.S.	b E	152
Lewistown, Mt., U.S.	c Q	160
Lewistown, Pa., U.S.	g I	146
Lewisville, Ar., U.S.	i C	152
Lewisville, Tx., U.S.	f J	154
Lewisville Lake ⊜1	f J	154
Lexa	h F	152
Lexington, Ga., U.S.	f C	150
Lexington, Il., U.S.	j G	148
Lexington, Ky., U.S.	c K	152
Lexington, Ma., U.S.	e O	146
Lexington, Mi., U.S.	h M	148
Lexington, Mo., U.S.	c C	152
Lexington, Ne., U.S.	k H	156
Lexington, N.C., U.S.	d F	150
Lexington, Ok., U.S.	d I	154
Lexington, Or., U.S.	f E	160
Lexington, S.C., U.S.	f E	150
Lexington, Tn., U.S.	g H	152
Lexington, Va., U.S.	b G	150
Lexington Park	i J	146
Leye	g G	100
Leyte I	d H	108
Leyte Gulf c	c H	108
Lezhë	h C	90
Lhokseumawe	l D	110
Lhorong	e M	114
Lhuntsi Dzong	d N	114
Liangananmakki Reservoir ⊜1	f C	116
Liao ≃	e J	110
Lianga	e J	110
Liangyen	m S	109b
Lianyungang (Xinpu)	i G	102
Liao ≃	a J	110
Liaocheng	c C	102
Liaodong Bandao (Liaotung Peninsula) ⋋1	a J	102
Liaodong Wan c	c K	100
Liaoning □4	c K	100
Liaotung Peninsula → Liaodong Bandao ⋋1	a J	102
Liaoyang	c K	102
Liaoyuan	a J	110
Liard ≃	e H	134
Lîbîyâ, Çahrâ' al- (Libyan Desert) ⋆2	d F	126
Libagon	d H	108
Libby	b H	160
Libenge	a C	128
Liberal, Ks., U.S.	n G	156
Liberal, Mo., U.S.	e B	152
Liberec	e O	80
Liberia	e G	168
Liberia □1	e D	124
Libertad General Bernardo O'Higgins □4	h C	178
Libertad General San Martín	b F	178
Liberty, Ky., U.S.	e L	152
Liberty, Mo., U.S.	c B	152
Liberty, Ms., U.S.	k F	152
Liberty, N.Y., U.S.	f L	146
Liberty, S.C., U.S.	e D	150
Liberty, Tx., U.S.	i K	154
Liberty Center	f B	146
Liberty Hill	i I	154
Libertyville	h H	148
Lîbîyâ, Çahrâ' as- (Libyan Desert) ⋆2	d F	126
Libourne	h F	84
Libramont	h H	82
Libreville	a A	128
Libya □1	c D	126
Libyan Desert → Lîbîyâ, Çahrâ' as- ⋆2	d F	126
Licata	l I	88
Licentén	d F	178
Lich	e H	80
Lichfield	i L	78
Lichinga	d G	128
Lichtenburg	f H	130
Lichtenfels	e K	80
Lichtervelde	f C	82
Licking	i B	148
Lida	h H	96
Lidgerwood	e J	156
Lidköping	l M	76
Lidzbark	b S	80
Lidzbark Warmiński	a T	80
Liechtenstein □1	f l	74
Liège (Luik)	g H	82
Liège □9	g H	82
Liegnitz → Legnica	d P	80
Lieksa	j V	76
Lienz	i L	80
Liepāja	e D	96
Lier (Lierre)	f F	82
Lierre (Lier)	f F	82
Lieshout	e H	82
Liestal	d H	83
Liévin	b I	84
Lièvre, Rivière du ≃	b K	146
Liezen	h N	80
Lifford	g F	78
Liffré	d E	84
Lifou I	s X	188f
Lighthouse Point	m F	150
Lighthouse Point ⋋	c E	156
Lignite	d L	156
Ligny-en-Barrois	d L	84
Ligonha ≃	e G	128
Ligonier, In., U.S.	a K	152
Ligonier, Pa., U.S.	g H	146
Ligui	e C	166
Liguria □4	e C	88
Ligurian Sea ⊤2	f D	88
Lihue	p N	163a
Lijiang	f G	100
Likasi (Jadotville)	d E	128
Likino-Dulevo	f U	96
Liknes	j K	76
Likoma Island I	d F	128
Likouala ≃	b C	128
Lilbourn	g J	152
L'Île-Rousse	j O	84
Lilienfeld	g O	80
Liling	h B	104
Lille	b J	84
Lillebonne	c G	84
Lillehammer	k L	76
Lillers	b I	84
Lillesand	l K	76
Lillestrøm	l L	76
Lillhärdal	k N	76
Lillington	d H	150
Lillooet	g M	140
Lillooet ≃	h L	140
Lilongwe	d F	128
Liloy	d G	108
Lily	b B	148
Lilydale	g B	184
Lima, Perú	f C	174
Lima, Sve.	k M	76
Lima, Mt., U.S.	f M	160
Lima, N.Y., U.S.	e I	146
Lima, Oh., U.S.	g B	146
Lima (Limia) ≃	d C	86
Lisbon Falls	d N	146
Lisburn	g G	78
Lisburne, Cape ⋋	b B	138
Limanowa	f T	80
Limassol → Lemesós	e E	118
Limavady	f G	78
Limay ≃	d C	176
Limbang	e F	108
Limbdi	i D	114
Limburg □4, Bel.	f G	82
Limburg □4, Ned.	f H	82
Limburg an der Lahn	e H	80
Limeira	b O	178
Limerick	i E	78
Limerick □6	i E	78
Lime Springs	g D	156
Limestone	f F	144
Limfjorden ⋃	m K	76
Limia (Lima) ≃	d C	86
Liminka	i S	76
Limmared	m M	76
Limmen Bight c3	b G	182
Límnos I	j l	90
Limoeiro	e K	174
Limoges	h H	84
Limogne	h H	84
Limón, C.R.	i G	168
Limón, Hond.	d I	168
Limon, Co., U.S.	l D	158
Limón □4	h K	168
Limón de Ramos	f E	166
Limoux	i I	84
Limpopo ≃	e K	130
Linares, Chile	h C	178
Linares, Esp.	g H	86
Linares, Méx.	e J	166
Lincang	a J	110
Linch	h L	158
Lincoln, Arg.	h E	178
Lincoln, Eng., U.K.	h M	78
Lincoln, Ca., U.S.	f D	162
Lincoln, Il., U.S.	b G	152
Lincoln, Ks., U.S.	l I	156
Lincoln, Me., U.S.	c R	146
Lincoln, Mi., U.S.	f K	148
Lincoln, Mo., U.S.	d D	152
Lincoln, Mt., U.S.	c M	160
Lincoln, N.H., U.S.	d O	146
Lincoln, Ne., U.S.	k J	156
Lincoln, Mount ∧	e J	158
Lincoln City	f B	160
Lincoln Park, Co., U.S.	f K	158
Lincoln Park, Ga., U.S.	g B	150
Lincoln Park, Mi., U.S.	h L	148
Lincoln Sea ⊤2	a N	132
Lincolnshire □6	h M	78
Lincolnton, Ga., U.S.	f D	150
Lincolnton, N.C., U.S.	d E	150
Lincoln Village	g C	148
Lind	d G	160
Linda	f D	162
Lindale, Ga., U.S.	e A	150
Lindale, Tx., U.S.	g K	154
Lindau	h I	80
Linden, Al., U.S.	j l	152
Linden, Guy.	c F	174
Linden, Mi., U.S.	h L	148
Linden, Tx., U.S.	i B	152
Lindesberg	l N	76
Lindesnes ⋋	m J	76
Lindi	c G	128
Lindian	b L	100
Lindley	f J	130
Lindsay, On., Can.	f G	148
Lindsay, Ca., U.S.	h F	162
Lindsay, Mt., U.S.	c S	160
Lindsay, Ne., U.S.	j I	156
Lindsay, Ok., U.S.	e l	154
Lindsborg	m J	156
Line Islands II	c K	180
Linesville	f F	146
Lineville, Al., U.S.	i K	152
Lineville, Ia., U.S.	j B	148
Linfen	d l	100
Linganamakki Reservoir ⊜1	f C	116
Lingao	e J	110
Lingayen	m S	109b
Lingayen Gulf c	k O	76
Lingbo	k O	76
Lingen	c G	80
Lingga, Kepulauan II	o H	110
Lingga, Pulau I	o H	110
Lingle	b L	158
Lingling	a K	110
Linguère	e C	124
Linh, Ngoc ∧	g I	110
Linhai	g J	104
Linhares	e H	177
Linhe	d B	102
Linjiang	b G	100
Linköping	l N	76
Linkou	b M	100
Linkuva	e F	96
Linlithgow	f J	78
Linn, Ks., U.S.	l J	156
Linn, Mo., U.S.	d E	152
Linqing	e C	102
Linru	a K	104
Lins	g F	177
Lintao	d G	100
Linth ≃	d K	83
Linton, In., U.S.	c J	152
Linton, N.D., U.S.	e G	156
Linville	c E	150
Linxi	c J	102
Linxia	d G	100
Linyanti ≃	b G	130
Linyi	h F	102
Linz	g N	80
Lion, Golfe du c	i K	84
Liozno	h I	96
Lipa	o S	109b
Lipari, Isola I	k I	88
Lipeck	i V	96
Lipetsk → Lipeck	i V	96
Lipez, Cerro ∧	h E	174
Lipki	h T	96
Lipno	c S	80
Lipno, údolní nádrž ⊜1	g N	80
Lipova	c E	90
Lippe ≃	d H	80
Lippstadt	d H	80
Lipscomb	c F	154
Liptovský Mikuláš	f S	80
Liptrap, Cape ⋋	l F	184
Lira	h G	126
Lisala	a D	128
Lisboa (Lisbon)	g B	86
Lisbon → Lisboa, Port.	g B	86
Lisbon, N.H., U.S.	c O	146
Lisbon, N.D., U.S.	e J	156
Lisbon, Oh., U.S.	g F	146
Lisbon Falls	d N	146
Lisburn	g G	78
Lisburne, Cape ⋋	b B	138
Lishui	g H	104
Lisianski Island I	a J	180
Lisičansk	h E	92
Lisieux	c G	84
L'Isle-sur-le-Doubs	e M	84
Lisman	j H	152
Lismore, Austl.	g J	184
Lismore, N.S., Can.	g K	144
Lisse	d F	82
Listowel, On., Can.	g D	148
Listowel, Ire.	i D	78
Lit	j N	76
Litang, Zhg.	f G	100
Litang, Zhg.	f G	100
Litang ≃	f G	100
Lîtânî, Nahr al- ≃	b D	120
Litchfield, Il., U.S.	c G	152
Litchfield, Mi., U.S.	h K	148
Litchfield, Mn., U.S.	e B	148
Litchfield, Ne., U.S.	k H	156
Litchfield Park	k D	158
Litchville	e H	156
Lithgow	l F	184
Lithonia	f B	150
Lithuania → Litovskaja Sovetskaja Socialističeskaja Respublika □3	g J	96
Lititz	g J	146
Litoměřice	e N	80
Litovskaja Sovetskaja Socialističeskaja Respublika □3	g J	96
Littau	d l	83
Little ≃, Al., U.S.	i B	152
Little ≃, Ga., U.S.	f D	150
Little ≃, Ky., U.S.	e K	152
Little ≃, Ok., U.S.	k D	154
Little ≃, Tn., U.S.	g C	150
Little Abaco Island I	m J	170
Little Andaman I	k E	110
Little Arkansas ≃	m l	156
Little Bear ≃	c E	158
Little Belt Mountains ⋌	d O	160
Little Bighorn ≃	d O	160
Little Bitterroot ≃	c L	160
Little Blackfoot ≃	d M	160
Little Blue ≃	l K	156
Little Buffalo ≃	d l	134
Little Cayman I	e E	170
Little Cedar ≃	g C	148
Little Chute	f G	148
Little Colorado ≃	h F	158
Little Cottonwood ≃	c D	160
Little Current	c D	148
Little Current ≃	o J	142
Little Deschutes ≃	g E	160
Little Desert ⋆2	l E	184
Little Diomede Island I	b B	138
Little Eau Pleine ≃	e F	148
Little Falls, Mn., U.S.	e B	148
Little Falls, N.Y., U.S.	e L	146
Littlefield	e l	154
Littlefork	b A	148
Little Fork ≃	b B	148
Little Humboldt ≃	c H	162
Little Inagua I	d I	170
Little Juniata ≃	g I	146
Little Kanawha ≃	h E	146
Little Karroo ⋌1	i E	130
Little Mecatina ≃	f T	135
Little Mexico	g E	154
Little Miami ≃	h B	146
Little Minch, The ⋃	d G	78
Little Missouri ≃, U.S.	c E	156
Little Missouri ≃, Ar.	i C	152
Little Muddy ≃, Il.	e G	152

Symbols in the index are identified on page 198.

Name | Map Ref. | Page

Little Muddy ≃, N.D., U.S. c D 156
Little Namaqualand ▫9 g C 130
Little Nemaha ≃ k K 156
Little Nicobar I k B 110
Little Osage ≃ d B 152
Little Pee Dee ≃ f G 150
Little Platte ≃ c B 152
Little Powder ≃ g B 156
Little Rann of Kutch ≍ i D 114
Little Red ≃ g E 152
Little River m I 156
Little Rock, Ar., U.S. h D 152
Little Rock, Ia., U.S. h L 156
Little Sable Point ≻ g I 148
Little Sac ≃ e C 152
Little Salkehatchie ≃ f F 150
Little Sandy ≃ i C 146
Little Scarcies ≃ g D 124
Little Sioux ≃ i L 156
Little Smoky ≃ b Q 140
Little Snake ≃ d H 158
Littlestown h I 146
Little Tallapoosa ≃ f A 150
Little Tennessee ≃ d B 150
Littleton, Co., U.S. e K 158
Littleton, N.H., U.S. c O 146
Littleton, N.C., U.S. c I 150
Littleton, W.V., U.S. h F 146
Little Traverse Bay ⊂ e J 148
Little Valley e H 146
Little Wabash ≃ d H 152
Little Washita ≃ e H 154
Little White ≃ h F 156
Little Wolf ≃ f F 148
Little Wood ≃ g K 160
Litvínov e M 80
Liucheng b J 110
Liuhe c G 104
Liuyang g B 104
Liuzhou b J 110
Lively d N 148
Live Oak, Ca., U.S. e D 162
Live Oak, Fl., U.S. i D 150
Livermore, Ca., U.S. g D 162
Livermore, Ia., U.S. h A 148
Livermore, Ky., U.S. e I 152
Livermore Falls c P 146
Liverpool, N.S., Can. h I 144
Liverpool, Eng., U.K. h K 78
Liverpool, Pa., U.S. g J 146
Liverpool Bay ⊂ b CC 138
Livingston, Guat. b F 168
Livingston, Al., U.S. j H 152
Livingston, Ca., U.S. g E 162
Livingston, Il., U.S. d G 152
Livingston, Ky., U.S. b B 150
Livingston, La., U.S. l F 152
Livingston, Mt., U.S. e O 160
Livingston, Tn., U.S. f K 152
Livingston, Tx., U.S. i L 154
Livingston, Wi., U.S. h E 148
Livingstone e E 128
Livingstone, Chutes de ⌞ b B 128
Livingstone, Lake ⊜1 i K 154
Livingstone Falls → Livingstone, Chutes de ⌞ b B 128
Livingstonia d F 128
Livingston Manor f L 146
Livno f L 88
Livny i T 96
Livonia, La., U.S. l E 152
Livonia, Mi., U.S. h L 148
Livonia, N.Y., U.S. e I 146
Livorno (Leghorn) f E 88
Liwale c G 128
Lixi f C 104
Liyang d H 104
Liyujiang j B 104
Lizard Head Peak ∧ h P 160
Lizard Point ≻ l H 78
Ljubljana c I 88
Ljubuški f L 88
Ljugarn m P 76
Ljungaverk j O 76
Ljungby m M 76
Ljusdal k O 76
Ljusnan ≃ j M 76
Llancanelo, Laguna ⊜ h D 178
Llandovery j J 78
Llandrindod Wells i J 78
Llandudno h J 78
Llanelli j I 78
Llanfyllin i J 78
Llangefni h I 78
Llangollen i J 78
Llanidloes i J 78
Llano i H 154
Llano ≃ i H 154
Llanos ≍ b E 174
Llanwrtyd Wells i J 78
Lleida d L 86
Llera f J 166
Lloydminster e D 142
Llucmajor f N 86
Llullaillaco, Volcán ∧1 c D 178
Loa f E 158
Loa ≃ a C 176
Loami c G 152
Loanda b L 178
Loange (Luangue) ≃ c C 128
Lobatse e G 130
Löbau d N 80
Lobaye ≃ h D 126
Lobelville g I 152
Lobenstein e K 80
Lobería j I 178
Lobito d B 128
Lobitos d B 174
Lobn'a e T 96
Lobos h I 178
Lobos de Afuera, Islas II e B 174
Lobos de Tierra, Isla I e B 174
Locarno f J 83
Lochaline e H 78
Lochboisdale d F 78
Lochem d I 82
Lochgilphead e H 78
Lochinver c H 78
Lochmaben f J 78
Lock i A 184
Lockeport i H 144
Lockerbie f J 78
Lockesburg i B 152
Lockhart, Austl. j G 184
Lockhart, Tx., U.S. j I 154
Lock Haven f I 146
Lockney e E 154
Löcknitz b N 80
Lockport, Il., U.S. i G 148
Lockport, La., U.S. m F 152
Lockport, N.Y., U.S. d H 146
Lockwood e C 152
Loc-ninh i I 110
Locri k K 88
Locust Fork ≃ h J 152
Locust Grove c K 154
Lod (Lydda) e C 120
Lodejnoje Pole a P 96
Lodève i J 84
Lodge Grass e R 160
Lodgepole j E 156
Lodi, It. d D 88
Lodi, Ca., U.S. f D 162
Lodi, Oh., U.S. f D 146
Lodi, Wi., U.S. g F 148
Lodja b D 128
Lodwar h H 126
Łódź d S 80
Loei f F 110
Loen k J 76
Loeriesfontein h D 130
Lofa ≃ g D 124
Lofer h L 80
Lofoten II g M 76
Logan, Ia., U.S. j L 156
Logan, Ks., U.S. l H 156
Logan, N.M., U.S. d C 154
Logan, Oh., U.S. h D 146
Logan, Ut., U.S. c E 158
Logan, W.V., U.S. j E 146
Logan ≃ c E 158
Logan, Mount ∧ f X 138
Logandale h K 162
Logan Martin Lake ⊜1 i J 152
Logan Pass)(b L 160
Logansport, In., U.S. b J 152
Logansport, La., U.S. k C 152
Loganville f C 150
Logojsk g J 96
Logone ≃ f D 126
Logroño c I 86
Løgstør m K 76
Lohatlha g F 130
Lohiniva h S 76
Lohja k S 76
Lohne c H 80
Lohr e I 80
Lohrville i M 156
Loi-kaw e D 110
Loimaa k R 76
Loire ▫5 g K 84
Loire ≃ e E 84
Loire-Atlantique ▫5 e E 84
Loiret ▫5 d I 84
Loir-et-Cher ▫5 e H 84
Loitz b M 80
Loja, Ec. d C 174
Loja, Esp. h G 86
Lokandu b E 128
Lokan tekojärvi ⊜1 h T 76
Løken l L 76
Lokeren f E 82
Lokka h T 76
Løkken m K 76
Lokn'a e M 96
Lokolama b C 128
Lokoro ≃ b C 128
Lol ≃ g F 126
Loleta d A 162
Loliondo b G 128
Lolita k J 154
Lolland I n L 76
Lolo d K 160
Lolo Pass)(d K 160
Lom, Blg. f G 90
Lom, Nor. k K 76
Lom ≃ g I 124
Lomami ≃ b D 128
Lomas de Zamora h I 178
Lomax j D 148
Lombardia ▫4 d D 88
Lomblen, Pulau I g G 108
Lombok I g F 108
Lomé g G 124
Lomela b D 128
Lomela ≃ b D 128
Lometa h H 154
Lomi h O 76
Lomira g G 148
Lommel f G 82
Lomond, Loch ⊜ e I 78
Lomonosov b L 96
Lompoc j E 162
Lom Sak f F 110
Łomża b V 80
Lonaconing h H 146
Loncoche d B 176
Londinières c H 84
London, On., Can. h N 148
London, Eng., U.K. j M 78
London, Ky., U.S. b B 150
London, Oh., U.S. h C 146
London, Tx., U.S. i G 154
Londonderry, N.S., Can. g J 144
Londonderry, N. Ire., U.K. f F 78
Londonderry, Cape ≻ b E 182
Londonderry, Isla I h B 178
Londrina b M 178
Lone Grove e I 154
Lone Mountain ∧ f H 162
Lone Oak, Ky., U.S. e H 152
Lone Oak, Tx., U.S. f K 154
Lone Pine h G 162
Lone Rock g E 148
Lone Star j B 152
Lone Tree i D 148
Lone Wolf e G 154
Longa ≃ d B 128
Longa, proliv ⌶ c AA 94
Long Bay ⊂ f H 150
Long Beach, Ca., U.S. k G 162
Long Beach, Ms., U.S. l G 152
Long Beach, N.Y., U.S. g M 146
Long Beach, Wa., U.S. d A 160
Longboat Key l D 150
Long Branch g M 146
Long Branch ≃ c D 152
Longchamps h H 82
Longchang f H 100
Long Creek f F 160
Long Eaton i L 78
Longeau e L 84
Longford, Austl. l G 184
Longford, Ire. h F 78
Longford ▫6 h F 78
Long Island I, Austl. d H 184
Long Island I, Ba. c G 170
Long Island I, N.Y., U.S. g N 146
Long Island Sound ⌶ f N 146
Longitudinal, Valle ∨ h C 178
Longjiang b K 100
Longkou d K 100
Long Lake d L 146
Long Lake ⊜ g G 156
Longleaf k D 152
Long Leaf Park e I 150
Longli a I 110
Longmeadow e N 146
Longmont d K 158
Longnawan e E 108
Longny m N 78
Long Pine i H 156
Long Point ≻1 h O 148
Long Prairie f M 156
Long Prairie ≃ e M 156
Longquan g H 104
Long Range Mountains ⩘ d P 144
Longreach d F 184
Long-Sault b L 146
Longsheng b K 110
Longs Peak ∧ d K 158
Long Tom ≃ f B 160
Longton n K 156
Longueuil b M 146
Longuyon c L 84
Longview, N.C., U.S. d E 150
Longview, Tx., U.S. j B 152
Longview, Wa., U.S. d C 160
Longwood Park e G 150
Longwy c L 84
Longxi e G 100
Long-xuyen i H 110
Longzhou c I 110
Lonigo d F 88
Löningen c G 80
Lonoke h E 152
Lønsdal h H 76
Lonsdale f B 148
Lons-le-Saunier f L 84
Loogootee d J 152
Looking Glass ≃ h K 148
Lookout, Cape ≻ e J 150
Lookout Mountain ∧, U.S. h K 152
Lookout Mountain ∧, Or., U.S. f E 160
Lookout Pass)(c J 160
Lookout Ridge ⩘ b O 138
Loomis k H 156
Loon Lake ⊜ c L 142
Loon op Zand e G 82
Loop g D 154
Lopatka, mys ≻ g W 94
Lop Buri g F 110
Lopez, Cap ≻ b A 128
López Collada b C 166
Lop Nur (Lop Nor) ⊜ c E 100
Lopori ≃ a D 128
Lora del Río h F 86
Lorain f D 146
Loraine g F 154
Lorca h J 86
Lord Howe Island I f K 182
Lordsburg l H 158
Loreauville l E 152
Loreley ♦ e G 80
Lorena g F 177
Lorenzo f E 154
Loreto, Bra. e I 174
Loreto, Méx. d D 166
Loreto, Méx. f I 166
Lorette h M 142
Loretto, Ky., U.S. e K 152
Loretto, Tn., U.S. g I 152
Lorica j G 170
Lorient e C 84
L'Orignal b L 146
Lorimor a B 152
Loris e H 150
Lorman k E 152
Lorne, Austl. l E 184
Lorne, N.B., Can. e G 144
Lörrach h G 80
Lorraine ▫9 d M 84
Lorris e I 84
Los Alamos, Méx. c H 166
Los Alamos, Ca., U.S. j E 162
Los Alamos, N.M., U.S. i J 158
Los Aldamas d J 166
Los Andes g C 178
Los Ángeles, Chile i B 178
Los Angeles, Ca., U.S. j G 162
Los Angeles Aqueduct ≚1 i G 162
Los Banos g E 162
Los Blancos b G 178
Los Burros e D 166
Los Coronados, Islas II l H 162
Los Cristianos o X 87b
Los Ebanos, Méx. e K 166
Los Ebanos, Tx., U.S. m H 154
Los Fresnos n I 154
Los Gatos g D 162
Los Herreras e G 166
Łosice c V 80
Los Lagos d B 176
Los Llanos de Aridane o W 87b
Los Lunas j J 158
Los Mochis e E 166
Los Molinos d C 162
Los Padillas j J 158
Los Palacios y Villafranca h F 86
Los Pinos ≃ g I 158
Los Reyes [de Salgado] h H 166
Los Rodríguez e H 166
Los Roques, Islas II i K 170
Los Santos ▫4 j N 168
Los Sauces o W 87b
Losser d K 82
Lossiemouth d J 78
Lost ≃, U.S. h D 160
Lost ≃, In., U.S. d J 152
Lost ≃, Mn., U.S. d L 156
Lost ≃, W.V., U.S. i H 146
Los Teques i K 170
Lost Hills i F 162
Lostine ≃ e H 160
Lost Nation l E 148
Los Tres Palos e J 166
Lost River Range ⩘ f L 160
Lost Trail Pass)(e L 160
Losuia a J 182
Los Vidrios b C 166
Los Vilos f C 178
Lot ▫5 h H 84
Lot ≃ h G 84
Lota i B 178
Lot-et-Garonne ▫5 h G 84
Lothair, S. Afr. f J 130
Lothair, Ky., U.S. b C 150
Lothian ▫4 f J 78
Lotofaga a B 188a
Lotsane ≃ d H 130
Lott h I 154
Lotung k J 104
Louangnamtha d F 110
Louangphrabang e G 110
Loudéac d D 84
Loudon d B 150
Loudonville g D 146
Loué d F 84
Louga e C 124
Loughborough i L 78
Loughrea h E 78
Louhans f L 84
Louin j G 152
Louisa, Ky., U.S. a D 150
Louisa, Va., U.S. a H 150
Louisbourg g N 144
Louisburg, Ks., U.S. m M 156
Louisburg, N.C., U.S. c H 150
Louisdale g L 144
Louise, Ms., U.S. j F 152
Louise, Tx., U.S. j J 154
Louise, Lake ⊜ e U 138
Louiseville a N 146
Louisiade Archipelago II b J 182
Louisiana c E 152
Louisiana ▫3 e H 136
Louis Trichardt d I 130
Louisville, Al., U.S. k K 152
Louisville, Ga., U.S. f D 150
Louisville, Il., U.S. d H 152
Louisville, Ky., U.S. d K 152
Louisville, Ms., U.S. i G 152
Louisville, Ne., U.S. k K 156
Louisville, Oh., U.S. g E 146
Louis-XIV, Pointe ≻ f Q 134
Loulé h C 86
Louny e M 80
Loup ≃ j J 156
Loup City j I 156
Lourdes, Nf., Can. d N 144
Lourdes, Fr. i F 84
Lourenço Marques → Maputo e K 130
Loures g B 86
Lourinhã f B 86
Lourosa e D 86
Lousã e C 86
Louth, Ire. h G 78
Louth, Eng., U.K. h M 78
Louth ▫6 h G 78
Loutre ≃ d E 152
Louvain (Leuven) g F 82
Louveigné g H 82
Louviers, Fr. c H 84
Louviers, Co., U.S. e K 158
Louwsburg f J 130
Lövånger i Q 76
Lovat' ≃ d N 96
Loveč f H 90
Lovelady h K 154
Loveland d K 158
Lovell f Q 160
Lovelock d G 162
Lovely b D 150
Lovere d E 88
Loves Park h F 148
Lovilia i C 148
Loving, N.M., U.S. g B 154
Loving, Tx., U.S. f H 154
Lovingston b H 150
Lovington, Il., U.S. c H 152
Lovington, N.M., U.S. g C 154
Lövstabruk k O 76
Low b K 146
Low, Cape ≻ d O 134
Lowa ≃ b E 128
Lowden i E 148
Lowell, Ar., U.S. f B 152
Lowell, In., U.S. a I 152
Lowell, Ma., U.S. e O 146
Lowell, Mi., U.S. h J 148
Lowell, Or., U.S. g C 160
Löwenberg c M 80
Lower Arrow Lake ⊜ h P 140
Lower Hutt h I 186
Lower Kalskag f N 138
Lower Klamath Lake ⊜ c D 162
Lower Post e G 134
Lower Red Lake ⊜ d L 156
Lower Trajan's Wall ⊥ d L 90
Lower West Pubnico i H 144
Lower Wood's Harbour i H 144
Lowestoft i O 78
Łowicz c S 80
Lowmoor b G 150
Lowrah (Pishīn Lora) ≃ e A 114
Low Rocky Point ≻ n F 184
Lowry City d C 152
Lowville d K 146
Loxley l I 152
Loxton, Austl. j D 184
Loxton, S. Afr. h F 130
Loyal f E 148
Loyalton e E 162
Loyalty Islands → Loyauté, Îles II s X 188f
Loyauté, Îles (Loyalty Islands) II s X 188f
Lozère ▫5 h J 84
Loznica e C 90
Lua ≃ h D 126
Lualaba ≃ b E 128
Luama ≃ b E 128
Lu'an d E 104
Luan ≃ c J 100
Luanda c B 128
Luando c C 128
Luang, Thale ⊂ k F 110
Luang Prabang → Louangphrabang e G 110
Luang Prabang Range ⩘ e F 110
Luangue (Loange) ≃ c C 128
Luanguinga ≃ d D 128
Luangwa ≃ d F 128
Luanshya d E 128
Luapula ≃ d E 128
Luba h H 124
Lubań, Pol. d O 80
L'uban', S.S.S.R. i J 96
Lubang Islands II c G 108
Lubango d B 128
Lubawa b S 80
Lübben d M 80
Lübbenau d M 80
Lubbock f E 154
L'ubča h I 96
Lubec c T 146
Lübeck b J 80
Lubefu b D 128
L'ubercy f T 96
Lubilash ≃ c D 128
L'ubim c W 96
Lubin d P 80
Lublin d V 80
Lubliniec e R 80
Lubnān, Jabal (Lebanon Mountains) ⩘ a E 120
Lubny g D 92
L'ubochna h Q 96
Luboń c P 80
Lubsko d N 80
Lübtheen b K 80
Lubudi c E 128
Lubudi ≃ c E 128
Lubumbashi (Élisabethville) d E 128
Lubutu b E 128
Lübz b L 80
Lucan g N 148
Lucania, Mount ∧ f X 138
Lucas, Ia., U.S. i B 148
Lucas, Ks., U.S. l I 156
Lucasville i D 146
Lucban n S 109b
Lucca f E 88
Lucedale l H 152
Lucena, Esp. h G 86
Lucena, Pil. o S 109b
Lučenec g S 80
Lucera h J 88
Lucerne → Luzern d I 83
Lucerne e C 162
Lucerne, Lake → Vierwaldstätter See ⊜ d I 83
Lüchow, B.R.D. c K 80
Luchow → Luzhou, Zhg. f H 100
Lucindale k D 184
Lucira d B 128
Luck, S.S.S.R. g C 92
Luck, Wi., U.S. e C 148
Luckau d M 80
Luckenwalde c M 80
Luckhoff g G 130
Luckiamute ≃ f B 160
Lucknow, On., Can. g N 148
Lucknow, India g I 114
Luçon f E 84
Lüdenscheid d G 80
Lüderitz f B 130
Ludhiāna e F 114
Lüdinghausen d G 80
Ludington g I 148
L'udinovo h Q 96
Ludlow, Eng., U.K. i K 78
Ludlow, Ma., U.S. e N 146
Ludlow, Vt., U.S. d N 146
Ludowici h E 150
Ludvika k N 76
Ludwigsburg g I 80
Ludwigsfelde c M 80
Ludwigshafen f H 80
Ludwigslust b K 80
Luebo c D 128
Lueders g G 154
Luena, Ang. d C 128
Luena, Zaïre c E 128
Luena ≃ d D 128
Lufeng, Zhg. m D 104
Lufeng, Zhg. b G 110
Lufira ≃ c E 128
Lufkin k B 152
Luga c L 96
Luga ≃ b L 96
Lugano f J 83
Lugano, Lago di ⊜ c D 88
Lugansk → Vorošilovgrad h E 92
Lugenda ≃ d G 128
Lugnaquillia Mountain ∧ i G 78
Lugo, Esp. b D 86
Lugo, It. e F 88
Lugoj d E 90
Luhit ≃ g P 114
Luik (Liège) g H 82
Luilaka ≃ b D 128
Luino c C 88
Luishia d E 128
Luisiânia a M 178
Luiza c D 128
Luján, Arg. g F 178
Luján, Arg. g D 178
Lukang k I 104
Lukanga Swamp ≡ d E 128
Lukenie ≃ b D 128
Lukeville m D 158
Luknovo e Y 96
Lukolela b C 128
Łuków d V 80
Lukuga ≃ c E 128
Lukulu d D 128
Lula h F 152
Luleå i R 76
Lüleburgaz b B 118
Lüliang Shan ⩘ d I 100
Luling j I 154
Lulonga ≃ a C 128
Lulua ≃ c D 128
Lumbala N'guimbo d D 128
Lumber ≃ e G 150
Lumber City h D 150
Lumberport h F 146
Lumberton, Ms., U.S. k G 152
Lumberton, N.C., U.S. e G 150
Lumberton, Tx., U.S. l B 152
Lumbres b I 84
Lumby g P 140
Lumding h O 114
Lumpkin g B 150
Lumsden, Sk., Can. g K 142
Lumsden, N.Z. l C 186
Lumut f F 110
Luna Pier i L 148
Lūnāvāda i E 114
Lund, Sve. n M 76
Lund, Nv., U.S. f J 162
Lundale j E 146
Lundazi d F 128
Lundi ≃ c J 130
Lundy I j I 78
Lüneburg b J 80
Lüneburger Heide ✦1 b J 80
Lunel i K 84
Lünen d G 80
Lunenburg, N.S., Can. h I 144
Lunenburg, Va., U.S. c H 150
Lunéville d M 84
Lunga ≃ d E 128
Lungi g D 124
Lungué-Bungo ≃ d D 128
Lūni ≃ h D 114
Luninec i I 96
Luo ≃ e I 100
Luohe b C 104
Luolong e Q 114
Luoyang e I 100
Lupeni d G 90
Luqu e G 100
Luray i H 146
Lure e M 84
Luremo c C 128
Lurgan g G 78
Lurín f C 174
Lúrio d H 128
Lúrio ≃ d G 128
Lusaka e E 128
Lusambo b D 128
Lusanga b C 128
Lushan e G 100
Lu Shan ∧ f J 100
Lushnje i C 90
Lushoto b G 128
Lüshun (Port Arthur) e I 102
Lusk h L 158
Luspebryggan h P 76
Lustenau h I 80
Luster k J 76
Lūt, Dasht-e ✦2 f Q 118
Lutcher l F 152
Lutesville e G 152
Luther, Mi., U.S. f J 148
Luther, Ok., U.S. d I 154
Luton j M 78
Lutong e E 108
Luttrell c C 150
Lutz k D 150
Lützow b K 80
Lützow-Holm Bay ⊂ b D 189
Lutzputs g E 130
Lutzville h D 130
Luuq h I 126
Luverne, Al., U.S. k J 152
Lu Verne, Ia., U.S. h A 148
Luverne, Mn., U.S. h K 156
Luvua ≃ c E 128
Luvuvhu ≃ d J 130
Luwegu ≃ c G 128
Luxembourg (Luxemburg) i I 82
Luxembourg ▫4 i G 82
Luxembourg ▫1 f I 74
Luxemburg f H 148
Luxeuil-les-Bains e M 84
Luxi (Mangshi) b E 110
Luxor → Al-Uqṣur j E 118
Luxora g G 152
Luzarches c I 84
Luzern d I 83
Luzern ▫3 d I 83
Luzhou f H 100
Luziânia d E 177
Luzon I n S 109b
Luzon Strait ⌶ a G 108
Luzy f J 84
L'vov h B 92
Lwówek c P 80
Lybster c J 78
Lycksele i P 76
Lycoming Creek ≃ f I 146
Lydd k N 78
Lydda → Lod e C 120
Lydenburg e J 130
Lydia ▫9 k L 90
Lydia Mills e E 150
Lyell, Mount ∧ f Q 140
Lyerly e A 150
Lyford m I 154
Lykens g J 146
Lyle g C 148
Lyles g I 152
Lyman, Ne., U.S. j C 156
Lyman, S.C., U.S. e D 150
Lyman, Wy., U.S. c F 158
Lyme Bay ⊂ k J 78
Lyme Regis k K 78
Łyna (Lava) ≃ g C 96
Lynch, Ky., U.S. c D 150
Lynch, Ne., U.S. i I 156
Lynchburg, Oh., U.S. h C 146
Lynchburg, S.C., U.S. e F 150
Lynchburg, Tn., U.S. g J 152
Lynchburg, Va., U.S. b G 150
Lynches ≃ f G 150
Lynden b C 160
Lyndhurst h C 184
Lyndon, Ks., U.S. m L 156
Lyndon, Ky., U.S. d K 152
Lyndonville c N 146
Lyndora g G 146
Lynd, The b F 184
Lyngdal l J 76
Lyngen g Q 76
Lyngør l K 76
Lynn, Al., U.S. h I 152
Lynn, In., U.S. b L 152
Lynn, Ma., U.S. e P 146
Lynn Canal ⊂ g AA 138
Lynndyl e D 158
Lynn Garden c D 150
Lynn Haven l K 152
Lynn Lake b M 142
Lynnville i C 148
Lynton j J 78
Lyon g K 84
Lyon Mountain c M 146
Lyonnais, Monts du ⩘ g K 84
Lyons, Co., U.S. d K 158
Lyons, Ga., U.S. g D 150
Lyons, In., U.S. d I 152
Lyons, Ks., U.S. m I 156
Lyons, Mi., U.S. h K 148
Lyons, Ne., U.S. j K 156
Lyons, N.Y., U.S. d J 146
Lyons ≃ d C 182
Lys (Leie) ≃ b I 84
Lysekil l L 76
Lyss d G 83
Lys'va f I 92
Lytham Saint Anne's h K 78
Lytle j H 154
Lyttelton j G 186

M

Ma ≃ d H 110
Maalaea Bay ⊂ q Q 163a
Ma'ān h E 120
Ma'anshan d G 104
Ma'arrat an-Nu'mān e G 118
Maas (Meuse) ≃ d E 80
Maaseik f H 82
Maasmechelen g H 82
Maasniel f I 82
Maassluis e E 82
Maastricht g H 82
Mababe Depression ⩱7 b G 130
Mabank g J 154
Maben i G 152
Mablethorpe h N 78
Mableton f B 150
Mabou f L 144
Mabton d F 160
McAdam g F 144
McAdoo g K 146
Macaé g H 177
McAlester e K 154
Macalister ≃ k F 184
Macalister, Mount ∧ j H 184
McAllen m H 154
Macão f C 86
Macao → Macau ▫2 g I 100
Macapá c H 174
Macará d C 174
Macarani c H 177
McArthur h D 146
Macau, Bra. e K 174
Macau (Aomen), Macau m B 104
Macau ▫2 g I 100
McBain f J 148
McBee e F 150
McCall f I 160
McCall Creek k F 152
McCamey h D 154
McCammon h M 160
McCaysville e B 150
McCleary c B 160
McClellanville f G 150
MacClenny i D 150
Macclesfield h K 78
McClintock, Mount ∧ d H 189
McCloud c C 162
McClure, Il., U.S. e G 152
McClure, Pa., U.S. g I 146
McClusky d G 156
McColl e G 150
McComas b E 150
McComb, Ms., U.S. k F 152
McComb, Oh., U.S. f C 146
McConaughy, Lake ⊜1 j F 156
McConnellsburg h I 146
McConnelsville h E 146
McCook k G 156
McCormick f D 150
McCrory g E 152
McCune n L 156
McCurtain d L 154
McDade i I 154
McDavid l I 152
McDermitt c H 162
McDermott i C 146
McDonald l F 156
Macdonnell Ranges ⩘ d F 182
McDonough f B 150
Macduff d K 78
Macedo de Cavaleiros d E 86
Macedonia → Makedonija ▫3 h E 90
Macedonia ▫9 h F 90
Maceió e K 174
Macenta g E 124
Macerata f H 88
McEwen f I 152
McFadden c J 158
McFarland, Ca., U.S. i F 162
McFarland, Wi., U.S. g F 148
MacFarlane ≃ e K 134
Macfarlane, Lake ⊜ h B 184
McGehee l E 152
McGill e K 162
McGrath e Q 138
McGraw e J 146
McGregor i P 142
McGregor, Ia., U.S. g D 148
McGregor, Tx., U.S. h I 154
McGregor ≃ c M 140
McGregor Range ⩘ f E 184
Machačkala i G 92
Machado a P 178
Machadodorp e J 130
Machagai d H 178
Machakos b G 128
Machala d C 174
Machattie, Lake ⊜ e C 184
McHenry, Il., U.S. h G 148
McHenry, Ms., U.S. l G 152
Machias c S 146
Machias ≃ c S 146
Machico m U 87a
Machilīpatnam (Bandar) d F 116
Machiques i H 170
Machupicchu f D 174
Machynlleth i J 78
McIntosh, Al., U.S. k H 152
McIntosh, Mn., U.S. d L 156
McIntosh, S.D., U.S. f F 156
Macintyre ≃, Austl. g H 184
Macintyre ≃, Austl. c H 184
Mackay, Id., U.S. g L 160
Mackay, Lake ⊜ d E 182
McKee b C 150
McKeesport g G 146
Mackenzie b G 174
McKenzie, Al., U.S. k J 152
McKenzie, Tn., U.S. f H 152
Mackenzie ▫5 c EE 138
Mackenzie ≃ f C 134
Mackenzie Bay ⊂ b Z 138
McKenzie Bridge f C 160
Mackenzie Delta ≚2 b AA 138
Mackenzie Island g U 142
Mackenzie Mountains ⩘ d CC 138
Mackinac, Straits of ⌶ e K 148
Mackinac Island e K 148
Mackinac Island I e K 148
Mackinaw j F 148
Mackinaw ≃ j F 148
Mackinaw City e K 148
McKinley, Mount ∧ e S 138
McKinleyville d A 162
McKinney f J 154
Mackinnon Road b G 128
Macklin f E 142
Macksville, Austl. h J 184
Macksville, Ks., U.S. m I 156
McLain k H 152
McLaughlin f G 156
McLaurin k G 152
Maclean g J 184
McLean, Il., U.S. b G 152
McLean, Tx., U.S. d F 154
McLeansboro d H 152
Maclear h I 130
McLennan b N 140
McLeod ≃ d S 140
Macleod, Lake ⊜ d B 182
McLoughlin, Mount ∧ h C 160
McLouth l L 156
Maclovio Herrera c G 166
Macmillan ≃ e AA 138
McMillan, Lake ⊜1 g B 154
McMinnville, Or., U.S. e B 160
McMinnville, Tn., U.S. g K 152
McMurdo ▫3 c H 189
McMurdo Sound ⌶ c H 189
McNary j G 158
McNeil i C 152
McNeill l G 152
Macomb j E 148
Macomer i C 88
Mâcon, Fr. f K 84
Macon, Ga., U.S. g C 150
Macon, Il., U.S. c H 152
Macon, Ms., U.S. i H 152
Macon, Mo., U.S. c D 152
Macon, Bayou ≃ j E 152
McPherson m J 156
McPherson Range ⩘ g J 184
Macquarie ≃, Austl. m G 184
Macquarie ≃, Austl. h G 184
Macquarie Harbour ⊂ n F 184
Macquarie Island I a H 189
McQueeney j H 154
McRae, Ar., U.S. g E 152
McRae, Ga., U.S. g D 150
McRoberts b D 150
Mac. Robertson Land ✦1 b E 189
Macroom j E 78
MacTier e P 148
Macuspana i M 166
McVeigh b D 150
McVille d I 156
McWilliams k I 152
Mad ≃, Ca., U.S. d B 162
Mad ≃, Oh., U.S. h B 146
Mad ≃, Vt., U.S. c N 146
Ma'dabā e E 120
Madagascar (Madagasikara) ▫1 e I 128
Madagascar Basin ✦1 l F 98
Madanapalle f E 116
Mādārīpur i N 114
Madawaska e E 144
Madawaska ≃ e R 148
Maddaloni h I 88
Maddock d H 156
Madeira I m U 87a
Madeira ≃ e F 174
Madeira, Arquipélago da II m U 87a
Mädelegabel ∧ e Q 84
Madeleine, Îles de la II e L 144
Madelia f A 148
Madeline Island I d E 148
Madera, Méx. c F 166
Madera, Ca., U.S. h E 162
Madhubani g L 114
Madhya Pradesh ▫3 i G 114
Madibogo f G 130
Madidi ≃ f E 174

Symbols in the index are identified on page 198.

Madi-Maue

Name	Map Ref.	Page
Madill	e J	154
Madimba	b C	128
Madīnat ash-Sha'b (Al-Ittihad)	h D	117
Madingou	b B	128
Madison, Al., U.S.	h J	152
Madison, Fl., U.S.	i C	150
Madison, Ga., U.S.	f C	150
Madison, In., U.S.	d K	152
Madison, Ks., U.S.	m K	156
Madison, Me., U.S.	c Q	146
Madison, Mn., U.S.	f K	156
Madison, Mo., U.S.	c D	152
Madison, Ne., U.S.	j J	156
Madison, N.C., U.S.	c G	150
Madison, Oh., U.S.	f E	146
Madison, S.D., U.S.	g J	156
Madison, Va., U.S.	i H	146
Madison, W.V., U.S.	i E	146
Madison, Wi., U.S.	g F	148
Madison ≃	e N	160
Madison Heights	b G	150
Madison Range ⋏	e N	160
Madisonville, Ky., U.S.	e I	152
Madisonville, La., U.S.	l F	152
Madisonville, Tn., U.S.	d B	150
Madisonville, Tx., U.S.	i K	154
Madiun	j O	109a
Madoc	f R	148
Mado Gashi	b G	128
Madoi	e F	100
Madrakah, Ra's al- ➤	e J	117
Madras, India	g K	112
Madras, Or., U.S.	f D	160
Madras → Tamil Nadu □³	g E	116
Madre, Laguna c, Méx.	e K	166
Madre, Laguna c, Tx., U.S.	m I	154
Madre, Sierra ⋏, N.A.	b B	168
Madre, Sierra ⋏, Pil.	m T	109b
Madre de Dios ≃	f E	174
Madre de Dios, Isla I	g A	176
Madre del Sur, Sierra ⋏	i J	166
Madre Occidental, Sierra ⋏	e F	166
Madre Oriental, Sierra ⋏	f I	166
Madrid, Esp.	e H	86
Madrid, Al., U.S.	k K	152
Madrid, Ia., U.S.	i B	148
Madrid, Ne., U.S.	k F	156
Madrid □⁴	e H	86
Madriz □⁵	d H	168
Madsen	h U	142
Madura I	j P	109a
Madurai	h E	116
Madyan ✦¹	i F	118
Maebashi	k N	106
Mae Hong Son	e D	110
Mae Klong ≃	g E	110
Maengsan	d N	102
Mae Sariang	e D	110
Maeser	d G	158
Mae Sot	f E	110
Maesteg	j J	78
Maestra, Sierra ⋏	d F	170
Maevatanana	p V	131b
Maéwo I	p Y	188f
Mafeteng	g H	130
Maffra	k G	184
Mafia Island I	c G	128
Mafikeng	e G	130
Mafra, Bra.	d N	178
Mafra, Port.	g B	86
Magadan	f V	94
Magadi	b G	128
Magallanes	o T	109b
Magallanes, Estrecho de (Strait of Magellan) ꭥ	g C	176
Magangué	j G	170
Magazine Mountain ⋏	g C	152
Magdalena, Bol.	f F	174
Magdalena, Méx.	g H	166
Magdalena, N.M., U.S.	j I	158
Magdalena ≃	b D	174
Magdalena, Isla I	e B	176
Magdalena de Kino	b D	166
Magdeburg	c K	80
Magdeburg □⁵	c K	80
Magee	k G	152
Magelang	j O	109a
Magellan, Strait of → Magallanes, Estrecho de ꭥ	g C	176
Magenta	d C	88
Maggia	f J	83
Maggiore, Lago ⊜	c C	88
Maghāghah	h D	118
Magione	f G	88
Maglaj	e B	90
Magnitogorsk	g I	92
Magnolia, Ar., U.S.	i C	152
Magnolia, Mn., U.S.	h K	156
Magnolia, Ms., U.S.	k F	152
Magog	b N	146
Magpie, Lac ⊜	a I	144
Magrath	h V	140
Maguari, Cabo ➤	d I	174
Magwe	d C	110
Mahābād	d K	116
Mahābaleshwar	f I	112
Mahābalipuram	g K	112
Mahābhārat Range ⋏	f J	114
Mahabo	s V	131b
Mahajamba, Helodranon' i c	o V	131b
Mahajanga	o V	131b
Mahakam ≃	e F	108
Mahalatswe	d H	130
Mahānadi ≃	e K	112
Mahanoro	q W	131b
Mahanoy City	g J	146
Mahārāshtra □³	c C	116
Maha Sarakham	f G	110
Mahbūbnagar	d D	116
Mahd adh-Dhahab	c B	117
Mahe	g C	116
Mahébourg	v R	131c
Mahé Island I	b K	128
Mahendra Giri ⋏	c H	116
Mahenge	c G	128
Mahi ≃	i E	114
Mahia Peninsula ➤¹	f L	186
Mahlabatini	g J	130
Mahnomen	d L	156
Mahoba	h H	114
Mahomet	b H	152
Mahone Bay	h I	144
Mahuva	b A	116
Maia	d C	86
Maîche	e M	84
Maicurú ≃	d H	174
Maiden	d E	150
Maidenhead	j M	78
Maidstone, Sk., Can.	e E	142
Maidstone, Eng., U.K.	j N	78
Maiduguri	f I	124
Maienfeld	d L	83
Maignelay	c I	84
Maiko ≃	b E	128
Maillezais	f F	84
Main ≃	f I	80
Mainburg	g K	80
Main Channel ꭥ	e N	148
Mai-Ndombe, Lac ⊜	b C	128
Maine □⁹	d F	84
Maine □³	b M	136
Maine, Gulf of c	c M	136
Maine-et-Loire □⁵	e F	84
Mainhardt	f I	80
Mainland I, Scot., U.K.	b J	78
Mainland I, Scot., U.K.	a L	78
Mainpuri	g H	114
Maintenon	d H	84
Maintirano	q U	131b
Mainz	e H	80
Maio I	e B	124
Maipo, Volcán ⋏¹	h D	178
Maipú, Arg.	i J	178
Maipú, Chile	g C	178
Maiquetía	i K	170
Maitengwe ≃	c H	130
Maitland, Austl.	j B	184
Maitland, Austl.	i I	184
Maitland, N.S., Can.	g J	144
Maíz, Islas del II	e K	168
Maizuru	l J	106
Maji	g H	126
Majkop	i F	92
Majorca → Mallorca I	f O	86
Makabana	b B	128
Makālu ⋏	g L	114
Makanza	a C	128
Makarakomburu, Mount ⋏	j Q	188e
Makarjev	d Z	96
Makarska	f L	88
Makasar, Selat (Makassar Strait) ꭥ	f F	108
Makassar Strait → Makasar, Selat ꭥ	f F	108
Makawao	q Q	163a
Makedonija □³	h E	90
Makejevka	h E	92
Makeni	g D	124
Makgadikgadi ≃	c G	130
Makindu	b G	128
Makinsk	g L	92
Makkah (Mecca)	d A	117
Makó	i T	80
Makokou	a B	128
Makoua	a C	128
Makrāna	g F	114
Maksaticha	d R	96
Makumbi	c D	128
Makung (P'enghu)	l H	104
Makurdi	g H	124
Makwassie	f G	130
Malabang	d G	108
Malabar Coast ⚓²	c C	116
Malabo	h H	124
Malacca, Strait of ꭥ	m F	110
Malacky	g Q	80
Malad ≃	c D	158
Malad City	h M	160
Málaga, Col.	b D	174
Málaga, Esp.	i G	86
Malaga, N.M., U.S.	g B	154
Malagash	g J	144
Malagasy Republic → Madagascar □¹	e I	128
Malaimbandy	r U	131b
Malaita I	j Q	188e
Malaja Višera	c O	96
Malaka → Melaka	e C	108
Malakāl	g G	126
Malakoff	g J	154
Malakula I	q X	188f
Malang	j P	109a
Malanje	c C	128
Malanville	f G	124
Mälaren ⊜	I O	76
Malargüe	h D	178
Malartic	b Q	148
Malaspina Glacier ⊓	g X	138
Malåträsk	i P	76
Malatya	c H	118
Malaut	e F	114
Malawi □¹	d F	128
Malawi, Lake → Nyasa, Lake ⊜	d F	128
Malaya □⁹	m G	110
Malaybalay	d H	108
Malāyer	e M	118
Malay Peninsula ➤¹	k F	110
Malay Reef ✦²	a H	184
Malaysia □¹	e C	108
Malazgirt	c J	118
Malbork	a S	80
Malchin	b L	80
Malchow	b L	80
Malcolm	e D	182
Malcom	i C	148
Maldegem	f C	82
Malden	f G	152
Malden I	d L	180
Maldive Islands II	b B	116
Maldives □¹	i H	98
Maldonado	h K	178
Malé, It.	c E	88
Male, Mald.	i H	98
Maléa, Ákra ➤	m G	90
Målegaon	b C	116
Malema	d G	128
Malente	a J	80
Måler Kotla	e F	114
Maleshèrbes	d I	84
Malestroit	e D	84
Malha Wells	e F	126
Malheur ≃	g H	160
Malheur Lake ⊜	g G	160
Mali □¹	e F	124
Mali ≃	a D	110
Malik, Wādī al- ∨	e F	126
Mali Kyun I	h E	110
Malin	h D	160
Malinaltepec	i J	166
Malindi	b H	128
Malines (Mechelen)	f E	82
Malin Head ➤	f F	78
Maljamar	g C	154
Malkāpur	b D	116
Malkapuram	d G	116
Malkaig	d H	78
Mallala	j C	184
Mallawī	i D	118
Mallersdorf	g L	80
Mallnitz	i M	80
Mallorca I	f O	86
Mallow	i E	78
Malmberget	h Q	76
Malmédy	h I	82
Malmesbury	i D	130
Malmö	n M	76
Malmöhus Län □⁶	n M	76
Malo I	p X	188f
Maloarchangel'sk	i S	96
Maloja	f L	83
Malolos	n S	109b
Malone, Fl., U.S.	i A	150
Malone, N.Y., U.S.	c L	146
Malonga	d D	128
Małopolska ✦¹	e U	80
Måløy	k I	76
Malpas	j D	184
Malpelo, Isla de I	c B	174
Malta, Mt., U.S.	b R	160
Malta, Oh., U.S.	h E	146
Malta □¹	h J	74
Malta I	n I	88
Malta Channel ꭥ	m I	88
Maltahöhe	e C	130
Malte Brun ⋏	j E	186
Malton	g M	78
Maluku (Moluccas) II	f H	108
Maluku, Laut (Molucca Sea) ⁻₂	f G	108
Malung	k M	76
Malvern, Ar., U.S.	h D	152
Malvern, Ia., U.S.	j L	156
Malvern, Oh., U.S.	g E	146
Malyj Jenisej ≃	g K	94
Malyj Kavkaz ⋏	i F	92
Mamberamo ≃	f J	108
Mambéré ≃	h D	126
Mamburao	o S	109b
Mamers	d G	84
Mamfe	g H	124
Mamie	c K	150
Mammoth, Az., U.S.	I F	158
Mammoth, W.V., U.S.	i E	146
Mammoth Cave National Park ♠	e J	152
Mammoth Lakes	g G	162
Mammoth Spring	f E	152
Mamoré ≃	f E	174
Mamou, Guinée	f D	124
Mamou, La., U.S.	l D	152
Mampikony	p V	131b
Mamry, Jezioro ⊜	a U	80
Man, C. Iv.	g E	124
Man, W.V., U.S.	b E	150
Mana	o N	163a
Mana ≃	b H	174
Manabique, Punta de ➤	b F	168
Manacapuru	d F	174
Manacor	f O	86
Manado	e G	108
Managua	e H	168
Managua □⁵	e H	168
Managua, Lago de ⊜	e H	168
Manakara	s W	131b
Manāli	c J	112
Manama → Al-Manāmah	a G	117
Mananara	p W	131b
Mananjary	r W	131b
Manapouri, Lake ⊜	l B	186
Manas	c D	100
Manās ≃	g N	114
Manas Hu ⊜	b D	100
Manāslu ⋏	f K	114
Manasquan	g L	146
Manassa	g K	158
Manassas	i I	146
Manatí	e K	170
Manaus	d F	174
Manawa	f G	148
Manbij	d G	118
Mancelona	f J	148
Manche □⁵	c E	84
Manchester, Eng., U.K.	h K	78
Manchester, Ct., U.S.	f N	146
Manchester, Ga., U.S.	g B	150
Manchester, Ia., U.S.	h D	148
Manchester, Ky., U.S.	b C	150
Manchester, Ma., U.S.	e P	146
Manchester, Mi., U.S.	h K	148
Manchester, N.H., U.S.	e O	146
Manchester, Oh., U.S.	i C	146
Manchester, Tn., U.S.	g J	152
Manchester, Vt., U.S.	d M	146
Manchuria □⁹	b L	100
Mancos	g H	158
Mancos ≃	g H	158
Mand ≃	h N	118
Manda	d F	128
Mandabe	r U	131b
Mandaguari	b M	178
Mandal	l J	76
Mandala, Puncak ⋏	f K	108
Mandalay	c D	110
Mandalgov'	b H	100
Mandalī	f K	118
Mandan	e G	156
Mandara Mountains ⋏	f I	124
Mandas	j D	88
Mandasor	h F	114
Mandeb, Bab el ꭥ	h C	117
Manderson	f R	160
Mandeville, Jam.	e F	170
Mandeville, La., U.S.	l F	152
Mandi	e G	114
Mandi Bahāuddīn	d E	114
Mandi Būrewāla	e E	114
Mandimba	d G	128
Mandioli, Pulau I	f H	108
Mandla	a F	116
Mandritsara	o W	131b
Manduria	i L	88
Māndvi	f D	116
Mandya	f D	116
Manfalūt	i D	118
Manfredonia	h J	88
Manfredonia, Golfo di c	h K	88
Mangabeiras, Chapada das ⋏²	f I	174
Mangakino	e J	186
Mangalagiri	d F	116
Mangalore	f C	116
Mangchang	f H	100
Mangham	j E	152
Mangochi	d G	128
Mangoky ≃	r U	131b
Mangole, Pulau I	f H	108
Māngrol	j D	114
Mangualde	e D	86
Mangueira, Lagoa c	g L	178
Mangum	e G	154
Mangya	d E	100
Manhattan, Ks., U.S.	l K	156
Manhattan, Mt., U.S.	e N	160
Manhuaçu	f G	177
Maniago	c G	88
Maniamba	d F	128
Manicoré	e F	174
Manicouagan ≃	c E	144
Manicouagan, Réservoir ⊜¹	a E	144
Manic Trois, Réservoir ⊜¹	b E	144
Manihiki I¹	e K	180
Manila, Pil.	n S	109b
Manila, Ar., U.S.	g F	152
Manila, Ut., U.S.	g D	158
Manila Bay c	n S	109b
Manilla, Austl.	h I	184
Manilla, Ia., U.S.	j L	156
Manipur □⁸	h O	114
Manisa	c B	118
Manistee	f I	148
Manistee ≃	f I	148
Manistique	e I	148
Manistique ≃	d I	148
Manito	b G	152
Manitoba □⁴	f M	134
Manitoba, Lake ⊜	g P	142
Manitou	i P	142
Manitoulin Island I	e M	148
Manitou Springs	f L	158
Manitowaning	e N	148
Manitowish Waters	d F	148
Manitowoc	f H	148
Manitowoc ≃	f G	148
Maniwaki	a K	146
Manizales	b C	174
Manja	r U	131b
Manjacaze	e K	130
Mānjra ≃	c D	116
Mankato, Ks., U.S.	l I	156
Mankato, Mn., U.S.	f B	148
Mankayane	f J	130
Manly	g B	148
Manmād	b C	116
Mannahill	i C	184
Mannar, Gulf of c	h E	116
Mannārgudi	g E	116
Männedorf	d J	83
Mannford	c J	154
Mannheim	f H	80
Manning, Ia., U.S.	j L	156
Manning, N.D., U.S.	d E	156
Manning, S.C., U.S.	f F	150
Mannington	h F	146
Mannville	d W	140
Manokotak	g O	138
Manono	c E	128
Manor	i I	154
Manorhamilton	g E	78
Manosque	i L	84
Manouane, Lac ⊜	b C	144
Manp'o	b N	102
Manresa	d M	86
Mānsa, India	f F	114
Mansa, Zam.	d E	128
Mānsehra	c E	114
Mansel Island I	d Q	134
Mansfield, Austl.	k G	184
Mansfield, Eng., U.K.	h L	78
Mansfield, Ar., U.S.	g B	152
Mansfield, Ga., U.S.	f C	150
Mansfield, Il., U.S.	b H	152
Mansfield, La., U.S.	j C	152
Mansfield, Ma., U.S.	e O	146
Mansfield, Mo., U.S.	e D	152
Mansfield, Oh., U.S.	g D	146
Mansfield, Pa., U.S.	f I	146
Mansfield, Tx., U.S.	g I	154
Mansfield, Mount ⋏	c N	146
Manson	i M	156
Mansura	k D	152
Manta	d B	174
Manteca	g D	162
Mantekamuhu ⊜	c M	114
Manteno	i H	148
Manteo	d K	150
Mantes-la-Jolie	d H	84
Manti	e E	158
Mantiqueira, Serra da ⋏	g F	177
Manton	f J	148
Mantorville	f C	148
Mantova	d E	88
Mantua → Mantova, It.	d E	88
Mantua, Oh., U.S.	f E	146
Manturovo	c AA	96
Mäntyharju	k T	76
Mäntyluoto	k Q	76
Manú ≃	f D	174
Manua Islands II	b D	188a
Manuel	f J	166
Manuel Benavides	c H	166
Manukau	d I	186
Manukau Harbour c	d I	186
Manus Island I	d F	180
Manvel	c J	156
Many	k C	152
Manyara, Lake ⊜	b G	128
Manyoni	c F	128
Manzanares	f H	86
Manzanillo, Cuba	d F	170
Manzanillo, Méx.	h G	166
Manzanillo, Punta ➤	h O	168
Manzanillo Bay c	e I	170
Manzano	j J	158
Manzanola	m D	156
Manzano Peak ⋏	j J	158
Manzhouli	b J	100
Manzini	f J	130
Maó, Esp.	f P	86
Mao, Rep. Dom.	e I	170
Mao, Tchad	f D	126
Maoke, Pegunungan ⋏	f J	108
Maoming	g I	100
Maouri, Dallol ∨	f G	124
Mapastepec	j M	166
Mapia, Kepulauan II	e I	108
Mapimí	e H	166
Mapimí, Bolsón de ✦²	d H	166
Maple ≃, U.S.	f I	156
Maple ≃, Ia., U.S.	i L	156
Maple ≃, Mi., U.S.	g K	148
Maple ≃, Mn., U.S.	g A	148
Maple ≃, N.D., U.S.	e J	156
Maple Creek	i E	142
Maple Lake	e A	148
Maple Mount	e I	152
Maplesville	j J	152
Mapleton, Ia., U.S.	i L	156
Mapleton, Mn., U.S.	g B	148
Mapleton, Or., U.S.	f B	160
Mapleton, Ut., U.S.	d E	158
Mapuera ≃	d G	174
Maputo	e K	130
Maputo ≃	f K	130
Maquela do Zombo	c C	128
Maquinchao	e C	176
Maquoketa	h E	148
Maquoketa ≃	h E	148
Mar, Serra do ⋏⁴	c N	178
Mara ≃	b F	128
Marabá	e I	174
Maracá, Ilha de I	c H	174
Maracaibo	i I	170
Maracaibo, Lago de ⊜	j I	170
Maracay	i K	170
Marādah	c D	126
Maradi	f H	124
Marāgheh	d L	118
Maragogipe	b I	177
Marahuaca, Cerro ⋏	c E	174
Marais des Cygnes ≃	d A	152
Marajó, Baía de c	d I	174
Marajó, Ilha de I	d I	174
Marakabei	g I	130
Maralal	a G	128
Marampa	g D	124
Maramureș □⁶	b H	90
Maran	m G	110
Marana	l E	158
Marand	c K	118
Marang	I G	110
Maranguape	d K	174
Maranoa ≃	e I	182
Marañón ≃	d C	174
Marapanim	d I	174
Maraș	d G	118
Marathon, Austl.	c E	184
Marathon, On., Can.	b I	148
Marathón, Ellás	k G	90
Marathon, N.Y., U.S.	e J	146
Marathon, Tx., U.S.	i C	154
Marathon, Wi., U.S.	f F	148
Maravillas	d G	166
Marawī	e G	126
Marbach	e H	83
Marble, Mn., U.S.	c B	148
Marble, N.C., U.S.	d C	150
Marble Bar	d C	182
Marble Canyon ∨	h E	158
Marble Falls	i H	154
Marble Hall	e I	130
Marblehead	f D	146
Marble Hill	e G	152
Marble Rock	h C	148
Marburg, B.R.D.	e H	80
Marburg, S. Afr.	h J	130
Marcali	i Q	80
Marcaria	d E	88
Marceline	c D	152
Marcellus	h J	148
March	i N	78
March (Morava) ≃	g P	80
Marcha ≃	e O	94
Marche □⁴	f H	88
Marche □⁹	f H	84
Marche-en-Famenne	h G	82
Marchegg	g P	80
Marchena	h F	86
Marchin	h G	82
Mar Chiquita, Laguna c	i J	178
Mar Chiquita, Laguna ⊜	f G	178
Marcigny	f K	84
Marcinelle	h E	82
Marcola	f C	160
Marcos Juárez	g G	178
Marcos Paz	h I	178
Marcus	i L	156
Marcus Baker, Mount ⋏	f U	138
Marcus Island → Minami-Tori-shima I	a G	180
Marcy, Mount ⋏	c M	146
Mardān	c E	114
Mar del Plata	j J	178
Mardin	d I	118
Maré I	s Y	188f
Mareeba	a F	184
Marengo, Il., U.S.	h G	148
Marengo, In., U.S.	d J	152
Marengo, Ia., U.S.	i C	148
Marenisco	d F	148
Marfa	i B	154
Margaree	f L	144
Margaree Harbour	f L	144
Margaretville	e L	146
Margarita, Isla de I	i M	170
Margate, S. Afr.	h J	130
Margate, Eng., U.K.	j O	78
Margate, Fl., U.S.	m F	150
Margate City	h L	146
Margecany	g U	80
Margherita Peak ⋏	a E	128
Margilan	i I	92
Mārgow, Dasht-e ✦²	c G	112
Marguerite Bay c	b L	189
María Elena	b D	178
Maria Gail	i M	80
Maria Island I	n H	184
Mariana Islands II	b F	180
Marianao	c C	170
Mariana Trench ✦¹	b F	180
Mariāni	g P	114
Marianna, Ar., U.S.	h F	152
Marianna, Fl., U.S.	i A	150
Mariánské Lázně	f L	80
Marias ≃	b O	160
Marías, Islas II	g F	166
Marias Pass ⁾⁽	b L	160
Mariato, Punta ➤	g H	164
Mariazell	h O	80
Maribor	c J	88
Marica (Évros) (Meriç) ≃	h J	90
Marico ≃	e H	130
Maricopa, Az., U.S.	k D	158
Maricopa, Ca., U.S.	i F	162
Marie Byrd Land ✦¹	c J	189
Marie-Galante I	g N	170
Mariehamn	k P	76
Mariembourg	h F	82
Marienbad → Mariánské Lázně	f L	80
Marienburg → Malbork	a S	80
Mariental	e C	130
Marienville	f G	146
Maries ≃	d D	152
Mariestad	I M	76
Marietta, Ga., U.S.	f B	150
Marietta, Mn., U.S.	f K	156
Marietta, Oh., U.S.	h E	146
Marietta, Ok., U.S.	f I	154
Marieville	b M	146
Mariga ≃	f H	124
Marignane	i L	84
Mariinsk	f I	94
Marikana	e H	130
Marília	b N	178
Marimba	c C	128
Marin, Esp.	c B	86
Marín, Méx.	e I	166
Marina di Ravenna	e G	88
Marinduque Island I	c G	108
Marine City	h M	148
Marinette	e H	148
Maringá	b M	178
Maringa ≃	a D	128
Maringouin	l E	152
Marinha Grande	f C	86
Marino	h G	88
Marion, Al., U.S.	j I	152
Marion, Ar., U.S.	g F	152
Marion, Il., U.S.	e H	152
Marion, In., U.S.	b K	152
Marion, Ia., U.S.	h D	148
Marion, Ks., U.S.	m J	156
Marion, Ky., U.S.	e H	152
Marion, La., U.S.	j D	152
Marion, Mi., U.S.	f J	148
Marion, Ms., U.S.	j H	152
Marion, N.C., U.S.	d D	150
Marion, N.D., U.S.	e I	156
Marion, Oh., U.S.	g C	146
Marion, S.C., U.S.	e G	150
Marion, S.D., U.S.	h J	156
Marion, Va., U.S.	c E	150
Marion, Wi., U.S.	f G	148
Marion, Lake ⊜¹	f F	150
Marion Junction	j I	152
Marion Lake ⊜¹	m J	156
Marion Reef ✦²	b J	184
Marionville	e C	152
Mariópolis	d L	178
Mariposa	g F	162
Mariscal Estigarribia	b H	178
Marissa	d G	152
Maritime Alps ⋏	h N	84
Marjina Gorka	h K	96
Marka	h I	126
Markaryd	m M	76
Markdale	f O	148
Marked Tree	g F	152
Markesan	g G	148
Market Weighton	h M	78
Markham, On., Can.	g P	148
Markham, Tx., U.S.	k J	154
Markham, Mount ⋏	d H	189
Markle	b K	152
Markleeville	f F	162
Markovo, S.S.S.R.	e Z	94
Markovo, S.S.S.R.	d W	96
Marks	h F	152
Marksville	k D	152
Marktheidenfeld	f I	80
Marktoberdorf	h J	80
Marktredwitz	e L	80
Mark Twain Lake ⊜¹	c E	152
Marlboro	f M	146
Marlborough, Austl.	d H	184
Marlborough, Eng., U.K.	j L	78
Marlborough, Ma., U.S.	e O	146
Marle	c J	84
Marlette	g L	148
Marlin	h J	154
Marlinton	i F	146
Marlow	e I	154
Marmaduke	f F	152
Marmande	h G	84
Marmara Adası I	i K	90
Marmara Denizi (Sea of Marmara) ⁻₂	b C	118
Marmarth	e D	156
Marmaton ≃	e B	152
Marmelos, Rio dos ≃	e F	174
Marmet	i E	146
Marmora	f R	148
Marnay	e L	84
Marne, B.R.D.	b I	80
Marne, Mi., U.S.	g J	148
Marne □⁵	d K	84
Marne ≃	c J	84
Marne au Rhin, Canal de la ≍	d M	84
Maroa, Il., U.S.	b H	152
Maroa, Ven.	c E	174
Maroantsetra	o W	131b
Maromokotro ⋏	o W	131b
Marondera	b J	130
Maroni ≃	c H	174
Maros (Mureș) ≃	c D	90
Maroua	f I	124
Marovoay	p V	131b
Marquand	e F	152
Marquard	g H	130
Marquesas Islands → Marquises, Îles II	i Z	190
Marquesas Keys II	o D	150
Marquette, Ks., U.S.	m J	156
Marquette, Mi., U.S.	d H	148
Marquise	b H	84
Marquises, Îles (Marquesas Islands) II	i Z	190
Marrah, Jabal ⋏	f C	126
Marrakech	b E	124
Marrawah	m F	184
Marree	g C	184
Marrero	m F	152
Marromeu	b L	130
Mars	g F	146
Marsā al-Burayqah	b D	126
Marsabit	h H	126
Marsala	l G	88
Marsā Maṭrūḥ	b F	126
Marsden	i G	184
Marseille	i L	84
Marseille-en-Beauvaisis	c H	84
Marseilles	i G	148
Marshall, Liber.	g D	124
Marshall, Ar., U.S.	g D	152
Marshall, Il., U.S.	c I	152
Marshall, Mi., U.S.	h K	148
Marshall, Mn., U.S.	g L	156
Marshall, Mo., U.S.	c C	152
Marshall, N.C., U.S.	d D	150
Marshall, Tx., U.S.	j B	152
Marshall, Va., U.S.	i I	146
Marshallberg	e J	150
Marshall Islands □²	b H	180
Marshall Islands II	c H	180
Marshalltown	h C	148
Marshallville	g C	150
Marshfield, Mo., U.S.	e D	152
Marshfield, Wi., U.S.	f E	148
Mars Hill, Me., U.S.	f F	144
Mars Hill, N.C., U.S.	d D	150
Marsh Island I	m E	152
Marsh Peak ⋏	d G	158
Marshville	e F	150
Marsing	g I	160
Märsta	l O	76
Mart	h J	154
Martaban	f D	110
Martaban, Gulf of c	f D	110
Martapura	f E	108
Martha's Vineyard I	f P	146
Martigny	f G	83
Martigues	i L	84
Martin, Ky., U.S.	b D	150
Martin, Mi., U.S.	h J	148
Martin, N.D., U.S.	d G	156
Martin, S.D., U.S.	h F	156
Martin, Tn., U.S.	f H	152
Martina Franca	i L	88
Martinborough	h J	186
Martindale	j I	154
Martinez, Ca., U.S.	f C	162
Martinez, Ga., U.S.	f D	150
Martínez de la Torre	g K	166
Martinho Campos	e F	177
Martinique □²	g N	170
Martin Lake ⊜¹	j K	152
Martinniemi	i S	76
Martinsberg	g O	80
Martinsburg, Pa., U.S.	g H	146
Martinsburg, W.V., U.S.	h I	146
Martins Ferry	g F	146
Martinsville, Il., U.S.	c I	152
Martinsville, In., U.S.	c J	152
Martinsville, Va., U.S.	c G	150
Martin Vaz, Ilhas II	g L	172
Marton	g J	186
Martos	h H	86
Martre, Lac la ⊜	d I	134
Martti	h U	76
Marudi	e E	108
Marugame	m H	106
Marungu ⋏	c E	128
Marv Dasht	h O	118
Marvell	h F	152
Marvine, Mount ⋏	f E	158
Mary	j J	92
Maryborough, Austl.	e J	184
Maryborough, Austl.	k E	184
Marydale	g F	130
Mary Kathleen	c C	184
Maryland □³	c K	136
Maryneal	g F	154
Maryport	g J	78
Marys ≃	c J	162
Marystown	e R	144
Marysvale	f D	158
Marysville, N.B., Can.	g G	144
Marysville, Ca., U.S.	e D	162
Marysville, Ks., U.S.	l K	156
Marysville, Mi., U.S.	h M	148
Marysville, Oh., U.S.	g C	146
Marysville, Pa., U.S.	g J	146
Marysville, Wa., U.S.	b C	160
Maryville, Mo., U.S.	b B	152
Maryville, Tn., U.S.	d C	150
Marzūq	c C	126
Marzūq, Ṣaḥrā' ✦²	d C	126
Masada → Meẓada, Ḥorvot ⊥	f D	120
Mas'adah (Cæsarea Philippi)	b E	120
Masai Steppe ⋏¹	b G	128
Masaka	b F	128
Masan	h P	102
Masasi	d G	128
Masatepe	f H	168
Masaya	f H	168
Masaya □⁵	e H	168
Masbate	c G	108
Masbate Island I	c G	108
Mascarene Islands II	f K	128
Mascot	c C	150
Mascota	g G	166
Mascoutah	d G	152
Maseru	g H	130
Mashaba Mountains ⋏	b J	130
Mashābih I	j G	118
Masherbrum ⋏	c G	114
Mashhad	d R	118
Māshkel, Hāmūn-i- ⊜	d G	112
Mashra'ur-Raqq	g F	126
Masi Manimba	b C	128
Masindi	h G	126
Maṣīrah I	d K	117
Maṣīrah, Khalīj c	e K	117
Masjed Soleymān	g M	118
Mask, Lough ⊜	h D	78
Maskanah	d H	118
Masoala, Cap ➤	o X	131b
Masoala, Presqu'île de ➤¹	o X	131b
Mason, Mi., U.S.	h K	148
Mason, Oh., U.S.	h B	146
Mason, Tn., U.S.	g G	152
Mason, Tx., U.S.	i G	154
Mason, W.V., U.S.	h D	146
Mason City, Il., U.S.	b G	152
Mason City, Ia., U.S.	g B	148
Mason City, Ne., U.S.	j H	156
Masqat (Muscat)	c K	117
Massa	e E	88
Massachusetts □³	c L	136
Massachusetts Bay c	e P	146
Massafra	i L	88
Massa Marittima	f E	88
Massangena	c K	130
Massarosa	f E	88
Massena, Ia., U.S.	j M	156
Massena, N.Y., U.S.	c L	146
Massenya	f D	126
Masset	c B	140
Masseube	i G	84
Massey	d M	148
Massillon	g E	146
Massina ✦¹	f F	124
Massinga	d L	130
Massive, Mount ⋏	e J	158
Masterson	d E	154
Masterton	g J	186
Mastung	f B	114
Masuda	m F	106
Masvingo	c J	130
Matachewan	c O	148
Mata de São João	b I	177
Matadi	c B	128
Matador	e F	154
Matagalpa	e I	168
Matagalpa □⁵	e I	168
Matagami	g Q	134
Matagorda	k K	154
Matagorda Bay c	k J	154
Matagorda Island I	k J	154
Matakana Island I	d K	186
Matale	i F	116
Matam	e D	124
Matamata	d J	186
Matamoras	f L	146
Matamoros	e K	166
Matamoros de la Laguna	e H	166
Matandu ≃	c G	128
Matane	d F	144
Matanuska ≃	f T	138
Matanzas, Cuba	c D	170
Matanzas, Méx.	g I	166
Mata Ortiz	b E	166
Matapalo, Cabo ➤	i K	168
Matara	j F	116
Mataram	g F	108
Mataró	d N	86
Matatiele	h I	130
Mataura	m C	186
Matāutu	a B	188a
Matehuala	f I	166
Matera	i K	88
Mátészalka	h V	80
Matewan	b D	150
Mathematicians Seamounts ✦³	h H	132
Mather	h F	146
Matheson	b O	148
Mathews	b J	150
Mathis	k I	154
Mathura	g G	114
Matías Romero	i L	166
Matignon	d D	84
Matlock	h L	78
Mato, Cerro ⋏	b E	174
Mato Grosso	g G	174
Mato Grosso □³	c B	177
Mato Grosso, Planalto do ⋏¹	g G	174
Mato Grosso do Sul □³	b K	178
Matopo Hills ⋏²	c I	130
Matosinhos	d C	86
Matou	I I	104
Matoury	c H	174
Matrah	c K	117
Matrei in Osttirol	h L	80
Matsapha	f J	130
Matsudo	l N	106
Matsue	l H	106
Matsumae	f O	106
Matsumoto	k L	106
Matsusaka	m K	106
Matsu Tao I	i H	104
Matsutō	k K	106
Matsuura	n E	106
Matsuyama	n G	106
Mattagami ≃	b N	148
Mattagami Heights	b N	148
Mattāncheri	h D	116
Mattawa, On., Can.	d Q	148
Mattawa, Wa., U.S.	d F	160
Mattawamkeag	b R	146
Mattawamkeag ≃	b R	146
Matterhorn ⋏, Europe	g N	84
Matterhorn ⋏, Nv., U.S.	c J	162
Mattersburg	h P	80
Mattighofen	g M	80
Mattoon, Il., U.S.	c H	152
Mattoon, Wi., U.S.	e F	148
Mattydale	d J	146
Maturín	j M	170
Maú ≃	f G	174
Maúa	d G	128
Maubeuge	b J	84
Ma-ubin	f C	110
Maud, Ok., U.S.	d J	154
Maud, Tx., U.S.	i B	152
Maude	j F	184
Maués	d G	174

Symbols in the index are identified on page 198.

220

Name	Map Ref.	Page

Symbols in the index are identified on page 198.

Name	Map Ref.	Page

Symbols in the index are identified on page 198.

Name	Map Ref.	Page

Symbols in the index are identified on page 198.

Name	Map Ref.	Page

Symbols in the index are identified on page 198.

Symbols in the index are identified on page 198.

Name	Map Ref.	Page
Podol'sk	f T	96
Podoz'orskij	d W	96
Podravska Slatina	d A	90
Pofadder	g D	130
Pogar	i P	96
Poggibonsi	f F	88
Pogradec	i D	90
P'ohang	g Q	102
Pohénégamook	e D	144
Pohjois-Karjalan lääni □⁴	j U	76
Poinsett, Cape ➤	b F	189
Point	g K	154
Point Arena	f B	162
Point Au Fer Island I	m E	152
Point Comfort	k J	154
Pointe a la Hache	m G	152
Pointe-à-Pitre	f N	170
Point Edward	g M	148
Pointe-Noire	b B	128
Point Fortin	i N	170
Point Hope	b K	138
Point Imperial ⋀	h E	158
Point Learnington	c R	144
Point Marion	h G	146
Point Pelee National Park ♦	i M	148
Point Pleasant, N.J., U.S.	g L	146
Point Pleasant, W.V., U.S.	i D	146
Point Sapin	f l	144
Poisson Blanc, Réservoir du ☒¹	a K	144
Poissy	d l	84
Poitiers	f G	84
Poix	c H	84
Pojoaque Valley	i J	158
Pokhara	f J	114
Pokrov	f V	96
Polacca	i F	158
Pola de Lena	b F	86
Poland (Polska) □¹	e K	74
Polanów	a P	80
Polcirkeln	h Q	76
Pol-e Khomrī	c C	114
Polesje ⬅¹	h D	80
Polessk [Labiau]	g D	96
Polevskoj	i J	92
Polgár	h U	80
Põlgyo	i O	102
Police	b N	80
Poligny	f L	84
Polillo Islands II	n T	109b
Polistena	k K	88
Polk, Ne., U.S.	j J	156
Polk, Pa., U.S.	f G	146
Polkton	d F	150
Polla	i J	88
Polláchi	g Q	116
Pöllau	h O	80
Pollock, La., U.S.	k D	152
Pollock, S.D., U.S.	f G	156
Polmak	f U	76
Polo, Il., U.S.	i F	148
Polo, Mo., U.S.	c B	152
Polochic ≃	b E	168
Polock	f K	96
Polonnaruwa	i F	116
Polotn'anyj	g S	96
Polson	c K	160
Poltava	h D	92
Poltimore	b K	146
Põltsamaa	c H	96
Polvijärvi	j U	76
Polynesia II	d L	180
Pomabamba	e C	174
Pomarkku	k R	76
Pomaro	h H	166
Pombal	f C	86
Pomerania □⁹	f C	86
Pomeranian Bay c	a N	80
Pomerene	m F	158
Pomeroy, Ia., U.S.	i M	156
Pomeroy, Oh., U.S.	h D	146
Pomeroy, Wa., U.S.	d H	160
Pomfret	e F	150
Pomme de Terre ≃, Mn., U.S.	f K	156
Pomme de Terre ≃, Mo., U.S.	e C	152
Pomona, Ca., U.S.	j H	162
Pomona, Ks., U.S.	m L	156
Pomona Park	j E	150
Pompano Beach	m F	150
Pompei ⊥	i l	88
Pompéia	i l	88
Pompéia	g C	177
Pompton Lakes	g L	144
Pomquet	g G	140
Ponape I	f G	180
Ponca	i K	156
Ponca City	c l	154
Ponce	e K	170
Ponce de Leon	l K	152
Ponchatoula	l F	152
Pond	e l	152
Pondcreek	c l	154
Pondicherry	g E	116
Pondicherry □⁸	g E	116
Pond Inlet	b Q	134
Pondoland □⁹	h l	130
Pondosa	c D	162
Ponferrada	c E	86
Pongolo ≃	f K	130
Ponnūru Nidubrolu	d F	116
Ponoka	e U	140
Ponorogo	j O	109a
Pons	g F	84
Ponta do Sol	m T	87a
Ponta Grossa	c M	178
Pontão	f C	86
Ponta Porã	b K	178
Pontarlier	f M	84
Pontassieve	f F	88
Pont-Audemer	e G	84
Pont-Aven	e C	84
Pont Canavese	d B	88
Pontchartrain, Lake ☒	l F	152
Pont-d'Ain	f K	84
Pont-de-Vaux	f K	84
Ponte da Barca	d C	86
Pontedera	f E	88
Ponte de Sor	f C	86
Ponte do Lima	d C	86
Ponteix	i G	142
Ponte Nova	f G	177
Pontevedra	c D	86
Ponte Vedra Beach	i E	150
Pontiac, Il., U.S.	i H	148
Pontiac, Mi., U.S.	h L	148
Pontianak	f D	108
Pontivy	e D	84
Pont-l'Abbé	e B	84
Pont-L'Évêque	c G	84
Pontoise	c l	84
Pöntorson	d E	84
Pontotoc, Ms., U.S.	h H	152
Pontotoc, Tx., U.S.	i H	154
Pontremoli	e E	88
Pontresina	f L	83
Ponts	d M	86
Pont-sur-Yonne	d l	84
Pontus Mountains ⋌	b l	118
Pontypridd	j J	78
Pony	e N	160
Ponziane, Isole II	i l	88
Poole	k L	78
Pooler	g E	150
Poolville	g l	154
Poona → Pune	c B	116
Poopó, Lago	g E	174
Poor Knights Islands II	c C	174
Popayán	c C	174
Pope	h G	152
Poperinge	g B	82
Popigaj ≃	c N	94
Popilta Lake ☒	i D	184
Poplar, Mt., U.S.	c B	156
Poplar, Wi., U.S.	d D	148
Poplar ≃, Can.	f R	142
Poplar ≃, Mn., U.S.	d K	156
Poplar Bluff	f F	152
Poplar Hill	f T	142
Poplarville	i G	152
Poplevinskij	h V	96
Popocatépetl, Volcán ⋀¹	h J	166
Popokabaka	c C	128
Popoli	g H	88
Popondetta	a l	182
Popovo	f J	90
Poppel	f G	82
Poppi	f F	88
Popple ≃	e G	148
Poprad	f T	80
Poprad ≃	f T	80
Pöptong	e O	102
Poquoson	b J	150
Porangatu	b D	177
Porbandar	j C	114
Porcher Island I	d D	140
Porcuna	h G	86
Porcupine ≃	d W	138
Pordenone	d D	88
Pori	k Q	76
Porirua	h l	186
Porlamar	i M	170
Poronajsk	h T	94
Porozovo	i Q	96
Porpoise Bay c	b G	189
Porrentruy	d C	83
Porsanger	i K	76
Porsgrunn	g F	74
Portachuelo	g F	174
Port Adelaide	i C	184
Portadown	g G	78
Portage, Mi., U.S.	h J	148
Portage, Ut., U.S.	c D	158
Portage, Wi., U.S.	g F	148
Portage ≃	f C	146
Portage-la-Prairie	i P	142
Portageville	f G	152
Portal, Ga., U.S.	g E	150
Portal, N.D., U.S.	c E	156
Port Alberni	h K	140
Portalegre	f D	86
Portales	e C	154
Port Alfred (Kowie)	i H	130
Port Alice	g G	140
Port Allegany	f H	146
Port Allen	l E	152
Port Angeles	b B	160
Port Antonio	e F	170
Port Aransas	l l	154
Portarlington	h F	78
Port Arthur → Thunder Bay, On., Can.	b F	148
Port Arthur, Austl.	n G	184
Port Arthur, Tx., U.S.	m C	152
Port Arthur → Lüshun, Zhg.	e l	102
Port Askaig	f G	78
Port Augusta	i B	184
Port au Port Peninsula ➤¹	d N	144
Port-au-Prince	e H	170
Port Austin	f M	148
Port Barre	l E	152
Port-Bergé	o V	131b
Port Blair	i B	110
Port Borden	f J	144
Port-Bouët	g F	124
Port Broughton	i B	184
Port Byron	i F	148
Port-Cartier	i M	114
Port Chalmers	l E	186
Port Charlotte	m D	150
Port Chester	f M	146
Port Clinton	f D	146
Port Clyde	d D	146
Port Colborne	h D	148
Port Coquitlam	h L	140
Port Credit	g P	148
Port-de-Paix	e H	170
Port Dickson	m F	109a
Port Dover	h O	148
Porte Crayon, Mount ⋀	i G	146
Port Edward, B.C., Can.	c D	140
Port Edward, S. Afr.	h J	130
Port Edwards	f F	148
Portel, Bra.	d H	174
Portel, Port.	g D	86
Port Elgin, N.B., Can.	f l	144
Port Elgin, On., Can.	f N	148
Port Elizabeth	h l	130
Port Ellen	f G	78
Port-en-Bessin	c F	84
Porter, Ok., U.S.	d l	154
Porter, Tx., U.S.	i K	154
Porterville, S. Afr.	i D	130
Porterville, Ms., U.S.	j H	152
Port-Étienne → Nouâdhibou	d C	124
Port Fairy	l E	184
Port Fitzroy	c E	186
Port Gamble	b C	160
Port Gentil	b A	128
Port Germain	i B	184
Port Gibson	k F	152
Port Graham	g S	138
Port Greville	g l	144
Port Harcourt	h H	124
Port Hardy	g G	140
Port Hawkesbury	g L	144
Port Hedland	d C	182
Port Henry	c M	146
Port Hill	f l	144
Port Hood	g L	144
Port Hope, On., Can.	g P	148
Port Hope, Mi., U.S.	g M	148
Port Huron	h M	148
Portimão	h C	86
Port Isabel	m l	154
Port Jervis	f L	146
Port Kembla	i l	184
Portland, Austl.	l D	184
Portland, Austl.	i E	184
Portland, Ar., U.S.	i E	152
Portland, In., U.S.	b L	152
Portland, Me., U.S.	d C	146
Portland, Mi., U.S.	h K	148
Portland, Or., U.S.	e C	160
Portland, Tn., U.S.	g J	152
Portland, Tx., U.S.	l l	154
Portland, Bill of ➤	k K	78
Portland, Cape ➤	m G	184
Portland Bay c	l D	184
Portland Bight c³	f F	170
Portland Canal ☒	b D	140
Portland Point ➤	f F	170
Port Laoise	h F	78
Port Lavaca	k J	154
Port Leyden	d K	146
Port Lincoln	j A	184
Port Lions	h K	138
Port Loko	g D	124
Port-Louis, Fr.	e C	84
Port Louis, Maus.	v R	131c
Port-Lyautey → Kenitra	b E	124
Port Macquarie	h J	184
Port Mahomack	d J	78
Port Maitland	i G	144
Port McNeill	g G	140
Port McNicoll	f P	148
Port Moody	h L	140
Port Moresby	a l	182
Port Morien	f N	144
Port Mouton	i l	144
Port Neches	m C	152
Portneuf ≃	h M	160
Port Nolloth	g C	130
Port Norris	h K	146
Porto	d C	86
Porto Alegre	f M	178
Porto Amazonas	c N	178
Porto Amboim	d B	128
Pôrto de Mós	f C	86
Porto de Moz	d H	174
Porto de Pedras	e K	174
Porto Empedocle	l H	88
Porto Esperança	g G	174
Porto Esperidião	g G	174
Porto Feliz	b O	178
Porto Ferreira	f E	177
Port of Spain	i N	170
Portogruaro	d G	88
Portola	e E	162
Porto Lucena	c N	178
Porto Mendes	c K	178
Porto Moniz	m T	87a
Porto Murtinho	h G	174
Porto Nacional	f l	174
Porto-Novo	g G	124
Port Orange	j F	150
Port Orchard	c C	160
Porto Recanati	f H	88
Port Orford	h A	160
Porto San Giorgio	f H	88
Porto Sant'Elpidio	f H	88
Porto Santo I	l U	87a
Porto Santo I I	l U	87a
Porto Seguro	d l	177
Porto Torres	i C	88
Porto União	d M	178
Porto-Vecchio	m X	85a
Porto Velho	e F	174
Portoviejo	d B	174
Port Perry	f P	148
Port Phillip Bay c	l F	184
Port Pirie	i F	184
Portree	d C	78
Port Richey	k D	150
Port Rowan	h D	148
Port Royal, Pa., U.S.	g l	146
Port Royal, S.C., U.S.	g F	150
Portrush	f G	78
Port Said → Bûr Sa'īd	g E	118
Port Saint Joe	j A	150
Port Saint Johns	h l	130
Port Saint Lucie	l F	150
Port Sanilac	g M	148
Port Saunders	b l	184
Portsea	i l	184
Port Shepstone	h J	130
Portsmouth, Eng., U.K.	k L	78
Portsmouth, N.H., U.S.	d P	146
Portsmouth, Oh., U.S.	i D	146
Portsmouth, Va., U.S.	c J	150
Portsoy	d K	78
Port Stanley	h D	148
Portstewart	f G	78
Port Sudan → Bûr Südän	e H	126
Port Sulphur	m G	152
Port Talbot	j J	78
Porttipahdan tekojärvi ☒¹	g T	76
Port Townsend	b C	160
Portugal □¹	h F	72
Portugalete	g P	148
Portuguese Guinea → Guinea-Bissau ⬅	f C	124
Port-Vendres	j J	84
Port Vila	q Y	188f
Port Waikato	d l	186
Port Wakefield	i B	184
Port Washington	g F	148
Port Weld	f G	150
Port Wentworth	g E	150
Port Wing	d D	148
Porum	d K	154
Porvenir	e B	176
Porz	f G	80
Porzuna	f G	86
Posada	d K	88
Posadas	d K	178
Poschiavo	f M	83
Posen	c P	80
Posen, Mi., U.S.	e L	148
Posio	h U	76
Positano	i l	88
Posse	c E	177
Possession Islands II	b K	189
Possneck	e K	80
Possum Kingdom Lake ☒¹	g H	154
Post	f E	154
Poste-de-la-Baleine	e Q	134
Postelle	d B	150
Post Falls	c l	160
Postmasburg	f F	130
Postojna	d J	88
P'ostraja Dresva	e G	94
Postville	g D	148
Potchefstroom	f H	130
Poteau	d K	154
Poteet	j H	154
Potenza	i l	88
Poteriteri, Lake ☒	m B	186
Potgietersrus	e l	130
Poth	j H	154
Potholes Reservoir ☒¹	c F	160
Poti	e J	92
Potiskum	f H	124
Potlatch	c l	160
Potomac ≃	b l	152
Potomac Heights	i l	146
Potosi, Bol.	g E	174
Potosi, Mo., U.S.	e F	152
Potrero Grande	e F	166
Potsdam, D.D.R.	c M	80
Potsdam, N.Y., U.S.	c L	146
Potsdam □⁵	c L	80
Potter	j D	156
Pottersville	h K	146
Potts Camp	h G	152
Pottstown	g K	146
Pottsville	h l	146
Potwin	m J	156
P'otzu	l l	104
Pouancé	e E	84
Pouce-Coupe	b N	140
Pouce Coupé ≃	a O	140
Pouch Cove	e U	144
Poughkeepsie	f M	146
Poulan	h C	150
Poulsbo	c C	160
Poultney	d M	146
Poún	g O	102
Pound	b D	150
Pouso Alegre	b P	178
Poutasi	b B	188a
Pouthisät	d P	148
Povážská Bystrica	f R	80
Póvoa de Varzim	d C	86
Povorino	h j	92
Povungnituk	d Q	134
Povungnituk, Rivière de ≃	d R	134
Powassan	d P	148
Powder ≃, U.S.	b E	156
Powder ≃, Or., U.S.	f H	160
Powderly, Ky., U.S.	e l	152
Powderly, Tx., U.S.	f K	154
Powell	c C	150
Powell ≃	g F	158
Powell, Lake ☒¹	g F	158
Powell, Mount ⋀	e J	158
Powellhurst	e C	160
Powell River	h j	140
Powellton	i E	146
Powers, Mi., U.S.	e H	148
Powers, Or., U.S.	h A	160
Powers Lake	c E	156
Powhatan, La., U.S.	k C	152
Powhatan, Va., U.S.	b l	150
Powhatan Point	h F	146
Powys □⁶	i J	78
Poxoréu	f E	104
Poyang Hu ☒	f E	104
Poyen	h D	152
Poygan, Lake ☒	f G	148
Poynette	g F	148
Poza Grande	e B	166
Poza Rica de Hidalgo	g K	166
Poznań	c P	80
Pozoblanco	g G	86
Pozo Colorado	b J	178
Pozo Negro	o AA	87b
Pozuelos	i L	170
Pozzallo	i l	88
Pozzuoli	i l	88
Prachin Buri	i E	110
Prachuap Khiri Khan	j E	110
Prades	j l	84
Prado	d l	177
Prague → Praha, Česko.	e N	80
Prague, Ne., U.S.	j K	156
Prague, Ok., U.S.	d J	154
Praha (Prague)	e N	80
Prahova □⁷	d J	90
Praia	f B	124
Praia Grande	e F	174
Prainha	e F	174
Prairie ≃, Mn., U.S.	c B	148
Prairie ≃, Wi., U.S.	e F	148
Prairie City, Il., U.S.	j E	148
Prairie City, Ia., U.S.	i B	152
Prairie City, Or., U.S.	f G	160
Prairie du Chien	g D	148
Prairie du Sac	g E	148
Prairie Grove	g B	152
Prairies, Lake of the ☒¹	g M	142
Prairie View	g K	154
Prairie Village	m K	156
Praslin Islands II	b l	128
Pratápgarh	h F	114
Pratas Island → Tungsha Tao I	g J	104
Prato	f F	88
Pratt	n l	156
Pratteln	c H	83
Prattsburg	e l	146
Prattville	j J	152
Pravdinsk	e z	96
Pravia	b F	86
Praya	g F	108
Predazzo	c F	88
Preditz [-Turrach]	h M	80
Preeceville	f G	142
Pré-en-Pail	d F	84
Pregarten	g N	80
Preili	e J	96
Prémery	e J	84
Premnitz	c L	80
Premont	l H	154
Prentice	d F	148
Prentiss	k G	152
Prenzlau	b N	80
Preparis Island I	g B	110
Preparis North Channel ☒	g B	110
Preparis South Channel ☒	g C	110
Přerov	f Q	80
Prescott, On., Can.	c K	146
Prescott, Az., U.S.	i D	158
Prescott, Ar., U.S.	j C	152
Prescott, Wi., U.S.	f D	148
Presho	g H	156
Presidencia Roque Sáenz Peña	b H	178
Presidente Epitácio	a l	178
Presidente Hayes □⁵	a J	178
Presidente Prudente	b M	178
Presidente Venceslau	b M	178
Presidio	j B	154
Presidio ≃	c H	154
Preslav	e H	90
Prešov	f S	80
Prespa, Lake ☒	i E	90
Presque Isle	b S	144
Presson	h G	158
Preston, Eng., U.K.	h K	78
Preston, Id., U.S.	h N	160
Preston, Ia., U.S.	i C	148
Preston, Ks., U.S.	n l	156
Preston, Mn., U.S.	g B	148
Prestonburg	b D	150
Prestonpans	f L	78
Prestwick	f l	78
Pretoria	e l	130
Pretty Prairie	n l	156
Préveza	k E	90
Prey Vêng	i l	110
Pribilof Islands II	e K	138
Priboj	f D	90
Příbram	f N	80
Price, Tx., U.S.	f l	154
Price, Ut., U.S.	e F	158
Price ≃	e F	158
Prichard	l H	152
Priddy	h H	154
Priego de Córdoba	h L	86
Prien	h L	80
Prieska	i E	130
Priest	h l	160
Priest Lake ☒	b l	160
Priest River	b l	160
Prievidza	g R	80
Prijedor	e K	88
Prikaspijskaja nizmennost' ≃	h G	92
Prilep	h E	90
Priluki	g D	92
Primera	m l	154
Primero ≃	f G	178
Primghar	i M	156
Primorsk, S.S.S.R.	a K	96
Primorsk, S.S.S.R.	a G	96
Primrose Lake ☒	f K	134
Prince Albert, Sk., Can.	e l	142
Prince Albert, S. Afr.	i F	130
Prince Albert Mountains ⋌	c H	189
Prince Albert National Park ♦	d H	142
Prince Albert Sound ☒	b l	134
Prince Alfred Hamlet	i E	130
Prince Charles Island I	c Q	134
Prince Charles Mountains ⋌	c E	189
Prince Edward Island □⁴	g T	134
Prince Edward Islands II	m G	190
Prince Frederick	i J	146
Prince George, B.C., Can.	d L	140
Prince George, Va., U.S.	b l	150
Prince of Wales, Cape ➤	d J	138
Prince of Wales Island I, Austl.	b H	182
Prince of Wales Island I, N.T., Can.	b M	134
Prince of Wales Island I, Ak., U.S.	i BB	138
Prince of Wales Strait ☒	b l	134
Prince Olav Coast ±²	b D	189
Prince Patrick Island I	b N	132
Prince Regent Inlet ☒	b N	134
Prince Rupert	c D	140
Princess Anne	i K	146
Princess Astrid Coast ±²	c C	189
Princess Martha Coast ±²	c B	189
Princess Ragnhild Coast ±²	c C	189
Princess Royal Channel ☒	d F	140
Princess Royal Island I	e F	140
Princes Town	i N	170
Princeton, B.C., Can.	h N	140
Princeton, Ca., U.S.	e C	162
Princeton, Il., U.S.	i H	148
Princeton, In., U.S.	d l	152
Princeton, Ky., U.S.	e l	152
Princeton, Me., U.S.	b S	144
Princeton, Mn., U.S.	e B	148
Princeton, Mo., U.S.	c D	152
Princeton, N.J., U.S.	g L	146
Princeton, N.C., U.S.	d H	150
Princeton, W.V., U.S.	b E	150
Princeton, Wi., U.S.	g F	148
Princeville, P.Q., Can.	a O	146
Princeville, Il., U.S.	i H	148
Princeville, N.C., U.S.	d l	150
Prince William Sound ☒	f U	138
Principe I	a A	128
Príncipe da Beira	f F	174
Prineville	f D	160
Prinzapolka	b K	168
Prinzapolka ≃	b K	168
Prior, Cabo ➤	b C	86
Pripet Marshes → Polesje ⬅¹	g C	92
Priština	g E	90
Pritchett	d E	156
Pritzwalk	b L	80
Privas	h K	84
Priverno	h H	88
Privolžsk	d X	96
Privolžskaja vozvyšennost' ≃¹	g G	92
Prizren	g E	90
Prizzi	l H	88
Probolinggo	j P	109a
Probstzella	e K	80
Proctor, Mn., U.S.	d C	148
Proctor, Vt., U.S.	d M	146
Proddatūr	e E	116
Proença-a-Nova	f C	86
Progreso	g O	166
Project City	e C	162
Prokopjevsk	g K	94
Prokuplje	f E	90
Proletarij	b G	96
Prome (Pyè)	d C	110
Promission	i D	177
Promontogno	f L	83
Pronsk	g V	96
Prophet ≃	b N	134
Prophetstown	i F	148
Propriá	f K	174
Proserpine	c l	182
Prosser	d G	160
Prostějov	f Q	80
Proston	f l	182
Protection	n H	156
Protem	k D	152
Provadija	e H	90
Provence □⁹	i L	84
Providence, R.I., U.S.	f N	146
Providence, Isla de ☒	c J	170
Providence Island I	c J	170
Providencetown	e N	146
Provins	d J	84
Provo	i D	158
Provost	f C	142
Prudhoe Bay c	a T	138
Prudhoe Island I	b l	182
Prudnik	f Q	80
Prüm	c F	80
Pruszków	c Q	80
Prut ≃	c J	90
Pružany	h C	80
Prydz Bay c	c F	189
Pryor	c K	154
Przasnysz	b T	80
Przedbórz	d S	80
Przemków	c N	80
Przemyśl	g W	80
Převal'sk	d X	92
Przeworsk	d X	80
Pskov	d K	96
Pszczyna	f R	80
Ptarmigan, Cape ➤	b l	134
Ptolemais	i E	90
Ptuj	d A	88
Puan	h N	102
Pubalco	i H	144
Pucallpa	e D	174
Pučež	d Z	96
Pucheng	h G	104
Puches	c A	86
Pudasjärvi	i T	76
Pudukkottai	g E	116
Puebla [de Zaragoza]	h J	166
Pueblo	f L	158
Pueblo Hundido	b B	176
Pueblo Viejo	i M	166
Puerco ≃	j J	158
Puerco, Rio ≃	j J	158
Puerto Acosta	g E	174
Puerto Aisén	e B	176
Puerto Ángel	i K	166
Puerto Armuelles	i L	168
Puerto Asís	c C	174
Puerto Ayacucho	b E	174
Puerto Baquerizo Moreno	j N	174a
Puerto Barrios	b F	168
Puerto Belgrano	j G	178
Puerto Bermúdez	f D	174
Puerto Berrío	b D	174
Puerto Cabello	a E	170
Puerto Cabezas	c K	168
Puerto Carreño	b E	174
Puerto Casado	b J	178
Puerto Chicama	c C	174
Puerto Cortés, C.R.	i K	168
Puerto Cortés, Hond.	b G	168
Puerto Cumarebo	i J	170
Puerto de la Cruz	o X	87b
Puerto del Rosario	o AA	87b
Puerto de San José	d D	168
Puerto Deseado	f C	176
Puerto Escondido	j K	166
Puerto la Cruz	a E	170
Puerto Leguízamo	d D	174
Puerto Libertad	c C	166
Puerto Lobos	e C	176
Puerto Madryn	e C	176
Puerto Maldonado	f E	174
Puerto Montt	e B	176
Puerto Morazán	g P	166
Puerto Morelos	g P	166
Puerto Natales	f B	176
Puerto Padre	d F	170
Puerto Páez	b E	174
Puerto Peñasco	b B	166
Puerto Pinasco	b J	178
Puerto Pirámides	e C	176
Puerto Princesa	d F	108
Puerto Real	i E	86
Puerto Rico	e K	170
Puerto Rico □²	e K	170
Puerto Rico Trench +¹	g M	132
Puerto Sastre	a J	178
Puerto Suárez	g G	174
Puerto Tejada	c C	174
Puerto Vallarta	g E	166
Puerto Varas	e B	176
Puerto Viejo	h G	168
Puerto Wilches	b D	174
Pueyrredón, Lago (Lago Cochrane) ☒	f B	176
Puget Sound ☒	c C	160
Pugwash	g H	144
Puhos	j U	76
Puigcerdá	c M	86
Puigmal ⋀	c M	86
Pukaki, Lake ☒	f C	186
Pukapuka I	c N	102
Pukch'ang	d N	102
Pukch'ŏng	c O	102
Pukë	h C	90
Pukekohe	b l	186
Puksubaek-san ⋀	c O	102
Pula	d A	88
Pulacayo	h E	174
Pulaski, N.Y., U.S.	d J	146
Pulaski, Tn., U.S.	b l	152
Pulaski, Va., U.S.	b E	150
Pulaski, Wi., U.S.	f G	148
Puławy	d U	80
Pulicat Lake c	f D	116
Puliyangudi	h D	116
Pulkkila	i T	76
Pullman	d H	160
Pullo	f D	174
Pulog, Mount ⋀	n l	109b
Pulsano	i l	88
Pultusk	c T	80
Pulu	n l	109b
Púlar, Cerro ⋀	c D	178
Puná, Isla I	d B	174
Punakha	f L	114
Punata	g E	174
Pünch	e B	114
Pune (Poona)	c B	116
P'ungsan	c O	102
Púngoè ≃	b P	130
Púnia	b D	128
Punitaqui	f C	178
Punjab □³	e F	114
Punjab □³	e G	114
Puno	g D	174
Punta Alta	j H	178
Punta Arenas	g B	176
Punta del Este	c M	178
Punta Delgada	e D	176
Punta Gorda	m D	150
Punta Gorda, Bahía de c ≃	f K	168
Punta Negra, Salar de ≃	c D	178
Punta Prieta	c B	166
Punta Prieta	c B	166
Puntarenas	i l	168
Punto Fijo	i l	170
Punxsutawney	g H	146
Puolanka	i T	76
Puqi	f l	100
Puquio	f D	174
Puri	k l	114
Purificación	c C	166
Purísima	c D	166
Purli	h B	114
Purmerend	c G	82
Purnea	i L	114
Purúlia	i L	114
Purus (Purús) ≃	d F	174
Purvis	k G	152
Purwakarta	j N	109a
Purwokerto	j N	109a
Pusan	g H	102
Pushkar	g F	114
Puškin	b M	96
Puškino	e T	96
Puškinskije Gory	d K	96
Püspökladány	h U	80
Pustoška	e L	96
Putao	g Q	114
Putaruru	e J	186
Putian	j H	104
Puting, Tanjung ➤	f E	108
Putnam, Ct., U.S.	f O	146
Putnam, Tx., U.S.	g G	154
Putney, Ga., U.S.	h C	150
Putney, Vt., U.S.	e M	146
Putorana, plato ≃¹	d Q	92
Putsonderwater	g E	130
Puttalam	h E	116
Puttgarden	a K	80
Putumayo (Içá) ≃	d E	174
Putuo	f K	104
Puula ☒	k T	76
Puumala	k U	76
Pu'upu'u	a A	188a
Puxico	f F	152
Puyallup	c C	160
Puyallup ≃	c C	160
Puy-de-Dôme □⁵	g J	84
Puylaurens	i l	84
Puyo, Ec.	d C	174
Puyŏ	g N	102
Puysegur Point ➤	m A	186
Pweto	c E	128
Pwllheli	i l	78
Pyapon	f C	110
Pye Islands II	g S	138
Pyhäjoki	i S	76
Pyhäselkä	j U	76
Pyhäselkä ☒	j U	76
Pyinmana	e D	110
Pymatuning Reservoir ☒¹	f F	146
Pyŏktong	c M	102
Pyŏlch'ang-ni	d N	102
P'yŏngan	e N	102
P'yŏngsan	e O	102
P'yŏngt'aek	f O	102
P'yŏngyang	d M	102
Pyote	h C	154
Pyramid Lake ☒	d E	162
Pyrenees ⋌	c M	86
Pyrénées-Atlantiques □⁵	i F	84
Pyrénées-Orientales □⁵	j l	84
Pyrzyce	b N	80
Pytalovo	d J	96
Pyu	d E	110

Q

Name	Map Ref.	Page
Qacentina	a H	124
Qâ'emshahr	d O	118
Qaidam Pendi ≃¹	d B	114
Qalāt	d B	114
Qal'at Bīshah	d C	117
Qal'eh-ye Kānsī	h C	112
Qallābāt	f H	117
Qamar, Ghubbat al- c	f H	117
Qamdo	e A	114
Qäna	h B	118
Qandahār	d B	114
Qandala	e A	126
Qardho	f D	126
Qarqan ≃	c C	114
Qārūn, Birkat ☒	h D	118
Qäsh, Nahr al- (Gash) ≃	h D	118
Qasr al-Farāfirah	c E	126
Qa'tabah	h D	117
Qatanā	d E	112
Qatar (Qatar) □¹	d E	112
Qattara Depression → Qattârah, Munkhafad al- ≃⁷	b F	126
Qattârah, Munkhafad al- ≃⁷	b F	126
Qāyen	f H	118
Qazvīn	d E	118
Qeshm	f H	118
Qeys, Jazīreh-ye I	d L	118
Qezel Owzan ≃	c G	118
Qianyang	g l	100
Qiemo	c B	114
Qijiang	e H	104
Qilian Shan ⋀	d E	100
Qilian Shan ⋌	d F	100
Qilihu	c l	100
Qin Ling ⋌	e G	100
Qingdao (Tsingtao)	d K	100
Qinghai (Tsinghai) □⁴	d D	114
Qinghai Hu ☒	d F	100
Qingjiang	h H	104
Qingjiang	j H	104
Qingshui ≃, Zhg.	k B	104
Qingtang		
Qingxu	d l	100
Qingyuan, Zhg.	k B	104
Qingyuan, Zhg.	c l	100
Qinhuangdao (Chinwangtao)	d J	100
Qiongzhou Haixia ☒	a D	110
Qiqian	a E	102
Qiqihar (Tsitsihar)	b K	100
Qiryat Bialik	c C	112
Qiryat Gat	e C	112
Qiryat Mal'akhi	d C	112
Qiryat Motzkin		
Qiryat Ono		
Qiryat Shemona	b D	112
Qiryat Tiv'on		
Qishon ≃		
Qitai	c D	114
Qnadsa	c E	124
Qom	f G	118
Qomsheh	f G	118
Qondūz (Kondūz)	b D	114
Qondūz ≃		
Quabbin Reservoir ☒¹	e M	146
Quakenbrück	c G	80
Quakertown	g K	146
Qualicum Beach	h K	140
Quambone	g H	184
Quamby	c G	182
Quanah	c G	154
Quang-ngai	h J	110
Quanzhou (Chuanchou)	k G	104
Qu'Appelle ≃	g L	142
Quarai	f J	178

Quar-Rock

Name	Map Ref.	Page
Quaraí (Guareim) ≃	f J	178
Quaregnon	h D	82
Quarryville	h J	146
Quartu Sant'Elena	j D	88
Quartz Hill	j G	162
Quartz Mountain ∧	g C	160
Quartzsite	k B	158
Qūchān	d R	118
Queanbeyan	j H	184
Québec	f B	144
Québec □[4]	f R	134
Quebeck	g K	152
Quedlinburg	d K	80
Queen Alexandra Range ⋏	d H	189
Queen Charlotte	d B	140
Queen Charlotte Islands II	d B	140
Queen Charlotte Mountains ⋏	d B	140
Queen Charlotte Sound ⊔	f E	140
Queen Charlotte Strait ⊔	g G	140
Queen City, Mo., U.S.	b D	152
Queen City, Tx., U.S.	i B	152
Queen Elizabeth Islands II	b I	132
Queen Mary Coast ●[2]	b F	189
Queen Maud Gulf ⊂	c L	134
Queen Maud Land ◆[1]	c C	189
Queen Maud Mountains ⋏	d I	189
Queenscliff	I F	184
Queensland □[3]	d I	182
Queensport	g L	144
Queenstown, Austl.	n F	184
Queenstown, N.Z.	I C	186
Queenstown, S. Afr.	h H	130
Queimados	g G	177
Quelimane	a M	130
Quelpart Island → Cheju-do I	e L	100
Quemado, N.M., U.S.	j H	158
Quemado, Tx., U.S.	k F	154
Quemado, Punta del ›	d G	170
Quemoy → Chinmen Tao I	k G	104
Quercy □[9]	h H	84
Querétaro	g I	166
Querobabi	b D	166
Quesada	h H	86
Quesnel	e L	140
Quesnel Lake ⊜	e M	140
Questa	h K	158
Quetta	e B	114
Quettehou	c E	84
Quevedo	d C	174
Quezaltenango	c C	168
Quezaltenango □[5]	c C	168
Quezaltepeque	d E	168
Quezon □[4]	n S	109b
Quezon City	n S	109b
Qufu	h E	102
Quibdó	b C	174
Quiberon	e C	84
Quilá	e F	166
Quilcene	c C	160
Quillacollo	g E	174
Quillan	j I	84
Quillota	g C	178
Quilon	h D	116
Quilpie	f F	184
Quilpué	g C	178
Quimby	i L	156
Quimilí	d G	178
Quimper	d B	84
Quimperlé	e C	84
Quinault ≃	c B	160
Quincemil	f D	174
Quincy, Ca., U.S.	e E	162
Quincy, Fl., U.S.	i B	150
Quincy, Il., U.S.	c E	152
Quincy, Ma., U.S.	e O	146
Quincy, Mi., U.S.	i K	148
Quincy, Wa., U.S.	c F	160
Quines	g F	178
Quinga	e H	128
Quinhagak	g N	138
Qui-nhon	h J	110
Quinlan	g J	154
Quinn ≃	c G	162
Quintana Roo □[3]	h O	166
Quinte, Bay of ⊂	f R	148
Quinter	I G	156
Quintin	d D	84
Quinto ≃	h F	178
Quinton	d K	154
Quirihue	i B	178
Quirindi	h I	184
Quirino □[4]	m S	109b
Quirinópolis	e C	177
Quiroga, Esp.	c D	86
Quiroga, Méx.	h I	166
Quissanga	d H	128
Quitaque	e E	154
Quita Sueño Bank ⊹[4]	g D	170
Quitman, Ga., U.S.	i C	150
Quitman, Ms., U.S.	j H	152
Quitman, Tx., U.S.	g K	154
Quito	d C	174
Quixadá	d K	174
Qujing	b G	110
Qulin	f F	152
Qumalai (Sewugou)	c P	114
Qumar ≃	d E	100
Qumarlêb	e F	100
Qumrān, Khirbat ⊥	e D	120
Quorn	i C	184
Qūṣ	j E	118
Quthing	h H	130
Quxian	g G	104
Quyon	b J	146
R		
Raab (Rába) ≃	h O	80
Raahe	i S	76
Raalte	d I	82
Ra'anana	d C	120
Raba	g F	108
Rába (Raab) ≃	h Q	80
Rabat, Magreb	b E	124
Rabat (Victoria), Malta	m I	88
Rabaul	d G	180
Rabbit Ears Pass)(	d J	158
Rābigh	c A	117
Rabka	f S	80
Rabkavi Banhatti	d C	116
Rabyānah, Ṣaḥrā' ◆[2]	d E	126
Raccoon ≃	a C	152
Race, Cape ›	f T	144
Raceland	m F	152
Race Point ›	e P	146
Rach-gia	i H	110
Racibórz (Ratibor)	e R	80
Racine	h H	148
Ráckeve	h R	80
Rădăuți	b I	90
Radcliff	e K	152
Radeberg	d M	80
Radebeul	d M	80
Radevormwald	d G	80
Radford	b F	150
Rādhanpur	i D	114
Radolfzell	h H	80
Radom	d U	80
Radomsko	d S	80
Radoviš	h F	90
Radstadt	h M	80
Radville	i J	142
Raḍwā, Jabal ∧	j H	118
Rae	d I	134
Rāe Bareli	g I	114
Raeford	e G	150
Rae Isthmus ●[3]	c O	134
Raetihi	f J	186
Rafaela	f H	178
Rafaḥ	f B	120
Raffadali	I H	88
Rafḥā'	h J	118
Rafsanjān	g Q	118
Raft ≃	h L	160
Raft River Mountains ⋏	c C	158
Rafz	c J	83
Raga	g F	126
Ragay Gulf ⊂	c G	108
Ragged Island Range II	c G	170
Raglan	d I	186
Ragland	i J	152
Ragusa	m I	88
Rahad, Nahr ar- ≃	f H	126
Rahīmyār Khān	f D	114
Rahway	g L	146
Rāichūr	d D	116
Raiford	i D	150
Raiganj	h M	114
Raigarh	j J	114
Railton	m G	184
Rainelle	j F	146
Rainier, Mount ∧	d D	160
Rainy ≃, N.A.	c N	156
Rainy ≃, Mi., U.S.	e K	148
Rainy Lake ⊜	b B	148
Rainy River	b A	148
Raipur	j I	114
Raisin ≃	i L	148
Rājahmundry	d F	116
Raja-Jooseppi	g U	76
Rajang ≃	e E	108
Rājapālaiyam	h D	116
Rājasthān □[3]	g E	114
Rājasthān Canal ≍	f E	114
Rajčichinsk	h Q	94
Rajka	g Q	80
Rājkot	i D	114
Rāj-Nāndgaon	j I	114
Rājpīpla	b B	116
Rājshāhi	h M	114
Rakaia ≃	j G	186
Rakamaz	g U	80
Rakaposhi ∧	b F	114
Rakata, Pulau I	j L	109a
Rakovník	e M	80
Råkvåg	j L	76
Rakvere	b I	96
Raleigh, Ms., U.S.	j G	152
Raleigh, N.C., U.S.	d H	150
Ralik Chain II	c H	180
Ralls	f E	154
Ralston, Ne., U.S.	j K	156
Ralston, Pa., U.S.	f J	146
Rama	e J	168
Ramacca	I I	88
Ramah	i H	158
Rām Allāh	e D	120
Rāmanāthapuram	h E	116
Ramasucha	i P	96
Ramat Gan	d C	120
Ramat HaSharon	d C	120
Rambervillers	d M	84
Rambouillet	d H	84
Ramea	e P	144
Ramenskoje	f U	96
Ramer	j J	152
Rāmeswaram	h J	112
Ramingstein	h M	80
Ramla	e C	120
Ramlu ∧	f I	126
Ramm, Jabal ∧	i D	120
Ramon, Har ∧	g C	120
Ramona, Ca., U.S.	k I	162
Ramona, Ok., U.S.	c K	154
Ramona, S.D., U.S.	g J	156
Ramos	f I	166
Ramos Arizpe	e I	166
Rampart	d S	138
Rāmpur	f H	114
Rāmpur Hāt	h L	114
Ramree Island I	e B	110
Ramsele	j O	76
Ramseur	d G	150
Ramsey, I. of Man	g I	78
Ramsey, Il., U.S.	c G	152
Ramsgate	j O	78
Ramsjö	j N	76
Ramu ≃	f K	108
Ramygala	f G	96
Rānāghāt	i M	114
Ranburne	i K	152
Rancagua	h C	178
Rance ≃	d D	84
Rancharia	b M	178
Ranches of Taos	h K	158
Ranchester	f R	160
Rānchī	i K	114
Rancho Cordova	f D	162
Randers	m L	76
Randleman	d G	150
Randlett	e H	154
Randolph, Az., U.S.	I E	158
Randolph, Me., U.S.	c Q	146
Randolph, Ne., U.S.	i J	156
Randolph, N.Y., U.S.	e H	146
Randolph, Ut,. U.S.	c E	158
Randolph, Vt., U.S.	d N	146
Randolph, Wi., U.S.	g F	148
Random Lake	g H	148
Rand, The → Witwatersvant ◆[1]	e H	130
Råneå	i R	76
Rāngāmāti	i O	114
Rangeley	c P	146
Rangely	d H	158
Ranger	g H	154
Rangiora	j G	186
Rangoon	f D	110
Rangpur	e D	114
Rānībennur	e C	116
Rānīganj	i L	114
Rānīkhet	f H	114
Rānipet	f E	116
Ranken ≃	c B	184
Ranken Store	b B	184
Rankin, Il., U.S.	b I	152
Rankin, Tx., U.S.	h E	154
Rankin Inlet	d N	134
Ranlo	d E	150
Ranong	j E	110
Ranongga Island I	j O	188e
Ransom	m H	156
Ranson	h I	146
Rantauprapat	m E	110
Rantekombola, Bulu ∧	f G	108
Rantoul	b H	152
Ranua	i T	76
Råö	m L	76
Raoping	I F	104
Raoul	e C	150
Raoul Island I	f J	180
Rapallo	e D	88
Rapid ≃, Mi., U.S.	d H	148
Rapid ≃, Mn., U.S.	b A	148
Rapidan ≃	i I	146
Rapid City, Mi., U.S.	f J	148
Rapid City, S.D., U.S.	g D	156
Rapid River	e I	148
Rappahannock ≃	b J	150
Rapperswil	d J	83
Rāpti ≃	g J	114
Rápulo ≃	f E	174
Raron	f H	83
Rarotonga I	f L	180
Ra's al-'Ayn	d I	118
Ra's an-Naqb	h D	120
Ras Dashen Terara ∧	f H	126
Raseiniai	f F	96
Rashīd	g D	118
Rasht	d M	118
Rāsipuram	g E	116
Raška	f D	90
Rasskazovo	i X	96
Rastatt	g H	80
Rastede	b H	80
Rat ≃	b O	142
Ratak Chain II	c I	180
Ratangarh	f F	114
Rätansbyn	j N	76
Rāth	h H	114
Rathbun Lake ⊜[1]	j B	148
Rathdrum, Ire.	i G	78
Rathdrum, Id., U.S.	c I	160
Rathenow	c L	80
Rathkeale	i E	78
Rathlin Island I	f G	78
Ráth Luirc	i E	78
Ratingen	d F	80
Rat Islands II	k D	139a
Ratlām	i F	114
Ratnāgiri	d B	116
Ratnapura	i F	116
Raton	c B	154
Raton Pass)(	o C	156
Rattlesnake	d L	160
Rättvik	k N	76
Ratz, Mount ∧	h BB	138
Ratzeburg	b J	80
Raub	m F	110
Rauch	i I	178
Raufarhöfn	a F	76a
Raukumara Range ⋏	e L	186
Rauma	k Q	76
Raurkela	i K	114
Ravanusa	I H	88
Raven	b E	150
Ravena	e M	146
Ravenna, It.	e G	88
Ravenna, Ky., U.S.	b C	150
Ravenna, Mi., U.S.	g J	148
Ravenna, Ne., U.S.	j I	156
Ravenna, Oh., U.S.	f E	146
Ravensburg	h I	80
Ravenshoe	a F	184
Ravensthorpe	f D	182
Ravenswood	i E	146
Rāvi ≃	e E	114
Rāwalpindi	d E	114
Rawa Mazowiecka	d T	80
Rawdon	a M	146
Rawicz	d P	80
Rawlinna	f E	182
Rawlins	c I	158
Rawson	e C	176
Raxaul	d K	112
Ray	c D	156
Ray, Cape ›	e N	144
Raya, Bukit ∧	f E	108
Rāyadrug	e D	116
Raymond, Ab., Can.	h V	140
Raymond, Il., U.S.	c G	152
Raymond, Mn., U.S.	f L	156
Raymond, Ms., U.S.	j F	152
Raymond, Wa., U.S.	d B	160
Raymond Terrace	i I	184
Raymondville	m I	154
Rayne	I D	152
Rayón	c D	166
Rayones	e I	166
Rayong	h F	110
Raytown	c B	152
Rayville	j E	152
R'azan'	g V	96
Ražanj	f E	90
Razgrad	f J	90
R'ažsk	h W	96
Ré, Île de I	f E	84
Reading, Eng., U.K.	j M	78
Reading, Ks., U.S.	m L	156
Reading, Mi., U.S.	i K	148
Reading, Oh., U.S.	h B	146
Reading, Pa., U.S.	g K	146
Readlyn	h C	148
Readstown	g E	148
Real, Cordillera ⋏	h E	174
Real del Castillo	b A	166
Realicó	h F	178
Realitos	I H	154
Reardan	c H	160
Reata	d I	166
Reay	c J	78
Rebun-tō I	b P	106a
Recanati	f H	88
Recherche, Archipelago of the II	f D	182
Rečica	i M	96
Recife	e L	174
Recklinghausen	d G	80
Reconquista	e I	178
Recreo	e F	178
Rector	f F	152
Red (Hong-ha) (Yuanjiang) ≃, Asia	c H	110
Red ≃, N.A.	g M	134
Red ≃, U.S.	e H	136
Red ≃, Ky., U.S.	b C	150
Red ≃, N.M., U.S.	h K	158
Red ≃, Wi., U.S.	e G	148
Redang, Pulau I	I G	110
Redange	i H	82
Red Bank, N.J., U.S.	g L	146
Red Bank, Tn., U.S.	g K	152
Red Banks	h G	152
Red Bay, Al., U.S.	h H	152
Redbay, Fl., U.S.	I K	152
Red Bluff	d C	162
Red Bluff Reservoir ⊜[1]	b H	166
Red Boiling Springs	f K	152
Red Bud	d G	152
Redcar	g L	78
Red Cedar ≃, Mi., U.S.	h K	148
Red Cedar ≃, Wi., U.S.	e D	148
Red Cliff, Co., U.S.	e J	158
Redcliff, Zimb.	b I	130
Redcliffe	f J	184
Red Cliffs	j E	184
Red Cloud	k I	156
Red Deer	e U	140
Red Deer ≃, Can.	f J	134
Red Deer ≃, Can.	f L	134
Red Deer Lake ⊜	f M	142
Reddersburg	g H	130
Red Devil	f P	138
Redding	d C	162
Redeye ≃	e L	156
Redfield, Ia., U.S.	j M	156
Redfield, S.D., U.S.	g I	156
Redford	j B	154
Red Hook	f M	146
Red Indian Lake ⊜	d Q	144
Redkey	b K	152
Red Lake, On., Can.	g U	142
Redlake, Mn., U.S.	d L	156
Red Lake ⊜	f N	134
Red Lake ≃	d K	156
Red Lake Falls	d K	156
Red Lake Road	i U	142
Redlands, S. Afr.	g F	130
Redlands, Ca., U.S.	j H	162
Redlands, Co., U.S.	e H	158
Red Level	k J	152
Red Lick	k F	152
Red Lion	h J	146
Red Lodge	e P	160
Redmond, Or., U.S.	f D	160
Redmond, Ut,. U.S.	e E	158
Redmond, Wa., U.S.	c C	160
Red Mountain ∧	c B	162
Red Mountain Pass)(	g I	158
Red Oak, Ia., U.S.	j L	156
Red Oak, Ok., U.S.	e K	154
Redon	e D	84
Redondo	g D	86
Redondo Beach	k G	162
Red Rock	b G	148
Red Rock ≃	f M	160
Red Rock, Lake ⊜[1]	i B	148
Redruth	k H	78
Red Sea ⊤[2]	d H	126
Red Springs	e G	150
Redvers	i M	142
Redwater	d U	140
Redwater ≃	d B	156
Redwillow ≃	b O	140
Red Wing	f C	148
Redwood ≃	g L	156
Redwood City	g C	162
Redwood Falls	g L	156
Redwood National Park ♠	c A	162
Redwood Valley	e B	162
Ree, Lough ⊜	h E	78
Reed City	g J	148
Reeder	e E	156
Reedley	h F	162
Reedsburg	g E	148
Reeds Peak ∧	k I	158
Reedsport	g A	160
Reedsville	f H	148
Reefton	i F	186
Reelfoot Lake ⊜	f G	152
Rees	d F	80
Reese	g L	148
Reese ≃	d H	162
Reeseville	g G	148
Reform	i H	152
Refugio	k I	154
Regen	g M	80
Regensburg	f L	80
Regent	e E	156
Reggâne	c G	124
Reggello	f F	88
Reggio di Calabria	k J	88
Reggio nell'Emilia	e E	88
Reghin	c H	90
Regina, Sk., Can.	h J	142
Régina, Guy. fr.	c H	174
Registro	c O	178
Regnéville	c E	84
Reguengos de Monsaraz	g D	86
Rehau	e L	80
Rehoboth	d C	130
Rehoboth Beach	i K	146
Reḥovot	e C	120
Reichenau	e K	83
Reichenbach	e L	80
Reidsville, Ga., U.S.	g D	150
Reidsville, N.C., U.S.	c G	150
Reigate	j M	78
Reigoldswil	d H	83
Reims	c K	84
Reina Adelaida, Archipiélago II	g B	176
Reinach, Schw.	d I	83
Reinach, Schw.	c H	83
Reinbeck	h C	148
Reindeer Lake ⊜	e L	134
Reinga, Cape ›	a G	186
Reinosa	b G	86
Reisdorf	i I	82
Reisterstown	h J	146
Reitz	f I	130
Reivilo	f G	130
Reliance, N.T., Can.	d K	134
Reliance, Wy., U.S.	c G	158
Remada	b I	124
Remagen	b N	84
Remanso	e J	174
Rembang	j O	109a
Remer	c B	148
Remington, In., U.S.	b I	152
Remington, Va., U.S.	i I	146
Remiremont	d M	84
Remoulins	i K	84
Remscheid	d G	80
Remsen	i L	156
Remus	g J	148
Rena	k L	76
Renaix (Ronse)	g D	82
Rende	j K	88
Rend Lake ⊜[1]	d H	152
Rendova Island I	j O	188e
Rendsburg	a I	80
Renens	e F	83
Renfrew	e S	148
Rengo	h C	178
Reng Tlāng ∧	j O	114
Renick	j F	146
Renkum	e H	82
Renmark	j D	184
Rennell I	b L	182
Rennes	d E	84
Rennick Glacier ⊓	c H	189
Reno	e F	162
Reno ≃	e F	88
Renous	f H	144
Renovo	f I	146
Rensjön	g P	76
Rensselaer, In., U.S.	b I	152
Rensselaer, N.Y., U.S.	e M	146
Rentería	b J	86
Renton	c C	160
Renville	g L	156
Renwick	h B	148
Répce ≃	h P	80
Repino	a L	96
Repton	k I	152
Republic, Ks., U.S.	I J	156
Republic, Mi., U.S.	d H	148
Republic, Mo., U.S.	e C	152
Republic, Wa., U.S.	b G	160
Republican ≃	I J	156
Repulse Bay	c O	134
Repulse Bay ⊂	c H	184
Repvåg	f S	76
Requena	f J	86
Réquista	h I	84
Reschenpass)(	f Q	84
Resen	h E	90
Reserve, La., U.S.	I F	152
Reserve, N.M., U.S.	k H	158
Resistencia	d I	178
Reșița	d E	90
Resolute	b N	134
Resolution Island I, N.T., Can.	d S	134
Resolution Island I, N.Z.	I A	186
Restigouche (Ristigouche) ≃	e F	144
Reston	i M	142
Retalhuleu □[5]	c C	168
Rethel	c K	84
Réthimnon	n H	90
Reunion (Réunion) □[2]	f K	128
Reus	d M	86
Reuss ≃	d I	83
Reuterstadt Stavenhagen	b L	80
Reutlingen	g I	80
Rev'akino	g T	96
Revda	f I	92
Revelstoke	g P	140
Reventazón	e B	174
Revigny-sur-Ornain	d K	84
Revillagigedo, Islas II	h D	166
Revillagigedo Island I	i CC	138
Revillo	f K	156
Revin	c K	84
Revuè ≃	b K	130
Rewa	h I	114
Rewāri	f G	114
Rexburg	g N	160
Rexford, Ks., U.S.	I G	156
Rexford, Mt., U.S.	b J	160
Rexton	f I	144
Rey	e N	118
Rey, Isla del I	g I	164
Reyes	f E	174
Reyes, Point ›	f B	162
Reykjanes ›[1]	c B	76a
Reykjavík	b C	76a
Reyno	f F	152
Reynolds, Ga., U.S.	g B	150
Reynolds, N.D., U.S.	d J	156
Reynoldsville	f H	146
Reynosa	d J	166
Rezé	e E	84
Rēzekne	e J	96
Rezovska (Mutlu) ≃	g K	90
Rhaetian Alps ⋏	f P	84
Rhame	e D	156
Rheda-Wiedenbrück	d H	80
Rheden	d I	82
Rheims → Reims	c K	84
Rhein → Rhine ≃	d F	80
Rheine	c G	80
Rheinfelden	h G	80
Rheinhausen	d F	80
Rheinland-Pfalz □[3]	e F	80
Rhenen	e H	82
Rhine	h C	150
Rhine (Rhein) (Rhin) ≃	d F	80
Rhinebeck	f M	146
Rhinelander	e F	148
Rhir, Cap ›	b E	124
Rho	d D	88
Rhode Island □[3]	c L	136
Rhode Island Sound ⊔	f O	146
Rhodes → Ródhos I	m L	90
Rhodesia → Zimbabwe □[1]	e E	128
Rhodope Mountains ⋏	h H	90
Rhön ⋏	e I	80
Rhondda	j J	78
Rhône □[5]	g K	84
Rhône ≃	h K	84
Rhône au Rhin, Canal du ≍	h G	80
Rhyl	h J	78
Riachão	e I	174
Riaño	c F	86
Riau, Kepulauan II	n H	110
Ribeauvillé	d N	84
Ribeirão do Pinhal	b M	178
Ribeirão Prêto	f E	177
Ribemont	c J	84
Ribera	I H	88
Riberalta	f E	174
Rib Lake	e E	148
Ribnitz-Damgarten	a L	80
Ricardo Flores Magón	c F	166
Riccarton	j G	186
Riccia	h I	88
Riccione	f G	88
Rice	g J	154
Rice Lake	e D	148
Riceville, Ia., U.S.	g C	148
Riceville, Tn., U.S.	d B	150
Richan	i V	142
Richards	i K	154
Richard's Bay	g K	130
Richard's Bay ⊂	g K	130
Richards Island I	b AA	138
Richardson	g J	154
Richardson ≃	e J	134
Richardson Mountains ⋏	c Z	138
Richardton	e E	156
Riche, Pointe ›	b P	144
Richelieu	e G	84
Richey	d B	156
Richfield, Id., U.S.	g K	160
Richfield, Mn., U.S.	f B	148
Richfield, Pa., U.S.	g I	146
Richfield, Ut,. U.S.	f D	158
Richfield Springs	e L	146
Richford	c N	146
Rich Hill	d B	152
Richibucto	f I	144
Richisau	d J	83
Richland, Ga., U.S.	g B	150
Richland, Mi., U.S.	h J	148
Richland, Mo., U.S.	e D	152
Richland, Tx., U.S.	h J	154
Richland, Wa., U.S.	d F	160
Richland Center	g E	148
Richlands, N.C., U.S.	e I	150
Richlands, Va., U.S.	b E	150
Richland Springs	h H	154
Richmond, Austl.	i I	184
Richmond, Austl.	c E	184
Richmond, B.C., Can.	h K	140
Richmond, On., Can.	b K	146
Richmond, P.Q., Can.	b N	146
Richmond, N.Z.	h H	186
Richmond, S. Afr.	h F	130
Richmond, S. Afr.	g J	130
Richmond, Eng., U.K.	g L	78
Richmond, Ca., U.S.	g C	162
Richmond, In., U.S.	c L	152
Richmond, Ks., U.S.	m L	156
Richmond, Ky., U.S.	b B	150
Richmond, Me., U.S.	c Q	146
Richmond, Mi., U.S.	h M	148
Richmond, Mn., U.S.	f M	156
Richmond, Mo., U.S.	c C	152
Richmond, Tx., U.S.	j K	154
Richmond, Ut,. U.S.	c E	158
Richmond, Vt., U.S.	c N	146
Richmond, Va., U.S.	b I	150
Richmond Heights	n F	150
Richmond Highlands	c C	160
Richmond Hill, On., Can.	g P	148
Richmond Hill, Ga., U.S.	h E	150
Richmondville	e L	146
Rich Square	c I	150
Richton	k H	152
Richwood, Oh., U.S.	g C	146
Richwood, W.V., U.S.	i F	146
Rico	g H	158
Ridderkerk	e F	82
Riddle	h B	160
Riddle Mountain ∧	g G	160
Ridgecrest	i H	162
Ridge Farm	c I	152
Ridgefield	f M	146
Ridgeland, Ms., U.S.	j F	152
Ridgeland, S.C., U.S.	g F	150
Ridgely	f G	152
Ridgetown	h N	148
Ridgeville	f F	150
Ridgeway, Mo., U.S.	b C	152
Ridgeway, Wi., U.S.	g F	148
Ridgway, Co., U.S.	f I	158
Ridgway, Il., U.S.	e H	152
Ridgway, Pa., U.S.	f H	146
Riding Mountain National Park ♠	h N	142
Ried im Innkreis	g M	80
Riegelwood	e H	150
Riehen	c H	83
Rienzi	h H	152
Riesa	d M	80
Riesco, Isla I	g B	176
Riesi	I I	88
Rietavas	f D	96
Rieti	g G	88
Rif ⋏	a F	124
Riffe Lake ⊜[1]	d C	160
Rifle	e I	158
Rifle ≃	f K	148
Rift Valley V	i I	122
Rīga	e G	96
Riga, Gulf of → Rižskij zaliv ⊂	d F	96
Rigby	g N	160
Rīgestān ◆[1]	c G	112
Riggins	e I	160
Rigi ∧	d J	83
Rigo	a I	182
Rigolet	f U	134
Riihimäki	k S	76
Riiser-Larsen Peninsula ›[1]	b D	189
Riisitunturin kansallispuisto ♠	h U	76
Rijeka	d I	88
Rijssen	d J	82
Rijswijk	d E	82
Riksgränsen	g P	76
Rikuzen-takata	h P	106
Riley	I K	156
Rillito	I E	158
Rima ≃	f H	124
Rimavská Sobota	g T	80
Rimbey	e T	140
Rimbo	I P	76
Rimersburg	f G	146
Rimforsa	I N	76
Rimini	e G	88
Rîmnicu Sărat	d K	90
Rîmnicu Vîlcea	d H	90
Rimouski	d E	144
Rincon, Ga., U.S.	g E	150
Rincon, N.M., U.S.	I I	158
Rinconada	b E	178
Rincón del Bonete, Lago Artificial ⊜[1]	g K	178
Rincón de Romos	f H	166
Rindal	j K	76
Ringebu	k L	76
Ringgold, Ga., U.S.	e A	150
Ringgold, La., U.S.	j C	152
Ringkøbing	m K	76
Ringling	e I	154
Ringsted	h M	156
Ringvassøy I	g P	76
Rinjani, Gunung ∧	g F	108
Rinteln	c I	80
Rio	g F	148
Río Balsas	i J	166
Riobamba	d C	174
Río Blanco	g C	178
Rio Branco	e E	174
Río Bravo	e J	166
Rio Brilhante	f A	177
Rio Claro, Bra.	b O	178
Rio Claro, Trin.	i N	170
Río Colorado	j F	178
Río Cuarto	g F	178
Rio de Janeiro	g G	177
Rio Dell	d A	162
Rio do Sul	d N	178
Río Gallegos	g C	176
Río Grande, Arg.	g C	176
Rio Grande, Bra.	g L	178
Río Grande, Méx.	f H	166
Rio Grande → Grande, Rio ≃	f G	136
Rio Grande City	m H	154
Rio Grande do Sul □[3]	e K	178
Ríohacha	i H	170
Rio Hondo	m I	154
Rioja	e C	174
Río Lagartos	g O	166
Rio Largo	e K	174
Riom	g J	84
Río Mayo	f B	176
Rio Negro	d N	178
Río Negro □[4]	j F	178
Rio Negro, Pantanal do ≡	g G	174
Rionero in Vulture	i J	88
Rio Pardo	e L	178
Rio Pardo de Minas	c G	177
Rio Rancho	i J	158
Río San Juan □[5]	f J	168
Río Tercero	g F	178
Rio Tinto	e K	174
Rio Verde, Bra.	d C	177
Ríoverde, Méx.	g J	166
Rio Vista	f D	162
Rioz	e M	84
Ripley, Ms., U.S.	h H	152
Ripley, N.Y., U.S.	e G	146
Ripley, Oh., U.S.	i C	146
Ripley, Tn., U.S.	g G	152
Ripley, W.V., U.S.	i E	146
Ripon, P.Q., Can.	b K	146
Ripon, Eng., U.K.	g L	78
Ripon, Ca., U.S.	g D	162
Ripon, Wi., U.S.	g G	148
Riposto	I J	88
Ririe	g N	160
Risbäck	i N	76
Riscle	i F	84
Rishiri-suidō ⊔	b P	106a
Rishiri-tō I	b P	106a
Rishon leẔiyyon	e C	120
Rising Star	g H	154
Rising Sun, In., U.S.	d L	152
Rising Sun, Md., U.S.	h J	146
Risingsun, Oh., U.S.	f C	146
Rison	i D	152
Risør	I K	76
Ristigouche (Restigouche) ≃	e F	144
Ristijärvi	i U	76
Ritchie	g G	130
Ritter, Mount ∧	g F	162
Rittman	g E	146
Ritzville	c G	160
Riva	d E	88
Rivadavia	e C	178
Rivanna ≃	b H	150
Rivas	f I	168
Rivas □[5]	f H	168
Rive-de-Gier	g K	84
Rivera	f K	178
Riverbank	g E	162
River Cess	g E	124
Riverdale, Ca., U.S.	h F	162
Riverdale, N.D., U.S.	d F	156
River Falls, Al., U.S.	k J	152
River Falls, Wi., U.S.	f C	148
Rivergaro	e D	88
Riverhead	g N	146
River Hébert	g I	144
Riverina ◆[1]	j F	184
River John	g J	144
Rivermont	d I	150
River Road	f B	160
Rivers	h N	142
Riversdale	j E	130
Riverside, Ca., U.S.	k H	162
Riverside, Ia., U.S.	i D	148
Riverside, Tx., U.S.	i K	154
Rivers Inlet	f G	140
Riverton, Mb., Can.	h R	142
Riverton, N.Z.	m C	186
Riverton, Il., U.S.	c G	152
Riverton, Ne., U.S.	k I	156
Riverton, Ut,. U.S.	d E	158
Riverton, Va., U.S.	i H	146
Riverton, Wy., U.S.	a H	158
Riverton Heights	c C	160
River View, Al., U.S.	j K	152
Riverview, Fl., U.S.	I D	150
Riverview, Ks., U.S.	n J	156
Rives	f G	152
Rivesaltes	j I	84
Rivesville	h F	146
Riviera, Az., U.S.	i B	158
Riviera, Tx., U.S.	I I	154
Riviera Beach	m F	150
Rivière-du-Loup	e D	144
Rivière du Rempart	v R	131c
Rivière-Verte	e E	144
Riviersonderend	j D	130
Rivoli	d B	88
Riyadh → Ar-Riyāḍ	b E	117
Rīz	f N	118
Rizal □[4]	n S	109b
Rize	b I	118
Rizhao	h G	102
Rižskij zaliv (Rīgas Jūras līcis) (Gulf of Riga) ⊂	d F	96
Roa	k L	76
Roachdale	c J	152
Road Town	e L	170
Roan Cliffs ●[4]	e G	158
Roan Mountain	c D	150
Roanne	f K	84
Roanoke, Al., U.S.	i K	152
Roanoke, Il., U.S.	j F	148
Roanoke, In., U.S.	b K	152
Roanoke, Va., U.S.	b G	150
Roanoke (Staunton) ≃	c I	150
Roanoke Island I	d K	150
Roanoke Rapids	c I	150
Roan Plateau ⋏[1]	e F	158
Roaring Spring	g H	146
Roaring Springs	f F	154
Roatán	a H	168
Roatán, Isla de I	a H	168
Robbins, N.C., U.S.	d G	150
Robbins, Tn., U.S.	c B	150
Robbins Island I	m F	184
Robbinsville	d C	150
Röbel	b L	80
Robeline	k C	152
Robersonville	d I	150
Roberta	g B	150
Roberta Mills	d F	150
Robert Lee	h F	154
Robert Louis Stevenson's Tomb ⊥	a B	188a
Roberts, Id., U.S.	g M	160
Roberts, Mt., U.S.	e P	160
Robert's Arm	c R	144
Roberts Creek Mountain ∧	e I	162
Robertsdale, Al., U.S.	I I	152
Robertsdale, Pa., U.S.	g H	146
Robertsfors	i Q	76
Robert S. Kerr Lake ⊜[1]	d K	154
Robertson	i D	130
Roberts Peak ∧	e N	140
Robertsport	g D	124
Roberval	g R	134
Robinson, Il., U.S.	c I	152
Robinson, Tx., U.S.	h I	154
Róbinson Crusoe, Isla (Isla Más A Tierra) I	c A	176
Robinson Range ⋏	e C	182
Robinvale	j E	184
Roblin	g M	142
Roboré	g G	174
Robson, Mount ∧	d O	140
Robstown	I I	154
Roby	g F	154
Roca, Cabo da ›	g B	86
Rocanville	h M	142
Roca Partida, Isla I	h C	166
Rocas, Atol das I[1]	d L	174
Roccastrada	f F	88
Rocciamelone ∧	d B	88
Rocha	h K	178
Rochdale	h K	78
Rochefort, Bel.	h G	82
Rochefort, Fr.	g F	84
Rochelle, Ga., U.S.	h C	150
Rochelle, Il., U.S.	i F	148
Rochelle, Tx., U.S.	h G	154
Rochester, Austl.	k F	184
Rochester, Eng., U.K.	j N	78
Rochester, In., U.S.	a J	152
Rochester, Mi., U.S.	h L	148
Rochester, Mn., U.S.	f C	148
Rochester, N.H., U.S.	d P	146
Rochester, N.Y., U.S.	d I	146
Rochester, Tx., U.S.	f G	154
Rochlitz	d L	80
Rock	d H	148
Rock ≃, U.S.	i F	148
Rock ≃, U.S.	h K	156
Rockall I	d E	74
Rockcastle ≃	b B	150
Rock Creek Butte ∧	f G	160
Rockdale, Il., U.S.	i G	148
Rockdale, Tx., U.S.	i I	154
Rockefeller Plateau ⋏[1]	d J	189
Rockenhausen	f G	80
Rock Falls	i F	148
Rockford, Al., U.S.	j J	152
Rockford, Il., U.S.	h F	148
Rockford, Ia., U.S.	g C	148
Rockford, Mi., U.S.	g J	148
Rockford, Oh., U.S.	g B	146
Rockford, Tn., U.S.	d C	150
Rock Hall	h J	146
Rockhampton	d I	184
Rock Hill	e E	150
Rockingham	e G	150
Rockingham Bay ⊂	b G	184

Symbols in the index are identified on page 198.

Rock-Sain

Name	Map Ref.	Page
Rock Island	i E	148
Rocklake	c H	156
Rockland, On., Can.	b K	146
Rockland, Id., U.S.	h M	160
Rockland, Me., U.S.	c Q	146
Rockland, Ma., U.S.	e P	146
Rockland, Mi., U.S.	d F	148
Rocklands Reservoir ⊜[1]	k E	184
Rockledge	k F	150
Rocklin	f D	162
Rockmart	e A	150
Rockport, Ky., U.S.	e J	152
Rockport, Me., U.S.	c Q	146
Rockport, Ma., U.S.	e P	146
Rock Port, Mo., U.S.	b A	152
Rockport, Tx., U.S.	k I	154
Rock Rapids	h K	156
Rock River	c K	158
Rocksprings, Tx., U.S.	i F	154
Rock Springs, Wy., U.S.	c G	158
Rockstone	b G	174
Rock, The	j G	184
Rockton	h F	148
Rock Valley	h K	156
Rockville, In., U.S.	c I	152
Rockville, Md., U.S.	h I	146
Rockwall	g J	154
Rockwell, Ia., U.S.	h B	148
Rockwell, N.C., U.S.	d F	150
Rockwell City	i M	156
Rockwood, Me., U.S.	b Q	146
Rockwood, Pa., U.S.	h G	146
Rockwood, Tn., U.S.	d B	150
Rocky	d G	154
Rocky ≃	d G	150
Rocky Ford	m D	156
Rocky Harbour	c P	144
Rocky Mount, N.C., U.S.	d I	150
Rocky Mount, Va., U.S.	c G	150
Rocky Mountain ∧	c M	160
Rocky Mountain House	e T	140
Rocky Mountain National Park ♠	k B	156
Rocky Mountains ⋀	e H	132
Roda	c D	150
Rodalben	f G	80
Rødbyhavn	n L	76
Roddickton	b Q	144
Rodeo, Arg.	f D	178
Rodeo, Méx.	e G	166
Rodeo, N.M., U.S.	m G	158
Rodewisch	e L	80
Rodez	h I	84
Ródhos (Rhodes)	m L	90
Ródhos (Rhodes) I	m L	90
Rodi Garganico	h J	88
Roding	f L	80
Rodney, On., Can.	h N	148
Rodney, Ms., U.S.	k E	152
Rodniki	d X	96
Rodrigues I	k G	98
Roebourne	d C	182
Roeland Park	l M	156
Roelofarendsveen	d F	82
Roermond	f I	82
Roeselare (Roulers)	g C	82
Roes Welcome Sound ⊔	d O	134
Roff	e J	154
Rogačevo	e T	96
Rogačov	h M	96
Rogagua, Laguna ⊜	f E	174
Rogaguado, Laguna ⊜	f E	174
Rogaland □[6]	l J	76
Rogatica	f C	90
Rogers, Ar., U.S.	f B	152
Rogers, Tx., U.S.	i I	154
Rogers, Mount ∧	c E	150
Rogers City	e L	148
Rogers Lake ⊜	j H	162
Rogers Pass)(	f Q	140
Rogersville, N.B., Can.	f H	144
Rogersville, Al., U.S.	h I	152
Rogersville, Tn., U.S.	c C	150
Rogliano	j P	84
Rogoźno	c Q	80
Rogue ≃, Mi., U.S.	g J	148
Rogue ≃, Or., U.S.	h A	160
Rogue River	h B	160
Rohri	g C	114
Rohtak	f G	114
Roi Et	f G	110
Roisel	c J	84
Rojas	h H	178
Rojo, Cabo ›	f K	170
Rokeby National Park ♠	b H	182
Rokiškis	f H	96
Rokuan kansallispuisto ♠	i T	76
Rokycany	f M	80
Roland, Ar., U.S.	h D	152
Roland, Ia., U.S.	h B	148
Rolândia	b M	178
Røldal	l J	76
Rolette	c H	156
Rolfe	i M	156
Roll	l C	158
Rolla, Ks., U.S.	n F	156
Rolla, Mo., U.S.	e E	152
Rolla, N.D., U.S.	c H	156
Rolle	f E	83
Rolleston	e H	184
Rolling Fork	j F	152
Rolling Fork ≃	e K	152
Rollingstone	b G	184
Roma, Austl.	f H	184
Roma (Rome), It.	h G	88
Roma, Leso.	g H	130
Roma, Tx., U.S.	m G	154
Romagna □[9]	h R	84
Romaine ≃	f T	134
Roman	c J	90
Romania (România) □[1]	f M	74
Romano, Cayo I	c F	170
Romanshorn	c K	83
Romans [-sur-Isère]	g L	84
Rome → Roma, It.	h G	88
Rome, Ga., U.S.	e A	150
Rome, Il., U.S.	j F	148
Rome, Ms., U.S.	i F	152
Rome, N.Y., U.S.	d K	146
Romeo	h L	148
Romilly-sur-Seine	d J	84
Romney	h H	146
Romont	e F	83
Romorantin-Lanthenay	e H	84
Rona I	b H	78
Ronan	c K	160
Roncador, Serra do ⋀[1]	f H	174
Roncador Bank ✦[4]	h D	170
Ronceverte	b F	150
Ronchamp	e M	84
Ronda	i F	86
Rønde	m L	76
Rondônia	f F	174
Rondonópolis	d A	177
Ronehamn	m P	76
Ronge, Lac la ⊜	c I	142
Rønne	n N	76
Ronneburg	e L	80
Ronneby	m N	76
Ronne Entrance ⊂	c L	189
Ronne Ice Shelf ⊓	c L	189
Ronse (Renaix)	g D	82
Ronuro ≃	f H	174
Roodhouse	c F	152
Rooiboklaagte ≃	c E	130
Roorkee	f G	114
Roosendaal	e E	82
Roosevelt, Az., U.S.	k E	158
Roosevelt, Mn., U.S.	c L	156
Roosevelt, Ok., U.S.	e G	154
Roosevelt, Ut,. U.S.	d G	158
Roosevelt ≃	e F	174
Roosevelt Island I	c I	189
Root ≃, Mn., U.S.	g D	148
Root ≃, Wi., U.S.	h H	148
Roper	d J	150
Roper ≃	b F	182
Ropesville	f D	154
Roquefort	h F	84
Roraima, Mount ∧	b F	174
Rorke Lake ⊜	d V	142
Røros	j L	76
Rorschach	d L	83
Rørvik	i L	76
Rosa, Monte ∧	g H	83
Rosales	c G	166
Rosalia	c H	160
Rosamond	j G	162
Rosamorada	f G	166
Rosana	g B	177
Rosario, Arg.	g H	178
Rosário, Bra.	d J	174
Rosario, Méx.	b B	166
Rosario, Méx.	f G	166
Rosario, Para.	c J	178
Rosario, Ven.	i H	170
Rosario Bank ✦[2]	e B	170
Rosario de la Frontera	c F	178
Rosario de Lerma	c F	178
Rosário do Sul	f K	178
Rosário Oeste	f G	174
Rosarito, Méx.	c B	166
Rosarito, Méx.	d D	166
Rosarno	k J	88
Roščino	a L	96
Roscoe, S.D., U.S.	f H	156
Roscoe, Tx., U.S.	g F	154
Roscommon, Ire.	h E	78
Roscommon, Mi., U.S.	f K	148
Roscommon □[6]	h E	78
Roscrea	i F	78
Rose, Mount ∧	e F	162
Roseau, Dom.	g N	170
Roseau, Mn., U.S.	c L	156
Roseau ≃	b K	156
Rosebery	m F	184
Roseboro	e H	150
Rosebud, Mt., U.S.	d S	160
Rosebud, S.D., U.S.	h G	156
Rosebud, Tx., U.S.	h J	154
Roseburg	g B	160
Rosebush	g K	148
Rose City	f K	148
Rosedale, Austl.	e I	184
Rosedale, In., U.S.	c I	152
Rosedale, La., U.S.	l E	152
Rosedale, Ms., U.S.	i E	152
Rosehearty	d K	78
Rose-Hill, Maus.	v R	131c
Rose Hill, N.C., U.S.	e H	150
Rose Hill, Va., U.S.	c C	150
Roseland	l F	152
Rosenberg	j K	154
Rosendal	l J	76
Rosenheim	h L	80
Rosepine	l C	152
Rose Point ›	c C	140
Rosetown	g F	142
Rosetta → Rashīd	g D	118
Roseville, Ca., U.S.	f D	162
Roseville, Il., U.S.	j E	148
Roseville, Mi., U.S.	h M	148
Roseville, Mn., U.S.	e B	148
Roseville, Oh., U.S.	h D	146
Rosewood	f J	184
Rosh Ha'Ayin	d C	120
Rosholt, S.D., U.S.	f K	156
Rosholt, Wi., U.S.	f F	148
Rosiclare	e H	152
Rosignano Marittimo	f E	88
Rosignol	b G	174
Roșiori de Vede	e I	90
Roskilde	n M	76
Roslavl'	h O	96
Roslyn	c E	160
Rosman	d D	150
Rosmead	h G	130
Rosporden	e C	84
Ross, Austl.	n G	184
Ross, N.Z.	i E	186
Ross ≃	e CC	138
Rossano	j K	88
Rossburn	h N	142
Rossford	f C	146
Ross Ice Shelf ⊓	d I	189
Rossijskaja Sovetskaja Federativnaja Socialističeskaja Respublika (Russian Soviet Federative Socialist Republic) □[3]	e N	92
Rossiter	g H	146
Ross Lake ⊜[1]	b D	160
Rossland	h Q	140
Rosslare	i G	78
Rosslau	d L	80
Rosso	e C	124
Rossön	j O	76
Ross-on-Wye	j K	78
Rossony	f K	96
Rossoš'	g E	92
Ross R. Barnett Reservoir ⊜[1]	j F	152
Ross River	f BB	138
Ross Sea ⊤[2]	c I	189
Rossville, Ga., U.S.	e A	150
Rossville, Il., U.S.	b I	152
Rossville, In., U.S.	b J	152
Rossville, Ks., U.S.	l L	156
Rosswein	d M	80
Røst II	h M	76
Rosthern	f H	142
Rostock	a L	80
Rostock □[5]	a L	80
Rostov	d V	96
Rostov-na-Donu	h E	92
Roswell, Ga., U.S.	e B	150
Roswell, N.M., U.S.	f B	154
Rota	i E	86
Rotan	g F	154
Rotenburg, B.R.D.	b I	80
Rotenburg, B.R.D.	d I	80
Roth	f K	80
Rothaargebirge ⋀	d H	80
Rothbury	f L	78
Rothenburg ob der Tauber	f J	80
Rotherham	h L	78
Rothes	d J	78
Rothesay, N.B., Can.	g G	144
Rothesay, Scot., U.K.	f H	78
Rothsay	e K	156
Rothschild	f F	148
Rothwell	f G	144
Roti, Pulau I	h G	108
Roto	i F	184
Rotoiti, Lake ⊜	e K	186
Rotondella	i K	88
Rotorua	e K	186
Rott am Inn	h L	80
Rottenburg	g H	80
Rottenburg an der Laaber	g L	80
Rottenmann	h N	80
Rotterdam, Ned.	e E	82
Rotterdam, N.Y., U.S.	e M	146
Rottweil	g H	80
Rotuma I	e I	180
Roubaix	b J	84
Roudnice	e N	80
Rouen	c H	84
Rougé	e E	84
Rougemont	e M	84
Rough ≃	e J	152
Rough River Lake ⊜[1]	e J	152
Rouillac	g F	84
Roulers (Roeselare)	g C	82
Roulette	f H	146
Round Hill Head ›	e I	184
Round Lake	h L	156
Round Mountain	f H	162
Round Mountain ∧	h J	184
Round Rock	i I	154
Roundup	d Q	160
Rouses Point	b M	146
Roussillon □[9]	j I	84
Rouxville	h H	130
Rouyn	b P	148
Rovaniemi	h S	76
Rovato	d E	88
Rovereto	d F	88
Rovigo	d F	88
Rovno	g C	92
Rovuma (Ruvuma) ≃	d G	128
Rowena	h F	154
Rowland	e G	150
Rowlesburg	h G	146
Rowley Island I	c Q	134
Roxas (Capiz)	c G	108
Roxboro	c H	150
Roxburgh	l D	186
Roxie	k E	152
Roxton	f K	154
Roy, N.M., U.S.	d B	154
Roy, Ut,. U.S.	c D	158
Roy, Wa., U.S.	c C	160
Royal	h L	156
Royal Canal ≍	h F	78
Royal Center	b J	152
Royal City	d F	160
Royale, Isle I	b G	148
Royal Gorge V	f K	158
Royal Leamington Spa	i L	78
Royal Oak	h L	148
Royalton	e A	148
Royal Tunbridge Wells	j N	78
Royan	g E	84
Roye	c I	84
Royse City	g J	154
Royston	e C	150
Rožňava	g T	80
Rrëshen	h C	90
Rrogozhinë	h C	90
Rtiščevo	g F	92
Ruabon	i J	78
Ruacana Falls ∟	a B	130
Ruahine Range ⋀	g K	186
Ruapehu, Mount ∧	f J	186
Rub'al Khali → Ar-Rub'al-Khālī ◆[2]	d G	117
Rubbestadneset	l I	76
Rubcovsk	g H	94
Rubežnoje	h E	92
Rubinéia	f C	177
Ruby	d Q	138
Ruby ≃	e M	160
Ruby Dome ∧	d J	162
Ruby Mountains ⋀	d J	162
Ruby Valley V	d J	162
Rudall	i B	184
Rudall River National Park ♠	d D	182
Ruda Śląska	e R	80
Rudensk	h J	96
Rüdersdorf	c M	80
Rüdesheim	f G	80
Rudkøbing	n L	76
Rudn'a	g N	96
Rudnyj	g J	92
Rudo	f C	90
Rudolf, Lake (Lake Turkana) ⊜	h H	126
Rudolstadt	e K	80
Rūd Sar	d N	118
Rudyard, Mi., U.S.	d K	148
Rudyard, Mt., U.S.	b O	160
Rue	b H	84
Ruen ∧	g F	90
Rufā'ah	f G	126
Ruffieux	g L	84
Ruffin	f F	150
Rufino	h G	178
Rufisque	f C	124
Rufus	e E	160
Rugao	c I	104
Rugby, Eng., U.K.	i L	78
Rugby, N.D., U.S.	c H	156
Rügen I	a M	80
Ruhpolding	h L	80
Ruhr ≃	f J	82
Rui'an	h I	104
Ruidoso	k K	158
Ruidoso, Rio ≃	k K	158
Ruidoso Downs	k K	158
Ruijin	j E	104
Ruinen	c I	82
Ruivo, Pico ∧	m U	87a
Ruiz	g G	166
Rukwa, Lake ⊜	c F	128
Rule	f G	154
Ruleville	i F	152
Rulo	k L	156
Rum ≃	e B	148
Ruma	d C	90
Rumbek	g F	126
Rumbeke	g C	82
Rum Cay I	c G	170
Rumford	c P	146
Rumia	a R	80
Rumigny	c K	84
Rum Jungle	b F	182
Rumoi	d P	106a
Runan	b C	104
Runanga	i F	186
Runge	k I	154
Rungwa	c F	128
Rungwa ≃	c F	128
Ruo ≃	c F	100
Ruoqiang	d D	100
Ruovesi	k S	76
Rupert, Id., U.S.	h L	160
Rupert, W.V., U.S.	j F	146
Rupert, Rivière de ≃	f Q	134
Rural Hall	c F	150
Rural Retreat	c E	150
Rurrenabaque	f E	174
Rurstausee ⊜[1]	g I	82
Rusape	b K	130
Ruse	f I	90
Rush ≃, N.D., U.S.	d J	156
Rush ≃, Wi., U.S.	f C	148
Rush Center	m H	156
Rush City	e C	148
Rushford	g D	148
Rushmore	h L	156
Rush Springs	e I	154
Rushville, Il., U.S.	b F	152
Rushville, In., U.S.	c K	152
Rushville, Ne., U.S.	i E	156
Rusk	h K	154
Ruskin	l D	150
Russas	d K	174
Russell, Mb., Can.	h M	142
Russell, On., Can.	b K	146
Russell, N.Z.	b I	186
Russell, Ia., U.S.	j B	148
Russell, Ks., U.S.	m I	156
Russell, Ky., U.S.	i D	146
Russell, Mn., U.S.	g L	156
Russell, Pa., U.S.	f G	146
Russell Islands II	j P	188e
Russells Point	g C	146
Russell Springs	e K	152
Russellville, Al., U.S.	h I	152
Russellville, Ar., U.S.	g C	152
Russellville, Ky., U.S.	f J	152
Russellville, Mo., U.S.	d D	152
Rüsselsheim	e H	80
Russian ≃	f B	162
Russian Soviet Federative Socialist Republic → Rossijskaja Sovetskaja Federativnaja Socialističeskaja Respublika □[3]	e N	92
Russiaville	b J	152
Rust	h P	80
Rustavi	i G	92
Rustburg	b G	150
Rustenburg	e H	130
Ruston	j D	152
Rute	h G	86
Ruteng	g G	108
Ruth, Ms., U.S.	k F	152
Ruth, Nv., U.S.	e K	162
Rutherford	f H	152
Rutherfordton	d E	150
Ruthin	h J	78
Ruthton	g K	156
Ruthven	h M	156
Rüti	d J	83
Rutland, N.D., U.S.	e J	156
Rutland, Vt., U.S.	d N	146
Rutledge, Ga., U.S.	f C	150
Rutledge, Tn., U.S.	c C	150
Rutog	e B	100
Rutshuru	b E	128
Rutter	d O	148
Ruukki	i S	76
Ruvuma (Rovuma) ≃	d G	128
Ruy Barbosa	b H	177
Ruza	f S	96
Ružany	i G	96
Ružomberok	f S	80
Rwanda □[1]	b F	128
Ryan	e I	154
Rybačje, S.S.S.R.	i M	92
Rybačje, S.S.S.R.	h H	94
Rybinskoje vodochranilišče ⊜[1]	c U	96
Rybnik	e R	80
Rybnoje	g V	96
Ryd	m N	76
Rydaholm	m N	76
Ryde	k L	78
Ryder	d F	156
Ryderwood	d B	160
Ryegate	d P	160
Rye Patch Reservoir ⊜[1]	d G	162
Ryes	c F	84
Ryfoss	k K	76
Rygnestad	l J	76
Rymanów	f U	80
Rypin	b S	80
Rysy ∧	f T	80
Ryūgasaki	l O	106
Ryukyu Islands → Nansei-shotō II	f L	100
Ržanica	h P	96
Rzeszów	e V	80
Ržev	e Q	96
S		
Saale ≃	d K	80
Saales	d N	84
Saalfeld	e K	80
Saar → Saarland □[3]	f F	80
Saarbrücken	f F	80
Saarburg	f F	80
Saaremaa I	c E	96
Saarijärvi	j S	76
Saaristomeren kansallispuisto ♠	l R	76
Saarland □[3]	f F	80
Saarlouis	f F	80
Saas Grund	f H	83
Saavedra	i G	178
Sab, Tônlé ⊜	h H	110
Saba I	f M	170
Saba Bank ✦[2]	f M	170
Šabac	e C	90
Sabadell	d N	86
Sabae	l K	106
Sabalān, Kūhhā-ye ∧	c L	118
Sabana, Archipiélago de II	c D	170
Sabanagrande	d G	168
Sabanalarga	i G	170
Sabancuy	h N	166
Sabang	e F	108
Sabanilla	e I	166
Sabará	e G	177
Sābarmati ≃	i E	114
Sabaudia	h H	88
Sabetha	l L	156
Sabhā	c C	126
Sabi (Save) ≃	b K	130
Sabie	e J	130
Sábiè ≃	e K	130
Sabile	d E	96
Sabina	h C	146
Sabinal	j G	154
Sabinas	d I	166
Sabinas ≃	d I	166
Sabinas Hidalgo	d I	166
Sabine ≃	e H	136
Sabine, Mount ∧	c H	189
Sabine Lake ⊜	m C	152
Sabine Pass ⊂	m C	152
Sabinosa	p V	87b
Sable, Cape ›	i H	144
Sable, Cape ›[1]	n E	150
Sable, Île de I	c K	182
Sable, Rivière du ≃	e S	134
Sable Island I	i N	144
Sablé-sur-Sarthe	e F	84
Sabres	h F	84
Sabrina Coast ⊥[2]	b G	189
Sabugal	e D	86
Sabula	h E	148
Şabyā	f C	117
Sabzevār	d Q	118
Sac ≃	e C	152
Sacajawea Peak ∧	e H	160
Sacaton	k E	158
Sac City	i M	156
Săcele	d I	90
Sachalin, ostrov (Sakhalin) I	g T	94
Sachalinskij zaliv ⊂	g T	94
Sachigo ≃	f N	134
Šachovskaja	e R	96
Šachrisabz	j K	92
Sachsenburg	i M	80
Sachs Harbour	b G	134
Šachty	h F	92
Sackets Harbor	d J	146
Säckingen	h G	80
Sackville	g I	144
Saco, Me., U.S.	d P	146
Saco, Mt., U.S.	b R	160
Saco ≃	d P	146
Sacramento	f D	162
Sacramento ≃, Ca., U.S.	f D	162
Sacramento ≃, N.M., U.S.	l K	158
Sacramento Mountains ⋀	l K	158
Sacramento Valley V	d C	162
Sacred Heart	g L	156
Sada	b C	86
Şa'dah	f C	117
Sada-misaki ›	n G	106
Saddle Mountain ∧	f K	158
Sa-dec	i H	110
Sādiqābad	f D	114
Sadiya	d N	112
Sado I	i M	106
Sado-kaikyō ⊔	j M	106
Šadrinsk	f J	92
Sadulgarh	f F	114
Sädvaluspen	h O	76
Saegertown	f F	146
Saeki	m I	106
Säffle	l M	76
Safford	l G	158
Safi	b E	124
Safīd ≃	d M	118
Safīd Kūh, Selseleh-Ye ⋀	c G	112
Safonovo	f D	92
Saga, Nihon	n E	106
Saga, Zhg.	f D	100
Sagae	i O	106
Sagaing	d C	110
Sagamihara	l N	106
Sagami-nada ⊂	l N	106
Saganthit Kyun I	i E	110
Sāgar	i H	114
Sagavanirktok ≃	b T	138
Sagerton	f G	154
Saginaw	g L	148
Saginaw ≃	g L	148
Saginaw Bay ⊂	g L	148
Saglek Bay ⊂	e T	134
Sagres	h C	86
Saguache	f J	158
Sagua de Tánamo	d G	170
Sagua la Grande	c D	170
Saguenay ≃	d C	144
Sagunt	f K	86
Sa'gya	f D	100
Sahara ◆[2]	f G	122
Sahāranpur	f G	114
Sahaswān	f H	114
Sahel → Sudan ◆[1]	f K	124
Sāhibganj	h L	114
Sāhiwāl (Montgomery)	e E	114
Sahuaripa	c E	166
Sahuarita	m F	158
Sahuayo	g H	166
Sai Buri	k F	110
Saïda	b G	124
Saidpur	h M	114
Saidu	c E	114
Saignelégier	d G	83
Sai-gon → Thanh-pho Ho Chi Minh	i I	110
Saijō	n H	106
Saiki	o F	106
Saimaa ⊜	k T	76
Saín Alto	f H	166
Saint-Affrique	i I	84
Sainte-Agathe-des-Monts	a L	146
Saint Alban's, Nf., Can.	e R	144
St. Albans, Eng., U.K.	j M	78
Saint Albans, Vt., U.S.	c M	146
Saint Albans, W.V., U.S.	i E	146
Saint Albert	d U	140
St. Aldhelm's Head ›	k K	78
Saint-Alexandre-de-Kamouraska	e D	144
Saint-Amand-Montrond	f I	84
Saint-Amour	f L	84
Saint-André, Cap ›	p U	131b
Saint-André-Avellin	b K	146
Saint Andrews, N.B., Can.	g F	144
St. Andrews, Scot., U.K.	e K	78
Saint Andrews, S.C., U.S.	g G	150
Saint Anne	i H	148
Sainte-Anne-de-Beaupré	e C	144
Sainte-Anne-de-Madawaska	e E	144
Sainte-Anne-des-Chênes	i R	142
Sainte-Anne-des-Monts	c G	144
St. Anne's	h J	78
Saint Ann's Bay	e F	170
Saint-Anselme	f C	144
Saint Ansgar	g C	148
Saint Anthony, N.B., Can.	f I	144
Saint Anthony, Nf., Can.	a R	144
Saint Anthony, Id., U.S.	g N	160
Saint Arnaud, Austl.	k E	184
Saint Arnaud, N.Z.	h G	186
Saint-Augustin ≃	f U	134
Saint Augustine	j E	150
Saint-Augustin-Saguenay	a O	144
St. Austell	k I	78
Saint-Avold	c M	84
Saint-Barthélemy I	f M	170
Saint-Basile	e E	144
Saint-Béat	j G	84
Saint-Blaise	d F	83
Saint-Bonnet	h M	84
Saint-Bonnet-de-Joux	f K	84
Saint-Brieuc	d D	84
Saint-Calais	e G	84
Saint Catharines	g P	148
Saint Catherines Island I	h E	150
Saint-Cergue	f E	83
Saint-Chamond	g K	84
Saint Charles, Ar., U.S.	h E	152
Saint Charles, Id., U.S.	h N	160
Saint Charles, Il., U.S.	i G	148
Saint Charles, Mi., U.S.	g K	148
Saint Charles, Mn., U.S.	g C	148
Saint Charles, Mo., U.S.	d F	152
Saint Charles Mesa	m C	156
Saint Christopher (Saint Kitts) I	f M	170
Saint Christopher-Nevis □[1]	f M	170
Saint Clair, Mi., U.S.	h M	148
Saint Clair, Mo., U.S.	d F	152
Saint Clair ≃	h M	148
Saint Clair, Lake ⊜	h M	148
Saint Clair Shores	h M	148
Saint Clairsville	g F	146
Saint-Claude	f L	84
Saint Cloud, Fl., U.S.	k E	150
Saint Cloud, Mn., U.S.	e A	148
Sainte-Croix	e F	83
Saint Croix I	f L	170
Saint Croix ≃, N.A.	g F	144
Saint Croix ≃, U.S.	e C	148
Saint Croix Falls	e C	148
Saint David, Az., U.S.	m F	158
Saint David, Il., U.S.	j E	148
St. David's	j H	78
St. David's Head ›	j H	78
Saint-Denis, Fr.	d I	84
Saint-Denis, Réu.	v Q	131c
Saint-Dié	d M	84
Saint-Dizier	d K	84
Sainte → Saint		
Saint Edward	j J	156
Saint Eleanor's	f J	144
Saint Elias, Cape ›	g V	138
Saint Elias, Mount ∧	f X	138
Saint Elias Mountains ⋀	f X	138
Saint-Élie	c H	174
Saint Elmo	c H	152
Sainte-Rose-du-Lac	g O	142
Saintes	g F	84
Saintes, Îles des II	g N	170
Saintes-Maries-de-la-Mer	i K	84
Saint-Étienne	g K	84
Saint-Eustache	b M	146
Saint-Fabien	d E	144
Saint-Félicien	g R	134
Saint-Félix-de-Valois	a M	146
Saint-Florent	l X	85a
Saint-Flour	g J	84
Sainte-Foy	f B	144
Sainte-Foy-la-Grande	h G	84
Saint Francis, Ks., U.S.	l F	156
Saint Francis, S.D., U.S.	h G	156
Saint Francis, Wi., U.S.	h H	148
Saint Francis ≃	h F	152
Saint Francis, Cape ›	j G	130
Saint Francis, Lake ⊜	b L	146
Saint Francisville	l E	152
Saint-François, Lac ⊜	b O	146
Saint-Gabriel	a M	146
Saint-Gaudens	i G	84
Sainte Genevieve	e F	152
Saint George, Austl.	g H	184
Saint George, N.B., Can.	g G	144
Saint George, On., Can.	g O	148
Saint George, S.C., U.S.	f F	150
Saint George, Ut,. U.S.	g C	158
Saint George Island	h J	138
Saint George Island I	j B	150
Saint George's, Nf., Can.	d O	144
Saint-Georges, P.Q., Can.	a P	146
Saint George's, Gren.	h N	170
Saint-Georges, Guy. fr.	c H	174
Saint George's Bay ⊂, Nf., Can.	d N	144
Saint Georges Bay ⊂, N.S., Can.	g L	144
St. George's Channel ⊔	j G	78
Saint Georges Head ›	j I	184
Saint-Germain	d I	84
Saint-Germain-du-Bois	f L	84
Saint-Gervais-les-Bains	g M	84
Saint-Géry	h H	84
Saint-Gilles (Sint-Gillis)	g E	82
Saint-Gingolph	f F	83
Saint-Girons	j H	84
Saint-Guénolé	e B	84
Saint Helena	f C	162
Saint Helena □[2]	j F	122
Saint Helena Sound ⊔	g F	150
Saint Helens, Austl.	m H	184
Saint Helens, Or., U.S.	e C	160
Saint Helens, Mount ∧[1]	d C	160
St. Helier	l S	78
Saint-Hilaire-du-Harcouët	d E	84
Saint-Hippolyte	e M	84
Saint-Hippolyte-du-Fort	i J	84
Saint-Hubert	h G	82
Saint-Hyacinthe	b N	146
Saint-Ignace, N.B., Can.	f H	144
Saint Ignace, Mi., U.S.	e K	148
Saint Ignace Island I	b H	148
Saint Ignatius	c K	160
Saint-Imier	d G	83
Saint-Isidore	e H	144
St. Ives	k H	78
Saint James, Mi., U.S.	e J	148
Saint James, Mn., U.S.	h M	156
Saint James, Mo., U.S.	e E	152
Saint James, N.Y., U.S.	g M	146
Saint James, Cape ›	f C	140
Saint-Jean, Lac ⊜	g R	134
Saint-Jean-d'Angély	g F	84
Saint-Jean-de-Losne	e L	84
Saint-Jean-de-Luz	i E	84
Saint-Jean-Pied-de-Port	i E	84
Saint-Jean-Port-Joli	e C	144
Saint-Jean-sur-Richelieu	b M	146
Saint-Jérôme	b L	146
Saint Jo	f I	154
Saint John, N.B., Can.	g G	144
Saint John, Ks., U.S.	m I	156
Saint John, N.D., U.S.	c H	156
Saint John, Wa., U.S.	c H	160
Saint John I	e L	170
Saint John ≃	g G	144
Saint John, Cape ›	b R	144
Saint Johns, Antig.	f N	170
Saint John's, Nf., Can.	e U	144
Saint Johns, Az., U.S.	j G	158
Saint Johns, Mi., U.S.	g K	148
Saint Johns ≃	i E	150
Saint Johnsbury	c N	146
Saint Joseph, N.B., Can.	g I	144
Saint Joseph, Il., U.S.	b H	152
Saint Joseph, La., U.S.	k E	152
Saint Joseph, Mi., U.S.	h I	148
Saint Joseph, Mn., U.S.	e A	148
Saint Joseph, Mo., U.S.	c B	152
Saint Joseph, Tn., U.S.	g I	152
Saint Joseph ≃, U.S.	i K	148
Saint Joseph ≃, U.S.	i I	148
Saint Joseph, Lake ⊜	f N	134
Saint-Joseph-de-Beauce	f C	144
Saint Joseph Island I	d L	148
Saint-Jovite	a L	146
Saint-Julien-en-Born	h E	84
Saint-Julien-en-Genevois	f M	84
Sainte-Julienne	b M	146
Saint-Junien	g G	84
Saint-Just-en-Chaussée	c I	84
Saint Kilda	l E	186
St. Kilda I	d E	78
Saint Kitts → Saint Christopher I	f M	170
Saint-Lambert	b M	146
Saint Landry	l D	152
Saint-Laurent-du-Maroni	b H	174
Saint Lawrence, Austl.	d H	184
Saint Lawrence, Nf., Can.	f R	144
Saint Lawrence ≃	g S	134
Saint Lawrence, Gulf of ⊂	d K	144
Saint Lawrence Island I	e I	138
Saint-Léonard	e F	144
Saint-Léonard-d'Aston	a N	146
Saint-Lô	c E	84
Saint-Louis, Sén.	e C	124
Saint Louis, Mi., U.S.	g K	148
Saint Louis, Mo., U.S.	d F	152
Saint Louis ≃	d C	148
Saint-Louis, Lac ⊜	b M	146
Saint-Louis-de-Kent	f I	144
Saint Louis Park	f B	148
Saint-Loup-sur-Semouse	e M	84
Saint Lucia □[1]	h N	170
Saint Lucia, Lake ⊜	g K	130
Saint Lucia Channel ⊔	g N	170
Sainte-Lucie	m X	85a
Saint Lucie Canal ≍	l F	150
Saint-Malo	d D	84
Saint-Malo, Golfe de ⊂	d D	84
Saint-Marc	e H	170
Sainte-Marguerite ≃	b G	144
Sainte-Marie, Cap ›	t U	131b
Sainte-Marie-aux-Mines	d N	84
Saint Maries	c I	160
Saint Marks	i B	150
Saint-Martin (Sint Maarten) I	e M	170
Saint Martin, Lake ⊜	g P	142
Saint Martins	g H	144
Saint Martinville	l E	152
Saint Mary	e G	152
Saint Mary Peak ∧	h C	184
Saint Mary Reservoir ⊜[1]	h U	140
Saint Marys, Austl.	m H	184
Saint Mary's, On., Can.	g N	148
Saint Marys, Ak., U.S.	e M	138
Saint Marys, Ga., U.S.	i E	150
Saint Marys, Ks., U.S.	l K	156
Saint Marys, Oh., U.S.	g B	146
Saint Marys, Pa., U.S.	f H	146
Saint Marys, W.V., U.S.	h E	146
Saint Marys ≃, N.A.	d K	148
Saint Marys ≃, U.S.	g B	146
Saint Marys ≃, U.S.	i E	150
Saint Mary's, Cape ›	f S	144
Saint Mary's Bay ⊂	f T	144
Saint-Mathieu	g G	84
Saint Matthew Island I	f H	138
Saint Matthews, Ky., U.S.	d K	152
Saint Matthews, S.C., U.S.	f F	150
Saint-Maur [-des-Fossés]	d I	84
Saint-Maurice ≃	g R	134
Sainte-Maxime	i M	84
Saint-Méen-le-Grand	d D	84
Saint Meinrad	d J	152
Sainte-Menehould	c K	84
Sainte-Mère-Église	c E	84
Saint Michael	e M	138
Saint Michaels	i J	146
Saint-Mihiel	d L	84
Saint-Moritz → Sankt Moritz	f P	84
Saint-Nazaire	e D	84
Saint Nazianz	f H	148
St. Neots	i M	78
Saint-Nicolas → Sint-Niklaas	f E	82
Saint-Omer	b I	84
Saintonge □[9]	g F	84
Saint-Pamphile	f D	144
Saint Paris	g C	146
Saint-Pascal	e D	144
Saint Paul, Ab., Can.	d W	140
Saint-Paul, Fr.	i N	84
Saint-Paul, Réu.	v Q	131c
Saint Paul, In., U.S.	c K	152
Saint Paul, Ks., U.S.	n L	156
Saint Paul, Mn., U.S.	f B	148
Saint Paul, Ne., U.S.	j I	156
Saint Paul, Va., U.S.	c D	150
Saint-Paul ≃, Can.	f U	134
Saint Paul ≃, Liber.	g D	124
Saint-Paul, Île I	l K	190
Saint Paul Island	h I	138
Saint Pauls	e H	150
Saint Peter	f B	148
Saint Peter Island I	f F	182
Saint Peter Port	c D	84
Saint Peters	g M	144
Saint Peters Bay	f K	144
Saint Petersburg	l D	150
Saint-Pierre, Mart.	g N	170
Saint-Pierre, Réu.	v Q	131c
Saint-Pierre, St. P./M.	f Q	144
Saint-Pierre I	f Q	144
Saint-Pierre, Lac ⊜	a N	146

Symbols in the index are identified on page 198.

Symbols in the index are identified on page 198.

Name	Map Ref.	Page
São Vicente, Cabo de (Cape Saint Vincent) ≻	h B	86
Sapé	e K	174
Sapele	g H	124
Sapello ≃	i K	158
Sapelo Island I	h E	150
Sapitwa ∧	e G	128
Sapožok	h W	96
Sapporo	d P	106a
Sapri	i J	88
Sapt Kosi ≃	g L	114
Sapulpa	d J	154
Saqqez	d L	118
Sarāb	d L	118
Sara Buri	g F	110
Saragosa	h C	154
Saragossa → Zaragoza	d K	86
Sarai	h X	96
Sarajevo	f B	90
Sarakhs	b G	112
Saraland	l H	152
Saran'	h L	92
Saranac	h J	148
Saranac ≃	c M	146
Saranac Lake	c L	146
Sarandë	j D	90
Sarangani Islands II	d H	108
Saransk	g G	92
Sarapul	f H	92
Sarasota	l D	150
Saratoga, Ca., U.S.	g C	162
Saratoga, Tx., U.S.	i L	154
Saratoga, Wy., U.S.	c J	158
Saratoga Springs	d M	146
Saratov	g G	92
Saratovskoje vodochranilišče ⊜[1]	g G	92
Saravan	g I	110
Sarawak □[3]	n K	110
Sarayköy	d C	118
Sárbogárd	i R	80
Sarcoxie	e B	152
Sārda (Kāli) ≃	f I	114
Sardārshahr	f F	114
Sardegna □[4]	i D	88
Sardegna (Sardinia) I	i D	88
Sardinia → Sardegna I	i D	88
Sardis, Al., U.S.	j J	152
Sardis, Ga., U.S.	g E	150
Sardis, Ms., U.S.	h G	152
Sardis, Tn., U.S.	g H	152
Sardis Lake ⊜[1]	h G	152
Sarek ∧	h O	76
Sarepta	j C	152
Sargans	d K	83
Sargent, Ga., U.S.	f B	150
Sargent, Ne., U.S.	j H	156
Sargodha	d E	114
Sarh	g D	126
Sārī	d O	118
Sáric	b D	166
Sarina	c H	184
Sariñena	d K	86
Sarita	b I	154
Sariwŏn	e M	102
Sark I	l K	78
Sarkad	i U	80
Sarles	c I	156
Sármellék	i Q	80
Sarmiento	f C	176
Sarmiento, Cerro ∧	g B	176
Särna	k M	76
Sarnen	e I	83
Sarnia	h M	148
Sarno	i I	88
Saron	i D	130
Saronikós Kólpos ⊂	l G	90
Saronno	d D	88
Sárospatak	g U	80
Sarpsborg	l L	76
Sarralbe	c N	84
Sarrebourg	d N	84
Sarreguemines	c N	84
Sarre-Union	d N	84
Sartang ≃	d R	94
Sartell	e A	148
Sartène	h C	88
Sarthe □[5]	d G	84
Sartilly	d E	84
Sárvár	h P	80
Sarykol'skij chrebet ⋏	a F	114
Sarysu ≃	h K	92
Sarzana	e D	88
Sasakwa	e J	154
Sasarām	h K	114
Sásd	i R	80
Sasebo	n D	106
Sasebo Naval Base ■	n D	106
Saskatchewan □[4]	f K	134
Saskatchewan ≃	f L	134
Saskatoon	f H	142
Saslaya, Cerro ∧	h B	170
Sasolburg	f H	130
Sasovo	g X	96
Saspamco	j H	154
Sassafras	b C	150
Sassafras Mountain ∧	d D	150
Sassandra	h E	124
Sassandra ≃	g E	124
Sassari	i C	88
Sassenheim	d F	82
Sassnitz	a M	80
Sassoferrato	f G	88
Sasso Marconi	e F	88
S'as'stroj	a O	96
Sassuolo	e E	88
Sastown	h E	124
Sata-misaki ≻	q E	106
Satanta	n G	156
Sátão	e D	86
Sātāra, India	d B	116
Satara, S. Afr.	e J	130
Sataua	a A	188a
Satellite Beach	k F	150
Säter	k N	76
Satna	h I	114
Sátoraljaújhely	g U	80
Sātpura Range ⋏	j G	114
Satsuma	l H	152
Satsunan-shotō II	r D	107b
Sattahip	h F	110
Satu Mare	b F	90
Satu Mare □[6]	b F	90
Şatun	k F	110
Satura	f V	96
Sauce	f I	178
Saucier	l G	152
Saucillo	c G	166
Sauda	l J	76
Sauđárkrókur	b D	76a
Saudi Arabia (Al-'Arabīyah as-Sa'ūdīyah) □[1]	d D	112
Saugatuck	h I	148
Saugerties	e M	146
Sauk ≃	e A	148
Sauk Centre	f M	156
Sauk City	g F	148
Sauk Rapids	e A	148
Saukville	g H	148
Saül	c H	174
Saulgau	g I	80
Saulieu	e K	84
Sault-au-Mouton	d D	144
Sault Sainte Marie, On., Can.	d K	148
Sault Sainte Marie, Mi., U.S.	d K	148
Saumarez Reef ✧[2]	c J	184
Saumur	e F	84
Sauquoit	d K	146
Saurimo	c D	128
Sausalito	g C	162
Sauveterre-de-Béarn	i F	84
Sauvo	k R	76
Sava	i L	88
Sava ≃	f K	74
Savage, Md., U.S.	h J	146
Savage, Mt., U.S.	d C	156
Savai'i I	a A	188a
Savanna, Il., U.S.	h E	148
Savanna, Ok., U.S.	e K	154
Savannah, Ga., U.S.	g E	150
Savannah, Mo., U.S.	c B	152
Savannah, Tn., U.S.	g H	152
Savannah ≃	g E	150
Savannakhét	f H	110
Savanna-la-Mar	e E	170
Savé	g G	124
Save (Sabi) ≃	b L	130
Sāveh	e N	118
Savelli	j K	88
Saverdun	i H	84
Saverne	d N	84
Savigliano	e B	88
Şavitaipale	k T	76
Savnik	g C	90
Savognin	e L	83
Savoie □[5]	g M	84
Savo Island I	j P	188e
Savona	e C	88
Savonlinna	k U	76
Savonranta	j U	76
Savoonga	e I	138
Savoy	f J	154
Sävsjö	m N	76
Savu Sea → Sawu, Laut ⊤[2]	g G	108
Sawai Mādhopur	h G	114
Sawākin	e H	126
Sawankhalok	f E	110
Sawara	l O	106
Sawata	i M	106
Sawatch Range ⋏	e J	158
Sawdā', Jabal as- ⋏[2]	c D	126
Sawdā', Qurnat as- ∧	e G	118
Sawel Mountain ∧	g F	78
Sawhāj	i D	118
Sawknah	c D	126
Şawqirah, Ghubbat ⊂	e J	117
Sawu, Laut (Savu Sea) ⊤[2]	g G	108
Sawu, Pulau I	h G	108
Şawwān, Arḍ aṣ- ≚	g H	120
Sawyer, Mi., U.S.	i I	148
Sawyer, N.D., U.S.	c F	156
Saxby ≃	b D	184
Saxis	b K	150
Saxmundham	i O	78
Saxon, Schw.	f G	83
Saxon, Wi., U.S.	d E	148
Saxton	g H	146
Sayan Mountains (Sajany) ⋏	g P	92
Sayaxché	i N	166
Saybrook	b H	152
Şaydā (Sidon)	a D	120
Şayhūt	g G	117
Saylorville Lake ⊜[1]	i B	148
Sayre, Ok., U.S.	d G	154
Sayre, Pa., U.S.	f J	146
Sayreville	g L	146
Sayula, Méx.	h H	166
Sayula, Méx.	c D	166
Saywūn	g F	117
Sazonovo	b R	96
Scafell Pikes ∧	g J	78
Scalea	j J	88
Scammon	n M	156
Scandia	l J	156
Scanlon	d C	148
Scapa Flow ⊂	c J	78
Scapegoat Mountain ∧	c M	160
Scappoose	e C	160
Scarborough, On., Can.	g P	148
Scarborough, Trin.	i N	170
Scarborough, Eng., U.K.	g M	78
Şcawfell Island I	c H	184
Ščelkovo	f U	96
Ščerbinka	f T	96
Schaerbeek (Schaarbeek)	g E	82
Schaesberg	g I	82
Schaffhausen	c J	83
Schaffhausen □[3]	c J	83
Schaller	i L	156
Schärding	g M	80
Schefferville	f S	134
Scheibbs	g O	80
Scheinfeld	f J	80
Schelde (Escaut) ≃	d D	80
Schenectady	e M	146
Schertz	j H	154
Schesslitz	f K	80
Scheveningen	d E	82
Schiedam	e E	82
Schiermonnikoog	b I	82
Schiermonnikoog I	b I	82
Schijndel	e G	82
Schiltigheim	d N	84
Schio	d F	88
Schkeuditz	d L	80
Schladming	h M	80
Schlater	i F	152
Schleiden	e F	80
Schleswig, B.R.D.	a I	80
Schleswig, Ia., U.S.	i L	156
Schleswig-Holstein □[3]	a I	80
Schleusingen	e J	80
Schlieren	d I	83
Schlitz	e I	80
Schlüchtern	e I	80
Schmalkalden	e J	80
Schmidmühlen	f K	80
Schmölln	e L	80
Schneeberg	e L	80
Schneverdingen	b I	80
Schodn'a	f T	96
Schofield	f F	148
Schoharie	e L	146
Schönebeck	c K	80
Schongau	h J	80
Schoolcraft	h J	148
Schopfheim	h G	80
Schorndorf	g I	80
Schoten	f F	82
Schouten Island I	n H	184
Schouwen I	e D	82
Schramberg	g H	80
Schreiber	b H	148
Schriever	m F	152
Schrobenhausen	g K	80
Schroffenstein ∧	f D	130
Schruns	h I	80
Schulenburg	j J	154
Schumacher	b N	148
Schüpfheim	e I	83
Schuyler, Ne., U.S.	j J	156
Schuyler, Va., U.S.	b H	150
Schuylkill ≃	g K	146
Schuylkill Haven	g J	146
Schwabach	f K	80
Schwaben □[9]	g J	80
Schwäbische Alb ⋏	g I	80
Schwäbisch Gmünd	g I	80
Schwäbisch Hall	f I	80
Schwabmünchen	g J	80
Schwanden	d K	83
Schwandorf	f L	80
Schwaner, Pegunungan ⋏	f E	108
Schwarza	e K	80
Schwarzach im Pongau	h M	80
Schwarzenburg	e G	83
Schwarzwald (Black Forest) ⋏	g H	80
Schwaz	h K	80
Schwechat	g P	80
Schwedt	b N	80
Schweinfurt	e J	80
Schweizer Nationalpark ♦	e M	83
Schweizer-Reneke	f G	130
Schwerin	b K	80
Schwerin □[5]	b K	80
Schwetzingen	f H	80
Schwyz	d J	83
Schwyz □[3]	d J	83
Sciacca	l H	88
Scicli	m I	88
Scilla	k J	88
Scilly, Isles of II	l G	78
Scio, Oh., U.S.	g E	146
Scio, Or., U.S.	f C	160
Scioto ≃	i C	146
Scipio	e D	158
Şcobey	b T	160
Ščokino	g T	96
Scone	i I	184
Scooba	j H	152
Scordia	l I	88
Scotia, Ne., U.S.	j I	156
Scotia, N.Y., U.S.	e M	146
Scotia Sea ⊤[2]	j J	172
Scotland, On., Can.	g O	148
Scotland, S.D., U.S.	h J	156
Scotland, Tx., U.S.	f H	154
Scotland □[8]	d I	78
Scotland Neck	c I	150
Scotlandville	l E	152
Scotsburn	g K	144
Scott	i E	152
Scott ≃	c C	162
Scott, Mount ∧	h C	160
Scott Base ⊌[3]	c H	189
Scottburgh	h J	130
Scott City, Ks., U.S.	m G	156
Scott City, Mo., U.S.	e G	152
Scottdale	g G	146
Scott Islands II	g F	140
Scott Mountain ∧	f J	160
Scott Reef ✧[2]	b D	182
Scottsbluff	j D	156
Scottsboro	h J	152
Scottsburg	d K	152
Scottsdale, Austl.	m G	184
Scottsdale, Az., U.S.	k E	158
Scotts Hill	g H	152
Scottsville	f J	152
Scottville	g I	148
Scourie	c H	78
Scranton, Ia., U.S.	i M	156
Scranton, N.D., U.S.	e D	156
Scranton, Pa., U.S.	f K	146
Screven	h D	150
Şcribner	j K	156
Ščučin	h G	96
Ščučinsk	g L	92
Scunthorpe	h M	78
Scuol (Schuls)	e M	83
Scurry	g J	154
Scutari → Üsküdar	h M	90
Scutari, Lake ⊜	g C	90
Seaboard	c I	150
Seadrift	k J	154
Seaford	i K	146
Seaforth	g N	148
Seagraves	g D	154
Seaham	g L	78
Seahorse Point ≻	d P	134
Sea Islands II	i E	150
Sea Isle City	h L	146
Seal ≃	e M	134
Sea Lake	j E	184
Seal Cove, N.B., Can.	h G	144
Seal Cove, Nf., Can.	c Q	144
Seale	j K	152
Sealevel	e J	150
Seal Lake ⊜	f T	134
Sealy	j J	154
Searchlight	i K	162
Searcy	g E	152
Searsport	c R	146
Seaside, Ca., U.S.	h D	162
Seaside, Or., U.S.	e B	160
Seaside Park	h L	146
Seattle	c C	160
Sébaco	e H	168
Sebago Lake ⊜	d P	146
Sebakwe Recreational Area ♦	b J	130
Sebastian	m I	154
Sebastián Vizcaíno, Bahía ⊂	c B	166
Sebastopol, Ca., U.S.	f C	162
Sebastopol, Ms., U.S.	j G	152
Sebeka	e L	156
Sebeş	d G	90
Sebes Körös (Crişul Repede) ≃	b E	90
Sebewaing	g L	148
Sebnitz	e N	80
Sebree	e I	152
Sebring	l E	150
Secas, Islas II	j L	168
Sechelt	h K	140
Sechura, Bahía de ⊂	e B	174
Secretary Island I	l A	186
Section	h K	152
Security	m C	156
Seda	e G	100
Sedalia	d C	152
Sedan, Fr.	c K	84
Sedan, Ks., U.S.	n K	156
Sedano	c H	86
Sederot	e C	120
Sedgefield	d F	150
Sedgewick	e W	140
Sedgwick, Co., U.S.	k E	156
Sedgwick, Ks., U.S.	n J	156
Sedgwick, Mount ∧	i H	158
Sedini	i C	88
Sedom (Sodom) ⊥	f D	120
Sedona	j E	158
Sedro Woolley	b C	160
Seeberg	d H	83
Seefeld in Tirol	h K	80
Seehausen	c K	80
Seeheim	f C	130
Seeley Lake	c L	160
Seelow	c N	80
Seelyville	c I	152
Seengen	d I	83
Sées	d G	84
Seesen	d J	80
Sefton, Mount ∧	j E	186
Segama ≃	d F	108
Segamat	m G	110
Segeža	e D	92
Segni	h H	88
Ségou	f E	124
Segovia	e G	86
Séguédine	d I	124
Seguin	j I	154
Segundo	n C	156
Segundo ≃	f G	178
Segura	f E	86
Segura ≃	g K	86
Seia	e D	86
Seibert	l E	156
Seiland I	f R	76
Seiling	c H	154
Sein, Île de I	d B	84
Seinäjoki	j R	76
Seine ≃, On., Can.	b C	148
Seine ≃, Fr.	c G	84
Seine, Baie de la ⊂	c F	84
Seine-et-Marne □[5]	d J	84
Seine-Maritime □[5]	c H	84
Seitsemisen kansallispuisto ♦	k R	76
Seixal	g B	86
Şeki, Nihon	l K	106
Şeki (Nucha), S.S.S.R.	i G	92
Sekondi-Takoradi	h F	124
Selah	d E	160
Selama	l F	110
Selangor □[3]	m F	110
Selaru, Pulau I	g I	108
Selatan, Tanjung ≻	f E	108
Selawik	c N	138
Selayar, Pulau I	g G	108
Selb	e L	80
Selbu	j L	76
Selby, Eng., U.K.	h L	78
Selby, S.D., U.S.	f G	156
Selbyville	i K	146
Selçuk	d B	118
Selden	l G	156
Seldovia	g S	138
Selenga (Selenge) ≃	g M	94
Selenge (Selenga) ≃	h L	94
Selenicë	i C	90
Selenn'ach ≃	d T	94
Sélestat	d N	84
Selfoss	c C	76a
Selfridge	e G	156
Şélibaby	e D	124
Šelichova, zaliv ⊂	f W	94
Seliger, ozero ⊜	d P	96
Seligman, Az., U.S.	i D	158
Seligman, Mo., U.S.	f C	152
Selinsgrove	g J	146
Sellišče	e P	96
Seližarovo	e P	96
Selje	j I	76
Seljord	l K	76
Selkirk, Mb., Can.	h R	142
Selkirk, Scot., U.K.	f K	78
Selkirk Mountains ⋏	f P	140
Selle, Chaîne de la ∧	e I	170
Sellers	e G	150
Sellersburg	d K	152
Sells	m E	158
Selm	d G	80
Selma, Al., U.S.	j I	152
Selma, Ca., U.S.	h F	162
Selma, N.C., U.S.	d H	150
Selmer	g H	152
Selmont	j I	152
Seltz	d O	84
Selva	e G	178
Selvas ◆[3]	e F	174
Selwyn	c D	184
Selwyn Lake ⊜	e L	134
Selwyn Mountains ⋏	d BB	138
Selwyn Range ⋏	c D	184
Seman ≃	i C	90
Semarang	j O	109a
Semeru, Gunung ∧	k P	109a
Semibratovo	d V	96
Seminary	k G	152
Seminoe Reservoir ⊜[1]	b J	158
Seminole, Ok., U.S.	d J	154
Seminole, Tx., U.S.	g D	154
Seminole, Lake ⊜[1]	i B	150
Semipalatinsk	g H	94
Semnān	e O	118
Sem'onovka	i O	96
Semporna	e F	108
Semuliki ≃	a E	128
Semur-en-Auxois	e K	84
Sena	e G	128
Senador Pompeu	e K	174
Sena Madureira	e E	174
Senanga	e D	128
Senath	f F	152
Senatobia	h G	152
Sendai	i O	106
Sendai ≃	p E	106
Seneca, Il., U.S.	i G	148
Seneca, Ks., U.S.	l K	156
Seneca, Mo., U.S.	f B	152
Seneca, Or., U.S.	f G	160
Seneca, S.C., U.S.	e D	150
Seneca Falls	e J	146
Seneca Lake ⊜	e J	146
Senecú	b F	166
Senegal (Sénégal) □[1]	f D	124
Sénégal ≃	e D	124
Senekal	g H	130
Senftenberg	d N	80
Senhor do Bonfim	f J	174
Senica	g Q	80
Senigallia	f H	88
Senise	i K	88
Senj	e I	88
Senja I	g O	76
Senlis	c I	84
Senmonorom	h I	110
Senneterre	b R	148
Sennori	i C	88
Senoia	f B	150
Sens	d J	84
Senta	d D	90
Sentinel	d G	154
Senyavin Islands II	c G	180
Seoni	i H	114
Seoul → Sŏul	f N	102
Šepetovka	g C	92
Sepik ≃	f K	108
Sępólno Krajeńskie	b Q	80
Sept-Îles (Seven Islands)	b G	144
Sepulga ≃	k J	152
Sequatchie ≃	d A	150
Sequeros	e E	86
Sequim	b B	160
Sequoia National Park ♦	h G	162
Seraing	g G	82
Seram (Ceram) I	f H	108
Seram, Laut (Ceram Sea) ⊤[2]	f H	108
Serang	g D	108
Serbia → Srbija □[3]	f D	90
Sered'	g Q	80
Seredejskij	g R	96
Seremban	m F	110
Serengeti Plain ≚	b F	128
Serenje	d F	128
Šereševo	i G	96
Sergeant Bluff	i K	156
Seria	e E	108
Serian	n K	110
Sérifos I	l H	90
Sérigny ≃	e S	134
Seringapatam	f D	116
Sermata, Pulau I	g H	108
Serov	f J	92
Serowe	d H	130
Serpa	h D	86
Serpents Mouth ⋓	j N	170
Serpuchov	g T	96
Serra do Navio	c H	174
Sérrai	h G	90
Serrana Bank ✧[4]	g D	170
Serranilla Bank ✧[4]	g E	170
Serra Talhada	e K	174
Serrezuela	f F	178
Serrinha	f K	174
Sersale	j K	88
Sertã	f C	86
Sertânia	e K	174
Sêrxu	e F	100
Sesfontein	b A	130
Sesheke	e D	128
Sesimbra	g B	86
Seskarö	i R	76
Sessa Aurunca	h H	88
Sestao	b H	86
Sestri Levante	e D	88
Şestroreck	a L	96
Šešupe ≃	g E	96
Setana	e N	106a
Sète	i J	84
Sete Lagoas	e F	177
Sete Quedas, Salto das ⌞	c K	178
Seth Ward	e E	154
Seto	l L	106
Seto-naikai ⊤[2]	m G	106
Settat	b E	124
Setté Cama	b A	128
Settlers	e I	130
Setúbal	g C	86
Setúbal, Baía de ⊂	g C	86
Seui	j D	88
Seul, Lac ⊜	h V	142
Seurre	e L	84
Sevagram	b E	116
Sevan, ozero ⊜	i G	92
Şevastopol'	i D	92
Ševčenko	i H	92
Severn ≃, On., Can.	e O	134
Severn ≃, U.K.	j K	78
Severnaja Dvina ≃	e F	92
Severnaja Sos'va ≃	e D	94
Severnaja Zeml'a II	b Q	92
Severna Park	h J	146
Severnyje uvaly ⋏[2]	b AA	96
Severodvinsk	e E	92
Severo-Sibirskaja nizmennost' ≚	c R	92
Severo-Zadonsk	g U	96
Severskij Donec ≃	h E	92
Severy	n K	156
Sevettijärvi	g U	76
Sevier ≃	e D	158
Sevier Desert ◆[2]	e D	158
Sevier Lake ⊜	f C	158
Sevierville	d C	150
Sevilla, Col.	c C	174
Sevilla (Seville), Esp.	h F	86
Seville → Sevilla, Esp.	h F	86
Seville, Fl., U.S.	j E	150
Seville, Oh., U.S.	f E	146
Sevlievo	f I	90
Sevsk	i Q	96
Sewanee	g K	152
Seward, Ak., U.S.	f T	138
Seward, Ne., U.S.	k J	156
Seward, Pa., U.S.	g G	146
Seward Peninsula ≻[1]	d M	138
Sewell	h C	178
Sexsmith	b P	140
Seybaplaya	h N	166
Seychelles □[1]	b K	128
Seyđisfjörđur	b F	76a
Seylac	f I	126
Seymour, Austl.	k F	184
Seymour, Ciskei	i H	130
Seymour, Ct., U.S.	f M	146
Seymour, In., U.S.	d K	152
Seymour, Ia., U.S.	j B	148
Seymour, Mo., U.S.	e D	152
Seymour, Tx., U.S.	f G	154
Seymour, Wi., U.S.	f G	148
Seymourville	l E	152
Seyssel	g L	84
Sezela	h J	130
Sfax	b I	124
Sfîntu-Gheorghe	d I	90
's-Gravenbrakel → Braine-le-Comte	g E	82
's-Gravenhage (The Hague)	d E	82
Shaanxi (Shensi) □[4]	d H	100
Shabeelle (Shebele) ≃	h I	126
Shache (Yarkand)	a G	114
Shackleton Ice Shelf ⊡	b F	189
Shaddādī	d I	118
Shady Cove	h C	160
Shady Grove	i C	150
Shadyside	h F	146
Shafer Butte ∧	g I	160
Shafter	i F	162
Shaftesbury	j K	78
Shageluk	e O	138
Shag Rocks II[1]	g H	176
Shāhābād, India	e G	114
Shāhābād, India	d D	116
Shah Alam	m F	110
Shahdād, Namakzār-e ≚	g R	118
Shahdol	i I	114
Shāhjahānpur	g H	114
Shāhpura	h F	114
Shakawe	b E	130
Shaker Heights	f E	146
Shaki	g G	124
Shakopee	f B	148
Shaktoolik	d N	138
Shala, Lake ⊜	g H	126
Shaler Mountains ⋏	b J	134
Shallotte	f H	150
Shallowater	f E	154
Shām, Bādiyat ash- ◆[2]	f I	118
Shām, Jabal ash- ∧	c J	117
Shamattawa	c V	142
Shāmli	f G	114
Shammar, Jabal ⋏	i I	118
Shamokin	g J	146
Shamrock, Fl., U.S.	j C	150
Shamrock, Tx., U.S.	d F	154
Shamva	e F	128
Shandī	e G	126
Shandong (Shantung) □[4]	d J	100
Shandong Bandao (Shantung Peninsula) ≻[1]	f H	102
Shangani ≃	b I	130
Shanghai	d J	104
Shanghai Shi □[7]	e K	100
Shangqiu (Zhuji)	a D	104
Shangrao	g F	104
Shangshui	b C	104
Shangxian	e H	100
Shangzhi	b L	100
Shanhaiguan	c G	102
Shannon, N.Z.	g J	186
Shannon, S. Afr.	g H	130
Shannon, Ga., U.S.	e A	150
Shannon, Il., U.S.	h F	148
Shannon, Ms., U.S.	h H	152
Shannon ≃	i D	78
Shannontown	f F	150
Shansi → Shanxi □[4]	d I	100
Shantou (Swatow)	l E	104
Shantung Peninsula → Shandong Bandao ≻[1]	f H	102
Shanxi (Shansi) □[4]	d I	100
Shanxian	i D	102
Shanyin	d I	100
Shaoguan	k B	104
Shaowu	h F	104
Shaoxing	e I	104
Shaoyang	f I	100
Shaqrā'	h D	117
Sharbatāt, Ra's ash- ≻	f J	117
Sharbīn, Jabal ∧	a F	120
Sharbot Lake	f S	148
Sharjah → Ash-Shāriqah	b I	117
Shark Bay ⊂	e B	182
Sharktooth Mountain ∧	e G	134
Sharm ash-Shaykh	i F	118
Sharon, N.D., U.S.	d J	156
Sharon, Pa., U.S.	f F	146
Sharon, Tn., U.S.	f H	152
Sharon, Wi., U.S.	h G	148
Sharon Springs	m F	156
Sharpe, Lake ⊜[1]	g H	156
Sharqī, Al-Jabal ash- (Anti-Lebanon) ⋏	a F	120
Sharqīyah, Aṣ-Ṣaḥrā' ash- (Arabian Desert) ◆[2]	c G	126
Shashe ≃	c I	130
Shashi	e I	100
Shasta	d C	162
Shasta ≃	c C	162
Shasta, Mount ∧[1]	c C	162
Shasta Lake ⊜[1]	d C	162
Shattuck	c G	154
Shaunavon	i F	142
Shaw	i F	152
Shawano	f G	148
Shawinigan	g R	134
Shawnee, Ks., U.S.	l M	156
Shawnee, Oh., U.S.	h D	146
Shawnee, Ok., U.S.	d J	154
Shawneetown	e H	152
Shawville	b J	146
Shaybārā I	j G	118
Shay Gap	d D	182
Shaykh, Jabal ash- (Mount Hermon) ∧	b E	120
Shaykh 'Uthmān	h D	117
Shebele (Shabeelle) ≃	g I	126
Sheberghān	b A	114
Sheboygan	g H	148
Sheboygan ≃	g H	148
Sheboygan Falls	g H	148
Shediac	f I	144
Sheenjek ≃	c W	138
Sheep Mountain ∧	g O	160
Sheet Harbour	h K	144
Shefar'am	c D	120
Sheffield, N.Z.	j G	186
Sheffield, Eng., U.K.	h L	78
Sheffield, Al., U.S.	h I	152
Sheffield, Il., U.S.	i F	148
Sheffield, Ia., U.S.	h B	148
Sheffield, Pa., U.S.	f G	146
Sheffield, Tx., U.S.	i E	154
Shegaon	b D	116
Shekhūpura	e E	114
Shelagyote Peak ∧	b G	140
Shelbina	c D	152
Shelburn	c I	152
Shelburne, N.S., Can.	i H	144
Shelburne, On., Can.	f O	148
Shelburne Falls	e N	146
Shelby, Ia., U.S.	j L	156
Shelby, Mi., U.S.	g I	148
Shelby, Ms., U.S.	i F	152
Shelby, Mt., U.S.	b N	160
Shelby, Ne., U.S.	j J	156
Shelby, N.C., U.S.	d E	150
Shelby, Oh., U.S.	g D	146
Shelbyville, Il., U.S.	c H	152
Shelbyville, In., U.S.	c K	152
Shelbyville, Ky., U.S.	d K	152
Shelbyville, Mo., U.S.	c D	152
Shelbyville, Tn., U.S.	g J	152
Shelbyville, Lake ⊜[1]	c H	152
Sheldon, Ia., U.S.	h L	156
Sheldon, Mo., U.S.	e B	152
Shelikof Strait ⋓	h Q	138
Shellbrook	e H	142
Shelley	g M	160
Shellharbour	j I	184
Shell Lake	e D	148
Shellman	h B	150
Shell Rock	h C	148
Shell Rock ≃	g B	148
Shellsburg	h D	148
Shelton, Ct., U.S.	f M	146
Shelton, Ne., U.S.	k I	156
Shelton, Wa., U.S.	c B	160
Shemogue	f I	144
Shemya Station	j B	139a
Shenandoah, Ia., U.S.	k L	156
Shenandoah, Pa., U.S.	g J	146
Shenandoah, Va., U.S.	i H	146
Shenandoah ≃	h I	146
Shenandoah National Park ♦	i H	146
Shengze	e I	104
Shensi → Shaanxi □[4]	d H	100
Shenyang (Mukden)	b K	102
Sheopur	h G	114
Shepherd, Mi., U.S.	g K	148
Shepherd, Tx., U.S.	l A	152
Shepherdstown	h I	146
Shepherdsville	e K	152
Shepparton	k F	184
Sheppey, Isle of I	j N	78
Sherard, Cape ≻	b P	134
Sherborne	k K	78
Sherbro Island I	g D	124
Sherbrooke, N.S., Can.	g L	144
Sherbrooke, P.Q., Can.	b O	146
Sherburn	h M	156
Sherburne	e K	146
Sheridan, Ar., U.S.	h D	152
Sheridan, In., U.S.	b J	152
Sheridan, Mt., U.S.	e M	160
Sheridan, Or., U.S.	e B	160
Sheridan, Tx., U.S.	j J	154
Sheridan, Wy., U.S.	f S	160
Sheringham	i O	78
Sherman, Ms., U.S.	h H	152
Sherman, N.Y., U.S.	e G	146
Sherman, Tx., U.S.	f J	154
Sherman Mills	b R	146
Sherman Station	b R	146
Sherpur	h N	114
Sherrard	i E	148
Sherridon	c M	142
Sherrill	d K	146
Shertallai	h D	116
's-Hertogenbosch	e G	82
Sherwood, P.E., Can.	f J	144
Sherwood, Ar., U.S.	h D	152
Sherwood, N.D., U.S.	c F	156
Sherwood, Oh., U.S.	f B	146
Sherwood, Tn., U.S.	g K	152
Sherwood Park	d U	140
Sherwood Shores	i H	154
Shetland □[4]	a L	78
Shetland Islands II	a L	78
Shexian	f G	104
Sheyenne	d H	156
Sheyenne ≃	e J	156
Shibām	g F	117
Shibata	j N	106
Shibetsu	c Q	106a
Shibīn al-Kawm	g D	118
Shibukawa	k N	106
Shicheng	i E	104
Shickley	k J	156
Shickshinny	f J	146
Shidao	g J	102
Shidler	c J	154
Shields ≃	e O	160
Shiga □[5]	l K	106
Shijiazhuang	e B	102
Shikārpur	g C	114
Shikohābād	g H	114
Shikoku I	n H	106
Shikoku-sanchi ⋏	n H	106
Shillelagh	i G	78
Shillington	g K	146
Shillong	h N	114
Shiloh	h B	146
Shilong	l B	104
Shimabara	o E	106
Shimada	m M	106
Shimane □[5]	m G	106
Shimber Berris ∧	f J	126
Shimian	f G	100
Shimizu	l M	106
Shimminato	k L	106
Shimodate	k N	106
Shimoga	f C	116
Shimoji-jima I	g M	188d
Shimokita-hantō ≻[1]	f P	106
Shimonoseki	n E	106
Shinano ≃	j M	106
Shīndand	c G	112
Shiner	j I	154
Shinglehouse	f H	146
Shingū, Nihon	m I	106
Shingū, Nihon	n J	106
Shingwidzi	d J	130
Shingwidzi (Singuédeze) ≃	d J	130
Shinjō	i O	106
Shinkolobwe	d E	128
Shinnston	h F	146
Shinshār	e G	118
Shinyanga	b F	128
Shiocton	f G	148
Shiogama	i P	106
Shiojiri	k L	106
Shiono-misaki ≻	n J	106
Shiping	c G	110
Shipman	b H	150
Shippegan	e I	144
Shippensburg	g I	146
Shiprock	h H	158
Ship Rock ∧	h H	158
Shirakami-misaki ≻	f O	106a
Shirakawa	j O	106
Shiranuka	e S	106a
Shiraoi	e P	106a
Shīrāz	h O	118
Shire ≃	e F	128
Shiretoko-misaki ≻	c T	106a
Shirley	c K	152
Shiroishi	i O	106
Shirone	j N	106
Shirpur	b C	116
Shīrvān	d Q	118
Shishmaref	c K	138
Shively	d K	152
Shivpuri	h G	114
Shivwits Plateau ⋏[1]	h C	158
Shizunai	e Q	106a
Shizuoka	m M	106
Shizuoka □[5]	l M	106
Shkodër	g C	90
Shoal Harbour	d T	144
Shoal Lake	h N	142
Shoal Lake ⊜	i S	142
Shoals	d J	152
Shōdo-shima I	m I	106
Sholāpur	d C	116
Shorewood	g H	148
Shortland Islands II	i N	188e
Shortsville	e I	146
Shoshone	h K	160
Shoshone ≃	f Q	160
Shoshone Basin ≚[1]	h Q	160
Shoshone Mountains ⋏	f H	162
Shoshong	d H	130
Shoshoni	a H	158
Shouxian	c E	104
Show Low	j F	158
Shreve	g D	146
Shreveport	j C	152
Shrewsbury, Eng., U.K.	i K	78
Shrewsbury, Ma., U.S.	e O	146
Shropshire □[6]	i K	78
Shuajingsi	e G	100
Shuangcheng	b L	100
Shuangliao	c K	100
Shuangyashan	b M	100
Shubrā al-Khaymah	g D	118
Shubuta	k H	152
Shuksan, Mount ∧	b D	160
Shule ≃	c F	100
Shullsburg	h E	148
Shunde	m B	104
Shungnak	c P	138
Shuqrah	g D	112
Shuqualak	j H	152
Shūr ≃	e N	118
Shūrāb ≃	g P	118
Shuraytah, Ra's ≻	a J	117
Shurugwi	b J	130
Shūshtar	f M	118
Shuswap Lake ⊜	g O	140
Shwebo	c C	110
Shyok ≃	c G	114
Siālkot	d F	114
Siam → Thailand □[1]	b C	108
Siam, Gulf of → Thailand, Gulf of ⊂	i F	110
Sian → Xi'an	e H	100
Şiasconset	f Q	146
Şiauliai, S.S.S.R.	f B	92
Šiauliai, S.S.S.R.	f F	96
Sibaj	e S	74
Sibasa	d J	130

Symbols in the index are identified on page 198.

Symbols in the index are identified on page 198.

Name	Map Ref.	Page

Symbols in the index are identified on page 198.

Name	Map Ref.	Page
Tobruk → Tubruq	b E	126
Tobyhanna	f K	146
Tocantínia	e I	174
Tocantinópolis	e I	174
Tocantins ≃	d I	174
Toccoa	e C	150
Toccoa (Ocoee) ≃	e B	150
Tochigi	k N	106
Tochigi □⁵	k N	106
Tochio	j N	106
Töcksfors	l L	76
Toco	b D	178
Tocoa	b H	168
Tocopilla	b C	178
Tocumwal	j F	184
Todi	g G	88
Todos Santos, Bol.	g E	174
Todos Santos, Méx.	f D	166
Todtnau	h G	80
T'oejo	d O	102
Tofield	d V	140
Togiak	g N	138
Togian, Kepulauan II	f G	108
Togo □¹	g G	124
Togwotee Pass)(	g O	160
Toiyabe Range ⋌	e H	162
Tokachi ≃	e R	106a
Tōkamachi	j M	106
Tokanui	m C	186
Tokara-rettō II	r D	107b
Tokat	b G	118
Tokelau □²	d J	180
Tokmak	i M	92
Toko Range ⋌	d C	184
Toksook Bay	f L	138
Toksovo	a M	96
Tok-to (Take-shima) II	j F	106
Toku Island I	e J	180
Tokuno-shima I	t C	107b
Tokushima	m I	106
Tokuyama	m F	106
Tōkyō	l N	106
Tōkyō Bay → Tōkyō-wan c	l N	106
Tōkyō-wan c	l N	106
Tolbuhin	f K	90
Toledo, Bra.	c L	178
Toledo, Esp.	f G	36
Toledo, Il., U.S.	c H	152
Toledo, Ia., U.S.	i C	148
Toledo, Oh., U.S.	f C	146
Toledo, Or., U.S.	f B	150
Toledo Bend Reservoir ⊜¹	k C	152
Tolentino	f H	88
Toliara	s T	131b
Tolima, Nevado del ⋀	e E	174
Toljatti	g G	32
Tolleson	k D	158
Tolmačovo	c L	36
Tolmezzo	c H	88
Tolna	i R	90
Tolna □⁶	i R	90
Tolo, Teluk c	f G	138
Točin	g L	36
Tolono	c H	152
Tolosa	b I	86
Tolten	d B	176
Tolú	j G	170
Toluca	i F	148
Toluca, Nevado de ⋀¹	h J	166
Toluca [de Lerdo]	h J	166
Tom' ≃	f I	94
Tomah	g E	148
Tomahawk	e F	148
Tomakomai	e P	106a
Tomanivi ⋀	m T	188g
Tomar	f C	86
Tomaszów Lubelski	e W	80
Tomaszów Mazowiecki	d T	80
Tomatlán	h G	166
Tomball	i K	154
Tombigbee ≃	k H	152
Tombouctou (Timbuktu)	e F	124
Tombstone	m F	158
Tombstone Mountain ⋀	d Y	138
Tombua	e B	128
Tom Burke	d I	130
Tomé	i B	178
Tomelilla	n M	76
Tomelloso	f H	86
Tomini, Teluk c	f G	108
Tomioka	k M	106
Tomo ≃	b E	174
Tompkinsville	f K	152
Tom Price	d C	182
Tomra	j J	76
Toms ≃	g L	146
Toms River	h L	146
Tomsk	f H	94
Tonalá	i M	166
Tonami	k K	106
Tonasket	b F	160
Tonawanda	d H	146
Tonbridge	j N	78
Tondano	e G	108
Tønder	n K	76
Tone ≃	k N	106
Tonekābon	d N	118
Tonga □¹	f J	180
Tongaat	g J	130
Tonganoxie	f K	152
Tongariro, Mount ⋀	f J	186
Tongatapu I	f J	180
Tongatapu Group II	f J	180
Tongcheng	g D	104
Tongchuan	d H	100
Tongeren (Tongres)	g G	82
Tongguan	e I	100
Tonghai	b G	110
Tonghua	b M	102
Tongjosŏn-man c	d P	102
Tongliao	c K	100
Tongling	f H	100
Tongnae	h Q	102
Tongo	h E	184
Tongoy	f C	178
Tongren	f H	100
Tongsa Dzong	g N	114
Tongtianhe ≃	d E	100
Tongtianheyan	d E	100
Tongue	e I	80
Tongue ≃, U.S.	e S	160
Tongue ≃, N.D., U.S.	c J	156
Tongue ≃, Tx., U.S.	f F	154
Tongue of the Ocean ✦	b F	170
Tongxian	d D	102
Tongyu	c K	100
Tongzi	f H	100
Tonica	i F	148
Tónichi	c E	166
Tonk	g F	114
Tonkawa	e I	154
Tonkin, Gulf of c	d J	110
Tonle Sap → Sab, Tônlé ⊜	h H	110
Tonnerre	h G	84
Tönning	b E	76
Tonopah	f H	162
Tonota	c H	130

Name	Ref.	Page
Tønsberg	l L	76
Tonstad	l J	76
Toobeah	g H	184
Tooele	d D	158
Toompine	f F	184
Toomsboro	g C	150
Toowoomba	f I	184
Topawa	m E	158
Topeka	i L	156
Topia	e F	166
Topki	f I	94
Topol'čany	g R	80
Topolobampo	e E	166
Toppenish	d E	160
Topsham	d Q	146
Torbalı	c B	118
Torbat-e Heydarīyeh	e R	118
Torbay → Torquay, Eng., U.K.	k J	78
Torbejevo	g Z	96
Torbrook	h I	144
Torch ≃	e K	142
Torch Lake	e J	148
Tordesillas	d F	86
Töre	i R	76
Torez	h E	92
Torgau	d M	80
Torhout	f C	82
Torino (Turin)	d B	88
Torit	h G	126
Torkestān, Selseleh-ye Band-e ⋌	c A	114
Torneälven (Tornionjoki) ≃	h R	76
Torneträsk ⊜	g P	76
Torngat Mountains ⋌	e T	134
Tornillo	e J	148
Tornio	i S	76
Tornionjoki (Torneälven) ≃	h S	76
Tornquist	i G	178
Toro	d F	86
Törökszentmiklós	h T	80
Toronto, On., Can.	g P	148
Toronto, Ks., U.S.	n L	156
Toronto, Oh., U.S.	g F	146
Toronto, S.D., U.S.	g K	156
Tororo	a F	128
Toros Dağları ⋌	d E	118
Torquay	k G	162
Torrance	k G	162
Torrão	g C	86
Torre de Moncorvo	d F	86
Torredonjimeno	h H	86
Torrejón de Ardoz	e H	86
Torrelavega	b G	86
Torremaggiore	h J	88
Torremolinos	i G	86
Torrens, Lake ⊜	h B	184
Torrens Creek	c F	184
Torrent	f K	86
Torreón	e H	166
Torres, Îles II	o X	188f
Torres Novas	f F	86
Torres Strait ⊔	b H	182
Torres Vedras	f F	86
Torridon	d H	78
Torriglia	e D	88
Torrington, Ct., U.S.	f M	146
Torrington, Wy., U.S.	l C	156
Torsby	k M	76
Tórshavn	d H	76b
Tortola I	e L	170
Tortoli	j D	88
Tortona	e C	88
Tortosa	e L	86
Tortue, Île de la I	d H	170
Toruń	b R	80
Torup	m M	76
Toržok	d D	96
Tosa	n H	106
T'osan	e N	102
Tosa-shimizu	o G	106
Tosa-wan c	n H	106
Tosca	b M	96
Toscana (Tuscany) □⁴	f E	88
T'osovo-Netyl'skij	c N	96
T'osovskij	c M	96
Tostado	h F	178
Tostón	o Z	87b
Tosu	n E	106
Totagatic ≃	d D	148
Tōteng	c F	130
Têtes	c F	130
Tot'ma	b Y	96
Totness	b G	174
Totonicapán □⁵	b C	168
Tototlán	g H	166
Tottenham, Austl.	i G	184
Tottenham, On., Can.	f P	148
Tottori	l I	106
Touba	g E	124
Toubkal, Jebel ⋀	b H	124
Touggourt	b I	124
Toul	d L	84
Touliu	l I	100
Toulnustouc ≃	c E	144
Toulon, Fr.	i L	84
Toulon, Il., U.S.	i F	148
Toulouse	i H	84
Tounan	l I	100
Toungoo	c G	110
Touques ≃	c G	84
Touraine ⬚	g G	84
Tourcoing	b J	84
Tournai (Doornik)	g C	82
Tournus	f G	84
Tours	g K	84
Tousside, Pic ⋀	d I	126
Toutle ≃	c C	160
Touwsrivier	i E	130
Tovarkovskij	h U	96
Tow ≃	i H	154
Towada	h G	106
Towanda, Ks., U.S.	n K	156
Towanda, Pa., U.S.	f J	146
Towcester	i K	78
Tower	c C	148
Tower City, N.D., U.S.	e I	156
Tower City, Pa., U.S.	g I	146
Tower Hill	c G	150
Town and Country	c G	150
Towner	c H	156
Townsend	d H	160
Townsend, Mount ⋀	k H	184
Townshend Island I	d I	184
Townsville	b G	184
Towson	h J	146
Toxkan ≃	c B	100
Toyah	h C	154
Tōya-ko ⊜	e N	106a
Toyama	k L	106
Toyama-wan c	k L	106
Tōyo	m I	106
Toyohashi	m L	106
Toyonaka	m J	106
Toyooka	l I	106
Toyosaka	j N	106
Toyota	m L	106
Tozeur	b I	124
Trabzon	b H	118
Tracadie	e I	144
Tracy, P.Q., Can.	a M	144

Name	Ref.	Page
Tracy, Ca., U.S.	g D	162
Tracy, Mn., U.S.	g L	156
Tracy City	g K	152
Tradewater ≃	e I	152
Traer	h C	148
Trafalgar, Cabo ⟩	i E	86
Traiguén	j B	178
Trail	h Q	140
Trakai	g G	96
Tralee	i D	78
Trammel	b D	150
Tramore	i F	78
Tranås	l N	76
Trancas	d F	178
Trancoso, Méx.	f H	166
Trancoso, Port.	e D	86
Tranebjerg	n L	76
Trang	k E	110
Trangie	i G	184
Trängslet	k M	76
Trani	h K	88
Transantarctic Mountains ⋌	d I	189
Transkei □¹	h I	130
Transvaal □¹	e I	130
Transylvania □⁹	c G	90
Transylvanian Alps → Carpaţii Meridionali ⋌	d H	90
Trapani	k G	88
Traralgon	l J	184
Trasacco	h H	88
Trasimeno, Lago ⊜	f G	88
Trás-os-Montes □⁹	d D	86
Traun	g N	80
Traun ≃	g N	80
Traunstein	h L	80
Travellers Lake ⊜	i E	184
Traverse, Lake ⊜	f K	156
Traverse City	f I	148
Travis, Lake ⊜¹	i H	154
Travnik	e L	88
Trbovlje	c J	88
Třebíč	f O	80
Trebinje	g B	90
Trebisacce	j K	88
Trebišov	g U	80
Treblinka	c V	80
Trecate	d C	88
Treene ≃	a I	84
Tregosse Islets II	a I	184
Tréguier	d C	84
Treherne	i P	142
Treinta y Tres	g K	178
Trélazé	e F	84
Trelew	e C	176
Trelleborg	n M	76
Tremblant, Mont ⋀	a L	146
Tremont, Il., U.S.	j F	148
Tremont, Pa., U.S.	f D	146
Tremonton	d D	158
Trempealeau	f D	148
Trempealeau ≃	f D	148
Trenčín	g R	80
Trenque Lauquen	h G	178
Trent → Trento	c F	88
Trent ≃	h M	78
Trente et un Milles, Lac des ⊜	a K	146
Trentino-Alto Adige □⁴	c F	88
Trento	c F	88
Trenton, On., Can.	f P	148
Trenton, Fl., U.S.	j D	150
Trenton, Ga., U.S.	a A	150
Trenton, Ky., U.S.	f I	152
Trenton, Mo., U.S.	b C	152
Trenton, Ne., U.S.	k F	156
Trenton, N.J., U.S.	i L	146
Trenton, N.C., U.S.	d I	150
Trenton, Tn., U.S.	h B	152
Trenton, Tx., U.S.	f J	154
Trentwood	c H	160
Trepassey	f T	144
Tres Arroyos	i H	178
Tres Esquinas	g C	174
Três Lagoas	f C	177
Três Marias, Reprêsa ⊜¹	e F	177
Três Montosas ⋀	d L	158
Três Passos	c F	177
Três Picos, Cerro ⋀	i H	178
Tres Puntas, Cabo ⟩	f C	176
Três Rios	k L	76
Tretten	g J	76
Treuchtlingen	g J	80
Treuenbrietzen	c L	80
Treviglio	d D	88
Trévoux	f G	84
Trevorton	g J	146
Trezevant	h H	152
Triabunna	n G	184
Triánda	m L	90
Triangle	i I	146
Triberg	g H	80
Tribune	m F	156
Tricase	j M	88
Trichardt	f I	130
Trichūr	g O	116
Trieben	h N	80
Trier	f F	80
Trieste	c H	88
Triglav ⋀	c H	88
Trigueros	h E	86
Trikala	j E	90
Trikora, Puncak ⋀	f J	108
Trilby	k D	150
Trim	h G	78
Trimont	h M	156
Trin	e K	83
Trincheras	b D	166
Trincomalee	h F	116
Trindade	f F	130
Trinidad, Bol.	f F	174
Trinidad, Col.	b D	174
Trinidad, Cuba	d E	170
Trinidad, Tx., U.S.	g J	154
Trinidad, Ur.	h I	170
Trinidad and Tobago □¹	i M	166
Trinitaria	i M	166
Trinity ≃, Ca., U.S.	d B	162
Trinity ≃, Tx., U.S.	i L	154
Trinity Bay c, Nf., Can.	e T	144
Trinity Bay c, Tx., U.S.	j L	154
Trinkat Island I	j B	110
Trino	c B	88
Triolet	v R	131c
Trion	e A	150
Tripoli → Tarābulus, Lībiyā	b C	126
Tripoli → Tarābulus, Lubnān	e F	118
Tripoli, Ia., U.S.	h C	148
Tripoli	l F	88
Tripp	h H	156
Tripura □⁴	i N	114
Tristan da Cunha Group II	l E	122

Name	Ref.	Page
Triumph	m G	152
Trivandrum	h D	116
Trnava	g Q	80
Trochu	f U	140
Trogir	f K	88
Troia	h J	88
Troick	g J	92
Troina	l I	88
Troisdorf	e G	80
Trois-Pistoles	d D	144
Trois-Rivières	a N	146
Trojan	g H	90
Trollhättan	l M	76
Trombetas ≃	c G	174
Tromelin, Île I	e J	128
Tromsburg	h G	130
Tromso ≃	g P	76
Tromsø	g P	76
Trona	i H	162
Tronador, Monte ⋀	j L	76
Trondheim	j L	76
Trondheimsfjorden c²	j L	76
Troodos Mountains ⋌	e B	118
Trooilapspan	g E	130
Tuli	c I	130
Tropea	k J	88
Tropic	g D	158
Tropojë	g D	90
Trosa	l N	76
Trotwood	h B	146
Troup	g K	154
Trout	k D	152
Trout Creek	f U	148
Trout Creek Pass)(	g U	158
Trout Lake	g U	142
Trout River	c O	144
Troutville	b G	150
Trouville [-sur-Mer]	c G	84
Troy, Al., U.S.	k K	152
Troy, Id., U.S.	d I	160
Troy, In., U.S.	e J	152
Troy, Ks., U.S.	i L	156
Troy, Mo., U.S.	d F	152
Troy, Mt., U.S.	b J	160
Troy, N.H., U.S.	e N	146
Troy, N.Y., U.S.	e M	146
Troy, N.C., U.S.	d G	150
Troy, Oh., U.S.	f B	146
Troy, Tn., U.S.	f G	152
Troy, Tx., U.S.	h I	154
Troy ⅃	c B	118
Troyes	d K	84
Troy Peak ⋀	f J	162
Trstenik	f E	90
Truc-giang	i I	110
Truchas	h K	158
Truchas Peak ⋀	i K	158
Trucial States → United Arab Emirates □¹	e E	112
Truckee	e E	162
Truckee ≃	e F	162
Trujillo, Esp.	f F	86
Trujillo, Hond.	b H	168
Trujillo, Perú	e C	174
Trujillo, Ven.	j I	170
Truk Islands II	c G	180
Trumann	g F	152
Trumansburg	e J	146
Trumbull	f M	146
Trundle	i G	184
Truro, N.S., Can.	e I	144
Truro, Eng., U.K.	k H	78
Truscott	f G	154
Trust Territory of the Pacific Islands □²	b G	180
Truth or Consequences (Hot Springs)	k I	158
Trutnov	e O	80
Tryon, Ne., U.S.	j G	156
Tryon, N.C., U.S.	d D	150
Trzcianka	b Q	80
Trzebiez	b N	80
Trzebnia	e S	80
Trzebnica	d S	80
Tsaratanana	p V	131b
Tsaratanana, Massif du ⋌	o W	131b
Tsau	c F	130
Tsavo	b G	128
Tsévié	g G	124
Tshabong	f F	130
Tshane	e E	130
Tshangalele, Lac ⊜	d E	128
Tshela	c B	128
Tshikapa	c D	128
Tshofa	c E	128
Tshuapa ≃	b D	128
Tshwaane	d F	130
Tsiafajavona ⋀	q V	131b
Tsihombe	t U	131b
Tsingtao → Qingdao	g H	102
Tsining Shan → Qin Ling ⋌	e H	100
Tsiribihina ≃	q U	131b
Tsiroanomandidy	q V	131b
Tsomo ≃	h H	130
Tsoying	m I	104
Tsu	m K	106
Tsubame	j M	106
Tsuchiura	k M	106
Tsugaru-kaikyō ⊔	f O	106a
Tsukumi	n E	106
Tsumeb	d C	130
Tsumis Park	d C	130
Tsuni → Zunyi	f H	100
Tsuruga	l K	106
Tsuruoka	i M	106
Tsushima	l I	106
Tsushima-kaikyō (Eastern Channel) ⊔	m D	106
Tsuyama	l I	106
Tuakau	d I	186
Tual	f I	108
Tuamotu, Îles (Tuamotu Archipelago) II	e M	180
Tuao ⋀	b M	106a
Tuapse	i F	92
Tuasivi	m B	186
Tuatapere	t U	186
Tubac	m E	158
Tuba City	h E	158
Tūbās	d D	120
Tubize (Tubeke)	g E	82
Tubarão	d E	177
Tubruq	b C	126
Tucacas	b H	170
Tuchola	b Q	80
Tucson	k E	158
Tucumán □⁴	d C	178
Tucumcari	c D	158
Tucupita	b H	170
Tucuruí	d I	174
Tudela	c K	86
Tudmur (Palmyra)	e H	118
Tugela ≃	g J	130
Tug Fork ≃	b D	150

Name	Ref.	Page
Tugidak Island I	h Q	138
Tuguegarao	m S	109b
Tuineje	o Z	87b
Tukangbesi, Kepulauan II	g G	108
Tuktoyaktuk	b BB	138
Tuktoyaktuk Peninsula ⟩¹	b BB	138
Tula, Méx.	f J	166
Tula, S.S.S.R.	g T	96
Tulaghi	j Q	188e
Tulancingo	g J	166
Tulare, Ca., U.S.	h F	162
Tulare, S.D., U.S.	g I	156
Tularosa	k H	158
Tularosa Valley ≃¹	l I	158
Tulbagh	i D	130
Tulcán	c C	174
Tulcea	d L	90
Tulcea □⁶	d L	90
Tule ≃	h F	162
Tulelake	c D	162
Tule Valley ⩔	e C	158
Tulia	e E	154
Tülkarm	d D	120
Tullahoma	g I	152
Tullamore, Austl.	i G	184
Tullamore, Ire.	h F	78
Tulle	g H	84
Tullibigeal	i G	184
Tulln	g N	80
Tullos	k D	152
Tullow	i G	78
Tully	c F	184
Tulsa	e I	154
Tulsequah	e F	134
Tuluá	c C	174
Tuluksak	f N	138
Tulum	g D	166
Tulumaya (Lavalle)	g D	178
Tulun	k O	109a
Tulungagung	k O	108
Tuma ≃	d J	168
Tumaco	c C	174
Tuman-gang (Tumen) ≃	a Q	102
Tumba, Lac ⊜	b C	128
Tumbarumba	j H	184
Tumbes	d B	174
Tumble Mountain ⋀	e O	160
Tumbotino	f Z	96
Tumby Bay	j B	184
Tumeremo	b F	174
Tumkūr	f D	116
Tummo	d C	126
Tumos ≃	b E	116
Tumpat	k G	110
Tumsar	b E	116
Tumuc-Humac Mountains ⋌	c G	174
Tumut	j H	184
Tumwater	c C	160
Tunduru	d G	128
Tundža ≃	g J	90
T'ung ≃	f P	94
Tunga ≃	f C	94
Tungabhadra ≃	e E	116
Tungabhadra Reservoir ⊜¹	e D	116
Tungkang	m I	104
Tungla	d J	168
Tungsha Tao (Pratas Island) I	g J	100
Tungshih	k I	104
Tuni	d G	116
Tunica	h F	152
Tunis	a I	124
Tunis, Golfe de c	a I	124
Tunisia (Tunisie) □¹	b H	124
Tunkhannock	f K	146
Tunnel Hill	b A	150
Tunnelton	h G	146
Tununak	f L	138
Tunuyán	g D	178
Tunuyán ≃	g D	178
Tunxi	f G	100
Tuo ≃	e F	100
Tuokusidawanling ⋀	b K	114
Tuolumne	g F	162
Tuolumne ≃	g E	162
Tupã	a M	177
Tupaciguara	e E	177
Tupanciretã	e D	177
Tupelo, Ms., U.S.	h E	152
Tupelo, Ok., U.S.	h I	154
Tupiza	h E	174
Tupper Lake	c L	146
Tupungato, Cerro ⋀	g D	178
Túquerres	c C	174
Tura	h N	114
Turabah	f E	112
Turangi	f J	186
Turbacó ⋀	b F	170
Turbat	d G	112
Turbo	b C	174
Turda	c G	90
Turek	c R	80
Turfan → Turpan	c D	100
Turfan Depression → Turpan Pendi ⪪⁷	c D	100
Turgaj	g J	92
Turgajskoje plato ⪪¹	g J	92
Turginovo	e S	96
Turgutlu	k F	86
Turia ≃	f K	86
Turin → Torino	d B	88
Turkestan	i K	92
Túrkeve	h T	80
Turkey	e F	154
Turkey ≃	h D	148
Turkey Creek ≃	i I	154
Turkmenskaja Sovetskaja Socialističeskaja Respublika □³	i I	92
Turks Islands II	d D	170
Turks Island Passage ⊔	d D	170
Turku (Åbo)	k R	76
Turkwel ≃	a F	128
Turlock	g E	162
Turnagain ≃	c G	138
Turnagain, Cape ⟩	f J	186
Turneffe Islands II	b C	168
Turner, Mt., U.S.	b N	160
Turner, Or., U.S.	f C	160
Turners Falls	e M	146
Turner Valley	f U	140
Türnitz	h O	80

Name	Ref.	Page
Turnor Lake ⊜	b F	142
Turnov	e O	80
Turnu-Măgurele	f H	90
Turon	n I	156
Turpan	c D	100
Turpan Pendi ⪪⁷	c D	100
Turquino, Pico ⋀	f F	170
Turrell	g F	152
Turrialba, Volcán ⋀¹	g K	168
Turriff	d K	78
Turskaja ložbina ⩔	j Q	188e
Turtle Creek	c L	144
Turtle-Flambeau Flowage ⊜¹	d E	148
Turtle Lake, N.D., U.S.	d G	156
Turtle Lake, Wi., U.S.	e C	148
Turtle Mountains ⋌	c G	102
Tuscaloosa	i I	152
Tuscany → Toscana □⁴	f E	88
Tuscarora Mountain ⋀	g I	146
Tuscarora Mountains ⋌	d I	162
Tuscola, Il., U.S.	c H	152
Tuscola, Tx., U.S.	h G	154
Tuscumbia, Al., U.S.	h I	152
Tuscumbia, Mo., U.S.	d D	152
Tuskegee	j K	152
Tustumena Lake ⊜	g S	138
Tutajev	d V	96
Tuticorin	h E	116
Tutóia	d J	174
Tutrakan	e J	90
Tuttle, N.D., U.S.	d H	156
Tuttle, Ok., U.S.	d I	154
Tuttle Creek Lake ⊜¹	i J	156
Tutuila I	b C	188a
Tutupaca, Volcán ⋀¹	g D	174
Tutwiler	h F	152
Tutzing	h K	80
Tuul ≃	b G	100
Tuurun-Poorin lääni □⁴	k J	76
Tuusniemi	j U	76
Tuvalu □¹	d I	180
Tuwayq, Jabal ⪪	d D	117
Tuxpan, Méx.	b C	166
Tuxpan, Méx.	g K	166
Tuxpan, Méx.	g K	166
Tuxtepec	i K	166
Tuxtla Chico	j M	166
Tuxtla Gutiérrez	i M	166
Tuyen-quang	d H	110
Tuy-hoa	h J	110
Tuz Gölü ⊜	c E	118
Tuzla	e B	90
Tweed	f R	148
Tweed Heads	g J	184
Tweeling	f G	130
Twee Rivieren	e E	130
Tweespruit	f F	130
Twentynine Palms	j J	162
Twillingate	c S	144
Twin Bridges	e M	160
Twin City	g D	150
Twin Falls	g K	160
Twin Lakes, Ga., U.S.	i C	150
Twin Lakes, Wi., U.S.	h C	148
Twinsburg	f E	146
Twin Valley	d K	156
Twisp	b E	160
Twofold Bay c	k H	184
Two Harbors	c D	148
Two Hills	d W	140
Two Medicine ≃	b M	160
Two Rivers	f H	148
Tybee Island	g E	150
Tychy	e S	80
Tydal	j J	76
Tye ≃	g G	154
Tygh Valley	d E	160
Tyler, Mn., U.S.	g L	156
Tyler, Tx., U.S.	g K	154
Tylertown	k F	152
Tym ≃	e O	94
Tyndall	h I	156
Tyne ≃	g L	78
Tynemouth	f L	78
Tynset	j L	76
Tyre → Sûr	b D	120
Tyrone, Ok., U.S.	c E	154
Tyrone, Pa., U.S.	g H	146
Tyrrell, Lake ⊜¹	j E	184
Tyrrhenian Sea (Mare Tirreno) ⫪²	i G	88
Tysse	k C	76
Tytuvėnai	f E	96
Ty Ty	h C	150
Tywyn	i I	78
Tzaneen	e G	130
Tzucab	g O	166

U

Name	Ref.	Page
Uatumã ≃	d G	174
Uaupés (Vaupés) ≃	c E	177
Ubá	f G	177
Ubangi (Oubangui) ≃	h J	124
Ube	g E	106
Úbeda	g I	86
Uberaba	e E	177
Überlândia	d E	177
Überlingen	h I	80
Ubly	g M	148
Ubombo	g K	130
Ubon Ratchathani	f H	110
Ubundu	b E	128
Ucayali ≃	e D	174
Uchiura-wan c	e O	106a
Uchiza	e C	174
Uchta	e H	92
Uckermark □⁹	b M	80
Ucluelet	h G	140
Ucon	g N	160
União da Vitória	d D	178
União dos Palmares	e L	174
Unicoí	c D	150
Unimak Island I	g L	138
Unimak Pass ⊔	h L	138
Union, Ia., U.S.	h B	148
Union, Mo., U.S.	d F	152
Union, Ms., U.S.	j E	152
Union, N.J., U.S.	i K	146
Union, Or., U.S.	f I	160
Union, S.C., U.S.	d E	150
Union, Wa., U.S.	c C	160
Union, W.V., U.S.	b E	150
Union City, Ca., U.S.	g D	162
Union City, Ga., U.S.	f B	150
Union City, Mi., U.S.	h K	148
Union City, Oh., U.S.	f A	146
Union City, Pa., U.S.	e F	146
Union City, Tn., U.S.	f G	152
Union de Tula	d E	160

Name	Ref.	Page
Ugie	h I	130
Uglegorsk	h T	94
Uglič	d V	96
Uglovka	c Q	96
Ugljan I	f I	88
Uherské Hradiště	f Q	80
Uhrichsville	g E	146
Úige	c C	128
Uijeongbu	f O	102
Uiju	c L	102
Uíl	h H	92
Uil ≃	h H	92
Uimaharju	j G	76
Uinta ≃	d F	158
Uinta Mountains ⋌	d F	158
Uísong	g P	102
Uitenhage	i G	130
Uithoorn	d F	82
Uithuizermeeden	b J	82
Uji	g J	106
Ujfehértó	h U	80
Uji-guntō II	p D	107b
Ujiji	b E	128
Ujjain	i F	114
Ujung Pandang (Makasar)	g F	108
Ukerewe Island I	b F	128
Ukiah, Ca., U.S.	e B	162
Ukiah, Or., U.S.	e G	160
Ukmergė	f G	96
Ukraine → Ukrainskaja Sovetskaja Socialističeskaja Respublika □³	h C	92
Ukrainskaja Sovetskaja Socialističeskaja Respublika (Ukraine) □³	h C	92
Ulaanbaatar	b H	100
Ulaangom	a E	100
Ulan	i H	184
Ulan Bator → Ulaanbaatar	b H	100
Ulan-Ude	e W	94
Ulaców	g G	96
Ulchin	g Q	102
Ulcinj	h C	90
Ulco	g G	130
Uleåborg → Oulu	i S	76
Ulft	e I	82
Ulhásnagar	c B	116
Uliastaj	b F	100
Ulindi ≃	b E	128
Ulithi I¹	c E	180
Uljanovsk	f J	96
Ulla ≃	f L	96
Ulladulla	j I	184
Ullapool	d H	78
Ullin	e H	152
Ullung-do I	j E	106
Ulm, B.R.D.	g I	80
Ulm, Mt., U.S.	c N	160
Ulmarra	g J	184
Ulongué	d F	128
Ulricehamn	m M	76
Ulrum	b I	82
Ulsan	h Q	102
Ulster □⁹	g F	78
Ulúa ≃	b F	168
Ulungur ≃	b D	100
Ulungur Hu ⊜	b D	100
Uluru National Park ⌖	e F	182
Ulverstone	m G	184
Ulysses, Ks., U.S.	n E	156
Ulysses, Ne., U.S.	n F	156
Ulzé	h C	90
Umán, Méx.	g O	166
Uman', S.S.S.R.	h D	92
Umarkot	h C	114
Umatilla, Fl., U.S.	k E	150
Umatilla, Or., U.S.	e F	160
Umba ≃	a I	130
Umbertide	f F	88
Umbria □⁴	g G	88
Umeå	i Q	76
Umeälven ≃	h O	76
Umfors	g M	76
Umfuli ≃	b I	130
Umhlanga Rocks	g J	130
Umkomaas	g J	130
Umm al-Qaywayn	b I	117
Umm Durmān (Omdurman)	e G	126
Umm el Fahm	c D	120
Umnäs	g M	76
Um'ot	g Y	96
Umpqua ≃	g B	160
'Umrān	e E	112
Umred	i G	116
Umreth	i E	114
Umsö	i O	102
Umtata	h I	130
Umtentweni	h J	130
Umuarama	b L	177
Umzinto	g J	130
Una ≃	e L	88
Unadilla, Ga., U.S.	g C	150
Unadilla, N.Y., U.S.	e K	146
Unalakleet	e N	138
Unalaska	h K	138
'Unayzah	f E	112
Uncia	g E	174
Uncompahgre ≃	f I	158
Uncompahgre Peak ⋀	f I	158
Uncompahgre Plateau ⪪¹	f H	158
Underberg	g I	130
Underwood	d F	156
Unecha	h P	96
Ungava, Péninsule d' ⟩¹	e R	134
Ungava Bay c	e S	134
Unggi	a R	102
Unión	i O	178
Union, S.C., U.S.	d E	150
Union Gap	d E	160

Name	Map Ref.	Page
Union Grove	h G	148
Unión Hidalgo	i L	166
Union of Soviet Socialist Republics □[1], Europe	e N	92
Union of Soviet Socialist Republics □[1], Europe	e L	94
Union Park	k E	150
Union Point	f C	150
Union Springs, Al., U.S.	j K	152
Union Springs, N.Y., U.S.	e J	146
Uniontown, Al., U.S.	j I	152
Uniontown, Ky., U.S.	e I	152
Uniontown, Pa., U.S.	h G	146
Unionville, Mi., U.S.	g L	148
Unionville, Mo., U.S.	b C	152
United	g G	146
United Arab Emirates □[1]	e E	112
United Arab Republic → Egypt □[1]	c G	126
United Kingdom □[1]	e G	74
United States □[1]	d G	136
Unity	f E	142
Universal City	j H	154
University	h G	152
University City	d F	152
University Park, N.M., U.S.	l J	158
University Park, Tx., U.S.	g J	154
Unjha	i E	114
Unna	d G	80
Unnão	g I	114
Unp'a	e M	102
Unsan	d N	102
Unterterzen	d K	83
Unterwalden □[3]	e I	83
Unža ≃	d Z	96
Uozu	k L	106
Upata	b F	174
Upemba, Lac ⊜	c E	128
Upham	c G	156
Upington	g E	130
Upland	k I	156
Upleta	j D	114
Upolu I	a B	188a
Upolu Point ≻	q R	163a
Upper Arlington	g C	146
Upper Arrow Lake ⊜	g Q	140
Upper Blackville	f H	144
Upper Darby	h K	146
Upper Hutt	h J	186
Upper Iowa ≃	g D	148
Upper Island Cove	e T	144
Upper Klamath Lake ⊜	h D	160
Upper Lake	e C	162
Upper Musquodoboit	g K	144
Upper Red Lake ⊜	c M	156
Upper Sandusky	g C	146
Upper Sheila	e I	144
Uppsala	l O	76
Upsala → Uppsala	l O	76
Upstart, Cape ≻	b G	184
Upton, Ky., U.S.	e K	152
Upton, Wy., U.S.	g C	156
Ur ⊥	g L	118
Urahoro	e R	106a
Urakawa	e Q	106a
Ural ≃	h H	92
Uralla	h I	184
Ural Mountains → Ural'skije gory ⩘	e I	92
Ural'sk	g H	92
Ural'skije gory (Ural Mountains) ⩘	e I	92
Urana	j G	184
Urandangi	c C	184
Urangan	e J	184
Urania	k D	152
Uranium City	e K	134
Uraricoera ≃	c F	174
Urasoe	u B	107b
Ura-T'ube	j K	92
Uravan	f H	158
Urawa	l N	106
Urbana, Ar., U.S.	i D	152
Urbana, Il., U.S.	b H	152
Urbana, Mo., U.S.	e C	152
Urbana, Oh., U.S.	g C	146
Urbandale	a C	152
Urbania	f G	88
Urbino	f G	88
Urečje	i J	96
Ures	c D	166
Urfa	d H	118
Urgenč	i J	92
Ürgüp	c F	118
Urho Kekkosen kansallispuisto ♠	g U	76
Uri □[3]	e J	83
Uriah	k I	152
Uribia	i H	170
Urich	d B	152
Urique	d F	166
Urk	c H	82
Urla	c B	118
Urmia → Orūmīyeh	d K	118
Urmia, Lake → Orūmīyeh, Daryācheh-ye ⊜	d K	118
Uroševac	g E	90
Urrao	b C	174
Ursa	b E	152
Uršel'skij	f W	96
Uruapan [del Progreso]	h H	166
Urubamba ≃	f D	174
Urubu ≃	d G	174
Uruguaiana	e J	178
Uruguay □[1]	g J	178
Uruguay (Uruguai) ≃	g I	178
Urumchi → Ürümqi	c D	100
Ürümqi	c D	100
Urun-Islāmpur	d C	116
Ur'upinsk	g F	92
Usa	n F	106
Usa ≃	d I	92
Ušači	f K	96
Uşak	c C	118
Usakos	d B	130
Usedom I	a N	80
Ushant → Ouessant, Île d' I	d A	84
Ushuaia	g C	176
Usingen	e H	80
Usk	b H	160
Usk ≃	j J	78
Üsküdar	b C	118
Uslar	d I	80
Usman'	i V	96
Usolje-Sibirskoje	g L	94
Ussuri (Wusuli) ≃	h R	94
Ussurijsk	i R	94
Ustaritz	i E	84
Uster	d J	83
Ust'-Ilimskoje vodochranilišče ⊜[1]	f R	92
Ústí nad Labem	e N	80
Ústí nad Orlicí	f P	80
Ustka	a P	80
Ust'-Kamenogorsk	h H	94
Ust'-Kut	f M	94
Uštobe	h M	92
Ust'urt, plato ⩘[1]	i I	92
Ust'užna	c S	96
Usu	c C	100
Usuki	n F	106
Usumacinta ≃	i N	166
Utah □[3]	d D	136
Utah Lake ⊜	d E	158
Utashinai	d Q	106a
Ute	i L	156
Utembo ≃	e D	128
Utena	f H	96
Utersum	a H	80
Utete	c G	128
Uthai Thani	g F	110
Utiariti	f G	174
Utica, Ks., U.S.	m G	156
Utica, Mi., U.S.	h L	148
Utica, Ms., U.S.	j F	152
Utica, Ne., U.S.	k J	156
Utica, N.Y., U.S.	d K	146
Utica, Oh., U.S.	g D	146
Utiel	f J	86
Utila	a H	168
Utila, Isla de I	a H	168
Uto	o E	106
Utopia	j G	154
Utrecht, Ned.	d G	82
Utrecht, S. Afr.	f J	130
Utrecht □[4]	d G	82
Utrera	h F	86
Utsjoki	g T	76
Utsunomiya	k N	106
Uttaradit	f F	110
Uttar Pradesh □[3]	g I	114
Utuado	e K	170
Utupua I	e H	180
Uudenmaan lääni □[4]	k S	76
Uusikaupunki (Nystad)	k Q	76
Uvá ≃	c E	174
Uvalda	f C	150
Uvalde	j G	154
Uvaroviči	i M	96
Uvdal	k K	76
Uvinza	c F	128
Uvira	b E	128
Uvongo Beach	h J	130
Uvs nuur ⊜	g J	94
Uwajima	n G	106
'Uwaynāt, Jabal al- ∧	d E	126
Uxbridge	f P	148
Uxmal	g O	166
Uxmal ⊥	g O	166
Uyuni	h E	174
Uyuni, Salar de ≃	h E	174
Už (Uh) ≃	g V	80
Uzbekskaja Sovetskaja Socialističeskaja Respublika □[3]	i J	92
Uzbek Soviet Socialist Republic → Uzbekskaja Sovetskaja Socialističeskaja Respublika □[3]	i J	92
Uzda	h J	96
Uzdin	d D	90
Užgorod	h B	92
Uzlovaja	h U	96
Uzunköprü	b B	118
Užur	f I	94
Užventis	f E	96

V

Name	Map Ref.	Page
Vääksy	k S	76
Vaal ≃	g F	130
Vaala	i T	76
Vaaldam ⊜[1]	f I	130
Vaalserberg ∧	g I	82
Vaalwater	e I	130
Vaanta (Vanda)	k S	76
Vaasa (Vasa)	j Q	76
Vaasan lääni □[4]	j R	76
Vaassen	d H	82
Vabalninkas	f G	96
Vác	h S	80
Vača	f Y	96
Vacaria	e M	178
Vacaville	f D	162
Vaccarès, Étang de ⊂	i K	84
Vach ≃	e G	94
Vacoas	v R	131c
Vado Ligure	e C	88
Vadsø	f U	76
Vaduz	e P	84
Vågåmo	k K	76
Vágar I	d H	76b
Váh ≃	g Q	80
Vaiden	i G	152
Vaihingen	g H	80
Vail, Co., U.S.	e J	158
Vail, Ia., U.S.	i L	156
Vailly-sur-Aisne	c J	84
Vaitupu I	d I	180
Vajgač, ostrov I	c I	92
Vākhān ◆[1]	b E	114
Vålådalen	j M	76
Valais (Wallis) □[3]	f G	83
Valašské Meziříčí	f Q	80
Valatie	e M	146
Valcheta	e C	176
Valdagno	d F	88
Valdaj	d P	96
Valdajskaja vozvyšennost' ⩘[2]	d P	96
Valdemārpils	d E	96
Valdemarsvik	l O	76
Valdepeñas	g H	86
Valders	f H	148
Valdés, Península ≻[1]	e D	176
Val-des-Bois	b K	146
Valdese	d E	150
Valdez	f U	138
Val-d'Isère	g M	84
Valdivia	d B	176
Valdobbiadene	d G	88
Val-d'Oise □[5]	c I	84
Val-d'Or	b R	148
Valdosta	i C	150
Vale	g H	160
Valemount	e O	140
Valença, Bra.	b I	177
Valença, Bra.	g G	177
Valença, Port.	c C	86
Valençay	e H	84
Valence	h K	84
València, Esp.	f K	86
Valencia, Ven.	i J	170
València □[4]	f K	86
València, Golf de ⊂	f L	86
Valencia de Alcántata	f D	86
Valenciennes	b J	84
Valentine, Ne., U.S.	i G	156
Valentine, Tx., U.S.	i B	154
Valenza	d C	88
Valera	j I	170
Valga	d I	96
Valiente, Península ≻[1]	j D	170
Valier, Il., U.S.	d G	152
Valier, Mt., U.S.	b M	160
Valjevo	e C	90
Valka	d I	96
Valkeakoski	k S	76
Valkenburg	g H	82
Valkenswaard	f G	82
Valladolid, Esp.	d G	86
Valladolid, Méx.	g O	166
Vallauris	i N	84
Valldal	j J	76
Valle	b G	86
Valle □[5]	d G	168
Vallecitos	h J	158
Valle d'Aosta □[4]	d B	88
Valle de Bravo	h I	166
Valle de la Pascua	j K	170
Valle de Olivos	d F	166
Valle de Santiago	g I	166
Valle de Zaragoza	d G	166
Valledupar	i H	170
Vallegrande	g F	174
Vallehermoso, Esp.	o W	87b
Valle Hermoso, Méx.	e K	166
Vallejo	f C	162
Vallenar	e C	178
Valles Caldera ⚲[6]	i J	158
Valletta	n I	88
Valley, Al., U.S.	j K	152
Valley, Ne., U.S.	j K	156
Valley Bend	i G	146
Valley Center	n J	156
Valley City	e J	156
Valley Falls	l L	156
Valley Farms	l E	158
Valley Head, Al., U.S.	h K	152
Valley Head, W.V., U.S.	i F	146
Valley Mills	h I	154
Valley of the Kings ⊥	j E	118
Valley Springs	h K	156
Valley Station	d K	152
Valley, The	e M	170
Valleyview, Ab., Can.	b Q	140
Valley View, Tx., U.S.	f I	154
Valliant	e K	154
Vallorbe	e E	83
Valls	d M	86
Valmaseda	b H	86
Valmeyer	d F	152
Valmiera	d H	96
Valognes	c E	84
Valona → Vlorë	i C	90
Valongo	d C	86
Valparai	g D	116
Valparaíso, Chile	g C	178
Valparaíso, Méx.	f H	166
Valparaiso, Fl., U.S.	l J	152
Valparaiso, In., U.S.	a I	152
Valparaiso, Ne., U.S.	j K	156
Valparaíso □[4]	g C	178
Valréas	h K	84
Vals, Tanjung ≻	g J	108
Valsbaai ⊂	j D	130
Valsetz	f B	160
Valsjöbyn	i N	76
Valthermond	c J	82
Valtimo	j U	76
Valverde del Camino	h E	86
Van, Tür.	c J	118
Van, Tx., U.S.	g K	154
Van Alstyne	f J	154
Van Buren, Ar., U.S.	g B	152
Van Buren, Me., U.S.	e F	144
Van Buren, Mo., U.S.	f E	152
Vanceboro	b S	146
Vanceburg	i C	146
Vancleave	l H	152
Vancouver, B.C., Can.	h K	140
Vancouver, Wa., U.S.	e C	160
Vancouver, Cape ≻, Austl.	g C	182
Vancouver, Cape ≻, Ak., U.S.	f L	138
Vancouver, Mount ∧	f Y	138
Vancouver Island I	h I	140
Vandalia, Il., U.S.	d G	152
Vandalia, Mo., U.S.	c E	152
Vandalia, Oh., U.S.	h B	146
Vanderbijlpark	f H	130
Vanderbilt, Mi., U.S.	e K	148
Vanderbilt, Tx., U.S.	k J	154
Vandergrift	g G	146
Vanderhoof	c J	140
Vanderlin Island I	c G	182
Vandervoort	h B	152
Van Diemen Gulf ⊂	b F	182
Vanegas	f I	166
Vänern ⊜	l M	76
Vänersborg	l M	76
Vangaindrano	s V	131b
Van Gölü ⊜	c J	118
Vangsnes	k J	76
Vangunu Island I	j P	188e
Van Horn	h B	154
Van Horne	h C	148
Vanier	b K	146
Vanimo	f K	108
Vāniyambādi	f E	116
Vankleek Hill	b L	146
Van Lear	b D	150
Vännäs	j P	76
Vanndale	g F	152
Vannes	e D	84
Van Reenen	g I	130
Van Rees, Pegunungan ⩘	f J	108
Vanrhynsdorp	h D	130
Vansant	b D	150
Vansbro	k N	76
Vanstadensrus	g H	130
Vanua Lava I	o X	188f
Vanua Levu I	m T	188g
Vanua Mbalavu Island I	m U	188g
Vanuatu □[1]	e H	180
Van Vleck	j K	154
Van Wert	g B	146
Vanwyksdorp	i E	130
Vanwyksvlei	h E	130
Vanzylsrus	f F	130
Var □[5]	i M	84
Var ≃	i M	84
Varallo	d C	88
Varāmīn	e N	118
Vārānasi (Benares)	h J	114
Varangerfjorden ⊂[2]	g V	76
Varangerhalvøya ≻[1]	f U	76
Varaždin	c K	88
Varazze	e C	88
Varberg	m M	76
Vardaman	i G	152
Vardar (Axiós) ≃	h F	90
Varde	n K	76
Vardø	f V	76
Varel	b H	80
Vareš	e B	90
Varese	d C	88
Varginha	f F	177
Varkaus	j T	76
Värmlands Län □[6]	l M	76
Varna	f K	90
Värnamo	m N	76
Varniai	f E	96
Varnsdorf	e N	80
Varnville	g E	150
Värö	m M	76
Várpalota	h R	80
Värtsilä	j V	76
Vas □[6]	h P	80
Vasai (Bassein)	c B	116
Vasilevič	i L	96
Vasiljevskij Moch	d R	96
Vaslui	c K	90
Vaslui □[6]	c K	90
Vass	d G	150
Vassar	g L	148
Västerås	l O	76
Västerbottens Län □[6]	i O	76
Västernorrlands Län □[6]	j O	76
Västervik	m O	76
Västmanlands Län □[6]	l O	76
Vasto	g I	88
Vas'uganje ⩩	f G	94
Vasvár	h P	80
Vatan	e H	84
Vathí	l J	90
Vatican City (Città del Vaticano) □[1]	h G	88
V'atka ≃	f H	92
Vatnajökull ⍓	b E	76a
Vatneyri	b B	76a
Vatomandry	q W	131b
Vatra Dornei	b I	90
Vättern ⊜	l N	76
Vatu Ira Channel ⩍	m T	188g
Vatukoula	m S	188g
Vaucluse □[5]	i L	84
Vaucouleurs	d L	84
Vaud □[3]	e F	83
Vaughan	g P	148
Vaughn	j K	158
Vaupés (Uaupés) ≃	c D	174
Vauvert	i K	84
Vauxhall	g V	140
Vava'u I	e J	180
Vava'u Group II	e J	180
Växjö	m N	76
V'azemskij	h R	94
V'az'ma	f Q	96
V'azniki	e Y	96
Veazie	c R	146
Veblen	f J	156
Vechta	c H	80
Vecsés	h S	80
Veddige	m M	76
Veedersburg	b I	152
Veendam	b J	82
Veenendaal	d H	82
Veenhuizen	b I	82
Veenoord	c J	82
Vega	d D	154
Vega I	i L	76
Veghel	e H	82
Vegreville	d V	140
Veguita	j J	158
Veinticinco de Mayo	h H	178
Veisiejai	g F	96
Vejer de la Frontera	i F	86
Vejle	n K	76
Velardeña	e H	166
Velas, Cabo ≻	g I	168
Velbert	d G	80
Velddrif	i D	130
Velden	g L	80
Veldhoven	f G	82
Veleka ≃	g K	90
Velet'ma	f Y	96
Vélez-Málaga	i G	86
Vel'gija	c P	96
Velhas, Rio das ≃	d F	177
Velikaja ≃	e Z	94
Velika Morava ≃	e E	90
Velika Plana	e E	90
Velikije Luki	e M	96
Velikij Ust'ug	e G	92
Velikodvorskij	f W	96
Veliko Gradište	e E	90
Veliko Târnovo	f I	90
Vélingara	f D	124
Velíž	f N	96
Vella Lavella I	i O	188e
Velletri	h G	88
Vellore	f E	116
Velma	e I	154
Velp	d H	82
Vel'sk	e F	92
Velten	c M	80
Velva	c G	156
Vemdalen	j M	76
Venaco	g D	88
Venado Tuerto	g H	178
Vence	i N	84
Venceslau Brás	b N	178
Vencimont	h F	82
Venda □[1]	d J	130
Venda Nova	d D	86
Vendas Novas	g C	86
Vendée □[5]	f E	84
Vendeuvre-sur-Barse	d K	84
Vendôme	e H	84
Venecia	g J	168
Veneto □[4]	g R	84
Venev	g U	96
Venezia (Venice)	d G	88
Venezuela □[1]	b E	174
Venezuela, Golfo de ⊂	a D	174
Venezuelan Basin ✦[1]	h M	132
Veniaminof, Mount ∧	h O	138
Venice → Venezia, It.	d G	88
Venice, Fl., U.S.	l D	150
Venice, La., U.S.	m G	152
Venice, Gulf of ⊂	d H	88
Vénissieux	g K	84
Venjan	k M	76
Venlo	f I	82
Venosa	i J	88
Venray	e H	82
Vent	i J	80
Ventersburg	g H	130
Ventersdorp	f H	130
Venterstad	h G	130
Ventimiglia	f B	88
Ventnor	k L	78
Ventspils	d D	96
Ventuari ≃	c E	174
Ventura	j F	162
Venus	l E	150
Venustiano Carranza, Méx.	i M	166
Venustiano Carranza, Méx.	h H	166
Vera	e H	178
Veracruz □[3]	h L	166
Veracruz [Llave]	h K	166
Veraguas □[4]	i M	168
Verāval	j D	114
Verbania	d C	88
Verbilki	e T	96
Verbovskij	f Y	96
Vercelli	d C	88
Vercel [-Villedieu-le-Camp]	e M	84
Verchn'aja Salda	f J	92
Verchn'aja Tajmyra ≃	c K	94
Verchnij Ufalej	f J	92
Verchojansk	d R	94
Verchojanskij chrebet ⩘	d Q	94
Verchovje	i T	96
Vercors ◆[1]	h L	84
Verde ≃, Bra.	f B	177
Verde ≃, Para.	b I	178
Verde ≃, Az., U.S.	k E	158
Verden, B.R.D.	c I	80
Verden, Ok., U.S.	d H	154
Verdi	e F	162
Verdigre	i I	156
Verdigris ≃	c K	154
Verdon	k L	156
Verdun, P.Q., Can.	b M	146
Verdun, Fr.	i H	84
Verdun-sur-le-Doubs	f L	84
Verdun-sur-Meuse	c L	84
Vereeniging	f H	130
Vereja	f S	96
Vergennes	c M	146
Verín	d D	86
Veríssimo	e D	177
Verkhoyansk → Verchojansk	d R	94
Vermejo ≃	h L	158
Vermilion, Ab., Can.	d X	140
Vermilion, Oh., U.S.	f D	146
Vermilion ≃, Ab., Can.	e C	142
Vermilion ≃, Il., U.S.	i G	148
Vermilion ≃, La., U.S.	m D	152
Vermilion ≃, Mn., U.S.	b C	148
Vermilion Bay	i U	142
Vermilion Bay ⊂	m D	152
Vermilion Lake ⊜	c C	148
Vermilion Pass)(	f R	140
Vermillion	i K	156
Vermillion ≃	h K	156
Vermont	b F	152
Vermont □[3]	c L	136
Vernal	d G	158
Vernayaz	f G	83
Verndale	e L	156
Verner	d O	148
Verneuil	d G	84
Verneukpan ≃	h E	130
Vernon, B.C., Can.	g O	140
Vernon, Fr.	c H	84
Vernon, Al., U.S.	i H	152
Vernon, Ct., U.S.	f N	146
Vernon, Fl., U.S.	l K	152
Vernon, In., U.S.	d K	152
Vernon, Tx., U.S.	e G	154
Vernon, Ut,. U.S.	d D	158
Vernonia	e B	160
Vernon River	f K	144
Verny	c M	84
Vero Beach	l F	150
Véroia	i F	90
Verona, On., Can.	f S	148
Verona, It.	d F	88
Verona, Ms., U.S.	h H	152
Verona, Wi., U.S.	h F	148
Versailles, Fr.	d I	84
Versailles, Il., U.S.	c F	152
Versailles, In., U.S.	c K	152
Versailles, Ky., U.S.	d L	152
Versailles, Mo., U.S.	d D	152
Versailles, Oh., U.S.	g B	146
Vert, Cap ≻	f C	124
Vertientes	d E	170
Vertou	e E	84
Verulam	g J	130
Verviers	g H	82
Vervins	c J	84
Vesanto	j T	76
Vescovato	g D	88
Vesjegonsk	c T	96
Vesoul	e M	84
Vesta	h K	168
Vest-Agder □[6]	l J	76
Vestavia Hills	i J	152
Vesterålen II	g N	76
Vestfjorden ⊂[2]	h N	76
Vestfold □[6]	l L	76
Vestmanna	d H	76b
Vestmannaeyjar	c C	76a
Vesuvio ∧[1]	i I	88
Vesuvius → Vesuvio ∧[1]	i I	88
Veszprém	h Q	80
Veszprém □[6]	h Q	80
Vésztő	i U	80
Vetlanda	m N	76
Vetralla	g G	88
Vetrino	f K	96
Vetschau	d N	80
Veurne (Furnes)	f B	82
Vevay	d K	152
Vevelstad	i M	76
Vevey	f F	83
Vézelise	d M	84
Viacha	g E	174
Viadana	e E	88
Vian	d L	154
Viana	d I	174
Viana do Alentejo	g C	86
Viana do Castelo	d C	86
Viangchan (Vientiane)	f G	110
Viareggio	f E	88
Viborg, Dan.	m K	76
Viborg, S.D., U.S.	h J	156
Vibo Valentia	k K	88
Vibraye	d G	84
Viburnum	e E	152
Vic (Vich)	d N	86
Vicco	b C	150
Vic-en-Bigorre	i G	84
Vicente Guerrero	b A	166
Vicente López	h I	178
Vicenza	d F	88
Vichada ≃	c E	174
Vichadero	f K	178
Vichy	f J	84
Vici	c G	154
Vicksburg, Mi., U.S.	h J	148
Vicksburg, Ms., U.S.	j F	152
Vico	l W	85a
Viçosa	f G	177
Victor, Id., U.S.	g N	160
Victor, Ia., U.S.	i C	148
Victor, Mt., U.S.	d K	160
Victor Harbor	j C	184
Victoria, Arg.	g H	178
Victoria, Cam.	h H	124
Victoria, B.C., Can.	i K	140
Victoria, P.E., Can.	f J	144
Victoria, Chile	j B	178
Victoria (Xianggang), H.K.	m C	104
Victoria, Malay.	d F	108
Victoria, Sey.	b K	128
Victoria, Ks., U.S.	m H	156
Victoria, Tx., U.S.	k I	154
Victoria, Va., U.S.	c H	150
Victoria □[3]	g I	182
Victoria ≃	c F	182
Victoria, Lake ⊜, Afr.	b F	128
Victoria, Lake ⊜, Austl.	i D	184
Victoria, Mount ∧	d B	110
Victoria de las Tunas	d F	170
Victoria Falls ∟	a G	130
Victoria Harbour	f P	148
Victoria Island I	b J	134
Victoria Lake ⊜[1]	d P	144
Victoria Land ◆[1]	c H	189
Victoria Nile ≃	h G	126
Victoria Peak ∧	i O	166
Victoria River Downs	c F	182
Victoriaville	a O	146
Victoria West	h F	130
Victor Manuel Bueno	e J	166
Victorville	j H	162
Vičuga	d X	96
Vicuña Mackenna	g F	178
Vidalia, Ga., U.S.	g D	150
Vidalia, La., U.S.	k E	152
Vidauban	i M	84
Vidigueira	g D	86
Vidin	f F	90
Vidisha	i G	114
Vidor	l B	152
Viðoy I	d H	76b
Vidsel	i Q	76
Vidzy	f I	96
Viechtach	f L	80
Viedma	e D	176
Viedma, Lago ⊜	f B	176
Vieira do Minho	d C	86
Viella	c L	86
Vienna → Wien, Öst.	g P	80
Vienna, Ga., U.S.	g C	150
Vienna, Il., U.S.	e H	152
Vienna, Md., U.S.	i K	146
Vienna, Mo., U.S.	d E	152
Vienna, S.D., U.S.	g J	156
Vienna, W.V., U.S.	h E	146
Vienne	g K	84
Vienne □[5]	f G	84
Vienne ≃	e G	84
Vientiane → Viangchan	f G	110
Vieques	e L	170
Vieques, Isla de I	e L	170
Vieremä	j T	76
Vierfontein	f H	130
Viersen	d F	80
Vierwaldstättersee ⊜	d I	83
Vierzon	e I	84
Viesca	e H	166
Vieste	h K	88
Vietnam □[1]	b D	108
Viet-tri	d H	110
Vievis	g G	96
Vigan	m S	109b
Vigeland	l J	76
Vigevano	d C	88
Vigneulles-lès-Hattonchâtel	d L	84
Vignola	e F	88
Vigo	c C	86
Vihti	k S	76
Viinijärvi	j U	76
Viitasaari	j S	76
Vijāpur	i E	114
Vijayawāda	d F	116
Vijosë (Aóös) ≃	i D	90
Vikajärvi	h T	76
Vikersund	l L	76
Viking	d W	140
Vikna	i L	76
Vikna I	c J	74
Vikramasingapuram	h D	116
Vila de Manica	b K	130
Vila de Rei	f C	86
Vila do Bispo	h C	86
Vila do Conde	d C	86
Vila Flor	d D	86
Vila Fontes	a L	130
Vilafranca del Penedès	d M	86
Vila Franca de Xira	g C	86
Vilaka	d J	96
Vilanculos	d L	130
Vila Nova de Famalicão	d C	86
Vila Nova de Foz Côa	d D	86
Vila Nova de Gaia	d C	86
Vilanova i la Geltrú	d M	86
Vila Novo de Ourém	f C	86
Vila Real	d D	86
Vila Real de Santo António	h D	86
Vilar Formoso	e E	86
Vila Velha	f H	177
Vila Velha de Ródão	f D	86
Vila Verde	d C	86
Vila Viçosa	g C	86
Vîlcea □[6]	e H	90
Vilhelmina	i O	76
Vilhena	f F	174
Viljandi	c H	96
Viljoenskroon	f H	130
Vil'kickogo, proliv ⩍	b R	92
Villa Ahumada	b F	166
Villa Ángela	d H	178
Villa Bella	f E	174
Villa Bruzual	j J	170
Villacañas	f H	86
Villa Carlos Paz	f F	178
Villacarrillo	g H	86
Villach	i M	80
Villacidro	j C	88
Villa Colón (Caucete)	c C	176
Villa Constitución	g H	178
Villada	c G	86
Villa de Arriaga	g I	166
Villa de Cos	f H	166
Villa de Cura	i K	170
Villa Delgado	d E	168
Villa de Méndez	e J	166
Villadiego	c G	86
Villa Dolores	f F	178
Villa Flores	i M	166
Villafranca de los Barros	g E	86
Villafranca di Verona	d E	88
Villa Frontera	d I	166
Village	d I	154
Villa González	f J	166
Villagrán	e J	166
Villa Grove	c H	152
Villaguay	f I	178
Villa Guerrero	h J	166
Villa Hayes	c J	178
Villahermosa	i M	166
Villa Hidalgo	g H	166
Villaines-la-Juhel	d F	84
Villa Juárez	d E	166
Villa Krause	f D	178
Villalonga	d D	176
Villa López	d G	166
Villa Madero	h I	166
Villa Mainero	e J	166
Villa María	g G	178
Villa Mazán	e E	178
Villamil	j M	174a
Villa Montes	h F	174
Villa Nueva, Arg.	g D	178
Villanueva, Méx.	f H	166
Villanueva, N.M., U.S.	i K	158
Villanueva de Córdoba	g G	86
Villanueva de la Serena	g F	86
Villanueva del Río y Minas	h F	86
Villa Ocampo	e I	178
Villa Orestes Pereyra	d G	166
Villarcayo	c H	86
Villa Regina	j E	178
Villa Rica	f B	150
Villarrica, Chile	d B	176
Villarrica, Para.	c J	178
Villarrobledo	f I	86
Villas	h L	146
Villa Sandino	e J	168
Villasayas	d I	86
Villasimius	j D	88
Villasor	j C	88
Villa Unión, Arg.	e G	178
Villa Unión, Méx.	f F	166
Villavicencio	c D	174
Villa Vicente Guerrero	f H	166
Villaviciosa	b F	86
Villazón	h E	174
Villé	d N	84
Villedieu	d E	84
Villefort	h J	84
Villefranche	g K	84
Ville-Marie	c P	148
Villena	g K	86
Villeneuve-d'Aveyron	h I	84
Villeneuve-Saint-Georges	d I	84
Villeneuve-sur-Lot	h G	84
Ville Platte	l D	152
Villers-Bocage, Fr.	c I	84
Villers-Bocage, Fr.	c F	84
Villersexel	e M	84
Villerupt	c L	84
Villeurbanne	g K	84
Villiers	f I	130
Villingen-Schwenningen	g H	80
Villisca	k M	156
Villupuram	g E	116
Vilnius	g H	96
Vilsbiburg	g L	80
Vilshofen	g M	80
Vil'uj ≃	e P	94
Vil'ujskoje vodochranilišče ⊜[1]	e T	92
Vilvoorde (Vilvorde)	g E	82
Vimianzo	b B	86
Vimmerby	m N	76
Vimoutiers	d G	84
Vina	e C	162
Vina ≃	g I	124
Viña del Mar	g C	178
Vinalhaven	c R	146
Vinaròs	e L	86
Vincennes	d I	152
Vincennes Bay ⊂	b F	189
Vincent	i J	152
Vindeln	i P	76
Vindhya Range ⩘	i G	114
Vinegar Hill ∧	f G	160
Vine Grove	e K	152
Vineland	h K	146
Vinemont	h J	152
Vineyard Haven	f P	146
Vinh	e H	110
Vinhais	d D	86
Vinh Cam-ranh ⊂	i J	110
Vinh-long	i H	110
Vinita	c K	154
Vinkovci	d B	90
Vinnica	h C	92
Vinson Massif ∧	c L	189
Vinton, Ia., U.S.	h C	148
Vinton, La., U.S.	l C	152
Vinton, Va., U.S.	b G	150
Viola, Il., U.S.	i E	148
Viola, Wi., U.S.	g E	148
Vipiteno	c F	88
Virac, Pil.	c G	108
Virac, Pil.	m S	109b
Viramgām	i E	114
Virbalis	g E	96
Virden, Mb., Can.	i N	142
Virden, Il., U.S.	c G	152
Virden, N.M., U.S.	l G	158
Vire	d F	84
Virelles	h E	82
Virgil	n K	156
Virgilina	c H	150
Virgin ≃	h B	158
Virgin Gorda I	e L	170
Virginia, S. Afr.	g H	130
Virginia, Il., U.S.	c F	152
Virginia, Mn., U.S.	c C	148
Virginia □[3]	d K	136
Virginia Beach	c K	150
Virginia City, Mt., U.S.	e N	160
Virginia City, Nv., U.S.	e F	162
Virginia Falls ∟	f FF	138
Virginiatown	b P	148
Virgin Islands □[2]	e L	170
Virojoki	k T	76
Viroqua	g E	148
Virovitica	d L	88
Virrat	j R	76
Virserum	m N	76
Virtaniemi	g U	76
Virton	i H	82
Virudunagar	h D	116
Virungu	c E	128
Vis	f K	88
Vis (Fish) ≃	e C	130
Vis, Otok I	f K	88
Visalia	h F	162
Visayan Sea ⩱[2]	c G	108
Visby	m P	76
Viscount Melville Sound ⩍	b K	134
Visé (Wezet)	g H	82
Višegrad	f C	90
Viseu	e D	86
Vishākhapatnam	d G	116
Vishoek	j D	130
Vislinskij zaliv ⊂	a S	80
Visnagar	i E	114
Viso, Monte ∧	e B	88
Visoko	f B	90
Visp	f H	83
Vissefjärda	m N	76
Visselhövede	c I	80
Vista	k H	162
Vistula → Wisła ≃	a R	80
Vitarte	f C	174
Vitebsk	f M	96
Viterbo	g G	88
Viti Levu I	m S	188g
Vitim ≃	f N	94
Vitória, Bra.	f H	177
Vitoria (Gasteiz), Esp.	c I	86
Vitória da Conquista	c H	177
Vitré	d E	84
Vitry-le-François	d K	84
Vittangi	h Q	76
Vitteaux	e K	84
Vittel	d L	84
Vittoria	m I	88
Vittorio Veneto	d G	88
Viver	f K	86
Vivian	j C	152
Vizianagaram	c G	116
Vizzini	l I	88
Vlaardingen	e E	82
Vladimir	e W	96
Vladivostok	i R	94
Vlasenica	e B	90
Vlasotince	g F	90
Vledder	c I	82
Vlieland I	b G	82
Vlissingen (Flushing)	f D	82
Vlonë → Vlorë	i C	90
Vlorë	i C	90
Vlorës, Gji i ⊂	i C	90
Vltava ≃	f N	80
Vnukovo	f T	96
Voca	h G	154
Vochtoga	c X	96
Vöcklabruck	g M	80
Vogelsberg ⩘	e I	80
Voghera	e D	88
Vohenstrauss	f L	80
Vohibinany	q W	131b
Vohimarina	n X	131b
Voi	b G	128
Void	d L	84
Voinjama	g E	124

Symbols in the index are identified on page 198.

Symbols in the index are identified on page 198.

Symbols in the index are identified on page 198.

Acknowledgments

A WORLD OF WONDERS

Toucan Books Limited, London, is grateful for the assistance of the following consultants in preparing the information that appears on pages 4-63.

Geoffrey W. Amery, F.R.A.S., British Astronomical Association

Prof. B.W. Atkinson, Queen Mary College, University of London

Dr. Tim Bayliss-Smith, Department of Geography, Cambridge University

Prof. D.Q. Bowen, Royal Holloway and Bedford New College, University of London

Cambridge Paleomap Services Ltd.

Dr. Alan Carr

Mark R. Chartrand, Ph.D.

Dr. Jenny Clack, Museum of Zoology, Cambridge University

B.A.L. Cranstone, Pitt Rivers Museum, Oxford University

Prof. P.C.W. Davies, Department of Theoretical Physics, University of Newcastle-upon-Tyne

Dr. W.J. Gould, Institute of Oceanographic Sciences

Herb Kawainui Kane

Dr. Jeremy Leggett, Imperial College of Science and Technology, University of London

Dr. J.S.G. McCulloch, Institute of Hydrology, Wallingford

Dr. Lance Miller, Royal Observatory, Edinburgh

Prof. Rosalind Mitchison, Dept. of Economic and Social History, University of Edinburgh

National Remote Sensing Centre, Farnborough

Stu Nishenko, National Earthquake Information Center, U.S. Geological Survey

Kevin Schurer, Wolfson College, Cambridge University

Dr. Roger Searle, Institute of Oceanographic Sciences

Dr. Andrew Sherratt, Ashmolean Museum, Oxford University

B.W. Sparks, Fellow of Jesus College, Cambridge University

Dr. C.B. Stringer, British Museum (Natural History), London

The editors acknowledge their indebtedness to the following books, which were consulted for reference.

The Universe: Iain Nicolson and Patrick Moore (Collins). *The Universe:* Lloyd Motz (Abacus). *The Left Hand of Creation:* John D. Barrow and Joseph Silk (Unwin Paperbacks). *Space and Time in the Modern Universe:* P.C.W. Davies (Cambridge University Press). *Superforce:* Paul Davies (Heinemann). *The Cambridge Atlas of Astronomy:* Cambridge University Press. *The New Astronomy:* Nigel Henbest and Michael Marten (Cambridge University Press). *100 Billion Suns:* Rudolf Kippenhahn (Counterpoint). *The Edge of Infinity:* Paul Davies (Oxford University Press). *Sun and Earth:* Herbert Friedman (Scientific American Library). *Exploring the Solar System* (Science Museum, London). *The Solar System:* Barrie William Jones (Pergamon Press). *Guide to Stars and Planets:* Ian Ridpath (Collins). *The Planets:* Heather Couper with Nigel Henbest (Pan Books). *The Cambridge Photographic Atlas of the Planets:* Geoffrey Briggs and Fredric Taylor (Cambridge University Press). *Moon, Mars and Meteorites* (Geological Museum, London). *The Moon—Our Sister Planet:* Peter Cadogan (Cambridge University Press). *The Moon:* Patrick Moore (Mitchell Beazley). *The Cambridge Encyclopedia of Earth Sciences:* Edited by David G. Smith (Cambridge University Press). *The Age of the Earth* (Geological Museum, London). *The Story of the Earth* (Geological Museum, London). *The Making of the Earth:* Edited by Richard Fifield (Basil Blackwell & New Scientist). *Earth:* Frank Press and Raymond Siever (W.H. Freeman and Company, San Francisco). *Gaia:* J.E. Lovelock (Oxford University Press). *Continental Drift:* D.H. and M.P. Tarling (Penguin Books). *The Pulse of the Earth:* J.H.F. Umbgrove (Marinus Nijhof). *The Making of a Continent:* Ron Redfern (BBC Books). *The Evolving Continents:* Brian F. Windley (John Wiley & Sons). *Understanding the Earth* (Artemis Press and Open University Press). *Volcanoes:* Peter Francis (Penguin Books). *Volcanoes:* (Geological Museum, London). *Earthquakes* (Geological Museum, London). *Corridors of Time:* Ron Redfern (Times Books). *The Evolving Earth:* Edited by L.M.R. Cocks (British Museum/Natural History and Cambridge University Press). *The Earth:* Edward J. Tarbuck and Frederick K. Lutgens (Charles E. Merrill Publishing Company). *Glaciers and Landscape:* David E. Sugden and Brian S. John (Edward Arnold). *Rivers and Landscape:* Geoff Petts and Ian Foster (Edward Arnold). *Rocks and Relief:* B.W. Sparks (Longman). *Coasts:* Eric C.F. Bird (Basil Blackwell). *The Times Atlas of the Oceans* (Times Books). *Exploration of the Oceans:* John G. Weihaupt (Macmillan). *Atmosphere, Weather and Climate:* R.G. Barry and R.J. Chorley (Methuen). *Earth's Aura:* Louise B. Young (Penguin Books). *Elementary Meteorology* (HMSO). *Climate and Weather:* Hermann Flohn (World University Library). *Modern Meteorology and Climatology:* T. J. Chandler (Nelson). *Meteorology:* Joe R. Eagleman (D. Van Nostrand Company). *The Weather Book:* R. Hardy, P. Wright, J. Gribbin, J. Kington (Michael Joseph Limited). *World Climate:* T.F. Gaskell and Martin Morris (Thames and Hudson). *Cambridge Encyclopedia of Life Sciences* (Cambridge University Press). *Man's Place in Evolution* (British Museum/Natural History and Cambridge University Press). *Human Evolution:* Roger Lewin (Blackwell Scientific Publications). *The Human Story* (Commonwealth Institute). *Ascent to Civilization:* John Gowlett (Collins). *The Times Atlas of World History* (Times Books). *Ecological Imperialism:* Alfred W. Crosby (Cambridge University Press). *World Population Prospects* (United Nations). *World Resources 1986:* World Resources Institute and the International Institute of Environment and Development (Basic Books Inc., N.Y.). *The World Bank Atlas 1986* (World Bank). *North-South: A Programme for Survival:* The Report of the Independent Commission on International Development Issues under the Chairmanship of Willy Brandt (Pan Books). *Ending Hunger* (Praeger). *The New State of the World Atlas:* Michael Kidron and Ronald Segal (Pan Books). *World Development Report 1986* (published for The World Bank by Oxford University Press). *The Atlas of Earth Resources* (Mitchell Beazley). *The Gaia Atlas of Planet Management:* Edited by Norman Myers (Pan Books). *Encyclopedia Britannica 1982.* Various editions of the following newspapers and magazines were also consulted: *Discover; Horizon; National Geographic; New Scientist; Scientific American; The New York Times.*